BELIEF AND CULTURE
IN THE MIDDLE AGES

OXFORD
UNIVERSITY PRESS

Great Clarendon Street, Oxford OX2 6DP
Oxford University Press is a department of the University of Oxford.
It furthers the University's objective of excellence in research, scholarship,
and education by publishing worldwide in

Oxford New York

Athens Auckland Bangkok Bogotá Buenos Aires Cape Town
Chennai Dar es Salaam Delhi Florence Hong Kong Istanbul
Karachi Kolkata Kuala Lumpur Madrid Melbourne Mexico City Mumbai
Nairobi Paris São Paulo Shanghai Singapore Taipei Tokyo Toronto Warsaw
and associated companies in Berlin Ibadan

Oxford is a registered trade mark of Oxford University Press
in the UK and certain other countries

Published in the United States
by Oxford University Press Inc., New York

British Library Cataloguing in Publication Data

Data available

Library of Congress Cataloging in Publication Data
Belief and culture in the Middle Ages: studies presented to Henry Mayr-Harting / edited by
Richard Gameson and Henrietta Leyser.
p. cm.
Includes bibliographical references and index.
1. Christianity and culture—Europe—History—Middle Ages, 600–1500.
2. Europe—Church history—600–1500. I. Mayr-Harting, Henry. II.
Gameson, Richard. III. Leyser, Henrietta.
BR252 .B45 2002 274'.03—dc21 00-051664

ISBN 0-19-820801-4

1 3 5 7 9 10 8 6 4 2

Typeset by Jayvee, Trivandrum, India
Printed in Great Britain
on acid-free paper by
T.J. International Ltd.,
Padstow, Cornwall

Henry Mayr-Harting

BELIEF AND CU
IN THE MIDDLE

STUDIES PRESENTED
HENRY MAYR-HARTIN

Edited by

Richard Gameson *and* Henriett

UNIVERSITY PRESS

PREFACE

This book was conceived as a tribute to Henry Mayr-Harting, Regius Professor of Ecclesiastical History in the University of Oxford, most distinguished of scholars, most generous of friends, and of colourful medievalists surely the most vivid.

Henry was born in Prague in 1936. Educated at Douai and Merton College, Oxford, he became Lecturer in Medieval History at the University of Liverpool in 1960, moving to St Peter's College, Oxford, eight years later.[1] St Peter's was still his academic home when we began planning our volume; what we did not, of course, know at that point was that his sixty-fifth birthday would find him down the road at Christ Church.

So broad is the range of Henry's interests and so large the circle of his academic friends that it was impossible for a single volume—even one of more generous proportions than the usual English *Festschrift*—fully to reflect the former and adequately to include the latter. Yet if one were to identify leitmotifs in the honorand's work they would surely be 'to take the religion of other people and other ages seriously as religious', and not to 'allow cultural and political life to float free of each other . . . By political life I do not mean only ideology, but also real politics, royal, aristocratic, ecclesiastical, monastic and missionary';[2] and it is these that lie behind the conception of the present collection. The resulting essays, treating subjects that range in date from late antiquity to the thirteenth century, exploring the activities of individual prelates, potentates, and patrons, drawing upon the evidence of Rules, vitae, letters, treatises, charters, palaeography, and art history, all in their different ways illuminate the interaction of Christian belief and culture, and illustrate their central role in the study of medieval history as a whole.

It is a pleasure to record the enthusiasm that, from its inception, this project elicited not only from all the authors here represented, but also from those other potential contributors whose field of work or suggested topic did not, regretably, suit the design and form of the volume—an enthusiasm which undoubtedly reflects the affection and admiration with which Henry is regarded. Equally worthy of note is the fact that amidst manifold other responsibilities and commitments, the participants in the finalized volume met the various requests and deadlines with efficiency and good humour.[3] It is a matter of satisfaction that the volume is published by Oxford University Press, thereby

---

[1] Henry is (with customary zest and good humour) chronicling his first decades in his memoirs.

[2] Henry Mayr-Harting, *Ottonian Book Illumination: An Historical Study*, 2 vols. (London, 1991), I, 7 and 9.

[3] Quaedam philomela non cecinit.

providing a fitting acknowledgement of the honorand's work for the Press over many years as an editor of the Oxford Historical Monographs series. Moreover, its production has been overseen by one of his former pupils, Anne Gelling. St Peter's College, Oxford, kindly contributed to defraying the cost of the illustrations.

In addition, R.G. would like to thank all the contributors for the equanimity with which, without exception, they responded to the editorial interventions that a volume of this size requires; and to acknowlege both the invaluable secretarial help he received from Sian Dixon of the School of History, University of Kent, and the never-failing, expert assistance of Christine Gameson with the proofs. H.L. would like to express heartfelt gratitude to R.G. for his editorial skill, and to thank Ruth Parr at the Press for her commitment to the volume. Special thanks go to Caroline Mayr-Harting for her support and encouragement, and for providing the photograph of Henry in Toledo.

R.G., H.L.

Feast of St Anselm, 2000

CONTENTS

LIST OF ILLUSTRATIONS

Henry Mayr-Harting   *Frontispiece*

(between pp. 176–177)

Photographs were supplied, and permission to reproduce them here was kindly granted by the following bodies: the Ashmolean Museum, Oxford (7); the Bayerische Staatsbibliothek, Munich (13 and 15); the Bibliothèque nationale de France, Paris (11 and 17); the Bodleian Library, Oxford (1, 2, 8, 9, 10, 12, 14, 16, 18, 21, 24); the British Library, London (3–5, 20, 22–3); Bundesdenkmalamt, Vienna (6); and the Herzog-August-Bibliothek, Wolfenbüttel (19).

ABBREVIATIONS

ANS	(*Proceedings of the Battle Conference*) *for Anglo-Norman Studies* (Woodbridge)
ASE	*Anglo-Saxon England* (Cambridge)
CLA	E. A. Lowe, *Codices Latini Antiquiores*, 11 vols. plus *Supplement* (Oxford, 1934–71), 2nd edn. of vol. II (Oxford, 1972)
CCCM	Corpus Christianorum, Continuatio Medievalis (Turnhout)
CCSL	Corpus Christianorum, Series Latina (Turnhout)
CSEL	Corpus Scriptorum Ecclesiasticorum Latinorum
EEMF	Early English Manuscripts in Facsimile (Copenhagen)
EHR	*English Historical Review*
HE	*Bede's Ecclesiastical History of the English People*, ed. B. Colgrave and R. A. B. Mynors (Oxford, 1969)
JEH	*Journal of Ecclesiastical History*
MGH	Monumenta Germaniae Historica (Berlin, Hanover, Munich)
PG	*Patrologia Graeco-Latina*, ed. J.-P. Migne, 161 vols. (Paris)
PL	*Patrologia Latina*, ed. J.-P. Migne, 221 vols. (Paris)
RS	Rolls Series (London)
SC	Sources chrétiennes (Paris)
TRHS	*Transactions of the Royal Historical Society*

THE CONTRIBUTORS

STUART AIRLIE is a Senior Lecturer in the Department of History, University of Glasgow. He is the author of a series of articles on kingship and the aristocracy in Carolingian and post-Carolingian Europe, and is currently completing a book on Carolingian political culture. He has profited from Henry's insights for over twenty years—ever since he heard him analysing Ottonian culture in a series of surprising but illuminating metaphors drawn from cricket!

CHRISTOPHER BROOKE was Professor of Medieval History at Liverpool, 1956–67; Professor of History, Westfield College, London, 1967–77; Dixie Professor of Ecclesiastical History at Cambridge, 1977–94; and has been a Fellow of Gonville and Caius College, 1949–56 and since 1977. He and Henry first met as colleagues at Liverpool in the 1960s.

KATHLEEN G. CUSHING is Lecturer in Medieval History at the University of Keele. Her research interests are canon law, eleventh-century ecclesiastical reform and hagiography. Her most recent book is *Papacy and Law in the Gregorian Revolution: The Canonistic Works of Anselm of Lucca* (1998). Henry provided vital support during her doctoral work, and in preparing her thesis for publication.

VALERIE I. J. FLINT is G. F. Grant Professor of History at the University of Hull. Her research focuses on the history of ideas in the Middle Ages, and her most recent book is *Honorius of Regensburg* (1995). As an undergraduate and graduate, she was a contemporary of Henry at Oxford.

RICHARD GAMESON is Reader in Medieval History at the University of Kent, Canterbury. He specializes in early manuscripts and cultural history. His most recent book is *The Manuscripts of Early Norman England c.1066–1130* (1999). Henry supervised his doctoral thesis, and has provided continuous encouragement thereafter.

DAVID GANZ is Professor of Palaeography at King's College, London, and has published widely on early medieval manuscripts. At Oxford he was inspired by Henry's historical geography lectures—and by his reminder that Julian Brown, Richard Hunt, and Beryl Smalley also got Oxford second-class degrees.

BRIAN GOLDING is Reader in Medieval History at the University of Southampton, and the author of *Gilbert of Sempringham and the Gilbertine*

Order c.1130–c.1300 (1995). He is currently working on an edition of Gerald of Wales's *Speculum Ecclesie* for Oxford Medieval Texts.

LAWRENCE GOLDMAN is Fellow and Tutor in Modern History at St Peter's College, Oxford, where, between 1990 and 1997, he was Henry's close colleague and taught with him. He specializes in British and American History in the nineteenth and twentieth centuries, and is the author of *Dons and Workers: Oxford and Adult Education since 1850* (1995).

JULIAN HASELDINE read History at St Peter's College, Oxford, between 1985 and 1988, and is now Lecturer in Medieval History at the University of Hull. He is currently editing the letters of Peter of Celle for Oxford Medieval Texts, and working on a book, *The Medieval Language of Friendship*.

ERIC JOHN was formerly Reader in History at the University of Manchester. A specialist in early English history, his latest book was *Re-assessing Anglo-Saxon England* (1996). He died on 25 April 2000.

MARTIN KAUFFMANN was, as an undergraduate at Merton College, Oxford, taught medieval history by Henry. He wrote his doctoral thesis on thirteenth-century illustrated saints' lives at the Courtauld Institute, London, and is now Assistant Librarian in the Department of Special Collections and Western Manuscripts in the Bodleian Library, Oxford. He has written mainly about thirteenth- and fourteenth-century manuscript illustration in England and France.

MATTHEW KEMPSHALL is Lecturer in the Department of History at the University of York, and the author of *The Common Good in Late Medieval Political Thought* (1999). Along with a generation of fellow undergraduates at Merton College, he had the great pleasure, and privilege, of being taught by Henry.

CONRAD LEYSER is Lecturer in Medieval History at the University of Manchester. His book, *Authority and Asceticism from Augustine to Gregory the Great* (2000), is based on a D.Phil. thesis supervised by Henry.

HENRIETTA LEYSER is a Fellow of St Peter's College, Oxford, where she now occupies the rooms that were formerly Henry's. She has published on the history of medieval women in England, and on twelfth-century religious history. Henry has long been her mentor and mainstay—not to mention organist.

R. A. MARKUS is Professor Emeritus in the University of Nottingham. A specialist in Late Antiquity and early Christianity, his most recent book is *Gregory the Great and his World* (1997). He was a colleague of Henry at Liverpool.

D. J. A. MATTHEW is Professor Emeritus in the University of Reading. The focus of his work is the Normans. He has known Henry since they were students at Merton.

R. I. MOORE is Professor of Medieval History at the University of Newcastle upon Tyne. He has published extensively on medieval heresy, his most recent book being *The First European Revolution* (2000). He and Henry were both pupils of Ralph Davis at Merton, and they co-edited his *Festschrift* (1985).

JANET L. NELSON is Professor of Medieval History at King's College, London. Her research interests are mainly in the Carolingian period, and her most recent book is *Rulers and Rulership in Early Medieval Europe* (1999).

VERONICA ORTENBERG was first taught by Henry in 1981. Her interest in Anglo-Saxon hagiography, which she explored in a book and numerous articles, has now expanded to include more general West European ecclesiastical and cultural history from the fifth to the eighth centuries. Formerly a lecturer at Lampeter, she has recently returned to Oxford as assistant editor, The Victoria County History of Oxford.

STELLA PANAYOTOVA is Assistant Keeper of Manuscripts and Printed Books at the Fitzwilliam Museum, Cambridge, having previously been working on a catalogue of the western illuminated manuscripts in the Cambridge University Library. Henry supervised her doctoral thesis on the interpretation and illustration of English psalters *c*.1150–1250.

ALISON PEDEN was a Fellow of St Hilda's College, Oxford, and is currently Honorary Lecturer at the University of Glasgow. She is editing Abbo of Fleury's *Commentary on the Calculus of Victorius of Aquitaine* for the British Academy.

FRANCES RAMSEY is Director of Studies and teaches History at Westminster School. As an undergraduate, she was taught by Henry; and her doctoral thesis, a collection and study of the *acta* of the bishops of Bath and Wells 1061–1205 (published in 1995), was prepared under his supervision.

TIMOTHY REUTER is Professor of Medieval History at the University of Southampton and Director of the Wessex Medieval Centre. He has published widely on medieval Germany, and is currently working on a comparative study of European bishoprics in the Middle Ages.

SUSAN J. RIDYARD is Associate Professor of History at the University of the South and Director of the Sewanee Mediaeval Colloquium. She has published

The Royal Saints of Anglo-Saxon England: A Study of West Saxon and East Anglian Cults (1988) and articles on Anglo-Saxon and Anglo-Norman church history. She is currently working on an edition and translation of the canonization process of St Thomas Cantilupe.

ANTON SCHARER is Associate Professor of Medieval History at the University of Vienna. His most recent book is *Herrschaft und Repräsentation: Studien zur Hofkultur König Alfreds des Grossen* (2000).

NICHOLAS VINCENT is Professor of Medieval History at Christ Church College, Canterbury, and director of the British Academy's Angevin *Acta* project. His most recent book is *The Holy Blood* (2000). He read history under Henry's direction at St Peter's College.

PATRICK WORMALD is college tutor and university lecturer at Christ Church, Oxford, having previously been Prize Fellow of All Souls College, Oxford, and a lecturer in Medieval History at the University of Glasgow. A specialist in early English history he is currently publishing his two-volume study *The Making of English Law* (1999–2002). Not formally a pupil of Henry and only recently a colleague, he owes him decades of insight, wisdom and friendship.

HENRY MAYR-HARTING AT LIVERPOOL

Christopher Brooke

One cannot truly separate Mayr-Harting at Liverpool from Mayr-Harting at Oxford; for he brought with him all that was best of Oxford and Merton in a zeal to teach, dedication to the needs of his students, training in research widely and deeply based, and an ideal of a college and university community—which never led him to patronize the provincial university, yet never let him accept its methods and values with complacency. When we fostered a research student of outstanding brilliance in Ian Kershaw, Henry strongly advised him to move to Oxford—and told his supervisor afterwards. Later on, by an attraction as near infallible as a historian can admit, he followed Ian back to Oxford himself, and has been there ever since. But Liverpool has always meant much to him; and it was not only a ripple of the Isis which he brought to the Mersey: he brought too his own special gifts of charm, brilliant imagination, and incisiveness of mind. It was said of a famous boxer that no one was ever quite the same who had once felt his glove. None of us, staff or students—or the wide circle of his friends on Merseyside—went unaffected by him.

Shortly after his arrival in Liverpool in 1960 as an Assistant Lecturer in Medieval History, he and I travelled to Oxford for his D.Phil. viva—which I had agreed to examine, after overcoming scruples of conscience in treating a colleague in this way. The thesis was first-rate and so was the hospitality of Oxford; only I was in quarantine for mumps and developed it the next day— and the Liverpool doctor completed the dismantling of our department by putting Henry in quarantine so as to prevent the plague from spreading. From this inauspicious start he went from strength to strength. He did not catch mumps; he established himself very rapidly as a brilliant teacher and a much-valued tutor in Derby Hall. A shrewd judge had indicated to me before he came that he had the promise of an exceptionally distinguished tutor: his words stick in my mind, for they impressed me at the time, and even more later when they came to be so clearly and marvellously fulfilled.

His admirable thesis on the *Acta* of the Bishops of Chichester was duly published by the Canterbury and York Society in 1964, and established his reputation as a scholar.[1] It enlisted him among the pioneers in editing these crucial documents—now the subject of twenty volumes or so of a British Academy major project. It also revealed the imagination and insight he brought to apparently routine documents. A by-product was a celebrated article on Bishop

---

[1] *The Acta of the Bishops of Chichester, 1075–1207* (Torquay, 1964).

Hilary of Chichester, in which he showed how the trained ecclesiastical royal servant spread ideas in the royal curia essential for understanding Henry II's legal reforms; a prophetic article.[2] The doctrine that the English Common Law owed anything significant to the *ius commune* of Canon and Roman Law was once anathema to secular-minded legal historians, but is now coming to be more widely appreciated.

Teaching and research have always been most intimately linked in Henry's faith and practice; and his Liverpool pupils enjoyed the first preview of his studies of Ottonian Germany which were to bear fruit many years later in the most original of his books (so far). Exigencies of the teaching programme led him back into the early Middle Ages in England as well as the continent; and in his later years at Liverpool the foundations were laid for *The Coming of Christianity to Anglo-Saxon England*, although this was not actually published until 1972. It is a model in the art of writing history that will appeal at once and equally to a wide audience and to the professional scholar: it is delightful to read, perceptive and enchanting; and it shows the sharp edge of his mind at every turn. It was paid a high compliment by the late Michael Wallace-Hadrill, who in earlier life had been Henry's tutor at Merton—where he had failed to detect the high promise of his pupil. In his last years Wallace-Hadrill wrote his great commentary on Bede's *Ecclesiastical History* (published posthumously in Oxford Medieval Texts, 1988). This book is also a commentary on a small club of eminent scholars whose comments on Bede were especially worth recording; and Henry's book is among them. Bede (*HE* II, 11) quotes a letter from the pope to King Edwin's queen saying he is sending her an ivory comb adorned with gold. Thus Wallace-Hadrill: 'Mayr-Harting . . . has a brief but useful survey of presents reaching England from the East. Apropos the comb, "we do not have to imagine travels between Britain and Egypt." Certainly not'—said the old tutor—'The comb came from Rome.'[3] In spite of these occasional flashes, Wallace-Hadrill gladly accepted that his former pupil had turned even ivory into gold.

Henry taught us much, and also entertained us—in a wide variety of ways: at the residential courses for students at Attingham Park (near Shrewsbury) he might act the heroic goalkeeper in a celebrated game of football before breakfast, and enchant us with Mozart sonatas on the grand piano after dinner; more domestically, he might give breakfast in his mother's house in Bristol to his head of department and all his family heading to a holiday in Cornwall. Some of his exploits entered into legend. On one occasion he lunched with us in the Wirral and set off by bicycle for dinner in Derby Hall—but was diverted to the History School instead in search of a book; and when eventually he came to light the

    [2] 'Hilary, Bishop of Chichester (1147–69) and Henry II', *EHR* 78 (1963), 209–24, shortly followed by 'Henry II and the Papacy, 1170–1189', *JEH* 16 (1965), 39–53.
    [3] J. M. Wallace-Hadrill, *Bede's Ecclesiastical History of the English People: A Historical Commentary* (Oxford, 1988), 70, commenting on *HE* II, 11 (p. 174), and quoting H. Mayr-Harting, *The Coming of Christianity to Anglo-Saxon England* (London, 1972), 126.

Warden of Derby Hall (a law professor and magistrate) was heard to say 'we had the police of five counties out in search of him'. More seriously, another book kept him so deep in its grip that he failed to answer a fire alarm—and had it not been a practice alarm he would have perished. He helped to make the History School a place of joy and laughter, as well as of earnest study and deep research.

I have spoken at length of what Henry gave to Liverpool. What, then, did Liverpool give in return? No doubt the experience of working in a small group of dedicated medievalists helped to foster and mature his own talents: the group was as friendly and harmonious as one could wish—but also comprised very varied personalities and interests, each freely and candidly expressing his and her individuality. It gave him experience of human relations among teachers and students; it gave him the opportunity to spread his wings in new fields of enquiry; it confirmed (what he never entirely lacked) confidence in his own powers; it confirmed, perhaps, his preference for Oxford. But it marked him too as a man (in Lytton Strachey's words) 'who was acquainted with the world as well as Oxford'[4]—vital experience if his talents were to be developed to the full after his return to the Isis.

It gave him something more. There came a time when we noticed with interest and pleasure fairly frequent visits to his room in the History School in Abercromby Square by a charming third-year classics student. In the School and in Derby Hall it was earnestly debated how soon he would announce his engagement. But Henry went on leave and was away for a while, and silence fell. When he returned he came to call on me, and said, 'I have some news that is going to surprise you: I am engaged to be married'. And we had the delight of welcoming Caroline to our company; and the assurance in later years that Henry's time in Liverpool had been well spent.

---

[4] *Portraits in Miniature* (London, 1931), 200, on J. A. Froude.

TEACHING WITH HENRY MAYR-HARTING

Lawrence Goldman

Henry returned to Oxford from Liverpool in 1968 on his election to a fellowship (and an associated university lectureship) at St Peter's College. Founded in 1929 for the education of poor men in the evangelical tradition, St Peter's had been granted its charter in 1961. Henry arrived at a singular moment, as the fellowship expanded rapidly during the late 1960s and as St Peter's moved from the more enclosed atmosphere of a permanent private hall to take its place as a full college of the university. Few members of St Peter's played a larger role than Henry in building up the reputation of the college, both in Oxford and outside. In three decades as a fellow he fashioned St Peter's into a centre for historical learning and established a tradition of undergraduate excellence. The statistics show it. Before Henry came to St Peter's no undergraduate at the college had taken a first-class degree in Modern History. Between 1968 and 1997, however, there were twenty-nine firsts in Modern History alone and several more in History and its associated joint schools. Henry would deny the credit for this; 'the firsts are made in heaven', I can hear him say. But generations of St Peter's historians know how much they owe to his enthusiasm and academic rigour—the able and the less able, both.

Henry arrived to partner the presiding History tutor, Eric Smith, until he retired in 1971. As Senior History Tutor, Henry then had three more historian colleagues in St Peter's: Tim Mason from 1971 to 1985, Rhodri Williams from 1985 to 1990, and myself between 1990 and 1997. Each pairing was different and each brought distinct qualities to the teaching of history in the college. But there can be little doubt that Henry's partnership with Tim Mason, the brilliant and much-lamented historian of modern Germany, established the college as a vital place to study history. Henry's own scholarship also played a crucial role, of course: the publication in 1972 of *The Coming of Christianity to Anglo-Saxon England* established his research reputation, and for more than two decades it drew prospective students to St Peter's—and now to Christ Church, no doubt. In the 1970s Henry was an energetic Admissions Tutor, using his associations with the north-west to build up the college's links with schools in that area, and was always ready to jump on a train and give a talk to sixth-form historians. He was also Chairman of the Faculty Board of Modern History in Oxford. It is a mark of how quickly things have changed that when Henry held this office in the early 1980s he combined it with a full load of tutorials and lectures. Administering a university faculty is a full-time job in itself today.

Of course, Henry loved and still loves teaching, and in Oxford this is how he is best known—as 'the crack tutor of the Oxford History School', as one of our colleagues once put it. I first heard of Henry (when I was a student in Cambridge) from an undergraduate friend of mine who had been taken for tutorials by him for the very successful course Henry devised in the 1980s on the Carolingian Renaissance. Henry, I learnt, loved Mozart, was often late, and was the most accomplished of tutors. All of this is true, as I was to discover for myself. Alas, even a close colleague can never penetrate the mysteries of another's tutorials: I have never seen Henry in full flow in response to an undergraduate essay. But I have heard tell many times of his careful questioning which leads students to the answer—and makes them think in the process; of his surprising and enlightening use of evidence in order to see a problem from a new angle; of his focus on the particular to illuminate the general; of the enjoyment to be had—and the privilege, also—while sitting in Henry's room and talking about the past.

Apart from the usual collaboration of subject tutors in a college as they go about the business of organizing the tuition of their undergraduates—a collaboration which usually involved a glass of whisky in Henry's room—I was fortunate enough to interact with Henry in two distinct contexts. For several years we taught introductory classes together for our first-year students on a variety of historical themes—'general historical problems' it would once have been called. In these I marvelled at Henry's range. Whatever the issue or subject—Weber's *Protestant Ethic*, Marx's theory of revolution, the methods of oral history, or even the role of rivers in history—Henry had an original view or a fresh critical perspective. If there was a linking theme in all his observations, it was to emphasize the uniqueness of every historical event and context. Comparisons were possible and should be made, but Henry emphasized more often that the study of history was the study of difference. I once asked him (in all the innocence of a modernist) why I had never heard him use the term 'feudal'. I received the most brilliant response not only on the limitations of such a word when applied to the vast complexity of medieval Europe but on the limitations of such terms in general. For Henry, in history as in life, it is the differences between places, people, and politics that are interesting and enlivening.

Our other great collaboration was in the admission of undergraduates each winter. These 'campaigns', as we called them, took several weeks and would come to a climax in Henry's room as we interviewed prospective students. In my inexperience I imagined that interviews were best conducted through strings of aggressive questions: the fittest would survive the barrage and demonstrate their capacity to stand up to the weekly rigours of the tutorial system. But Henry showed me that it was possible to learn all that we required about a candidate by courtesy and careful probing. Interviewing is difficult: to test a student's capacity for historical analysis and discover whether he or she is capable of thinking about an issue requires a line of questioning that has a clear direction and terminus—some sort of correct answer—but which does not constrain the interviewee or deter authentic and original responses. Time after

time Henry set the hare racing and gently guided students in such a way that it
very soon became clear if they had picked up the scent and were in hot pursuit
or if they were lost on the moor without a clue where to go next. Each student
was treated with the greatest respect; each in turn received Henry's full attention. Many interviewees turned and thanked him as they left the room for such
an interesting discussion. And at the end of two intensive days we were left in
no doubt as to the best among them: while other tutors were still toiling over
their lists we were in the Randolph Hotel having tea—surely Henry's favourite
meal of the day. Henry is a fine judge of character and personal capacity—he
would say that a good historian has to be—and it was always evident in his
gentle but incisive handling of the new recruits.

Henry is one of those fortunate individuals who have been allowed to pursue
the career that suits them best. It is difficult to think of him in any role other
than that of university lecturer and college tutor. He has educated generations
by his example alone; his intellectual energy, curiosity, and commitment to history have rubbed off on all those around him. In the 1990s as I worked with him
it was a great satisfaction to see him rewarded for all of this. First came a University Readership, then a Fellowship of the British Academy, and finally his
translation to Christ Church as Regius Professor of Ecclesiastical History.
Rarely has any academic appointment met with such universal approval as
Henry's to this distinguished chair. And rarely has a more unusual appointment
been made to a canonry of Christ Church or any other cathedral, as the *Daily
Telegraph* was quick to recognize on its announcement.[1] But to many of his
friends and colleagues Henry's elevation seemed entirely appropriate: such a
remarkably gifted teacher and scholar deserved a remarkable appointment, and
a man who can so easily make his companions laugh merited an office and position which brought broad smiles to so many Oxford faces. For me personally it
was little short of a disaster: to lose Henry felt like losing a limb. But for the university, the historical profession, and for learning in general it was a brilliant
coup. It is an indication of the affection in which he was held by the students
that the St Peter's historians had the excellent photograph of Henry which
appeared in the *Telegraph* printed on to a mass-produced tee-shirt bearing the
legend: 'Henry Mayr-Harting, St Peter's College, The Glory Years 1968–1997.'
They sold like the proverbial hot cakes among the students, and more than one
medieval historian in the Oxford Modern History Faculty now counts the
garment as a treasured possession.

The contributions to this volume pay tribute to Henry as a wonderfully creative historical scholar with a broad range of interests across many centuries. In
an age when teaching no longer seems so central to academic life it is also a pleasure to honour someone for whom it has always been an essential part of the job,
and who does it so well and makes it so much fun.

[1] *Daily Telegraph*, 5 Mar. 1997, p. 6.

PRINCIPAL PUBLICATIONS OF
HENRY MAYR-HARTING (TO 2000)

BOOKS

The Bishops of Chichester, 1075–1207: Biographical Notes and Problems (Chichester, 1963).

(ed.), *The Acta of the Bishops of Chichester 1075–1207*, Canterbury and York Society, 56 (1964).

The Coming of Christianity to Anglo-Saxon England (London, 1972; 2nd edn., 1977; 3rd edn., 1991).

(ed. with R. I. Moore), *Studies in Medieval History Presented to R. H. C. Davis* (London, 1985).

(ed.), *St Hugh of Lincoln: Lectures Delivered at Oxford and Lincoln To Celebrate the Eighth Centenary of St Hugh's Consecration as Bishop of Lincoln* (Oxford, 1986).

Ottonian Book Illumination: An Historical Study, 2 vols. (London, 1991; 2nd edn., 1999).

ARTICLES AND PAMPHLETS

'Hilary, Bishop of Chichester (1147–1169) and Henry II', *EHR* 58 (1963), 209–24.

'Henry II and the Papacy 1170–1189', *JEH* 16 (1965), 39–53.

'Functions of a Twelfth-Century Recluse', *History*, 60 (1975), 337–52.

The Venerable Bede, the Rule of St Benedict and Social Class, Jarrow Lecture (Jarrow, 1976).

'St Wilfrid in Sussex', in *Studies in Sussex Church History*, ed. M. J. Kitch (Chichester, 1981), 1–17.

'England bis 1066', *Theologische Realenzyklopadie*, Band IX (Berlin and New York, 1982), 617–26.

'Functions of a Twelfth-Century Shrine: The Miracles of St Frideswide', in *Studies in Medieval History Presented to R. H. C. Davis*, ed. Mayr-Harting and Moore (London, 1985), 193–206.

'Saxons, Danes and Normans, 409–1154: Overview', in *The Cambridge Historical Encyclopaedia of Great Britain and Ireland*, ed. C. Haigh (Cambridge, 1985), 54–8.

Saint Wilfrid, Archbishop of York 634–709 (London, 1986).

What To Do in the Penwith Peninsula (Cornwall) in Less Than Perfect Weather (Oxford, 1987; 2nd edn., 1988).

'The Foundation of Peterhouse, Cambridge (1284) and the Rule of St Benedict', *EHR* 103 (1988), 318–38.

'The West: The Age of Conversion (700–1050)', in *The Oxford Illustrated History of Christianity*, ed. J. McManners (Oxford, 1990), 92–121.

'Two Abbots in Politics: Wala of Corbie and Bernard of Clairvaux', *TRHS* 5th ser., 40 (1990), 217–37.

'The Church of Magdeburg: Its Trade and Its Town in the Tenth and Early Eleventh

Centuries', in *Church and City: Essays Presented to Christopher Brooke*, ed. D. Abulafia, M. Franklin, and M. Rubin (Cambridge, 1992), 129–50.

'Ruotger, the Life of Bruno and Cologne Cathedral Library', in *Intellectual Life in the Middle Ages: Essays Presented to Margaret Gibson*, ed. L. Smith and B. Ward (London and Rio Grande, 1992), 33–60.

'Charlemagne as a Patron of Art', in *The Church and the Arts*, Studies in Church History, 28, ed. D. Wood (Oxford, 1992), 43–77.

'Odo of Deuil, the Second Crusade and the Monastery of Saint-Denis', in *The Culture of Christendom: Essays in Medieval History in Commemoration of Denis L. T. Bethell*, ed. M. Meyer (London, 1993), 225–41.

Two Conversions to Christianity: The Bulgarians and the Anglo-Saxons, Stenton Lecture (Reading, 1994).

'Bede's Patristic Thinking as a Historian', in *Historiographie im frühen Mittelalter*, ed. A. Scharer and G. Scheibelreiter (Munich, 1994), 367–74.

'Charlemagne, the Saxons, and the Imperial Coronation of 800', *EHR* III (1996), 1113–33.

'Karl Joseph Leyser 1920–1992', *1996 Lectures and Memoirs: Proceedings of the British Academy*, 94 (1997), 599–624.

Perceptions of Angels in History, An Inaugural Lecture Delivered in the University of Oxford on 14th November 1997 (Oxford, 1998).

'Artists and Patrons', in *The New Cambridge Medieval History III, c.900–c.1024*, ed. T. Reuter (Cambridge, 1999), 212–30.

'Warum 799 in Paderborn?', in *799—Kunst und Kultur der Karolingerzeit*, ed. C. Stiegemann and M. Wemhoff, 3 vols. (Mainz, 1999), III, 2–6.

'Charlemagne's Religion', in *Am Vorabend der Kaiserkrönun. Das Epos 'Karolus Magnus et Leo Papa' und der Papstbesuch in Paderborn*, ed. J. Jarnut *et al.* (forthcoming).

1

ANGELS, MONKS, AND DEMONS IN THE EARLY MEDIEVAL WEST

Conrad Leyser

If the monk wants to spit, or to blow mucus from his nose, he should not aim in front of himself, but behind—because there are angels standing in front of him, as is shown by the prophet, 'In the sight of angels, I will sing psalms for you Lord, and I will worship at your sacred temple' [Ps. 137.1].

So states the *Rule of the Master*, an anonymous early sixth-century Italian text for the regulation of the cenobitic life, in discussing the monk's deportment while engaged in singing the office or in verbal prayer.[1] The prescription is repeated twice, along with warnings against continual coughing or heavy breathing. As he sings, the monk must stand upright, perfectly still, head bowed, so as to show the angels before him that his praise for the Lord is not empty, but that his lips speak directly to the condition of his heart.

Angels were, literally, within spitting distance in this early medieval community. To a modern audience the *Rule of the Master*'s angels are a source of amusement, or even embarrassment. They seem out of place: it is not only that they are intimately and unexpectedly close, but also that they are there at all in a monastic Rule. We tend to assume that angels, supernatural and volatile beings, do not belong in a text that seeks to legislate systematically for a human community.[2] The temptation is to dismiss the Master's angels as a 'cameo appearance', epiphenomenal to the serious constitutional purpose of the text.

---

[1] *Regula Magistri* 47.21–23, 48.6–9, ed. A. de Vogüé, 3 vols. (Paris, 1964), SC 105–7: II, 216–18 (hereafter *RMag*: SC). These passages, and the ubiquity of angels in the *Rule*, are noted by R. Markus, *The End of Ancient Christianity* (Cambridge, 1990), 22 and n. 4. The present essay was first presented as a paper at the Thirteenth International Conference on Patristic Studies, held at Oxford in August 1999, under the title 'Angels, Monks, and Demons in the Latin West, *c.*500'. The text as printed is largely unaltered from that of the lecture. I thank Kate Cooper, Ian Wood, Klaus Zelzer, and the editors of this volume for their inspiration and correction. It did not escape my notice that almost two years previously, on the same podium in Oxford, Henry Mayr-Harting delivered his inaugural lecture as Professor of Ecclesiastical History, *Perceptions of Angels in History* (Oxford, 1998).

[2] Guiding this assumption might be two influential models of the development of moral authority: Max Weber's analysis of the routinization of charisma, in *Economy and Society: An Outline of Interpretive Sociology*, ed. G. Roth and C. Wittich, trans. E. Fischoff *et al.*, 3 vols. (New York, 1968), I, 246–54; III, 1121–3 (on which see Markus, *End of Ancient Christianity*, 25–6); or, alternatively, Michel Foucault's account of public spectacle followed by institutionalization in his *Discipline and Punish: The Birth of the Prison*, trans. A. Sheridan (London, 1977); see also id., 'The Battle for Chastity', in *Western Sexuality*, ed. P. Ariès and A. Béjin (Oxford, 1985), 14–25.

This would be a mistake. Angels, as we shall see, were central to the Master's vision of authority and community. At the moment of the crystallization of the regular cenobitic tradition in the West, and for long thereafter, angels were present in ways we have yet to apprehend. Five hundred years after the Master wrote, startling corroboration of his insistence on the physical proximity of angels is provided by the Burgundian monk, Rodolfus Glaber († 1047). In his *Histories*, Glaber relates that he knew a monk who was in the habit of expectorating heavily at the altar—until, that is, a figure clad in white materialized before him in his sleep, and asked 'Cur me sputis propriis verberando inlinis?' ('Why do you shower me with spittle?') This was no way to treat one who carried his prayers up to God, remonstrated the long-suffering angel.[3] Such stories prompt the suspicion that the 'magical realism' of modern Latin American fiction would be a better guide to early medieval monastic culture than some of the categories of twentieth-century sociology or hermeneutics.

For monks in the West, then, angels were not only startling emanations of divine charisma: they were, in the same moment, part of the routine of everyday life. In this sense, the monastic experience of angels may have differed from that of the laity, for whom angels tended to appear at extraordinary moments of social drama. Henry Mayr-Harting has shown how an angel could resolve otherwise impossible tensions in the honour–shame culture of the early medieval aristocracy by offering a gift that did not need to be returned, or a rebuke that could be accepted without loss of face.[4] The appearance of a supernatural being broke a deadlock in the natural or the cultural order of things. For monastic communities, however, a daily concourse with angels may have diminished the role of the *angelus ex machina*. This is not to say that familiarity bred contempt. There were social tensions aplenty within early medieval ascetic groups that called down the ministrations of angels. The point is rather, that in the regular commerce with supernatural powers sustained in monasteries, angels did not only represent the solution to earthly problems: they were, in themselves, part of the problem.

Not the least difficulty was in determining the nature of angels. How 'supernatural' were these creatures? Did they have bodies? Then there was the question of character: how could a monk tell the difference between a good angel and a bad one—a demon? Since the Creation fallen angels had beguiled humans into following the errors of their ways. For Latin monks at the turn of the sixth century the answers to these and other questions lay most readily to hand in the writings of John Cassian († *c.*435), the spiritual expert who had settled in Marseilles some three generations previously, and whose self-appointed task had been to instruct westerners in the ascetic ways of the desert.[5] I begin

[3] Glaber, *Historiarum Libri Quinque*, V.1, ed. N. Bulst and J. France (Oxford, 1989), 224.
[4] Mayr-Harting, *Perceptions of Angels*, 4–13.
[5] On Cassian, see now C. Stewart, *Cassian the Monk* (New York, 1998).

with Cassian on angels and demons, and with his reception by two early sixth-century texts: the *Rule of the Master* and, for comparison, the *Lives of the Jura Fathers*. This text, composed *c.*510–20 by an anonymous monk at Condat for two monks at the community of St Maurice at Agaune, recalls the opening up of the Alpine wilderness by ascetic pioneers.[6] Here, angels are notable by their absence: the tension we moderns might expect between supernatural beings and human institutions seems in the Jura to have resulted in the tacit avoidance of the former, and a countermanding emphasis on the naturalistic operation of authority within the community. The naturalism of the *The Life of the Jura Fathers* throws into stronger relief, however, the magical realist landscape evoked by the Italian Master. In Campania monks and angels were to be housed together: how, we must ask, did the Master make use of the angelic tradition he inherited, and how plausible did the living arrangements he prescribed appear to his own readers?

Angels have always tended to prompt unanswerable questions. 'How many angels can dance on the head of a pin?' was the conundrum preoccupying late medieval scholastics, or so their detractors claimed.[7] Many topics—such as the tradition of high angelology stretching back to the Hebrew Bible and Jewish Apocrypha, for example, or the Graeco-Roman context for Christian demonology—are not even broached here.[8] Furthermore, in speaking exclusively of monks—so saying nothing of nuns—I can only be telling half the story, if that. My limited goal, to rephrase the pseudo-scholastic question, is to assess how many angels there may have been dancing in the monastery as envisaged by the best-known early medieval reader of the *Rule of the Master*, namely St Benedict.

THE ANGELIC LIFE

The association of monks and angels was as old as the monastic life itself. Admirers of the desert ascetics of Egypt and Syria repeatedly referred to them as 'our angels' or 'angels of God'.[9] Their ascetic endeavour—unremitting and sometimes spectacular feats of denial and endurance—had transformed them, in particular their bodies. The desert fathers were literally 'otherworldly' figures, on the point of dematerialization. Like the angels, they did battle with demons, the bad angels, joining the warfare raging in the middle air.

[6] For this dating and attribution, see *Vita Patrum Iurensium* (hereafter *VPJ*), ed. F. Martine (Paris, 1968), SC 142, 14–57. An English translation of the text is forthcoming in the Cistercian Studies Series.

[7] B. Hamilton, *Religion in the Medieval West* (London, 1986), 88.

[8] For brief discussion and further bibliography, see articles 'Angels' and 'Demons' in *Encyclopedia of the Early Church*, ed. A. di Berardino, 2 vols. (Cambridge, 1992), 38–40, 226–7; and for a recent medieval survey, D. Keck, *Angels and Angelology in the Middle Ages* (Oxford, 1998).

[9] See K. Frank, *Angelikos Bios: begriffsanalytische und begriffsgeschichtliche Untersuchung zum 'engelgle-ichen Leben' im frühen Mönchtum* (Munster, 1964); and P. Brown, *The Body and Society: Men, Women, and Sexual Renunciation in Early Christianity* (New York, 1988), 324–38.

Many Christians had been bemused by the sudden flowering in the desert of ascetic practices which had previously taken place in the Christian household. To characterize the monastic life as the angelic life, therefore, resolved a problem of classification for observers of the new monastic movement. At the same time there were dangers inherent in this identification. If men could become angels, fighting invisible demons on their own, this threatened to cast in a poor light the remaining 'terrestrial' Christians; and to place an unendurable burden of expectation on those who might themselves be considering discipleship of the desert fathers. If the association between monks and spiritual beings was made immediately, it also immediately generated ambivalence.[10]

Two centuries later Latin discussion of angels continued to reflect these uncertainties. On the one hand, we find in the *Life of the Jura Fathers* the confident assertion that Romanus, the first to venture as a recluse into the forests and mountains of the Jura, lived the *vita angelica*.[11] On the other hand, the *Rule of the Master*, in its very last chapter, specifically disavowed the notion of monks as angels, its author clearly mindful of the social pressures on the monastic community exerted by friends and enemies alike. Monks were not allowed to go wandering outside the cloister, mixing with the laity. They risked not only the crude mockery of detractors, but also the over-zealous veneration of the devout. 'Under their eyes, we may be worshipped as angels. . . . Perhaps they will take us for the saints we are not.'[12] To take advantage of this pious naivety is to invite demonic temptation. If monks seek the company of angels, they must with meticulous obedience apply themselves to the techniques of sanctity as set out in the *Rule*. In this sense, close as angels seem in the *Rule of the Master*, they stand in fact at a carefully judged remove from the human domain. This contrast between the enthusiasm of the hagiographer and the caution of the author of a Rule is, perhaps, only to be expected: all the more surprising, then, to find that overall the Master is more committed to angels than is the author of the *Life of the Jura Fathers*.

Both *Rule* and *Life* are grounded in the ascetic teaching of John Cassian; indeed, their angelogical uncertainties can be understood to derive from this source. In his *Conferences*, constructed as a series of dialogues between himself, his companion Germanus, and the desert fathers, Cassian seems to equivocate on the subject of angels. On the one hand, he avers, he had seen monks as angels, men who had undergone seraphic transformation.[13] On the other hand, speaking directly to his western audience, he insists that eastern practices are too difficult to follow—indeed, that the age of real achievement in terms of

---

[10] On this issue more broadly, see Markus, *End of Ancient Christianity*, 63–83.

[11] *VPJ* 12: SC 142, 252.   [12] *RMag* 95.17–21: SC 106, 446.

[13] Cassian, *Collationes*, VII.1–2, ed. E. Pichery, 3 vols. (Paris, 1955–9), SC 42, 58, 64: I, 244–6 on the suprahuman *castitas* of Abba Serenus, vouchsafed him by an angel. Appropriately enough, it is Serenus who speaks on angels and demons.

sanctity was effectively over.[14] In the past, in the desert, monks had communed with angels, wrestled with demons; now, in Gaul, the level of holiness was so low that demons could scarcely be bothered to engage in temptation, and angelic contact was at a low ebb.[15]

These pronouncements hardly account for Cassian's later influence as an angelological or ascetic authority. It is important not to mistake his withering critique of western asceticism in the light of his own desert experience for a detached verdict on the spiritual capacities of western ascetics: it was rather a warning to westerners to avoid the fate of their eastern counterparts. Although Cassian depicted his days and nights in the desert as a timeless encounter with the sources of spiritual wisdom, in fact he had witnessed his two most important mentors, Evagrius Pontus and John Chrysostom, condemned in the bitter feud over Origenism.[16] When Cassian arrived in Gaul he found local ascetics embroiled in rivalries with each other and in the vagaries of military and ecclesiastical politics. If he expressed scepticism about the possibility of leading the angelic life in the West, this was to give himself a rhetorical platform from which to warn of the demons of self-destructiveness that had overcome the ascetic movement in the eastern Mediterranean.[17]

In the substance of his analysis, applying the lessons taught him by Evagrius, Cassian set out a demonology and an angelology as a basis for a reconstructed asceticism that was better able to withstand the temptations of faction and polemic.[18] His starting-point was not whether ascetics could resemble angels, but whether or not demons could penetrate the recesses of the human mind. Cassian went to great lengths to explain how they could not: although spiritual beings, they were not actually incorporeal, for only God was truly without body. A demon seeking to tempt an ascetic had, therefore, to read the state of mind of the prospective victim from exterior signs—body language or verbal language—just as a thief creeping into a house at night throws fine sand around the room, and by the sound judges what is of value to steal.[19] Demons, then, no less than spiritual directors, were in the position of having to discern the contents of an ascetic's heart. Cassian went on to develop his own 'fine sand'—a science of the assessment of moral progress, to be used by the ascetic, and those more expert than he, to measure the contents of his heart and the extent to which it had been infiltrated by demons. Cassian's extremely well-known taxonomy of

[14] Cassian, *Institutiones*, pref. 8, ed. J.-C. Guy (Paris, 1965): SC 109, 30.

[15] Cassian, *Collationes*, VIII.23: SC 42, 265–6.

[16] See E. Clark, *The Origenist Controversy: The Cultural Construction of an Early Christian Debate* (Princeton, 1992).

[17] See further C. Leyser, '*Lectio divina, oratio pura*: Rhetoric and the Techniques of Asceticism in the *Conferences* of John Cassian', in *Modelli di santità e modelli di comportamento: contrasti, intersezioni, complementarità*, ed. G. Barone, M. Caffiero, and F. Scorza Barcellona (Turin, 1994), 79–105.

[18] On Cassian and Evagrius, see D. Marsili, *Giovanni Cassiano ed Evagrio Pontico* (Rome, 1936), and Stewart, *Cassian, passim*.

[19] Cassian, *Collationes*, VII.16: SC 42, 259–60.

the eight vices, from gluttony to pride, should therefore be understood in its demonological context.

By insisting that vice was demonic, Cassian offered ascetics a means of retaining a sense of objectivity. A man's sense of hopelessness, and no less his feeling of elation, as he made his laborious way along the path of moral virtue— both of these could represent diabolic illusion. Forearmed with such know-ledge, the ascetic could avoid falling prey to his every mood-swing. But while Cassian established a *modus vivendi* with the demonic, he did not entirely resolve how the individual ascetic might cohabit with his fellow humans, espe-cially those who were not of equal virtue. It was impossible, believed Cassian, for the morally weak to live in the same community as the spiritually strong without experiencing catastrophic discouragement.[20] While he saw many pit-falls to the life of the recluse and many advantages to the cenobitic life, he could not fix on either one as the institutional context for the ascetic technique which he had explained.[21] The tension between standards of perfection and the exigencies of community living—a tension arising from the moral charge of identifying the ascetic with the angelic life—continued to disrupt Cassian's attempt satisfactorily to conclude his argument. This was the problem his subsequent Latin readers had to solve.

THE MUTING OF ANGELS

The author of the *Life of the Jura Fathers* is keen to present himself and his *con-frères* as punctilious disciples of Cassian, fully accepting the need to adapt east-ern practices for a western audience.[22] The mention in the *Life* of a Rule has prompted scholars to speculate that the Jura communities represent the 'miss-ing link' between the fifth-century Rules of the island monastery of Lérins and the sixth-century Italian Rules of the Master, Eugippius of Lucullanum, and Benedict.[23] That this suggestion has met with little support need not deter us from comparing the *Life of the Jura Fathers* with the *Rule of the Master* for its treatment of angels and monastic community.[24]

[20] Cassian, *Collationes*, XVI.23–26: SC 58, 242–4.

[21] This argument is further developed by Leyser, '*Lectio divina, oratio pura*'.

[22] *VPJ* 174: SC 142, 426–8.

[23] See F. Masai, 'La "Vita Patrum Iurensium" et les débuts du monachisme à Saint-Maurice d'Agaune', in *Festschrift Bernhard Bischoff*, ed. J. Autenrieth and F. Brunhölzl (Stuttgart, 1971), 43–69; and 'Recherches sur le texte originel du de humilitate de Cassien (Inst. IV.39) et des Règles du Maître (RM X) et de Benoît (RB VII)', in *Latin Script and Letters A.D. 400–900: Festschrift Presented to Ludwig Bieler*, ed. J. J. O'Meara and B. Naumann (Leiden, 1976), 236–63.

[24] For critiques of Masai's work, see A. de Vogüé, 'Les Recherches de Francois Masai sur le Maître et saint Benoît. I. Inventaire et analyse II. Essai de synthèse et de bilan', *Studia Monastica*, 24 (1982), 7–42, 271–309; and K. Frank, 'Das Leben der Juraväter und die Magisterregel', *Regulae Benedicti Studia*, 13 (1986), 35–54. I. Wood, 'A Prelude to Columbanus: The Monastic Achievement in the Burgundian Territories', in *Columbanus and Merovingian Monasticism*, ed. H. B. Clarke and M. Brennan (Oxford, 1981), 3–32, offers an ingenious solution to the problem of the *Regula Eugendi*.

Angels attend the first and the last of the three Jura Fathers. The protagonists of the *Life* are: Romanus; his brother Lupicinus, who follows him into the wilderness; and their successor in the next generation, Eugendus, whose death the author himself witnessed. Romanus, as we have seen, is presented as a latter-day Antony, leading the angelic life.[25] A surrogate kinship is established between Romanus and Eugendus, who as a boy was granted a vision of angels descending and ascending to heaven, modelled on that of Jacob's dream (Gen. 28.12): 'Little by little, with great care, the troop of angels begins to mingle with the crowd of mortals; the angels pick up these mortal creatures, join together with them, and singing in unison go back up towards the heavens from whence they came.'[26] Eugendus' vision serves, perhaps, to demonstrate his worthiness as a successor to the founding fathers, and also to underscore the narrator's claim that the angelic holiness of the desert fathers has been definitively recreated in the Jura: from there mortals ascend into heaven to join the celestial hosts.

In the course of the narrative between Romanus' entry into the wilderness and the vision of Eugendus, however, we look in vain for an angelic presence. Granted the dangers of an argument *ex silentio caeli*, this muting of angels seems to represent a conscious decision on the part of the narrator. As his account unfolds it appears that the harmony of monastic community, and the proper functioning of abbatial authority, can best be maintained without the disruptive presence of supernatural beings. In the course of describing miracles of healing performed by Romanus and Lupicinus, the narrator tacitly observes a move on the part of the brothers to exclude both angels and demons from their monasteries.

Romanus lives, as it were, the textbook life of the charismatic. He enters the desert alone, attracts many followers, and returns to the city—in this case Geneva—in triumph. Two lepers cured by the holy man ensure that news of their healing is made public; Romanus is brought before the assembled clergy and people; the expulsion of disease from the bodies of the lepers becomes a cure of the ills of the social body.[27] Here is the holy man as bearer of supernatural objectivity, driving out sickness and social tension alike.[28]

Then comes a twist to the conventional plot. The *Life* starts to observe the moral 'fallout' from Romanus' conduct of the angelic life. The band of his disciples grows: many flocked to the holy man 'in rabid ambition . . . walking tall on their proud high heels'—the reference is to the theatre—with the intention of taking clerical office as soon as they can.[29] An old man comes to Romanus to complain about the uncontrolled incorporation into the community of too

---

[25] *VPJ* 12: SC 142, 252.   [26] *VPJ* 123: SC 142, 370–2.   [27] *VPJ* 45–50: SC 142, 288–94.
[28] The model established by P. Brown, 'The Rise and Function of the Holy Man in Late Antiquity', *Journal of Roman Studies*, 61 (1971), 80–101. For a sample of the extensive and ongoing discussion generated by this article, see the essays collected in *Journal of Early Christian Studies*, 6: 3 (1998).
[29] *VPJ* 21: SC 142, 262.

many new members, producing an unhealthy mix of young and old, the ascetically committed and fellow travellers. Surely it would be best to separate out an elite of true monks and expel the rest.[30] Romanus' impassioned answer denounces the pride of the old man, and insists that the community remain a mixed body: only God is in a position to make the segregation proposed by the elder.[31]

These tensions spill over into the career of Lupicinus, who joins Romanus in the wilderness and establishes a community of his own a few miles away. Lupicinus' asceticism is more extreme than that of his brother—during the last eight years of his life he refuses even water[32]—and Romanus has occasion to call on him to drive out a boisterous faction of gluttonous monks.[33] After Romanus' death Lupicinus took sole charge of the Jura communities, but the discontent of the elders over declining standards of observance rumbled on. One old monk in particular strove to emulate Lupicinus in the severity of his regime.[34] His body was so weak and debilitated that he looked like a leper. For seven years all he had eaten was the crumbs he could collect from the tables of the brethren once they had finished, moistened with water. The old man's physical sickness bespoke his demonic affliction with *cenodoxia*, vanity—diagnosed by the narrator in the terminology used by Cassian.[35]

In extraordinary circumstantial detail the *Life* describes the cure of this elder. Lupicinus 'came to his help with a healing touch so delicate that he did not seem to be blaming or in any way publicly censuring the excessive abstinence of the man'.[36] One day he took him outside into the garden, where he put a sheepskin on the ground in the middle of the vegetables and lay down on it, pretending to be suffering from the same affliction as the old man. Then Lupicinus began to stretch his arms and legs, rolling from side to side; he encouraged the old man to do the same, and he leant over him to stretch him out. With the old man beginning to move, Lupicinus ran into the cellar, picked up some pieces of bread, and dipped them in wine. He poured a generous helping of oil over a whole plate of food, and in the name of monastic obedience charged the old man to eat. This dietary and exercise programme continued for a week, until the old man was fully restored to physical and spiritual health. The narrator comments: 'Everyone who is engaged in the monastic profession must avoid the steep drop to the right of them or the crevasses to the left: all must keep strictly to the middle.'[37]

At one level, the story of the old man's cure can be read as a successful disabling of an ascetic rival whose austerity threatened Lupicinus' pre-eminence.

---

[30] *VPJ* 27–8: SC 142, 268–70. [31] *VPJ* 29–34: SC 142, 270–8, striking a notably Augustinian tone.
[32] *VPJ* 66, 116: SC 142, 312, 360. [33] *VPJ* 36–41: SC 142, 278–84.
[34] See *VPJ* 71–8: SC 142, 318–24 for the whole incident.
[35] Cassian, *Institutiones*, XI: SC 426–46. [36] *VPJ* 72: SC 142, 318.
[37] *VPJ* 77: SC 142, 322–4. For the image of the *via regia* in monastic tradition, see J. Leclercq, *L'Amour des lettres et le désir de Dieu* (Paris, 1957), 102–5.

In the process, however, the character of Lupicinus' authority is itself transformed. The narrator's 'middle way' is not simply a euphemism for abbatial power. The cure involves a renunciation of excessive asceticism by the old man—but also the refusal of the extravagant public celebration attendant on Romanus' cure of the lepers outside Geneva. Lupicinus' miracle remains one of persuasion in relative secrecy, with no spectacular revelation before a crowd; it is a cure, not an exorcism, in which both demons and angels have quietly dropped out of view.[38]

While the humane perspective of the *Life of the Jura Fathers* may charm its modern readers, in the sixth century such studious naturalism may have seemed eccentric. The banishing of angels to the heavens, their confinement to a contemplative role, and the systematic articulation of a natural sphere largely exempt from angelic intervention—all of this lay far in the medieval future.[39] The Italian contemporaries of the Jura author devoted their best efforts to developing an account of the monastery fully inclusive of angels.

ANGELIC SUPERVISION

In the *Rule of the Master* Latin angelology was definitively conscripted to support an institutionalized asceticism—the cenobitic life under an abbot and a Rule. The Master knew his Cassian at least as well as the Jura author, and was no less committed to an approach that removed Cassian's lingering reserve about the achievement of cenobitic community. Rather than evade supernatural beings, however, the Master decided to invoke their ministrations whenever possible, although he was far from indiscriminate. As we have seen at the outset, in his discussion of the monk's deportment during psalmody the Master laid less emphasis on the hovering presence of demons than of angels, and he paid less attention to the eradication of vice than to the attainment of virtue. The dominant image of the first part of the text, setting out the spiritual basis for the administrative arrangements which follow, is the ladder of humility, based on Jacob's vision of angels ascending and descending between heaven and earth. The monk is urged to make of his own body and soul a ladder, which he may hope to ascend as he grows in lowliness, conscious that angels watch his every move and report daily to the Lord on his progress.[40]

The regime of angelic vigilance subtends the structure of human authority within the community. The Master envisages his monks divided into groups of

[38] The same shift from charismatic exorcism to 'bureaucratic' cure is recapitulated in the account of Eugendus as a healer: see *VPJ* 141–8: SC 142: 388–98. Cf. the restraint on his own powers of cursing exercised by John Gualbert in eleventh-century Tuscany, as interpreted by R. I. Moore, 'Family, Community and Cult on the Eve of the Gregorian Reform', *TRHS* 30 (1980), 49–69, at 54–5.

[39] See Mayr-Harting, *Perceptions of Angels*, 13–21.

[40] *RMag* 10.5–13: SC 105, 418–20. See S. Pricoco, 'La scala di Giacobbe—L'interpretazione ascetica di Gen. 28, 12 da Filone a San Benedetto', *Regulae Benedicti Studia*, 14–15 (1985/6), 41–58.

ten; each group is supervised by a prior, whose scrutiny of words and gestures must be as close as that of the angels.[41] Those who visit the community are no less subject to this regime: lodged apart, in quarters with no monastery tools or utensils, they are to be accompanied by two monks on a twenty-four-hour basis.[42] *Custodia, custodire, cautela custodiendi*: these are the watchwords of the text.[43] A renunciation of the identity of the monastic and the angelic life, the *Rule of the Master* is, by the same token, an extraordinary attempt to imagine in relentless detail what life would be like when lived in the company of guardian angels, who were indefatigably on guard.

The role of angels in the *Rule of the Master* is not only to discipline or punish. The pressure of angelic supervision felt in the *Rule* coexists with an equally powerful evocation of the way in which the inmate of the community could return the watchful gaze of the angels, like Jacob in his dream. Refusing to countenance the attainment of angelic status in this life, the *Rule* is expansive upon the celestial rewards for ascent of the ladder of humility. In the eternal life to come true monks may expect to dwell in a garden of unimaginable sensory delight. Willed deprivation in this world entitles the monk in paradise to satiety at will: in the heavenly garden he has only to set eyes upon something and he will taste it in his mouth. 'One hears there the sounds of instruments on the banks of the rivers, accompanying the hymns which the pure and holy angels and archangels, antiphonally singing the psalms in a choir, chant in praise of the Lord.'[44] On earth monks had laboured to attain perfect deportment in their psalmody. In heaven the angels would sing for the monks.

In this evocation of paradise the Master drew from the *passiones* of the Roman martyrs and from apocalyptic visionary literature, and it is vividly juxtaposed with the passages of ascetic exhortation derived from Cassian.[45] While the rhetorical effect is one of variation of tone, substantively, the texts of the visionary tradition are no less didactic than the *Institutes* or *Conferences*, and they serve to reinforce the *Rule*'s moral caution in its handling of angels. As an example, we can take the so-called *Apocalypse* or *Vision of Paul*, one of the Master's principal sources for his description of paradise. The anonymous author of the *Vision* presents his text as a manuscript discovered in Tarsus, a supposedly long-hidden account by Paul of his experience of the third heaven, briefly described in the correspondence with the Corinthians (2 Cor. 12). The unearthing of the manuscript is said to have taken place during the reign of the

---

[41] *RMag* 11.35–6: SC 106, 14–16.   [42] *RMag* 79: SC 106, 322–8.

[43] See e.g. *RMag* 11: SC 106, 6, announcing the programme for the rest of the *Rule*: 'Incipit ordo monasterii: modus, observatio, gradus, continentia, custodia et mensura . . .'

[44] *RMag* 3.90: SC 105, 374 at the conclusion of the *ars sancta*; cf. *RMag* 10.94–117 and 90.17–27: SC 105, 438–44, concluding the chapter on humility, and drawing on the *Passio Sebastiani* 13: PL 17, 1117–19, and on the *Visio Pauli*, 23: *Apocrypha Anecdota*, ed. M. R. James, Texts and Studies, II.3 (Cambridge, 1893), 24.

[45] See SC 105, 214–20 for comment on the Master's use of these sources; and now K. Cooper, 'The Widow as Impresario: The Widow Barbaria in Eugippius's *Vita Severini*', in *Eugippius und Severin: Der Autor, der Text, und der Heilige*, ed. M. Diesenberger (Vienna, forthcoming 2000).

emperor Theodosius, and in fact a Latin version of the text seems to have been in circulation in the early fifth century.[46] The apostle is conducted by an angel around the domains of the saved and the damned. Among their ranks he sees figures who would have been instantly recognizable to a late Roman audience—ascetics, bishops, priests, deacons, lectors, the whole array of the recently empowered Christian establishment. In other words, as the Master appreciated, the *Vision of Paul* is an explicit attempt to draw upon familiar apocalyptic and angelogical material in order to address contemporary issues of power and responsibility in the church.

The apocalyptic tradition was, from its inception in the second century BC, a scholarly vehicle for criticism of the priesthood, and at first glance the *Vision* seems to conform to the genre, setting off the purity of the ascetic life against the mismanagement and corruption of church officialdom.[47] Angels rejoice as they carry word to God of those who have left the world 'to wander as strangers and live in a cave of the rocks; they weep every hour they are on the earth'.[48] On the apostle's tour of hell, meanwhile, he sees clerics languishing for their neglect of their responsibilities and their vicious abuse of power.[49] Then Paul observes that the status of ascetics is also open to abuse. He is guided to men and women who are 'clothed in rags full of tar and sulphurous fire . . . and angels with fiery horns confined them, and struck them and closed up their nostrils'. The apostle asks: 'Who are these, sir? And [the angel] said to me: They are those who seemed to renounce the world by wearing our raiment, but the tribulations of the world made them miserable . . . They did not take in the stranger or the pilgrim . . . nor show mercy to their neighbour. Not even for one day did their prayer go up pure to the Lord.' The false ascetics are rebuked by the lay sinners for their pretensions: 'We knew that we were sinners; we saw you in holy clothing and we called you blessed . . . but now we have seen that in vain you were called by the name of God.'[50]

The *Vision of Paul* may have been generated in a literate lay circle suspicious of the public posturing both of churchmen and of ascetics; or it may represent a self-critical discourse from these same newly prominent groups. Whatever the source, the message is clear enough: ascetics in particular had to beware of

[46] For discussions of the dating and the textual tradition of the *Visio Pauli*, see R. Casey, 'The Apocalypse of Paul', *Journal of Theological Studies*, 34 (1933), 1–32, and T. Silverstein, *Visio sancti Pauli* (London, 1935). For an English translation of the oldest extant Latin version (to be found in an eighth-century Fleury manuscript, and transcribed in *Apocrypha Anecdota*, ed. James), see E. Hennecke, *New Testament Apocrypha*, II (hereafter *NTA* II), ed. W. Schneemelcher and R. Wilson (Philadelphia, 1965), 755–98. For full bibliography, see now K. Zelzer, art. *Acta Pauli*, in *Handbuch der Lateinischen Literatur der Antike*, IV, ed. R. Herzog and P. L. Schmidt (Munich, 1997), sec. 470.8.
[47] See M. Himmelfarb, *Ascent to Heaven in Jewish and Christian Apocalypses* (Oxford, 1993).
[48] *Visio Pauli*, 9: ed. James, 14; *NTA* II, 762.
[49] *Visio Pauli*, 34–6: ed. James, 29–30.
[50] *Visio Pauli*, 40: ed. James, 32; *NTA* II, 784–5. While not directly used in *RMag*, this passage is repeatedly cited by the Master's contemporary, Caesarius of Arles: see B. Fischer, 'Impedimenta mundi fecerunt eos miseros', *Vigiliae Christianae*, 5 (1951), 84–7.

overstating their case. The angels with whom they claimed intimacy could easily turn against them if they fell short of the mark. This was a message fully assimilated by the Master. At dawn and at dusk, he reminds his readers, 'our angels' report to the Lord on the good deeds of the just. 'As the holy Paul says in his Revelation: "Sons of men, praise the Lord without ceasing, but above all at sunset."'[51] In the *Rule of the Master* the angelic life of the desert recluse is modulated for cenobites who moved among angels, 'thousands upon thousands of them'.[52] It is a society monks can expect to enjoy in perpetuity, so long as their vigilance with regard to their own conduct matches that of the heavenly hosts.

How many angels are there, then, in the *Rule of St Benedict*? It is now all but universally accepted that Benedict composed his own *Rule* with a copy of the *Rule of the Master* before him. One of his central concerns was to do more than the Master to prevent differences of social or moral status between individual monks from disrupting the overall harmony of the community.[53] Whether he regarded angels as a help or a hindrance is less clear. On the one hand, in his clauses on psalmody Benedict omitted the Master's condemnation of spitting and coughing. He also excised wholesale the evocation of the angelic choirs in paradise.[54] Similarly, his prescriptions for the treatment of the sick and the correction of sinners eschew the dramatic language of exorcism, and recall rather the tactful, callisthenic approach of Lupicinus.[55] On the other hand, Benedict affirmed without hesitation the Master's basic premiss that the monastic community coexisted with the community of angels, and that each monk has an angel personally assigned to him who reported continually to God on his actions, in particular at dawn and at dusk.[56] We are left with two possibilities. The first is that Benedict has intentionally minimized the angelic emphasis of the *Rule of the Master*; and leans towards the humanism of the Jura author. The second is that he assumes in his reader a knowledge of the Master, in which case we must accord to the Master's angels a central place in the Benedictine community.

Benedict is the best-known early reader of the Master: we may turn to the best-known reader of the *Rule of St Benedict* for an adjudication of the question of angels. In his account of St Benedict in the *Dialogues*, Pope Gregory the Great, the most influential angelological writer of the early Middle Ages, depicts

---

[51] *RMag* 34.9–10: SC 106, 188–90, citing *Visio Pauli*, 7: ed. James, 13. See also *RMag* 10.13, 10.39 on angels at dawn and dusk.

[52] *Visio Pauli*, 16: ed. James, 18.

[53] See on this theme, H. Mayr-Harting, *The Venerable Bede, the Rule of St Benedict, and Social Class*, Jarrow Lecture (Jarrow, 1976).

[54] See *RBen* 19.5–6: SC 182, 536 on psalmody; and *RBen* 4.76; 7.70: SC 181, 462–4; 490 for the excision of paradise. Cf. the much less stringent abridgements of *RMag* made in *Regula Eugippii*, ed. F. Villegas and A. de Vogüé (Vienna, 1976), CSEL 87: *REug* 24.22: CSEL 87, 42 repeats the clause against spitting, and *REug* 28.87–112: CSEL 87, 59–60 repeats *RMag* 10.92–117 on the heavenly rewards for humility.

[55] See *RBen* 36: SC 106, 570–2 on cure; *RBen* 46.5: SC 106, 596 on secret rebuke.

[56] *RBen* 7.13–28: SC 181, 476–80.

his subject as living in a landscape that swarms with angels and demons.[57] His informants, whom Gregory is careful to identify, were Benedict's disciples at Subiaco and Montecassino: in their memory at least, Benedict was no stranger to the supernatural.

It would be fair to add that the *Dialogues* tell us at least as much about Gregory's relationship to angels as about that enjoyed by Benedict. Gregory rarely missed an opportunity to discourse about angels. In his *Homilies on the Gospels*, for example, delivered in a liturgical context before the people of Rome, the pope did not hesitate to involve the congregation in a lengthy discussion of the angelic hierarchy. Anticipating the accusation of irrelevance, Gregory argued:

But what good does it do to speak briefly of these angelic spirits, if we are not zealous to turn them to our profit by appropriate reflection on what we have said . . . Since we believe that the multitude of humans that is going to ascend to the heavenly city is equal to the multitude of angels that never left, it remains for those humans who are returning to their heavenly homeland to imitate some of these bands of angels, in the process of their return.[58]

The ethical imperative of Gregory's angelology applied not only to monks, but to all the faithful.

Gregory's angels have many ranks and, as is well known, he drew on the *Celestial Hierarchy* of Pseudo-Denys to enumerate them—a source which appears to take him far from the crowded intimacy of the angels in the *Rule of the Master*.[59] But while the neoplatonic Pseudo-Denys stressed the resonance between cosmic and ecclesiastical hierarchies, Gregory's point was, in fact, grounded in the angelology of the western ascetic tradition. His interest lay in the moral character of authority, be it on earth or in heaven. Angels for Gregory were not only the embodiment of the divine contemplation toward which all must strive; crucially, they were also models of virtuous leadership. Here is his description of the Seraphim, taken from the same passage in the *Homilies on the Gospels*:

And some are set on fire by supernal contemplation, and are filled with eager desire for their Creator alone. They no longer long for anything in this world, they are nourished by love of eternity alone, they thrust aside all earthly things; their hearts transcend every temporal thing; they love, they are on fire, they find rest in this fire; loving speech sets them on fire, and they enkindle others too with their speech: those they touch with their words they instantly set on fire with love of God. What then should I call these people whose hearts, which have been turned into fire, are shining and burning, but Seraphim?[60]

[57] See e.g. Gregory, *Dialogorum Libri Quattuor*, II.4; II.35.3: SC 260, ed. A. de Vogüé (Paris, 1979); 150–2, 238. For further discussion, see S. Boesch Gajano, 'Demoni e miracoli nei *Dialoghi* di Gregorio Magno', in *Hagiographies, cultures, sociétés IVᵉ–XIIᵉ siècles* (Paris, 1981), 398–445.

[58] Gregory, *Homiliae in Evangelia*, II.34.11: PL 76, col. 1252C; tr. D. Hurst, Cistercian Studies Series 123 (Kalamazoo, 1990), 289.

[59] See C. Micaelli, 'L'angelologia di Gregorio Magno tra oriente e occidente', *Koinonia*, 16 (1992), 35–51.

[60] Gregory, *HEv* II.34.11: PL 76, col. 1253B; tr. Hurst, 291.

One begins here to see the magnetism of angels for Gregory, for he is able in discussing them to strike simultaneously two themes which are central to his moral writing: the interdependence of action and contemplation, and the urgency of the preacher's task in extending inspiration to the community around him. For all that he owes to neoplatonic cosmology and to monastic tradition, Gregory's angels carry their own message.

In this respect, however, angels resemble any other element of the patristic legacy handed down to the medieval church. The intimacy of a tradition well-studied, and even internalized, coexists with a readiness to take flight in new directions, to respond to altered contexts and changed human needs. So viewed, every early medieval monk *was* an angel, a messenger from another country, whether from heaven or from the past.

2

GREGORY THE GREAT'S PAGANS

R. A. Markus

'Pagan' is a notoriously difficult word for historians. We think we know what we mean by it, and only the most pernickety among us keep insisting that we don't, and that we had better be clear and define it. I have been as tiresomely insistent as anyone that we must at least begin with a preliminary clarification: we should be clear as to whether we are speaking of 'pagans' in our own terms, in which case we must be prepared to say what *we* mean by the word; or of 'pagans' as they were conceived by whoever is the subject of our discussion—early or medieval Christians, bishops, writers, missionaries—in which case we must be clear as to what *they* meant by it.[1] For one thing is certain: the word has been slippery in the extreme, and its history—which is, of course, by no means over—is complex, interesting, and largely uninvestigated.

The author of *The Coming of Christianity to Anglo-Saxon England*[2] knows much more about pagans in Britain than did Gregory the Great, or, for that matter, than Bede thought edifying enough to put in his *Ecclesiastical History*. But even if we are clear that what we are to discuss is what other people, at some particular time and place, have meant by paganism, we are far from out of the wood. Often they were not much clearer about it than are we modern historians. Gregory the Great is a case in point: he may have thought he knew what he meant when he spoke of pagans, but, if he did, he has certainly not made it easy for us to discover what he meant. We must be on our guard against assuming that the lack of a clear, unambiguous vocabulary is 'only' a matter of linguistic usage. Yet if we can elucidate the way Gregory used his language, we shall certainly be closer to understanding the manner in which he perceived the reality. I shall therefore begin by surveying his vocabulary, and then examine the way he thought of pagans and paganism in practice; in a final section I shall briefly raise some questions about missionary homiletics.

---

[1] I have discussed these problems at length in *The End of Ancient Christianity* (Cambridge, 1990), esp. 1–17; 'L'Autorité épiscopale et la définition de la chrétienté', *Studia Ephemeridis Augustinianum*, 58 (1997), 37–43 (for the late fourth and early fifth centuries); and for the sixth and seventh centuries, in 'From Caesarius to Boniface: Christianity and paganism in Gaul', in *Le Septième Siècle: Changements et continuités / The Seventh Century: Change and Continuity*, ed. J. Fontaine and J. N. Hillgarth (London, 1992), 154–72.
[2] H. Mayr-Harting, *The Coming of Christianity to Anglo-Saxon England* (London, 1972), 22.

THE WORDS

There is a cluster of words Gregory uses to designate people who are not Jews or Christians: *gentiles, infideles, impii, iniqui, idolorum cultores, pagani*. The words are not exact synonyms, though they overlap in use. Little would be gained by a complete survey of Gregory's usage. I confine myself here to mapping some of its more significant features.

The commonest of these terms, *gentilis*, has biblical resonances, and usually bears the biblical meaning 'gentiles', the Old Testament's *goyim*. They are destined to be, and sometimes already have been, converted to Christ, thus helping to constitute the Church composed of 'two peoples', Jews and Gentiles.[3] The *gentiles* can of course also be those who have rejected him.[4] The latter are sometimes described as *idolorum cultores*.[5] All this corresponds to well-established usage. Gregory's term *gentiles* ('gentiles' or 'heathen', as I shall translate it) is in fact a quasi-theological designation of the non-Jewish world as called to salvation by Jesus. The gentile world (*gentilitas*) is the *locus* of God's *misericordia*;[6] it has a continuing role in the economy of salvation which does not end with the apostolic times in which the group was split in two—into those who believed in, and those who rejected Jesus. Thus discussing Job's 7,000 sheep and 3,000 camels (Job 1.3), Gregory makes the former stand for 'the perfect innocence of some of those who have come to the perfection of grace from the pastures of the Law'; while the latter stand for 'the twisted wickedness of the heathen (*torta gentilium vitiositas*) who have come to the fullness of the faith'. A little further into this passage these camels are not only morally twisted, but have not yet come to the faith, never mind to its fullness: these gentiles are burdened with the cult of idols.[7] The *gentiles* have either already entered the *ecclesia* or have still to do so.[8] Thus they are not only the people from whom the *ecclesia ex gentilibus* has been recruited, they are also those from whom it is still to be recruited, or who may refuse to be recruited. In this sense they merge into present-day, living non-Christians. So, for example, Gregory speaks of Italy during the Lombard wars as 'ravaged by gentile swords'.[9] He habitually uses the

---

[3] e.g. *Mor.* (*Moralia*, ed. Adriaen, CCSL 143, 143A, 143B) XIX.23.40. For some further examples of this commonplace in Gregory's writings, see *Mor.* II.29.48; VII.10.11; XIX.23.39–40; XXV.14.32; *HEv* (*Homiliae in Evangelia*, PL 76) I.14.4; *In Cant.* (*Expositio in Canticum Canticorum*, ed. Verbraken, CCSL 146) 39.

[4] This theme is very frequent in Gregory's work. For good extended examples, see e.g. *Mor.* XXVII.43.71–44.73; XXIX.25.50–26.51; 27.54–29.56; *HEz* (*Homiliae in Hiezechielem*, ed. Adriaen, CCSL 142), I.2.11–14; Fr. II (= Paterius, *In Gen.*, c. 53).

[5] e.g. *Mor.* I.15.21.   [6] *Mor.* XXVII.34.58.

[7] *Mor.* I.15.21: 'quia igitur per oves, Hebraeos pascuis legis ad fidem venientes accipimus, nihil obstat ut per camelos tortos moribus atque onustos idolorum cultibus gentilium populos sentiamus'. Cf. XXXV.16.36–41.

[8] e.g. '... aggregandam Deo gentilitatem ...' (*Mor.* II.29.48).

[9] *HEv* I.1.1. Here the word comes close to synonymity with 'barbarian'; cf. also e.g. *Dial.* (*Dialogorum libri IV*, ed. A. De Vogüé, SC 251, 260, 265), III.37.2; III.1.3. *Ep.* (*Epistola[e]* ed. Norberg, CCSL 140, 140A), II.2 is interesting in that *gentiles* among the Lombards are distinguished from heretics.

word in its biblical sense, and allows it a contemporary application: the biblical category can embrace existing pagans. For Gregory, *gentiles*, heathen, are all about us still.

Moreover, his favoured moral exposition of the scripture pushed him relentlessly towards finding the 'gentile' within the Church itself. Thus, for instance, after an extended discussion of the calling of the gentiles, he remarks:

> These things, which we have said generally concerning the gentiles, we may also, if we consider the matter closely, see among individuals within the bosom of the Church. For there are many here who are heedless of God's words, who, though claiming the name of faith, hear the words of life with their ears but do not let it penetrate into the inner chambers of their hearts . . .[10]

Gregory comes close to saying that *gentiles* are not only all about us, but are also within the Church; however, it is important to note that he does not actually call these Christians 'heathens': he says only that they are very like them. The biblical sense of the word seems to have had a powerful enough hold on Gregory's usage to prevent such an extension. *Gentiles* are outsiders. The term functions as a theological category—to define those not within the faithful community.

Much the same pattern can be observed in Gregory's alternative vocabulary: the term *infidelis* refers to outsiders, contrasted with *fideles*, the faithful. Gregory appears to want to map the logical relations between the labels with a clarity and care unusual for him: '"Impious" (*impius*) stands for "infidel" (*pro infideli ponitur*), that is to say for one who is alien to the piety of religion; whereas one is said to be wicked (*iniquus*) who deviates from righteousness by the wickedness of his works, though perhaps he bear the name of Christian.'[11] *Infidelis* is the outsider, the *iniquus* can be an insider; and *impius* in scriptural usage, Gregory says, is equivalent to 'infidel', both implying 'faithlessness', which says more than mere sinfulnes or iniquity.[12] Thus the faithless and persecuting people—here the Jews—can be designated by the title of 'impious'.[13] The *impii* who are 'the prey of inner vice' will in the time of trial readily fall into the whirlpool of overt *infidelitas*.[14] The saints pray neither for the defunct *infideles* nor the *impii*.[15] *Infidelis* and *impius*, to summarize, tend to be synonymous and to stand for the outsider; whereas *iniquus* is wider in meaning, and can refer to bad Christians as well.

Once again, however, we can observe Gregory's penchant for blurring the boundaries: although he does, as we have just seen, distinguish between Christians and 'infidels' (or the 'impious'), the distinction is apt to be rapidly

---

[10] *Mor.* XXIX.26.53.
[11] *Mor.* XVIII.6.12: 'impius namque pro infideli ponitur, id est a pietate religionis alienus; iniquus vero dicitur, qui pravitate operis ab aequitate discordat, vel qui fortasse christianae fidei nomen portat.'
[12] *Mor.* XXV.10.25; *HEz* I.11.11.
[13] *Mor.* IX.28.44: 'potest ergo nomine impii infidelis ac persecutor populus designari.'
[14] *Mor.* XXIX.6.11.   [15] *Mor.* XXXIV.19.38; *Dial.* IV.46.8.

subverted and the dichotomy blurred. The sins of the *infideles* are also to be found among carnally minded, or proud Christians within the Church, who are like the infidel.[16] The cloud which hides the truth from the infidel does not do so only for 'those placed outside', but also for those living carnally within the Church.[17] Many who now seem to be among the *fideles*, will turn out to be enemies of the faith;[18] many things show that some who are 'placed within the Church's peace, are in fact infidels'.[19]

Only in the last of these examples is the distinction between 'infidels' and members of the Church breached. As in the case of 'gentile' (or 'heathen': *gentilis*), Gregory prefers to keep *infidelis* to designate outsiders; members of the Church are often *like* 'infidels', and Gregory fondly dwells on qualities which make them so. He is reluctant actually to call a Christian an 'infidel'. The difference between the two vocabularies of *gentilis* and *infidelis* is thus not drastic. Both *gentilis* and *infidelis* are opposed to *fidelis*, but whereas *gentiles* cannot be found within the christian community, *infideles*, in occasional passages, can. The doublet *fidelis/gentilis* functioned as a theological category, its terms taken as mutually exclusive. *Fidelis/infidelis* was largely similar, but functioned a little more widely, in a manner which allowed application of both terms to (bad) contemporary Christians.

Although Gregory had the vocabulary to allow him to distinguish them, the boundary between wicked Christians and faithless outsiders was very labile, easily effaced. As we shall see, this precariousness of the dichotomy between 'pagan' and 'Christian' had serious implications for Gregory's missionary ideas, which I now turn to examine.

THE FACTS

To discuss Gregory's missionary concerns we need to turn to his correspondence. The word *paganus* occurs only in his letters; but it is not the only one he uses to refer to the objects of his missionary enterprises. All the words we have already considered, as well as phrases such as *idolorum cultores* and the like, crop up to designate the unbeliever. But what precisely is this unbeliever? The answer, as we shall see, is not at all straightforward. What Gregory refers to, and how the word relates to the language of 'faithful/infidel', is the subject of this second part of my enquiry.

---

[16] e.g. *Mor.* III.19.35: 'sed quid ista de infidelibus dicimus, cum ipsa quoque ecclesia multos carnalium, pravis moribus contra redemptoris vitam pugnare videamus?'

[17] *Mor.* XXVIII.17.37: 'Haec nubes non solum solet infideles extra positos premere; sed quosdam etiam viventes carnaliter intra ecclesiam tenebrare.' Cf. *Mor.* XXXI.5.7.

[18] *Mor.* XXIX.6.12–7.14.

[19] *Mor.* XXIX.7.16: 'sunt praeterea plurima, quae quosdam in ipsa pace ecclesiae constitutos infideles esse renuntient.' The theme of Christians 'in name' only is, of course, a Gregorian commonplace: e.g. *HEv* II.32.5.

It has been remarked that Gregory hardly ever speaks of pagans in concrete terms: he leaves it to his reader to decide what exactly he is referring to.[20] He was aware of pockets of paganism remaining in Italy. Only a generation ago St Benedict had discovered 'foolish rustic people worshipping Apollo in the manner of the ancients', at a very old sanctuary; all round the shrine 'an insane multitude of infidels sweated at sacrilegious sacrifices' in honour of the demons. Benedict, Gregory tells us, after destroying the idol and upturning the altar, built an oratory dedicated to St Martin in the shrine and one to St John on the site of the altar (where he was to be buried); and he then called the multitude to the faith by constant preaching.[21] Was Gregory thinking of the 'insane multitude' who sacrificed to demons as unbaptized pagans? Were the 'poor foolish rustics' worshipping Apollo perhaps baptized Christians, who, being country bumpkins, knew no better than to follow ancient cult practices? Were there in fact two such distinct groups? Did Gregory believe there were? The kindly indulgence of his language in regard to the former ('poor foolish rustics') compared with the greater savagery of his denunciation of the latter ('insane multitude . . .') suggests that he was thinking of two distinct groups; but we cannot be sure. In any case, they tend to coalesce in his narrative, as they probably did in reality—if indeed there were two.

This uncertainty also infects what Gregory has to say about pagans of his own day. Sometimes the meaning of *paganus* is unambiguous: for instance, when he made arrangements for the purchase of English slaves in Provence, Gregory wanted a priest to travel with them to Rome so that if any of them were to fall ill on the journey they could be baptized in case of imminent death, 'for they are pagans' (*pagani*).[22] Here clearly 'pagans' are unbaptized persons. Similarly, quite often Gregory uses the word with legal precision to distinguish people who are neither Jews nor Christians,[23] or to describe Roman emperors before Constantine.[24]

So far as these examples go, as a term of exclusion, *paganus* may seem to be precise enough to define a category—non-Christians and non-Jews—without ambiguity. Gregory certainly could, when he wanted to, discriminate between pagans in this narrow sense and others of whose religious observance he

---

[20] P. Benkart, 'Die Missionsidee Gregors d. Grossen', Diss., Leipzig, 1946, ch. I/2.

[21] *Dial*. II.8.10–11: 'ubi uetustissimum fanum fuit, in quo ex antiquorum more gentilium ab stulto rusticorum populo Apollo colebatur. Circumquaque etiam in cultu daemonum luci succreverant, in quibus adhuc eodem tempore infidelium insana multitudo sacrificiis sacrilegis insudabat. Ibi itaque vir dei perveniens, contriuit idolum, subvertit aram, succidit lucos, atque in ipso templo Apollinis oraculum beati Martini, ubi vero ara eiusdem Apollinis fuit, oraculum sancti construxit Iohannis, et commorantem circumquaque multitudinem praedicatione continua ad fidem vocabat'. Similarly in II.19.1. On Benedict's burial site, II.37.

[22] *Ep*. VI.10. The slaves to be purchased from among the Barbaricini in Sardinia are not identifiable as pagan or as baptized: *Ep*. IX.124. Slaves purchased *de externis finibus* (apparently this includes Gaul: *Ep*. IX.105) were evidently often pagan: *Ep*. VI.29.

[23] e.g. *Ep*. VI.29, 30 (referring to slaves who are neither Christian nor Jewish); VIII.35.

[24] *Ep*. V.36.

disapproved. Corsica is a case in point. The area seems to have been full of people whose Christian faith was dubious or non-existent. Writing to a bishop in the recently revived Corsican see of Aleria, Gregory clearly distinguished 'those who were once faithful, but have relapsed into the cult of idols from their own negligence or through no fault of their own (*neglegentia aut necessitate faciente*)' from those who have not been baptized. The bishop was to deal differently with these two different groups. The lapsed he should try to bring back to the faith (*ad fidem reducere*) they had deserted, by imposing several days of penance, so that repenting their guilt and returning to their faith they might, with the Lord's help, hold to it the more firmly for their repentance. The unbaptized, by contrast, were to be 'gathered to the Lord, by admonishing, by entreaty, by the threat of the coming judgement, by explaining why they ought not to worship sticks and stones'.[25] The distinction between the two kinds of people is here absolutely clear. It is echoed in a remarkable passage of the *Moralia* to which I shall return below, where the Church is said 'now to preach knowledge of the Trinity to infidels, now to preach the four [cardinal] virtues to the faithful'; for 'the holy Church accommodates its preaching carefully to the state of the hearers' minds'.[26]

Evidently, Gregory appreciated the distinction between baptized Christians who had relapsed into their former bad ways, and persons who had never been baptized; and he knew the two categories needed two correspondingly different sorts of preaching. This seems to anticipate the modern missiological distinction between mission to pagans (*Heidenmission*) and spiritual care of converts (*Neophytenseelsorge*; *innerkirchliche Nacharbeit*).[27] In practice, however, it was only in this single case of Aleria and never in any other missionary situation that Gregory actually applied this distinction between unbaptized pagans and other people whose religion was in some manner suspect or objectionable. Evidently we need to examine his language in relation to what he tells us about particular situations.

Gregory uses the word *paganus* only twice in letters concerning the conversion of non-Christians, and they both relate to Sardinia.[28] In Sardinia, as in Corsica, a recently revived bishopric (Fausiana) was intended to deal with the problem that had apparently been caused by a cessation of episcopal ministry over some considerable time. As a consequence, Gregory wrote to the archbishop of Caralis, saying 'we know that some pagans have remained in those regions, living in the manner of beasts; they are altogether ignorant of the

[25] *Ep.* VIII.1. I have translated *necessitate faciente* as 'through no fault of their own'; in the light of *Ep.* IV.29 *pro rerum necessitate* may refer to inadequate pastoral care in difficult times, as in Sardinia.
[26] *Mor.* XXIX.31.72. See below, at n. 53.
[27] Cf. H.-D. Kahl, 'Die ersten Jahrhunderte des missionsgeschichtlichen Mittelalters. Bausteine für eine Phänomenologie bis ca. 1050', in *Kirchengeschichte als Missionsgeschichte*. Band 2: *Die Kirche des frühen Mittelalters*, ed. K. Schäferdiek ([Erster Halbband] München, 1978), 11–76, at 40–2: 'Christianisierung' and 'Entpaganisierung'.
[28] *Ep.* IV.26 and 29. (Ep. VI.10 has been referred to above, n. 22).

worship of God'.[29] The archbishop was instructed to provide a bishop for them who would have the required pastoral zeal and would be equal to the task of 'bringing to the Lord's flock those who have strayed'.[30] Gregory had spoken of 'pagans' here; but we may suspect that the situation would not have differed very much from what we (and Gregory) have seen to be the case in Corsica. Another, later letter to the same archbishop confirms the suspicion: now there is no mention of pagans. Gregory admonishes the archbishop

to keep zealous guard with pastoral care against worshippers of idols or soothsayers and sorcerers (*idolorum . . . cultores vel aruspicum atque sortilegorum*); to preach publicly before the people against men guilty of this sort of thing; to recall (*revocare*) them, with persuasive exhortation, from the taint of so great a sacrilege and the danger they court of the divine judgement as well as to their life here [on earth].[31]

'Worshippers of idols' leaves all possibilities open; *idolorum cultores* could well refer to people whom elsewhere Gregory calls 'pagans', or could at any rate include such people among a more mixed group. The others here referred to are more specific, and look like baptized Christians indulging in traditional rituals still widely practised in what appears to be a rural society. They are all to be 'called *back*' (*revocare*) by the bishop's preaching from their sinful ways. The bishop is clearly warned against quite a range of practices unacceptable in a respectable Christian society, within which it is impossible to distinguish outright paganism. Those who refuse to be corrected and to mend their ways (*emendare se a talibus atque corrigere nolle*) are to be seized—with fervent zeal!—and, if they are of servile status, punished by beating and torture; if they are free men, they are to be locked up and given appropriate penance, so that 'those who spurn to listen to the words which save from the peril of death, might at least be brought back (*reducere*) to sanity of mind by punishment of the body'.[32]

This is the only letter concerning the Sardinian 'pagans' in which Gregory specifies the people to be converted or corrected more exactly. But when, elsewhere, he writes about *pagani, infideles, idolorum cultores* without such exactitude he is certainly not referring to 'pagans' in the strict, exclusive, sense of unbaptized infidels. He knew perfectly well that some of the people suspected

---

[29] *Ep.* IV.29: 'quia autem nunc sacerdotum indigentia quosdam illic paganos remanere cognovimus, et ferino degentes modo Dei cultum penitus ignorare . . .' Cf. *Ep.* IV.27: 'dum enim Barbaricini omnes ut insensata animalia vivant, Deum verum nesciant, ligna autem et lapides adorent . . .'

[30] *Ep.* IV.29: 'qui ad hoc opus moribus atque verbo aptus existat et aberrantes ad gregem Dominicum pastorali studeat aemulatione deducere . . .'

[31] *Ep.* IX.205.

[32] Ibid. Kahl, 'Die ersten Jahrhunderte', 55, n. 99, has rightly noted that words like *corrigere* and *paenitentia* belong to the vocabulary of ecclesiastical penitential discipline. He also states that Gregory's vocabulary distinguishes between *vocare*, *adducere* on the one hand and *revocare*, *reducere* on the other. Although this contrast is not absolute (see e.g. *Ep.* XI.37, where the emperor Constantine is said to have 'recalled' (*revocans*) pagan Romans from the cult of idols), Kahl's conclusion that the present letter is not aimed at 'außerkirchliches Heidentum' may be accepted. I would not, however, exclude the possibility that unbaptized heathen were in fact included, without being specifically distinguished.

of sacrificing to idols or worshipping such things as trees and animal-heads were in fact Christians who went to church but had not given up 'the cult of demons'.[33] Lapsed Christians were to be found among idolaters,[34] and so was even a misbehaving priest.[35] Gregory habitually spoke, if only following good scriptural rhetoric and Pauline usage (Colossians 3.5), of avarice as *idolorum servitus*.[36] All this should prevent us from assuming that in the absence of qualification, 'pagan', 'idolater', and the like are to be taken in their strict sense. They will, in most cases, refer either to Christians of unacceptable habits or to groups that include such people along with unbaptized persons. Distinguished at Aleria, 'those who were once faithful, but have relapsed into the cult of idols' and those 'who have not yet been baptized'[37] are elsewhere inextricably mixed up in an undifferentiated mass that needs recalling to Christian respectability.

THE STRATEGIES

As we have seen, Gregory's first line of attack on 'pagans', whatever they were, was through bishops and their preaching. But preaching was not all. In principle, Gregory opposed forced baptism, though he only asserted the principle in the context of the conversion of Jews.[38] In reality, however, he recommended resort to coercion. Thus landlords had a special responsibility for the souls of their tenants. On the properties belonging to the see of Cagliari itself, for instance, Gregory knew of peasants 'who have been allowed to this day to remain in infidelity' through the archbishop's negligence. He must be careful to watch over their conversion.[39] And other bishops were to do likewise: Gregory promises to be tough with any Sardinian bishops on whose lands he discovers pagan peasants. Moreover, if any peasant was found to be so obstinate in his perfidy as to refuse 'to come to God', he was to be so burdened with rent that he would think again and 'hasten to righteousness'.[40] At the same time Gregory wrote to local dignitaries and landowners: he had been informed that 'almost all of [them] had peasants given to idolatry living on their properties'.[41] They were

---

[33] *Ep.* VIII.4 (in Gaul: to be restrained by Queen Brunhild).

[34] *Ep.* VIII.1 (cf. above, n. 25).

[35] *Ep.* X.2: he was accused to be *idolorum venerator ac cultor*, and also suspected of sodomy, and was to be jailed.

[36] e.g. *Mor.* XXVI.6.7; XXX.25.72; *RP* (*Liber Regulae Pastoralis*, ed. Rommel, SC 381, 382), II.10; *Epp.* IX.219; XI.38; 47 (the last three referring to simony in Gaul).

[37] See above, n. 25.

[38] *Ep.* I.45: the principle is enunciated for Jews, but its validity seems to be unrestricted. As Kahl, 'Die ersten Jahrhunderte', 55–6, n. 100, points out, although Gregory referred the text of Luke 14.23 to *gentiles*, he backed off using it to justify coercion.

[39] *Ep.* IV.26: 'ipsos rusticos quos habet ecclesia nuncusque in infidelitate remanere neglegentia fraternitatis vestrae permisit . . .' The *extranei* referred to in this paragraph are tenants on estates other than those of the archbishop.

[40] *Ep.* IV.26: 'tantae fuerit perfidiae et obstinationis inventus ut ad Deum venire minime consentiat . . .'

[41] *Ep.* IV.23: 'cognovi paene omnes vos rusticos in vestris possessionibus idolatriae deditos habere'.

told that they were responsible for their tenants' souls, that the end of this world was near, and that they, as worshippers of the true God, were not to permit those committed to their care to worship stones. It is from another letter that we learn the true state of things: Gregory was aware that 'in the island of Sardinia there are many heathen (*gentiles*) and that they still worship idols with sacrifices in the manner of depraved heathen';[42] it was bribes to local officials that made this possible. It must have been this practice that Gregory was aiming at in his exhortation to Sardinian landowners and dignitaries.[43] Landowners, ecclesiastical and lay, were thus expected to enforce the bishops' admonitions. And not only landowners: also military commanders, local chieftains, and civil officials—all were expected to exert themselves to 'bring [pagans] to the service of Christ'.[44] Preaching was to be backed with coercion by the available powers.

This was the general pattern of Gregory's expectations in all missionary situations. We may consider the remaining cases briefly. The Lombard settlers in Italy were something of a special case. Compulsion, even had Gregory wanted to resort to it, was not practicable. Where they were settled among the Roman population, as at Narni, the local bishop was to preach to them along with the Roman members of his flock, whether they were Arian heretics or pagans.[45] Sicily, an area that was particularly well policed by Gregory's patrimonial staff, and hence perhaps one we are especially well informed about, was a hotbed of various sorts of worshippers of idols, Manichees and their like, soothsayers and sorcerers, and practitioners of witchcraft.[46] Ecclesiastical and secular

---

[42] *Ep.* V.38 (to the empress Constantina): 'dum in Sardiniae insula multos esse gentiles cognovissem, eosque adhuc pravae gentilitatis more idolorum sacrificiis deservire . . .' In this letter Gregory is protesting against unjust exactions by local *iudices*. It reveals that they not only exacted bribes to permit pagan practices, but that they continued to exact them after their practitioners had converted to Christianity. Does this imply that such payments had become customary exactions, or that Christian converts were required to pay to be allowed to continue practising 'pagan' rites?

[43] *Ep.* IX.204 complains about peasants deserting ecclesiastical estates for the possessions of lay landowners. This may well be a consequence of the greater tolerance of objectionable practices by the latter. On this question, see S. Boesch Gajano, 'Teoria e pratica pastorale nelle opere di Gregorio Magno', in *Grégoire le Grand*, ed. J. Fontaine, R. Gillet, and S. Pellistrandi (Paris, 1986), 181–8, esp. 185–6. Clients of wealthy lay people were assumed to be candidates for conversion: *Ep.* VII.8.

[44] *Ep.* IV.25: *ad Christi servitium adducatis* (to a *dux* victorious over pagan Barbaricini). In *Ep.* XI.12 the *praeses Sardiniae* is bidden to assist the bishop of Fausiana in 'converting and baptizing' the many 'barbarians [= Barbaricini] and provincials who are reported to be hastening with great devotion to the christian faith'. Similarly, the converted *dux* of the Barbaricini, Hospito, in *Ep.* IV.27. *Ep.* IX.103 (Luni): it is not clear whether the *magister militum* mentioned here is to assist the priests and deacons who are bidden 'adhortationis suae sollicitudine degentem illic populum ab infidelitate revocare . . . ac a gentilium cultu suspendere . . .' It may be that this is an instance where clergy are to act on their own. On coercion, see *Ep.* IX. 205, quoted above p. 29, with n. 32.

[45] *Ep.* II.2: 'admonitione sive exhortatione . . . maxime gentilium et haereticorum' (cf. *Ep.* I.17). *Ep.* IX.103 speaks of clergy who are to recall inhabitants of a town (retaken from Lombard control?) from infidelity and to end heathen rites ('ab infidelitate revocare ac . . . a gentilium cultu suspendere . . .').

[46] *Ep.* III.59 (praetor and rector to deal with *idolorum cultores atque Angelliorum dogmatis*); *Ep.* V.7 (the rector to deal with Manichees); Ep. XI.33 (the rector to deal with *incantatores atque sortilegos*); *Ep.* XIV.1 (a *scholasticus* praised for his severity against *maleficos*).

authorities, and especially the staff of the papal patrimonies, were to seek them out and 'correct' them. In Frankish Gaul Queen Brunhild was expected to 'restrain' her subjects from the cult of demons;[47] and Gregory evidently envisaged King Æthelbert acting on the same lines in Kent. The Anglo-Saxon king, following the example of the Christian emperor Constantine, was told to promote the work of Gregory's missionaries, and to back it up with his own coercive measures, just as the *dux* Hospito had been instructed to do among the Barbaricini of Sardinia; even the language of Gregory's exhortation recalls that of his letters to the Corsican chieftain.[48] It was only when Gregory realised that coercion by the court was not a practical option in Kent that he rethought the missionary strategy he had originally envisaged.[49] It is unlikely that Gregory imagined the English 'worshippers of idols'[50] to whom he sent his missionaries as Christians who had 'gone native', reverted to ancient, heathen rites. He assumed that the *Angli*, like the slave boys to be purchased in Provence,[51] were unbaptized pagans. He did not, however, feel it necessary to distinguish them in his terminology from the mixture of unbaptized heathen and rustic Christians clinging to their pre-christian customs with which he had been familiar in the Italian islands. He interpreted—until better informed later on—the unfamiliar in terms of what was familiar. And the ways in which he intended to deal with these heathen were identical.

It has sometimes been thought that Gregory distinguished missions to remedy deficiencies (*labes*) in religion which cause it to fall short of 'christian norms and principles' from missions to unbaptized pagans, and that he reserved compulsion for the former class, excluding it from the latter.[52] This cannot be maintained in the face of the situations we have examined, and even less so in the face of the missionary strategy he had originally laid down for the English mission. It is clear that in Kent, in Italy, in Sicily, in Sardinia—though not, perhaps, in Corsica—Gregory wished the available authorities to lend their weight and whatever force they could exert to reinforce the salutary preaching of the word. He did not generally discriminate between real thick-blooded 'pagans' and nominal 'rude' Christians, any more than he distinguished different ways of dealing with them.

[47] *Ep.* VIII.4; cf. above, n. 33.

[48] *Ep.* XI.37. In addition to the general likeness of Gregory's admonitions, note especially CCSL 140A, lines 9–11 and *Ep.* IV.27 (see above, n. 44), CCSL 140, lines 6–10 and lines 63–4; cf. *Ep.* IV.25, lines 10–11.

[49] I have discussed this in some detail in my 'Gregory the Great and the Origins of a Papal Missionary Strategy', *Studies in Church History*, 6 (1970), 29–38 (repr. in *From Augustine to Gregory the Great: History and Christianity in Late Antiquity* (London, 1983), no. XI; and in *Gregory the Great and His World* (Cambridge, 1997), 76–82, where I also touch on the case of the Jews and Gregory's attitudes towards them, and the missionary procedures he advocated in their regard.

[50] *Ep.* XI.36, 37, 56: 'gens Anglorum in mundi angulo posita in cultu lignorum ac lapidum perfida nuncusque remaneret . . .': *Ep.* VIII.29.

[51] See above, n. 22.

[52] e.g. Kahl, 'Die ersten Jahrhunderte'; the quotation is from p. 55, n. 99. For the argument, see 42–5.

THE WORD OF PREACHING

I drew attention to the statement in the *Moralia* where Gregory distinguishes external missionary from intra-ecclesial parenetic preaching. He says that the Church 'preaches knowledge of the Trinity to infidels', but to the faithful 'she preaches the four [cardinal] virtues'; for 'the holy Church accommodates its preaching carefully to the state of the hearers' minds'.[53] It is a remarkable passage, and so far as I know it is unique in the Gregorian corpus. Gregory does sometimes refer to preaching to *infideles*, especially when speaking of the apostle Paul;[54] but he does not distinguish what or how to preach to them from what is to be preached, or how, to the faithful. Nor does this dichotomy figure in his long list of the different sorts of people to whom the preacher should adapt his preaching. The nearest he comes to this is in a chapter on 'admonishing those who do not rightly understand the sacred scripture, and those who do understand it but do not speak with humility' (III.24). It is clear, however, that he is not concerned here—or anywhere else—with insiders and outsiders.[55] Throughout, he is concerned with the pastor's duty to adapt his preaching to different sorts within his Christian flock. When Gregory was giving serious thought to the manner and content of preaching, it is clear that he was always thinking of a congregation of essentially faithful, baptized Christians, even if it included more or less unsatisfactory Christians, perhaps shading off at its margins into a minority of unbaptized pagans. The distinction between preaching to *infideles* and to *fideles* made here is unique. Why is it made here, and nowhere else?

The answer is provided by considering the context of the statement. Gregory is commenting on the text (as he had it), 'Can you bind the glittering stars of the Pleiades, or loose the turning bands of Orion?' (Job 38.31: *numquid conjungere valebis micantes stellas Pleiades, aut gyrum Arcturi poteris dissipare?*). In their rotation (*gyrum*), the seven stars of Orion alternate between the position in which three are at the top while four are at the bottom, and the reverse: four on top, three below. So the holy Church, obviously, 'changes its state as if by turning round its preaching' (*quasi rotatu praedicationis status sui speciem quodammodo immutat*). So at one time she preaches the three divine persons to the infidel, at another the four virtues to the faithful. Gregory is not interested in the

---

[53] *Mor.* XXIX.31.72 (above, n. 26). The importance of the passage has been emphasized by Kahl, 'Die ersten Jahrhunderte' (cf. above, n. 27) at p. 48.

[54] e.g. *RP* II.5.30; II.5.34.

[55] Excepting, of course the *Moralia* passage cited. For parallels to *RP* III in the *Moralia*, see my *Gregory the Great*, 21, n. 10. The Revd Dr Edward Yarnold has suggested (in a personal communication) that the *infideles* referred to here are not really outsiders, but catechumens, distinguished from the baptized members of the congregation. This is possible, but I cannot see how one could tell. If this were the case, it would imply that catechumens received instruction separately from the main congregation—not as in Augustine's time, when it seems that catechumens received much of their instruction at the ordinary Sunday liturgy: cf. W. Harmless, *Augustine and the Catechumenate* (Pueblo, Collegeville, 1995); I am grateful to Dr Yarnold for this reference.

question: what is to be preached to different hearers? His interest is to find some figurative meaning for the three and the four of Orion's rotation, corresponding to the Church's *gyrus*. We can understand why it took so complex an image to suggest the idea of distinguishing preaching to pagans from preaching to the faithful. Gregory never made this distinction on any other occasion—not even where we might particularly have expected to find it, in the *Regula Pastoralis*—because, quite simply, he was not interested in it—something that is apparent even on this one occasion when he did make it.

I have searched in vain for precedents for a corresponding distinction in earlier patristic literature. Gregory had almost certainly read Augustine's *De Catechizandis Rudibus*;[56] but the nearest parallel he would have found there was the differentiation between *rudes ac simplices* and *liberalibus doctrinis exculti*.[57] For Augustine, the distinction here was between two kinds of unbaptized persons—educated and uneducated catechumens awaiting baptism. Gregory made use of the contrast between educated and uneducated, but applied it to preaching to a congregation of the faithful. When Augustine did discuss how people were to be instructed before and after baptism, it is noteworthy that his recommendation is quite different from Gregory's, indeed it is quite the opposite: some people, he says, would prefer to have catechumens baptized first, and instructed in the good life and the virtues only after baptism—on the lines of Gregory's distinction. But Augustine would not have this (except in emergencies); let people be told what they are in for, what standards of behaviour will be expected of them, before being baptized.[58]

How are we to account for such a change in assumptions between Augustine and Gregory? Did Gregory—and his episcopal colleagues, for that matter—not have to give catechetical addresses to unbaptized pagans? I know of no catechetical sermons after those Quodvultdeus seems to have preached in Carthage in the 430s and Peter Chrysologus in Ravenna perhaps a little later; nothing of the kind has been preserved. In general, it is clear that Gregory was living, imaginatively even more than in reality, in a more thoroughly and radically christianized society than had been Augustine. His lack of interest in distinguishing pagans from unsatisfactory Christians, and his correspondingly much stronger concentration on moral preaching, must be related to his assumptions about the nature of his society.[59] And linked with these assumptions is his propensity to think of missionary activity as a facet of pastoral responsibility.[60]

---

[56] See V. Paronetto, 'Une présence augustinienne chez Grégoire le Grand: le *De catechizandis rudibus* dans la *Regula pastoralis*', in *Grégoire le Grand*, ed. Fontaine *et al.*, 511–19.

[57] *De Catechizandis Rudibus*, 8.12–9.13.   [58] *De Fide et Operibus*, 9.

[59] See my *Signs and Meanings: World and Text in Ancient Christianity* (Liverpool, 1996), esp. 46–7.

[60] Cf. my 'Augustine and Gregory the Great', in *St Augustine and the Conversion of England*, ed. R. G. Gameson (Stroud, 1999), 41–9.

3

THE ANNOTATIONS IN OXFORD, BODLEIAN LIBRARY, AUCT. D. II. 14

David Ganz

Oxford, Bodleian Library, Auct. D. II. 14 is one of two surviving Italian gospel books which had reached Anglo-Saxon England by the end of the seventh century (pls. 1–2).[1] The other, Cambridge, Corpus Christi College, 286 has long been called the Gospels of St Augustine, and fanciful accounts of its place of origin and its arrival in England have ensured that it has recently kept company with England's primates.[2] Oxford, Bodleian Library, Auct. D. II. 14 was given to Sir Thomas Bodley by Robert Cotton in 1603, and clear evidence of its earlier history is lacking.[3] It contains an Italian text of the gospels, now incomplete,[4] which editors have long called O.[5] The frequent annotations found in this manuscript make it possible to explore its history and use from the seventh to the twelfth century.

The volume measures 250 × 195 mm, copied in quaternions with the flesh sides outside. The gospel text is set out in two columns of twenty-seven lines,

[1] I am grateful to Dr Martin Kaufmann for allowing me to examine the manuscript on several occasions, to Dr Carol Farr for generously lending me her own notes on the annotations, to Professor Simon Keynes for advice on Anglo-Saxon charter hands, to Professor Malcolm Parkes for several helpful discussions of the scripts in O, to Dr Susan Rankin for advice on the neumes and the identification of hands, and to Dr Alan Thacker for discussion of the cult of St Chad. I have also benefited from advice from Julia Crick, Patrick McGurk, and Chris Verey. Richard Gameson generously allowed me access to forthcoming papers by himself and Richard Marsden in *St Augustine and the Conversion of England*, ed. R. Gameson (Stroud, 1999), which also treat of this manuscript. None of these scholars are responsible for errors of fact or interpretation which may be present.

[2] See now M. Budny, *Insular, Anglo-Saxon and Early Anglo-Norman Manuscript Art at Corpus Christi College Cambridge: An Illustrated Catalogue*, 2 vols. (Kalamazoo, 1997), I, no. 1. Both manuscripts were apparently first linked to Augustine of Canterbury by Wanley, *Catalogus Librorum Septentrionalium* (Oxford, 1689), in G. Hickes, *Institutiones . . .*, 173. See further, *Letters of Humphrey Wanley*, ed. P. Heyworth (Oxford 1989), 69 and 144, noting distinctive textual readings in O.

[3] The late eleventh-century Bury St Edmunds booklist on the endleaf, edited by Lapidge, 'Surviving Booklists from Anglo-Saxon England', in *Learning and Literature in Anglo-Saxon England: Studies Presented to Peter Clemoes*, ed. M. Lapidge and H. Gneuss (Cambridge, 1985), 74–6, was rightly regarded by Ker, Julian Brown, and Lapidge as a later insertion. There is no valid reason to suggest that this manuscript was ever at Bury.

[4] The text begins at Matthew 4.14 and ends at John 21.15. A leaf is missing after fol. 6 with the text of Matthew 8.29–9.18.

[5] *Novum Testamentum Domini nostri Iesu Christi latine secundum editionem S. Hieronymi*, I: *Quattuor Evangelia*, ed. J. Wordsworth and H. J. White (Oxford, 1898), p. xiii and *passim*.

copied by one hand, writing a balanced uncial, which has been dated to the seventh century. The script is hard to parallel, and is clearly not typical of Rome. The most distinctive letter is the D, which starts with a curving headstroke followed by the round body of the letter; this is made in a separate movement, with the result that the headstroke creates a marked shoulder at the join. X has a cross-stroke which descends deeply to the left and curves round at the top right, and G a slender tail which curves slightly to the left. F and P sit low, with the crossbar of F and the bow of P on the baseline, and there are triangular serifs on the crossbar of T.[6] At line-ends there are elegant NS, NT, US, and UR ligatures. Each gospel opens with elaborate uncial, with an enlarged and decorated initial, and with a *Criste fave* invocation above the start of the text. The opening lines and the first word of each chapter are in red, as are the gospel explicits, which are copied in a clumsy enlarged *capitalis*. Orthography is poor: some examples are **cyto** for *cito*, **estes** for *estis*, **parulos** for *parvulos*, **pussum** for *possum*, **dicibatur** for *dicebatur*, **inhoriatis** for *inhonoratis*, **sautem** for *ambulans autem*, **mecari** for *moechari*, and frequent **b/v** confusion. The gospel of Matthew was copied in continuous lines, the other three gospels are set out *per cola et commata*. The gospel text of Matthew and the first two chapters of Mark have been heavily corrected, and the text of Matthew has been supplied with word division.

The gospel texts have marginal annotations by two Italian scribes (one of whom is the main scribe of the volume), indicating passages to be read on feast days. The gospels were corrected in England by a scribe writing insular minuscule; the same scribe was responsible for the distinctive English uncial used to correct Luke 7.21 on fol. 74r and John 16.33 on fol. 164v.[7] Many of his corrections bring the text closer to the Irish gospel text found in the Book of Kells and the MacRegol Gospels.[8] On fols. 26v and 27r at Matthew 22.32 and 37 this corrector also identified two quotations from Exodus.[9] An unskilful scribe writing insular minuscule entered brief liturgical texts on fol. 34r and, upside down, on fol. 149v, which appear unrelated to the gospel text[10] (see Plates 1 and 2). One of

---

[6] Italian paleographers have been unable to localize this uncial script, but agree that it is not Roman. A. Petrucci, 'L'onciale romana' *Studi medievali*, 12 (1971), 75–131 at 115, n. 116. Cf. E. Condello, *Una scrittura e un territorio: L'onciale dei secoli V–VIII nell'Italia meridionali* (Spoleto, 1994).

[7] The annotations on fol. 32v are shown in the plate in *CLA* II, no. 230.

[8] Respectively Dublin, Trinity College, 58; and Oxford, Bodleian Library, Auct. D. II. 19. At Matthew 20.16 (fol. 23r) *vero* is added; on fol. 35r at Matthew 26.61 *hoc* is added, and on fol. 36v at Matthew 27.32 (the interpolation about Simon of Cyrene), *venientem obviam sibi* is added. At Luke 22.27 two Old Latin additions have been supplied in a passage about hypocrites who pretend to fast. For a detailed account of the textual family of O, which establishes that it had no progeny, see Richard Marsden, 'The Gospels of St Augustine', in *St Augustine*, ed. Gameson, 285–312. The hand illustrated by Marsden at fig. 12.4 is that of the tenth-century annotator and not that of the insular annotator discussed here.

[9] This identification is not found in any early commentary known to me, implying that the scribe was a biblical scholar.

[10] Fol. 149v is illustrated in E. A. Lowe, *English Uncial* (Oxford, 1960), pl. IV. Fols. 79r, 149r, and 149v were illustrated by E. W. B. Nicholson, *Early Bodleian Music III: Introduction to the Study of Some of the Oldest Latin Music Manuscripts in the Bodleian Library Oxford* (London, 1913), and discussed on pp. xvii–xix.

these refers to St Chad. Later hands added further liturgical annotations, chiefly to Matthew. The letters **l** and **t** as well as neumes were added to the genealogy of Christ in Luke 3.23–38.[11] In the early twelfth century a very small hand, writing in black ink, copied passages from Ambrose and Augustine relating to the text, made further corrections, and altered the chapter titles to Mark and Luke.[12] This may be the hand which supplies word division to the text of passages of the gospels and the chapters. The gospel text has been re-inked in places, notably on fols. 166v–167r. Because the manuscript is copied in pale ink and is tightly bound, some of the annotations are not visible on microfilm.[13] In this study I transcribe all annotations, and offer a tentative account of the history of the manuscript from the seventh to the twelfth century. For each of the liturgical annotators, a table lists the exact wording of each marginal note, the first verse of the gospel passage beside which the note appears, and the standard Roman feast for which this lection was used.[14]

The first liturgical annotator was the original main scribe, but his marginal annotations are written in a tiny uncial script:

---

[11] The opening column of neumes is reproduced by Nicholson, *Early Bodleian Music*, pl. 3. For the letters see M. Huglo, *Les Livres de chant liturgique*, Typologie des sources du moyen âge occidental, 52 (Turnhout, 1988), 17–20. Neumes appear on fols. 79r–80r and 158v. The neumes on fol. 158r appear in the upper margin; unaccompanied by text, they nevertheless seem to represent a melody rather than a pen-trial. These neumes are typically insular, the axis of upwards and downwards strokes close to perpendicular, and the hook at the top of the *clives* fully rounded. On fols. 79r–80r three different hands have added neumatic notation. Two of these, one following after the other, notate the genealogy of Christ (Luke 3.21, 'Factum est autem . . .', as far as 4.1, '. . . egressus est a Iordane'); this was sung on the feast of the Epiphany, either at the end of Matins or during the Mass. Both neume hands are probably insular (rather than French), although neither has the classic calligraphic style typical of Winchester hands, and seen also on fol. 158r; here the *clives* are more hooked, and the relation between upward and downward strokes more angled than parallel. Here the second hand took over from the first somewhere before fol. 79v, col. 1, line 9. Although less neatly written, the neumes of the first hand convey more diastematic information (by means of *virgae* of differing lengths) than those of the second. However, since the melody for singing the genealogy is completely formulaic and repetitive (on this see David Hiley, *Western Plainchant: A Handbook* (Oxford, 1993), 56–8), a lack of diastematic information towards the end of the notation need not surprise us. The reason for adding these neumes was merely to indicate how a repeated melodic pattern could be moulded to text phrases of varying lengths. All of these hands could have been written at any time between the late tenth and the end of the third quarter of the eleventh century; all probably date from the first half of the eleventh century. The last set of neumes, written conspicuously later, appear, together with the text 'Dominus vobiscum et cum spiritu tuo initium sancti evangelii secundum Lucam', in the right-hand margin of fol. 79r, beside the beginning of the Luke genealogy. Appearing with a texthand which can be dated as late as the early twelfth century, these neumes are noticeably of a new kind: their cross-strokes are beginning to develop into 'petits points', and their formation much more like Norman notations of the late eleventh century.

[12] The liturgical annotations were printed by Dom J. Chapman, *Notes on the Early History of the Vulgate Gospels* (Oxford, 1908), 192–3 and 200, with discussion at 181–202. They were discussed by W. H. Frere, *Studies in Early Roman Liturgy 2: The Roman Gospel Lectionary*, Alcuin Club Collections, 30 (Oxford, 1934), 224; and by U. Lenker, *Die Westsächsische Evangelienversion und die Perikopenordnungen im Angelsächischen England* (Munich, 1997), 406–11 and *passim*.

[13] Lenker, *Evangelienversion*, 407, n. 22.

[14] The identifications follow Lenker's table, 298–383.

fol. 76r	IN NATALE DNI	Luke 2.1	1st Mass of Christmas (at night)
fol. 87v	AD N N	Luke 7.19	Advent
fol. 144r	IN MEDIO PENTICOSTE	John 7.14	Lent IV[15]
fol. 152r	IN DIDICATIONE	John 10.22	Dedication of church
fol. 160v	IN SABBATO PENTECOSTE	John 14.15	Vigil of Pentecost
fol. 161r	IN PENTECOSTE	John 14.23	Pentecost
fol. 165v	PASSIO	John 18.1	Good Friday

This first set of marks indicates lections for the liturgical seasons of Advent, Christmas, Easter, and Pentecost as well as the standard Italian lection for the Dedication of a church.[16]

The second Italian liturgical annotator wrote in a slanting script which combines uncial and cursive letter forms: **b**, **d**, and **e** are always minuscule, while **a** may be minuscule or uncial. There are seldom more than three or four letters per line, set off with a curving penstroke at the end, and often having a cross at the start. These notes were entered after the book had been bound. Notes in the outer margins have been trimmed by the binder. In my transcription, / indicates a binding cut, and + a marginal cross. The conventions are as before, but where the marginal note in O is not in agreement with Roman usage, an indication of the latter appears in brackets. Abbreviation marks are not shown.

fol. 1r	in natale sci andree	Matthew 4.18	St Andrew (30.11)
fol. 2r	*Chi rho* symbol	Matthew 6.9[17]	?
fol. 7v	in ordinatione episc/	Matthew 10.1	Ordination of a bishop
fol. 8r	in scorum	Matthew 10.16	Common of a martyr or confessor
fol. 8v	+ in scorum	Matthew 10.32	Common of a martyr or confessor
fol. 9r	+ de adventu	Matthew 11.2	Advent
fol. 10r	+ in x lect/ de pe/	Matthew 12.1	(Pentecost VIII, Friday)
fol. 12r	+ in sci pauli	Matthew 13.3	St Paul (30.6)
fol. 15v	/octabas sci petri	Matthew 14.23	Octave of SS Peter and Paul (6.7)
fol. 17v	+ in nat sci petri	Matthew 16.13	St Peter (29.6)
fol. 18r	+ in scor/	Matthew 16.24	Common of a martyr
fol. 23r	+ de passione	Matthew 20.17	(Lent II, Wednesday)
fol. 24r	+ in dedicatione Ecclsiae	Matthew 21.10	Dedication of church
fol. 28v	in sci stefa[ne]	Matthew 23.34	St Stephen (26.12)
fol. 30v	/n confessoru	Matthew 24.45	Common of confessors
fol. 30v	+ de martyras	Matthew 25.1	Common of a martyr
fol. 31r	+ in martyras	Matthew 25.14	Common of martyrs
fol. 34v	(traces of annotation)	Matthew 26.52	Palm Sunday
fol. 38r	+ in nocte sca +	Matthew 28.1	Vigil of Easter Day
fol. 64r	pas[sione]	Mark 14.1	Palm Sunday

---

[15] On the use of this Lent reading in another period of fasting, see Frere, *Gospel Lectionary*, 224.

[16] Lenker, *Evangelienversion*, 301, 408. Lenker notes that this is also a Gallican pericope.

[17] The meaning of this annotation is unclear: the passage is not recorded as a lection in Lenker.

fol. 69r	+ in doca sca	Mark 16.1	Easter Day
fol. 70r	+ in ascensa	Mark 16.14	Ascension
fol. 73r	In vigilias sci iohannis baptistae	Luke 1.5	Vigil of St John Baptist (23.6)
fol. 74r	+ de adventu	Luke 1.26	Advent III, Wednesday
fol. 74r	adventu	Luke 1.39	Advent
fol. 75r	+ in natale sci ioh	Luke 1.57	St John Baptist (24.6)
fol. 76r	in nat dni	Luke 2.1	1st Christmas Mass (at night)
fol. 76v	in octabas dni	Luke 2.21	Advent
fol. 78r	de adventu	Luke 3.1	Advent
fol. 125r	in secunda firia	Luke 24.1	Easter Monday
fol. 126r	+ in tertia feria	Luke 24.13	Easter Tuesday
fol. 130r	in nle dni	John 1.1	3rd Christmas Mass (in the day)
fol. 130v	de adventu	John 1.19	Advent IV
fol. 131r	in vigilias sci andree	John 1.35	Vigil of St Andrew (29.11)
fol. 145r	*Chi Rho* symbol	John 7.37	Lent V, Thursday

Here there are five lessons for Advent, two for Christmas, four for Lent, six for the Easter season, and others for the feasts of SS Andrew, Peter, Paul, Stephen, and John the Baptist, and six for the common of saints, all of which correspond to readings used at Rome. Whether inclusion of the lection for the ordination of a bishop suggests the home of the annotator was an episcopal see is unclear.

While the insular corrector of the text only writes very brief passages,[18] he used some distinctive letter-forms, which provide a clue to the date of his activity. On fol. 26v at Matthew 22.19 he copied the word **numisma** using an **mi** ligature. On fol. 32v he added the Irish reading *pretio* to Matthew 26.9.[19] The **tio** ligature has a very remarkable curve, which is also found in Anglo-Saxon charters and in some Mercian manuscripts.[20] It is first used in the letter of Bishop Wealdhere datable to 704–5,[21] and is frequent in Mercian charters of the first third of the ninth century.[22] This corrector used the insular abbreviation for *per* in *percusserunt* at Matthew 26.52, which is also found in some Mercian charters.[23]

[18] Cf. n. 7 above.

[19] As in the Book of Armagh (Dublin, Trinity College, 52), the Lichfield Gospels (Lichfield Cathedral, 1), and the Book of Kells (Dublin, Trinity College, 58).

[20] M. P. Brown, *The Book of Cerne* (London, 1996), esp. fig. 14, showing the ligature in Oxford, Bodleian Library, Hatton 93.

[21] P. Chaplais, 'The Letter from Bishop Wealdhere of London to Archbishop Brihtwold of Canterbury: The Earliest Original "letter close" Extant in the West', in *Medieval Scribes, Manuscripts and Libraries, Essays presented to N.R. Ker*, ed. M. B. Parkes and A. G. Watson (London, 1978), 3–23, esp. 20 and pl. 1. The ascenders and descenders in this letter are much longer than in O.

[22] ti appears in the charters of Uhtred regulus of the Hwicce dated 770 (P. Sawyer, *Anglo-Saxon Charters: An Annotated List and Bibliography* (London, 1968) [henceforth: S], 59), Cenwulf of Mercia dated 798 (S 153), Archbishop Wulfred of Canterbury dated 811 (S 1264), Cenwulf dated 812 (S 169), Cenwulf dated 814 (S 173), Wiglaf king of Mercia dated 831 (S 188). I have not found it in the royal charters of Wessex or Kent. It is also used by glossator B in Fulda, Hessische Landesbibliothek, Bonifatius I, and in manuscripts from Würzburg.

[23] Offa dated 793–6 (S 139), Wulfred of Canterbury dated 811 (S 1264).

The insular scribe responsible for the Chad annotation used his own distinctive letter-forms: a clumsy 3-shaped **g** with a curving cross-stroke, a very angular **s** composed of a headstroke which slants up from below the top of the shaft, a round **d**, curved cross-strokes on **t** and **g**, and pronounced serifs on **b** and **l**. A more accomplished version of the script he was trying to write is found in the vernacular interlinear gloss in the Vespasian Psalter (London, British Library, Cotton Vespasian A. 1), and in the main script of the Aldhelm manuscript (London, British Library, MS Royal 5 F. III).[24] The entries read:

fol. 39v   ut umana fragilitas quae pro se proclivis est/ (see pl. 1)
fol. 149v   Elegite dns sacerdote sibi et sacrificandu vis laudis ic est sacerdos magnos
               qui in diebus suis placuit do confersor sci et saecerdos magni beati sce
               ceadda (see pl. 2).

The first entry represents a passage from a prayer in the votive Mass 'in time of tribulation' *Deus humilium consolator*. The Mass is found in both Gelasian and Gregorian sacramentaries.[25] The second entry comprises two separate liturgical chants: *Eligit te dominus* is a responsory from the common of a confessor pontiff; *hic est sacerdos magnus* must represent a chant proper to the feast of St Chad, but it is not recorded elsewhere.[26] It builds on a text often used in the liturgy for confessor pontiffs in the form, 'Ecce sacerdos magnus qui in diebus suis placuit deo', and present in Roman-Gregorian books in three chant genres (Gradual, Office responsory, and Office antiphon). Given the length of the chant beginning '[H]ic est sacerdos', as well as its juxtaposition to the responsory 'Eligit te dominus', it probably also represents a responsory for the feast of St Chad.

This scribe's orthography is poor: he wrote *sacerdos magnos* and *confersor*, *laudis* was originally copied as *ladis*, *hic* is written *ic*, and *Elegite* is probably a misreading of *Elegit te*. But the **ae** ligature used in *sacerdos* in line 3 may represent an Old English ash spelling,[27] and non-aspirate H in *hic* might also be a vernacular feature. Malcolm Parkes notes that in the upper left-hand margin of this folio the letters 'seco' are just visible. The text on this page, John 9.10–20, was not a standard lection for a confessor.

The feast of St Chad was celebrated on 2 March, and is found in the Old English Martyrology and in tenth-century and later Anglo-Saxon calendars, including those in the Leofric Missal, the Bosworth Psalter, and the Salisbury

[24] *The Vespasian Psalter*, ed. D. H. Wright, EEMF 14 (Copenhagen, 1967); E. Temple, *Anglo-Saxon Manuscripts 900–1066* (London, 1976), no. 2.

[25] *Le Sacramentaire Grégorien II*, ed. J. Deshusses (Fribourg, 1988), 159.

[26] See R.-J. Hesbert, *Corpus Antiphonalium Officii*, 7 vols. (Rome, 1963–79). The first text is very close to 'Elegit te dominus sacerdotem sibi ad sacrificandum ei hostiam laudis' (*CAO* no. 6649). The second text combines standard phrases used in liturgical chants for saints' feasts: cf. 'Ecce sacerdos magnus qui in diebus suis placuit deo' (*CAO* no. 6609) and the several responsory openings: 'Hic est N', 'Hic est vere martyr', 'Hic est vir sanctus'.

[27] I am grateful to Malcolm Parkes for this suggestion.

Psalter.[28] Chad is also included among confessors in Anglo-Saxon litanies of the saints. There is a Mercian homily on his life, to be read on his feast-day, which Napier and Vleeskruyer believed to be the translation of a Latin homily.[29] The language of this homily was localized to the West Midlands, and most probably 'in the saint's own see of Lichfield'.[30] Given that Chad is the only Anglo-Saxon saint whose name appears in a book that is well supplied with lections for the feasts of apostles and unspecified martyrs and confessors, it seems as probable that this entry, and the sacramentary extract copied by the same scribe, were also made in the see of Lichfield.[31] Churches with medieval dedications to Chad are only found in Mercia.[32]

The final liturgical notes, made by two Anglo-Saxon hands, are almost exclusively within the gospel of Matthew.[33] The script of the entries—'unius MR' and 'de martiribus' on fol. 8v, 'de virginibus' on fol. 14v, and 'de petro' on fol. 53v—is a distinctive uncial, and may well pre-date the other entries. They were copied in a very black ink, using an alphabet which is chiefly uncial, with a distinctive uncial **M** whose first bow is completely closed, and an uncial **N**, but with a square minuscule **e** and **b**, and with ligatures for **en** and **LX**. There are abbreviations for '-bus' (in the form b;) and for 'post', as well as 'DOM' and 'FR'. Several lection markings start with a cross with a small curve on the left-hand crossbar. The gospel text corresponding to these lection markings has often been carefully punctuated, and later hands have inserted **ct** and **st** ligatures between the uncial letters, and drawn lines to indicate word division. The *feria* marks ('FR') are often in the lower margin, and not clearly linked to a particular verse. The lection entries read:

fol. 6v	Dom iiii post theoph	Matthew 8.23	4th Sunday after Epiphany
fol. 7r	FR VI	Matthew 9.23	[no recorded Roman usage]
fol. 7r	in sab xii[ue]l m	Matthew 9.27	[not in Lenker][34]
fol. 7r	FR	Matthew 9.32	[not in Lenker]

---

[28] Oxford, Bodleian Library, Bodley 579; London, British Library, Add. 37517; and Salisbury Cathedral, 150. See F. Wormald, *English Kalendars before A.D. 1100*, Henry Bradshaw Society, 72 (London, 1934).

[29] *The Life of St Chad: An Old English Homily edited with Introduction, Notes, Illustrative Texts and Glossary*, ed. R. Vleeskruyer (Amsterdam, 1953), 16–18. Vleeskruyer suggests that the lost Latin text may also have been the work of the homilist. Janet Bately suggests the homily may date 'before the second quarter of the ninth century'; see her 'Old English Prose Before and During the Reign of Alfred', *Anglo-Saxon England*, 17 (1988), 93–138.

[30] *Life of St Chad*, ed. Vleeskruyer, 70–1.

[31] For a list of the Anglo-Saxon bishops of Lichfield, see the *Handbook of British Chronology*, ed. E. B. Fryde, D. E. Greenway, S. Porter, and I. Ray, 3rd edn. (Cambridge, 1986), 218–9 (entries by S. Keynes). O was first linked to Lichfield by Nicholson.

[32] F. Arnold-Foster, *Studies in Church Dedications of England's Patron Saints*, I (London, 1899), 398–400.

[33] Chapman, Vogels, and Lenker, the last of whom worked from microfilm, ascribe these notes to a single tenth-century hand.

[34] The marginal note clearly refers to a 'Sabbato in xii lectionibus', that is, the Saturday of an Ember week.

fol. 7v	Apostolorum	Matthew 10.7	(Common of saints)
fol. 8r	de martyribus	Matthew 10.16	Common of martyrs
fol. 8v	FR	Matthew 10.23	(SS Protus and Jacintus (11.9))
fol. 8v	unius martyris	Matthew 10.25	(Common of a martyr)
fol. 9r	dom de adventu dni	Matthew 11.1	Advent III
fol. 9v	FR	???	
fol. 10r	de sapientia	Matthew 11.19	[not in Lenker][35]
fol. 10v	FR	Matthew 12.9–12	(Epiphany VII)
fol. 11r	dom in xl	???	Quadragesima
fol. 12r	dom in lx	Matthew 13.3	Sexagesima
fol. 13r	FR	Matthew 13.24	(Pentecost XIX, Wednesday or Friday)
fol. 13v	FR	Matthew 13.31	(five uses)
fol. 14r	de virginib	Matthew 13.44	Common of virgins
fol. 15v	in octabas apla petri et pauli	Matthew 14.22	Octave of SS Peter and Paul (6.7)
fol. 16r	FR I XL	Matthew 15.1	(Epiphany VIII, Wednesday or Lent III, Wednesday)
fol. 16v	m in ii et in XL	Matthew 15.21–8	Lent II
fol. 18r	unius mar	Matthew 16.24	Common of a martyr
fol. 18v	sabb i XL	Matthew 17.1	(Lent II)
fol. 19r	FR in xii[ue]l	Matthew 17.14	(Lent II, Wednesday)
fol. 19v	FR	Matthew 17.24	(Pentecost XXIV, Wednesday or Friday)
fol. 19v	de sco mihaele	Matthew 18.1	St Michael (29.9)
fol. 20r	I XL FR iii ebd iii	Matthew 18.15	Lent III, Tuesday
fol. 20v	dom xxii post pent.	Matthew 18.23	Pentecost XXII
fol. 21v	ad parvulos Fr	Matthew 19.16	(Pentecost VIII)
fol. 22r	in festo sci petri	Matthew 19.27	St Peter (29.6)
fol. 22v	in dom LXX	Matthew 20.1	Septuagesima
fol. 23r	FR iiii in XL	Matthew 20.17	Lent II, Wednesday
fol. 23r	de iac	Matthew 20.20	St James (25.7)
fol. 23v	in sabb xii[ue]l post pent	Matthew 20.29	Saturday after Pentecost
fol. 24r	dom I in adventu dni	???	
fol. 24r	in I FR I in x[l]	Matthew 21.10	Lent I, Tuesday
fol. 24v	FR	Matthew 21.18	[no recorded Roman usage]
fol. 24v	FR	Matthew 21.23	Pentecost V, Wednesday
fol. 25r	FR vi in XL in ii F	Matthew 21.33	(Lent V)
fol. 26r	dom xx post pen.	Matthew 22.1–10[36]	(Pentecost XXI)
fol. 26v	m xxv p pe.	Matthew 22.15–23	(Pentecost XXIV)
fol. 27r	EB xviii dom. Post pen	Matthew 22.34	(Pentecost XIX)
fol. 28r	FR	Matthew 23.15	(no recorded Roman usage)
fol. 29r	de martib	Matthew 24.1–9	Common of martyrs

[35] On this entry see below.   [36] The end of the passage to be read is marked.

fol. 29v	FR vi	Matthew 24.27	Saturday, Vigil of Advent I
fol. 30v	de virginib	Matthew 25.1	Common of Virgins
fol. 53v	de petro FR	Mark 8.22	(five uses)
fol. 53v	de petro	Mark 8.27	St Peter (29.6)
fol. 54r	unius mart.	Mark 8.37	(St Menas, feast on 11.11)

Many of the gospel passages marked as lections have been re-punctuated—by two different scribes, one of whom uses an early form of interrogation mark. Since the lection markings appear chiefly in Matthew, with three in Mark, they are likely to derive from a gospel book. If they had been copied from a lectionary or a lection list the scribe would have had to move through all of the gospels as he went from one feast to the next through the liturgical year. The lections follow the later Roman system of pericopes, which continued to specify readings until the 25th week after Pentecost. But the readings for weekday services, indicated by FR for Feria, do not correspond to any clear set. Lections for votive feasts include the entries 'De sapientia' (Matthew 11.25) and 'ad parvulos' (Matthew 19.13), neither of which is found in any other Anglo-Saxon source.[37] The Gregorian Sacramentary includes a votive mass entitled 'Missa de Sapientia' (with the lection John 17.1–3), while the lection from Matthew 11 is one of two rubricated 'De Sapientia' in the late ninth-century St Amand Sacramentary (Paris, Bibliothèque nationale de France, lat. 2291), presumably with a votive function.[38]

The late eleventh-century textual annotator has copied on fol. 3v a passage from Ambrose, *De Sacramentis* (V.4), under a heading which ascribes the text to Augustine. The passage discusses 'panem nostram superstantialem'. On fol. 23r the same scribe has added a note on the long interpolation at Matthew 20.28 which reads: 'Mirum unde istud additum cum Lucas parabolam de invitatis ad nuptias et primos accubitus eligentibus decimo canone ubi Mattheus sua non communia dicat referat.'[39] This note depends in part on the account of differences between the gospel narratives in Augustine, *De Consensu Evangelistorum*, LXXII. On fol. 135v at John 3.34 ('non enim ad mensuram'), a marginal note quotes Augustine, *In Johannem, Sermo* CXXIV. 10, 6, on the difference between God's gifts to men and to Christ.[40] On fol. 158r a marginal note at John 17.1 reads, 'Hoc evangelium legitur in cena domini ad collationem sicut consuetudines docent', implying that at this date the gospel book was in a monastic house. The lection is indeed that for Maundy Thursday.[41] The scribe of these

---

[37] Lenker, *Evangelienversion*, 410–11.

[38] Deshusses, *Sacramentaire Grégorien*, II, 41, III, 299.

[39] *Quattuor Evangelia*, ed. Wordsworth and White, 124, print this entry. Chapman, *Vulgate Gospels*, 192, quotes Madan's view that this is the hand of the Anglo-Saxon liturgical annotator. I cannot agree.

[40] PL 31, col. 1508.

[41] Lenker, *Evangelienversion*, 317. The notes were discussed briefly by H. H. Glunz, *History of the Vulgate in England from Alcuin to Roger Bacon, Being an Inquiry into the Text of some English Manuscripts of the Vulgate Gospels* (Cambridge, 1933), 304–5.

marginal notes wrote in a small script with Anglo-Norman features and distinctive **d** and **g**, which may be compared with the hands found in the early
twelfth-century Worcester copy of Smaragdus' *Diadema Monachorum* (London, British Library, Royal 8 D. XIII). This may also be the hand which, in several places, revised the gospel texts to incorporate Theodulfian readings.[42]

That this gospel book has survived may suggest that it was regarded with
veneration, although there is no surviving evidence that it was regarded as a
relic. It is not clear whether the book was copied in Italy (or even Gaul) for
export, or whether it was used on the continent before the insular corrector
altered the text to conform with the Irish gospel family. But the various series of
lection marks and neumes entered between the seventh and the twelfth centuries show that this book was used as the source of gospel lections for one or
more communities which followed Roman use. Both the script used by the
insular corrector of the text and the Chad entry suggest that this was in Mercia.
If the suggested connection with Lichfield is accepted, then the fourteenth-
century tradition that in 822 Lichfield had twenty canons, of whom eleven were
priests and nine deacons, may shed light on the community which made use of
this manuscript.[43] The entry from a sacramentary provides rare evidence of
early knowledge of the Gelasian Sacramentary in England around the year
800.[44]

As a rare instance of a gospel book which shows continuous use throughout
the pre-conquest period and into the twelfth century, this early Italian manuscript adds to the body of evidence reminding us that concern with text, liturgy,
music, and exegesis was not confined to Theodore's Canterbury, Bede's Jarrow,
or to the reforms of the tenth century. From a concern with the correct textual
readings, especially of passages read on feast days, the annotations move to
exegesis and to the explanation of the Lord's Prayer and of the celebrated textual
interpolation in the gospel of Matthew. As so often, the examination of a manuscript can enhance the diet of historians, and even reduce its homogeneity.

[42] This is Wordsworth and White's O gl. at Matthew 5.24 and Luke 9.54.
[43] A. J. Kettle and D. A. Johnson, 'The Cathedral of Lichfield', in *A History of the County of
Staffordshire, III*, ed. M. W. Greenslade, Victoria County History (Oxford, 1970), 140.
[44] For sacramentaries used in England, see D. A. Bullough, *Carolingian Renewal* (Manchester, 1991),
211–12.

4

WHY DID EADFRITH WRITE THE LINDISFARNE GOSPELS?

Richard Gameson

The Lindisfarne Gospels is—thanks to the colophon that was added to it in the tenth century—one of the few relatively secure footholds in the shifting sands of Insular book production, palaeography, and illumination (pls. 3–5).[1] Written, we are told, by Eadfrith, 'bishop of the Lindisfarne Church', bound by Æthelwald, 'bishop of the Lindisfarne islanders', and (subsequently) encased in precious metal and gems by Billfrith the anchorite, this deservedly famous manuscript establishes Lindisfarne at the end of the seventh century as a supremely accomplished scriptorium.[2] It shows, moreover, something of the resources and activities of that centre at the time. The scriptorium evidently had access, for instance, to a good Italian Vulgate text, and to a set of evangelist portraits. It was able to obtain and prepare a wide range of pigments, including the exotic lapis lazuli and—admittedly in very small quantities—gold ink. It could call upon the animal resources and technical skill needed to make parchment of the highest order. Furthermore, it was a place where Insular half-uncial was refined under the influence of Italian uncial; and where elements of Insular, Germanic, and Mediterranean art were synthesized in a masterly way.

[1] London, British Library, Cotton Nero D. iv: E. A. Lowe, *Codices Latini Antiquiores*, 11 vols. plus *Supplement* (Oxford, 1934–71); 2nd edn. of vol. II (Oxford, 1972) (henceforth: *CLA*), II, no. 187; J. J. G. Alexander, *Insular Manuscripts 6th to 9th Century* (London, 1978), cat. 9; G. Henderson, *From Durrow to Kells: The Insular Gospel-books 650–800* (London, 1987), 99–122. Facsimile: *Codex Lindisfarnensis*, ed. T. Kendrick, T. J. Brown, R. L. S. Bruce-Mitford *et al.*, 2 vols. (Olten and Lausanne, 1956–60) (henceforth: *Cod. Lind.*).

[2] Fol. 259r: discussed in *Cod. Lind.*, II, 5–16 (the case for dating it to 687 x 98, 'probably nearer the latter date', is put on 12–16), and Book ii, 5–11. See also Henderson, *Durrow to Kells*, 112. The full text (as trans. in *Cod. Lind.*, II, Book ii, 10) reads: 'Eadfrith, bishop of the Lindisfarne church, originally wrote this book, for God and for St Cuthbert and—jointly—for all the saints whose relics are in the island. And Æthelwald, bishop of the Lindisfarne islanders, impressed it on the outside and covered it—as he well knew how to do. And Billfrith, the anchorite, forged the ornaments which are on it on the outside and adorned it with gold and with gems and also with gilded-over silver—pure metal. And Aldred, unworthy and most miserable priest, glossed it in English between the lines with the help of God and St Cuthbert. And by means of the three "sections" he made a home for himself: the section of Matthew was for God and St Cuthbert; the section of Mark for the bishop; the section of Luke for the members of the community (in addition, eight ores of silver for his induction); and the section of St John was for himself (in addition four ores of silver for God and St Cuthbert) so that, through the grace of God, he may gain acceptance into heaven, happiness and peace, and through the merits of St Cuthbert, advancement and honour, wisdom and sagacity on earth. Eadfrith, Æthelwald, Billfrith, Aldred made or, as the case may be, embellished this gospel book for God and Cuthbert.'

Inevitably, in view of the lack of comparably reliable information for the early history of most other Insular gospel books, such manuscripts tend to be dated, placed, and interpreted in relation to the Lindisfarne Gospels. Correspond- ingly, the community of Lindisfarne is firmly fixed in scholarly (and popular) perception as a place—*the* place, indeed—where masterpieces of Insular callig- raphy and book illumination were produced; and Lindisfarne has attracted into its orbit a constellation of fine books.[3] The various attributions and their strengths and weaknesses do not really concern us here—except to the extent that they may lead us to forget both how exceptional the Lindisfarne Gospels is, and that the community of Lindisfarne did not inevitably and continuously produce such volumes. Moreover, the relatively high survival rate of fine, decor- ated Insular gospel books, the very low survival rate of their humbler but undoubtedly once infinitely more numerous counterparts, and the general paucity of ordinary reading texts can further encourage us to regard the wholly extraordinary as the norm.[4] The fact that so many modern works reproduce the Lindisfarne Gospels and so few reproduce the lesser volumes, understandable though it is, nevertheless perpetuates the myth. This is not to minimize the standards of Lindisfarne as a scriptorium: on the contrary, the Lindisfarne Gospels itself—clearly the mature work of an accomplished and well-practised scribe-artist who had ready access to materials of the highest quality—provides unshakeable evidence for the excellence of its work (pl. 3). It is important, how- ever, to avoid the temptation to regard this manuscript as the standard (which it very definitely is not), and thus to lose sight of its wholly exceptional qualities. Even taking the most generous view of the late seventh- and early eighth- century manuscripts which may be attributed to Lindisfarne, only the Durham Gospels approaches the quality of our book;[5] the Cambridge–London Gospels[6] and the Echternach Gospels,[7] fine though they may be, are of a lesser grade. Indeed, among all the early English or Insular gospel books that have come

---

[3] *Cod. Lind.*, II, esp. 89–106, was fundamental in this; and, though criticized in various respects, its view still largely holds the field. The most important recent contributions to the debate, materially advancing knowledge of the textual relationships between the various books, are C. Verey, 'The Gospel Texts at Lindisfarne at the Time of St Cuthbert', in *St Cuthbert, His Cult and His Community to 1200*, ed. G. Bonner, D. Rollason, and C. Stancliffe (Woodbridge, 1989), 143–50; 'A Northumbrian Text Family', in *The Bible as Book: The Manuscript Tradition*, ed. J. Sharpe and K. Van Kampen (London, 1998), 105–22; and 'Lindisfarne or Rath Maelsigi? The Evidence of the Texts', in *Northumbria's Golden Age*, ed. J. Hawkes and S. Mills (Stroud, 1999), 327–35.

[4] See further R. G. Gameson, 'The Royal 1 B. vii Gospels and English Book Production in the Seventh and Eighth Centuries', in *The Early Medieval Bible: Its Production, Decoration and Use*, ed. Gameson (Cambridge, 1994), 24–52.

[5] Durham Cathedral Library, A. II. 17 etc.: *CLA* II, no. 149. Facsimile: *The Durham Gospels*, ed. C. Verey, T. J. Brown and E. Coatsworth, EEMF 20 (Copenhagen, 1980).

[6] Cambridge, Corpus Christi College, 197B + London, British Library, Cotton Otho C. v + Royal 7 C. xii: *CLA* II, no. 125; Alexander, *Insular Manuscripts*, cat. 12; Verey, 'Northumbrian Text Family'.

[7] Paris, Bibliothèque nationale de France, lat. 9389: *CLA* V, no. 578; Alexander, *Insular Manuscripts*, cat. 11. See more generally N. Netzer, *Cultural Interplay in the Eighth Century: The Trier Gospels and the Making of a Scriptorium at Echternach* (Cambridge, 1994).

down to us, Lindisfarne has only two peers: the Codex Aureus[8] and the Book of Kells.[9] Scriptoria have their own dynamics, linked to the history of their respective centres, and Lindisfarne evidently reached a peak in the generation around 700; nevertheless, even then it is unlikely to have operated like the 'Court School' of Charlemagne, turning out a steady stream of highly opulent gospel books. On the contrary, we should have clearly in view that fact that the Lindisfarne Gospels, a superlatively fine manuscript, is and was altogether extraordinary; and it was, therefore, almost by definition, the product of exceptional circumstances.

The motive for the work is stated unequivocally at the start of the lengthy Old English colophon that was added in the tenth century by Aldred, the 'unworthy and most miserable priest' who supplied an interlinear gloss to the entire text, and who subsequently became provost of the community (then at Chester-le-Street).[10] This says: 'Eadfrith, bishop of the Lindisfarne church, originally wrote this book for God and for St Cuthbert and—jointly—for all the saints whose relics were in the island.'[11] There follows a lengthy account of Aldred's own labours; and the note concludes with a brief restatement (in Latin) of the original rationale, wherein the glossator joins himself to his predecessors: 'Eadfrith, Æthelwald, Billfrith, Aldred made or, as the case may be, embellished this gospel book for God and Cuthbert' (pls. 4–5). Whether one believes that, when talking about his predecessors, Aldred was echoing the words of a now lost earlier record, or rather that he was finally preserving in writing what had formerly been an oral tradition,[12] it is notable that the expressed rationale is purely spiritual and altruistic. Although, in view of the late date of the record, one should avoid placing too much weight on the words themselves, the general tone remains suggestive, particularly given that the recorded motivations associated with other early Insular or Anglo-Saxon books are rather different. The colophon in the Book of Durrow, for instance (itself

---

[8] Stockholm, Kungliga Bibliotek, A. 135: *CLA* XI, no. 1642; Alexander, *Insular Manuscripts*, cat. 30. Facsimile: *Codex Aureus*, ed. R. G. Gameson, 2 vols., EEMF 28–9 (Copenhagen, 2000–1).

[9] Dublin, Trinity College, 58: *CLA* II, no. 274; Alexander, *Insular Manuscripts*, cat. 52. Facsimile: *Evangliorum Quattuor Codex Cenannensis*, ed. P. Meyer, 3 vols. (Olten and Lausanne, 1951); also *The Book of Kells*, ed. P. Fox, 2 vols. (Luzern, 1990).

[10] N. R. Ker, 'Aldred the Scribe' repr. in his *Books, Collectors and Libraries: Studies in the Medieval Heritage*, ed. A. G. Watson (London, 1985), 3–8; W. J. Boyd, *Aldred's Marginalia* (Exeter, 1975); G. Bonner, 'St Cuthbert at Chester-le-Street', in *St Cuthbert*, ed. Bonner *et al.*, 387–95, esp. 392–3.

[11] The other main relics were the head of King Oswald, some part of the bones of Aidan, along with the bodies of Eadberht, Æthelwald, and Eadfrith himself: cf. Symeon of Durham, *Libellus de exordio et procursu istius hoc est Dunelmensis ecclesiae*, II, 6, ed. D. Rollason (Oxford, 2000), 102.

[12] In favour of the former interpretation is the fact that, by the time Aldred was writing, the community had been away from Lindisfarne itself for the best part of a century. The putative original could not pre-date Billfrith's contribution—done at an uncertain point in the eighth century—and might even have been associated with it in some way. One might compare the case of the eighth-century copy of canons, Toulouse, Bibliothèque municipale, 364 + Paris, Bibliothèque nationale de France, lat. 8901, whose colophon, now lost, was included in a tenth-century copy of the MS, Albi, Bibliothèque municipale, 2: see *CLA* VI, no. 836.

seemingly copied from, or based on an earlier note), beseeches the blessing of St Patrick and begs the reader's prayers for the scribe ('Columba').[13] A similar philosophy appears in a simpler form in the colophon of the Barberini Gospels which, written in the hand of the final scribe, states bluntly: 'Pray for Wigbald.'[14] The luxurious gospel book written in gold on purple parchment which Wilfrid offered to Ripon had been commissioned, so Stephen of Ripon tells us, for the good of that bishop's soul; and it was kept in his church as a memorial to him, mention of it even being made in the epitaph that was inscribed on his tomb there.[15] A golden copy of the Petrine epistles was commissioned from Minster-in-Thanet by St Boniface († 754) 'to secure honour and reverence for the holy scriptures' from the heathen amongst whom he laboured;[16] while the anonymous Life of Ceolfrith († 716), abbot of Wearmouth-Jarrow, explains thus the function of the three great pandects whose production he organised: 'two . . . he had placed in the churches of his two monasteries, so that it should be easy for all who wished to read any chapter of either testament to find what they wanted; while the third he resolved to offer as a gift to Peter, prince of the apostles, when he was about to go to Rome.'[17]

Such records are inevitably simplifications, and doubtless conceal as much as they reveal. Nevertheless, the contrast between these cases—where the work was recorded as a gift, or to have a didactic or proselytizing function, or was expressly hoped to benefit the soul of the scribe or patron—and the documented function of our manuscript remains noteworthy. There is no shortage of medieval books which are said to have been written for the patron saint of the house in question (sometimes implying both the saint and the community);[18]

---

[13] Dublin, Trinity College, 57, fol. 247v: reproduced in colour, B. Meehan, *The Book of Durrow* (Dublin, 1996), 78. Further on the MS see *CLA* II, no. 273; Alexander, *Insular Manuscripts*, cat. 6; facsimile: *Evangelium Quattuor Codex Durmachensis*, ed. A. A. Luce, G. O. Simms, P. Meyer, and L. Bieler, 2 vols. (Olten and Lausanne, 1960).

[14] 'Ora pro Wigbaldo.' Vatican City, Biblioteca Apostolica Vaticana, Barb. lat. 570, fol. 153r: *CLA* I, no. 63; Alexander, *Insular Manuscripts*, cat. 36. Cf. e.g. *CLA* I, no. 18 and V, no. 608.

[15] *The Life of Bishop Wilfrid by Eddius Stephanus*, ed. B. Colgrave (Cambridge, 1927), 36; *HE* V, 19 (p. 528).

[16] 'Sic et adhuc deprecor, ut augeas quod cepistis, id est, ut mihi cum auro conscribas epistolas domini mei sancti Petri apostoli ad honorem et reuerentiam sanctarum scripturarum ante oculos carnalium in praedicando, et quia dicta eius, qui me in hoc iter direxit, maxime semper in presentia cupiam habere': *Die Briefe des heiligen Bonifatius und Lullus*, ed. M. Tangl, MGH Epistolae Selectae I (Berlin, 1916), no. 35 (p. 60). Cf. *English Historical Documents I c.500–1042*, ed. D. Whitelock, 2nd edn. (London, 1979), no. 172.

[17] 'quorum duo per totidem sua monasteria posuit in aecclesiis, ut cunctis qui aliquod capitulum de utrolibet Testamento legere uoluissent, in promtu esset inuenire quod cuperent; tertium autem Romam profecturus donum beato Petro apostolorum principi offerre decreuit'. *Vita Ceolfridi*, c. 20: *Venerabilis Baedae Opera Historica*, ed. C. Plummer, 2 vols. (Oxford, 1896), I, 388–404, at 395.

[18] e.g. Douai, Bibliothèque municipale, 306 (Gregory, *In Ezechielem*, etc.; Marchiennes; s. xi). The original scribe wrote L[iber] S[anctae] R[ic]t[ru]d[is] prominently on several folios (3r, 16v, 17r, 24v, 25r) and concluded his work (94r, col. 1) with the following colophon: 'Huius libri scriptoris fratris Amandi cunctorum monachorum infimi. memor esto sancta Rictrudis. eique ueniam scelerum suorum apud terribilem iudicem impetra ut tecum sine fine mereatur regnare in supera regna' ('Be mindful, St Rictrude,

yet the emphasis that is placed in Aldred's note on God, Cuthbert, and the Lindisfarne saints as co-dedicatees commands attention. Doubtless Eadfrith, Æthelwald, and Billfrith did hope that their labours would benefit their own souls—and as the first two both became bishop of Lindisfarne, some would claim that it may also have helped their 'careers'. Moreover, the memory of their involvement in the project was evidently kept golden; and a prayer added by Aldred to the end of Matthew's Gospel begs: 'Thou living God, remember Eadfrith and Æthelwald and Billfrith and Aldred, a sinner; these four with God were concerned with this book.'[19] Be that as it may, the primary purpose of the Lindisfarne Gospels, at least as it has been transmitted to us, was to honour the divine, thereby establishing a direct relationship with heaven, one that was channelled through 'St Cuthbert and all the saints whose relics are on the island'. Assuming that the tradition embodied in the colophon is broadly reliable, it lends considerable weight to the conjecture that the Lindisfarne Gospels was produced shortly before the translation of Cuthbert's body in 698. But whatever the truth of this point, the manuscript was clearly believed to have been written as an act of devotion, expressing the community's veneration of God, of Cuthbert, and of other local saints. Given the superlative quality of the book, the honour it represented—not to mention the investment of resources— was very considerable. Why was such an investment made at this time? The translation of St Cuthbert, though part of the story, is not in itself the answer: it is a symptom of the circumstances that lie behind the manuscript, not its cause. To understand *that* we must consider the history and situation of Lindisfarne itself.

Founded in 635, when King Oswald of Northumbria (634–42) gave the island to Aidan, the missionary monk from Iona, the community of Lindisfarne initially enjoyed a commanding position within the Northumbrian church.[20] Although the first Christian king of Northumbria, Edwin († 633), had been a Deiran, and the new faith initially took root, therefore, in the southern part of the kingdom,[21] on Edwin's death at the hands of Penda of Mercia the see of York lapsed and the Roman mission was abandoned. As Oswald, the next Christian king to support missionary endeavours, had Bernician roots and had been in exile among the Irish, the centre of gravity for ecclesistical power moved north, and it was monks from Iona whom he sponsored. Bishop Aidan († 651) enjoyed particularly close relations with Oswald; and the intimate connection

---

of Brother Amand, the scribe of this book, lowliest of all monks; grant him pardon for his sins before the dread judge so that he may be worthy to reign with you for ever in the heavenly realms').

[19] 'ðu lifigiende god gemyne ðu eadfrið 7 æðilwald 7 billfrið 7 aldred peccator ðas feowero mið gode ymbwᵒeron ðas boc.' Fol. 89v: cf. *Cod. Lind.*, Book ii, 10–11 (whose translation and edition are reproduced here).

[20] *HE* III, 3–6.

[21] Edwin does not appear to have founded any churches in Bernicia: Oswald is credited with having been the first to do so: *HE* III, 2 (p. 216).

between Lindisfarne and the Bernician monarchy is underlined by the island's physical proximity to the royal stronghold of Bamburgh. Yet at the same time the community remained a daughter house of Iona, and Aidan's immediate successors as abbot of Lindisfarne (and bishop of Northumbria), the Irish monks Finan (651–61) and Colman (661–4), were not elected from within the Lindisfarne community but came directly from the mother house, having been consecrated there.[22] Lindisfarne prospered under Finan, who both augmented its internal resources, building a church 'suitable for an episcopal see', and enhanced its external authority. It is clear that he enjoyed a mutually beneficial relationship with King Oswy, a Bernician 'who had been educated and baptized by the Irish and was well versed in their language', and who gradually extended his *imperium* first into Deira and then into Mercia.[23] Finan baptized both Peada of Mercia and Sigeberht of Essex as they accepted Christianity under Oswy's spreading influence, and the bishop consolidated the footholds thus gained by dispatching his protégés Cedd and Diuma as bishop of the East Saxons and Mercians respectively.[24] As Northumbrian power waxed strong—especially after Oswy's defeat of Penda of Mercia in 655—while the influence of the church of Canterbury (along with the political power of Kent) was waning, Lindisfarne became the pre-eminent ecclesiastical force in England. Yet there were already storm clouds on the horizon—Finan was forced to defend his Irish customs in the face of criticism from a certain Ronan, a fellow Irishman who had spent some time in Italy and Francia.

To note that Irish and Roman Christians in England had to some extent intermingled by this point should not lead one to minimize the ideological and doctrinal divide between them. After all, the fact that in our own day the pope and the archbishop of Canterbury could pray together in Canterbury Cathedral in no way implied a rapprochment in their respective views on, for instance, birth control, homosexuality, and women priests, nor an imminent reunification of their churches! Moreover, whether or not Bede overstressed the divisions between the Roman and the Irish christians, there can be no doubt that this 'golden age' of spiritual authority and political influence for Lindisfarne came to an end at the Synod of Whitby in 664.[25] When King Oswy decided in favour of the Roman faction he dealt a harsh blow to the Irish party in general and to Lindisfarne in particular, a blow which is likely to have been felt all the more keenly for being unexpected. The fact that Colman, the abbot-bishop of Lindisfarne, had been the spokesman for the Irish customs at the Synod (reflecting the central role of Lindisfarne at that point) focused the impact of the decision on Holy Island and its reputation. Colman himself retreated to Iona, moving thence to Ireland, taking with him, we are told, all the Irish from

---

[22] *HE* III, 25 (p. 294).   [23] Ibid.   [24] *HE* III, 21–2.
[25] *HE* III, 25. The discussion of H. Mayr-Harting, *The Coming of Christianity to Anglo-Saxon England*, 3rd edn. (London, 1991), 103–13 (with 7–9), remains fundamental here as elsewhere.

Lindisfarne plus thirty English members of the community.[26] Even allowing
for some exaggeration, the effect of depopulation on this scale must have been
devastating to the house at every level—a situation which can only have been
exacerbated by the great plague which struck in the same year. As Lindisfarne's
prestige plummeted, so that of the Roman party was in the ascendant. This is
reflected in the circumstance that when Colman's immediate successor, Tuda,
died of the plague shortly after taking office in 664, the Roman party's
spokesman, Wilfrid, was chosen as archbishop of the Northumbrians—with
his see at York.[27] It is equally embodied in the establishment of major houses
whose connections with Rome (and Gaul) were particularly strong: Hexham,
founded by Wilfrid in 671–3, Wearmouth, set up by Benedict Biscop *c.*673–4,
followed by its counterpart, Jarrow, some eight years later. Above all, it is illustrated by the fact that shortly before the Synod of Whitby Alhfrith, Oswy's son,
had reassigned to Wilfrid the foundation of Ripon which he had formerly given
to Eata of Melrose; the Irish, 'when given the choice, preferred to renounce the
site rather than change their customs'.[28]

If the ecclesiastical landscape of Northumbria was thus being redrawn to the
disadvantage of Lindisfarne, the judgement at Whitby had equally serious
implications for the less tangible but even more significant matter of its spiritual prestige. Conviction of erroneous ritual practices, particularly in relation to
the celebration of the prime Christian feast, must inevitably have undermined,
if not exactly discredited, Lindisfarne's spiritual status. As Bede observed,
quoting from Galatians 2.2, the dispute 'naturally troubled the minds and hearts
of many people who feared that, though they had received the name of Christian, they were running or had run in vain'.[29] Moreover, the Irish defence of their
practices at Whitby had centred on the authority of their great patronal saint,
Columba, the founder of Iona—an authority which was, in the event, overruled
by that of St Peter. The Synod thus shook the spirituality and sanctity of Lindisfarne to its very roots. The circumstance that its mother house, Iona, the epi-
centre of Columban monasticism, persisted in the Irish observances until the
early eighth century cannot have helped;[30] and nor can the fact that political
relations between Northumbria and Ireland seem to have been deteriorating.
They reached their nadir in 684 when King Ecgfrith (670–85), Oswy's son and

---

[26] *HE* IV, 4.

[27] A post which he held stormily (at first *in absentia*) until 678. Further on Wilfrid, see Mayr-Harting,
Coming of Christianity, 129–47—which may be supplemented by his *Saint Wilfrid* (London, 1986); D. P.
Kirby, 'Northumbria in the Time of Wilfrid' and D. H. Farmer, 'Saint Wilfrid', both in *Saint Wilfrid at
Hexham*, ed. Kirby (Newcastle, 1974), 1–34 and 35–59; and C. Cubitt, 'Wilfrid's Usurping Bishops: Epis-
copal Elections in Anglo-Saxon England *c.*600–800', *Northern History*, 25 (1989), 18–38.

[28] *HE* III, 25 (p. 298); Bede, *Vita Cuthberti*, c. 7: *Two Lives of St Cuthbert*, ed. B. Colgrave
(Cambridge, 1940), 174–6.

[29] *HE* III, 25 (p. 296).

[30] *HE* V, 22. For the repercussions of the Synod of Whitby on Iona itself, see M. Herbert, *Iona, Kells
and Derry: The History and Hagiography of the Monastic Familia of Columba* (Oxford, 1988), esp. 44–6.

successor, dispatched an army to Ireland, whose leader 'wretchedly devastated a harmless race that had always been most friendly to the English, and his hostile bands spared neither churches nor monasteries'.[31]

Eata, abbot of Melrose (a foundation with close links to Holy Island), succeeded Colman in the role of abbot of Lindisfarne, with the formidable task of leading the refuted, depopulated, and demoted community. An Englishman, trained at Lindisfarne by Aidan but who now accepted the Roman Easter, Eata represented the maximum continuity that was possible in the circumstances. That in the long term contacts with the Irish church were to continue is clear;[32] however, in the short term there seems no reason to doubt that the composition of the community had changed fairly dramatically—and we may note in passing that all three craftsmen associated with the Lindisfarne Gospels have Anglo-Saxon as opposed to Irish names. Similarly, a symbolic reorientation may be seen in the dedication of the 'episcopal' church that had been built by Finan to St Peter, the ceremony being conducted by Archbishop Theodore of Canterbury.[33] Eata seems to have discharged his responsibilities well, and in 678 he was awarded the Bernician half of the newly divided diocese of Northumbria. He continued to serve as the bishop based at Lindisfarne when the diocese was subdivided again three years later; and in 685 the companion diocese, Hexham, was offered to another Melrose-Lindisfarne man, Cuthbert—who exchanged posts with Eata in order to remain at Holy Island. If the hagiographical portraits of Cuthbert underline his asceticism, it is nevertheless apparent that he enjoyed personal contacts with the great and the good.[34] Moreover, this seems to have been a period of growing financial strength for Lindisfarne, in common with other Northumbrian foundations.[35]

Yet if such developments imply a resurgence in Lindisfarne's external status, while the Lives of Cuthbert provide appealing portraits of its spiritual hero, this remained a period of crisis for the community in terms of its internal composition, its role within Northumbria, and its relationship with the royal court. The community was again ravaged by plague c.680, and 'nearly the whole of that renowned congregation of spiritual fathers and brethren departed to be with the

---

[31] *HE* IV, 26. For an explanation of the event see A. P. Smyth, *Warlords and Holy Men: Scotland A.D. 800–1000* (London, 1984), 26.

[32] See in general K. Hughes, 'Evidence for Contacts Between the Churches of the Irish and English from the Synod of Whitby to the Viking Age', in *England Before the Conquest: Studies in Primary Sources Presented to Dorothy Whitelock*, ed. P. Clemoes and K. Hughes (Cambridge, 1971), 49–67.

[33] *HE* III, 25 (p. 294).

[34] Cf. e.g. the Anonymous *Vita Cuthberti*, cc. 6 and 8: *Two Lives*, ed. Colgrave, 102–4 and 122; and Bede's *Vita Cuthberti*, cc. 24 and 27: *Two Lives*, ed. Colgrave, 234–6 and 242–4. Fundamental on Cuthbert himself is C. Stancliffe, 'Cuthbert and the Polarity Between Pastor and Solitary', in *St Cuthbert*, ed. Bonner *et al.*, 21–44.

[35] See M. Roper, 'Wilfrid's Landholdings in Northumbria', in *St Wilfrid*, ed. Kirby, 61–79 at 64. If Bede may be believed (*HE* III, 26), Colman and his predecessors at Lindisfarne had no money, only cattle, and would only accept lands or possessions to build monasteries if compelled to do so!

Lord in that pestilence'.[36] Cuthbert's rule at Lindisfarne was not universally popular within the community; and after his death there was a period of upheaval which once again resulted in the departure of 'many' of the monks.[37] Moreover, the house faced stiff competition from Wilfrid who, having been restored to York in 669 by Archbishop Theodore, was until 678 at the height of his power and influence.[38] Restored to York, Ripon, and Hexham in 686, he actually administered the see of Lindisfarne itself immediately after Cuthbert's death, until Archbishop Theodore intervened and consecrated Eadbert as bishop of Lindisfarne (688). The extent to which the status and reputation of Lindisfarne—and of the Irish contribution to the Anglo-Saxon church in general—still hung in the balance is perhaps suggested by the Life of Gregory the Great that was written at Whitby c.700.[39] Although it originally had strong Irish connections, Whitby was then being ruled by Ælfflæd, daughter of King Oswy and Queen Eanflæd, and a supporter of Wilfrid. Northumbrian history is a major preoccupation of the anonymous author, yet there is no word of the Irish contribution to the conversion of the kingdom.[40]

In such circumstances the promotion of the cult of Lindisfarne's great holy man, Cuthbert, after his death in 687 and, above all, subsequent to the revelation eleven years later that his body had remained incorrupt, was of central importance to the status, spiritual identity, and possibly also the internal unity of the community, which seems to have applied itself to the task with great energy and acumen.[41] The political climate was favourable for a resurgence of a foundation with strong Irish connections, for the new king of Northumbria, Aldfrith (686–705), had an Irish mother, had been in exile in Ireland, and was on friendly terms with Adomnán of Iona.[42] Cuthbert's body was elevated and enshrined in 698, and his story and sanctity were then immortalized in no fewer than three accounts, two of them being written by the greatest scholar in Christendom.[43] Bede clearly admired the spiritual heritage, the asceticism, and the evangelistic spirit of Lindisfarne; and whilst underlining his disapprobation of its initial erroneous observance of Easter—excusable through ignorance—he included a glowing portrait of the community, in Aidan's day no less than

---

[36] Bede, *Vita Cuthberti*, c. 27: *Two Lives*, ed. Colgrave, 246–8.

[37] Ibid., cc. 16 and 40: ed. Colgrave, 210 and 286.

[38] See in general Farmer, 'St Wilfrid', 44–6; Mayr-Harting, *St Wilfrid*, 6–8.

[39] *The Earliest Life of Gregory the Great*, ed. B. Colgrave (Kansas, 1968).

[40] Significantly, the anonymous Lindisfarne *Vita Cuthberti* of 699 x 704 plays down the saint's Ionan heritage: Stancliffe, 'Cuthbert', 23.

[41] A. Thacker, 'Lindisfarne and the Origins of the Cult of St Cuthbert', in *St Cuthbert*, ed. Bonner *et al.*, 103–22; D. P. Kirby, 'The Genesis of a Cult: Cuthbert of Farne and Ecclesiastical Politics in Northumbria in the Late Seventh and Early Eighth Centuries', *JEH* 46 (1995), 383–97, esp. 395–7.

[42] *HE* IV, 26; V, 15 and 19. See also H. Moisl, 'The Bernician Royal Dynasty and the Irish in the Seventh Century', *Peritia*, 2 (1985), 103–26, esp. 120–4.

[43] On the different *raisons d'être* of the Lives, see Thacker, 'Cult of St Cuthbert', 117–21; S. J. Coates, 'The Bishop as Pastor and Solitary: Bede and the Spiritual Authority of the Monk-Bishop', *JEH* 47 (1996), 601–19, esp. 612–18.

Cuthbert's, in his *Historia Ecclesiastica* of 731, which undoubtedly furthered its cause and disseminated its reputation. That such factors were ultimately successful in re-establishing Lindisfarne's paramount status—at least spiritually—is confirmed by the most distinguished son of the house's estwhile 'rival', York. Writing to King Æthelred of Northumbria in 793, Alcuin characterized the island community as the most sacred place in Britain.[44]

The broad setting in which the Lindisfarne Gospels was produced was thus one of turmoil and ferment, intimately bound up with religious and cultural change. Our manuscript was made at a delicate juncture in the history of the Lindisfarne community, as it was striving to defend its status, to define a new identity, and to find a new role in a Northumbria whose church and state were rapidly evolving. Moreover, if, following Bede, it is the dispute between the Roman and Irish parties that one perceives most clearly, there is no doubt that further tensions—such as the relations between Bernicia and Deira, between Wilfrid and other clerics, between Canterbury and other dioceses, not to mention between church and state as a whole—also came into play.

The opulence of the Lindisfarne Gospels would have been inconceivable without the material prosperity and—no less important—the more open-minded approach to the issue of ecclesiastical grandeur that followed the debacle of 664, something which undoubtedly reflected the influence of the Roman church. Equally, many aspects of the manuscript presuppose an availability of Mediterranean models which can only have materialized in the later seventh century—above all, after the book-collecting activities of Benedict Biscop and Ceolfrith for Wearmouth-Jarrow—and a receptiveness to them which is likely to have been a direct result of the outcome of the Synod of Whitby. The contents or 'architecture' of the Lindisfarne Gospels, its Italian Vulgate text, the layout *per cola et comata*, the reformed Insular half-uncial, the type of evangelist portraits, all advertise a foundation that had ready access to, and drew willingly upon Italian resources.[45] Yet, it need hardly be said, the result does not look at all like an Italian manuscript: the script is a reformulated variety of *Insular* half-uncial; greater emphasis is, in true Insular tradition, given to the incipits than to the explicits; the ornament is an elegant and refined version of the *Insular* vocabulary; and the portraits have been interpreted in a distinctively *Insular* way (pls. 3–4). This is a response to, rather than an adoption of Mediterranean

---

[44] 'locus cunctis in Brittannia uenerabilior': Alcuin, *Epistolae*, ed. E. Dümmler, MGH Epistolae IV (Berlin, 1895), no. 16 (p. 42).

[45] The evidence for this is set out in *Cod. Lind.* II, esp. 56–8, 93–4, 105–6, and 126–73. Brown refined his view of the importance of Roman uncial as a model for the script of the Lindisfarne Gospels, and its relationship to Eadfrith's Insular heritage, in 'The Irish Element in the Insular System of Scripts to A.D. 850', in his *A Palaeographer's View*, ed. J. Bately, M. Brown, and J. Roberts (London, 1993), 201–20 at 207–9; and, more generally, in *Durham Gospels*, ed. Verey *et al.*, esp. 43–4 and 46–9. Debate on the exact nature of the Italian model(s) for the portraits (and by implication the text) has been advanced by P. Michelli, 'What's in the Cupboard? Ezra and Matthew Reconsidered', in *Northumbria's Golden Age*, ed. Hawkes and Mills, 345–58.

models. If some elements of the book advertised a community that accepted the importance of the Mediterranean world and its interpretation of Christianity, plenty of others showed that it maintained a fundamental relationship to Irish and Insular traditions.

Such formal features are often discussed in a rather abstract way—as the result of the accessibility of models and of scribal evolution, or as a phenomenon of style. But this is, at best, only part of the story: it is naive in the extreme to assume that early medieval scribes and artists, particularly those of the highest order, were passive conduits for the material that happened to be at their disposal, and were unable to transcend their training and background if they so wished. On the contrary, they had pronounced tastes and preferences, and made deliberate choices about which models to follow, what to combine, and how to do so. No one would seriously doubt that the nature and appearance of the Codex Amiatinus and its sister pandects—grand volumes written in a skilled imitation of Roman uncial, whose sparing decoration and visual articulation accords with late antique rather than Insular canons—were declarations of Wearmouth-Jarrow's particular affiliation to Italian, specifically Roman, traditions.[46] Correspondingly, it is highly likely that the carefully balanced 'specifications' of the Lindisfarne Gospels (which no other putative Lindisfarne manuscript exactly matches[47]) represented a deliberate choice, and were conceived to make a statement about the community that sponsored and produced it. The two general points that no informed contemporary could have failed to perceive were that the manuscript combined the best of the Mediterranean and Insular worlds, and that its overall quality was exceptionally high. In sum, the creation of a superlative gospel book, whose text, script, figural decoration, and initial ornament all showed a receptiveness to Mediterranean models, subsumed into a continuing appreciation of Insular ones, and that was seemingly written in honour of God, St Cuthbert, and the saints of Holy Island, made a forthright declaration about Lindisfarne, its traditions, and its identity in post-Synod of Whitby Northumbria.

What was the point of such a gesture? It was a wholly religious act; but as such, like private prayer and public liturgy, it potentially had the power to move mountains. In the first place, such a splendid offering demonstrated to the heavenly recipients the devotion of the brothers, while subtly laying them under an obligation to reciprocate the gift by extending their support to this model

---

[46] Florence, Biblioteca Medicea Laurenziana, Amiatino 1: *CLA* III, no. 299; Alexander, *Insular Manuscripts*, cat. 7. London, British Library, Add. 37777 and 45025; also Loan 81: *CLA* II, no. 177; B. Bischoff and V. Brown, 'Addenda to *Codices Latini Antiquiores*', *Mediaeval Studies*, 47 (1985), 317–66 at 351–2. See further T. J. Brown, 'Tradition, Imitation and Invention in Insular Handwriting of the Seventh and Eighth Centuries', in his *A Palaeographer's View*, 179–200 at 197; also R. Marsden, *The Text of the Old Testament in Anglo-Saxon England* (Cambridge, 1995), 76–201.

[47] Cf. *Cod. Lind.*, II, 105–6, including Brown's statement: 'It may be that Eadfrith with his passion for what was best in the Italian book was an innovator whose example was not very widely followed by his contemporaries and successors in the Lindisfarne scriptorium.'

community. A good number of early medieval books (and artefacts) with donor images and inscriptions fulfilled the same function. The point is spelled out by the example in a fine volume comprising a gospel lectionary and the Passion of St Denis that was written by Dodolinus and decorated by Abbot Odbert at Saint Bertin in Saint-Omer around the millenium. This states:

> O bountiful Denis, accept this little gift
> Which your servant Dodolinus offers to you as a suppliant
> And watch over Father Odbert and all your servants
> And, in association with St Bertin, extend the hand of peace. Amen.[48]

Secondly, the work could, by extension, make an important contribution to the prestige and eminence of Holy Island, both physically and metaphysically. The case of Archbishop Egbert of Trier (977–93) provides an illuminating parallel here. Egbert's elaborate artistic patronage undoubtedly reflected a personality that loved art, who sought out highly skilled craftsmen (including the finest illuminator of the Ottonian empire), and had at his disposal a workshop of international renown; but it also fits into a context of competing for primatial status with the sees of Mainz and Cologne. The adornment of the episcopal staff that had reputedly been given by St Peter to Eucharius, the first bishop of Trier, the manufacture of the altar-like sandal reliquary of St Andrew, the creation of a psalter decorated with a sequence of the fourteen archbishops of Trier and preceded by an image of Egbert receiving the book from the scribe and presenting it to St Peter, and the possession of a de luxe gospel lectionary that was prefaced by a commanding image of Egbert of Trier himself, all this apotheosized his see, its venerable history, and himself, placing their collective merits before the eyes of God and man.[49] Moreover, as Henry Mayr-Harting has observed: 'The fact is that in the whole period of Egbert's archiepiscopate, after decades of greatness, Trier was under pressure. His art must be seen more as a response to that pressure than as a victory salute.'[50] The creation of the Lindisfarne Gospels was a similar exercise.

It is occasionally suggested that writing the Lindisfarne Gospels represented an astute 'career move' for Eadfrith, who became bishop of Lindisfarne shortly thereafter.[51] This is both an exaggeration and a minimization. Eadfrith's

---

[48] 'Alme Dyonysy paruum tu suscipe munus | Hoc tibi quod supplex offert seruus Dodolinus | Odbertumque patrem cunctosque tuere famellos | Bertinoque sacro sociante manum date pacem. Am[e]n.' Saint-Omer, Bibliothèque de l'agglomération, 342 *bis*, fol. 1r. Further on the MS see J. Porcher, *Manuscrits à peintures du VIIᵉ au XIIᵉ siècle* (Paris, 1954), no. 112.

[49] *Egbert Erzbischof von Trier 977–993*, ed. F. J. Ronig, 2 vols. (Trier, 1993), I, nos. 43, 41, 3, and 10 respectively. The MSS are Cividale, Museo Archeologico Nazionale, 136; and Trier, Stadtbibliothek, 24. See further, in general, H. Mayr-Harting, *Ottonian Book Illumination: An Historical Study*, 2 vols. (London, 1991), II, 57–83.

[50] Mayr-Harting, *Ottonian Book Illumination*, II, 83.

[51] Cf. M. P. Brown, 'The Lindisfarne Scriptorium from the Late Seventh to the Early Ninth Century', in *St Cuthbert*, ed. Bonner *et al.*, 151–63 at 154.

masterpiece advertised both his skill and his spirituality, and may to that extent have contributed to singling him out as the logical candidate for the see. The case of Ultán, the Irish scribe at a cell of Lindisfarne in the earlier eighth century who was immortalized in verse a century later, shows how highly calligraphic ability was regarded in such contexts, and how it could be considered to embody spiritual merit.[52] However, the 'careerist' interpretation of the Lindisfarne Gospels wholly underestimates the importance of the gesture, whose *raison d'être* was not to further the cause of one man, but rather to elevate a whole foundation spiritually and materially. The book, like the cult of Cuthbert with which it was associated, proclaimed the outstanding holiness of Lindisfarne. Indeed, this luxurious copy of the four gospels (itself a symbol of Christ) was, along with the body of the saint, the physical spirituality in its midst: these things became the essence of the community in a very real way—this is why, when the brothers abandoned Holy Island in the ninth century in the face of the Viking threat, these were what they took with them on their migrations.

It is easy to misunderstand the nature of early medieval Christianity, to misconstrue its practitioners, and to underestimate their actions. That the early Middle Ages was a period when what we tend to distinguish as 'political' and 'spiritual' were fundamentally and inextricably interwoven is often said; yet it is frequently forgotten that this did not just mean that holy men were involved in politics, nor even that spiritual movements interlocked with political factors, but equally that 'political' acts were shot through, even determined, by spiritual motivations. This was an age whose churchmen firmly believed that the Lord would help those who helped themselves; an age in which 'history' was written to show how things *should* have happened according to the divine plan as understood by the community or individual in question; and one in which many works of art were a forceful demonstration of devotion to the divine, a powerful advertisement of its favour, and a sincere and optimistic attempt to curry more. Furthermore, the sense of a common Christian purpose in planting and nourishing the faith in a given area in no way impeded a strong, primary commitment to one's own particular foundation, and to promoting its fortunes within a fallen world. Even in our own age of ecumenism (or interminable discussions about it), when most of the faithful would probably, if questioned, describe themselves as Christians first and as Anglicans (say) second, a sense of commitment and devotion to a preferred denomination or indeed to a particular church community runs strong; and not infrequently the more fervent the individual's faith, the more specific its locus. Only those who lack first-hand experience of this

---

[52] Æthelwulf, *De Abbatibus*, c. 8, ed. A. Campbell (Oxford, 1967), 18–23; to be read with L. Nees, 'Ultán the Scribe', *ASE* 22 (1993), 127–46. One should distinguish the case of Ultán (whose spiritual merit came from his work and skill as a scribe) from the more common book miracles, where the spirituality emanated from the independent holy status of the copyist or of the text copied (cf. e.g. *Adomnan's Life of Columba*, II, 8–9, ed. A. O. and M. O. Anderson (Edinburgh, 1961); *Vita Anselmi Episcopi Lucensis*, c. 80, ed. G. H. Pertz, MGH SS XII (Hannover, 1856), 1–35 at 34).

can doubt the reality of the tensions between Irish and Roman that came to a
head at Whitby, can be insensitive to the spirit of rivalry within unity that characterized the great monastic houses of Northumbria thereafter, and can fail to
perceive the strength of the feelings of local spiritual identity that activitated
Lindisfarne in the late seventh century. Doctrinal conformity, friendly relations, exchange of resources, and even transfer of personnel was in no way
incompatible with fierce local pride and competitiveness.

We are rarely in a position to comprehend the context in which, and the reasons why a de luxe early medieval manuscript was made with such clarity as in
relation to the Lindisfarne Gospels; and it is clear that these were extremely
complex. Above all, however, the creation of this extraordinary book presup-
posed not only exceptional skill and resources, but also unusually strong motivation. The Lindisfarne Gospels made a statement about the identity of
Lindisfarne and its synthesis of Roman and Irish traditions in the generation
after the Synod of Whitby; it incarnated the revived and reformulated spirituality of the community; it associated it with God, the local saints, and the great
new holy man, Cuthbert, in the most permanent way possible; and it laid these
parties under an obligation to support their faithful servants. It was the result of,
and a response to, very particular circumstances, needs, and aspirations; and
was the expression of localized, focused spirituality.

We can safely presume that, even though documentary details are lacking,
much the same was true of the comparably magnificent Codex Aureus and
Book of Kells. Correspondingly, they are themselves pointers to remarkable—
though, sadly, now irrecoverable—circumstances in the communities that produced them. More generally, the case of the better-documented Lindisfarne
Gospels reminds us of the breadth, depth, and paradoxes of early medieval spirituality which, while everything came within its remit, had very particular and
potentially competitive local applications and manifestations. Moreover, it
underlines the fundamental point that, if we do not take medieval religion seriously and try to comprehend it on its own terms, we will never understand the
ecclesiastical and political history, not to mention the art and culture of the
period.

5

VIRGIN QUEENS: ABBESSES AND POWER
IN EARLY ANGLO-SAXON ENGLAND

Veronica Ortenberg

'Scta Eormenhild virg'; 'scta Sexburga virg': thus do Anglo-Saxon calendars, litanies, and various other liturgical, narrative and hagiographical texts describe several women, ex-queens or royal widows who retired to monasteries after divorcing their husbands or after their husbands' deaths. I have long been struck by the deliberate choice of 'virgo', 'virgines', to designate women who were clearly anything but virgins, technically speaking. It is true, of course, that 'virgo' can just mean '(young) woman'; however, there can be little doubt, in view of the context and the way the word is deployed, that the intended sense in these cases was indeed 'virgin'. Why then were these women so described?

The power and influence of queens, princesses, and aristocratic women is a well-established feature of early Anglo-Saxon society.[1] The classic perspective on the subject is that these women had a great deal of power in the secular world, which was not questioned by their contemporaries, and, like their noble male counterparts, when they took charge of a monastic house they continued to exert this power. This is the current interpretation, which traditionally contrasts the power of 'Germanic' women with their much diminished status in a Christian society. To it I should like to add, if not substitute, another model. While not necessarily negating the first, this hopes to show that Anglo-Saxon ecclesiastical writers were not only describing a political and social reality, but were, more or less deliberately, attempting to fashion it according to their own perspective, and, sometimes, to meet their own needs.

Anglo-Saxon well-born women had power. What is not always appreciated

[1] Out of a fairly vast recent literature on the subject, see C. Fell, *Women in Anglo-Saxon England* (London, 1984), 111–27; P. Stafford, *Queens, Concubines and Dowagers: The King's Wife in the Middle Ages*, 2nd edn. (Leicester, 1998); J. T. Rosenthal, 'Anglo-Saxon Attitudes: Men's Sources, Women's History', in id. (ed.), *Medieval Women and the Sources of Medieval History* (Athens, Ga., 1990), 259–84; and H. Leyser, *Medieval Women: A Social History of Women in England 450–1500* (London, 1995), esp. 20, 24–30, 33–9, 47, and 56–64. A few studies refer more specifically to individual women of great renown and power, see e.g. J. Nicholson, '"Feminae gloriosae": Women in the Age of Bede', in *Medieval Women*, ed. D. Baker, Studies in Church History, Subsidia 1 (Oxford, 1978), 15–29; and S. Hollis, *Anglo-Saxon Women and the Church: Sharing a Common Fate* (Woodbridge, 1992), *passim*. Several important studies are in *New Readings on Women in Old English Literature*, ed. H. Damico and A. Hennessey Olsen (Bloomington, 1990).

is the fact that this power was principally respected and praised in women who
were either virgins (i.e. unmarried and having taken the veil) or who had come
to be regarded as 'honorary' virgins. Some, like the abbesses Æbbe of Colding-
ham, Æthelburh and Hildelith of Barking, Ælflæd of Whitby, Mildrith,
Mildgyth, and Eadburh of Minster-in-Thanet, or Mildburh of Wenlock were
nuns (virgins) in the traditional sense, women who had rejected the world in
order to take the veil. However, numerous English monastic foundations, both
male and female, were set up and/or led by women who, in view of their marital status as we know it, could not have been, technically speaking, virgins (with
the possible exception of Æthelthryth). Many were widows, like Eangyth and
her daughter, not to mention the famous abbess of Streonæshalch/Whitby,
Hild. Many again were the widows of kings: to cite but a few, we have Eanflæd,
Oswiu of Northumbria's widow, who ruled Whitby jointly with her daughter
Ælflæd; Sexburh, the widow of Eorconberht of Kent, who was abbess of
Minster-in-Sheppey then of Ely; and Eormenhild, the widow of Wulfhere of
Mercia, who became abbess of Minster-in-Sheppey. Others, however, were
divorced women, ex-queens, like Cuthburh of Wimborne, separated from
King Aldfrith of Northumbria and famous among her contemporaries for her
learning; Cyneburh, once wife of Alcfrith of Northumbria and later abbess of
Castor; and Osgyth, wife of Sighere of Essex and abbess of Chich.[2] Most of
these royal women ruled over monasteries which they themselves or other
women of their family had founded. In some cases, they retired there with their
daughters.[3] Many of these women were related to each other, and the tradition
of founding, endowing, and ruling a monastery was a family 'business': Sexburh
and Eormenhild went to Ely when Sexburh's sister Æthelthryth died; Mildrith,
Mildgyth, and Mildburh were sisters.

Why then were they all called 'virgines' in the texts? Clearly, defining widows
and kings' wives (as well as unmarried women) in this way was meant to emphasize the fact that they had, in effect, finished doing their job as women (namely
to marry and have children) and, having put this behind them, had placed
themselves outside the scope of that which made them women—they had
become asexual beings who were no longer regarded as specifically female.
Their choice of chastity, 'virginity of the soul' as Aldhelm put it,[4] was deliberate—akin to that of Mary Magdalene, a dearly loved model for Anglo-Saxon

---

[2] On most of these women, see *HE*.

[3] As did Sexburgh and Eormenhild, or Eanflæd and Ælflæd.

[4] Aldhelm, *Opera Omnia*, ed. E. Ehwald, MGH AA XV (Berlin, 1919), 226–323 (Prose) and 350–471
(Poem). *De Virginitate*, trans. in M. Lapidge and J. Rosier, *Aldhelm: The Poetic Works* (Cambridge, 1985)
and M. Lapidge and M. Herren, *Aldhelm: The Prose Works* (Cambridge, 1979). Aldhelm, using Augustine's words, says: 'The sanctity of the body is not lost provided that the sanctity of the soul remains',
Prose Works, 129. On Aldhelm's original treatment of this concept to take into account the Anglo-Saxon
situation and to create a parallel with the warrior-like queens through his insistance on showing nuns as
'soldiers of Christ', see Hollis, *Anglo-Saxon Women*, 75–112.

monastics, to whom they could likewise apply the title only as a matter of courtesy.[5] These abbesses, who were arguably no longer specifically female, acquired some of the functions of men in society, including that of exercising political power.

One might then say that, in a significant number of cases, personal political power and influence became open to women once they had ceased to be specifically female and had reached the ambiguous stage of asexuality through virginity, real or constructed. While political power was regarded as unseemly and tyrannical in a reigning queen by the likes of Bede or Stephen of Ripon, it was accepted and acceptable for women in this context. The unnamed wife of Rædwald of East Anglia who, after his conversion to Christianity on a visit to Kent, brought him back to paganism when he returned home; Eadburh, wife of Beohtric of Wessex, whose influence in government was such that she succeeded in removing her husband's other advisers and eventually had him murdered; and Iurminburh, King Ecgfrith of Northumbria's second wife, who persecuted Bishop Wilfrid and led the king to send him away, are illuminating examples.[6] Here are the few named queens who exercised real power, as opposed to being simply good Christian wives, and their press in the writings of Stephen of Ripon or Bede is all too clearly negative. We, of course, have no way of knowing whether they were really guilty of the deeds with which they are credited, or merely presented as such. Before ascertaining how this relative hostility to powerful secular women became an entrenched feature of English society as defined by its early ecclesiastical writers, it is worth looking at the concept of virginity before the Anglo-Saxon period, in particular in the Ancient World.

In Greek society, and indeed language, this status and word are somewhat ambiguous.[7] The definition of 'parthenia' applies to women before they marry, before they join the ranks of the *gynē*, and thus become fully fledged members of society as wives and mothers. The 'parthenos' is not necessarily a non-deflowered

[5] On the importance of the model of Mary Magdalene for Anglo-Saxon monks, such as her depiction on the highly devotional Ruthwell Cross, see M. Shapiro, 'The Religious Meaning of the Ruthwell Cross' (1940), repr. in his *Late Antique, Early Christian and Medieval Art* (London, 1980), 150–95 at 164; and C. A. Farr, 'Worthy Women on the Ruthwell Cross', in *The Insular Tradition*, ed. C. Karkov, R. T. Farrell, and M. Ryan (New York, 1997), 45–61. Also my own discussion in V. Ortenberg, 'Le Culte de Ste Marie Madeleine dans l'Angleterre anglo-saxonne', *Mélanges de l'École Française de Rome: Moyen Age*, 104 (1992), 13–35.

[6] *HE* II, 15 (pp. 188–191), and *The Life of Bishop Wilfrid by Eddius Stephanus*, ed. B. Colgrave (Cambridge, 1927), ch. 24, pp. 48–9. In the case of Eadburh, the story has it that her act caused such ill-feeling that the wives of the kings of Wessex were not allowed to hold the title of 'queen' until Æthelwulf revived its use in the later ninth century.

[7] A vast literature exists on this subject, from S. B. Pomeroy, *Goddesses, Whores, Wives and Slaves: Women in Classical Antiquity* (London, 1975), 1–204, to S. Blundell, *Woman in Ancient Greece* (Cambridge, Mass., 1995), 43–6 and 160–1. More specifically on virginity and its meaning, see G. Sissa, *Greek Virginity* (Cambridge, 1990), 35–81; L. Viitaniemi, '"Parthenia": Remarks on Virginity and its Meaning in the Religious Context of Ancient Greece', in *Aspects of Women in Antiquity: Proceedings of the First Nordic Symposium on Women's Lives in Antiquity*, ed. L. Larsson Loven and A. Stromberg (Jonsereed, 1998), 44–57; and A. Rousselle, *Porneia: On Desire and the Body in Antiquity* (Oxford, 1988), 131–89.

girl, since some are in fact mothers: she can be an unmarried mother, whose sons are called 'sons of a parthenos', 'parthenoi'. The girl's change of status is due to marriage rather than to physical deflowering. Similarly, the 'parthenos' par excellence, Apollo's Pythia at Delphi, while originally a young girl, rapidly came to be an old woman dressed in a young girl's clothes. Here too virginity is postulated as a necessary condition for the relationship between the prophetess and the god, the condition for her gift of prophecy being that the god alone is allowed to 'fill' her. 'Virginity' is therefore linked to a woman who has put relationships with men behind her in order to devote herself exclusively to the god—which is not the same as having never known men.

If this was the case for the best-known Greek priestess, it was certainly not so in Roman society.[8] Mary Beard, in what should still be regarded as a seminal article,[9] discussed the status of the Vestal Virgins, keepers of the city's sacred flame and hence of the welfare of the whole Roman state. Having analysed the prerogatives, judicial, economic, and political, of the Vestals, as well as their archaic duties, apparel, and hairstyle—which were closely associated with those of the traditional Roman bride (the mark of transition between the status of virgin girl and married woman on her wedding day)—Beard concludes that virginity gave the Vestals a status which was not only beyond that of women, but also beyond that of men in their rights in society. They were more powerful than both, in fact, precisely because of this abnormal status. Their virginity, however, had to be real in sexual terms, on pain of death for the defaulter and of catastrophic consequences for the whole *res publica*. It is because they were sexually untouched that these creatures could have access to supernatural power; they could only be a channel for the power of the gods because they had been set aside from wordly concerns.

Whether Tacitus was influenced by the case of the Vestals, or whether he was just reporting to the best of his understanding what he had been told about the position of women prophetesses like Veleda in the ancient 'Germanic' world, is a moot point. The Germanic prophetess in Tacitus' account is strikingly similar: she lives in the forest of 'Germania', isolated in a tower, leading her people and transmitting the will of the gods to them;[10] she too is dependent for her power on her sexual purity, that is, her lack of sexual experience.

In both these examples the assumption is that the power which these women possessed arose from their privileged link with the Other World: their alien-

[8] Pomeroy, *Goddesses*, 204–26, and esp. the remarkable work by A. Staples, *From Good Goddess to Vestal Virgins* (London, 1998), 129–56.

[9] 'The Sexual Status of Vestal Virgins', *Journal of Roman Studies*, 70 (1980), 12–27; although Beard herself changed her mind later in the wake of Gender Studies, in 'Re-reading (Vestal) Virginity', in *Women in Antiquity: New Assessments*, ed. R. Hawly and B. Levick (London, 1995), 166–77, her first reading seems to me still outstandingly valid and sharp.

[10] Tacitus, *Germania*, ch. 8: *The Agricola and the Germania*, ed. and tr. M. Hutton, rev. M. Winterbottom (Harvard, 1963).

ation from sex gave them a special channel to supernatural power. Anglo-Saxon attitudes, however, are not directly related to access to the supernatural, but to political power and influence in *this* world. Hence virginity is not a *source* of power, but only the *means* of it. This explains why such a powerful role could perfectly well be played by persons who were beyond womanhood, past it, rather than only by those who had set themselves aside from it.

Can it be said, however, that the model that was put forward reluctantly by Bede and more wholeheartedly by Aldhelm and Boniface, the 'virginity of the soul', is closer to that of patristic or christian authors? Christian society as a whole, from the fourth century onwards at least, linked the concept of virginity very firmly with the Virgin Mary herself. The doctrine of the Virgin Birth, propounded by the likes of Jerome and Ambrose of Milan, and supported by popular devotion in both East and West, led to the Virgin Mary becoming the patroness of virgins in the great ascetic fervour of the early centuries.[11] Treatises on virginity were popular especially from the fourth century onwards—witness the writings on this subject by Tertullian, Origen, Cyprian, Methodius of Olympus, Ambrose, Augustine, John Chrysostom, Gregory of Nyssa, and Basil of Ancyra, all of whom distinguish it as the highest state for a woman, above even that of widowhood. Jerome and Gregory of Nyssa do indeed commend the state of virginity as chastity in relation to both nuns and widows, and occasionally specify that the woman in question (the virgin Macrina, for example) came to be equal to a man.[12] In their case, though, the most highly praised women are those who behaved like a man in spiritual terms, in their religious life and spiritual asceticism. The idea that they could possibly have taken on the worldly jobs of a man—advisors to kings, leaders of major administrative, economic, and cultural institutions like Whitby, Ely, or Barking, scholars, teachers, missionaries and, some claim, responsible for carrying out sacerdotal duties, on the model of Hild, Ælflæd, Cuthburh, or Leoba—could hardly have been popular with the likes of Jerome, for example: while he happily allowed his disciples Melania, Paula, and Eustochium to live a monastic life and direct other women like them, this would not have included the possibility that they should act as men in a worldly context, let alone actually rule over men. Bede

[11] *A Dictionary of Mary*, ed. D. Attwater (London, 1957), 298-300; *Mary in the Documents of the Church*, ed. P. F. Palmer (London, 1953), 24-9; G. Miegge, *The Virgin Mary: The Roman Catholic Doctrine* (London, 1955), 36-52; and D. Edwards, *The Virgin Birth in History and Faith* (London, 1943), *passim*.

[12] This is another widely studied topic; see e.g. J. Bugge, *'Virginitas': An Essay in the History of a Medieval Ideal* (The Hague, 1975), 42-133; S. Elm, *Virgins of God: The Making of Asceticism in Late Antiquity* (Oxford, 1994), 44-169; G. Paterson Corrington, 'The "Divine Woman"? Propaganda and the Power of Chastity in the New Testament Apocrypha', in *Rescuing Creusa: New Methodological Approaches to Women in Antiquity*, ed. M. Skinner, Special Issue of *Helios*, NS, 13:2 (Lubbock, Tex., 1987), 151-62; D. F. Sawyer, *Women and Religion in the First Christian Centuries* (London, 1996), 148-9; A. Rousselle, *Porneia*, 130-3 and 186-9; P. Brown, *The Body and Society: Men, Women and Sexual Renunciation in Early Christianity* (London, 1988); and esp. G. Cloke, *'This Female Man of God': Women and Spiritual Power in the Patristic Age A.D. 350-450* (London, 1995), 57-70, 82-99, and 214-21.

himself, while greatly praising the spiritual example and rule of such women, did not always spend a great deal of time on detailing their political activities.[13] All the same, hagiographers do mention them, the 'blessed virgin [who] . . . was held in veneration by all who knew her, even by kings, [who] treated her with profound respect'; 'The princes loved her, the nobles received her, the bishops welcomed her with joy [on account of her wisdom and "prudence in counsel"]'; and, in the case of Hild, 'so great was her prudence that not only ordinary people but also kings and princes sometimes sought and received her counsel when in difficulties'.[14]

A parallel could be made here with the case of Æthelflæd, Lady of the Mercians († 918), ruler, administrator, and war leader. She had been married to Ealdorman Æthelred, by whom she had a daughter.[15] The *Anglo-Saxon Chronicle* begins to show her as a leader, including on the battlefield, even before her husband's death. (Of the daughter little is said, except to mention her existence and, after her mother's death, her removal by her uncle, after which she completely vanishes from the texts, as indeed she possibly did from her terrestrial existence.) Æthelflæd's role and presence are greatly enhanced, however, after Æthelred's death. This could well be due simply to her position then as sole commander and ruler. But, if her political power was obviously accepted fairly gracefully by her entourage, hardly renowned for being a 'soft touch', could it not be that, in addition to the hard reality, Æthelflæd, a widow, seemed to match the style and tradition of the abbesses of old? It is also possible that we see, in Æthelflæd's case, an association with the Scandinavian tradition of women heroines who were left alone in the world to defend the honour of their kin, without a man to protect them—virgins in the mould of Hervör, Gudrun, and other saga 'maiden warriors', or indeed of the Valkyries Brunhild and Sigrun, all forceful fighters on the battlefield also.[16]

---

[13] Hollis, 'Aldhelm's *De Virginitate*', 107–11; 'Confessors and Spiritual Mentors: Hagiographical Ideals and the Boniface Circle', in *Anglo-Saxon Women*, 119–136; 'A Beautiful Friendship Ruined: Bede's Revisionist Writing of Aelffled in the *Life of Cuthbert*', *ibid.* 179–207; 'Rewriting Female Lives: Hild of Whitby and Monastic Women in Bede's *Ecclesiastical History*', *ibid.* 243–70; and 'Rudolph of Fulda's *Life of Leoba*: An Elegy for the Double Monastery', *ibid.* 271–300 (Bischofsheim in Germany, under the powerful rule of Leoba, Boniface's friend, was another example of a major institution led by a woman, the missionary Leoba).

[14] 'The Life of St Leoba by Rudolf, monk of Fulda', in *The Anglo-Saxon Missionaries in Germany*, trans. C. H. Talbot (London, 1954), 222–3; *HE* IV, 23 (pp. 408–9).

[15] On Æthelflæd's life see F. T. Wainwright, 'Æthelflæd, Lady of the Mercians', in his *Scandinavian England*, ed. H. R. P. Finberg (Chichester, 1974), 305–24, repr. in *New Readings*, ed. Damico and Olsen, 44–55.

[16] An ironic twist, if ever there was one, since the people Æthelflæd was fighting were none other than the representatives and descendants of these 'heroines'—but it is in no way surprising to note the psychological, and literary, impact of a well-entrenched Viking tradition on English soil on the mentality of its own opponents. On these 'maiden warriors' and heroines of Scandinavian literature, see e.g. C. J. Clover, 'Maiden Warriors and Other Sons', in *Matrons and Marginal Women in Medieval Society*, ed. R. R. Edwards and V. Ziegler (Woodbridge, 1995), 75–87; M. Clunies Ross, 'Women and Power in the Scandinavian Sagas', in *Stereotypes of Women in Power: Historical Perspectives and Revisionist Views*, ed.

Commentators used to associate the Old English poem *Judith* with
Æthelflæd, seeing the Old Testament figure as a parallel type of saviour of her
people; however, it is now accepted that there is no demonstrable link between
the two.[17] Nevertheless, the work, which deals with the theme of a woman
fighting for her people, remains relevant to our enquiry in general terms.
Although Aldhelm in the *De Virginitate* had already treated Judith as a chaste
widow, it is in the poem that we see most clearly the transformation of the
widow-courtesan of the Old Testament into an heroic virgin warrior assuming
the leadership of her people.[18] The poem uses the words *mægð* and *ides* (with its
military connotations) no less than eight and four times respectively, repeatedly
referring to the divinely inspired wisdom, nobility, and bravery of the virgin
Judith—who is *torhtan, scyppendes, ellenrôf, snotere, searoðoncol, glēaw on geðonce,
ferhðglēawe, glēawhyðig wîf, gearoðoncolre, modigre*. The transition from courte-
san to virgin is significant: military power and political wisdom are clearly
acceptable in the second, but not in the first. An interesting association of virginity and military prowess is found again much later with Joan of Arc, whose
connections with the English, however inimical, make one wonder whether
some of her success may not have been due precisely to her enemies' awe of this
particular combination of powers.

The extant texts, one remembers, come from an ecclesiastical, and more
specifically monastic, milieu. Are we therefore talking about a view put forward
by the likes of Bede, Stephen of Ripon, or Leoba's biographer Rudolf, who can
only accept women in power if they can be subsumed into a specifically Christian model?[19] We may indeed have here an example of the Christian writers'
gloss on a reality of Anglo-Saxon society which they do not much like and
refuse to accept as such, wishing instead to mould it into a Christian tradition.
This reality is the genuine political influence of Anglo-Saxon queens and
aristocratic women like Eadburh or Sexburh, advisors to, and co-rulers with,
their husbands. It is because of their habit of being involved in the public life of

B. Garlick, S. Dixon, and P. Allen (New York, 1992), 105–19; J. Jochens, 'Old Norse Sources on
Women', in *Medieval Women*, ed. Rosenthal, 155–87. Especially illuminating on both the role of the
heroic tradition of armed and wise maiden-warriors, and on the role of the 'Germanic' queen as power-
sharer and counsellor (based on the idealized model of Wealhtheow in Beowulf) are J. Chance, *Woman
as Hero in Old English Literature* (Syracuse, NY, 1986) and H. Damico, *Beowulf's Wealhtheow and the
Valkyre Tradition* (Madison, Wis., 1984). One may well see Rædwald's queen, and indeed Iurminburh,
who accompanied her husband Ecgfrith near the battlefield where he fought the Picts, as belonging to
this tradition.

[17] Pringle, 'Judith: The Homily and the Poem', *Traditio*, 31 (1975), 83–97.

[18] *Judith*, ed. M. Griffith (Exeter, 1997); see also F. Gameson, 'Women in Anglo-Saxon Poetry', in
Women in Ancient Societies: An Illusion of the Night, ed. L. J. Archer, S. Fischler, and M. Wyke (London,
1994), 204–32 at 219–21.

[19] We have already noticed how negative the early Anglo-Saxon view of queens who exercise power
actually was; see n. 6. An additional illustration, should one be needed, is the case of Sexburh's life, the
wife of Cenwalh of Wessex; no mention is made anywhere of the fact that, after Cenwalh's death in 672,
she actually held power and reigned on her own for a year, until the much later Anglo-Saxon Chronicle,
which alone mentions this: *The Anglo-Saxon Chronicle*, trans. D. Whitelock *et al.* (London, 1961), 22.

the kingdom, both secular and ecclesiastical, through their influence in councils that women like Hild, Ælflæd, and Leoba, clearly prime movers at Whitby,
Nidd, and German councils, were used to exercising power and authority both
outside and inside their monasteries. But monastic writers in England, Bede
above all, seem less happy with this than other chroniclers in Italy (with Amala-
suntha and Theodelinda) and especially in Merovingian Gaul.[20] Frankish
queens were allowed to exercise the full political power of kingship, even
though they did so in the name of their sons or grandsons. The aristocracy
obeyed their political rule and government. They may have been regarded as
tyrants on an individual basis, but the texts show the authors' willingness to
loathe one or the other of these queens on merit, and not simply for exerting
power: while Brunhild, and later Balthild, were seen as tyrants, Nanthild was
not. Power was defined as being well or badly exercised according to the specific
policies followed by individual queens. English texts, as we saw earlier, have a
tendency to define *good* female power as being linked to the status of virginity,
and *bad* power to that of womanhood.

To this possible interpretation, therefore, I should like to add another, drawn
not from medieval history but from a comparison with the Greek and Roman
models described previously and from modern anthropological studies of the
concept of virginity.

Three concepts are directly associated with virginity in the classical models:
fertility, motherhood, and maleness. Virginity and fertility are linked because the
first is in no way an impediment to the second: virginity means the potential for
fertility preserved for the future, and hence is especially powerful since it is as yet
unspent (or spent in an alternative way). The link between virginity and motherhood is particularly noticeable among the Vestals, whose attire comprises several
pieces, including the *stola*, which were specifically reserved to matrons; the offi-
cially recognized and even divinely enhanced role of the 'parthenia' as a mother
has already been mentioned.[21] We must not forget that Mary herself, the ultimate virgin, is, through her privileged position in relation to her son, described as
mother and bride. Finally, the association of virginity and maleness, again so evident in the Vestals' judicial, economic, and political rights and privileges, and
taken over by patristic writers with their definition of the 'female Man of God',[22]
is an obvious one. As Mary Beard has shown, the power of the Vestals' virginity

---

[20] See e.g. I. Wood, *The Merovingian Kingdoms* (London, 1994), ch. 8; *Late Merovingian France: His-
tory and Hagiography 640–720*, ed. P. Fouracre and R. A. Gerberding (Manchester, 1996); and *Sainted
Women of the Dark Ages*, trans. J. A. McNamara *et al.* (Durham and London, 1992), on the relevant vitae;
J. Tibbetts Schulenburg, 'Saints' Lives as a Source for the History of Women', in *Medieval Women*, ed.
Rosenthal, 285–320; and the still-unrivalled paper by J. Nelson, 'Queens as Jezebels: Brunhild and
Balthild in Merovingian History' (1978), repr. in her *Politics and Ritual in Early Medieval Europe*
(London, 1986), 1–48.

[21] Most of Zeus' conquests among princesses, nymphs, and others were called this, and their half-
divine children were 'parthenioi' or 'partheniai'.

[22] See n. 12.

is due, not to one or other of these elements, but to the combination of the three, because all three statuses are fundamentally anomalous—in anthropological terms 'interstitial', in-between states which appertain to all these categories in part without actually being fully integrated in any single one completely.[23]

If we look at the description of several of the Anglo-Saxon abbesses mentioned above, we find a striking parallel with these features. Hild, Cuthburh, and Leoba are repeatedly credited with 'spiritual sons', who were educated by them in their monasteries or outside them: future bishops (at least five in Hild's case!), learned men, and missionaries. To them, but also to their whole community, they are said to be 'mothers', caring for them with 'motherly love': Hild again, and Ælflæd. Their acceptance as active members in the world of male authority and politics was based, in no small measure, on their ability to act as men, because they were 'virgines' and not women. This explains why the model of the Virgin Mary, or other real female virgins, cannot entirely match the Anglo-Saxon type described above. Mary expresses the prototype for the Christian ideal of womanhood: sexual purity, and submission to men in society. The point about the Anglo-Saxon nuns mentioned here is precisely that they do not show either. Therefore, unless they are to be depicted by their hagiographers, and accepted by them, as simply powerful individuals in a wordly context, bearing in reality no relation to the hagiographers' model of womanhood provided by the Virgin Mary, these writers *must* depict the women they write about as virgins, so that they can fit their model of a Christian woman. Altogether, we might pursue the parallel with the Vestals, women who are on the brink between virgin and woman, between woman and man, potential but not actual brides (in a Christian context, of course, nuns are called 'brides of Christ'); it is this abnormal status which gives them their power.

The combinations of virginity and potential fertility and of virginity and motherhood are powerful ones, found also in non-European societies.[24] In addition, and even more interestingly perhaps, girls and in some cases men also accept the power of an older, post-menopausal woman, who exerts a communal maternal function, largely because she is beyond the age of conceiving herself (though part of such women's authority probably relies also on their perceived general experience of life). This older woman also takes on a male function— for example, taking a man's name and exercising specifically masculine privileges, like that of speaking on public occasions (a point specifically made about Ælflæd and Leoba). It does not take a great deal of imagination to see the possible similarities, in anthropological terms, of such women to the most powerful Anglo-Saxon abbesses like Hild, Ælflæd, and Leoba.

[23] On the definition of this status and its considerable importance in the understanding of 'purity' in society, see the still-valid work by M. Douglas, *Purity and Danger* (London, 1966).

[24] Blundell, *Women in Ancient Greece*, 45, about the Bimin-Kuskumin tribe of Papua-New Guinea; and K. Hastrup, 'The Semantics of Biology: Virginity', in *Defining Females: The Nature of Women in Society*, ed. S. Ardener (Oxford, 1993), 34–50, esp. 42–4, about the Tewa Indians.

This type of woman continues to exert a similar influence in medieval and indeed early modern England: a famous example is that of Elizabeth I, the 'Virgin Queen', once again an honorary virgin whose political power was well accepted for other reasons, but was also, significantly, associated both by herself in the way she constructed her image, and by her biographers, with this status. In early modern England witchcraft accusations were directed at women with a similar profile, either young girls or older women, notably widows, living alone and perceived as having power over their fellow villagers. As late as the mid-nineteenth century, leading women on the social and political scene, such as Octavia Hill and Florence Nightingale, were unmarried, and were in some cases specifically said to have rejected marriage in order to exert influence in the world.[25] As indeed did the formidable female dons of Oxbridge colleges, so well portrayed by D. L. Sayers at the turn of the twentieth century.[26] Some have argued that, marriage and family notwithstanding, in deference to the late twentieth-century changes in attitudes, Lady (then Mrs) Thatcher, of whom a minister once famously said (rather less elegantly) that she was the only man in the Cabinet, belonged to the same breed. To what extent the choice of political and intellectual success at the expense or in place of 'womanhood' is one made by such women themselves, who see it as the only way to achieve their goal—as opposed to being imposed upon them by tradition, and internalized—is a matter for debate. What could be regarded as remarkable is the extraordinary length of time that this attitude, which was still to be observed during the first decades of the twentieth century, survived in English society. Despite numerous transformations on the way, the model put forward for—possibly sometimes by—early Anglo-Saxon nuns has had a long life.[27]

[25] See e.g. N. Boyd, *Josephine Butler, Octavia Hill, Florence Nightingale: Three Victorian Women Who Changed Their World* (London, 1982); J. Parker, *Women and Welfare: Ten Victorian Women in Public Social Service* (London, 1988), 94–117; and M. Vicinus, *Independent Women: Work and Community for Single Women 1850–1920* (London, 1985). I owe these references to Dr A. Borsay.

[26] Most famously in *Gaudy Night*. See also Vicinus, *Independent Women*, 121–62, on women's colleges.

[27] I should like to thank Dr W. Marx and Mr K. Hopwood for their help with bibliographical references and for their illuminating comments on and discussions of this paper.

6

DUKE TASSILO OF BAVARIA AND THE ORIGINS OF THE RUPERTUS CROSS

Anton Scharer

The confidence to embark in new directions and to attempt as a historian to interpret a work of art I owe to the honorand, who has in such a grand and convincing manner illuminated our understanding 'of the interaction of religion and politics in an art closely connected with the court of the Saxon emperors',[1] and of Charlemagne as a patron of art.[2] But my personal and intellectual debts to him, incurred over decades, are much greater than can be expressed here. May he accept the following as a modest expression of gratitude. I shall begin with a brief discussion of the Rupertus Cross itself. I shall then put forward some suggestions as to its function and context, which will lead us finally to the wider issues of works of art connected with Duke Tassilo and their significance for court culture.

The Rupertus Cross is a masterpiece of Insular metalwork of impressive dimensions (now 158 cm high and 94 cm wide), which is generally agreed to date from the second half of the eighth century (pl. 6).[3] With its natural radiance enhanced by jewel-like insets, this *crux gemmata* ultimately echoes the cross that was erected in Jerusalem at the site of the crucifixion.[4] The Rupertus Cross has apparently been preserved since the early Middle Ages in the Salzburg area, specifically the parish church of Bischofshofen (Salzburg). In the most recent English publication it was described thus by Leslie Webster: 'The cross consists

---

[1] H. Mayr-Harting, *Ottonian Book Illumination: An Historical Study*, 2 vols. (London, 1991), II, 7. I wish to thank Richard Gameson for his boundless patience and editorial help.

[2] H. Mayr-Harting, 'Charlemagne as a Patron of Art', in *The Church and the Arts*, ed. D. Wood, *Studies in Church History*, 28 (1992), 43–77.

[3] From the vast literature on the Cross I wish to single out the following: W. Topic-Mersmann, 'Das Kreuz von Bischofshofen als Crux gemmata', in *Bischofshofen: 5000 Jahre Geschichte und Kultur* (Bischofshofen, 1984), 125–52; H. Fillitz and M. Pippal, *Schatzkunst: Die Goldschmiede- und Elfenbeinarbeiten aus österreichischen Schatzkammern des Hochmittelalters* (Salzburg, 1987), 53–7 (no. 1), pls. 1.1–9; *The Making of England: Anglo-Saxon Art and Culture AD 600–900*, ed. L. Webster and J. Backhouse (London, 1991); *Geschichte der Bildenden Kunst in Österreich. Band 1: Früh- und Hochmittelalter*, ed. H. Fillitz (Munich, 1998), 196 (no. 1) and pl. 1 at p. 34.

[4] R. N. Bailey, *England's Earliest Sculptors* (Toronto, 1995), 46–7, 123; Topic-Mersmann, 'Kreuz von Bischofshofen', 131, noting the 'Constantinian context'; *Making of England*, 171, on the different layers of meaning.

of an equal-armed cross-head with square centre and arms which expand gradually to shovel-shaped ends, surmounting an integral straight-sided shaft.'[5] A
wooden core (definitely a later replacement) is covered by 'repoussé and chased
gilt-bronze sheets' on the one face and the two narrow sides; no covering for the
other face survives. Parts 'of the beaded frame which binds the edges are missing'; and the narrow side strips are likewise incompletely preserved. At some
stage the shaft was shortened at the bottom end;[6] the wooden tenon at the foot
of the cross is thus a secondary feature and provides no clue to the original
function of the artefact;[7] equally there may originally have been more settings
for glass insets than the thirty-eight which remain (nine of them are still filled
by glass insets).

The metal sheets of the face of the cross are decorated with delicate 'inhabited vine-scrolls in which birds and quadrupeds clamber and feed, and
where scrolls terminate in a variety of animal heads'. As for the sheets covering
the sides, they were 'die-impressed in a triple pattern: one panel each of interlaced mesh, interlaced knotwork, and a highly stylised spiral vine-scroll'. This
ornamental vocabulary is our primary evidence for characterizing and dating
the cross.

The closest stylistic parallels in metalwork for the face of the cross appear on
the Ormside Bowl, which has been dated to the second half of the eighth century.[8] On the bowl and cross alike the animals inhabiting the plant scroll
partly straddle the scroll with their legs; and there is also an example of 'leg
lock', 'the curious and characteristically Anglo-Saxon mannerism of bringing
the far leg of the animal over the front of the containing scroll, the near leg being
tucked behind it',[9] a widespread phenomenon in Northumbrian and Mercian
sculpture of the time.[10] The closest comparisons for the scrolls that terminate in
a beast's head are provided by two Anglo-Saxon ivories, for which a late eighth-
century date has been proposed,[11] and which have, moreover, been tentatively

---

[5] *Making of England*, 170. Not being a native English speaker, I shall return to the wording of this
excellent, subtle account from time to time.
[6] Clearly indicated by the abrupt end of the ornament; Topic-Mersman, 'Kreuz von Bischofshofen',
128, assumes the missing piece to have measured 5 cm, hence the original height would have amounted
to 163 cm.
[7] Contra Webster in *Making of England*, 171; cf. Topic-Mersmann, 131.
[8] On which see *Making of England*, 173 (no. 134). For comparison with the cross, *ibid.* 171 and 173;
D. M. Wilson, *Anglo-Saxon Art* (London, 1984), 134; Topic-Mersmann, 'Kreuz von Bischofshofen', 138,
141–2; Fillitz, *Früh- und Hochmittelalter*, 196.
[9] T. D. Kendrick, *Anglo-Saxon Art To A.D. 900* (London, 1938), 141, although Kendrick refers to it as
Anglo-Saxon 'lock'.
[10] *Making of England*, 171.
[11] John Beckwith, *Ivory Carving in Early Medieval England* (London, 1972), 119, no. 8 ('decorative
panel'; London, Victoria and Albert Museum), and no. 9 ('ascension'; Munich, Bayerisches Nationalmuseum), ills. 23 and 24 at pp. 24 and 25; see also the illustration of the former in Wilson, *Anglo-Saxon
Art*, 66 (ill. 61), and of the latter in C. R. Dodwell, *Anglo-Saxon Art: A New Perspective* (Manchester,
1982), 87 (ill. 16).

linked with the artistic milieu of our cross.[12] The closest metalwork equivalent to the spiral vine scroll (one of the die-impressed ornaments on the sheets covering the narrow sides of the cross) is provided by 'sheet-metal fragments from Dumfriesshire' which have been assigned to the second half of the eighth century.[13] The beaded frame (running along the edges) calls to mind the 'collar of beaded wire' between the cup and the knop of the Tassilo Chalice (769/777–88) from the abbey of Kremsmünster.[14] Thus, comparison with metalwork and ivories suggests a date for the cross in the second half of the eighth century, possibly later rather than earlier in this period.

Previous discussions of the Rupertus Cross have drawn parallels with the Barberini Gospels, a manuscript that is generally ascribed to the later eighth century:[15] the inhabited scroll on the face of the cross has been compared to the similar one on the *Chi-rho* page[16] while the foliate scroll on the cross face has been likened to that in the evangelist portraits.[17] It may also be noted in passing that the decoration on the narrow sides of the cross (a triple pattern of interlaced mesh, interlaced knotwork, and stylized scrolls) has some interesting similarities to the ornament in the St Petersburg Gospels, an under-studied manuscript which is believed to date from the late eighth century.[18] For our enquiry to be comprehensive, we should also, in theory, consider stone sculpture; however, given the dearth of securely dated work in the medium,[19] along with the more immediate relevance of portable objects to our cross,[20] we have examined more than enough for the present purposes. And it is clear that the Rupertus Cross sits comfortably within the corpus of Insular art (broadly defined) from the second half of the eighth century.

Although the copper that was used was probably of Southumbrian origin,[21] the Rupertus Cross could have been assembled or produced by an Insular artist on the continent. As for the possible event that may have occasioned the commissioning or acquisition of the cross in the Salzburg area, the consensus of scholarly opinion points to the building of the cathedral around 774 by Bishop

---

[12] By Leslie Webster in *Making of England*, 180 (no. 140), who tentatively attributes these ivories to the 'Salzburg *Kulturkreis*'.

[13] *Making of England*, 173–5 (no. 135).   [14] Ibid. 168 (no. 131).

[15] J. J. G. Alexander, *Insular Manuscripts* 6th to the 9th Century (London, 1978), 61–2 (no. 36), ills. 169–78; *Making of England*, 205–7 (no. 160).

[16] Topic-Mersmann, 'Kreuz von Bischofshofen', 142–6, ill. 54 at p. 145 (= Alexander, *Insular Manuscripts*, ill. 170). Alexander, *Insular Manuscripts*, ill. 174, 176, esp. 177 (St John) [= *Making of England*, 206 (no. 160)] and 178.

[17] Topic-Mersmann, 'Kreuz von Bischofshofen', 146.

[18] St Petersburg, Public Library, MS F. v. 1. 18: Alexander, *Insular Manuscripts*, 64 (no. 39), col. frontispiece, ills. 188–95. See esp. the panels in the Canon Tables and initial pages and the dot patterns on the opening pages to Mark (fol. 78r) and Luke (fol. 119r): ills. 193 and 194. For the sides of the cross, see the colour plate (no. 14) in Topic-Mersmann, 'Kreuz von Bischofshofen', 140.

[19] See the pessimistic comments of Wilson, *Anglo-Saxon Art*, 53–60.

[20] Though some major monuments, such as 'Acca's Cross' at Hexham, are believed to have imitated metalwork: see Bailey, *England's Earliest Sculptors*, esp. 121–3.

[21] Topic-Mersmann, 'Kreuz von Bischofshofen', 151, n. 6; Fillitz, *Früh- und Hochmittelalter*, 196.

Virgil of Salzburg.[22] There is, however, no evidence to support this conjecture; while an altogether more intelligible—and better-documented—context for the production of this *crux gemmata* is provided by Tassilo of Bavaria.

Let us turn to a letter by one *Clemens Peregrinus*,[23] addressed to Duke Tassilo and the bishops and nobles of the Bavarian people, which prays for Tassilo's victory against a heathen enemy.[24] This letter was transmitted in a now lost, ninth-century Salzburg *Liber Traditionum* (collection of formularies and letters), wherein it was part of a subgroup of material that had special significance for Tassilo and his family. The collection as a whole was transcribed by Frobenius Forster in the eighteenth century; Forster's transcript of the letter also subsequently disappeared, but happily this happened after the publication of the *editio princeps* by Zirngibl in 1779.[25] The historical circumstances in which the letter was written are obvious: it must refer to Tassilo's dealings with the Carantanians in the early 770s.[26] After the local prince, Cheitmar, a Christian, had died in 769, a heathen reaction set in among the Carantanians, escalating into a war which ended in a great victory for Tassilo in 772.

Many years ago Bernhard Bischoff tentatively suggested that the writer of the letter could be one and the same person as Peregrinus of Freising,[27] an Insular scribe who worked at the scriptorium of Freising in the time of Bishop Arbeo (764–84)[28] and hence, in all probability had some connection with the circle of Bishop Virgil of Salzburg (746/7–84). This hypothesis is further supported by the circumstance that the *Clemens Peregrinus* of the letter quotes a few words of a prayer which also appear in the *Florilegium Frisingense* that was written and compiled by Peregrinus of Freising.[29] If, at first glance, Peregrinus'

---

[22] See the works cited in n. 3 above; and H. Wolfram, *Salzburg, Bayern, Österreich* (Vienna, 1995), 274.

[23] Which can be understood as 'Clemens the pilgrim' or 'gentle Peregrinus', see following note.

[24] *Epistolae Karolini Aevi* 2, ed. E. Dümmler, MGH Epistolae IV (Berlin, 1895), 496–7 (no. 1). For recent, superb comment see M. Garrison, 'Letters To a King and Biblical Exempla: The Examples of Cathwulf and Clemens Peregrinus', *Early Medieval Europe*, 7 (1998), 305–28. May I note here that some of the following results were reached independently, prior to the publication of Garrison's article.

[25] Fundamental, not just on the question of transmission, is B. Bischoff, *Salzburger Formelbücher und Briefe aus Tassilonischer und Karolingischer Zeit* (Bayer. Akad. d. Wiss., phil.-hist. Kl., Sitzungsberichte Jahrgang 1973, Heft 4, Munich, 1973), 9, 16–26, esp. 19–20.

[26] H. Wolfram, *Grenzen und Räume. Geschichte Österreichs vor seiner Entstehung* (Vienna, 1995), 89 and 124.

[27] B. Bischoff, *Die südostdeutschen Schreibschulen und Bibliotheken in der Karolingerzeit*, I (Wiesbaden, 1974), 61, n. 1.

[28] *Ibid.* 60–2, 73–5 (nos. 6–8: Munich, Bayerische Staatsbibliothek, Clm 6237, 6297, and 6433).

[29] *Angeli Dei boni ante vos et post vos, a dextris et a sinistris vestris*: Letter, MGH Epistolae IV, 497, l.10; *Angeli Dei a dextris et a sinistris nostris perducant nos in viam rectam*, *Florilegia: Florilegium Frisingense (Clm 6433)*, *Testimonia divinae scripturae <et patrum>*, ed. A. Lehner, CCSL 108D (Turnhout, 1987), 39, no. 455, ll. 23–4. See Garrison, 'Letters', 310, for the comparison and for Peregrinus as compiler of the Florilegium; cf. also Lehner, p. xxxvi. The quotation appears ultimately to derive from a 'Reisegebet', a prayer for safe voyage, which B. Bischoff, *Anecdota novissima: Texte des vierten bis sechzehnten Jahrhunderts* (Stuttgart, 1984), 161, App. II to no. XIX, edited from a late ninth-century MS.: *Angeli Dei almi a dextris et a sinistris nostris perducant nos in viam rectam*. Incipit of the whole prayer: *Dirige, Domine, famulos tuos in via tua....* It should be noted that the *Florilegium Frisingense* ends (in no. 455) with a peculiar assemblage of devotional texts (a prayer and formulae derived from other prayers) which appears in

letter seems to comprise a drab series of Old Testatment quotations strung together in a prayer-like fashion, closer inspection reveals that it is much more than this. The biblical citations themselves are well chosen, and they are so arranged as to solicit God's help for the fight against a heathen enemy, and more specifically to invoke his support for Duke Tassilo's victory. After the invocation and address comes a salutation which, taking up 'a phrase from the salutations in the Pauline epistles'[30] and ending with 'amen', sounds like a liturgical formula. The ensuing first part of the epistle, directed, as it were, to the addressees at large, exhorts them in their cause by assuring them that God is on their side against the pagans. Then, in the second part of the letter the focus shifts more explicitly to Tassilo with a series of intercessions on his behalf. The style, no less than the content, of these intercessions enhances the prayer-like character of the text. They have the appearance of benedictions: 'Sit Dominus noster cum Daissilone, sicut fuit cum Abraham . . . Sit Dominus omnipotens pugnator pro vobis, sicut fuit cum Moysi et cum Iosue . . . Percutiat Dominus inimicos vestros ante conspectum vestrum, sicut percussit gentes multas ante conspectum filiorum Israel. . . . Tribuat vobis Dominus victoriam de inimicis vestris, sicut dedit ad Gedion ducem populi Dei . . . Det Dominus fortitudinem duci nostro domino Daissiloni, sicut dedit fortitudinem Samson . . .'[31] The letter continues in this vein. Finally, after the valediction, comes the call to sing Psalms 113.1–3 (*Non nobis, Domine, non nobis; sed nomini tuo da gloriam . . .*) and 67.2–4 (*Exsurgat Deus, et dissipentur inimici eius . . .*).[32] The themes of praising the Lord, and his triumph over his enemies (i.e. the pagans),[33] are therefore brought home to the reader once again. In what we have termed benedictions, God's help for Tassilo is invoked and developed by analogy with a series of figures drawn, with one significant exception, from the Old Testament. Abraham, Moses, Joshua, Gideon, Samson, Jonathan, David, and Constantine are all mentioned with reference to a specific victory (generally against a heathen foe) that was achieved with God's help. This array of analogues is greater than that used in contemporary Ordines,[34] and reveals Peregrinus' single-mindedness. It also transcends the common cast of Old Testament *exempla* used in the genre of

almost identical form in the later Bayerische Staatsbibliothek, Clm 14248, fol. 164v, ed. M. Frost, 'A Prayer Book from St Emmeran, Ratisbon', *Journal of Theological Studies*, 30 (1929), 32–45, at 36; on the MS see Bischoff, *Schreibschulen*, I, 175 and 193 (no. 13). Peregrinus then provides in his *Florilegium* some of the earliest evidence for Insular, specifically Irish-inspired devotional texts. At this point one cannot but mention Henry Mayr-Harting's fine appreciation of 'Private Prayer' in his fundamental *The Coming of Christianity to Anglo-Saxon England*, 3rd edn. (London, 1991), 182–90.

[30] Garrison, 'Letters', 322.   [31] Letter, 496.   [32] Garrison, 'Letters', 322.

[33] Tellingly the Letter, p. 497, ll. 15–16, has *sic pereant* **gentiles** *a facie Dei nostri* for the Vulgate's (Ps. 67.3) *sic pereant peccatores a facie Dei*.

[34] See the formula *Deus inenarrabilis auctor mundi* in the Sacramentaries of Gellone and Angoulême and the Collection of Sankt Emmeram, *Ordines Coronationis Franciae: Texts and Ordines for the Coronation of Frankish and French Kings and Queens in the Middle Ages*, I, ed. R. A. Jackson (Philadelphia, 1995), 53, 59, and 67.

Mirror of Princes.[35] This leads one inevitably to the related questions of the nature of the source on which Peregrinus drew, and the extent to which he was himself responsible for the compilation of this array of Old Testament figures along with Constantine as an analogy for Tassilo. Taking account also of the many quotations that are woven into the text, it appears that Peregrinus culled most of his examples from Pseudo-Augustine's[36] *De mirabilibus sacrae scripturae*, especially from the last chapter of the second book, *De bellis praecipuis quae Domini auxilio peracta sunt.*[37] This would tally with other indications which suggest that the writer of the letter had an Irish background.[38]

Of particular relevance to the present enquiry is the long reference to the emperor Constantine which is the last of the comparisons coming towards the end of the 'benedictions'. Peregrinus seems to have drawn on the *Inventio sanctae crucis.*[39] The passage reads as follows: 'Tribuat Dominus victoriam Daissiloni et omni populo eius, sicut dedit regi Constantino filio Helenae, cui Dominus ostendit signum crucis in coelo nocte ante pugnam et audivit vocem dicentem sibi: "Constantine, in hoc signo vinces"? Hinc portata est crux ante eum in pugnam et omnes barbari fugerunt ill.[*for* illam *or* illum].'[40] Here an explicit and detailed evocation of Constantine, his vision, and the victory against the pagan barbarians that was bestowed by the cross serves both as an invocation for Tassilo and as a flattering and inspiring comparison. And here too, I suggest, lie the origins of the Rupertus Cross: it was designed as an evocation of Constantine's victory cross, and was a symbol of Tassilo's quasi-royal authority. As such it may even have been part of his insignia. And here one can advance the analogy of the representation of Louis the Pious († 840) in Hrabanus Maurus' *De laudibus sanctae crucis*: the emperor is depicted as *miles Christi* holding the cross in his right hand.[41] In brief, though incapable of proof, the theory of an association between Duke Tassilo and the Rupertus Cross fits the known circumstances extremely well, and has rather more to recommend it than the wholly hypothetical association with the foundation of Salzburg Cathedral.

---

[35] H. H. Anton, *Fürstenspiegel und Herrscherethos in der Karolingerzeit* (Bonn, 1968), esp. 419 ff.
[36] On the seventh-century 'Irish Augustine' see D. Ó Cróinín, *Early Medieval Ireland 400–1200* (London, 1995), 187–9.
[37] PL 35, col. 2192.   [38] Bischoff, *Salzburger Formelbücher*, 20.
[39] Cf. *Inventio sanctae crucis*, ed. A. Holder (Leipzig, 1889), i, ll. 11–27; *Cynewulfs Elene: (Kreuzauffindung)*, ed. F. Holthausen, 4th edn. (Heidelberg, 1936), 3–6 and pp. xi–xii on the source; E. Ewig, 'Das Bild Constantins des Großen in den ersten Jahrhunderten des abendländischen Mittelalters', *Historisches Jahrbuch*, 75 (1955), 1–46, at 21–2.
[40] 'May the Lord grant victory to Tassilo and to all his people, just as he gave it to King Constantine, son of Helena, to whom the Lord showed the sign of the cross in the sky on the night before the battle, and he heard a voice saying to him: "Constantine, in this sign you will conquer". Wherefore the cross was carried before him into battle, and all the barbarians fled from it [*or* him].' Letter, 497, ll. 4–8.
[41] P. E. Schramm, *Die deutschen Kaiser und Könige in Bildern ihrer Zeit 751–1190*, ed. F. Mütherich, 2nd edn. (Munich, 1983), 158–9 (no. 16) and pl. 16 at 293–4.

Assuming this was the case, we may presume that the cross survived Tassilo's downfall because of its religious nature. Treasures with an overtly religious meaning passed into the care of the church either, presumably, as donations from Tassilo and his family, or subsequently by undocumented routes. The Tassilo Chalice and the Montpellier Psalter are cases in point,[42] as are the short *Speculum principis* and the letters that were preserved in the now lost Salzburg *Liber traditionum*.[43] Tassilo's sceptre, on the other hand, has not survived.[44]

Whatever the circumstances surrounding the creation of the Rupertus Cross, the material we have considered leads us to a couple of related issues which we can usefully air in conclusion. First, in view of the artistic achievements that may, with varying degrees of certainty, be associated with Duke Tassilo and his circle, one is entitled to wonder whether the beginnings of the court culture of his famous cousin and opponent, Charlemagne, were in some part a response to this. Secondly, it would be interesting to know if there was more than coincidence behind the strength of the Insular contribution to the culture of both courts. Consideration of these and other questions must, however, await another occasion.

---

[42] Montpellier, Bibliothèque de l'Université, 409: Bischoff, *Schreibschulen*, II (Wiesbaden, 1980), 16–18. V. Leroquais, *Les Psautiers manuscrits latins des bibliothèques publiques de France*, 3 vols. (Macon, 1940–7), I, 273–7; III, pls. I–II.

[43] Bischoff, *Salzburger Formelbücher*, 42–57.

[44] See the Murbach Annals *sub anno* 787, ed. G. H. Pertz, MGH Scriptores I (Hannover, 1826), 43.

7

THE VOICE OF CHARLEMAGNE[1]

Janet L. Nelson

Modern historians might well sympathize with the difficulty medieval people had in gaining access to kings. In our case, the reasons have nothing to do with obtrusive favourites or officious *ostiarii*, or with the *magnum impedimentum in palatio* caused by the throng of *clamatores*, seekers of redress.[2] Our direct evidence on rulers' aims and characters is so inadequate that we are likely to despair of ever scenting human flesh (to borrow Marc Bloch's phrase).[3] Yet we occasionally have a sense of contact with the individuals in question which may not be mere illusion. In the case of Charlemagne, Einhard's *Life* is an obvious *entrée*. Einhard does say—and the detail is the more credible because it is both unexpected and not borrowed from Suetonius—that the voice of Charlemagne 'was clear, but it was less than would have fitted the scale of his body (*voce clara quidem, sed quae minus corporis formae conveniret*)'.[4] Einhard also reports that Charlemagne was 'quite skilled in both reading lessons and chanting psalms in church, yet he never read the lesson in public (*publice*) and only chanted along with everyone else (*in commune*) and softly (*submissim*)'.[5] In context, this sounds like a sign of piety rather than deficiency: and we can infer that outside church Charlemagne could make himself audible enough, speaking clearly if not at the mighty volume his exceptionally large physique might have led contemporary observers to expect.

But where, metaphorically speaking, can we hear his voice now?[6] Various possibilities have been suggested: in the *arengae* and the titles of his

---

[1] My thanks, for comment, encouragement and patience, to David Ganz, Henrietta Leyser and Richard Gameson.
[2] MGH Capitularia Regum Francorum I, edd. A. Boretius and V. Krause (Hanover, 1883), no. 64, p. 153.
[3] 'Like the giant in the fairy-tale': M. Bloch, *The Historian's Craft* (Manchester, 1954), 22.
[4] *Vita Karoli*, c. 22, ed. O. Holder-Egger, MGH Scriptores rerum germanicarum in usum scholarum (Hannover, 1911), 27.
[5] Ibid., c. 26, pp. 27, 31.
[6] Virginia Woolf, looking back from the 1930s to her own childhood, imagined that voices might be recoverable: H. Lee, *Virginia Woolf* (London, 1997), 98: 'Is it not possible—I often wonder—that things we have felt with great intensity have an existence independent of our minds, are in fact still in existence? And if so, will it not be possible, in time, that some device will be invented by which we can tap them? . . . I shall fit a plug into a wall; and listen in to the past. I shall turn up August 1890 . . .'

charters;[7] in the formulae of the oaths so carefully specified in 789 and 802;[8] in his one surviving letter to his wife Fastrada;[9] in the prologue to the *Admonitio Generalis* and the prefaces to Paul the Deacon's Homiliary, the Codex Carolinus, and the Gregorian Sacramentary (the 'Hadrianum');[10] above all, in marginal annotations ('True', 'Shrewd') to the text of the *Libri Carolini* discussed and finalized at court.[11] None of these recordings is as direct, or as unproblematic, as modern connoisseurs would like (though the last comes close). There is no finer connoisseur of the material than Henry Mayr-Harting, nor has anyone done more in recent years to make Charlemagne more accessible.[12] In this contribution to a thank-offering for Henry, I explore yet another possibility: that we may be able to catch in a few capitularies of the latter years of Charlemagne's reign, sounding more clearly and insistently than in any evidence from the earlier years, echoes of a distinctive voice.

The distribution of capitulary evidence through Charlemagne's forty-seven-year reign (768–814) is notoriously uneven, with some thirteen of the texts in the Monumenta edition dating from before 802, and no fewer than fifty-six between 802 and the end of the reign.[13] And while this disproportion may result

[7] H. Fichtenau, *Arenga. Spätantike und Mittelalter im Spiegel von Urkundenformeln*, Mitteilungen der Instituts für österreichische Geschichtsforschung Ergänzungsband, 18 (Vienna, 1957), 56, 160; H. Wolfram, *Intitulatio I. Lateinische Königs- und Fürstentitel bis zum Ende des 8 Jhdts*, Mitteilungen der Instituts österreichische Geschichtsforschungen Erganzungsband, 21 (Vienna, 1967), 213–44.

[8] M. Becher, *Eid und Herrschaft. Untersuchungen zum Herrscherethos Karls des Grossen* (Sigmaringen, 1993), 16–20, 87, 210–2.

[9] J. L. Nelson, 'The Siting of the Council at Frankfort', in *Das Frankfurter Konzil von 794*, ed. R. Berndt, 2 vols. (Mainz, 1997), I, 149–65, at 159; and cf. in the same volume, F. Staab, 'Die Königin Fastrada', 183–218, at 197–8. Charlemagne would have dictated the letter to a scribe, of course. It survives, uniquely, in a St-Denis manuscript: see J. Story, 'Cathwulf, Kingship, and the Royal Abbey of St Denis', *Speculum*, 74 (1999), 1–21, at 11–21.

[10] P. Bernard, 'Benoît d'Aniane est-il l'auteur de l'avertissement "Hucusque" et du Supplément au sacramentaire "Hadrianum"?', *Studi medievali*, 39 (1998), 1–120, at 48–9, 55–6; cf. 116–7.

[11] W. von den Steinen, 'Karl der Große und die Libri Carolini. Die tironischen Randnoten zum Codex authenticus', *Neues Archiv*, 49 (1932), 207–80; A. Freeman, 'Further Studies in the *Libri Carolini*, III. The Marginal Notes in Vaticanus latinus 7207', *Speculum*, 46 (1971), 597–612, esp. 607, pointing to Alcuin's complaint in 799 (Ep. 172, ed. E. Dümmler, MGH Epistolae IV (Berlin, 1895), 284), that Charlemagne has not been critical enough in annotating his *Adversus Felicem Libri VII*, and the implication that such annotations were expected. See now Freeman's splendid new edition of the *Libri Carolini*, *Opus Caroli Regis Contra Synodum (Libri Carolini)*, MGH Concilia, Tomus II, Supplementum I (Hanover, 1998), 48–50.

[12] See H. Mayr-Harting, 'Charlemagne As a Patron of Art', *Studies in Church History*, 28 (1992), 43–77; id.,'Charlemagne, the Saxons, and the Imperial Coronation of 800', *EHR* 111 (1996), 1113–33; and id., 'Charlemagne's Religion', in *Am Vorabend der Kaiserkrönung. Das Epos 'Karolus Magnus et Leo Papa' und der Papstbesuch in Paderborn*, ed. J. Jarnut *et al.* (forthcoming, 2000), which includes characteristically perceptive comments on c. 52 of the decrees of the Council of Frankfurt, MGH Capitularia I, no. 28, p. 78.

[13] The definition of the term capitulary needs to be kept (as contemporaries kept it) broad; and these texts need to be set, as to their origins, in assemblies, and, as to their purposes, in a governmental context: see the fundamental study of H. Mordek, 'Karolingische Kapitularien', in *Überlieferung und Geltung normativer Texte der frühen und hohen Mittelalters*, ed. Mordek, Quellen und Forschungen zum Recht im Mittelalter, 4 (Sigmaringen, 1986), 25–50; cf. id., art. 'Kapitularien', in *Lexikon des Mittelalters*

in part from accidents of survival, there can be no doubting the reality of a huge increase in the documenting of the business of government in the years from 802 onwards. The later capitularies themselves attest such an intent on the part of Charlemagne and his advisers. A striking increase, now, in the numbers of personnel in his writing-office can hardly have been a coincidence.[14] The regime's enhanced use of the written word had a context. Charlemagne now had an imperial title, and an effectively fixed capital at Aachen. His sights were set higher than before, and his agenda had grown. The forty-chapter *Capitulare Missorum Generale* issued early in 802, when *demoravit domnus Caesar Carolus apud Aquis palatium quietus cum Francis sine hoste*,[15] was indeed, as F.-L. Ganshof said, programmatic.[16] The programme's watchword was justice: hence the meeting constituted, at the same time, a selection panel to appoint agents of justice *in regno*.[17] What the programme first generated was presumably lists of names of *missi*; and the key outcome of their activity was lists of names of oath-swearers.[18] In the years that followed, written instructions and regulations proliferated in secular administration, especially on military matters (for these years were far from 'quiet'). Ecclesiastical councils met more often and enacted far more legislation.[19] It is in the nature of capitularies to expose problems before providing solutions. Ganshof and, following him, many other historians have used the capitulary evidence after 802 to argue that Charlemagne was 'checkmated', that his government was overwhelmed by mounting difficulties, and that Charlemagne himself, old and ill, his bodily decline aptly mirroring the state's dissolution, was no longer able to inspire and run an effective

5 (1990), cols. 943–6; and, on the stages of a capitulary's creation, id., 'Recently Discovered Capitulary Texts Belonging To the Legislation of Louis the Pious', in *Charlemagne's Heir: New Perspectives on the Reign of Louis the Pious*, ed. P. Godman and R. Collins (Oxford, 1990), 437–53, and id., 'Kapitularien und Schriftlichkeit', in *Schriftkultur und Reichsverwaltung unter den Karolingern*, ed. R. Scheiffer, Abhandlungen der Nordrhein-Westfälischen Akademie der Wissenschaften, 97 (1996), 34–66. See further A. Bühler, '*Capitularia Relecta*. Studien zur Entstehung und überlieferung der Kapitularien Karls des Grossen und Ludwigs des Frommen', *Archiv für Diplomatik*, 32 (1986), 305–501; J. L. Nelson, 'Literacy in Carolingian Government', in *The Uses of Literacy in Early Medieval Europe*, ed. R. McKitterick (Cambridge, 1990), 258–96, repr. in Nelson, *The Frankish World* (London, 1996), 1–36; and now the invaluable discussion in P. Wormald, *The Making of English Law* (Oxford, 1999), part I, ch. 2, esp. 45–53. The unpublished M.Litt. dissertation (Cambridge, 2000) of Jennifer Davis, 'Conceptions of Kingship under Charlemagne', adds insights.

[14] See my contribution to *Places of Power*, ed. M. de Jong (forthcoming, Leiden, 2000).

[15] *Annales Laureshamenses* (Lorsch Annals), s.a. 802, ed. G.-H. Pertz, MGH Scriptores I (Berlin, 1826), 38.

[16] MGH Capitularia I, no. 33, pp. 91–9; Ganshof, 'Charlemagne's Programme of Imperial Government', in his *The Carolingians and the Frankish Monarchy*, trans. J. Sondheimer (London, 1971), 55–85. See also id., *Recherches sur les capitulaires* (Paris, 1958), 81, 87.

[17] P. J. Fouracre, 'Carolingian Justice: The Rhetoric of Improvement and Contexts of Abuse', *La Giustizia I*, Settimane di Studio del Centro Italiano di Studi sull'alto Medioevo di Spoleto, 42 (1995), 771–803.

[18] Nelson, 'Literacy', in *The Frankish World*, 20, 22, 26, 36.

[19] R. McKitterick, *The Frankish Church and the Carolingian Reforms* (London, 1977), ch. 1; W. Hartmann, *Die Synoden der Karolingerreich* (Paderborn–Munich, 1986).

regime.[20] That same evidence can be read differently: I take it to reflect an imperial regime certainly newly ambitious and arguably newly effective.

The term 'capitularies' is elastic, and the Monumenta editor's *additamenta* stretch the category to include miscellaneous lists and other administrative or regulatory material, ecclesiastical as well as secular. If, in the years from 802, the capitulary form was bursting at the seams, that was due in part to the ongoing implementation of the programme of 802 itself. A rather full and well-written record of orders given by Charlemagne, and formally confirmed by *omnes fideles*, at an assembly at Aachen targets local notables (*homines boni generis*) who act *inique vel iniuste*: these men are to be brought to the king, who will then punish them by imprisonment and exile.[21] Another capitulary has similar intent: bishops and abbots, counts and *potentiores*, who may be in dispute and refuse to settle peacefully are to be commanded to come *ad nostram praesentiam*; further, the count of the palace is to deal only with disputes involving the claims of *pauperes* and *minus potentes*: he is not to judge cases involving the more powerful *sine nostra iussione*.[22] One of a number of orders about military mobilization required four copies of these orders to be made, the first and second for the regular *missi* and count of the region, the third for the military commanders, and the fourth to be retained by 'our chancellor'.[23]

Other capitularies seem to reflect Charlemagne's enhanced personal role in the formulation of policy.[24] He not only gives instructions to his administrative agents, but at the same time instructs, in the sense of educates, them. Orders given at Nijmegen in March 806 to *missi*, bishops, abbots and abbesses, counts and benefice-holders, change gear halfway through to become a set of critical reflections on usury in time of famine.[25] One remarkable text is the 'admonition of Lord Charles the emperor' as transmitted by one *missus*: it is a little sermon not only summarizing the duties of clergy and office-holders but enjoining true belief and responsible social conduct on men, women, and children generally.[26] Another capitulary extends its target audience far beyond *missi* and notables: it requires *seniores* to exercise self-control in alcohol-consumption in order to show an example to their inferiors, and then calls on all in the *vulgaris populus*

---

[20] Ganshof, 'L'Échec de Charlemagne', translated as 'Charlemagne's Failure', and id., 'The Last Period of Charlemagne's Reign: A Study in Decomposition', in *The Carolingians and the Frankish Monarchy*, chs. 12 and 13; H. Fichtenau, *The Carolingian Empire* (Oxford, 1957; originally published in German in 1949), 177–87; J. M. Wallace-Hadrill, *The Barbarian West* (London, 1952), 114, 163; R. Le Jan, *Histoire de la France: origines et essor* (Paris, 1996), 92–3; R. Collins, *Charlemagne* (London, 1998), 173–4; J. Favier, *Charlemagne* (Paris, 1999), 582, 584–7. M. Becher, *Karl der Grosse* (Munich, 1999), excellent in other respects, curiously ducks the question.

[21] MGH Capitularia I, no. 77 (801 x 813), pp. 170–3, cl. 12.

[22] Ibid., no. 80 (811 x 813), pp. 176–7, cl. 2.   [23] Ibid., no. 50, of early 808, p. 138, cl. 8.

[24] Wormald, *Making of English Law*, 50, captures 'the "off-the-record" air of such nonetheless ostensibly mandatory texts'.

[25] MGH Capitularia I, no. 46, p. 130–2, from cl. 11 to cl. 18.   [26] Ibid. no. 121, pp. 238–40.

to discipline their inferiors too.[27] A capitulary of 811 shows the consequences of Charlemagne's listening: he lists categories of complaints that pit *homines* and *pauperes* against their social superiors, ecclesiastical (bishops, abbots and abbesses) or lay (counts and hundredmen). *Pauperiores* allege they have been compelled to perform host-service, while the clients of *potentes* contrive to evade it. Yet Charlemagne has also heard from the other side: counts have told of problems posed for them by *pagenses* who know how to play off *missi*, or their own lords, against them, and hence evade service altogether. The *missi*, say the counts, have become rival sources of authority: '*pagenses* tend to run to *missi* more than before.'[28] It takes a certain wilfulness, surely, to read this as evidence of Charlemagne's failure.

Nevertheless, Charlemagne's own voice can be heard only imperfectly in all these capitularies. Even though his will is plain enough, and the subject-matter often reflects his own particular concerns, the styles remain typical of the genre, and the writing up is done by *consiliarii* at court, or by private individuals.[29] The sermonizing *missus* may be giving his own gloss on Charlemagne's orders. Multiple other voices resound in the reported complaints of *pauperes* and counts.

In three capitularies, though, Charlemagne can perhaps be 'heard' without interference. First, an oddity: a set of replies from Charlemagne to a *missus* somewhere in Gaul. Evidently this is not the first time that the emperor has heard from this man; nor is he hearing some of the queries for the first time, and on these points the tone of the replies becomes accordingly tetchy: 'we have given you orders time after time, in fact, that it is quite impossible for anyone to free himself from servitude by false evidence'; and 'about unlawful tolls, this order too we have given you before, by our own mouth, and you have not understood it at all'.[30] There is a directness here—indeed at one point Charlemagne even forgets the royal 'we' and uses the first person singular (. . . *me interrogasti*)—and a clearly personal relationship between ruler and agent. Counterposed to that familiarity is the smack of command, and the repeated *praecipimus*, or *volumus*.

Two further capitularies belong together in the two extant manuscripts.[31] In

---

[27] MGH Capitularia I, no. 64 (810), p. 153, cll. 7, 17. For Charlemagne's personal moderation in alcohol-consumption, see Einhard, *Vita Karoli*, c. 24, pp. 28–9. Einhard's striking emphasis on this partly follows Suetonius' *Life of Augustus*, cc. 76, 77.

[28] MGH Capitularia I, no. 73, pp. 164–5.

[29] Bernard, 'Benoît d'Aniane', 55–61, for the role of *consiliarii*, *capellani*, and notaries, without specifically considering capitulary-production.

[30] MGH Capitularia I, no. 58, p. 145, cll. 3, 6.

[31] Ibid., nos. 71 and 72, pp. 162–5. These, along with nos. 20, 21, 23, 34, 36, 39, 40–4, 46, 48, 49, 51–3, 55–9, 61–6, 71, 75, 77, 78, 80, and 119, all from Charlemagne's reign (as well as 5 earlier and 20 later ones, plus the Ansegis Collection) are in Paris, Bibliothèque nationale de France lat. 9654 and Vatican City, Biblioteca Vaticana, pal. lat. 582, which derive from 'a collection [that] originated in the Sens archives', as Wormald, *Making of English Law*, 51, observes. Thus, no. 71, presumably, represents the letter sent to Archbishop Magnus (801–18). For these MSS, and for capitularies nos. 71 and 72 therein, see Ganshof, *Recherches*, 48–9; id., 'Note sur les "Capitula tractanda de causis cum episcopis et abbatibus tractandis" de

both, new and arresting tones can be heard, one of them set at the very beginning of no. 71 by the word *volumus*, and continued in a series of gerundives (*interrogandi sunt*; *discutiendum est atque interveniendum*; *interrogandum est acutissime* (clause 5); *nobis despiciendum est* (clause 9); *inquirendum est* (clause 12))), the other conveyed in direct and insistent questions (*unde illae frequentissimae causationes? Quid sit quod unusquisque christianus in baptismo loquitur?*). No. 71's form is hybrid: it is a list that ends with the envoi of a letter (*Bene valete in Domino*). It is in effect a briefing paper for participants in an upcoming assembly. Each recipient will prepare by pondering Charlemagne's agenda and asking himself Charlemagne's questions.

Charlemagne requires further information as the basis for correction of life and conduct. As a prior condition, he wants bishops, abbots, and counts to be 'separated', by which he seems to mean, not, perhaps, that they should meet separately, for some agenda items concern ecclesiastics and laymen alike, but that they should sit in distinct blocs, and then he may wish to inquire of them *singulariter*—individually.[32] Charlemagne is determined to engage his leading men in collective and individual self-examination, to expose the roots of sin— what makes men selfish, greedy, competitive, hypocritical, complacent—and to eradicate them. Charlemagne raises the most fundamental, and uncomfortable, of questions: *utrum vere christiani sumus?* Equally, he is confident answers can 'very easily' be found: *quod . . . facillime cognosci potest, si diligenter conversationem coram discutere voluerimus*. That last first-person plural is a collective, not a royal, 'we'. Each one is capable of this act of will to confess derelictions; now that the gap between profession and practice has been exposed, all must act together to close it. Individual interrogations are to be followed by shared investigations in each other's presence and hearing (*coram*). The atmosphere Charlemagne wants for this remorseless probing and exposing of individual *conversatio*, that is, motivation and conduct, sounds like a cross between Quaker meeting and quality inspection, with traces of confessional, lawcourt, touchgroup, and management training session. If those terms sound anachronistic, that is because we confuse the radical with the modern, and so we fail to recognize Charlemagne's prescriptions for what they really were—fail, that is, to hear not only what he was saying but how he said it. *Hic interrogandum est acutissime.*

81r', *Studi Gratiani*, 13 (1967), 1–25, at 5, with an edition of no. 72 at 20–5; and now Mordek, *Bibliotheca capitularium regum Francorum manuscripta. Überlieferung und Traditionszusammenhang der fränkischen Herrscherlasse*, MGH Hilfsmittel XV (Munich, 1995), 562–3, 569–70, 780–1, 789, and G. Schmitz's comments in his fine edition of Ansegis, *Die Kapitulariensammlung des Ansegis*, MGH Capitularia NS I (Munich, 1996), 133–5, 156–8. No. 71's importance as evidence for Charlemagne's reform agenda was noted by Ganshof, 'Note', 4–5. P. D. King, *Charlemagne: Sources* (Kendal, 1987) translates no. 71 but not no. 72. I have found his translation of no. 71 very helpful, but made my own (see Appendix).

[32] King, *Charlemagne*, 263 translates 'in distinct groups', following Ganshof, 'Note', 4; but cf. *Admonitio generalis* (789), cl. 70, MGH Capitularia I, p. 59: 'non admittantur testes ad juramentum antequam discutiantur; et si aliter discuti non possint, separentur adinvicem et singulariter inquirantur.'

In the context of private conscience and public morals, had anyone spoken like that since Socrates?

No. 72 pursues this agenda but in some ways is more radical still, and its tone more urgent. It is also, as the MGH editor tartly observed (and as his annotated emendations indicate), *magis neglenter conceptum*.[33] It is clearly a sequel—but its themes, and some of its details too, are so closely related to no. 71's, and pursue them so insistently (gerundives multiply), that no. 72 should be seen as a series of afterthoughts, or further thoughts, set down in some haste as a postscript, perhaps following a night's reflection. We might imagine *vassi*-messengers waiting, booted and spurred, as notaries dashed off the requisite copies. The gap here between conception and dictation seems exceptionally small—these look like reflections uttered and written almost as soon as thought: 'fideles nostros episcopos et abbates alloqui volumus et commonere de communi omnium nostrorum utilitate'. *Alloqui et commonere*: the burden of responsibility for the well-being of 'all our people' could be shared or delegated only to a limited extent. In the end it weighed—increasingly heavily—on Charlemagne. He was (as Lord Randolph Churchill said of Gladstone in his seventies) an old man in a hurry.

Dated by its first clause to 811 (with its reference to a previous year's three-day fast which other evidence securely dates to 810[34]), no. 72's set of instructions was apparently first conceived with the same intended audience as that of no. 71, namely, counts as well as ecclesiastics. Clause 2 says that 'enquiry is *first* to be made concerning ecclesiastics', but in fact all the subsequent clauses are likewise addressed *only* to ecclesiastics. Secular questions slip from Charlemagne's mind, as, in clauses 7–11, he seems to be pursuing a personal quest.[35] What emerges is something resembling a stream of consciousness, with more than a hint of introspection.

---

[33] Ganshof, 'Note', 6, with n. 11, distinguishes between the extant text in the two MSS (cf. above, n. 31), which was indeed 'copié avec une certain négligence', and the original text, which need not have been. Yet, given the difference in this respect between no. 71 and no. 72, it seems more likely that the original was indeed produced, and reproduced in multiple copies, in exceptional haste, to reach participants just in time for consideration before the assembly. The interest of no. 72 was briefly noted by A. Hauck, *Kirchengeschichte Deutschlands*, II (Leipzig, 1912), 219–20, finding here 'die herbsten und spitzigsten Äusserungen Karls, welche überhaupt auf uns gekommen sind', and E. Amann, *L'Époque carolingienne*, vol. 6 of *Histoire de l'Église*, ed. A. Fliche (Paris, 1937), 90–1, suggesting that it was composed by Charlemagne 'un jour de mauvaise humeur'! But only Ganshof has given it the attention it deserves. His 'Note', which David Ganz kindly brought to my attention only after I'd completed a first draft of the present paper, is a characteristically penetrating analysis, whose full force is, to my mind, weakened only by the determined setting of the text in the context of 'les dernières années du règne de Charlemagne ... marquées par des phenomènes de désordre et de désobéissance', and perhaps too by heavy insistence on the role of the 'counsellor' who drafted the text ('Note', 4, 13). Where Ganshof hears the counsellor's voice, I hear the master's.

[34] MGH Capitularia I, no. 127, a letter of Riculf of Mainz (786–813) transmitting Charlemagne's orders to organize fasting on 'Monday 9 December' and the subsequent two days, must belong to 810.

[35] Ganshof, 'Note', 7: here, 'l'interrogation n'est qu'une figure de style employée de manière soutenue: l'empereur est fixé sur ce qu'il doit savoir: il attaque ...'

Charlemagne addresses subordinates, *de haut en bas* (this is less Socrates than the philosopher-king). Nevertheless, he speaks in a peculiarly direct, unmediated fashion. As in no. 71, what begins as a harangue turns into a series of reflections. Charlemagne addresses himself, thinks aloud, voices questions that are on his mind. God had evidently answered the collective prayers of the previous year, and the improvement of each one's *conversatio*, way of living, is this year to be not merely contemplated but undertaken—*quod nunc facere desideramus*. The inquiry of no. 71, clause 5, is repeated urgently, in light of further pondering on St Paul's words, and on what it should mean to 'quit the world'. For in this same year of 811, after all, Charlemagne pondered the option of a *voluntaria saecularium rerum carentia*.[36] That might entail much more than '*only* not bearing arms and not being publicly married'. But Charlemagne's most insistent enquiry was to *ecclesiastici* under the illusion that they could reconcile 'leaving the world' with extremes of worldliness. Charlemagne in clause 2 pointedly alludes to the gap between principle and practice as he reminds his bishops and abbots that 'they are called, and ought to be, shepherds of the church'. He shudders perceptibly as he recalls and explores, in clauses 5, 6, 7, and 8, the varieties of ecclesiastical corruption, from tricking the innocent, especially the weak, the unlearned, the 'more simple', and forcing them into crime through poverty, to perverting the course of justice by encouraging perjury, and involving venal subordinates in their crimes. Worse still, the relics of the saints themselves are manipulated in pursuit of the same acquisitive ends, while even bishops are deceived by the perpetrators' faked piety. In clause 6 Charlemagne sounds as if he's been roused to wrathful irony (*miramur!*) by the thought of churchmen who keep military retinues as well as private estates, 'usurping' both the things themselves and the status of world-renouncers. Clause 9 returns to the theme briefly mentioned in no. 71, clauses 6 and 7: the meaning of every Christian's renunciation in baptism, and of the special obligation of churchmen to set an example to the laity. The voice reaches a crescendo: *Hic diligentissime considerandum est et acutissime distinguendum . . .*, as the lay–ecclesiastical distinction is transcended and 'every single one of us' is summoned not only to self-inspection but to confrontation of the reality of Satan himself at work in the world.

The tone of no. 72's final sections, on right living for those in religious orders, is less fraught, but the issues raised are nonetheless fundamental, the consequence of no less remorseless inquiry. Recruits to a community of monks or canons must be voluntary (clause 10). Those in charge of such communities must seek to recruit, 'not many men but good men. . . . Imperfection in chanting is more tolerable than imperfection in living . . . [and] the adornment and splendour of virtuous living is to be preferred to the adornment and splendour of buildings'. These injunctions, while in part they echo older (patristic and

---

[36] Einhard, *Vita Karoli*, p. 39, cl. 33.

conciliar) models, also evoke such highly topical concerns as those of the monks
of Fulda, who in 812 protested against their abbot's ruinously expensive building projects,[37] or those of the assembled bishops who, at the five great councils
of 813, recalled canons and monks to their respective regular ways of life, bishops
and counts to mutual peace, and priests and monks to avoid involvement in
secular business.[38] At the same time, there is a notable contrast to the *Epistola
de Litteris Colendis*:[39] then, in perhaps 789/90, living well and reading (aloud)
well had been cheerfully paired; now, in 811, they are compared, and living rated
higher than reading, 'the adornment and splendour of good conduct' than the
beauty of church buildings. 'For so far as we can see, the construction of
churches draws in a way on the custom of the Old Law, whereas the improving
of conduct properly pertains to the New Testament.' Theodulf in the *Libri
Carolini* had encapsulated the New Law's transcendence of the Old in a single,
phrase: *nova antiquitas et antiqua novitas*. Charlemagne's response had been:
acute![40] Now, twenty years on, he was engaged in the translation of Theodulf's
insight into a social and political programme to be extended from court to
regions. What was called for now was a more individually responsible, and also
more active, approach to ethics—in other words, and quite explicity, a super-
seding of Old Testament by New Testament values: *morum autem emendatio
proprie ad novum testamentum et christianam pertinet disciplinam*. Churchmen
were called upon to follow Christ and the apostles, but responsibility for getting
'ecclesiastical discipline' right was Charlemagne's, and the corollary was that
'the ruler was of necessity a theologian'.[41] As an afterthought, he picks up the
last question raised in no. 71: were there monks in Gaul before Benedict's Rule
reached there. In no. 72 Charlemagne recalls having 'read that Martin was a

[37] *Supplex Libellus*, ed. J. Semmler, in *Corpus Consuetudinum Monasticarum*, I, ed. K. Hallinger,
Monumenta aevi Anianensis (Siegburg, 1963), 321-7.
[38] Council of Arles, c. 6, MGH Concilia aevi Karolini, Teil I, ed. A. Werminghoff (Hanover, 1906),
p. 251, and cll. 12, 13, pp. 251-2; Council of Reims, cl. 30, p. 256; Council of Mainz, cll. 14, 16, pp. 264-5;
Council of Chalon cl. 5, p. 275. Werminghoff, 'Arles', 246, n. 1, suggests the influence of Capitulary
no. 72, and Ganshof, 'Note', 15-19, shows the extent to which these councils pursued the agenda of 811.
[39] MGH Capitularia I, no. 29, p. 79. For the date, see T. Martin, 'Bemerkungen zur "Epistola de litteris colendis"', *Archiv für Diplomatik*, 31 (1985), 227-72, at 266-70, followed by D. Bullough, *Carolingian
Renewal* (Manchester, 1992), 158, n. 58.
[40] *Libri Carolini*, II, c. 27, p. 295: 'perceptively!' (or, to translate more colloquially, 'spot on!'). For the
marginal annotation as embodying Charlemagne's reaction, see above n. 10. See further the excellent
commentary of E. Dahlhaus-Berg, *Nova antiquitas et antiqua novitas. Typologische Exegese und isidori-
anisches Geschichtsbild bei Theodulf von Orléans* (Cologne and Vienna, 1974), 35-8. Dahlhaus-Berg (pp.
13-4, 221-35) makes a compelling case for Theodulf's authorship of the decrees of the Council of Chalon
(813), noting (p. 235) that he was 'the very man to transmit the experiences and desires of the region to the
court, and the court's reform programme to the region'. To Dahlhaus-Berg's evidence for Theodulf's
influence in the Aachen years should be added his presence in 811 as a witness of Charlemagne's will:
Einhard, *Vita Karoli*, c. 33, p. 41.
[41] D. Ganz, 'Theology and the Organisation of Thought', in *The New Cambridge Medieval History*,
II, ed. R. McKitterick (Cambridge, 1995), 758-85, at 784: Ganz's comment made in a broader context
seems equally apt for this one.

monk, and had monks', and he correctly adds that Martin lived long before Benedict. This rings true as a characteristically direct, and independent-minded, approach to the question of what might be an original, homegrown monastic Rule *in Gallia*. Finally, the ways of life of (enclosed) nuns and (house-dwelling) *ancillae Dei* are included in the list of matters to be discussed. Perhaps Charlemagne was more sympathetic than his bishops to the *conversatio* of the *ancillae Dei*.[42]

In the end, no proof is possible that Charlemagne himself was personally responsible for the wording of these capitularies, nor is it certain that he laid down their agendas. What seems clear, though, is that their content is in part new, and unparalleled, and their tone distinctive. All that can be offered is an interesting possibility. But if no. 72, especially, sounds a shade anachronistic—a twelfth-century appeal *avant la lettre?*—that may be because we have yet to attune our ears to authentic tones of Carolingian spirituality,[43] and, as ground-bass, the voice of Charlemagne.

APPENDIX

Capitulary on Matters To Be Discussed With Counts, Bishops, and Abbots,
ed. A. Boretius, MGH Capitularia I (Hanover, 1883), no. 71, pp. 161–2.

1. First, we wish to separate our bishops, abbots, and counts and to speak to them individually (*singulariter*).
2. What are the reasons that cause one man to refuse to give help to another, whether in a border-region (*in marcha*), or in the army, where he ought to perform any useful act for the defence of the fatherland (*patria*)?
3. Whence have arisen those very frequent disputes in which one man demands from another whatever he sees his peer (*par*) possessing?
4. About what happens when someone receives someone else's man who flees to him?
5. They are to be asked in what matters, or what places, ecclesiastics impede laymen, or laymen ecclesiastics, in their carrying out of their office (*ministerium*). In this place it has to be discussed and intervention has to be made [to find out] about how far a bishop or abbot ought to involve himself in secular affairs or how far a count or any other layman ought to involve himself in ecclesiastical affairs. Here enquiry is to be made most searchingly: what did the Apostle [Paul] mean in saying: 'let no one who serves God involve himself in secular affairs' (2 Tim. 2.4), and to whom does that saying apply?
6. What is it that every Christian says in baptism, and what does he renounce?

---

[42] Cf. Nelson, 'The Wary Widow', in *Property and Power in the Early Middle Ages*, ed. W. Davies and P. J. Fouracre (Cambridge, 1995), 82–113, at 90–2.
[43] Cf. R. Sullivan, 'What Was Carolingian Monasticism? The Plan of St Gall and the History of Monasticism', in *After Rome's Fall. Narrators and Sources of Early Medieval History. Essays presented to Walter Goffart*, ed. A. Murray (Toronto and London, 1998), 251–87, at 255–61; and C. Chazelle, *The Crucified Christ* (forthcoming, Cambridge, 2000).

7. When a man makes his renuncation or abrogation null and void, what is he following, or neglecting, instead?

8. That a man who thinks he can despise God's precepts with impunity, or despises what God has threatened on the grounds that it won't happen, does not truly believe in God.

9. That investigation must be made into ourselves, whether we are really Christians. This can very easily be recognized by considering our [way of] life and our conduct, if we are willing conscientiously to discuss in front of each other [our] *conversatio*.

10. About the life and conduct of our pastors, that is, our bishops, who ought to give a good example to the people of God not only by teaching but by living. For we think that the Apostle spoke to them when he said: 'Be imitators of me and observe those who walk thus, just as you have our model' (Philipp. 3.17).

11. About the life of those who are are called canons, what sort ought it to be?

12. About the *conversatio* of monks, and whether any can be monks except those who observe the Rule of Benedict. It must also be asked if there were monks in Gaul before the tradition of the Rule of St Benedict reached these dioceses.

13. Keep these instructions as you should: and I have confidence in you, most pious pontiffs, and insofar as I can find things out, I shall not hesitate to send [messengers to] you and to write to you. Farewell in the Lord.

Capitula About Matters To Be Discussed With Bishops and Abbots, ed. A. Boretius, MGH Capitularia I (Hannover, 1883), no. 72, pp. 162–4 (811); better edition by F. L. Ganshof, 'Note sur les "Capitula de causis cum episcopis et abbatibus tractandis" de 811', Studia Gratiana, 13 (1967), 20–5.

Short list of points on which we wish to speak to our faithful bishops and abbots and to warn them about the common interests of all our people.

1. First, it's to be recalled, that in the previous year we made a three-day fast, praying God to deign to show us in what respects our *conversatio* ought to be improved in his sight: this we now wish to do.

2. Enquiry is first to be made into ecclesiastics, that is, bishops and abbots, so that they can set out for us their *conversatio*, how they ought to live, so that we can know to whom among them we ought to believe either good or something else in need of restraint. And that we may know how far it is permitted to any ecclesiastic, whether bishop, abbot, or monk, to involve himself in secular affairs, and what properly pertains to those who are called, and ought to be, pastors of the church and fathers of monasteries, so that we ought to demand of them no other than what it is permitted to them to do, and none of them should seek from us those things in which we ought not to give them our consent.

3. We wish to question those ecclesiastics and those who should not only learn the Holy Scriptures themselves but teach them to others, who are those to whom the Apostle said: 'Be my imitators', and who it was of whom he said: 'no one serving God should involve himself in secular business', and how the Apostle must be imitated, and how a man should serve God.

4. Again they must be questioned, so that they explain clearly to us what it means when it is said in respect of them that they are 'to leave the world (*saeculum*)', and in what ways those who have left the world can be distinguished from those who still follow the world: is the difference only that they don't bear arms and they are not publicly married?

5. Also they must be questioned as to whether a man has left the world if he doesn't stop increasing his possessions every day by whatever means and whatever tricks, by persuading about the blessedness of the heavenly kingdom, and threatening about the eternal suffering of hell, and in the name of God or of some saint despoiling of his property either a rich man or a poor man who are known to be simpler by nature and less learned and discrete: these people disinherit their legitimate heirs and thus force many to commit misdeeds and crimes out of the sheer neediness to which they've been reduced, so that they perpetrate thefts and acts of brigandage, they say on grounds of necessity, because the inheritance of their forefathers' property has been taken away by someone else and does not therefore pass to them.

6. Again, they must be questioned as to how a man has 'left the world', if led by greed to acquire property which he sees someone else possessing leads men, by paying them, into perjury and false witness, and seeks an advocate or a provost who is not just and God-fearing but cruel and greedy and not taking perjury at all seriously, and who when inquiring about property asks not 'how?' but 'how much?'

7. What is to be said about those who, allegedly on the grounds of love of God and the saints and martyrs and confessors, transfer the bones and relics of the bodies of saints from one place to another and build new churches there and most pressingly encourage whoever they can to hand over their property to those places. Such a man wishes to seem as if he performs a good action and to present himself as becoming through that action well-deserving before God, by which he can persuade bishops: clearly such a thing has been done in order to get hold of someone else's property.

8. We are amazed how it has come about that a man who professes himself to have 'renounced the world' and in no way to agree to being called 'secular' by anyone, can be willing to keep armed men and private property, when that pertains to those who have not yet wholly renounced the world: but how that can rightly pertain to ecclesiastics, we have absolutely no idea, unless those men who have no doubt they are taking what doesn't belong them, though they make [false] claims to legality, can give us some clues!

9. What each person promises to Christ in baptism and what things they have renounced: so that, although every Christian ought seriously to think about this, it is especially by ecclesiastics that enquiry ought to be made, since it is they who ought to offer layfolk an example of that promise and that renunciation in their own lives. This is something to be most carefully considered and most rigorously investigated, what things each one of us ought to follow, or spurn, in order to keep what they've promised or renounced, or alternatively make it null and void. And who is that Satan or Enemy whose works and whose pomp we have renounced in baptism? This is to be investigated, so that none of us should follow, by wrongdoing, him whom we long since renounced in baptism.

10. In which of the Canons or in the Rule of which holy father is it laid down that anyone can be made a cleric or monk against his will? And where did Christ command, or which apostle preached, that a community should be formed in a church of canons or monks consisting of persons unwilling or refusing or low-born?

11. What small benefit does it bring to the Church of Christ that he who should be a pastor or teacher (*magister*) of some venerable place should strive in his way of life to have more men rather than good men, and who takes pleasure not so much in virtuous men but in large numbers of men, and makes more effort to ensure that a cleric or monk

should chant and read well than that he should live a just and blessed way—although the
discipline of chanting and reading is not only something least to be despised in a church,
it's even to be wholly exercised. But if one can come to some holy place, it seems to us
that imperfection in chanting is something that ought to be put up with rather than
imperfection in living. And however much it may be a good thing that the buildings of
a church should be beautiful, nevertheless the adornment and splendour of virtuous living is to be preferred to adornment and splendour of the buildings; because, so far as we
can see, the construction of churches draws in a way on the custom of the Old Law,
whereas the improving of conduct properly pertains to the New Testament and to christian discipline. If Christ and the apostles and those who have rightly followed the apostles are those who must be followed in ecclesiastical discipline, then we ought to do
otherwise in many respects than we have been doing up to now, and many things in our
practice and custom must be done away with, and no less must many things be done
which we have not done.

12. By what rule did monks live in Gaul before the Rule of St Benedict was brought
there? For we read that St Martin was a monk, and had monks under him, and he was
long before St Benedict.

13. About the way of life of nuns and serving-women of God.

8

TRUE TEACHERS AND PIOUS KINGS: SALZBURG, LOUIS THE GERMAN, AND CHRISTIAN ORDER

Stuart Airlie

The church of Salzburg in the Carolingian era can easily appear as a missionary station focused on the frontiers of the empire. Writing to his friend Arn, bishop and after 798 archbishop of Salzburg, Alcuin referred to the latter's proximity to the 'frontiers of the Christian empire'. Alcuin was concerned with the work of conversion among the pagan Avars, whose military power had just been broken by Carolingian might. A century later one of Arn's successors, Archbishop Theotmar (873–907), wrote to the pope to express his anger at the savage behaviour of the pagan Hungarians which threatened the Christian culture of Pannonia. Theotmar, together with two other Bavarian bishops and a host of warriors, was in fact to perish in battle against the Hungarians at Pressburg (Bratislava) in 907.[1]

The interest of the church of Salzburg in what we would call missionary work thus appears unsurprising, though the shifting fortunes of Salzburg archbishops—from sharing in victories over the Avars to falling in battle against the Hungarians—warn us against seeing such work in purely linear terms of progress and success. It is from this perspective of missionary work that scholars have usually viewed a remarkable text produced in Salzburg in the late ninth century. This is the *Conversio Bagoariorum et Carantanorum* (Conversion of the Bavarians and Carantanians), composed in Salzburg in 870, possibly by Archbishop Adalwin (859–73). In the words of modern commentators, this text provides 'one of the most lively accounts of an early medieval mission station', and is 'unparalleled in its emphasis on the nitty-gritty: the dispatch of priests,

---

[1] Alcuin, *Epistolae*, no. 184, ed. E. Dümmler, MGH Epistolae Karolini Aevi II (Berlin, 1895), 309. Theotmar's letter is edited as *Epistola Theotmari episcopi* in F. Lošek, *Die Conversio Bagoariorum et Carantanorum und der Brief des Erzbischofs Theotmar von Salzburg*, MGH Studien und Texte XV (Hanover, 1997), 138–56; its authenticity is defended by Lošek, ibid. 73–87; there is a partial English translation in C. Bowlus, *Franks, Moravians and Magyars: The Struggle For the Middle Danube 788–907* (Philadelphia, 1995), 336–9. The contrast between Arn and Theotmar is noted by H. Wolfram, *Grenzen und Räume: Geschichte Österreichs vor seiner Entstehung* (Vienna, 1995), 187, 272–3.

the foundation of churches', etc.[2] As such, the *Conversio*, together with other sources (not least archaeological), has proved to be an invaluable source for scholars charting the spread of Christianity in south-east central Europe, and it has generated a prodigious body of commentary.[3]

Yet Salzburg was not simply an outward-looking missionary outpost. Arn inherited a flourishing cultural centre that had been built up (not least under his Irish predecessor Virgil) under the Agilolfing dukes who had ruled Bavaria before the Carolingian takeover in 788. Arn himself spent most of his time, not on far-flung missions, but in the service of his master Charlemagne. He built up a fine library in Salzburg itself, where collections of canon law and penitential material stemmed from northern Gaul and Ireland, and his work was success-fully continued by the archbishops who followed.[4] Salzburg, then, looked inward to the great cultural centres of Christendom, of which it was itself one, as much as it looked outward.

In fact, the *Conversio* is in many ways a very inward-looking text. Its intended audience was almost certainly the east Frankish king Louis the German, and its aim was to rehearse Salzburg's claims to the Slav lands to the south-east, specif-ically to Carantania and lower Pannonia. Salzburg did indeed have sound claims over Carantania, and eighth-century popes had recognized Salzburg's missionary activity there. Pannonia, however, was (in Herwig Wolfram's words) a no-man's land, the 'wild east', yet the Salzburg author was determined to describe it as a coherent territory over which Salzburg had claims.[5] The specific trigger for the writing of the text was the appearance in Pannonia of the Greek churchman Methodius, whose very presence there, not to mention his use of the Slavonic vernacular for the liturgy, outraged Bavarian churchmen. Their anger at seeing this intruder in their 'patch' went beyond the writing of

[2] R. Fletcher, *The Conversion of Europe* (London, 1997), 345; M. Innes, 'Franks and Slavs c.700–1000: The Problem of European Expansion Before the Millennium', *Early Medieval Europe*, 6 (1997), 201–16, at 211; both commentators are aware of the tendentious nature of the text. The latest edition of the text itself, with German translation, is in Lošek, *Die Conversio Bagoariorum et Carantanorum*; there is a valu-able commentary in H. Wolfram, *Conversio Bagoariorum et Carantanorum. Das Weissbuch der Salzburger Kirche über die erfolgreiche Mission in Karantanien und Pannonien* (Vienna, Cologne, and Graz, 1979); this is not entirely superseded by Wolfram's revised version of it in his *Salzburg Bayern Österreich: Die Con-versio Bagoariorum et Carantanorum und die Quellen ihrer Zeit* (Vienna and Munich, 1995).

[3] In addition to the work of Wolfram as at n. 2 above, see, from a vast bibliography, B. Wavra, *Salzburg und Hamburg. Erzbistumsgründung und Missionspolitik in karolingischer Zeit* (Berlin, 1991); *Karantanien und der Alpen-Adria-Raum im Frühmittelalter*, ed. G. Hödl and J. Grabmayer (Vienna, Cologne, and Weimar, 1993); broader perspectives are available in *Das Christentum im bairischen Raum von den Anfängen bis ins 11. Jahrhundert*, ed. E. Boshof and H. Wolff (Cologne, Weimar, and Vienna, 1994).

[4] On Salzburg's history and culture see, again selected from a large bibliography, B. Bischoff, *Die südostdeutschen Schreibschulen in der Karolingerzeit*, 2 vols. (Wiesbaden, 1974, 1980), esp. at II, 52–179; *Geschichte Salzburgs. Stadt und Land*, ed. H. Dopsch, vols I.1, I.2, I.3 (Salzburg, 1981–4); R. Meens, 'Kanonisches Recht in Salzburg am Ende des 8. Jahrhunderts', *Zeitschrift der Savigny-Stiftung für Rechtsgeschichte, Kanonistische Abteilung*, 83 (1996), 13–34; H. Löwe, *Deutschlands Geschichtsquellen im Mittelalter*, VI (Weimar, 1990), 811–20.

[5] I here follow the deft summary of Wolfram, *Conversio*, 15–16.

texts. In 870 Methodius was brought before a stormy synod at Regensburg, found guilty of having infringed diocesan rights, and then bundled off to monastic custody, probably in Swabia.[6]

Scholarly concentration on these topics has meant that the *Conversio*'s inward-looking features may not have been fully appreciated as an integral part of its design. Yet we would do well to remember that those early medieval churchmen whom we may be tempted to classify as missionaries often saw themselves as imposers of Christian order upon communities within Christendom as well as on its borders. A figure such as Boniface was just as concerned with the correction of backsliding Christians within Francia as with the preaching of the faith to pagans.[7] Correspondingly, the *Conversio* is as much concerned with the business of reformation and correction as with the spreading of the faith in Carantania and Pannonia. As such, it reflects the general concerns of the Carolingian renaissance as well as the concerns of other Christian authorities, such as Bede. To say this is not to deny that the text's focus is on Carantania and Pannonia. But the *Conversio*'s focus is not exclusively on these territories, and an examination of the text that bears this in mind can cast light on its overall structure and thus add to our understanding of its meaning as a contemporary document produced by a great centre of the Carolingian renaissance. The achievements of the Christian leaders so eloquently described in this text need to be seen as a whole, as that is how the *Conversio* presents them. The author of the *Conversio* also saw Louis the German as one of these Christian leaders. What this text reveals is how the work of kings and bishops was conceptualized in the mind-set, so to speak, of the great churches of the Carolingian world. This paper will be concerned, not so much with the details of the christianization of Pannonia and Carantania or with the rights and wrongs of Salzburg's claims to authority there, as with this text's vision of the foundations of authority in the Christian society of the Carolingian period. One of the foundations of authority was the Carolingian king himself whose office was so much more than a secular one.

We lose a dimension of the historical meaning of the *Conversio* if we see it as a text exclusively concerned with 'missionary' effort. The title was given to the text in the post-medieval period.[8] It does correspond to the text's content, but

---

[6] The sources for this synod are conveniently available in *Die Konzilien der Karolingischen Teilreiche 860–874*, ed. W. Hartmann, no. 35, MGH Concilia IV, Concilia Aevi Karolini DCCCLX–DCCCLXXIV (Hannover, 1998), 402–5; Wolfram, *Grenzen und Räume*, 263–4; Fletcher, *The Conversion of Europe*, 359. On the 870 date of the text and for Louis the German as its intended audience, Wolfram, *Salzburg Bayern Österreich*, 193 and Lošek, *Die Conversio*, 5–8.

[7] T. Reuter, 'Saint Boniface and Europe', in *The Greatest Englishman*, ed. T. Reuter (Exeter, 1980), 69–94. As Henry Mayr-Harting has written, 'no real distinction can be made between internal and external missionizing': 'The West: The Age of Conversion (700–1050)', in *The Oxford Illustrated History of Christianity*, ed. J. McManners (Oxford, 1990), 92–121, at 99.

[8] Wolfram, *Conversio*, 21–2.

above all it signals that the christianization of the Bavarians is an integral feature of the narrative. Before turning to the story of 'how the Slavs were instructed in the sacred faith and were made Christian', the author sums up the story so far: 'Up to now we have written of how the Bavarians became Christians and likewise written up the sequence of the bishops and abbots in the see of Salzburg.'[9] Although the story of the Carantanians and the Pannonians marks a new sequence in the text, the author's inclusion of the Bavarian section, and his summary of it, shows that the text's overriding concern was with the authority of Salzburg and the building of a Christian world in Bavaria as well as elsewhere. In this light, the *Conversio*'s links with texts written between 700 and 800 to record and confirm the history and property-holdings of the church of Salzburg are instructive.[10] The *Conversio* can thus take its place in a sequence of texts produced in Salzburg from the late eighth century onwards in which the history of the church of Salzburg was described, its fabric secured, and its identity articulated.[11]

The *Conversio* reflects the ambition of the Carolingian church to create a fully christianized landscape. In describing Rupert's evangelical activities, it goes beyond its sources, the *Gesta Hrodberti* and the *Breves Notitiae*, to stress that not only the 'nobles' but also the common people ('ignobiles') received baptism at his hands.[12] Rupert goes on to build and dedicate churches such as St Peter's at Salzburg, and ensures that the divine offices are properly celebrated there. Such activities foreshadow those undertaken by his successors whose construction of churches in Pannonia thus becomes part of the *Conversio*'s general image of christianizing the landscape.[13]

Despite its focus on Salzburg's claims to authority in Pannonia, the *Conversio* is, at another level, less concerned with such particularities than with the all-embracing nature of the Christian community. This enables us to appreciate an important dimension of one of the *Conversio*'s best-known anecdotes, the story of Ingo, a priest from Salzburg active in Carantania in the days of Archbishop Arn (785–821).

He summoned those servants who were Christian believers to his table while he made their unbelieving masters sit outside like dogs, placing before them bread and meat together with shabby wine vessels, so that they might eat thus. He ordered, however, that the servants be given golden vessels. Then the nobles who had been cast outside asked: 'Why are you behaving like this to us?' And he replied: 'You with your unwashed

---

[9] Lošek, *Die Conversio*, c. 3, 100–2.

[10] On the relationship of such Salzburg property texts as the *Notitia Arnonis* and *Breves notitiae* together with the Salzburg confraternity-book to the *Conversio*, see Wolfram, *Salzburg Bayern Österreich*, 197–226 and Lošek, *Die Conversio*, 33, 35–6.

[11] H. Dopsch, 'Die Zeit der Karolinger und Ottonen', in *Geschichte Salzburgs*, ed. Dopsch, I.1, 157–228, at 172–3; Lošek, *Die Conversio*, 21–36.

[12] Lošek, *Die Conversio*, c. 1, 92 with notes.

[13] Ibid., c. 1, 90–8; compare the activities of, for example, Archbishop Liupram, ibid., c. 11, 126.

bodies are unworthy to communicate with those who have been reborn through the sacred font, but deserve to eat your food outside the house like dogs.' Once this was done they were instructed in the holy faith and rushed to be baptized.[14]

This is not a story about the clash of pagan and Christian customs per se. Although it revolves round motifs of feasting, it does not involve a clash between an austere Christian missionary and pagan feasting practices, as in the story of Columbanus detonating a barrel of beer dedicated to pagan gods.[15] Nor does it involve quite the same sort of gulf between the pagan world and the Christian food of the consecrated host as is found in Bede's story of the demands made by the sons of King Sabert of the East Saxons to be given the 'white bread which you gave to our father Saba'.[16] Rather, it is a story about community and about how only common religious identity could permit the existence of full social community.[17] As Ian Wood has pointed out, Ingo deploys 'traditional social values' to bring about conversion. It is the lords' love of fine gold goblets that brings them into the fold.[18] Nonetheless, the story surely also contains an implied rebuke to earthly expressions of social status, in that it is the very fact that their servants have been given golden vessels that shocks the lords. It points to the sharp tensions between the claims of social hierarchy and the essential equality of members of the Christian community of believers, and thus fits into the mainstream of the Carolingian reform movement. Carolingian reformers were keenly aware of such tensions and, undeterred by the fact of their own noble origins, lambasted noble arrogance in a series of texts, such as Bishop Jonas of Orléans's *De Institutione Laicali*.[19] The Ingo story eschews description of pagan customs in Pannonia but asserts the universal norms of the Carolingian church.

The *Conversio* is also a rather serene text that betrays little concern for the difficulties faced on the ground in recently or lightly christianized areas. The absence of a sense of the unruliness of the Christian frontiers is striking. True, there are references to revolts in eighth-century Carantania which impede the efforts of bishops such as Virgil at christianization, but such events are only temporary setbacks and the steady stream of priests from Salzburg into the area

---

[14] Ibid., c. 7, 112–14; Wolfram, *Conversio*, 96–102; id., *Salzburg Bayern Österreich*, 287–9.

[15] I. Wood, 'Pagans and Holy Men, 600–800', in *Irland und die Christenheit*, ed. P. Ni Chathain and M. Richter (Stuttgart, 1987), 347–61, at 354; id., 'Pagan Religion and Superstitions East of the Rhine From the Fifth to the Ninth Century', in *After Empire: Towards an Ethnology of Europe's Barbarians*, ed. G. Ausenda (Woodbridge, 1995), 253–68, at 259; see also Wavra, *Salzburg und Hamburg*, 175.

[16] *HE* II, 5; noteworthy here is the reference to the life-giving waters of baptism.

[17] A. Angenendt, *Kaiserherrschaft und Königstaufe* (Berlin and New York, 1984), 72–5.

[18] Wood, 'Pagans and Holy Men', 357.

[19] See e.g. Jonas of Orleans's *De institutione Laicali*, II, c. 22 and c. 23, PL 106: cols. 214–5, 216; general discussion of Carolingian context in S. Airlie, 'The Anxiety of Sanctity: St Gerald of Aurillac and his Maker', *JEH* 43 (1992), 372–95 at 377–8, and J. Smith, 'Religion and Lay Society', in *The New Cambridge Medieval History II c.700–c.900*, ed. R. McKitterick (Cambridge, 1995), 654–78, at 664–5. For an intense meditation on such tensions in early medieval religious thought, see H. Mayr-Harting, *The Venerable Bede, the Rule of St Benedict and Social Class*, Jarrow Lecture (1976).

quickly resumes.[20] Inhabitants of Carantania and Pannonia are not depicted as particularly uncivilized or resistant to Christian teaching. The political upheavals in the south-east in the 860s, upheavals that directly involved the church of Salzburg, leave little or no imprint on the text, which relentlessly lists the building and dedicating of Christian churches under the eager patronage of Priwina and Chozil, princes of Pannonia.[21] This contrasts strongly with other texts of the period. Archbishop Theotmar, for example, disdainfully compares the glorious Christian kings of the Franks to the Slavs who stem from pagans, skulk in their remote strongholds, and persecute the true faith. He also refers to outlandish heathen customs, such as swearing by dog or wolf, and accuses the Slavs of shaving their heads as a sign of their alliance with the pagan Hungarians.[22] The world on Salzburg's frontiers appears as remote, hostile, and repulsive. The Synod of Mainz in 852, which was attended by Archbishop Liupram (836–59) and his suffragans, included a case which associated poor Christian standards with the fringes of the Carolingian Christian world. One Albgis had carried off the wife of one Patrichus 'to the extreme limits of the kingdom . . . to the still rough Christianity of the people of the Moravians'.[23] Some generations previously Archbishop Arn had been much concerned with the difficulty of baptizing an unlettered and ignorant people in the Avar regions.[24]

Such anxieties and contemporary anthropological expressions of cultural otherness are on the whole conspicuous by their absence from the *Conversio*. But such concerns did circulate among the Salzburg clergy who were active in Carantania in the 860s. Letters from Pope Nicholas I in reply to queries from Osbald, an assistant bishop (*chorepiscopus*) in Carantania, cast a vivid light on conditions among the Salzburg clergy there. What should happen, asked Osbald, if a priest should slay a heathen; can he still remain a priest? Further, what should happen if a priest, during a dispute with a deacon, should strike him so that the deacon fell off his horse and died?[25] The events and dilemmas that triggered such letters find no place in the *Conversio*. Even Osbald's attempt to 'outflank' his superior, the archbishop of Salzburg, by contacting the pope directly makes little or no dent on the smooth surface of the *Conversio*'s narrative, though it did trigger disciplinary action from an angry archbishop.

---

[20] Lošek, *Die Conversio*, c. 5, 106–8; noteworthy, however, is the text's discriminating political-religious vocabulary.

[21] Ibid., c. 12; c. 13, 128–32; on the political upheavals, see below.

[22] *Epistola Theotmari episcopi*, in ibid. 146–50.

[23] *Die Konzilien der Karolingischen Teilreiche 843–859*, ed. W. Hartmann, no. 26, c. xi, MGH Concilia Aevi Karolini III, DCCCXLIII–DCCCLIX (Hanover, 1984), 248–9; the phrase is not unique to this synod.

[24] *Concilia Aevi Karolini I*, ed. A. Werminghoff, no. 20, MGH Concilia II (Hanover and Leipzig, 1906), 172–6; on Arn's attendance here, Wolfram, *Salzburg Bayern Österreich*, 286–7. Alcuin's letters to Paulinus of Aquileia and to Arn are relevant here, Alcuin, *Epistolae*, nos. 99 and 107, ed. Dümmler, 143–4, 153–4; D. Bullough, 'Alcuin and the Kingdom of Heaven: Liturgy, Theology, and the Carolingian Age', in *Carolingian Essays*, ed. U.-R. Blumenthal (Washington, DC, 1983), 1–69, at 42–5.

[25] Dopsch, 'Die Zeit der Karolinger', 184.

The *Conversio* has minimal interest in such problems. Instead, it offers a 'can-do' approach to early medieval mission work which reveals much about itself. Consideration of some aspects of the *Conversio*'s picture of Rupert is instructive here. Rupert was one of the founding fathers of the diocese of Salzburg in the late seventh and early eighth centuries. He had been bishop of Worms, but political circumstances drove him to Salzburg where he co-operated with the duke of Bavaria in restoring the Christian faith in Salzburg itself and on the boundaries of Avar and Slav territory.[26] Rupert is an important figure in the *Conversio*, which indeed opens with an account of his career. This is paralleled in the so-called *Gesta Hrodberti* (Deeds of Rupert), which was probably written in Salzburg some time after 793, and a tangled thicket of scholarship has grown out of the study of the relationship of the *Conversio*'s mini-biography to the *Gesta* and both texts' relationship to a now lost version.[27] The point that needs to be stressed here, however, is that no matter what sources were available to the *Conversio*'s author, he produced an account of Rupert's career that in many respects reflected the concerns of Salzburg in the late ninth century rather than those of the early eighth.

A striking aspect of the *Conversio*'s account of Rupert's career is its serenity. Backed by the duke of Bavaria, Rupert encounters neither opposition nor setback in his preaching of the gospel. Moreover, the *Conversio* includes lower Pannonia as a site of Rupert's activity, but no reference to Pannonia appears in the parallel section of the earlier *Gesta* or the other eight-century sources. The author of the *Conversio* is here quietly adding an unhistorical extension to Rupert's activities. The reasons for this are clear enough. The text was written for a secular ruler and was designed to buttress Salzburg's claims in precisely this area. The author was intending to root the church of Salzburg's claims to lower Pannonia in the venerable past, and Rupert's activities there are said to unfold with the permission of the secular ruler, the duke of Bavaria: 'Then the man of the Lord, after receiving permission, journeyed by ship through the Danube valley as far as lower Pannonia to sow the seeds of life.'[28]

The *Conversio*'s Rupert not only travels further than the historical Rupert, he encounters none of the problems that bedevilled other far-travelled clergymen of the Carolingian era. Rupert's calm and prosperous Danube voyage stands in stark contrast to that undertaken by Anskar, for example, whose ninth-century mission to Sweden enjoined upon him by the emperor Louis the Pious encountered disaster at the hands of pirates.[29] Further, Rupert's journey to Lorch,

---

[26] Wolfram, *Grenzen und Räume*, 105–7.

[27] Lošek, *Die Conversio*, 21–7, gives the current state of play of scholarship on this question as well as including the *Gesta Hrodberti* as a parallel to the *Conversio*'s account of Rupert in his edition, ibid. 90–8; it is also available as *Vita Hrodberti episcopi Salisburgensis*, ed. W. Levison, MGH Scriptores rerum Merovingicarum VI (Hannover and Leipzig, 1913), 140–62.

[28] Lošek, *Die Conversio*, c. 1, 92–4 and NB 93, n. 9; see Wavra, *Salzburg und Hamburg*, 142.

[29] *Vita Anskarii auctore Rimberto*, ed. G. Waitz, c. 10, MGH Scriptores in rerum Germanicarum in usum scholarum separatim editi (Hanover, 1884), 31–2.

undertaken according to the *Conversio* on his return from lower Pannonia, is also presented with a calm lack of comment. Yet while Lorch, the site of a bishopric in antiquity, might have been a suitable place for Rupert to re-establish a bishopric, it was in fact too exposed and dangerous a location because of its closeness to Avar territory. Successful missions to the Avars were not a realistic possibility before their political power had been checked.[30] Nor is this insight confined only to modern-day scholars. According to the eighth-century *Life of Emmeram* by Arbeo, bishop of Freising in western Bavaria, duke Theodo actually forbade Emmeram from going on a mission to the land of the Avars because there was *discordia* between them and the Bavarians.[31]

What the *Conversio* offers us, then, is an account of Rupert's activity that is shaped by hindsight and the concerns of the late ninth century. The text is both tendentious and, in its careful attention to telling (from Salzburg's point of view) detail, artful. As such it is compromised as a source for the history of missionary work in the south-east. The role of the Agilolfing dukes as eighth-century patrons is, despite Theodo's appearance as supporter of Rupert, passed over. The author's focus was the kings of the Franks and the role of the church of Salzburg. Accordingly, Duke Tassilo, whose great victory over the Carantanians in 772 and establishing of monasteries as centres for mission in the south-east deserve mention in any account of missionary activity in Caranatania, is completely absent from the *Conversio*.[32] The other great churches of Bavaria, such as Regensburg and Freising, which had a significant stake in this area, are invisible in its pages.[33] The *Conversio* does mention, for example, a priest called Dominicus as active in the service of Priwina of Pannonia. Dominicus transferred into the service of Archbishop Liupram of Salzburg, who then gave him permission to celebrate Mass in his diocese and entrusted church and people to him. The *Conversio*'s stress on the following of due ecclesiastical procedure and the active authority of the archbishops of Salzburg is typical, but equally typical is its failure to refer to the fact that Dominicus originally came not from Pannonia but from the church of Regensburg.[34]

---

[30] Lošek, *Die Conversio*, c. 1, 94 with n. 11 at 95; H. Dopsch, 'Die Salzburger Slavenmission im 8./9. Jahrhundert und der Anteil der Iren', in *Irland und die Christenheit*, ed. Ni Chathain and Richter, 421–44, at 427; W. Pohl, 'Das sanfte Joch Christi: Zum Christentum als gestaltende Kraft im Mitteleuropa des Fruhmittelalters', in *Karantanien und der Alpen-Adria-Raum im Frühmittelalter*, ed. Hödl and Grabmayer, 259–80, at 266, 269.

[31] *Vita Haimhrammmi Episcopi*, ed. B. Krusch, c. 4, *Arbeonis Episcopi Frisingensis Vitae Sanctorum Haimhrammi et Corbiniani*, MGH Scriptores rerum germanicarum, 33–4; on textual echoes of Arbeo's text in the *Conversio*, see Lošek, *Die Conversio*, 93, n. 10.

[32] Wavra, *Salzburg und Hamburg*, 168–75.

[33] W. Störmer, 'Zur Frage der Funktionen des kirchlichen Fernbesitzes im Gebiet der Ostalpen vom 8. bis 10. Jahrhundert', in *Die transalpinen Verbindungen der Bayern, Alemannen und Franken bis zum 10. Jahrhundert*, ed. H. Beumann and W. Schroeder (Sigmaringen, 1987), 379–403; Wavra, *Salzburg und Hamburg*, 185–8; Wolfram, *Grenzen und Räume*, 124.

[34] Lošek, *Die Conversio*, c. 11, 124, with n. 134 at 125; Wolfram, *Salzburg Bayern Österreich*, 323–4.

Other absences and silences are yet more significant. There is no mention of the see of Aquileia in northern Italy. Its patriarch Paulinus (787–802) had been a friend of Arn of Salzburg and of Alcuin, but his successor Ursus (802–11) was too interested in Carantania for Salzburg's comfort. A dispute between Arn and Ursus was ended by a division of interest decreed by Charlemagne himself in 811. The *Conversio* makes no explicit reference to all this and offers a studiedly bland account of Arn's area of spiritual jurisdiction in the disputed zone.[35] Again, the *Conversio*'s attention to detail is noteworthy. Its author reports that Pippin, Charlemagne's son and king of Italy, granted part of lower Pannonia to the spiritual care of the church of Salzburg during the Avar campaigns of 796, but he refers to Pippin simply as a son of Charlemagne; he makes no mention of Pippin's Italian kingship, lest the shadow of Aquileia fall across his text at this point.[36]

Silence and discretion hold sway even where the history of the church of Salzburg itself is concerned. We have already encountered Osbald, assistant bishop in Carantania, and his worries over unruly priests. As we have seen, such worries have no place in the text of the *Conversio*. But Osbald himself had been unruly. He had attempted to assert his independence vis-à-vis the archbishop of Salzburg, and the tensions between the assistant bishops and archbishop had led to the production in Salzburg of a book, now lost, regulating their relations. It is possible that Osbald was in fact deposed by Archbishop Adalwin some time in the 860s. The *Conversio*, whose author, it will be remembered, may have been Adalwin himself, refers to Osbald in the following terms: 'In the time of archbishops Liupram and Adalwin, Bishop Osbald directed the people of the Slavs as in earlier times the previously mentioned bishops did, as subjects of the bishops of Salzburg.'[37] Perhaps the insistence on subordination to Salzburg here suggests that the author is protesting too much and thus reveals something of the conflict. Essentially, however, this passage deliberately highlights qualities of discipline and order and passes over conflict as unedifying.

This vision of Salzburg as disciplined, well ordered, and entitled to carry out its work among the Slavs was a vision destined for a king. It is not the only text which Louis would have received from Salzburg. Archbishop Adalram (821–36) sent him a copy of Pseudo-Augustine's *Sermo de Symbolo Contra Iudaeos* some time in the 820s when Louis was a youthful king in Bavaria.[38] We also have a

[35] Lošek, *Die Conversio*, c. 6, 110–12; c. 8, 114–6; Wolfram, *Conversio*, 17, 107–13; Dopsch, 'Das Erzbistum Salzburg und der Alpen-Adria-Raum', 102–3.

[36] Lošek, *Die Conversio*, c. 6, 110–12; Wolfram, *Conversio*, 148; H. Wolfram, 'Einleitung oder Lügen mit Wahrheit—Ein historiographisches Dilemma', in *Historiographie im frühen Mittelalter*, ed. A. Scharer and G. Scheibelreiter (Vienna, 1994), 11–25, at 14.

[37] Lošek, *Die Conversio*, c. 9, 118; *Vita Gebehardi archiepiscopi*, c. 2, MGH Scriptores XI (Hannover, 1854), 26; Dopsch, 'Die Zeit der Karolinger', 184.

[38] See the dedicatory verse in *Carmina Salisburgensia*, ed. E. Dümmler, no. xv.1, MGH Poetae Aevi Carolini II (Berlin, 1884), 647; B. Bischoff, 'Bücher am Hofe Ludwigs des Deutschen und die Privatbibliothek des Kanzlers Grimalt', *Mittelalterliche Studien*, III (Stuttgart, 1981), 187–212, at 188.

Stuart Airlie

poem, purporting to come from Louis himself, thanking Baldo, a distinguished
Salzburg scribe and scholar, for his 'pious writings' and expressing the hope that
Baldo would go on to expound them. The poem appears to refer to continuing
cultural contact between Baldo and Louis's court, and the text of Louis's poem
of thanks was preserved in Salzburg.[39] Baldo's consciousness of Louis's links
with Salzburg may find expression in his copy of the account of the 851 *translatio* of St Hermes to Salzburg, where Louis's royal title is highlighted in
uncials.[40]

   If the *Conversio* thus takes its place in a series of texts directed from Salzburg
to the royal court, and Louis often held court in Bavaria, other texts had helped
prepare a place for it. Hrabanus Maurus, abbot of Fulda and later archbishop of
Mainz, had addressed a whole series of commentaries on books of the Old
Testament to Louis in the 830s and 840s. Such commentaries were intended to
serve as a form of 'mirror for a prince' in which Louis could contemplate the
deeds of Old Testament kings and prophets as models for his own actions.[41]
Two of them deserve mention here. First, in his letter to the king accompanying his commentary on Chronicles, Hrabanus tells Louis that the history of the
kings of Judah has a spiritual sense that is well worth the contemplation of a
Christian king.[42] In the commentary itself Hrabanus naturally has much to say
on Solomon, his wisdom, and the building of the temple. Commenting on
Solomon's adorning of the house of God with gold, he points out that the king
decorated the rafters with gold just as God has 'raised up the holy teachers
('sanctos doctores') with the light of wisdom and contemplation', while the
golden doorposts and doorways of the temple stand for the true approach to the
faith, and the door of the temple is the Lord, since no one comes to the Father
except through him.[43] Splendour, orthodoxy, and wisdom are the hallmarks of
Solomon's temple here, and the doughty Salzburg churchmen of the *Conversio*
fit into this pattern. For what were they if not teachers ('doctores') of orthodoxy
and builders of splendid churches? Thus the *Conversio* describes how the
'doctor' Rupert built and dedicated churches and how Archbishop Liupram sent
'masters' from Salzburg to build a fine church for Prince Priwina in Mosapurc.[44]

   One of the main objects of the *Conversio* is, as we shall see, to contrast true
teachers with slippery 'philosophers', and Louis had also received warnings
about philosophers in the second text of Hrabanus that concerns us. In a letter
written some time between 842 and 846 to accompany the encyclopedia which

   [39] *Carmina Salisburgensia*, no. ix, 643–4; Bischoff, *Die südostdeutschen Schreibschulen*, II, 78–9; Löwe,
Deutschlands Geschichtsquellen, VI, 814.
   [40] Bischoff, *Die südostdeutschen Schreibschulen*, II, 160, no. 175; this dates from the 850s.
   [41] Bischoff, 'Bücher am Hofe Ludwigs des Deutschen', 190–1; Löwe, *Deutschlands Geschichtsquellen*,
VI, 661–2, 702.
   [42] Hrabanus, *Epistolae*, no. 18, ed. E. Dümmler, MGH Epistolae Karolini Aevi III (Berlin, 1899),
422–4.
   [43] *Commentarium in Libros II Paralipomena*, III, c. 3: PL 109, col. 427.
   [44] Lošek, *Die Conversio*, c. 1, 96–8; c. 11, 126; cf. Bede, *HE* V, 21.

he presented to the king, Hrabanus says that he has included in it 'much of the catholic faith and Christian religion; and also, by contrast, much on the superstition of the nations, on the error of heretics, and on philosophers, wizards, and false gods'. In the encyclopedia itself philosophers receive a better press and are praised for their love of wisdom. Hrabanus is careful, however, to stress that true wisdom is rooted in humility, and that the pride of philosophers can bracket them with the obstinacy of Jews and heretics.[45]

The *Conversio* is not only consistent with the views adumbrated by Hrabanus but also fits into a stream of advice directed to a Christian ruler throughout his reign. Louis was addressed as Solomon by the poet Sedulius Scottus in a text that appears to date from 870 itself.[46] Writing after Louis's death, both Notker of St Gallen and Regino of Prüm stressed the king's piety and his knowledge of the Bible and the faith as key aspects of his rule.[47] The representation of Louis's kingship at court appears to have combined military sternness with strikingly austere religious devotion. As Christian king, Louis presided over the baptism of fourteen Bohemian princes at Regensburg in 845.[48] There is, then, a consistent context of Christian culture into which the *Conversio* can fit as a text intended for Louis the German. A final, secular piece may be added to the jigsaw here. As a text dealing with the peoples on the eastern frontiers of the east Frankish kingdom, the *Conversio* would not have been an isolated specimen at Louis's court. We possess what appears to be a tribute-list focused on the lands north of the Danube which should be associated with court circles of the reign of Louis.[49]

It is clear that Louis the German was a fitting and a well-prepared recipient for a text such as the *Conversio*. Let us now switch our focus to Salzburg itself. What was its relation to Louis and, more specifically, what view was taken of Christian rulership in the text of the *Conversio*? Louis spent much time in Bavaria, where Regensburg was an important royal palace, and he twice visited Salzburg on major feast days, namely on St Martin's Day in 861 and on Easter

---

[45] Hrabanus, *Epistolae*, no. 37, 472–4; *De Universo Libri Viginti Duo*, XV, c. 1: PL iii, cols. 418–19.

[46] Sedulius, *Carmina*, no. 30, ed. L. Traube, MGH Poetae Latini Aevi Carolini III (Berlin, 1896), 196; P. Godman, *Poets and Emperors* (Oxford, 1987), 158; Löwe, *Deutschlands Geschichtsquellen*, VI, 907.

[47] Notker, *Gesta Karoli Magni Imperatoris*, II, c. 11, ed. H. Haefele, MGH Scriptores rerum Germanicarum, ns XII (Berlin, 1959), 67–70; Regino, *Chronicon*, a.876, ed. F. Kurze, MGH Scriptores in usum scholarum (Hanover, 1890), 110.

[48] *Annales Fuldenses*, a.845, ed. F. Kurze, MGH Scriptores rerum Germanicarum in usum scholarum (Hannover, 1891), 35; Angenendt, *Kaiserherrschaft und Königstaufe*, 237. Valuable new insights into Louis's kingship are provided by E. Goldberg, 'More Devoted to the Equipment of Battle than the Splendor of Banquets: Frontier Kingship, Military Ritual and Early Knighthood at the Court of Louis the German', *Viator*, 30 (1999), 41–78.

[49] *Descriptio civitatum et regionum ad septentrionalem plagam Danubii*, in *Magna Moraviae Fontes*, III (Brno, 1969), 285–91; Löwe, *Deutschlands Geschichtsquellen*, VI, 790, 800; Goldberg, 'More Devoted to the Equipment of Battle', 57; cf. H. Schwarzmaier, 'Ein Brief des Markgrafen Aribo an König Arnulf über die Verhältnisse in Mähren', *Frühmittelalterliche Studien*, 6 (1972), 55–66.

Day, 863.[50] Archbishop Liupram had served as one of Louis's court chaplains before becoming archbishop in 836.[51] The author of the account of the *translatio* of the relics of St Hermes is careful to tell us that Liupram set out for Rome with the permission of Louis.[52]

Our most important evidence for the relationship of Salzburg to the king is the series of ten royal charters which record grants or confirmations issued by Louis for the church of Salzburg.[53] Though many of these are conventional, even conventions can be instructive. For example, Louis's 837 confirmation of immunity for the church of Salzburg contains a clause requesting that the archbishop, his clergy, and the people pray for the king and for the stability of the kingdom. Such prayer clauses were a standard feature of many royal charters, but it was through such prayers that often-distant kings could make themselves present in the liturgy of the churches across their domains.[54]

Louis was thus very much a presence in the church of Salzburg. Salzburg, in fact, played an important role in maintaining security for him in the south-east of the kingdom. It was disturbances there, involving the loyalty of his own son Carloman, that triggered the important charter of 860 in which Louis made rich grants to Salzburg and converted a number of estates which the see had hitherto held as benefices into its property. Salzburg was being marked out as a key player in Louis's strategy for the region.[55]

More relevant here, however, is the fact that Louis's charters reveal that the royal court was well informed about the church of Salzburg's work in the southeast, and this information must have come from the churchmen of Salzburg whose activities would have been well known in royal circles. Thus, in 837 Louis granted to Salzburg territory in Sclavinia, including a church built there by Archbishop Adalram. This church has been identified as Winklarn in what is now lower Austria, and the charter tells us that Adalram had built it 'in accordance with our permission'.[56] The grant of 864 proclaims that Archbishop

---

[50] *Annales ex Annalibus Iuvavensibus antiquis excerpti*, a.861, a.863, ed. H. Bresslau, MGH Scriptores XXX (Leipzig, 1934), 741; Dopsch, 'Die Zeit der Karolinger', 185. Near to Salzburg was the royal villa of Mattighofen and Louis was there in 860, 862 and 864; see his charters, nos. 102, 107, and 115, *Die Urkunden Ludwigs des Deutschen, Karlmanns und Ludwigs des Jüngeren*, ed. P. Kehr, MGH Diplomata regum Germaniae ex stirpe Karolinorum I (Berlin, 1934); on Mattighofen, see Bowlus, *Franks, Moravians and Magyars*, 83–4, and on Louis' itinerary here, C. Brühl, *Fodrum, Gistum, Servitium Regis*, 2 vols. (Cologne and Vienna, 1968), I, 34.

[51] J. Fleckenstein, *Die Hofkapelle der deutschen Könige*, I. Teil: *Grundlegung. Die karolingische Hofkapelle* (Stuttgart, 1959), 179.

[52] *Translatio Sancti Hermetis*, ed. G. Waitz, MGH Scriptores XV (Hanover, 1887), 410.

[53] *Die Urkunden Ludwigs des Deutschen*, ed. Kehr, nos. 4, 7, 21, 22, 23, 25, 60, 102, 112, 115. See also no. 46 which stems from the text of the *Conversio*; see Lošek, *Die Conversio*, c. 12, 128.

[54] *Die Urkunden Ludwigs des Deutschen*, ed. Kehr, no. 22; the purpose of such prayers was not, of course, primarily political.

[55] *Die Urkunden Ludwigs des Deutschen*, ed. Kehr, no. 102; on the political context, Dopsch, 'Die Zeit der Karolinger', 179–81, and Bowlus, *Franks, Moravians and Magyars*, 133–40.

[56] *Die Urkunden Ludwigs des Deutschen*, ed. Kehr, no. 25; Dopsch, 'Die Zeit der Karolinger', 175; Dopsch, 'Das Erzbistum Salzburg und der Aplen-Adria-Raum', 128.

Adalwinus had informed the king on the situation in Carantania, and the charter records much detail on the financial arrangements necessitated there by the archbishop's preaching tours. The timing of its issue, just after the capture of Louis's rebellious son Carloman, together with what it reveals of the activities of the redoubtable Gundachar, count in Carantania, means that the grant took place in a highly charged political context.[57] Tough questions of politics and finance were as important as the work of preaching and church-building, and on all these questions the royal court was kept informed.

Our sources give us a clear picture of Louis's interest in this region, an interest that became more urgent in the 860s. Political upheavals brought Salzburg's potential role in his political strategy for the region into focus, but this did not mean that its pastoral and missionary work was lost sight of. On the contrary, Louis's grants and redefinitions of property for Salzburg ensured that the church gained rich resources in Carantania and Pannonia.[58] The *Conversio* also presents this decade as one in which Archbishop Adalwin was pursuing his pastoral activities in this area with great dedication. In 864, for example, he celebrated Christmas at the fortress of Moosburg, a stronghold of Prince Chezilo, and he went on to dedicate some twelve churches in Pannonia in 865 (dedicated to figures such as Stephen, Peter, Paul, and John the Baptist), appointing a priest to each church.[59] And it was in this same period that Adalwin stamped his authority on the independent-minded assistant bishop Osbald, as we have seen. It is in the midst of all this positive activity that Methodius makes his unwelcome appearance in the text of the *Conversio*. The deftly placed contrast between his irregular meddling and the majestic, orthodox activity of the archbishops of Salzburg could not be greater.[60] At a synod held in Worms in 868 at which both Louis and Adalwin had been present, the assembled clergy denounced the heretical thinking of the Greek Church on the Trinity, as well as differences in discipline.[61] The great project of co-operation between king and archbishop in this area was now threatened by this disturbing newcomer.

The archbishops and Louis had been working together here. In fact Louis and Adalwin had recently been made aware of Greek unsoundness. The historical situation therefore meant that Louis was a fitting recipient for the text of the *Conversio*. But the *Conversio*'s author did not simply assume that Louis would be a sympathetic audience. He skilfully portrayed rulership in his text so as to shape the king's response. His picture is designed to act as both a record of,

---

[57] *Die Urkunden Ludwigs des Deutschen*, ed. Kehr, no. 112; Dopsch, 'Die Zeit der Karolinger', 184; Bowlus, *Franks, Moravians and Magyars*, 139–40; Wolfram, *Grenzen und Räume*, 253–4.

[58] *Die Urkunden Ludwigs des Deutschen*, ed. Kehr, nos. 102, 112, and 115.

[59] Lošek, *Die Conversio*, c. 13, 130–4; see also ibid., c. 9, 118 and c. 12, 130, with Dopsch, 'Die Zeit der Karolinger', 185–6, and Bowlus, *Franks, Moravians and Magyars*, 155–6.

[60] Lošek, *Die Conversio*, c. 12, 130; c. 14, 134.

[61] *Die Konzilien der karolingischen Teilreiche 860–874*, no. 25.

and a blueprint for the behaviour of right-thinking Frankish rulers. As such it reveals much of what the great churchmen on active pastoral service in the Caro-lingian world expected of their rulers, as well as demonstrating how the latter sought to fulfil these expectations. Relations between Salzburg and Louis were a two-way street.

If the *Conversio* is to some extent a mirror for a prince, it is one with a very clear reflection. Historical material is shrewdly deployed by the author, who moulds it to fit his overall purposes. Much of the *Conversio* highlights the power and authority of the kings of the Franks in the areas of the Slav world that interested Salzburg. The Merovingian king Dagobert is said forcefully to have asserted his royal authority over the Slav Samo, who was *dux* of the Carantan-ians in the seventh century. Earlier sources, such as the Chronicle of Fredegar, suggest that Samo was of Frankish origin, that he is to be associated with the Wends, and that Dagobert's military strike against him failed.[62] But the Salzburg author was not drawing on Fredegar but on the later *Gesta Dagoberti*, and was less concerned with accurately depicting the seventh century than with using the putative victory of the 'glorious' King Dagobert as symbol of, and his-torical explanation for, the deep-rooted hegemony of Frankish kings in this area.[63] This account of Dagobert lays the ground for the appearance of other Frankish kings as masterful figures in the territories that are the *Conversio*'s theatre. The establishment of the true faith is presented as taking place in tandem with the establishment of the lordship of the Frankish kings.[64] Carantanian princes who had lived as hostages among the Bavarians in the eighth century and had become Christians were returned to their people 'by the command of the Franks' and 'by the permission of King Pippin'.[65] Archbishop Arn was com-manded by Charlemagne himself 'to go to the territories of the Slavs and to preach the word of God there', and the assistant bishop Theodericus was ordained by Arn on the orders of Charlemagne. Theodericus was escorted into the lands of the Carantanians by Arn and Count Gerold, prefect of Bavaria.[66] The text of the *Conversio* is suffused with the language of royal diplomata. The text ends by looking back to the time 'when by the gift and command of the lord emperor Charles the people of eastern Pannonia began to be ruled by the Salzburg prelates'.[67]

All this not only expresses the view of the great pillar of the Carolingian *Reichskirche* that Salzburg undoubtedly was. It echoes the views that kings

[62] *The Fourth Book of the Chronicle of Fredegar with its Continuations*, ed. J. M. Wallace-Hadrill (London, 1960), 56–8; F. Curta, 'Slavs in Fredegar and Paul the Deacon: Medieval *gens* or Scourge of God?', *Early Medieval Europe*, 6 (1997), 141–67, at 144–55.
[63] See the minimal but telling change to Fredegar's text in *Gesta Dagoberti I. regis Francorum*, c. 27, ed. B. Krusch, MGH Scriptores rerum Merovingicarum II (Hannover, 1888), 410; Wolfram, *Conversio*, 73–5, 85–6.
[64] Lošek, *Die Conversio*, c. 3, 102.   [65] Ibid., c. 4, 104.   [66] Ibid., c. 8, 114–16.
[67] Ibid., c. 14, 134; on charters as models for and elements of this text, ibid. 111, n. 78.

themselves took of their role as supporters of spreading the word of God in these territories. Charlemagne's work in converting the Avars was recalled by Louis the Pious in the *narratio* of a charter for the church of Passau, issued in 823.[68] What the text of the *Conversio* does with some skill is to place Louis the German, its intended audience, in a precise context. We have seen that the *Conversio's* author stresses the role of kings in the south-east as supporters of Salzburg's efforts to spread the Christian faith. It is worth noting that the text's focus is specifically on kings. The great achievements of the Agilolfing dukes are belittled or ignored.[69]

Instead, the achievements of Louis the German's predecessors and ancestors as kings of the Franks are celebrated. It is kings such as Dagobert and Charlemagne who impose *servitium* on the south-east.[70] Louis the German is made to fit into this framework of royal authority, appearing in the text as dispatcher of a powerful army against Prince Ratimar and as generous lord of property in the region.[71] References in the text reveal the existence of a relationship between Salzburg and such sites of Frankish royal power as Worms, Quierzy, and Regensburg.[72] Salzburg belongs to an imperial structure actively presided over by the kings of the Franks.

Furthermore, these kings are not simply muscular exemplars of secular lordship. Pippin III does not only exert control over the princes of the Carantanians; he has the spiritual insight to recognize the good qualities of Virgil, and the intellectual rigour to let him become bishop of Salzburg only when he has satisfied himself that Virgil is sufficiently learned ('bene doctus').[73] Royalty and holiness are brought together at the very start of the text, which refers to Rupert as 'stemming from the royal dynasty of the Franks'. If Rupert was of royal descent, then he was of Merovingian rather than Carolingian stock.[74] The affiliations of the historical Rupert are, however, of less importance than the fact that Louis the German probably believed that he himself was descended from the Merovingians. He bore a name of Merovingian origin, and a mid-ninth-century east-Frankish genealogy reveals that the creative ancestor-hunting of those Metz genealogists who had linked the Carolingians and the Merovingians found a ready echo in Louis's kingdom.[75] Through Rupert, at the very

---

[68] K. H. Krüger, 'Neue Beobachtungen zur Datierung von Einhards Karlsvita', *Frühmittelalterliche Studien*, 32 (1998), 124–45, at 141.

[69] Wolfram, *Conversio*, 67, 95, and cf. H. Kahl, 'Virgil und die Salzburger Slawenmission', in *Virgil von Salzburg Missionar und Gelehrter*, ed. H. Dopsch and R. Juffinger (Salzburg, 1985), 112–21, at 112–14.

[70] Lošek, *Die Conversio*, c. 4, 102; c. 10, 120; on the creative deployment of the term *servitium* in the text, see ibid. 103, n. 45, and Pohl, 'Das sanfte Joch Christi', 271–2.

[71] Lošek, *Die Conversio*, c. 10, 122; c. 11, 122; c. 12, 128.　　　[72] Ibid., c. 1, 90, 92; c. 2, 100; c. 12, 128.

[73] Ibid., c. 2, 100; c. 4, 104.

[74] Ibid., c. 1, 90; Wolfram, *Salzburg Bayern Österreich*, 237–8.

[75] *Commemoratio genealogiae domni Karoli gloriosissimi imperatoris*, ed. G. Waitz, MGH Scriptores XIII (Hannover, 1881), 245–6; O. G. Oexle, 'Die Karolinger und die Stadt des heiligen Arnulf', *Frühmittelalterliche Studien*, 1 (1967), 250–364, at 253–4, and 297, on links between Metz and Bavaria; see also

opening of the *Conversio*, Salzburg was associated with Frankish royalty which was itself thus associated with the holy 'teacher of the gospel.'[76] It is no surprise to find Louis appearing in the *Conversio* not simply as a lord of land and men, but as a prince by whose command the Pannonian duke Priwina could be instructed in the Christian faith and baptized.[77]

The *Conversio* thus describes, rather relentlessly, the great partnership between the church of Salzburg and the kings of the Franks in the south-east. Their work there appears as legitimate, well ordered, and disciplined. It is this sober world that is threatened by the sudden appearance of Methodius, who appears out of nowhere with the unwelcome novelty of church offices in Slavonic. Such novelty was only to be expected from a 'philosopher', a term not intended as a compliment; this Greek 'philosopher' stands in lurid contrast to the 'outstanding teacher' from Salzburg whom he disturbed in Pannonia.[78] The whole weight of the text falls in condemnation on Methodius here. The great prelates of Salzburg, such as Rupert, Vitalis, and Adalrammus, had all been labelled 'doctor' in the text, paving the way for the confrontation between Salzburg's 'doctor', the priest Swarnagal, and Methodius.[79]

The *Conversio*'s main target was not the deployment of Slavonic language in the liturgy.[80] Methodius had trespassed into territory that Salzburg regarded as its own. As we have seen, the Salzburg author was not willing to give even other Bavarian churches much of a part in his narrative. Methodius was carefully represented as a lone, unlicensed incomer; his true status was ignored. His appearance in the text is as surprising to the reader as it is represented as being to the Salzburg priest Swarnagal. In the *Conversio*'s world of disciplined and sober churchmen, subject to control from Salzburg and operating in a world brought into being by the church of Salzburg and the Frankish kings, Methodius, with his Greekness, his philosophy, and his novelties, appears as a dangerously charismatic figure intruding in what is almost a bureaucratized landscape. As such, he recalls Aldebert, the undisciplined and individualistic 'holy man' disciplined by Boniface and Rome in 745.[81] The *Conversio*'s view of Methodius shows that the churchmen of Salzburg, the heirs of Virgil, were also the heirs of Boniface.

J. M. Wallace-Hadrill, 'History in the Mind of Archbishop Hincmar', in *The Writing of History in the Middle Ages: Essays Presented to Richard William Southern*, ed. R. H. C. Davis and J. M. Wallace-Hadrill (Oxford, 1981), 43–70, at 55.

[76] Lošek, *Die Conversio*, c. 1, 92; on kings as teachers of orthodoxy, J. M. Wallace-Hadrill, *Early Germanic Kingship in England and on the Continent* (Oxford, 1971), 101–2.

[77] Lošek, *Die Conversio*, c. 10, 120; there are, however, limits to royal patronage of what are primarily church activities even in the *Conversio*, Angenendt, *Kaiserherrschaft und Königstaufe*, 231–2.

[78] Lošek, *Die Conversio*, c. 12, 130; c. 14, 134. On the term 'philosopher' see ibid. 45–6.

[79] Ibid., c. 1, 92; c. 2, 98; c. 9, 116; c. 12, 130. On the contrast, Wolfram, *Conversio*, 137–8.

[80] F. Dvornik, *Byzantine Missions Among the Slavs* (New Brunswick, 1970), 154.

[81] H. Mayr-Harting, *The Coming of Christianity to Anglo-Saxon England*, 3rd edn. (London, 1991), 269–70.

The text had been designed to help Salzburg's case in the eyes of Louis the German. In Slavonic sources describing his 870 'trial' at Regensburg in the presence of Louis and the Bavarian bishops, Methodius refers to himself, in a positive sense and with a dig at his persecutors, as a 'philosopher'.[82] One wonders if this is an echo of the tendentious briefing that Salzburg had laboured to give the king. It is of course the very limitations of this source, its very partial perspective, that give it its value. It was not concerned to provide an accurate picture of Salzburg's work in the south-east, but to celebrate and defend what it saw as Salzburg's rights and achievement there. In doing so, it can reveal much about the self-perception of a great church of the Carolingian empire. Above all, it reveals that Salzburg saw its status and activities in the south-east as dependent on its connections with that empire and how that empire was perceived to be Christian. The Salzburg of the *Conversio* is no far-flung outpost but a fully integrated member of a universal Christian world.

---

[82] Dvornik, *Byzantine Missions*, 153; M. Kantor, *Medieval Slavic Lives of Saints and Princes* (Ann Arbor, Mich., 1983), 117. The narrow Bavarian view of Methodius was not universal; it was not, for example, shared by the pope; see Wolfram, *Grenzen und Räume*, 261–4, and Innes, 'Franks and Slavs c.700–1000', 211–12. I am grateful to Richard Fletcher for much helpful advice and to Ian Wood for sharing his ideas on medieval missions with me. I am more generally grateful to Henry Mayr-Harting himself for a whole range of insights into early medieval culture generously given over a long span of time. Research for this paper was carried out during a period of study leave awarded by the University of Glasgow.

9

NO BISHOP, NO KING:
THE MINISTERIAL IDEOLOGY OF KINGSHIP
AND ASSER'S *RES GESTAE AELFREDI*

Matthew Kempshall

Writing about the character and achievements of a distinguished individual can
constitute more than just an encomium. It can also acknowledge the nurture an
author has received, discharge a debt of friendship, present an instructive exemplar for imitation, and ensure that a testament will be handed down to the
memory of posterity.[1] The consequences for writing about the life and conduct
of an early medieval king are considerable. If it is not just a vehicle for praise but
also a means of instruction, then a modern categorization as 'historiography'
should not be allowed to conceal the different possibilities which may have
underpinned the original composition. Given the subtlety of the connection
between a prescriptive and a descriptive *vita*, between the presentation of an
ideal and the historical reality to which it may, or may not, have corresponded,[2]
the recovery of such meaning frequently depends on identifying the audience
for which a text was written. For Asser's narrative of the life, character, conduct,
and achievements (*de vita et moribus . . . et conversatione atque . . . res gestas*) of
King Alfred,[3] this task is therefore made particularly problematic by the
absence of evidence for its circulation. As a result, historians have been divided
over whether to classify the text simply as a rough-hewn and incomplete celebration of its subject, or to attempt to uncover a more learned, even sophisticated, didactic purpose.

One solution to this impasse has been to identify an appropriate intellectual
and literary context for Asser's work and to read it, accordingly, as both a
Carolingian royal *vita* and *speculum principis*, a combination designed to
communicate a specific royal ideology.[4] However, given the intertwining of

1 Einhard, *Vita Karoli Magni Imperatoris*, ed. L. Halphen (Paris, 1981), prologue, 2–6.
[2] H. Mayr-Harting, 'Two Abbots in Politics—Wala of Corbie and Bernard of Clairvaux', *TRHS* 40
(1990), 217–37.
[3] Asser, *De Rebus Gestis Aelfredi*, ed. W. H. Stevenson, rev. D. Whitelock (Oxford, 1959), 73, p. 54
(henceforth *Asser*).
[4] J. Campbell, 'Asser's Life of Alfred', in *The Inheritance of Historiography 350–900*, ed. C.
Holdsworth and T. P. Wiseman (Exeter, 1986), 115–35 at 115–19; A. Scharer, 'The Writing of History at
King Alfred's Court', *Early Medieval Europe*, 5 (1996), 177–206.

Frankish, Irish, Roman, and indigenous traditions within earlier 'Anglo-Saxon' culture,[5] it is an open question whether the influence of these two genres stems directly from their ninth-century continental exponents. The element of a *speculum principis* in Asser's 'life' of Alfred, for example, may derive either from Carolingian Francia,[6] from Northumbria,[7] or from its original sources in Irish advice-literature and ecclesiastical *florilegia*.[8] A similar range of alternatives applies to the ideological tradition within which any designation as *speculum principis* would then locate Asser's work. It is because such literature comprises a patchwork of biblical and patristic extracts that 'it is so difficult to disentangle the immediate from the more distant sources of ninth-century political thought'.[9] It therefore remains an equally open question whether Asser's exposition of the virtues appropriate to kingly status came directly from the Old Testament, from Augustine, or from Isidore.[10] In each case, privileging one potential influence over another, or polarizing them as mutually exclusive alternatives, risks obscuring the complexities of the original context in which the text was written.

To recognize the proximity, even equivalence, of royal and episcopal ideology is one vital means of avoiding any anachronistic separation of temporal from spiritual authority in early medieval society.[11] Central to such a political theology is the way in which one text in particular, Gregory the Great's *Regula Pastoralis*, could be applied to all those who exercised authority, kings as well as bishops.[12] Given what *is* known about the authorship and chronology of the *Res Gestae Aelfredi*, therefore, it is perhaps surprising that a fuller appreciation of the connections with Gregory's text has not been made before. Asser himself, after all, reveals that he was writing for Alfred in 893, that is, whilst or immediately after helping the king produce an English version of the *Regula Pastoralis* which was notable for both the fullness and accuracy of its translation.[13] The effects of

[5] H. Mayr-Harting, *The Coming of Christianity to Anglo-Saxon England*, 3rd edn. (London, 1991).

[6] Smaragdus of Saint-Mihiel, *Via Regia*: PL 102, 933–70; Jonas of Orléans, *De Institutione Regia*, ed. A. Dubreucq, SC 407 (Paris, 1995); Sedulius Scottus, *Liber de Rectoribus Christianis*, ed. S. Hellmann (Munich, 1906); Hincmar of Reims, *De Regis Persona et Regio Ministerio*: PL 125, 833–56; id., *De Ordine Palatii*: MGH Fontes Iuris Germanici Antiqui III.

[7] Cathwulf, *Epistola*: MGH Epistolae IV, 502–5; Alcuin, *Epistolae*, nos. 16, 18, 30, 61, 64, 109, 119, 123, 171, 188, 217: MGH Epistolae IV, 18–481.

[8] *Tecosca Cormaic*, ed. K. Meyer (Dublin, 1909); *Audacht Morainn*, ed. F. Kelly (Dublin, 1976); Pseudo-Cyprian, *De Duodecim Abusivis Saeculi*, ed. S. Hellmann (Leipzig, 1910); *Proverbia Grecorum*, ed. D. Simpson, 'The *Proverbia Grecorum*', *Traditio*, 43 (1987) at 10–18; *Collectio canonum Hibernensis*, ed. H. Wasserschleben, *Die Irische Kanonensammlung* (Leipzig, 1885).

[9] J. M. Wallace-Hadrill, 'The *Via Regia* of the Carolingian Age', in *Trends in Medieval Political Thought*, ed. B. Smalley (Oxford, 1965), 22–41 at 25.

[10] Augustine, *De civitate Dei*, V.24–6 (CCSL 47), 160–3; Isidore, *Etymologiae*, IX.3.1–5, ed. W. M. Lindsay, 2 vols. (Oxford, 1911), I, 362.

[11] H. Mayr-Harting, *Ottonian Book Illumination: An Historical Study*, 2 vols. (London, 1991).

[12] Gregory the Great, *Regula Pastoralis*, ed. F. Rommel, SC 381–2 (Paris, 1992) (henceforth *RP*). Cf. R. A. Markus, 'Gregory the Great's *rector* and his Genesis', in *Grégoire le Grand*, ed. J. Fontaine, R. Gillet, and S. Pellistrandi (Paris, 1986), 137–46.

[13] *King Alfred's West-Saxon Version of Gregory's Pastoral Care*, ed. H. Sweet, 2 vols. (London, 1871), I, 7 (henceforth 'Sweet').

a detailed knowledge of Gregory's conception of *rector* and *regimen* can certainly be traced in Alfred's own theory and practice of kingship,[14] in education and legislation, as well as in the ritual washing of his hands before judgement.[15] If the *Regula Pastoralis* also provided the pattern for Asser's 'life' of Alfred, however, then this may help to explain not just the form which the *Res Gestae Aelfredi* was given but even why it was written at all.

The ninth century witnessed the development of a concept of kingship as a ministry (*ministerium*), as an office (*officium*) which was charged with responsibility for the spiritual and material well-being of the people within its care (*cura*). This profound sense of duty and, more significantly, an acute awareness of the consequences of its neglect (*negligentia*), increasingly governed the way in which Frankish bishops and Carolingian kings came to interpret a succession of political and social crises.[16] That Alfred's court was directly conversant with such an ideology is suggested by existing dynastic connections (the marriages of Charles the Bald's daughter, Judith, to Alfred's father and brother respectively) and by the presence of Grimbald of St Bertin.[17] Asser's exposition of Alfred's wisdom (*sapientia*) and righteousness (*iustitia*), and his discussion of Alfred's truthfulness (*veritas*), forbearance (*patientia*), generosity (*largitas*), affability (*affabilitas*), and friendship (*amicitia*), have thus been found convincing parallels in Sedulius Scottus' *Liber de Rectoribus Christianis*.[18] Evidence for Frankish influence, however, necessarily carries the caveat that some political and cultural connections may, in fact, represent a shared response to common stimuli based on similar resources. This is certainly applicable to Sedulius Scottus, since he was himself drawing on his native Irish sources, such as the *Proverbia Grecorum*, to which Asser too had direct access.[19] Given Asser's own background in St David's, and given the possibility that he also knew the *Collectio Canonum Hibernensis*,[20] the suggestion that his royal virtues may be as much

---

[14] J. M. Wallace-Hadrill, *Early Germanic Kingship in England and on the Continent* (Oxford, 1971), 143–5; A. Crépin, 'L'Importance de la pensée de Grégoire le Grand dans la politique culturelle d'Alfred, roi du Wessex', in *Grégoire le Grand*, 579–87; A. P. Smyth, *King Alfred the Great* (Oxford, 1995), 530–4, 589–92; P. Wormald, *The Making of English Law—King Alfred to the Twelfth Century* (Oxford, 1999), 428–9.

[15] *RP* II.5, pp. 200–2; Sweet, 105. Cf. Wormald, *Making of English Law*, 144–8; S. Keynes, 'The Fonthill Letter', in *Words, Texts and Manuscripts: Studies in Anglo-Saxon Culture Presented to Helmut Gneuss*, ed. M. Korhammer (Cambridge, 1992), 53–97 at 73–4.

[16] H. H. Anton, *Fürstenspiegel und Herrscherethos in der Karolingerzeit* (Bonn, 1968).

[17] J. M. Wallace-Hadrill, 'The Franks and the English in the Ninth Century: Some Common Historical Interests', in his *Early Medieval History* (Oxford, 1975), 201–16; J. L. Nelson, 'The Franks and the English in the Ninth Century Reconsidered', in *The Preservation and Transmission of Anglo-Saxon Culture*, ed. P. E. Szarmach and J. T. Rosenthal (Kalamazoo, 1997), 141–58.

[18] Scharer, 'Writing of History', 193–206.   [19] Ibid. 197–9.

[20] *Asser*, 106, p. 93: 'pro aliquorum amore vel timore aut aliorum odio aut etiam pro alicuius pecuniae cupiditate'; *Hibernensis* XXI.13, 66 (quoting Isidore, *Sententiae*, III.54.7: PL 83, 537–738 at 726–7): 'quatuor modis iudicium hominis pervertitur, timore, cupiditate, odio, amore'. Cf. Wormald, *Making of English Law*, 123.

Irish in origin as they are Carolingian deserves reinforcing. A demonstration of the evils which are consequent upon a wicked woman,[21] a connection between truthfulness and righteousness in judgement,[22] and an emphasis on alms-giving,[23] judicial protection of the poor,[24] and rule of the royal household,[25] would all provide cases in point.[26] So too might Asser's famous image of the king's lantern whose flame is prevented from being extinguished by the force of a hostile wind. In Irish texts, a lantern on a lampstand signifies the ruler, its flame the light of learning.[27]

By the same token, each of these virtues and themes has a firm, often explicit, basis in Scripture and, as the interest in the etymology of place-names and the comparison of Alfred to the penitent thief both demonstrate, Asser's exegetical expertise should not be underestimated.[28] Solomon provides an important case in point.[29] When Smaragdus of Saint-Mihiel wanted to demonstrate the centrality of wisdom to royal *ministerium*, he gave a detailed exposition of Solomonic kingship, equating righteousness with wisdom (fear of the Lord and obedience to his Law), and connecting wisdom with prosperity.[30] Solomon was thus a king who prayed for discernment in administering justice to his people and, in return, he received both wisdom and wealth from God.[31] This correspondence of *sapientia* with *iustitia*, and its causal connection with wealth, both bear close comparison with Asser,[32] but neither *requires* Carolingian mediation. The Old Testament was, *inter alia*, a practical handbook of government for all early medieval kings. It was, for example, Solomon's division of his workforce into three parts so that each spent one month in service and two months at

---

[21] *Asser*, 14–15, pp. 12–14; *Tecosca Cormaic*, XVI.1–122; *Proverbia Grecorum*, 62, p. 14; *De Duodecim Abusivis*, 40–3.

[22] *Asser*, 105, p. 91; *De Duodecim Abusivis*, 51; *Hibernensis*, XXXI.8, 107, LXVII.3, 241; *Proverbia Grecorum*, 33, 35, 38, 45, pp. 12–13. For the truth or righteousness of the ruler (*fír flathemon*) as the source of both his own virtues and prosperity for his people, see *Tecosca Cormaic*, I.7, 10, 14, 33, 38, 45–6, III.28, VI.22, 28, 32, XIX.16; *Audacht Morainn*, 12–21, 24–8, 51; *De Duodecim Abusivis*, 52–3. Cf. Psalm 72.3, 6, 16; Alcuin, *Ep.* 18, p. 51; *Via Regia*, XX. 960 (quoting Eccles. 37.19–20); *De Institutione Regia*, III. 186 (quoting Proverbs 20.28), 188, VI. 212; *De Ordine Palatii*, II. 44, IV. 66; *De Regis Persona*, II. 835.

[23] *Asser*, 102, pp. 88–9; *De Duodecim Abusivis*, 38–40; *Hibernensis*, XXVII.12, 89, XXV.4, 77, XXV.15, 81. Cf. Alcuin, *Ep.* 18, p. 50; 61, p. 105; 119, p. 174; *De Institutione Regia*, III, 188; *De Regis Persona*, II. 835.

[24] *Asser*, 105, pp. 91–2; *De Duodecim Abusivis*, 51; *Hibernensis*, XXXVII.13–15, 134–5. Cf. *Cathwulf*, 503; *Via Regia*, IX, 949; *De Institutione Regia*, III, 186 (quoting Proverbs 29.14), IV, 198–200, V, 204–6; *De Regis Persona*, II. 835.

[25] *Asser*, 76, p. 60; *De Duodecim Abusivis*, 36–8, 52; *Hibernensis*, XXXVII.25, 138. Cf. *De Institutione Regia*, III. 184; *De Regis Persona*, II. 835.

[26] For Asser's emphasis on Alfred as *secundarius*, see D. A. Binchy, *Celtic and Anglo-Saxon Kingship* (Oxford, 1970), 26–7, 29; D. N. Dumville, 'The Aetheling—A Study in Anglo-Saxon Constitutional History', *ASE* 8 (1979), 1–33. Cf. P. Wormald, 'Celtic and Anglo-Saxon Kingship—Some Further Thoughts', in *Sources of Anglo-Saxon Culture*, ed. P. E. Szarmach (Kalamazoo, 1986), 151–83.

[27] *Asser*, 104, pp. 90–1; *Hibernensis*, XXXVII.23; 137; XXXVIII.4, 142; XXXVIII.13, 145; *Proverbia Grecorum*, 110, p. 11; 29, p. 12. Cf. Alcuin, *Ep.* 116, p. 171.

[28] *Asser*, 89–90, pp. 75–6; Scharer, 'Writing of History', 189–90, 204.

[29] Scharer, 'Writing of History', 191–3; D. R. Howlett, *British Books in Biblical Style* (Dublin, 1997), 273–333; Wormald, *Making of English Law*, 121–2.

[30] *Via Regia*, IV–V. 941–6.   [31] 1 Kings 3.9–14; 2 Chronicles 10–12.   [32] *Asser*, 76, pp. 60–1.

home which provided Alfred with the model for his own division of his house-hold.[33] The connection does not stop there. Solomon was not only a wise king, but one who wrote and taught, acted as a judge, replaced traditional tribal boundaries with administrative districts, rebuilt cities as fortified centres and economic stores, built ships, and recruited craftsmen from other kingdoms. He also constructed *lucerna* and *candelabra*.[34]

As a model for the exercise of early medieval kingship, Solomon was, above all, a king who understood the conditions under which he was to exercise his royal authority. Observance of the laws of God would ensure the continuation of the king's own dynasty; failure to do so would mean the ejection of his people (whether through famine, plague, or defeat by their enemies) from the land which God had given to them.[35] This was why, according to Deuteronomy 17.18–20, when a king took the throne of his kingdom he was to write for him-self, on a scroll, a copy of God's Law. It was to be with him, and he was to read it, all the days of his life, carefully following all its decrees so that he and his descendants would rule over the kingdom. Hezekiah (a king who, like Alfred, was distinguished by his piety and his reform of religious practice, but also by being spared from illness by God's mercy) accordingly reaffirmed the covenant between God and his people.[36] Likewise, Josiah, a king comparable to Solomon in his wisdom, wealth, and righteousness, renewed the covenant and pro-claimed the Law to his people.[37] The prescription was explicit: '. . . in accord-ance with the wisdom of your God which you possess, appoint magistrates and judges to administer justice to all the people . . . all who know the laws of your God. And you are to teach any who do not know them. Whoever does not obey the law of your God and the law of the king must surely be punished by death, banishment, confiscation of property, or imprisonment'.[38] The signifi-cance of the conditional nature of this Old Testament kingship was not lost on Insular writers in the eighth century, nor on Carolingian bishops in the ninth.[39] It is this covenant which was renewed by Alfred. In his own law-code Alfred wrote for himself a copy of God's Law and expressly combined it with the law of the king, appending his own judgements to a digest of Exodus 20.1–23.13 and observing that the latter had been delivered by God to Moses with the com-mand that they should be kept.[40] Such an explicit conjunction indicates that it might be a mistake to underestimate the immediate historical import of Asser's

---

[33] 1 Kings 5.13–14; *Asser*, 100, pp. 86–7; H. Mayr-Harting, 'Saxons, Danes and Normans 409–1154: Overview', in *The Cambridge Encyclopedia of Great Britain and Ireland*, ed. C. Haigh (Cambridge, 1985), 54–8 at 57.

[34] 1 Kings 3.28, 4.7, 4.29–33, 7.49, 9.17–19, 26; 2 Chronicles 2.7, 8.5–6.

[35] 1 Kings 6.12–13, 9.4–9; 2 Kings 21.7–9; 1 Samuel 12.14–15; Psalm 132.11–12; Deuteronomy 28.15–25.

[36] 2 Chronicles 29.3, 30.26; 2 Kings 20; Isaiah 38.

[37] 2 Kings 23.2–3; 2 Chronicles 34.　　　[38] Ezra 7.25–6; *Hibernensis*, XXV.13, 80.

[39] *De Duodecim Abusivis*, 52–3; *Cathwulf*, 503; *Via Regia*, II. 938; *De Institutione Regia*, III. 186, 190–2; *De Rectoribus Christianis*, XV, 70–1; XX, 91; *De Regis Persona*, VIII. 840.

[40] Alfred, *Laws*, 1–48, ed. F. Liebermann, *Die Gesetze der Angelsachsen*, 3 vols. (Halle, 1903–16), I, 16–123 at 26–46. Cf. Wormald, *Making of English Law*, 417–29.

own comparison (*aequiparans*) between Alfred and Solomon. For Asser to insist on such an equivalence is not necessarily dependent on a Carolingian source and may have been suggested directly from Asser's own reading of the Old Testament. It may also reflect an ideology which, in theory *and* in practice, was wholeheartedly embraced by Alfred. The question is naturally raised, therefore, whether the same can also be said of the ideology which is contained in the *Regula Pastoralis*.[41]

Gregory the Great's own summary of the *Regula Pastoralis* identified four distinct parts to his work: how individuals should rise to a position of rule over others, how they should lead their lives once they are in office, how they should teach, and what they need to do in order to maintain their humility.[42] Wisdom is thus the primary qualification on which Gregory insisted; but it is a wisdom which has an intrinsic connection with teaching, in that it is the responsibility of those upon whom God has bestowed the gifts of grace to be 'useful' to their fellow humans.[43] It is this sense of duty which prompted Gregory to hold up Ezekiel as a model, not just for pastors and teachers, but for *all* those in authority (*praepositi*),[44] and which he denoted by the terms ministry (*ministerium regiminis*) and care (*cura regiminis*).[45] It was on this basis, therefore, that the *Regula Pastoralis* became the primary inspiration behind the Carolingian conception of *ministerium*. Reform councils enjoined the text upon bishops as a 'mirror' (*speculum*) for their conduct,[46] Thegan cited it as the touchstone of a good bishop,[47] whilst Hincmar of Reims insisted that familiarity with the text should guide every aspect of episcopal ministry and used it himself as part of the ritual cross-examination with which to prove a candidate's suitability for office.[48]

Alfred's recognition of the centrality of the *Regula Pastoralis*, therefore, his explicit connection of its translation to the transmission of God's Law, and his distribution of the text to individual bishops as a means of reforming both church and society, all have clear precedents in ninth-century Francia. Grimbald of St Bertin is again a prime candidate for the transmission of these ideas, not just because his services were secured from Fulk, Hincmar's successor at Reims, but specifically because his recruitment was said to have been

---

[41] For the influence of Boethius and Orosius, see J. L. Nelson, 'The Political Ideas of Alfred of Wessex', in *Kings and Kingship in Medieval Europe*, ed. A. Duggan (London, 1993), 125–58.

[42] *RP*, praef. p. 124; Sweet, 23. Cf. *De Ordine Palatii*, III. 44.

[43] *RP* I.1, pp. 128–32; I.5, pp. 144–8; I.6, p. 150; II.4, pp. 186–94, III.25, pp. 428–38; Sweet, 25–9, 41–7, 89–97, 375–85. Cf. 1 Corinthians 12.7; *Dialogues*, ed. A. de Vogüé, 3 vols., SC (Paris, 1978–80) II.16.6, 188.

[44] *RP* II.10, pp. 240, 246; Sweet, 153 (*scirmenn*), 161 (*lareowas*). Cf. Sweet, 41 (*rice ond . . . lareowdom*).

[45] *RP* II.6, p. 214, I.4, p. 140; Sweet, 121 (*ðegnung ðæs ealdordomes*), 37 (*bisgung ðæs rices ond ðæs recedomes*). Cf. *Via Regia*, XVIII. 958 (*ministerium regale*); *De Institutione Regia*, IV. 198 (*regale ministerium*); *De Rectoribus Christianis*, III. 29 (*regimen ministerii*); *De Regis Persona*, praef. 833 (*regium ministerium*).

[46] MGH Concilia II, 255, 274, 287; MGH Capitularia Regum Francorum II, 29–30. Cf. ibid. I 110, 235; B. Judic, 'Introduction' (*RP* 88–102).

[47] *Vita Hludowici*, XX: MGH Scriptores Rerum Germanicarum LXIV, 168–277, at 208.

[48] *Ep.* 52: PL 126, 271–6 at 275; MGH Concilia IV, 322.

'to supervise the administration of pastoral care'.[49] Once again, however, along-side Carolingian influence can be set a powerful Insular tradition, stemming primarily from Bede's personal admonition to an archbishop of York to fill his mind and speech with Gregory's *Regula Pastoralis*, but also from Bede's histor-ical account of how Pope Honorius had exhorted King Edwin of Northumbria to busy himself with frequent reading from Gregory's works.[50] Alcuin had accordingly never tired of insisting that prelates should always have a copy of the *Regula Pastoralis* at their side, reading and rereading it as frequently as possible, and using it as both a handbook and a mirror of the episcopal life.[51] Taking these Frankish and Insular traditions together, it becomes clear why Alfred should have considered the *Regula Pastoralis* to be a book 'most necessary for *all* men to know'. If it was the primary means of reforming both ecclesiasti-cal and secular *mores*, then it could mitigate the scourge of divine punishment. Gregory's text would therefore be just as efficacious in saving Alfred's *populus* from Scandinavian captivity as any number of fyrd levies, burhs, ships, and recoinages.[52] In 893, with Asser working alongside Grimbald in expounding the *Regula Pastoralis* for Alfred to turn it into English, it also becomes clear why Gregory's conception of *ministerium* might have provided the basis for Asser to compose a complementary work on Alfred's *own* exercise of his pastoral authority.

In Asser's account, the defining quality of Alfred's character is his wisdom. Not only does this mark Alfred out for office from his youth, but it is then com-municated to those within his care by means of personal tuition.[53] Gregory the Great took pains to underline that this critical connection between wisdom and teaching should be construed more widely than verbal instruction. A life of exemplary virtue, performing virtuous actions so that they may be imitated by others, is just as, if not more, efficacious than words alone, particularly when there are people for whom a knowledge of 'the praiseworthy deeds of others' (*laudabilia aliorum facta*) is sufficient.[54] In the history of the Church, something which is achieved (*res gesta*) signifies something which should be achieved (*gerendum*), such that when people hear of what has been done (*facta*) they will

[49] *Councils and Synods With Other Documents Relating to the English Church*, ed. D. Whitelock, M. Brett, and C. Brooke, 2 vols. (Oxford, 1981), I, 6–12, 10: 'ad hoc officium destinandum et curae pastoralis regiminis praeficiendum'. Cf. S. Keynes and M. Lapidge, *Alfred the Great—Asser's Life of King Alfred and Other Contemporary Sources* (Harmondsworth, 1983), 331–3; J. L. Nelson, '. . . *sicut olim gens Francorum . . . nunc gens Anglorum*: Fulk's Letter to Alfred Revisited', in *Alfred the Wise—Studies in Honour of Janet Bately*, ed. J. Roberts, J. L. Nelson, and M. Godden (Woodbridge, 1997), 135–44.

[50] *Epistola ad Ecgbertum*, ed. C. Plummer, *Baedae Opera Historica*, 2 vols. (Oxford, 1896), I, 405–23, at 406; *HE* II.17–18, pp. 194–6. Cf. Wallace-Hadrill, *Early Medieval History*, 107.

[51] Alcuin, *Ep.* 113, p. 166 (*enchiridion*); 116, p. 171 (*speculum . . . pontificalis vitae*). Cf. *Ep.* 39, p. 83; 124, p. 182; 209, p. 348. For the bishop himself as a *speculum* showing the road to be travelled, see *Ep.* 17, p. 46.

[52] R. H. C. Davis, 'Alfred the Great, Propaganda and Truth', *History*, 56 (1971), 169–82 at 180.

[53] *Asser*, 22, p. 20; 42, p. 32; 76, p. 60; 88, p. 73; 106, p. 95. Cf. *Preface*, Sweet, 3–4.

[54] *RP* I.2, pp. 134–6; II.2, p. 178; II.3, pp. 180–2; II.6, p. 212 (quoting 1 Peter 5.3); III.4, pp. 276–80; III.6, pp. 284–6; III.10, p. 308; III.40, p. 530; Sweet, 29–33, 77, 81, 119, 191–5, 203–5, 229–31, 461.

consider what should be done (*facienda*) in imitation of these deeds.[55] This was why Gregory himself set down a series of exemplary lives in his *Dialogues*.[56] Asser takes the general point and spells out the didactic function of recounting an individual's deeds. As in Scripture, good actions are recorded so that they may be imitated, bad actions so that they may be avoided.[57] However, he also takes the specific point about the lives of those who rule over others. Gregory illustrated this principle by enjoining those in authority to heed the scriptural injunction not to hide their light (*lucerna*) under a bushel but to place it on a *candelabrum*.[58] Like Scripture itself—a lantern (*lucerna*) set so that we can see in the midst of the night of this present life[59]—a ruler's actions should illuminate all around him. Asser's detailed account of Alfred's lantern is not necessarily dependent upon Irish sources for its symbolic importance. In Gregorian terms too, the image implied more than just the product of practical intelligence.[60]

Instruction through word and deed was reinforced by instruction through admonition. Indeed, according to Gregory, reproof was the key to discovery,[61] the most critical part of *ministerium* and one to which he accordingly devoted more than half of his treatise. The wisdom of those in authority is given its defining test by the need to deliver finely calibrated admonition, advice carefully adjusted to suit the particular needs of the people who are being corrected.[62] Asser's Alfred therefore teaches gently, flatters, exhorts, commands, and only as a last resort does he bitterly castigate.[63] The final chapter of Asser's work accordingly paints a vivid tableau of Alfred administering admonition to his judges.[64] Wisely scrutinizing all the judgements delivered in his absence, Alfred does not simply rebuke but, once again, inquires gently into the reason behind any iniquitous judgement before chastizing the guilty party with both discernment and moderation.[65] And the substance of his rebuke? The abuse of the position and *ministerium* of wise men through neglect of the study and practice of wisdom.

[55] *XL Homiliae in Evangelia*, II.21.2, ed. R. Étaix (CCSL 141), 174. Cf. *Moralia in Job* XIX.20.29, ed. M. Adriaen (CCSL 143), 981.

[56] *Dialogorum Libri IV de Miraculis Patrum Italicorum*, ed. A. de Vogüé, SC 260, 265 (Paris, 1979–80), I. prol. 9, 16. Cf. III.37.22, 426; *Asser*, 77, p. 62; M. Godden, 'Waerferth and King Alfred: The Fate of the Old English *Dialogues*', in *Alfred the Wise*, 35–51.

[57] *Asser*, 95, p. 82. Cf. Romans 15.4; *Boethius*, XL, 139; *HE*, praef. 2; *The Old English Version of Bede's Ecclesiastical History of the English People*, ed. T. Miller, 2 vols. (London, 1890–1), praef. 2.

[58] *RP* I.5, pp. 144–6; Sweet, 43. Cf. Matthew 5.15.

[59] *RP* III.24, p. 420; Sweet, 365. Cf. *RP* II.7, p. 220 (*lumen veritatis*); III.12, p. 330 (*lucerna domini*); III.16, p. 360; III.25, p. 430 (*supernus lumen*); III.39, p. 530 (*lux veritatis*); Sweet, 129, 259, 295, 379, 461. Cf. Proverbs 6.23; *Dialogues*, II.1.6, 134.

[60] *Asser*, 104, pp. 90–1. Cf. 77, p. 62 (*veluti quaedam luminaria*).

[61] *RP* II.4, p. 188 (*correptio*); Sweet, 91.

[62] *RP* II.8, pp. 230–6; II.10, pp. 238–52; III.1, pp. 258–60; III.36, pp. 518–22; Sweet, 141–7, 151–67, 173–9, 453.

[63] *Asser*, 91, p. 78.

[64] *Asser*, 106, p. 93. Cf. Scharer, 'Writing of History', 186; Wormald, *Making of English Law*, 118–25.

[65] *Asser*, 106, p. 93 (*leniter . . . discrete et moderanter*). Cf. *RP* II.6, pp. 216–18; II.10, pp. 238–44 (where *discretio* is exercised in reproof and *moderamen* is shown in combining the severity of justice with the *lenitas* of mercy); Sweet, 125–7, 151–3.

The response is complete terror. The capacity to instil fear was a characteristically royal virtue,[66] but it is particularly appropriate in this context because, as Gregory suggested, it is necessary for rulers to be feared whenever God's judgement is not enough to prevent their subjects from sinning.[67] Alfred's admonition on the connection between wisdom and *ministerium* is a carefully staged finale. Coupled with the imagery of the lantern and the account of justice in the preceding two chapters, it provides a fitting climax to Asser's work. It is not an abrupt end to an incomplete text; it is a particularly Gregorian meditation on the nature of authority as *ministerium*, on the 'pious care of ruling'.[68]

In expounding the connection between *sapientia* and *ministerium*, Gregory had no illusions as to the gravity of the responsibility placed upon those charged with this care. It is a burden and, as such, will be assumed with unwillingness and, if necessary, under compulsion.[69] Nevertheless, those whose gifts and character mark them out to assume such authority have a duty to do so, and in such a way that they combine the active and the contemplative lives, devoting themselves to prayer and to the study of wisdom but also to the spiritual and material needs of others.[70] This discussion of the caution with which individuals should assume authority over others formed the basis of a long and influential literary tradition. However, its broad correspondence with Asser's depiction of Alfred should not preclude a more immediate appropriation of Gregory's precepts. Asser has certainly taken to heart each part of Gregory's analysis: rule over others is a burden,[71] it is accepted by Alfred almost unwillingly[72] (and by Asser under compulsion),[73] and it is exercised by maintaining a careful balance between the active and the contemplative lives.[74] Gregory's image was that of the helmsman, steering his ship through the storms of this life, guiding his heart and body through the waves and tempests of the temporal world and towards the shore of perfection.[75] Once again Asser picks up the image. Alfred is the chief (*praecipuus*) helmsman, struggling to bring his ship through to its heavenly port, not allowing it to be diverted by the waves and tempests of the present life.[76]

---

[66] *De Duodecim Abusivis*, 43; *Hibernensis*, XXV.9, 28–9, XXXVII.3, 132; *De Institutione Regia*, IV, 198; *De Rectoribus Christianis*, II. 26; *De Ordine Palatii*, III. 52.

[67] *RP* II.6, p. 204; Sweet, 109.

[68] *Asser*, 90, p. 75: 'sicut a quodam sapiente iamdudum scriptum est, invigilant animi quibus est pia cura regendi'. The source of the proverb remains obscure. Cf. *De Regis Persona*, III. 836: 'cum ergo potentiae temporalis ministerium suscipitur, summa cura vigilandum est'; Scharer, 'Writing of History', 200–1, quoting *De Rectoribus Christianis*, I. 22.

[69] *RP* praef., pp. 124–6, I.3, pp. 136–8; I.6, pp. 148–50; I.7, pp. 150–4; I.9, p. 160; III.25, p. 434; Sweet, 23–5, 33, 47–53, 59, 383. Cf. *Dialogues*, II.3.2 140; *De Duodecim Abusivis*, 33–4, 44.

[70] *RP* II.1, p. 174; II.7, pp. 218–30; II.11, p. 252; Sweet, 75, 127–41, 169.

[71] *Asser*, 25, p. 25. Cf. *De Institutione Regia*, V, 206.

[72] *Asser*, 42, p. 32. Cf. *King Alfred's Old English Version of Boethius De Consolatione Philosophiae*, ed. W. J. Sedgefield (Oxford, 1899), XVII, 40.

[73] *Asser*, 79, p. 64.   [74] *Asser*, 25, p. 25; 81, p. 67; 92, p. 79.

[75] *RP* I.9, pp. 158–60; II.5, p. 200; III.28, p. 464; III.32, p. 492 (glossing Proverbs 23.34), III.34; p. 508; Sweet, 59, 103, 409, 431–3, 437.

[76] *Asser*, 91, p. 77. Cf. *Boethius*, XXXIV, 89, XXXV, 97, XLI, 144; Scharer, 'Writing of History',

In describing how those in authority should conduct themselves once in office, Gregory used 1 Timothy 3.2–7 and Titus 1.6–8 as the basis for a detailed description of the necessary virtues. Rulers require chastity, abstinence, learning, forbearance, humility, bravery, compassion, benevolence, and righteousness.[77] Dead to the passions of the flesh, they must disregard both worldly prosperity and adversity; they must overcome bodily infirmity as well as spiritual disdain; they must be generous, compassionate, merciful, do nothing wrong themselves, lament the sins of others, but also show sympathy for others' weakness. Rulers must provide instructive examples and they must pray.[78] Rulers will be pure in thought but chief (*praecipuus*) in action, discerning (*discretus*) in their silences but useful (*utilis*) in their words, close to people in compassion but raised above them in contemplation, humble companions of those who do good but zealous judges of those who sin. They must not lessen their care of the inner life through being preoccupied with exterior matters, but nor should they relinquish foresight (*providentia*) over exterior matters through their concern for the inner life.[79]

Given the widespread influence of Gregory's prescriptions on hagiography, *vitae*, and *specula principum*, Asser's account of Alfred's wisdom (*sapientia*),[80] practical wisdom (*prudentia, peritia*),[81] righteousness (*iustitia*),[82] foresight (*providentia*),[83] discernment (*discretio*),[84] compassion (*pietas*),[85] gentleness (*lenitas*),[86] and benevolence (*benevolentia*)[87] cannot, and perhaps should not, be given one single source. Nevertheless, there are certain features of Gregory's account which seem to have left a distinct impression on Asser's portrait. Two of Gregory's catalogues of virtues, for example, opened with the stipulation that the individual in authority must be free from lust. Gregory then proceded to discuss not just celibacy but marital chastity, setting out the type of admonition which should be delivered to those who are married, to those who have experienced the sins of the flesh as well as those who have not.[88] Asser takes some pains to describe Alfred's concern to avoid the snares of concupiscence within his own marriage,[89] relating Alfred's prayer that he might be given a disease

201–3. For Gregory's application of the metaphor to himself, see *RP* IV.1, p. 540; Sweet, 467; *Dialogues*, I. prol. 5, 12–14. Cf. *Asser*, 21, p. 19; 73, p. 54.

[77] *RP* I.5, p. 144 (*castitas, abstinentia, doctrina, patientia, humilitas, fortitudo, pietas, benignitas, iustitia*); Sweet, 41.

[78] *RP* I.10, pp. 160–2; Sweet, 61–3. [79] *RP* II.1, p. 174; Sweet, 75.

[80] *Asser*, 22, p. 20; 42, p. 32; 88, p. 73; 89, p. 75; 91, p. 79; 99, p. 86. Cf. *RP* III.6, pp. 284–6; III.14, p. 342 (quoting Proverbs 5.1); Sweet, 203–5, 273.

[81] *Asser*, 16, p. 15; 103, p. 89; 106, p. 93. Cf. *RP*, III.11, p. 316; Sweet, 237.

[82] *Asser*, 76, p. 61; 105–6, pp. 91–3. Cf. *RP* II.6, pp. 202–4, 214–18; III.16, pp. 354–6; Sweet, 107–9, 123–7, 291.

[83] *Asser*, 75, p. 58. Cf. *RP* III.17 p. 368; III.32, pp. 490–2; Sweet, 305, 431–3.

[84] *Asser*, 106, p. 93. Cf. *RP* II.6, p. 216; III.32, p. 494; III.35, p. 518; Sweet, 432.

[85] *Asser*, 99, p. 86. Cf. *RP* I.5, p. 198; II.6, pp. 216–18; Sweet, 101, 123–7.

[86] *Asser*, 91, p. 78, 106, p. 93. Cf. *RP* II.6, p. 216; Sweet, 125.

[87] *Asser*, 79, p. 64, 88, p. 73. Cf. *RP* III.9, p. 302; Sweet, 222.

[88] *RP* III.27–8, pp. 446–68; Sweet, 393–413. [89] Cf. *Dialogues*, I.4.1, 38; *Boethius*, XXXI. 70.

which would free him from carnal sin whilst not making him useless (*inutilis*) or despised by his subjects.[90] One of the two diseases which Asser takes from the list of disqualifications from priestly office in Leviticus is leprosy, an affliction which Gregory explicitly connected with lechery.[91] Likewise, in emphasizing the connection between Alfred's wisdom and his righteousness,[92] Asser appears mindful of how Gregory had moderated a ruler's zeal for justice with clemency (*clementia*), gentleness (*lenitas*), and forbearance (*patientia*), all of which stem from humility (*humilitas*).[93] Thus, Alfred's father is praised for his clemency, Alfred's children are held up for their humility and gentleness, whilst Alfred himself is only driven to rebuke after gentle inquiry and a long period of forbearance (*post longam patientiam*).[94] In the case of generosity, the link with Gregory is made explicit. Staple virtues for any medieval ruler, the *liberalitas* and *largitas* of Asser's Alfred are also expressed as *iocunditas* on the grounds that 'God loves a cheerful giver' (2 Corinthians 9.7).[95] Gregory cited the same verse in the same context.[96] Indeed, Asser follows his own quotation with his one direct reference to the *Regula Pastoralis*.[97] For Gregory, almsgiving to the poor was not simply an example of generosity or mercy. Strictly speaking, it was an expression of justice.[98]

If a direct relation between Gregory and Asser accounts for the prominence afforded to Alfred's marital chastity and for the connection of Alfred's forbearance and generosity to the overarching virtue of *iustitia*, then it may also lie behind the depiction of other aspects of his character. Gregory insisted, for example, that a ruler should be vigilant in attending both to his own needs and to those of others, avoiding the sleep of the slothful and remaining ever alert to the care of the soul, particularly during the night.[99] Asser likewise repeatedly emphasizes that Alfred's *ministerium* continued both day and night (*die noctuque*).[100] Gregory not only underlined the responsibility to speak the truth,[101] but connected speaking the truth with *iustitia*.[102] Asser has Alfred speaking the truth (*veredicus*)[103] and calls him an arbiter of truth in his judgements (*in iudiciis*

[90] *Asser*, 74, pp. 54–7.
[91] *RP* I.11, p. 170; Sweet, 69–71. Cf. 2 Kings 15.5. For blindness, see below, n. 169.
[92] *Asser*, 76, pp. 60–1. Cf. *RP* I.11, p. 168 (*sapientia seu iustitia*); Sweet, 203 (*ryht wisdom*).
[93] *RP* II.6, pp. 202–18; III.9, pp. 296–302; III.17, pp. 360–4; Sweet, 107–27, 215–22, 299–303.
[94] *Asser*, 12, p. 10; 13, p. 11; 75, p. 58; 91, p. 78.
[95] *Asser*, 76, p. 59; 81, p. 67; 101, p. 88; 102, p. 88.
[96] *RP* III.20, p. 384; Sweet, 323. Cf. *Via Regia*, X, 950–1.
[97] *Asser*, 102, p. 88, paraphrasing *RP* III.20, p. 384. Cf. Sweet, 321.
[98] *RP* III.21, pp. 394–6; Sweet, 335–7. Cf. Psalm 72.4, 12–13; *De Duodecim Abusivis*, 51.
[99] *RP* III.4, p. 278; III.15, p. 350; III.32, pp. 490–2; Sweet, 193–5, 283, 431.
[100] *Asser*, 22, p. 20; 76, pp. 59–60; 77, p. 63; 81, p. 67; 89, p. 75; 90, p. 75; 92, p. 79; 99, p. 86; 103, p. 89.
[101] *RP* II.8, pp. 234–6; III.11, pp. 314–22; Sweet, 145–7, 237–47. Cf. 2 Corinthians 6; Isidore, *Etymologies*, X.276, 424.
[102] *RP* III.25, p. 432 (quoting Psalm 39.10–11); Sweet, 381. Cf. above, n. 22.
[103] *Asser*, 13, p. 12; 37, p. 28; 105, p. 91.

veritatis arbiter).[104] There are still clearer parallels in the particular vices which should be avoided by those in authority. The converse of ministry is negligence,[105] of wisdom ignorance,[106] of truth falsehood,[107] and of benevolence envy.[108] It is thus specifically for their negligence and ignorance that Asser has Alfred rebuking his judges.[109] Ceolwulf of Mercia is condemned for his ignorance, the populace for their stupidity, the Vikings for their customary deceit, the Devil and the assailants of Abbot John for their envy.[110] Once again, however, there are two sins in particular which appear to have had a special resonance for Asser—sloth (*pigritia*) and pride (*insolentia*).

For Gregory, sloth is the vice most closely associated with negligence, the exact opposite of vigilance and foresight.[111] He was therefore particularly concerned to emphasize that, in admonishing the slothful, a ruler should point out the consequences of their failure to accomplish what they had the ability to do. He quotes Solomon: the slothful who do not plough in winter will receive nothing in the summer even though they beg for it (Proverbs 20.4). Likewise, those who begin to do good but neglect to carry it through to completion will end up losing the benefit of what they have started. Despite the belated realization of their error, such entreaties will be rejected by God.[112] Slothfulness and belated repentance are precisely what characterize Asser's criticism of Alfred's subjects for their unwillingness to act for the common needs of the kingdom. Alfred's orders are either not fulfilled or, having been acted upon too late, are useless. Asser appeals to the same scriptural principle. Belated repentance for their negligence is futile because it cannot bring back those who have died or been taken into captivity, nor can it be of benefit to the people themselves since they are now bereft of the means of subsistence.[113]

Even more pernicious than the effects of negligence and sloth are the effects of pride and vainglory.[114] Although pride lies at the root of so many other sins, Gregory drew a particularly close connection with stubbornness (*pertinacia*).[115] Asser follows suit. It is stubbornness as well as pride (*insolentia*) which drives Alfred's brother to commit the crime of rebelling against his father. Æthelbald is a stubborn son (*pertinax filius*), a wicked and stubborn son (*iniquus et pertinax*

---

[104] *Asser*, 105, p. 91. For the connection between truth and justice, see Exodus 23.1 (*Laws* 40, 44, p. 40) and, for equity of judgement concerning the poor, Exodus 23.6 (*Laws* 43, p. 40).
[105] *RP* II.10, p. 248; Sweet, 165. Cf. *De Duodecim Abusivis*, 45, 53, 56.
[106] *RP* I.1, pp. 128–32; Sweet, 25–9.   [107] *RP* III.11, pp. 314–22; Sweet, 237–47.
[108] *RP* III.10, pp. 308–14; Sweet, 229–37.
[109] *Asser*, 106, p. 93. Cf. 22, p. 20; 75, p. 59 (*otiose et incuriose*).
[110] *Asser*, 46, p. 35 (*insipientia*); 91, p. 78 (*stultitia*); 49, p. 37 (*fallacia*); 96, p. 82 (*invidia*).
[111] *RP* III.4, pp. 276–8; III.25, p. 430; Sweet, 191–5, 377.
[112] *RP* III.12, pp. 322–4; III.15, pp. 348–52; III.34, pp. 508–10; Sweet, 247–9, 281–7, 441–7.
[113] *Asser*, 91, pp. 78–9.
[114] *RP* I.9, pp. 156–8; II.6, pp. 206–12; III.2, pp. 268–72; III.5, p. 284; III.9, p. 298; III.14, p. 340; III.17, pp. 360–6; III.19, pp. 372–4; III.20, p. 382; III.24, pp. 422, 426; III.33, p. 500; III.38, p. 526; Sweet, 55–7, 109–19, 181–7, 201, 217, 271, 299, 304, 309–11, 321, 367, 373, 437, 457.
[115] *RP* III.18, 368–70; Sweet, 305–7.

filius), in seeking the kingdom while Æthelwulf is still alive.[116] It is with stubbornness as well as stupidity that Asser also charges Alfred's negligent subjects.[117] It is stubbornness which characterizes their disagreements, while it is pride which leaves Alfred amazed at his negligent judges.[118] Gregory's primary concern with pride, however, was as *the* occupational hazard for rulers, even for those who had hitherto been blameless in their conduct. Saul, David, and Solomon were thus his examples of virtuous rulers who came to be corrupted by their authority. Saul initially fled government because of his unworthiness, but as soon as he attained supreme rule he became puffed up with pride; he was elevated on account of his humility but cast down because of his pride.[119] David may have pleased God in almost all of his actions but, once in power, he too turned from righteousness, in his case to lasciviousness.[120] Even Solomon, for all his wisdom, descended into idolatry.[121] Who, then, Gregory asked, can seek wealth, power, or glory if these prove so harmful, even to those who do not seek them in the first place? Pre-eminence over others frequently results in pride as the praise and flattery (*adulatio*) of subjects encourage rulers to believe that they do indeed excel in the virtue and wisdom with which they were being credited.[122]

Faced with such a bleak assessment of the inherent temptations facing people in authority,[123] not least from those who seek to praise their virtue and wisdom, Gregory devoted considerable effort to prescribing the safeguards which rulers should observe if they are to avoid succumbing to the sin of pride: meditating daily on Scripture, recognizing that God is the source of their power, submitting to adversity and tribulation, regularly considering their physical infirmity, and constantly attending to rule over themselves as a prerequisite for rule over others.[124] Thus, whilst Asser is keen to indicate the pitfalls of negligence, sloth, pride, and stubbornness for Alfred's subjects, he is equally concerned to demonstrate the steps which the king himself has taken to avoid them in his own life. Alfred keeps with him at all times a book of prayers, psalms, and services; he assiduously visits saints' places for the sake of prayer and almsgiving; he listens to divine services daily, celebrating the daytime and night-time offices, and he visits churches at night to pray.[125] At every point

---

[116] *Asser*, 12, p. 10; 13, p. 11.   [117] *Asser*, 91, p. 78.   [118] *Asser*, 106, pp. 92–3.

[119] *RP* I.3, p. 138; II.6, pp. 206–8; III.2, p. 270; Sweet, 35, 113, 185. Cf. *De Duodecim Abusivis*, 44–5, 49; *Via Regia*, XVI, 957; *De Institutione Regia*, X, 234; *De Rectoribus Christianis*, III, 29; *De Ordine Palatii*, epil. 96–8.

[120] *RP* I.3, pp. 138–40; III.26, p. 444; Sweet, 35–7, 393.

[121] *RP* III.26, pp. 444–6; Sweet, 393.

[122] *RP* I.4, p. 142; II.6, p. 206; Sweet, 39, 111. Cf. *Dialogues*, I.4.11, 48.

[123] Cf. *Boethius*, XXVII, 61.

[124] *RP* I.3, pp. 136–40; II.2, pp. 176–80; II.3, pp. 182–4; II.11, p. 252; III.4, pp. 274–80; III.5, p. 284; III.12, pp. 326–32; III.13, pp. 334–8; III.20, p. 382; III.24, pp. 424–6; III.26, pp. 444–6; III.40, pp. 530–2; IV.1, p. 534; Sweet, 33–7, 75–9, 83, 169, 189–95, 201, 251–61, 263–7, 323, 369–73, 391–3, 461–3. Cf. *De Duodecim Abusivis*, 45.

[125] *Asser*, 24, p. 25; 74, p. 55; 76, pp. 59–60.

Asser ascribes Alfred's actions to his dependence on God, whether this is fighting in battles, acceding to the kingdom, defeating the Danes, hunting and praying, educating his youngest son, learning to read and translate, imbibing the rudiments of holy Scripture, or dividing his revenue and his time.[126] All power in Alfred's kingdom is subject to God, as Alfred himself is again quick to remind his negligent judges: they have received their *ministerium* from him but also from God (*Dei dono et meo*).[127]

In holding up the cautionary, and not just exemplary, model of Solomon's kingship, Gregory pointed out that his final descent from wisdom was unprompted by any adversity. Wisdom departed from the king's heart because it was not protected by the discipline of tribulation.[128] Likewise, in citing the example of David, Gregory observed that the king was only brought back to pardon by scourges sent from God.[129] The *Regula Pastoralis* was thus just as sensitive to the salutary effects of adversity as it was to the benefits of peace and material security. Prosperity can pollute the heart with vainglory, whereas adversity can purge it through grief. Those who are wearied by temporal adversity should accordingly be comforted by the hope of the eternal inheritance for which they are being educated through such discipline.[130] For Asser the lesson could not have been more apposite, as he describes the *magna tribulatio* of Alfred's time in Somerset and his subsequent return *post tantas tribulationes*.[131] Of the many 'nails of tribulation' with which Alfred is transfixed, however, it is the series of diseases with which his body is racked that he chooses to highlight ahead of the unremitting 'infestations' of foreign invasion. As Asser's language implies (*infestatione ... infestationibus*), the two are not unconnected.[132] Indeed, according to Gregory, not only will the nature of a people determine the nature of their ruler,[133] but the ruler can even transfer to himself the infirmities and sufferings of others through the 'bowels' of his compassion (*viscera pietatis*).[134] Nevertheless, the emphasis and priority which Asser gives to the particular tribulations of Alfred's physical infirmity require an explanation.

Asser's detailed and repeated references to Alfred's illnesses have long troubled historians, even to the extent of calling into question the authenticity of the text. When reassurance has been proffered, it has tended to take the form of appealing to the general hagiographical topos of a demonstration that divine favour is present.[135] A direct comparison with the *Regula Pastoralis*, however,

---

[126] *Asser*, 38, p. 29; 39, p. 30; 42, p. 32; 54, pp. 43–4; 56, p. 45; 69, p. 52; 74, p. 55; 75, p. 58; 91, p. 77; 76, p. 61; 87, p. 73; 89, p. 75; 99, p. 86; 103, p. 90.

[127] *Asser*, 106, p. 93. Cf. 91, p. 78.

[128] *RP* III.26, pp. 444–6; Sweet, 393.   [129] *RP* I.3, p. 140; Sweet, 37.

[130] *RP* III.26, pp. 438–44; Sweet, 387–91. Cf. *Boethius*, XX, 48; XL, 137; *De Duodecim Abusivis*, 52.

[131] *Asser*, 53, p. 41; 55, p. 45.   [132] *Asser*, 91, p. 76.

[133] *RP* II.7, p. 222 (quoting Hosea 4.9); Sweet, 132.

[134] *RP* II.5, p. 196. Cf. *RP* I.10, p. 162; II.6, p. 214. The principle, but not the image, appears in Alfred's translation (Sweet, 61, 99, 123). Cf. *RP* II.10, p. 248 (quoting 2 Corinthians 11.29); Sweet, 165.

[135] *Asser*, 25, p. 21; 74, pp. 54–7; 76, p. 59; 91, p. 76. Cf. *Dialogues*, IV.11.2, 46; *Boethius*, XXXIX, 133. For

suggests that a much more precise point is being made by Asser. According to Gregory, the sick are to be admonished that 'many are the tribulations of the righteous' (Psalm 33.20), because God chastizes those whom he has chosen with the scourge of discipline. Physical suffering washes away those sins which have been committed and restrains those which might be committed in the future. However, the *recollection* of bodily affliction (*memoria infirmitatis*) targets one sin in particular since, by recalling the infirmity of the body, the spirit is prevented from becoming puffed up with pride. A proud heart is thus reminded by the affliction of the flesh of the humility which it ought to maintain.[136] For Alfred, the lesson could not have been more pertinent. Not only did his disease save him from concupiscence, but it also acted as a powerful corrective against the besetting sin of rulership which had already brought down David and even Solomon.

There is one final reason why Asser should have discussed Alfred's physical infirmity so often and in such detail. In many respects it is the most important. In giving his work the form of a *vita* rather than a *speculum principis*, Asser would have been aware of the advantages of using *exempla* rather than *verba*, the praiseworthy deeds of others rather than words of instruction, in order to fulfil a moral-didactic function.[137] He may also have been responding to the lament that it was through sloth (*slæwð*), negligence (*gymeleast*), and irresponsibility (*reccelest*), that the lives (*lif*), character (*ðeawas*), and achievements (*dæde*) of men who were foremost in renown and most eager for glory had been left unwritten.[138] He may even have been prompted by the *vitae* of Louis the Pious.[139] Asser's familiarity with the *Regula Pastoralis*, however, yields another, more private explanation. A point which was made throughout Gregory's text

concerns, see e.g. Stevenson, *Asser*, pp. cxxx–cxxxi; and for doubts, V. H. Galbraith, 'Who Wrote Asser's Life of Alfred?', in his *An Introduction to the Study of History* (London, 1964), 88–128, at 113: 'No chapter [74] has done more to discredit Asser, for the hagiographical picture of Alfred as a neurotic invalid is irreconcilable with all we really know about him from the Chronicle and the prefaces to his translations, and to suppose that such a narrative was ever read by the king is pure absurdity'; Smyth, *Alfred the Great*, 199–216, 599–600. For response to this specific point, see D. Whitelock, *The Genuine Asser* (Reading, 1968), 15–17; Scharer, 'Writing of History', 187–90; and, more generally, S. Keynes, 'On the Authenticity of Asser's Life of King Alfred', *JEH* 47 (1996), 529–51.

[136] *RP* III.12, pp. 326–32; Sweet, 255–9.   [137] Above, n. 54.   [138] *Boethius*, XVIII, 43–4.
[139] D. A. Bullough, 'The Educational Tradition in England from Alfred to Aelfric—Teaching *utriusque linguae*', *Settimane di Studio del Centro Italiano di Studi sull' Alto Medioevo*, 19 (1972), 453–94, 455, n. 2. The formal parallels with these works are certainly striking. Thegan's *vita et mores* was written whilst his subject was still alive, opens with paternal and maternal genealogies, emphasizes that the youngest son was superior in merit to his elder brothers, and proceeds to describe his deeds (including the baptism of a Danish king), his hunting, and his daily prayer. The Astronomer, too, surrounds his *vita et actus* with a 'choir of virtues', but this time supports the veracity of his account (which includes a description of the king's illnesses) by emphasizing the reliability of his eyewitness historiography, detailing his own involvement with the king, using direct speech and, where necessary, appealing to the 'truth-telling' (*veredicus*) authority of his sources. Then again, Asser could also have turned directly to the Old Testament, where David protests his personal unworthiness, could have become king earlier than he did, withdraws to desert strongholds and hills (1 Samuel 23.14) to fight invaders with a small band of followers, and is likened to a lamp (2 Samuel 21.17).

is that individuals who exercise authority over others should first exercise authority over themselves.[140] This means that their lives should provide an exemplary demonstration of the content of their teaching (so that they practise what they preach) and that, in being zealous against the vices of others, they will also remove their own. Vigilant care of others must not prevent vigilant care of themselves. Once again, this is a necessary precaution against pride but it is achieved, first and foremost, by a ruler looking at himself.[141] In the first instance this process will involve calling to mind his past actions, remembering what he has done as a subject in order to assess his suitability to assume a position of authority.[142] Thereafter it becomes a matter of self-examination (*studium suae inquisitionis*), such that he will never be ignorant of his own self but will always be brought back to a memory of who and what he is (*memoria sui*). In reproving the infirmity of others, he must never be forgetful of his own (*oblitus sui*).[143] In Gregory's account, therefore, the act of remembering a ruler's virtues is a vital component of exercising office, for the ruler's self-knowledge and not just for the edification of others.

Gregory was quick to recognize, however, that such recollection can also become a pitfall of the soul (*fovea mentis*) in that the *memoria virtutis* can readily serve as a temptation to pride.[144] As with the performance of any good action by the ruler, there is a balance to be struck between keeping that action secret in order to preserve his own humility and making it public so that it can serve as an example to others.[145] The solution, for Gregory, was to accompany the recollection of virtue with the recollection of infirmity (*memoria infirmitatis*). The memory of the physical weakness to which an individual has been subject is thus the means by which the mind is brought to a knowledge of itself *without* succumbing to the sin of pride.[146] This is the point with which Gregory chose to open and close the argument of his entire treatise. For some people, he argues, the greatness of their virtue has become the occasion of their fall, when the Devil lists all the things which that individual has done well (*omne quod bene gessit*). Such an individual falls prey to pride as soon as his soul starts to seek its own praise rather than that of God, attributing to itself the good which it has received from God, and disseminating the glory of its own reputation through its lust for praise. Whenever an individual is thereby endangered by the abundance of his own virtues, he needs to recall, not the things which he has done, but the things which he has left undone. This is why God often leaves some imperfection in rulers so that when they shine in outstanding virtues they may also be repelled by their own weakness. Their struggle against the lowest and

---

[140] Cf. *Boethius*, XXIX, 67–8.   [141] *RP* I.2, pp. 134–6; I.4, pp. 140–2; Sweet, 29–33, 37–9.
[142] *RP* I.9, p. 158; Sweet, 57. Cf. *Tecosca Cormaic*, VII–VIII.
[143] *RP* I.3, p. 138; I.4, p. 140; II.6, p. 206; II.10, p. 244; Sweet, 35, 37, 63, 111, 159, 371, 393.
[144] *RP* IV.1, p. 534; Sweet, 463.
[145] *RP* III.35, pp. 512–18; Sweet, 447–53. Cf. *Dialogues*, I.9.7, 80–2.
[146] *RP* III.12, p. 328; Sweet, 255.

the least of difficulties will thus keep them humble even amidst the greatest of their achievements. It is this *memoria infirmitatis* which prevents the ruler from taking pride in the virtues which he has received from God.[147]

Gregory's strictures on the way in which virtue should be remembered provide a compelling motivation for Asser's distinctive approach to Alfred's *res gestae*. In calling to memory Alfred's good deeds, in laying them before the king's own eyes, Asser defends himself against the accusation of flattery (*adulatio*).[148] He points out that Alfred's piety was often conducted in secret.[149] Above all, he juxtaposes praise of Alfred's virtues and achievements with details of his infirmity. If Asser's recollection of the king's virtues was designed to provide Alfred with the requisite self-knowledge for all those who exercise authority, then the recollection of physical infirmity with which it was accompanied provided the necessary safeguard against pride, against the king forgetting himself. Alongside an object-lesson in the nature of true wisdom and the responsibilities of *ministerium*, therefore, alongside a demonstration of the centrality of *sapientia* and *iustitia*, Asser was taking great care to prevent this particular *memoria virtutis* from becoming a pitfall for Alfred's own soul.

Placed in its widest context, the *Res Gestae Aelfredi* has been read as a work directed towards a predominantly Welsh audience, either as Asser's *apologia pro vita sua* or as a political demonstration of Alfred's wealth and generosity, making available an account of the king's deeds for an audience which knew no English in order to encourage and reassure Welsh kings of the superiority of West Saxon, as opposed to Hiberno-Norse, overlordship.[150] Asser's Alfred certainly remains a heroic figure: victorious, wealthy, generous, fighting bravely like a wild boar, engaging his enemies in combat whilst his brother remains in prayer, and raiding hostile territory for the sake of plunder.[151] Even the pursuit of wisdom and justice is couched within a warrior-aristocratic frame of reference. Alfred displays avarice towards the wealth of wisdom,[152] he is generous in distributing the proceeds to his followers and to the poor, whilst in his judgements, as in all other things, Alfred is a most astute hunter, tracking justice down.[153] Set in a more restricted, 'courtly', context, the *Res Gestae Aelfredi* has been seen as Asser's response to the particular political tensions of the 890s.[154]

---

[147] *RP* praef., pp. 124–6, IV.1, pp. 534–40; Sweet, 23–5, 461–7. Cf. *Dialogues*, III.14.13, 312–14.

[148] *Asser*, 81, p. 68.   [149] *Asser*, 76, p. 59. Cf. 97, p. 83.

[150] D. P. Kirby, 'Asser and his Life of King Alfred', *Studia Celtica*, 6 (1971), 12–35; Keynes and Lapidge, *Alfred the Great*, 41–2, 56; S. Keynes, 'King Alfred and the Mercians', in *Kings, Currency and Alliances—History and Coinage of Southern England in the Ninth Century*, ed. M. A. S. Blackburn and D. N. Dumville (Woodbridge, 1998), 1–45, at 41–4.

[151] *Asser*, 38, pp. 29–30; 67, p. 50.

[152] *Asser*, 78, p. 63. Cf. J. L. Nelson, 'Wealth and Wisdom—the Politics of Alfred the Great', in *Kings and Kingship*, ed. J. Rosenthal (New York, 1987), 31–52.

[153] *Asser*, 106, p. 93 (*discretissimus indagator*). Cf. *Via Regia*, XXX, 968 (*in perquirendo iustitiam . . . sollicitus indagator*).

[154] J. L. Nelson, 'Reconstructing a Royal Family: Reflections on Alfred, From Asser, Chapter 2', in

For Alfred, it is thus a timely reminder of the virtues of good lordship and kingship; for his sons, a timely reminder of the wickedness of filial rebellion, the sin of *pertinacia*, the integrity of a father's testamentary deposition, and the perils of a divided kingdom;[155] for his bishops, meanwhile, it recalls the reality of the 'pagan' menace (*non sine materia*)[156] and the penalties of sloth and negligence. At its most intimate, however, the composition of the *Res Gestae Aelfredi* reflects very private concerns.[157] In itself, the absence of evidence for an audience wider than the ruler himself does not make a text any less of an ideological statement or an instrument of power.[158] Composed in the immediate aftermath of the exposition and translation of the *Regula Pastoralis*, addressed and dedicated to Alfred himself, Asser's 'life' of Alfred is the expression of a specifically ministerial conception of kingship. As such, the *Res Gestae Aelfredi* draws on material familiar from Carolingian and Irish texts, in *florilegia*, *vitae*, and *specula principum*, but much of what is distinctive about Asser's work stems from what is derived directly from the sources which underpinned them all: Solomonic kingship from the Old Testament and, above all, *ministerium* from Gregory the Great. Viewed in this light, the *Res Gestae Aelfredi* should be read as a highly personal text, a *memoria virtutis* which combined exemplary didacticism with precisely the safeguard against pride on which Gregory had insisted in his opening and closing chapters. If the *memoria infirmitatis* is the aspect of Asser's work which has caused modern historians the most difficulties, then it is the *memoria infirmitatis* which may lead directly back to Asser's original intention in writing.

Once a thorough knowledge of the *Regula Pastoralis* is made central to Alfred's conception of his own authority and, as a consequence, to Asser's presentation of Alfred's achievements to the king himself, it can also provide a pointer to the visual symbolism with which it was communicated. At the end of his treatise Gregory decribed himself as a 'painter' who had 'depicted' the type of man a pastor should be.[159] His immediate concern was to contrast his own imperfection with the ideal he was holding up for imitation, but it also echoed the imagery which he had earlier invoked in describing the Levitical priesthood (Exodus 28–9). Stipulating that a ruler should be pure in thought, Gregory described how his heart should be constrained by reason in the same way that Aaron wore the breastplate of judgement (*rationale*) containing both doctrine and truth. The ruler is therefore to think upon the exemplary lives of the fathers and the saints and to reflect that he is acting in the place of God. Mindful of his

---

People and Places in Northern Europe—Essays in Honour of P. H. Sawyer, ed. I. Wood and N. Lund (Woodbridge, 1991), 47–66.

[155] *Asser*, 12–13, pp. 9–11; 85, pp. 71–2.   [156] *Asser*, 91, p. 76.

[157] Davis, 'Alfred the Great', 177; Campbell, 'Asser's Life of Alfred', 127–8.

[158] Mayr-Harting, *Ottonian Book Illumination*, I, 16, 158, 176.

[159] *RP* IV.1, p. 540 (*pictor . . . depinxi*); Sweet, 467. This comparison is quoted, and expanded, by Aldhelm, *De Virginitate*, LX, ed. R. Ehwald: MGH Auctores Antiquissimi XV, 226–323 at 321–2. For Asser's debt to Aldhelm, see Keynes and Lapidge, *Alfred the Great*, 258–9, 269.

own faults, he is to combine zeal for correction with calmness of judgement.[160] Gregory pursued this Old Testament typology still further when insisting that the ruler should be foremost in action, advancing with the weapons of right-eousness in his right hand and in his left.[161] For Gregory, the robe of the Leviti-cal priesthood was to be understood as a sign of how a pastor should be protected against both prosperity and adversity by the ornament of the virtues. Each of the colours of the ephod is accordingly given a particular significance: gold indicates the understanding of wisdom (*intellectus sapientiae*); blue jacinth indicates the understanding of the truth which transcends earthly matters (and earthly praise) to reach the love of heavenly things; white, meanwhile, indicates chastity and the purity of the flesh.[162] With the pastor clothed in righteousness (Psalm 131.9),[163] his judgement is symbolized by carrying a rod (*virga*) in one hand and a staff (*baculus*) in the other, striking with the severity of justice but also supporting with the comfort of mercy.[164] Finally, in stipulating the requisite combination of the active and contemplative lives, Gregory expounded the significance of hair which is neither shaven (indicating a complete absence of temporal concerns) nor allowed to grow too long (indicating an excess of worldly cares) but which is maintained in moderation, long enough to cover the scalp but short enough not to impede the eyes.[165] And the significance of such unobstructed vision? Just as the sense of smell is the discernment with which a ruler chooses virtue and avoids sin, the sense of sight is the understanding with which he sees wisdom, the light of truth.[166] This comparison of sight with wisdom is thus an association to which Gregory repeatedly returned throughout his treatise. Those in the highest authority are like eyes, using the light of knowledge to see ahead (*providere*);[167] they should have eyes everywhere (Revelation 4.6), including within, so that they can be watchful over themselves but also detect what is in need of correction in others.[168] This is why blindness is a symbol of ignorance and why Gregory could speak of the eye, or the eyes, of the mind (*oculus mentis, oculi mentis*).[169]

---

[160] *RP* II.2, pp. 176–8; Sweet, 77–9. For Aaron as the prefiguration of bishops, see *Hibernensis*, I.3, 4. Cf. Mayr-Harting, *Ottonian Book Illumination*, II, 96–7.

[161] *RP* II.3, p. 182; Sweet, 83.

[162] *RP* II.3, pp. 182–6; Sweet, 83–9. Cf. *RP* II.7, p. 224; II.11, p. 254; III.24, p. 422; Sweet, 133, 171, 369, where gold signifies the excellence of holiness, the shining splendour of an exemplary life, and an understanding of the supreme splendour.

[163] *RP* II.4, p. 190; Sweet, 93.

[164] *RP* II.6, pp. 216–18; Sweet, 125–7. Cf. above, n. 65. For the same gloss on Psalm 23.4 ('Thy rod and thy staff they have comforted me'), see *Liber Psalmorum: The West Saxon Psalms*, ed. J. W. Bright and R. L. Ramsay (Boston, 1907), 47. For the budding of Aaron's rod as the symbol of his priestly authority, see Numbers 17; for the *baculus* of Exodus 12.11 as the symbol of pastoral care, see Gregory the Great, *XL Homiliae in Evangelia*, II.22.9, 191; *Hibernensis*, I.6, 5.

[165] *RP* II.7, pp. 228–30; Sweet, 139–41.

[166] *RP* I.11, pp. 166–8; Sweet, 65. Cf. *Hibernensis*, XXI.12, 66.

[167] *RP* I.1, p. 132; II.7, p. 222; III.32, p. 494; Sweet, 29, 131, 432.

[168] *RP* III.4, pp. 278–80; Sweet, 195.

[169] *RP* I.11, pp. 164, 168; I.9, p. 158; III.35, p. 512; IV.1, p. 538; Sweet, 57, 65–9, 99, 129, 259, 412, 447, 467. Cf. III.15, 352 (*palebra consilii*); Sweet, 287.

In the case of wisdom and sight, Gregory bequeathed symbolism which is picked up in Asser's portrait of Alfred. Blindness is the first of the two diseases which Alfred fears as a disqualification from office; it is his *oculi mentis* that Alfred directs afar in order to bring back the fruits of learning.[170] In the case of the pastoral judgement for which wisdom and sight are essential prerequisites, however, Gregory's iconography appears to have left its mark on a more striking image still. If the Alfred Jewel (pl. 7a–b) is indeed to be identified as the head of one of the *aestels* which Alfred distributed with each copy of the *Regula Pastoralis*, then the imagery within the text which it would then have accompanied deserves close examination.[171] Here is a depiction of a robed figure, with white flesh and hair, seated in judgement,[172] set within a casement of gold and against a blue background,[173] which was intended to be, literally, instrumental to a bishop's understanding of a text in which a priest's robe, eyes, and hair, and the colours gold, blue, and white, are all given an allegorical pastoral significance. Furthermore, if the inscription on the Alfred Jewel ('Alfred caused me to be made') can plausibly identify it as one of the treasures which were made by goldsmiths and craftsmen on the king's instructions and even to Alfred's own design,[174] then the potential ideological significance of such a close connection is considerable.

The iconography of the figure on the front of the Alfred Jewel is usually interpreted in one of two ways, either as a personification of Sight (on the basis of the Fuller Brooch) or as Christ personifying wisdom (1 Corinthians 1.24).[175] The back-plate, meanwhile, has been interpreted as a symbol of wisdom on the basis of Proverbs 3.18 (wisdom as the tree of life) or, better still, Revelation 22.2 (a tree of life which has twelve crops of fruit and whose leaves are for the healing of the nations).[176] Set in the context of the *Regula Pastoralis*, these interpretations are clearly not mutually exclusive. Far from Sight having little relevance to the text from which Alfred forbade his *aestel* to be removed, the contents of the *Regula Pastoralis* prove how sight and wisdom were, in fact, intimately connected and therefore how the jewel can be interpreted as *both* sight *and* wisdom within a single, coherent design. That overall design is the pastor's exemplary demonstration of wisdom in the act of judgement, in the exercise of his *ministerium*. Significantly, this is one point on which Alfred's English version of the

---

[170] *Asser*, 74, p. 55; 76, p. 61. Cf. 89, p. 75 (*corporales oculi*). Cf. the way in which the same image is drawn out from, and added to, the original, in *Boethius*, XXXIII, 82; XXXIV, 89; XXXVIII, 121.

[171] Cf. Crépin, 'L'Importance de la pensée de Grégoire le Grand', 584.

[172] For this association, see *RP* II.2, 180; III.32, 496; Sweet, 79, 435.

[173] D. A. Hinton, *A Catalogue of the Anglo-Saxon Ornamental Metalwork 700–1100 in the Department of Antiquities, Ashmolean Museum* (Oxford, 1974), 29–48.

[174] *Asser*, 76, p. 59.

[175] E. Bakka, 'The Alfred Jewel and Sight', *Antiquaries Journal*, 46 (1966), 277–82; D. R. Howlett, 'The Iconography of the Alfred Jewel', *Oxoniensia*, 39 (1974), 44–52.

[176] Cf. Psalm 52.8; *RP* III.21, p. 398; Sweet, 337 (for the fig tree bearing the fruit of good deeds); *Audacht Morainn*, 17 and *Tecosca Cormaic*, I.22 (for tree-fruit as a sign of just rule); *Proverbia Grecorum*, 22, p. 11 (*pomarium fertile*), 29, p. 12.

Regula Pastoralis chooses to elaborate on Gregory's original. According to Alfred's translation, a pastor's discernment between good and evil is expressed in instruction, in judgement, and in truth. Mindful of the divine judge who sits over all, he is to recognize that he has been set in authority in order to serve as a similitude (*bisen*) and likeness (*anlicness*) of Christ.[177] Such Christomimesis might, in itself, be sufficient to explain why the Alfred Jewel should portray a figure who is not only seated in judgement but also clothed in a robe of green, a vestment which was taken to signify the discipline of the Church and a colour which was understood to symbolize the divinity of Christ.[178] For Gregory the Great, however, a connection between the colour green and pastoral care was, if anything, even tighter. Once again Ezekiel provides the key, not just in virtue of the fact that he served as a type for all those in authority over others,[179] but because of the significance of his prophetic vision of the restored Temple of Jerusalem.

By expounding the words and events recorded in the Old Testament as a shadow of things which were to come in the New, it was a commonplace of patristic exegesis to regard the physical building of the Temple in Jerusalem as a prefigurement of the spiritual building of the Church. According to Augustine and Jerome, for example, the Temple of Solomon was to be read allegorically, as a symbol of the spiritual house in which Christians would become the 'living stones' (1 Peter 2.5). The prophetic visions of the second Temple in Ezekiel 40–2, of the restored Jerusalem in Isaiah 54, and of the heavenly Jerusalem in Revelation 21, were therefore all interpreted as anticipations of the holy community into which Christians were being gathered in this life and in the next. For Gregory the Great, however, the particular significance of Ezekiel's vision of a Temple rebuilt after its destruction by the Babylonians, a vision to which he devoted all ten of his homilies on this book, lay in its interpretation as the scriptural paradigm for a *reformed* Church, for a Christian community which was punished for its sins by invasion and captivity but which was to be rebuilt through the guidance of its pastors and teachers.[180] This was an exposition which was subsequently given vivid contemporary application, and circulation, amongst the Anglo-Saxons by the writings of Bede.[181] In connecting

---

[177] Sweet, 79.

[178] For the robe of Christ as the discipline of the Church, see e.g. *De Duodecim Abusivis*, 58; *De Regis Persona*, XXV, 850. For the greenness of jasper and emerald as a symbol of the divinity of Christ in the enthroned figure of Revelation 4.3–6, a figure who is seated in heaven behind a sea of glass 'as clear as crystal', see e.g. Haimo of Auxerre, *Expositio in Apocalypsin*, II.4: PL 117, cols. 937–1220, at 1004–5; anon., *Commentariorum in Apocalypsin Libri Quinque*, III.4: PL 100, cols. 1087–156 at 1116–17. Cf. Dublin, Trinity College, 58 (The Book of Kells), fol. 202v; also K. Veelenturf, *Dia Brátha: Eschatological Theophanies and Irish High Crosses* (Amsterdam, 1997), ch. 5.

[179] Above, n. 44.

[180] Gregory the Great, *Homiliae in Hiezechielem Prophetam*, ed. C. Morel, SC 327, 360 (Paris, 1990, 1996).

[181] H. Mayr-Harting, *The Venerable Bede, the Rule of St Benedict, and Social Class* (Jarrow Lecture, 1976), 12–13, 19–22; A. G. Holder, 'New Treasures and Old in Bede's *De Tabernaculo* and *De Templo*',

Ezekiel, Isaiah, and Revelation, therefore, Gregory paid particular attention to the meaning of precious stones since, according to Isaiah 54.11–12, the boundary walls of the new Jerusalem would be made of precious stones, its gates of cut stones, and its bastions of jasper, whilst according to Revelation 21.18–19, the heavenly Jerusalem of gold, jasper, and crystal would have walls whose foundations were precious stones, the first of which was jasper. For Gregory, the significance of precious stones (*lapides desiderabiles*) is thus as a symbol of those within the Church who are strong in faith and love. The significance of cut stones (*lapides sculpti*), meanwhile, is as a symbol of those within the Church through whose words we enter into eternal life. They are cut, rather than uncut, because such individuals must themselves exhibit the precepts which they enjoin upon others, displaying in their own lives the performance of God's commands as if they were fashioned into them. The significance of jasper, finally, is that the colour green (*viridis*) symbolizes the minds of those within the Church who teach. These *doctores* have been strengthened by a love of interior vitality (*viriditas*) in the sense that they despise everything transitory and seek nothing from a world which will come to an end, treating all its joys with disdain, as barren compared to the green pastures (*pascua ... viriditatis*) of an eternal inheritance which will never corrupt or fade away (Psalm 23.2; 1 Peter 1.3–4). It is these teachers who are therefore represented by the 'treasure-rooms' of Ezekiel 40.17, dispensing the riches of knowledge through the example of their lives and through the wisdom of their instruction.[182] As with Asser's profile of Alfred in the *Res Gestae Aelfredi*, the precious stone of the Alfred Jewel appears to have been cut, and coloured, in a distinctively Gregorian image.

Revue Bénédictine, 99 (1989), 237–49; and, more generally, A. Thacker, 'Bede's Ideal of Reform', in *Ideal and Reality in Frankish and Anglo-Saxon Society: Studies Presented to J. M. Wallace-Hadrill*, ed. P. Wormald, D. Bullough, and R. Collins (Oxford, 1983), 130–53.

[182] *Homiliae in Hiezechielem*, II.6.1–4, 272–8; *Moralia in Job*, XVIII.33, 919–20. Cf. Jerome, *Commentariorum in Esaiam Libri XII–XVIII*, ed. M. Adriaen (CCSL 73A), XV 612–13. Cf. Bede, *Explanatio Apocalypsis*, III.21: PL 93, cols. 129–206, at 197: *per jaspidem ergo fidei viror immarcescibilis indicatur*. Cf. P. Kitson, 'Lapidary Traditions in Anglo-Saxon England: Part II, Bede's *Explanatio Apocalypsis* and Related Works', *ASE* 12 (1983), 73–123; C. Meier, *Gemma Spiritalis—Methode und Gebrauch der Edelsteinallegorese vom frühen Christentum bis ins 18. Jahrhundert* (Munich, 1977), 135, n. 473. According to Isidore (*Etymologies*, XIV.7.1, 190), meanwhile, emerald is capable of reflecting images like a mirror (*speculum*). And the Latin for emerald? *Smaragdus*.

10

THE STRANGE AFFAIR OF THE
SELSEY BISHOPRIC, 953–963

Patrick Wormald

In the middle of the tenth century, just before the eruption of the crisis which has for a millennium been considered (somewhat optimistically) a 'Tenth-Century Reformation', two curious things happened in the English Church. First, there was an unparalleled outburst of bishops with the name Brihthelm. The best-known was briefly archbishop of Canterbury in 959 before being elbowed out in a shameless *putsch* by Edgar and Dunstan. There also seem to have been Brihthelms at London (*c.*951–7), Wells (?956–73/4), and Winchester (958/9–63), while (an)other(s) feature(s) in documents of 956–7, first as 'bishop elect' and then with no title. Most important for present purposes, a Brihthelm appears as bishop of Selsey in two charters of 956 and 957, one highly questionable, the other not above suspicion but of great importance: yet he is not in the Selsey episcopal list, which offers no name between a bishop whose last attestation was in 953 and one whose dated debut was 963. That brings us to our second phenomenon. In the charter of 957 (S 1291), 'Bishop Brihthelm' tells how he had induced King Eadwig to agree that a series of estates should be restored to Selsey. The lands in question were so extensive that they would have amounted to almost half the bishopric's eventual Domesday endowment, including its entire geographical core on the Selsey peninsula. At no other moment in Anglo-Saxon history was the viability of a (southern) see so gravely impaired. How did this come about? This paper offers a solution for both puzzles together; one that may cast further light on the somewhat fraught politics of Eadwig's reign.[1]

---

[1] For earlier attempts to resolve this crux, see J. A. Robinson. *The Saxon Bishops of Wells* (London, 1918), 62–7; D. Whitelock, 'The Appointment of Dunstan as Archbishop of Canterbury', in *Otium et Negotium: Studies . . . presented to Olof von Feilitzen*, ed. F. Sandgren (Stockholm, 1973), 232–47; N. Brooks, *The Early History of the Church of Canterbury* (Leicester, 1984), 237–44; and *Charters of Selsey* (*Ch. Sel.*). ed. S. E. Kelly, Anglo-Saxon Charters, VI (Oxford, 1998), pp. lxix–lxxiii, xci–xcii, 5–13, 88–91. It has been the subject of unpublished research by Professor Keynes into the crisis of Eadwig's reign, and by Dr Kelly into the circumstances surrounding S 1291, and I am grateful to both for showing me their studies. I acknowledge gladly that Dr Kelly's work first put me on to the solution proffered here and that she generously made me a 'gift' of her ideas; while it will be obvious that the exercise would have been quite impossible without constant recourse to Professor Keynes's colossal *Atlas of Attestations in Anglo-Saxon Charters, c.670–1066* (Cambridge, 1998). Each of these scholars kindly read my paper, as did Lesley Abrams, Nicholas Brooks, Shashi Jayakumar, and Jenny Wormald; which does not of course

The gist of S 1291 (the earliest copy of which dates from the thirteenth century) is this: Brihthelm, 'divina dispensatione episcopus', announces in Eadwig's second year that he proposes to improve his prospects in a future life by restoring land, 'which was fraudulently seized from the church by someone named Ælfsige against the decree of the holy fathers of the Council of Nicaea, when he was seen to have been raised as bishop to the episcopal seat of the Gewisse, that is of the South Saxons (*per quendam Ælfsinum nomine, contra decretum sanctorum patrum Niceni concilii ab ecclesia arrepta fuerat ubi Geuuissorum, id est Australium Saxonum, presul episcopali cathedra sublimari videbatur*)'. The estates comprised forty-two hides at Selsey, Itchenor, Birdham, *Egesawyda*, Brinfast, Sidlesham, and Wittering, and another thirty-two (or thirty-four) hides distributed between Aldingbourne and Lidsey, *Geinstidesgate*, Houghton, Coldwaltham, and Mundham. The inducement whereby Brihthelm procured Eadwig's agreement that the lands be restored 'to the aforesaid monastery' was 100 mancuses of gold; in return for which, the king ordered a charter to be written, and, with the consent of the bishops, ealdormen, and other leading men, assured Brihthelm (in direct speech) that he could have the lands for the duration of his life, but that its inheritance was to devolve, 'in unshaken right', on the South Saxon episcopal see for the uses of Selsey's bishops. The charter then gives the bounds of the first set of estates, and it is witnessed by Kings Eadwig and Edgar, Archbishop Oda, Bishops Ælfsige and Brihthelm, the bishops of Dorchester/York, Worcester, Ramsbury, and Elmham, six leading ealdormen (including the future hero, Byrhtnoth), and fifteen of the most prominent thegns of the time.[2]

This charter has a number of singularities. The first that need detain us is that the same estates and a couple of others appear together, assessed at eighty-seven hides, in a celebrated forgery whereby in 673(= 683?) King Cædwalla of the West Saxons is said to have granted them for Bishop Wilfrid to build a monastery at Selsey—this with the consent of 'Archbishop' Wilfrid, Bishop (or sub-king) Ecgwald, 'Bishop Wilfrid'. Eadberht, appointed bishop of Selsey *c.*710, and Ealdulf *dux*, who appeared as king of the South Saxons in the 760s, and then as *dux* after Offa's conquest of the kingdom.[3] One immediately suspects that Cædwalla's charter was cooked up to effect the happy outcome recorded in Brihthelm's, especially as eighty-seven hides is the very total of Selsey's original endowment in the accounts of Eddius Stephanus and Bede.[4]

mean that any of them in any way endorse my views. Two other prolegomena are that 'S ooo' usual designates charters as listed in P. H. Sawyer, *Anglo-Saxon Charters: An Annotated List and Bibliography*, Royal Historical Society Guides and Handbooks, 8 (London, 1968), whose revised version by Dr Kelly I cite (S*) for new or significantly reassessed documents; and that for consistency's sake I use the spelling Brihthelm throughout, though 'Byrhthelm' is no doubt more accurate.

[2] *Ch. Sel.* 20; Keynes, *Atlas*, XLVIII, L–LI.

[3] S 232 (*Ch. Sel.* 1); S 50 (*Ch. Sel.*, App. 2B), S 49, 1178, 1183–4 (*Ch. Sel.* 10–13); and *Ch. Sel.*, pp. lxxiii–lxxv, lxxx, lxxxviii–lxxxix.

[4] *The Life of Bishop Wilfrid by Eddius Stephanus*, ed. B. Colgrave (Cambridge, 1927), pp. xli, 82–5; *HE* IV, 13 (pp. 374–5).

There is, however, a problem about the assessment of the estates even in Brihthelm's charter. For one thing, the hidage of the first set of properties corresponds with suspicious precision to that which they have in Domesday Book, even though half were then in the hands of Earl Roger and only came into the bishop's possession in the early twelfth century.[5] For another, the total hidage allocated to the second group of estates in Brihthelm's charter is thirty-two just as in Cædwalla's, even though Brihthelm's figures actually add up to thirty-four.[6] It is as if Brihthelm's total had been adjusted to reflect that claimed for Cædwalla, and also the endowment as it was perceived in or soon after 1086.

It could therefore be that none of the assessments in any of the extant documents is reliable.[7] However, it is quite another matter to suppose that a record of a dispute between Bishop Brihthelm and Ælfsige about other property was rewritten to back up the claims already put by Cædwalla's charter. The Cædwalla text should have sufficed on its own. Why—unless perhaps to provide some sort of precedent for a bishop at odds with a local magnate (as hypothetically in 1086)—should Chichester's archivists have doctored a second document as well as fabricating the first?[8] Besides, half the properties itemized in Brihthelm's charter were unrecorded in 1086, as were two more that appear in Cædwalla's. Without the assistance of Domesday, whence did its draftsmen derive their view that six, though not all, of the estates proffered in '673/83' were also at stake in 957—unless in fact they were? There are a number of more or less suspect charters along the lines of Brihthelm's (not to mention a few that are substantially genuine), but none comes from a foundation with such modest resources and ambitions as Selsey's.[9] In short, the concoction by whatever means of a document like Brihthelm's charter would have created supererogatory difficulties for its authors unless something very like the crisis it recalls had truly occurred.

So what did actually happen? In point of fact, S 1291 gives a more straightforward answer than has usually been appreciated. It says that 'a certain Ælfsige' seized the lands, against the canons of a Council of Nicaea, 'when (*ubi*) . . .

---

[5] *Domesday Book*, ed. A. Farley (London, 1783), fols. 17a, 24b (*Domesday Book. Sussex*, ed. J. Mothersill (Chichester, 1976), 2:6–8, ii:44–7); *Ch. Sel.*, pp. lvii–lix, with Brooks's map, *Canterbury*, 242.

[6] *Ch. Sel.*, pp. lxiv–lxv, lxix–lxx, 11–12, 21–2. The assessments in the charter whereby King Nothelm/Nunna of the South Saxons granted most of these lands to his sister Nothgyth in 692 (S 45, *Ch. Sel.* 2) are different; again, the total in this essentially authentic document is given as thirty-three though it actually came to thirty-eight, but for an explanation of the discrepancy, see H. Edwards, *The Charters of the Early West Saxon Kingdom*, British Archaeological Reports, British Series, 198 (Oxford, 1988), 295–6.

[7] There could also be evidence of tampering in the phrase 'praefato monasterio' (above, 129), as there had been no previous mention of Selsey as such. But this could equally well be a case of loose drafting by a Selsey scribe who habitually thought in those terms.

[8] That some of the relevant lands were not in Selsey's possession in 1066/86 need not of course mean that they never had been; this was, after all, the heartland of the notoriously acquisitive Godwine kin: *Ch. Sel.*, pp. lvi–lix.

[9] S 1244 (St Augustine's), 1250–1 (Evesham), 1293, 1295 (post-conquest Westminster), 1378 (Christ Church), 1477 (Chertsey), 1480 (Worcester), 1481 (Peterborough).

raised to the episcopal seat of the Gewisse, that is the South [*sic*] Saxons' (above. p. 129). 'South' Saxons is clearly nonsense; 'Gewisse' was the ancient name for the *West* Saxons, and its currency at this late date is indicated by its use in the problematic but undoubtedly tenth-century record of the division of the south-western bishoprics.[10] A Selsey archivist was presumably startled to find a reference to the West Saxon see in this context and made the requisite amendment. Otherwise, the text states unequivocally that Ælfsige took the lands when promoted to the West Saxon bishopric. There was indeed a Bishop Ælfsige of Winchester at just this time (951–8). What is more, the reference to Nicaean canons is a loud signal that episcopal manoeuvre was afoot. The fifteenth decree of the first Council of Nicaea (325) was a standard Canon Law interdict on invading another bishop's see.[11] Many other canons could have been cited against run-of-the-mill annexation of church property.[12] Furthermore, there would be reason for Bishop Ælfsige to have moved in on Selsey. Bede said that after St Wilfrid's recall, the South Saxon Church 'was subject to the bishop of the Gewisse, that is the West Saxons, whose see was in the city of Winchester', and that before the promotion of its first bishop *c*.710, 'the province of the South Saxons belonged to the diocese of Winchester'. Additionally, there are grounds for thinking that Winchester's bishops had administered the see during a series of vacancies, the last as recent as *c*.900.[13] The warrant for doubting so dramatic a reading of the evidence is that one might not expect Winchester's bishop to be identified as 'a certain Ælfsige', nor to find him witnessing the charter that rebuffed him. Yet it was not unknown for litigants to attest documents recording their defeat, wherein they were not always politely described.[14] All things

---

[10] S* 1451a, cf. S 1296.

[11] 'Neither bishops nor presbyters nor deacons shall transfer from city to city (*civitatem*). If after this decision . . . anyone shall attempt such a thing . . . the arrangement shall be totally annulled, and he shall be restored to the church of which he was ordained bishop or presbyter or deacon': *Decrees of the Ecumenical Councils, I. Nicaea I to Lateran V*, ed. N. P. Tanner (London, 1990), xv, p. 13; *Ecclesiae Occidentalis Monumenta Iuris Antiquissima*, ed. C. H. Turner and E. Schwartz, 2 vols. (Oxford, 1899–1939), I, 134–5, 222–3, 268. Cf. e.g. the so-called 'Canons of the Apostles', xiv, Turner and Schwartz, I, 14; H. R. Percival, *The Seven Ecumenical Councils*, A Select Library of the Nicene and Post-Nicene Fathers, 2nd ser., 14 (Oxford and New York, 1900), 594; or Chalcedon v, ed. Tanner, 90.

[12] Brooks, *Canterbury*, 376 (n. 113) adduces a canon of the *second* (787) Nicaean Council 'against alienation of the lands of episcopal churches' (xii, ed. Tanner, 147–8); but this is a ban (again standard) on alienation of diocesan or monastic revenues by incumbents, so less obviously pertinent than Nicaea (325). Nor is there a sign that any record of Nicaea (787) got as far as England, for all the fuss that its rehabilitation of images provoked at Charlemagne's court.

[13] *HE* IV, 15 (pp. 380–1); V, 18 (pp. 514–15); cf. V̇, 23 (pp. 558–9); *Ch. Sel.*, pp. lxxxvii–xci, 90–1.

[14] P. Wormald. 'A Handlist of Anglo-Saxon Lawsuits', *ASE*, 17 (1988), 5 (Bynna), 14 (Abbess Cwenthryth), 19 (Æthelwulf, 'venatissimus anguis' in the text, but two so named in the witness-list), 21 (Æthelwald and Alhmund), 24, 26 (Æthelhelm), 69 (Leofwine?) 77 (Wulfstan and Wulfric). For all that, I should record here that Professor Keynes would translate 'ubi' as 'where', so giving the sense that 'a certain Ælfsige' removed property of the church 'where the bishop of the *Gewissae* . . . was seen to be raised to the episcopal throne'. In that case, it would mere coincidence that an otherwise unknown Ælfsige made his move when a namesake occupied the see of Selsey; but apart from the likelihood or otherwise of this, there remains the Nicaean canon's implication that a *bishop* was guilty.

considered, there is no good reason to doubt that a bishop of Winchester attempted to close down the see of Selsey in the mid-tenth century.

Who, then, was Brihthelm, and how did he get involved? When answering this sort of question, would-be Anglo-Saxon prosopographers have one great asset and two major handicaps. In early medieval England, unlike the continent, royal as well as private charters were witnessed by the leading figures of the kingdom—and sometimes of the locality too. On the other hand, the bishopric or office held by the people in question was rarely specified; and there was a marked tendency for the same names to be shared by different people.[15] So a first step is to tabulate the incidence of multiple or otherwise relevant Brihthelms in charters of the mid-tenth century.[16]

953	560 Witnessed by Bishop Brihthelm (6)
955	566 Witnessed by Bishop Brihthelm (9)
	565 Witnessed by Bishop Brihthelm (4)
	[*Accession of Eadwig*]
	582 Witnessed by Bishop Brihthelm (5) and by Deacon Brihthelm
956	614 (I, ?Jan.) Granted to Eadwig's 'faithful priest', Brihthelm; (cf. S 1292 below)
	615 (II, Feb.) Granted to Eadwig's 'dear relative', Bishop-elect Brihthelm; witnessed by Bishop Brihthelm (4)
	630 (?) Witnessed by Bishop Brihthelm (5), and by Brihthelm placed (7) but not identified as a bishop
	602 (IV. Nov.) Witnessed by two Bishops Brihthelm (2, 6)
	610 (IV. Nov.) Witnessed by two Bishops Brihthelm (2, 6)
	611 (IV. Nov.) Witnessed by Bishop Brihthelm of London (1) and by another Bishop Brihthelm (7)
	612 (IV. Nov.) Witnessed by two Bishops Brihthelm (2, 6)
	613 (IV. Nov.) Witnessed by two Bishops Brihthelm (2, 6)
956 x 7	1292 Exchange by Bishop Brihthelm with Abbot Æthelwold of land in S 614 above
957	645 Witnessed by two Bishops Brihthelm (2, 6)
	646 Witnessed by two Bishops Brihthelm (2, 6)
	1291 Granted by/to Bishop Brihthelm; witnessed by BishopBrihthelm (2)
	1794 Granted to Bishop Brihthelm; in St Paul's memorandum

[15] For the methodological issues, see, S. Keynes, *The Diplomas of King Æthelred 'the Unready', 978–1016* (Cambridge, 1980), 154–62; but also Dr Kelly's *Charters of Abingdon*, 2 vols., Anglo-Saxon Charters, VII (Oxford, forthcoming). Introduction, secs. 4(c)–(d).

[16] For ease of reference, the order of charters within a year is by S number; this is not chronological, but 956 texts are when possible assigned to the group (I, II, IV) and month wherein they are gathered by Keynes, *Diplomas*, 48–69, and by S*. Bracketed numbers after names indicate place in the sequence of bishops in each witness-list. For the details, see (naturally) Keynes, *Atlas of Attestations*, XLIV, XLVIII–XLIX, LIV. All roughly authentic lists are covered, whatever the unreliability of associated texts; but S 616 (956), a grant to Bishop Brihthelm and the 'brothers of Chichester' in the Chichester cartulary, is highly dubious (*Ch. Sel.* 19), so the single Brihthelm among its witnesses may have no significance and is disregarded.

[*Division of the kingdom between Eadwig and Edgar*]
639 Witnessed by Bishop Brihthelm (3), and by Brihthelm placed (5) but not identified as a bishop
642 Witnessed by two Bishops Brihthelm (3, 5)
647 Witnessed by two Bishops Brihthelm (2, 4)
958 575, 577 Witnessed by two Bishops Brihthelm (2, 5)
650 Witnessed by two Bishops Brihthelm (2, 4)
651 Witnessed by two Bishops Brihthelm (1, 3)
653 Witnessed by two Bishops Brihthelm (2, 4)
654 Witnessed by two Bishops Brihthelm (2, 5)
656 Witnessed by two Bishops Brihthelm (2, 4)
959 658 Witnessed by two Bishops Brihthelm (2, 4)
586 Witnessed by two Bishops Brihthelm (1, 3)
652 Witnessed by Archbishop Brihthelm of Canterbury and Bishop Brihthelm of Winchester (1)
660 Witnessed by Archbishop Brihthelm of Canterbury and Bishop Brihthelm of Winchester (1)
[*Accession of Edgar*]
960 680 Witnessed by two Bishops Brihthelm (3, 5)
683 Granted to Edgar's relative, Bishop Brihthelm, with reversion to Winchester
684 Witnessed by two Bishops Brihthelm (1, 3)
961 691 Witnessed by Bishop Brihthelm of Winchester (1)
692 Witnessed by two Bishops Brihthelm (1, 3)
693 Witnessed by Bishop Brihthelm of Winchester (1)
694 Witnessed by two Bishops Brihthelm (2, 4)
695 Granted to Edgar's relative, Bishop Brihthelm; land was Winchester's in 1086; witnessed by Bishop Brihthelm (2)
697 Witnessed by two Bishops Brihthelm (1, 4)
962 701 Witnessed by two Bishops Brihthelm (2, 4)
704 Witnessed by two Bishops Brihthelm (1, 3)
709 Witnessed by two Bishops Brihthelm (2, 4)
963 713 Witnessed by two Bishops Brihthelm (2, 4)
715 Witnessed by two Bishops Brihthelm (1, 3)
717 Witnessed by two Bishops Brihthelm (2, 5)
964 726 Witnessed by Bishop Brihthelm of Wells (8)

Faced with this swirl of homonomy, one reaches for handholds of comparative security. This much seems (relatively) certain:

a) There were at least two Bishops Brihthelm from some time in 956 until 963, but at no point before or after.

b) Edgar's charters have no one of that name until his accession to sole power (959). So any Brihthelm must either have held firm to Eadwig's regime when the kingdom was divided or soon left the scene.

c) One of these figures was bishop of London in 956–7 (S 611, 1794); and since his predecessor, Theodred, ceased to attest in 951, this Brihthelm should be the one who first appears in 953.[17] However, he can hardly have retained that post for long after the division of the kingdom, since London was Edgar's and he made Dunstan its bishop ((b) above).

d) At the time when one Brihthelm was archbishop of Canterbury in 959, another was bishop of Winchester (S 652, 660), the latter's date of accession being fixed by Ælfsige's promotion to Canterbury in the second half of 958.[18]

e) This Brihthelm still held Winchester in 961 (S 693, cf. S 683, 695), but was replaced by the great Æthelwold before 29 November 963.[19]

f) Alfred was bishop of Selsey until 953 (S 560), and Eadhelm was in place by 963 (S 717, cf. 726), so there can have been no Selsey Brihthelm before or after those dates.[20]

g) Finally, the Brihthelm who appears as bishop of Wells in 964 (S 726) lasted until 973/4, and can have acceded no earlier than 956, the last attestation of the Wulfhelm who had held the post since 938.[21] In addition, Dunstan's first biographer says that it was Brihthelm '(bishop) of Dorset' who was appointed to Canterbury by Eadwig, then sent back by Edgar; and in repeating this, John of Worcester emends 'Dorset' to 'Somerset'.[22]

Moving from virtual certainties to likelihoods, it is important to note that during the seven years when there were at least two Brihthelms in circulation, thirty-five distinct lists (rather over half) feature only one.[23] In other words, there is a better than even chance that any Brihthelm will be *absent* from a charter of these years. It follows, despite the relative rarity of the name, that it may be hasty to conclude that *only* two Brihthelms were involved. The odds can be further refined. Regularity of attendance must in part have been determined by personal importance, but we might assume that the top people got the best sees. So it is significant that bishops of Winchester very unusually missed a list; that most bishops of London were not much less punctilious; but that Wells's bishops skipped at least a quarter of relevant lists in the thirty years before 956, and over half in the twenty after 975; and that two-fifths of the lists lack both predecessors of Selsey's putative Brihthelm, while of two successors (ignoring a

[17] Theodred: S 558, 573; Brihthelm *sc.* of London: S 560–1. Here and in following notes, S references are given for charters not tabulated above, S numbers in the text referring to that table.

[18] Archbishop Oda died on 2 June, and S 650 is his sole 958 attestation; Kelly, *Charters of Abingdon*, Introduction, sec. 4(d), resolves his problematic appearance in S 658 (17 May 959), in noting his name's absence from the earlier cartulary version of this text.

[19] *The Anglo-Saxon Chronicle, MS A*, ed. J. M. Bately (Cambridge, 1986), *sub anno* 963, 75; *English Historical Documents, I. c.550–1042*, ed. D. Whitelock, 2nd edn. (London, 1979), 226.

[20] S 669, ostensibly an Edgar charter though dated 951/900(!), may draw on an authentic witness-list, but one that need not be earlier than 963. On the implications of S 717, see further below, 140.

[21] S 440–1, 608, 790, S* 794a; *Chronicle of John of Worcester*, ed. P. McGurk, 2 vols. (Oxford, 1995–), II, 424–5.

[22] *S. Dunstani Vita Auctore B*, 26: *Memorials of St Dunstan*, ed. W. Stubbs, RS, 63 (London, 1874), 38; *Chronicle of John of Worcester*, ed. McGurk, II, 410–11; cf. Robinson, *Saxon Bishops of Wells*, 64–6; Whitelock, 'Appointment of Dunstan', 233–4.

[23] This excludes obviously truncated lists, and includes November 956 charters (Group 'IV') (cf. n. 16 above), plus 963 diplomas bar the four featuring Bishop Æthelwold ((d) above).

future archbishop), one missed much more than half, though the other just a seventh.[24] We may conclude that any absent Brihthelm in the critical period could well be bishop of Wells or Selsey, but is probably not bishop of Winchester or London.

That impression is upheld by attestation sequence. As soon as a Brihthelm is likely to be the bishop of Winchester (S 651, *later* 958), he attests first or second, and maybe third in two cases.[25] Twenty-nine lists from late in Eadwig's reign onwards have a single Bishop Brihthelm so placed. The years of a probable London Brihthelm (953–7, (b) above) find individuals of that name listed from seventh to second (once first, once ninth). Five 957 pre-partition lists (including S 1291) have a single Brihthelm at second or third. The Wells candidate seems to oscillate between third and ninth under Edgar; some twenty full lists 959–63 have no Brihthelm in a corresponding position.

A final question of probability concerns the name itself. Apart from the two decades after 953, there were some nine other Brihthelms in the Old English period.[26] It seems scarcely likely that there were *four* more in the mid-tenth century. It is questionable that there were as many as three. If there were three, the odds are surely against more than one having been a royal relative, as in S 615, 683, and 695.[27] Name-giving habits in Germanic nobilities being what they were, kinly name-clusters are to be expected; but the Ecgberhting family's preferred prefixes were overwhelmingly Æthel-, Ælf-, and Ead-.

Returning, therefore, to the Brihthelm list, it can be seen that there *is* a 'spare' Brihthelm in at least seven lists (S 639, 642, 647, 575/577, 653–4, 656) between the likely disappearance of the bishop of London at or soon after the partition of (?mid-) 957 and the debut of Winchester's Brihthelm at least a year later (S 651, 658, 652, etc.).[28] The second candidate in eight charters running from November 956 ('IV') to the partition (S 602, 610–13, 630, 645–6) could, if not Wells's bishop, be this man too. It as yet remains possible that London's Brihthelm lost his see for preferring Eadwig, and was given some other see—or retained his title with no see—until a death before the end of the reign. If not, however, a

[24] Of *Winchester* bishops, Ælfheah I missed 4, Ælfsige 2, Ælfheah II 1, and Æthelwold none at all; for *London*, Wulfsige missed 2, Theodred 13 (out of a possible 100+), Wulfstan none, and Ælfhun 4, while the position with Ælfstan (959–96) is complicated by the existence of a Rochester namesake—but under 10% of post-963 lists have neither. *Wells's* Ælfheah missed 5/23, Wulfhelm 22/65 (also absent 946–8, 953), Cyneweard 3/6, and Sigegar 32/63; and *Selsey's* Wulfhun 11/24, Ælfred 15/42, Eadhelm 38/62, and (ignoring the future Archbishop Æthelgar) Ordbriht 6/43. Fabricated or duplicated lists are here bypassed in an exercise that must of course remain subjective and superficial.

[25] For the significance of S 651's dating from later 958 (Kelly, *Charters of Abingdon*, 79), cf. n. 18.

[26] This total is excavated from W. G. Searle, *Onomasticon Anglo-Saxonicum* (Cambridge, 1897), 89–90—a work badly needing detailed revision but quite reliable for trends.

[27] Endowments in Eynsham's foundation charter (S 911) included lands given to Æthelweard the historian, father of the founder Æthelmær, by a kinsman, Bishop Brihthelm; Æthelweard was himself of royal descent and may first have come to notice under Eadwig (below, n. 39).

[28] Winchester is excluded for the 958 Brihthelms other than that in S 651 by the fact that Ælfsige was still in post.

third Brihthelm did come on the scene from mid-957 at the latest, and perhaps from the latter part of 956. This could be the Selsey protagonist of S 1291.

Four remaining pieces of the jigsaw remain to be slotted in. First, there was a 'bishop-elect' Brihthelm, a royal kinsman, by February 956 (S 615), apparently a priest back in January (S 614, 1292), and probably a deacon in 955 (S 582); this man seemingly became bishop of Winchester by 960 (S 683, 695).[29] If, as William of Malmesbury averred, Brihthelm of Wells was an ex-monk of Glastonbury, he can hardly have been the 'faithful priest' and future bishop of S 614, 1292, nor S 582's deacon.[30] A 'dear relative' seems so natural an appointment for Eadwig to have made to Canterbury in 959 that we might be tempted to disregard William's evidence, and suppose that it was the Wells Brihthelm who was the royal kinsman achieving such visible promotion in 955–6.[31] It is therefore important that a strikingly high proportion of archbishops after 900 had previously been bishops of Wells or Ramsbury, especially if they were former monks of Glastonbury. Nor need we linger over the concentrations of royal demesne in central Somerset and west Berkshire to realize why.[32] Wells's Brihthelm required no royal kinship to commend him.

Second, a Brihthelm turns up twice in 956–7 (S 630, 639) at the end of the list of bishops but without being so styled; such a thing sometimes happened in witness-lists, but it is interesting that this particular bolt of lightning struck twice in about a year. Third, Ælfsige and Brihthelm are each absent from lists of archbishops, as one might expect of men who never collected a *pallium*.[33] And given the problem being investigated here, there might be several reasons why Selsey's list has no Brihthelm. But why should there be none in any version of Winchester's list bar one? It may be significant that all lists except that one (from Bath, *c*.1100) are closely akin and ultimately derive from Canterbury.[34] Fourth and finally, there is a patent connection, extending to details of wording, between Selsey's Cædwalla forgery (129–30) and one in the name of the same king and also for Wilfrid, but with an endorsement whereby Wilfrid transfers to Archbishop Theodore the Pagham estate that it conveys. The Pagham

---

[29] Cf. nn. 18–19, 27–8, above. That deacons occur in witness-lists only in obviously special circumstances favours the identification.

[30] *De Antiquitate Glastonie Ecclesie*, 67, ed. J. Scott: *The Early History of Glastonbury* (Woodbridge, 1981), 138–9.

[31] Cf. nn. 20–1. This is Dr Kelly's hypothesis, its main problem being that it gives us two princely Bishops Brihthelm; cf. n. 27.

[32] D. Hill. *An Atlas of Anglo-Saxon England* (Oxford, 1981), 101; D. Knowles. *The Monastic Order in England*, 2nd edn. (Cambridge, 1963), 697, 699–700.

[33] Ælfsige froze to death in the Alps en route to fetch it, *S. Dunstani vita auct. B*, 26: *Memorials*, ed. Stubbs, 38; Brihthelm can have had no time to do so before Edgar's accession on 1 October 959, and Dunstan's consequent usurpation: Brooks, *Canterbury*, 239–40.

[34] R. I. Page, 'Anglo-Saxon Episcopal Lists', *Nottingham Medieval Studies*, 9–10 (1965-6), 71–95, 2–24; D. N. Dumville, 'The Anglian collection of royal genealogies and regnal lists', *ASE* 5 (1976), 23–50; S. Keynes, 'Episcopal Lists', *The Blackwell Encyclopaedia of Anglo-Saxon England*, ed. M. Lapidge (Oxford, 1999), 172–3.

charter is extant in a hand ('s.x$^{med/2}$') that also wrote a Canterbury Offa forgery. Furthermore, the Pagham estate lies right between the Selsey peninsula and the other lands 'Cædwalla' gave to Selsey.[35] Together, the two documents give off a strong aroma of a mid-century 'deal' hatched by a harassed Selsey and an archbishop.

Before proffering a hypothesis about the meaning of these jagged shards of evidence, it may be helpful to summarize what they rule *out*:

a) The Brihthelm being promoted in 955–6 was obviously not the bishop of London on the scene from 953 (133–4, 136).

b) He was not the bishop of Wells if William of Malmesbury is to be believed. That this bishop is said to have been subsequently translated to Canterbury is no reason to disbelieve him (136).

c) As a royal kinsman, he most likely was the Brihthelm who ended up at Winchester. But this cannot have been before later 958 (134–5). Nor can the princely Winchester Brihthelm have been Eadwig's candidate for the archiepiscopate (134).

(a)–(c) seem to require three Brihthelms. A bishop newly elected in 956 with no known see until 958 looks the best bet for Selsey's man.[36]

It is now possible to essay a reasoned and informed guess as to what did happen at Selsey between 953 and 963. A number of indications, cumulatively rather than individually telling, suggest that Eadwig's accession in November 955 marked a resurgence of branches of the royal house that had been marginalized after Edward the Elder succeeded in 899, and after he and his son Ælfweard died within weeks of each other in summer 924—much as senior branches of the Saxon Liudolfings were shut out by the success of Henry the Fowler and Otto I.[37] One sign of a political shift was that Eadwig would be the first king since Ælfweard to be buried in Edward's royal shrine at the New Minster.[38] Another was the fall of dowager Queen Eadgifu, the most obvious beneficiary of her sons' regime since 939, followed by that of Dunstan, a confidante of Eadred's last years. Yet another was that Eadwig received his only sympathetic write-up (the New Minster *Liber Vitae* apart) from the historian Æthelweard, a descendant of King Alfred's elder brother, and possibly the brother of Eadwig's new queen.[39] Especially relevant for present purposes was the new

---

[35] S 230; on this, see Brooks, *Canterbury*, 240–3, and *Ch. Sel.*, pp. lxxii–lxxiii, 99–103. The related 'Offa' charter is S 111 ('774').

[36] Cf. Brooks, *Canterbury*, p. 239 and n. 107.

[37] The best general account of all this is B. Yorke, 'Æthelwold and the Politics of the Tenth Century', in *Bishop Æthelwold: His Career and Influence*, ed. Yorke (Woodbridge, 1988), 65–88, at 74–81. Her line convinces overall, but note Professor Keynes's caution in his exemplary facsimile, *The Liber Vitae of the New Minster and Hyde Abbey*, EEMF 26 (Copenhagen, 1996), 19–24. For Liudolfing tensions, see K. J. Leyser, *Rule and Conflict in an Early Medieval Society: Ottonian Saxony* (London, 1979), 11–14.

[38] *Liber Vitae*, ed. Keynes, 24, 81.

[39] *Chronicle of Æthelweard*, IV, 8, ed. A. Campbell (Edinburgh, 1962), 55; cf. n. 27. An Ælfgifu seems to have a brother Æthelweard: *Anglo-Saxon Wills*, VIII, ed. D. Whitelock (Cambridge, 1930), 20–2, and

prominence of men whose kinship with the king is stressed by his charters; Ælfgar and his brother Byrhtferth, and the famous brothers Ælfhere and Ælfheah.[40] Bishop Ælfsige of Winchester was not apparently a royal kinsman but was close to Ælfheah.[41] As lord of the city that resumed political centrality for the first time in a generation he must have been another of the government's key men. There is evidence that this group made its political presence felt as Eadred's powers waned.[42] However, Ælfsige was not only politically well placed to shut down Selsey when it fell vacant and take over its emoluments.[43] Crucially, the circumstances of its origin and subsequent history gave him some justification for doing so. Bede was a much-consulted authority in the new England. His report of the Anglian retreat from Abercorn after 685 may even have warranted the cession of Lothian to the Scots.[44] His account of how Selsey was carved out of Winchester's *parrochia* could have given any self-respecting tenth-century diocesan licence to restore what he saw as his church's immemorial entitlement.[45]

Another royal kinsman receiving notice by February 956 was 'bishop-elect' Brihthelm (S 615), very probably the 'faithful priest' attesting in January that year (S 614) and the deacon of late 955 (S 582); he shared his 'Briht-' prefix with one of the new regime's royal thegns.[46] In the political circumstances, his advance to a bishopric must have seemed highly desirable. Selsey was vacant but had been swallowed by Ælfsige. From the evidence as it stands it is possible to distil the following resolution of this dilemma:[47]

(1) In 956 the princely Brihthelm attained the title of bishop but as yet no see; hence, a Brihthelm appears in two charters among bishops but not so titled

this lady was probably the consort from whom Eadwig was separated for consanguinity (though cf. Keynes, *Diplomas*, 192, n. 139).

[40] S 582 (seemingly the king's first charter), S 585–6, 651; such references in diplomas are rarer than one might think. A. Williams, '*Princeps Merciorum gentis*: The Family Career and Connections of Ælfhere, Ealdorman of Mercia, 956–83', *ASE* 10 (1982), 143–72, esp. 147–54, 157–8. Cf. below, n. 46.

[41] See his will (a New Minster text): *Wills*, IV, ed. Whitelock, 16–17; and for Wulfric 'Cufing', another beneficiary, below, 140.

[42] e.g. S 554–5 (951), 564 (955); cf. S. Keynes, 'The "Dunstan B" Charters', *ASE* 23 (1994), 165–93, at 185–6, 188–90. Mr Shashi Jayakumar draws my attention to a passage in *The Chronicle Attributed to John of Wallingford*, ed. R. Vaughan, Camden Society, 3rd ser. 21 (London, 1958), 50, strongly implying that the young prince and his pack were on the prowl as his uncle Eadred waned.

[43] Ælfred of Selsey lasts attest in S 560–2 (953). Ælfsige's first secure attestations are S 559–60, and *John of Worcester*'s statement, 402–3, that he acceded as soon as 951 may be a deduction.

[44] *HE* IV, 26 (pp. 428–9); cf. P. Wormald, '*Engla Lond*: The Making of an Allegiance', *Journal of Historical Sociology*, 11–24, at 16; repr. in Wormald, *Legal Culture in the Early Medieval West* (London, 1999), 359–82, at 378.

[45] Above, n. 13, and see further below, 141.

[46] Cf. n. 40. Given the relative rarity of the name Brihthelm (cf. above, nn. 26–7), it may be noted that this does establish the existence of a *second* kin favouring the 'Byrht-/Briht-' prefix, the other being the evidently distinct family of the great ealdorman Byrhtnoth; I owe enlightenment on this to Shashi Jayakumar.

[47] For the outlines of this reconstruction, I am indebted to personal correspondence from Professor Brooks.

(S 630, 639). Any fully episcopal Brihthelm listed before late 958 could be that of London (or *emeritus* London) or Wells.

(2) Shortly before the kingdom's partition, Ælfsige conceded Brihthelm much of Selsey's endowment (S 1291)—even a suffragan role?—but would not allow the see to be formally reconstituted for the time being. Royal intervention brought agreement about, which is why it was Eadwig who was paid, and why the sum was a mere £12½: almost inconceivably low as the 'price' of some seventy-five lush hides.[48]

(3) What was in it for Ælfsige (aside from (5) below and no doubt other unspecified sweeteners) was the promise of the primacy itself when an ageing Oda at last vacated it. For Brihthelm, the deal was likewise that he would then succeed to Winchester. Each got far more than the minor bishopric in dispute or a share of its property. The king got key supporters in key posts. But all three had to wait.

(4) Brihthelm was nevertheless under no obligation to resurrect the see of Selsey once installed at Winchester. S 1291 did not even oblige him to hand over Selsey's lands until after his death.[49] The reasoning that had carried weight for Ælfsige would by then have made sense to him too. There is thus no further sign of a bishop of Selsey till sometime in 963.

(5) As leader-designate of the English Church, however, Ælfsige in 958 required further inducement to give the scheme his blessing; namely, that Canterbury should now become the accredited beneficiary of Selsey estates he had possessed since 953. The 'Cædwalla' charter that had provided leverage for S 1291 was therefore refabricated as a transfer (in the name of 'Wilfrid') of Pagham, a prime slice of *quondam* Selsey endowment, to Canterbury (in that of 'Theodore'). Brihthelm's clerks could provide the formulae, Canterbury scribes the penmanship.[50]

Whatever its strategems, Eadwig's regime lacked the muscle or luck of the party rallying to his formidable brother. Ælfhere and Ælfheah had already, like the Beaumonts in the 1140s, secured the family position by taking opposite sides. Archbishop Oda's witnessing became intermittent after the partition. But the old warhorse showed that he could still kick when in 958 he obliged Eadwig to separate from his queen 'because they were too much akin'. Ælfgifu's position seems to have been politically pivotal.[51] (Her sole attestation,

---

[48] The 'going-rate' at the time was a lot higher, but Ælfswith, wife of Ealdorman Ælfheah, could 'buy' 40 hides from Edgar for just £5, S 866. On this problem, see J. Campbell, 'The Sale of Land and the Economics of Power in Early England: Problems and Possibilities', *Haskins Society Journal*, 1 (1989), 23–37, esp. 31–3.

[49] *Ch. Sel.* pp. 86, 88.

[50] S 230 and see n. 35 above. Professor Brooks's published theory is that the forgery was the outcome of a Brihthelm–Oda pact, while Dr Kelly looks to a Wells/Selsey/Canterbury Brihthelm (above, n. 31). But were the reforming Oda or the 'gentle, modest, humble, and kindly' Brihthelm of Wells (*S. Dunstani vita auct. B*, 26: *Memorials*, ed. Stubbs, 38), such likely dealers as Ælfsige?

[51] *Two of the Saxon Chronicles Parallel*, ed. J. Earle and C. Plummer, 2 vols. (Oxford, 1892–9), I, 113.

revealingly for these purposes, was to Bishop Brihthelm's exchange with Abbot
Æthelwold of the land he had received when a 'faithful priest', S 1292, 614).
Within a year of Ælfsige's death in the Alps, Eadwig was dead himself.
Brihthelm, his Canterbury appointment, was back at Wells by late 959, Dunstan
in his place. Wulfric Cufing, a leading Eadwig lay adherent (and Ælfsige associate), had to pay Edgar £15 to recover his lands, before lapsing into obscurity.[52]
The Winchester Brihthelm may have been harder to reach. To judge from
S 683, 695, Edgar had his reasons to keep him on-side. Yet a sign of his waning
influence is that Selsey was reactivated in 963, before his death (S 717). Once he
was replaced by Æthelwold, another 'Winchester man' but Edgar's one-time
guardian, his politics and/or episcopal record could be punished by the *dam-
natio memoriae* visited on Archbishops Ælfsige and Brihthelm. It may not be
chance that the sole episcopal list with a Brihthelm in Winchester's sequence
was the one that does not apparently emanate from Dunstan's Canterbury.[53] On
a concluding note: it may surely be that the unique ferocity of Æthelwold's
assault on the Winchester 'clerks' in 964 was a comment on the questionable
churchmanship of his predecessors, Ælfsige and Brihthelm, and on their
hardly less suspect politics.

It goes without saying that this reading of the 'Brihthelm crux' is speculative
and leaves loose ends. Speculation and loose ends are inseparable from the study
of European protohistory. This particular flight accommodates most aspects of
an intractable body of evidence. It understands faction under Eadwig and his
brother much as one does under Henry VIII (in curious ways Edgar's mirror-
image), or any strong pre-modern government; that its contours are now vesti-
gial is no basis to deny its relevance. But an added virtue of this approach is that
it gives England's monochrome ecclesiastical politics the colour of the pre-
Gregorian Church at large. No Anglo-Saxon prelate bar Stigand stands in
lower repute than Ælfsige. He had a son.[54] So did tenth-century popes. As
framed by a propagandist of genius like Liutprand of Cremona, their behaviour
did the see of Peter as much long-term harm as those of the Renaissance, and

See n. 39 above; her political electricity must underlie Dunstan's fury at Eadwig's 'dalliance' with her
(and her mother) at his coronation banquet: *S. Dunstani vita auct. B*, 21: *Memorials*, ed. Stubbs, 32–3.

[52] S 687 (960); Keynes, *Atlas of Attestations*, LI (4–6), LVII (11); and n. 41 above. For a slightly differ-
ent reading of Wulfric attestations, see N. Brooks, 'The Career of St Dunstan' in *St Dunstan: His Life,
Times and Cult*, ed. N. Ramsay *et al.* (Woodbridge, 1992), 1–23, at 8–10. Æthelgeard, another partisan and
'Winchester man' at that, was eclipsed a bit earlier: *Liber Vitae*, ed. Keynes, 24, 86–7.

[53] See above, n. 34; nor indeed, given one theme of this paper, that 'Dunstan' lists are the first to insert
Wilfrid as initial bishop of Selsey (Keynes, 'Episcopal Lists', 173). For Æthelwold and Edgar, see E.
John, 'The King and the Monks in the Tenth-Century Reformation', *Bulletin of the John Rylands
Library*, 42 (1959–60), 61–87, at 67; repr. in his *Orbis Britanniae* (Leicester, 1966), 154–80, at 159–60.

[54] *Wills*, as n. 41, and cf. *Anglo-Saxon Chronicle MS A*, ed. Bately, *sub anno* 1001, 79–80, *English Historical Documents I*, ed. Whitelock, 237; the former's 'mægcnafa' is presumably Ælfsige's son, and if its
'maga' is not a daughter, she may be the boy's mother. That aside, the *Vita Oswaldi*, *Historians of the
Church of York*, ed. J. Raine, 3 vols., RS 71 (London, 1871–94), I, 408–9, has Ælfsige crowing on Oda's
tomb; one can now see that he had reason to do so.

for the same reason. It fell prey to family politics. Yet as Barchester's chronicler observed of Archdeacon Grantly's ambition to succeed his father as bishop, 'if we look to our clergymen to be more than men, we shall probably teach ourselves to think that they are less'.

This is in any case only one angle from which to view the Selsey crisis. A central contention of this paper is that Winchester's bishops did have a case. Their hostility to a Selsey diocese matches that of Cologne's archbishops, sustained for over half a century, to the Hamburg archbishopric's takeover of their suffragan see of Bremen, when Hamburg itself was flattened by the Danes in 845. Mainz's archbishop was no better pleased by Otto I's cherished plan for a Magdeburg metropolitanate.[55] One theme of the looming eleventh-century Reformation was the moral reform that exposed the deadliness of Ælfsige's sins. Another was the reassertion of ancestral church rights, which persuaded such men that they had a duty to the glory of God and the traditions of their sees, as well as to class and kin.

The teacher, colleague, and friend whom this volume celebrates launched his career with a study of Hilary, first in the line of distinguished Chichester bishops that ran on through Richard Poore and Lancelot Andrews to George Bell. His remains the finest account of St Wilfrid, Selsey's founder. He showed that Wilfrid was not just a haughty Northumbrian aristocrat with an eye for treasure and its uses, but also a churchman whose position at York and Hexham could be defended on principle, and whose biographer might understand his life-style in terms of an unexampled range of Old Testament imagery. Today's historians delight in discovering political and otherwise worldly motivation in the Church's history. Ecclesiastical history that leaves it at that, as no one has ever understood better than Henry Mayr-Harting, contributes little to the understanding of the Church, and not much more to that of humanity.

---

[55] *Adam of Bremen, Gesta Hammaburgens is Ecclesiae Pontificum*, ed. B. Schmeidler, MGH, Script. Rer. Germ. in us. schol., 3rd edn. (Hannover, 1917), pp. xlix–li, 48–52; T. Reuter, *Germany in the Early Middle Ages, c.800–1056* (London, 1991), 163–4.

11

THE CHURCH OF WORCESTER
AND ST OSWALD

Eric John

St Oswald's part in the revival of monasticism known as the Tenth-Century Reformation was the subject of an important study by Dean Armitage Robinson.[1] He was mainly concerned with the part Oswald played in the transformation of the cathedral community at Worcester into a fully Benedictine monastery. This transformation has since been the subject of varying interpretations. The present enquiry reconsiders the question in a broad chronological framework, continuing across the Norman conquest. The outcome will, I hope, be a clearer view of the history of the *mensa*, extending from Oswald's pontificate to the twelfth century.

Some post-conquest accounts say that Oswald did not use force to change the Worcester community but relied instead on 'holy guile'; other sources deny this. We can test the quality of the former accounts by looking at one of them: Eadmer's Life of Oswald.[2] Eadmer is famous as the biographer of St Anselm, but he also wrote this tendentious and partisan Life of Oswald. He did, however, have close Worcester contacts. According to Eadmer, Oswald tried and failed to make the clerks of Worcester change their lifestyles. He circumvented them by founding a rival, true Benedictine community in his cathedral city. The new monastery was dedicated to St Mary, the cathedral to St Peter. The people of Worcester were left to choose: even in the tenth century market forces operated! Eadmer says, 'Hoc itaque modo a beato Petro in matrem Domini Salvatoris, a clericos in monachos, translata est sedes pontificalis honoris'.[3] In spite of his preamble, it does look as though Eadmer thought that St Mary and the new monastery got the episcopal throne. Elsewhere he says that Oswald set up seven

---

[1] *St Oswald and the Church of Worcester*, British Academy Supplementary Papers (London, 1919). Oswald was commemorated in a conference held at Worcester in 1992, whose proceedings have been published as *St Oswald of Worcester: Life and Influence*, ed. N. Brooks and C. Cubitt (London, 1996). See esp. Julia Barrow, 'The Community of Worcester 961–c.1100'. Barrow also addressed the topic in 'How the Twelfth-Century Monks at Worcester Perceived their Past', in *The Perception of the Past in Twelfth-Century Europe*, ed. P. Magdalino (London, 1992), 53–74.

[2] *Vita et Miracula S. Oswaldi* in *Historians of the Church of York*, ed. J. Raine, 3 vols., RS 71 (1879–94), II, 1–59.

[3] 'In this way the bishop's throne was translated from Blessed Peter to the mother of the Saviour, from clerks to monks.'

monasteries in his diocese, 'ejectis clericis feminarum consortium ecclesiis antepotentibus'.[4] These must surely include Worcester. It is Eadmer and William of Malmesbury who promulgate the gentle image of Oswald: this image is not found in Worcester sources.

The traditional view of the three monk-bishops—the vigorous, uncompromising Æthelwold, the gentle Oswald, and the super-gentle Dunstan—was very largely the creation of Robinson. This picture cannot survive study of the sources. Michael Lapidge has some important comments apropos B's Life of St Dunstan. 'It reveals to us a Dunstan far different from the kindly elder statesman normally portrayed by modern scholarship. B's Dunstan is a difficult and tormented figure, now thrown by his colleagues into a duck pond, now pursued by the devil in the shape of a bear, a madman relentlessly swinging his staff at ever-present demons and thus disturbing the sleep of his monks by whacking the walls of the cloister, a man much given to illness and excessively given to visions.'[5]

We have no such intimate portrait of what Oswald was like. Although this paper is an attempt to elucidate his dealings with the Worcester community, we also have a fair amount of information about what Oswald did with the endowment of the church of Worcester, and it is difficult to avoid the conclusion that he dispossessed sitting tenants on some scale, replacing them by East Anglians.[6] I do not think a comparison between Oswald's *læns* and Æthelwold's *Liber Eliensis* suggests that Oswald was any more gentle than Æthelwold with his military tenants. Equally, if we look at the continental background to the Tenth-Century Reformation, we find that sweetness and light were not much in evidence there either. The career of Abbo of Fleury culminating in his murder, the letters of Rather of Verona, the lives of the Cluny saints, the savage lampoons of Adalberon of Laon, all show that the hard-liners were not confined to one party. Similarly, some of the reforming monks in England were harsh to their unreformed neighbours, who could reciprocate their ferocity.

Robinson did not accept the post-conquest sources entirely at face value, although they certainly influenced his thinking. In any case, Eadmer's account is not as unambiguous as some modern scholars seem to think. Robinson decided on some statistical considerations that the post-conquest sources were right: Oswald did convert his clerks gradually. Florence (now usually called John[7]) of

---

[4] 'Having ejected the clerks, who cohabited with women and were previously dominant in the churches', ibid. 20.

[5] 'B and the Vita Dunstani', *St Dunstan: His Life, Times and Cult*, ed. N. Ramsey, M. Sparks, and T. Tatton-Brown (Woodbridge, 1992), 247–59.

[6] Andrew Wareham, 'St Oswald's Family and Kin', in *St Oswald of Worcester*, ed. Brooks and Cubitt, 46–63, points out that Oswald used his family to create a network of clients he could trust to help him protect Worcester. It was so extensive a network and such a personal one as to make it certain it could only be created by dispossession.

[7] *The Chronicle of John of Worcester*, II, ed. R. R. Darlington and P. McGurk (Oxford, 1995). We have John of Worcester's own testimony that a Worcester monk called Florence, who died in 1118 (*s.a.* 1118, vol. III) had played a great part in the compilation of the Chronicle. There are few if any stylistic

Worcester claims, *sub anno* 969, that he has Oswald's own testimony to prove that clerks were expelled from Worcester and replaced by monks in that year. Robinson pointed out that this testimony was probably an Oswald charter of the same year (Birch, *Cartularium Saxonicum*, no. 1243), which alleges, in place of the usual witness-list, that the grant was witnessed by Wynsige the first prior of Worcester and all the monks of Worcester. He thought this and a similar charter of 969 were fabricated. So do I.[8] Wynsige was an important Worcester clerk, converted by Oswald and sent to the saint's other great foundation, Ramsey, for his monastic education. Robinson thought that Ramsey was founded in 968 at the earliest, though it seems possible that it was in fact established a few years before then.[9] Oswald issued no charters between 969 and 977.[10] When the series resumes, Wynsige witnesses most of them in a position of honour. The charters of 969 do not suggest that there was any upheaval in the community. He therefore concluded that the Worcester Latin Chronicle was giving a false date based on a forged charter. So far so good, but he went on to conclude that we could dismiss Oswald's alleged forcible conversion of his cathedral community by guile, holy or otherwise. He never considered any other 'crisis date', despite the fact that some Worcester sources give an alternative, 964, which I will consider in a moment. Before I do, it is worth airing a general objection to the notion of a gradual conversion. The conversion of Worcester to monasticism meant that the former clerks had to abandon their wives and children. I do not see how anyone can convert to celibacy gradually. Is it a tenth-century version of Augustine's prayer: 'Oh Lord make me chaste, but not yet'?

Patrick Wormald, in a remarkable paper setting Edgar's reforms in their continental context,[11] distinguishes between the attitudes of Dunstan and Oswald

---

differences between the pre- and post-1118 annals, but the editors do not attempt to elucidate the respective parts of John and Florence in their edition. Dr Hart's suggestion that we call it the 'Worcester Latin Chronicle' has much to commend it.

[8] *Orbis Britanniae* (Leicester, 1966), 250–62. My objections to CS 1243 are its use of formulas of the later notification charters and the fact that there are several other indubitably genuine charters of 969 not witnessed by Wynsige.

[9] C. R. Hart, 'The Foundation of Ramsey Abbey', *Revue Bénédictine*, 104 (1994), 295–327 at 313, points out that Oswald's concern for the little community of Westbury on Trim, sitting precariously on lands belonging to Worcester Cathedral, was part of the motivation behind Edgar's council of 964. The community of Westbury was reconstituted as the great abbey of Ramsey. Obviously his cathedral was at this time Oswald's primary concern, but it seems likely that Westbury would be the next item on his agenda.

[10] Why this long gap? Although nothing similar occurs in the rest of the series, it is not difficult to explain. From 964 to 969 the Benedictine reforms were being pushed through. By 969 the monks were triumphant. In 975 King Edgar died, or according to the *Vita Oswaldi* was murdered, and the monks were forced to fight a tough rearguard action. Is it a coincidence that a few months later the series of written grants to lay tenants was resumed? I would suggest that from 969 until the death of Edgar, Oswald had no need to give his tenants written title; after that it was very necessary indeed. Oswald's *indiculum*, CS 1136, records the outcome of a lawsuit between Oswald and his lay tenants. It says they should have tenure for three lives (not the same as three generations), but it never says they should have these arrangements recorded in written pseudo-landbook form.

[11] 'Æthelwold and his Continental Counterparts: Contact, Comparison, Contrast', in *Bishop Æthelwold: His Career and Influence*, ed. B. Yorke (Woodbridge, 1988), 13–42.

on the one hand, and that of Æthelwold on the other. Dunstan and Oswald had both had experience of continental monasteries and cathedrals, Oswald's experience being much greater than Dunstan's. They would thus have known that on the continent monastic cathedral chapters were unthinkable (the only one I can think of is Monreale in Sicily). Consequently, in Wormald's opinion neither Dunstan nor Oswald tried to turn their cathedrals into monasteries. He gives a first-class example, Magdeburg, where the cathedral and the monastery were created more or less simultaneously, despite the fact that it would have been simpler and very much cheaper if they could have been combined—as at Æthelwold's Winchester. Wormald is not arguing that Æthewold was ignorant or heedless of continental custom, but rather that he was so deeply imbued with English customs going back to Bede and possibly beyond, that he believed the English Church must rest on monasteries.

Now Dunstan certainly never attempted to turn his cathedral, Christ Church, into a monastery. It is possible that Wormald's explanation as to why he did not is correct. There could, however, have been local reasons—just as it is possible that local conditions at Magdeburg explain why cathedral and monastery were created separately.[12] Dunstan had very limited experience of continental monastic life and none at all of cathedral life. His own monastery had certainly been a monastery of a sort in the early ninth century and was to become a full Benedictine monastery before the death of Æthelred II (1016). Is it not, perhaps, the legacy and memory of the days of the Mercian hegemony over Kent and Canterbury that explain Dunstan's inaction? That hegemony was partly destroyed by Offa's attempts to ride roughshod over the men of Kent, both clerical and lay. Offa's West Saxon successors, on the other hand, always behaved with great care for Kentish sensibilities, especially where Canterbury Cathedral was concerned. Perhaps this is why Dunstan made no attempt to monasticize his cathedral: the king did not favour it. No such considerations apply to Worcester in Oswald's day.

Wormald and others, have been convinced by Sawyer's arguments that Oswald made no attempt to monasticize his cathedral community.[13] I had claimed some years earlier that Oswald treated his cathedral much as Æthelwold treated his;[14] this view Sawyer thought he had disproved. Yet there is a basic point that Sawyer and others seem to have overlooked. That somebody made Worcester cathedral into a monastery is not in doubt: if it were not Oswald, who was it?

[12] They perhaps served two very different purposes. Magdeburg lay in a frontier province both politically and ecclesiastically. The cathedral was the head of the province of East Saxony, the monastery the centre of the eastward-looking mission.

[13] 'Charters of the Reform Movement: The Worcester Archive', in *Tenth-Century Studies*, ed. David Parsons (Chichester, 1975), 84–93.

[14] 'St Oswald and the Church of Worcester', *Orbis Britanniae*, 234–48.

Eric John

The first Life of Oswald, written soon after his death, is adamant that Oswald did eject clerks from his cathedral, replacing them by monks: 'De loco in quo ejus pontificalis cathedra posita est, quid referam, quidque dicam? Nonne in eo quo quondam mansitabant diacones et struciones fecit Deo servire monachos?'[15] The *Vita Oswaldi* was a Ramsey source, and it is not alone in its opinion.[16] The *Historia* of Ramsey, or the relevant part of it, was put together in its present form about 1170. The author had excellent sources, judging by what can be checked and the plausibility of what cannot, and he was a man of discernment.[17] He had no doubt that Edgar did use force against the recalcitrant members of the Worcester community, 'Ut aut prebendis suis renunciarent vel habitum religionis . . . susciperent'.[18] The author claims that his account rests on contemporary documents which were still lying in the Ramsey archives in his day. One might have thought that this evidence was formidable, even conclusive.

There is, of course, a complication. This is a large, single-sheet charter written in the mid-twelfth century but purporting to have been given by Edgar to Oswald at Christmas 964. Known as *Altitonantis* from its first word,[19] it created a new kind of liberty for the bishop and his successors, in return for which they were required to furnish a ship and its crew for a national fleet; it created judicial

---

[15] 'Concerning the place in which his pontifical throne was placed what shall I set down, what shall I say? For where once dwelt deacons and evil creatures did he not make monks to serve God?', *Historians of York*, ed. Raine, I, 462. Barrow, 'Community of Worcester', 96, argues that this passage refers to Ripon and the antecedent of *eius* is Wilfrid whose relics are referred to in the previous sentence. Grammatically she ought to be right, but grammar isn't everything. Ripon in Oswald's day was not a monastery, nor was the cathedral church at York—which makes Dr Barrow's suggestion hard to accept. Wilfrid did not eject clerks from either Ripon or York. I cannot see that anyone thought Ripon was Wilfrid's see—indeed a see at all—before R. L. Poole enthroned him there. I argued against Poole in 'Social and Economic Problems of the English Church', in *Land, Church and People: Essays Presented to H. P. R. Finberg, Agricultural History Review* 18, supplement (1971), 30–63.

[16] S. J. Crawford first suggested that Byrhtferth of Ramsey was the author of the *Vita*, and Michael Lapidge and C. R. Hart have independently proved him right. The *Vita* makes two important points about the death of Edgar that have been overlooked. It says that Edgar was murdered—*interfecit*, which is hardly ambiguous. It also says that Edgar was decorated with lilies and roses at his delayed coronation. I suggested (*Re-assessing Anglo-Saxon England* (Manchester, 1996), 135–6) that this refers to items of regalia. By the tenth century roses and lilies had come to symbolize chastity and martyrdom. I took the lilies of chastity to refer to the new lily crown, used for the first time at Edgar's coronation: but there is nothing in the regalia that suggests roses. I think I misunderstood Byrhtferth here: he does not mean that Edgar wore roses literally; the lilies were the crown that represented the summit of Edgar's earthly success, and the roses were the crown of martyrdom that followed Edgar's coronation so closely.

[17] He had an unusual concern for his sources: in his preface (4) he claims the authority of ancient charters and writings supplemented by oral traditions based on the memories of the older members of the community; he worked out the dates for his short biography of Æthelstan 'Half-king' from the witness-lists of the diplomas and says so (11–12); the source for the descent of King Edgar is ascribed to the chronicles (13); and there is even rudimentary diplomatic criticism: we are told that Edgar did not use a seal (65). It is true that, unless he issued no writs, he must have done: what we know of Edgar's military and naval arrangements required the issue of writs. I think the author notices that Edgar's diplomas are never sealed (nor were any other king's) and drew the wrong conclusion.

[18] 'In order that they should either renounce their preferment or take up the habit of religion.'

[19] CS 1135.

privileges for the bishops of Worcester that enabled them to exert authority over the crews of the ships.[20] As Oswald's relations with his military tenants are only marginally relevant in the present context, I shall largely ignore the question of the status of the charter as a whole and concentrate on the two provisions which say what Oswald did in his cathedral church and with his cathedral chapter. No one claims that either provision is wholly genuine. Indeed they seem dubious at best.

The first provision is meant to authorize the conversion of the cathedral community into a Benedictine monastery. *Altitonantis* claims: 'Unde nunc in presenti monasterium quod predictus reverendus episcopus Oswaldus in sede episcopali Weogreceastre[21] in honore sancti dei genetricis Marie amplificavit et eliminatis clericorum neniis et spurcis lasciviis religiosis dei servis monachis meo et consensu et favore.'[22] The charter asserts that Edgar authorized Oswald to expel the clerks who were in some way sexually lax, even if only to the extent of having married. It credits Oswald with founding the monastery in his cathedral city, putting his episcopal throne in it, and dedicating the reformed monastery to St Mary. The old cathedral had been dedicated to Peter: this re-dedication to Mary is something we can check. The charter claims that the cathedral was dedicated to St Mary in 964. If this is true, then the re-dedication is part of the monastic conversion. This seems to be confirmed by an Oswald charter (CS 1166), dated 965 but probably rather later, which says that the transaction it records was done: 'cum consensu ac licencia monastecae conversationis sancte et intemeratae virginis Mariae.'[23] A charter of Oswald dated 966 has for the first time a formula of benediction that is frequently found in post-964 charters, where a blessing is invoked by St Mary and St Michael with St Peter and all God's saints on those keeping the provisions. The old dedication was to St Peter, the new to St Mary. (It is not altogether clear where St Michael comes

[20] F. Maitland (*Domesday Book and Beyond* (Cambridge, 1897)) thought the charter partly genuine, and so did F. Harmer (*Anglo-Saxon Writs*, 267, n. 2): 'In a twelfth-century copy of an alleged charter of King Edgar for Worcester (B. 1135) which may be founded on authentic material, Edgar is made to declare that the three hundreds of Oswaldslow shall constitute a naucupletionem, scypfylleth or scypsocne.' It may be added that the *scypsocne* was rather tagged on to the other two terms. The charter clearly assumes that the normal name for the liberty was *naucupletio* or *scypfylleth*. *Scypsocne* is, of course, a Scandinavian word. All are synonyms and best translated as 'shipful'. But *naucupletio* and *scypfylleth* are unique words that never occur again. In the *Leges Henrici Primi* of the early twelfth century the normal word is *shipsoke*. The inclusion of the first two terms thus points to a period long before, while *shipsoke* was the normal word when the charter was actually written down. This was why Harmer thought the charter could be based on authentic materials. Such evidence does not prove that any of the charter was authentically Edgarian, but it does suggest that some of it existed long before *Altitonantis* was written down.
[21] The g disappeared in the next generation and no twelfth-century forger would have spelt the name in this way.
[22] '. . . whence now in the present monastery that the aforesaid reverend bishop Oswald raised in his episcopal see of Worcester in honour of Mary the mother of holy God, having expelled the corrupt and lustful clerks, established holy monks to serve God with my agreement and favour.'
[23] 'With the consent and permission of the monastic community of the holy and incorrupt Virgin Mary.'

into the picture, though Julia Barrow makes some persuasive suggestions.[24]) CS 1136, Oswald's *indiculum*, which Maitland thought contemporary with *Altitonantis* and datable to 964,[25] deals with grants of land limited to three lives that the saint made to his military tenants. At the expiry of the third life the land had to be returned to the power of St Mary, 'in cujus nomine hoc monasterium dicatum est'. The texts of the surviving individual loan charters, most datable between 977 and 992, show that this provision was almost always included. Thus the association of St Mary as patron of Worcester cathedral, the date 964, and the coming of the monks does not depend on the testimony of one dubious charter. There can be no doubt that the re-dedication of Worcester cathedral to St Mary does date from the time of Oswald.

There is little so far that I did not say thirty years ago,[26] but the re-dedication of the cathedral and the likelihood that 964 was a significant year in the history of Worcester have been ignored in the subsequent discussions. Though, as Robinson pointed out, the witness-lists of the charters fail to provide evidence of a purge of the Worcester community in 969, the situation is rather different if one looks at them with the date 964 in mind. Between 963 and 966 seven witnesses disappear (four of them regulars) and seven new ones appear. The fact that seven went and seven came must suggest this was not natural wastage. Sawyer, whilst not disputing the figures, thinks them inadequate to constitute a purge.[27] But nobody knows how large the original community at Worcester was; and it is likely that only the senior members served as witnesses. The testament in the *Vita Oswaldi* that a great council was held at Winchester by King Edgar should also be examined here. It seems likely that this was convoked as a consequence of Æthelwold's expulsion of clerks from his cathedral at Winchester and their replacement by monks. The clerks seem to have appealed, but Edgar went along with Æthelwold and decreed that all the lands of the English church should be held by monks. The council was most probably held at Easter 964. Now, given that the *Vita Oswaldi* was mainly interested in events at Worcester and Ramsey, the purge of Worcester (or mini-purge if preferred), the re-dedication of Oswald's *sedes* to St Mary, and the probable holding of a revolutionary council by Edgar form an arresting collocation.

Altitonantis states: 'Habeatque Winsinus reverendus sacerdos ipse episcopus Oswaldus me favente ac auctoritatem regiam prestante in sede episcopali monachis preposuit quandiu ipse viexerit prepositi fuerint.'[28] The charter is claiming that Edgar appointed a senior priest, Wynsige, as *prepositus* (a normal title for the second-in-command of a monastic community until Lanfranc introduced the title 'prior' that has prevailed ever since). The monks of Worcester

[24] 'Community of Worcester'.   [25] *Domesday Book and Beyond*, 268.
[26] 'The Beginning of the Benedictine Reform in England', *Orbis Britanniae*, 249–64.
[27] 'Charters of the Reform Movement', 92.
[28] '... Wynsige the reverend priest ... by my favour and royal authority was set to rule over the monks in the episcopal see so long as he might live ...'

were, for reasons that will presently become clear, very anxious to deny that Oswald ever ruled the cathedral community directly, preferring to have him do so through the intermediary of a *prepositus*. This seems to be false: although Wynsige was the first *prepositus* of Worcester, he was not appointed until Oswald became archbishop of York in 972. In an *actum* of 1092 making his peace with his monks, Bishop Wulfstan of Worcester would not accept that Wynsige had been made prior as part and parcel of the conversion of Worcester cathedral, as *Altitonantis* alleged. He did concede that Wynsige was elevated in 972 when Oswald was made archbishop of York in *commendam* with Worcester.

We must now consider further arguments that Sawyer adduced against the putative purge of 964. He pointed out that Oswald granted seventy-nine *læns* as bishop of Worcester, and seventy-one of these 'have lists of witnesses who were probably members of the community, and the implication is the witnesses were its consenting members. These are normally described as clerk, deacon, priest, or—rarely—monk.' Sawyer compared the witness-lists in 969 (when the series temporarily ceases) with those of 977 and after (when the series resumes, to continue until the end of the pontificate), and showed that over the years there was a steady increase of new names. However, this increase is neither puzzling nor problematic: its implication is surely that Oswald attracted new men to the community. It was not uncommon on the continent for something similar to happen. In the church of Liège it is possible not only to identify the increase, but also to show both that the new regime was cheaper to run than the old, so that more recruits could be supported, and that contemporaries knew this.[29]

Sawyer and others also seem to think that the fact that the members of the Worcester community were almost never called monks, but priests or deacons instead, is significant, and that it has implications for the nature of the Worcester community. Knowles remarked apropos this point in 1940: 'In England, however, where there was an ancient tradition of monastic priesthood, it would seem to have been usual by the time of Dunstan for the majority of the community to proceed to orders.'[30] Sawyer's position is that there was a dichotomy between monks on the one hand and priests and deacons on the other. The titles 'priest' or 'deacon' were—as a tenth-century Lady Bracknell might have said—bases from which a position in good society might be secured. I doubt if

---

[29] Surviving Liège sources show that increasing economy and prosperity made it possible for the community to expand. Prior Udalrich of Cluny's letter to Abbot Wilhelm of Hirsau advising him on how to reform his community after the fashion of Cluny suggests that this increase was not simply a consequence of reform but an essential part of the strategy. See E. John, '*Secularium Prioratus* and the Rule of St Benedict', *Revue Bénédictine*, 75 (1965), 212–39.

[30] The *Monastic Order in England* (Cambridge, 1940), 468. D. Bullough, 'St Oswald: Monk, Bishop and Archbishop', in *St Oswald of Worcester*, ed. Brooks and Cubitt, 1–22 at 14, writes: 'The "gradualism" of Oswald, proposed by Dean Armitage Robinson and canonized by Sir Frank Stenton in contrast to Æthelwold's ruthlessness was challenged by Mr Eric John, whose alternative reading of a total change c. 964 unexpectedly commended itself to Professor David Knowles, when he revised his monumental *Monastic Order in England* in 1963.' Might it not be the case that he remembered what he wrote in 1940, which none of the other protagonists to the debate have?

the word *monachus* had much of a cachet in Oswald's day, although it is abundantly plain that the monastic life (as the great monk-bishops presented it and the Rule of St Benedict prescribed it) had an attraction for some young Englishmen and their families. Knowles pointed out that Archbishop Lanfranc required monks to be referred to by their clerical grades, and he was obviously not innovating here[31]—as the passage from *The Monastic Order* quoted above underlines. The *Liber Vitae* of the New Minster Winchester suggests that tenth-century Winchester practice was much the same as Worcester's, and that the Winchester monks were normally referred to by their clerical grades.[32] No one is going to argue that Winchester was a mixed community: yet if Sawyer's argument were applied to Winchester, it would suggest that the community was totally composed of non-monastic, secular clergy!

Perhaps the most important point here is that after 969 almost every witness-list is headed by Wynsige, who, though undoubtedly a monk, is almost always called 'priest'. Then a man called Æthelstan 'priest', who had hitherto witnessed immediately after Wynisge, took over as chief witness, sometimes with the title *primus*. A community ruled by a prior, *prepositus*, or *primus* is what most of us call a monastery.[33] Wynsige and Æthelstan were certainly monks, and it seems likely that the priests and deacons who follow them were also monks.

The *Altitonantis* charter confers another privilege on the new monks, to the effect that if they find themselves unjustly hurt or oppressed they may apply to the king or the archbishop for redress. This is not a general right for the church of Worcester but one for the monks alone. They are given the right to appeal to the king and the archbishop against Oswald. At first sight this seems preposterous, but the wording seems to suggest it was a right for future use. It is unlikely that anyone expected trouble in Oswald's day (although in fact it came); however, the monks had challenged the status quo, and it made sense to anticipate that the status quo might one day strike back, and to provide the monks with some means of defence.

Although it is not possible to claim that this was a genuine privilege granted by Edgar to Oswald, it was certainly in existence—and used—at an early date. It could not have been devised when the charter was written in the middle of the twelfth century, because by that time the forum for this sort of dispute was Rome and the papal curia.[34] At some point in William's reign the monks made an appeal to the king that must have been, in part, aimed against Bishop

---

[31] *The Monastic Constitutions of Lanfranc*, ed. M. D. Knowles (London, 1961), 112.

[32] *The Liber Vitae of the New Minster and Hyde Abbey Winchester*, ed. S. D. Keynes, EEMF 26 (Copenhagen, 1996).

[33] The title 'prior' seems to have been first introduced at Canterbury by Lanfranc: see Gervase of Canterbury, *Opera*, ed. W. Stubbs, RS 73, 2 vols. (London, 1879–80), II, 361; and cf. Lanfranc, *Monastic Constitutions*, ed. Knowles, 75.

[34] The first bull protecting the community's rights and property is *The Cartulary of Worcester Cathedral Priory*, ed. R. R. Darlington, Pipe Roll Soc. (London, 1962–3), no. 80, dated 1136–43. It is not the first bull of its kind, merely the first Worcester bull.

Wulfstan. The terminal dates for this appeal are 1066–80, when Prior Ælfstan of Worcester (Wulfstan's brother) gave way to Prior Thomas; and Darlington thought it was made early in the Conqueror's reign. The writ was granted in the interest of the monks, and Bishop Wulfstan and the sheriff of Worcester (Urse d'Abetot) are named:[35] the sheriff had no authority over Worcester's churches and tithes. Yet though the monks had plenty of complaints against the sheriff, the writ can scarcely have been aimed only or mainly at him. It reads: 'omnes suas consuetudines seu dignitates que ad ipsum prioratum pertinent in terris, ecclesiis, decimis seu ceteris possessionibus tam ecclesiasticiis quam secularis . . . et nolo, ut aliquis se intromittat de rebus monachorum nisi per priorem ecclesie.'[36] The amount of forgery—the *Altitonantis* charter, the Worcester Latin Chronicle, and the two charters of 969—which sought to show that the installation of a *prepositus* was part and parcel of the initial conversion of the cathedral community suggests a prolonged controversy over the respective powers of bishop and prior. When St Wulfstan became bishop of Worcester he seems to have retained the powers that he had hitherto had as prior.[37] In 1092, realizing he was nearing the end of his life, Wulfstan summoned a synod that issued a solemn *actum* resolving the dispute between himself and his monks, almost entirely in the latter's favour. This *actum* throws important light on what happened in the initial conversion of Worcester, and to it we must now turn.[38]

---

[35] *Worcester Cartulary*, ed. Darlington, no. 2 esp. p. 7, n. 1 for the date. Unlike the right of appeal granted to the monks in *Altitonantis*, the archbishop is not mentioned. This is easily explained if the writ were issued before 1070 and the deposition of Archbishop Stigand. Darlington thought the writ was 'a confirmation of that of Edward the Confessor (Harmer, *Writs*, no. 116)'; and he based his rejection of my interpretation of the *actum* of 1092 on this and on complete silence about the myriad forgeries designed to prove that the monks held their rights completely independent of the bishop. His claim is false. The Confessor's writ is addressed to both the bishop and Earl Ælfgar and grants to the monk Ælfstan: 'that he be entitled to his sake and soke and to toll and team over his land and his men within town and without.' What Darlington thought was a mere confirmation addressed to both bishop and sheriff reads: 'Know that I have conceded to Ælfstan dean and the monks of Worcester all their customs and their dignities that pertain to that authority in land, churches, and tithes and the rest of their property both ecclesiastical and secular.' The Confessor's writ was solely concerned with secular property and the monks' authority over it; the Conqueror's writ adds an ecclesiastical dimension to the grant: 'churches and tithes.' It seems obvious that the ecclesiastical dimension takes precedence here. The Confessor used what was becoming a standard formula (sake and soke, etc.) which had a purely secular implication; the Conqueror did not. The sheriff had at best a minor 'back-up' role where churches and tithes were concerned. It is to be noted that the Conqueror calls Ælfstan 'dean', though the body of the document does refer to a *prioratus*. Again this argues, as Darlington thought, for an early date for the writ before Lanfranc's new title of prior had taken effect.

[36] 'All their customs and dignities which pertain to their authority in lands, churches, and tithes or the rest of their possessions both ecclesiastical and secular . . . and I am unwilling that anyone should intrude into the goods of the church except through the prior of the church.'

[37] *Vita Wulfstani*, ed. R. R. Darlington, Camden Soc., 40 (London, 1928), p. xxxviii.

[38] Although the original text survived until the late seventeenth century at least and was edited by H. Wharton, *Anglia Sacra*, I (London, 1691), 542–3; cf. *English Historical Documents*, II, 1042–189, ed. D. C. Douglas and G. Greenaway, 2nd edn. (London, 1981), no. 85; it has since been lost. The most convenient edition is *Worcester Cartulary*, ed. Darlington, no. 52. Wharton's text is better but Darlington had to print the cartulary version he was editing (he gives a list of variant readings from Wharton).

The *actum* tells us that Wulfstan ordered a synod to be held at the monastery of St Mary. He summoned all the wisest people of the three shires that comprised the diocese of Worcester to give evidence on the matters that were under dispute. The immediate occasion seems to have been a disagreement between the Worcester priests Ælfnoth (incumbent of St Helen's) and Alam (incumbent of St Alban's) concerning their parishes and their customary rights. Wulfstan says he ordered certain well-informed elders to declare the truth about the ancient constitution of the two parishes in question, as also about that of all the parishes in the city of Worcester. The monks complained that they had suffered loss of revenues owing to a long-standing controversy between Ælfnoth and Alam. The elders all affirmed 'nullum esse parochiam in tota urbe nisi tantum matris aecclesiae. Ecclesiam vero sanctae Helenae vicariam hujus matris aecclesiae extitisse' from the time of King Æthelred of Mercia (ruled 674/5–704). Archbishop Theodore then went on to found the see of Worcester and established Bosel as its first bishop.[39] This situation remained unchanged until the time of Archbishop Oswald who, with the mandate of King Edgar and the authority of St Dunstan, 'de irregulari conversatione clericorum in regularem conversationem et habitum monachorum transtulit et mutavit hujus ecclesiae congregationem anno domini incarnationis 969'.[40]

In the time of Oswald[41] Wynsige was the vicar of St Helen's, the most prestigious church in Worcester after the cathedral, which also dated back to the creation of the diocese. Advised by Oswald ('advised' is probably too weak a word here), Wynsige renounced the world. He assumed the garb of monastic discipline

et claves ecclesiae sanctae Helenae, quarum ipse, sicut vicarius extiterit cum terris, decimis ceterisque redditibus ad communem usum monachorum reddidit. Winso proinde monacho facto cum ceteris qui secum sponte elegerunt converti, tam supradicta ecclesia, quam ceterae quae nunc usque monachorum sunt, ecclesiae, terrae, decimae sepulturae vel quelibet aliae consuetudines seu dignitates ecclesiasticae quae clericorum quasi propria hactenus extiterit in jus monachorum tunc transierunt et in communem usum illorum redactae sunt.[42]

---

[39] 'The elders all affirmed that there was no parish in the whole city except only the mother church. The church, to be sure, of St Helen existed as a subsidiary of this mother church.' Although Bede calls the ruler of the Hwicce 'king', it does sound as though there was an ancient degree of dependence between the kingdom of the Hwicce and Mercia.

[40] 'transferred and changed the community of this church from the irregular habits of clerks to the regular behaviour and habit of monks in the year of the Lord 969.'

[41] It is obvious from the documentation up to the *actum* of 1092 that there was never any doubt at Worcester that Oswald did create the cathedral monastery.

[42] 'He assumed the garb of monastic discipline; and the keys of the church of St Helen's of which he was formerly vicar with lands, tithes, and the rest of the incomings he handed over to the common use of monks. After Wynsige had become a monk (together with others who chose conversion of their own free will) both the aforesaid church and the rest of the churches, lands, tithes, burial fees, which now pertain to the monks or whatever other customs and ecclesiastical dignities had been in the hands of clerks as their own, now passed into the right of monks and were subject to their common use.'

This was done with the assent of Edgar, the blessed Dunstan, and the holy Oswald.

This long-windedness is not the mark of a repetitive literary style, but an indication of the importance the synod attached to the events narrated. According to the *actum*, the incumbent (*vicarius*) of St Helen's was Wynsige. This does not mean 'vicar' in the comparatively humble sense of stipendary priest that it acquired by the second half of the twelfth century.[43] Wynsige was plainly the incumbent in the full sense, with command of all the rights and revenues which he handed over to the cathedral community. Yet before we can accept this with confidence, we must consider Julia Barrow's arguments that the synod was mythical and the *actum* a fabrication dating from the mid-twelfth century, that is, from the same period as she supposes the *Altitonantis* charter to have been fabricated and written down.[44]

Barrow regards the very idea of a synod in 1092 as preposterous, though does not explain why. This allegedly mythical synod pronounced on matters at issue between the bishop and the community, offering very little comfort to the bishop. It did agree with him that Oswald did not appoint Wynsige *prepositus* at the same time as he monasticized the community, but on all the other considerations the community won hands down. The *actum* says the synod and all its works were instigated by St Wulfstan. Why did not his successors denounce it as a forgery and seek to recover the rights? Why did they ever surrender the rights in deference to a monastic forgery? But after Wulfstan's day I can find no evidence that the issues were ever raised again. Barrow refers with pride to the fact that she is the first scholar to question the *actum*'s authenticity; she admits she cannot prove with certainty that the *actum* was a forgery, and then proceeds to assume that it was.

Barrow never examines the document as a whole, and her case rests entirely on the use of just two words, *vicarius* and *diaconus*, in the *actum*. She assumes they were being employed in their mid- to late twelfth-century sense, which would be quite out of place in a document of 1092 (and this also seems to be the reason why the synod has to be declared mythical). But are the words being used in this later sense? Though Barrow quoted Cheney as saying, 'The process whereby large numbers of parish churches were appropriated by religious houses, which thereby became rectors of these churches and were required to appoint vicars to serve them, began only in the middle of the twelfth century', she has not done full justice to his position. For he cites no appropriation to a

[43] The Fourth Lateran Council required vicars to be paid £5 a year (with the implication that they had been getting considerably less), which shows how insignificant they were. Before the twelfth century *vicaria* had a wider meaning than it later merited. A useful example comes from Fleury in the time of Abbot Abbo. Arnulf, lord of Yèvre, claimed rights as *vicaria* over an estate Fleury held at Yèvre. (Mostert, *The Political Theology of Abbo of Fleury* (Hilversum, 1987), 39). It seems to mean the same as *advocatia*. Lord Arnulf was supposed to render services to Fleury as vicar and advocate, but in practice the offices were merely an excuse to claim fees from the monks.

[44] 'How the Twelfth-Century Monks at Worcester Perceived their Past', 60–9.

vicarage before 1182–4, while the earliest reference to a rural dean at Canterbury is dated 1181–3.[45] Though it might be argued (improbably) that Canterbury and the cathedral community were late-developers in this matter, the Worcester Cartulary does not suggest that Worcester was any quicker off the mark than the southern archbishopric. There is only one charter of appropriation before the reign of Henry III; this is for St Helen's church itself and can be dated 1214–5.[46] The grantor of the charter was the reigning bishop of Worcester, Walter de Gray. He mentions Oswald's dedication of his cathedral to St Mary, and says:

Noverit igitur universitas vestra nos autenticum scriptum sanctisimi confessoris Wlstani sepius inspexisse per quod ecclesia sancte Elene in Wigorn' cum pertinentiis eiusdem ecclesie monachis Wigorn' in usus proprios conceditur et auctoritate pontificalis confirmatur. [Bishop Walter then by his own episcopal authority:] ecclesiam predictam sancte Helen in Wigorn' cum omnibus que ad ipsam pertinent dilectis filiis nostris in Christo prior Wigorn' et eiudem loci conventui in proprios usus convertandam concessimus et confirmavimus. Salva vicaria honesta et competenti ad valentiam quincedim marcarum . . .[47]

In other words Walter de Gray, relying on Wulfstan's 'treaty' with his monks, points out that they have since Wulfstan's time enjoyed the use of the church and its revenues. He now authorizes them to convert all these to their own uses, but they must appoint a vicar and pay him fifteen marks a year. It would seem, then, that the incumbent of St Helen's did not become a vicar in Dr Barrow's sense until the end of John's reign.

It is much more likely that the author of the *actum* is using neither *vicaria* nor *decanus* in the late twelfth-century sense. The *actum* reveals that St Helen's had, since the time of the first bishop of Worcester, been dependent on the mother church—that is, the cathedral—and this dependence was denoted by the term *vicaria*. It is perfectly plain that Wynsige's position as incumbent was utterly different from that of the vicar of St Helen's after 1214–15. He was not a stipendiary: his preferment was given him by the church of Worcester, while his income came from the revenues of St Helen's. It is less clear what the *actum* means by *decanus*. The problem is that in pre-conquest documents the head of a monastic community is sometimes called *decanus*.[48] The *actum* speaks of the prior *summus decanus episcopi*. The dean is given precedence over the

[45] *English Episcopal Acta II: Canterbury 1162–90*, ed. C. R. Cheney and B. E. A. Jones (Oxford, 1986), nos. 66 and 50.

[46] *Cartulary of Worcester*, ed. Darlington, no. 57.

[47] 'All you therefore know we have frequently inspected the authentic writing of the most holy confessor Wulfstan by which the church of St Helen in Worcester with what pertains to the same church is granted and confirmed to the monks of the same church of Worcester for converting to their own use, . . . saving an honest and adequate vicar at a salary of fifteen marks.'

[48] In the Conqueror's writ, discussed above, Ælfstan is called dean of Worcester, although his power is expressed as a *prioratus*; I think here *prioratus* simply means authority. This is a good example of the problem of nomenclature in a time of fluidity about titles.

archdeacon in another section. It hardly seems that rural deans were part of the picture.

St Odo of Cluny put the programme of the reformers succinctly. He wanted monks to live chastely, to abstain from meat, and hold all their property in common.[49] That Odo must have had some influence over the English reformers is scarcely in doubt. He himself had in some sort reformed Fleury, and the importance of Fleury for the English reformers is well known.[50] Odo's first two provisos present no problems—you either live chastely and abstain from meat or you do not—but it is not so obvious what holding property in common actually entailed. How this was interpreted at Cluny has yet to be elucidated. The evidence from Worcester, more than any other English community, gives some idea of what was involved.

After the conquest it becomes apparent that monastic property was divided between two property-holding corporations, called the *mensa* of the abbot and the *mensa* of the monks.[51] The individual estates that comprised the bulk of these *mensae* were said to be held *ad usum monachorum* or *ad usum abbatis*; in a monastic cathedral the abbot's portion would be held *ad usum episcopi* or *presulis*. Though it was once thought that this was a post-conquest development, part of the feudalization of monastic property, this was not the case.[52] Returning to Wynsige, the *actum* says that he handed over the keys of his church, St Helen's—which is plainly assumed to imply the transfer of every form of revenue to the community. The other members of that community (who, it is stressed, had also chosen to become monks of their own free will) did likewise. The property which had been held in severalty under the old order was now held in common by the new monks: a concrete example of what Odo meant in his prescriptions.

In the third year after Wynsige had become a monk Oswald made him *prepositus* over Worcester. This is perfectly plausible: in 972 Oswald had been appointed archbishop of York as well as bishop of Worcester, so a local head was clearly necessary. Wynsige was either summoned back from Ramsey (where, we know, he received his monastic education) or, if the foundation of that house was nearer 964, he might have been *in situ* already. As *prepositus* (according to the *actum*), he was in charge of the lands, burial rights, and other ecclesiastical perquisites that had passed into the hands of the monks who now occupied the mother church. What had formerly been held in severalty was now held in common: there was in existence probably from 972, and certainly before the conquest,[53] what would be later called a *mensa*.

---

[49] John of Salerno, *Vita Odonis*: PL 133, col. 81.

[50] John Nightingale, 'Oswald, Fleury and Continental Reform', in *St Oswald of Worcester*, ed. Brooks and Cubitt, 23–45 at 23–4.

[51] Knowles, *Monastic Order*, 173 and 614.

[52] E. John, 'The Division of the Mensa in Anglo-Saxon England', *JEH* 9 (1958). In that article I overlooked the strongest piece of evidence: *Writs*, ed. Harmer, 116.

[53] *Writs*, ed. Harmer, 116.

What was at issue in 1092, then, emerges. Oswald, Wulfstan agrees, had granted to Wynsige and subsequent priors of the church of Worcester that they should be dean over all their churches and priests; no one could intervene in this small but significant clerical empire unless through the prior. The prior must, however, pay all ecclesiastical customs that were due to the bishop. When Wulfstan was promoted from prior to bishop he retained many, if not all, of the powers of the prior. The newly elected prior, Ælfstan, was awarded the conventional rights over the lands of the monks expressed in what was to become a common formula 'sake and soke', and these do not seem to have been disputed. By the end of Wulfstan's pontificate, however, the ecclesiastical patronage appears to have been at issue; and the conflict between prior and bishop was exemplified by the dispute over their oldest church, St Helen's. This is what their quarrel with Alam, incumbent of St Alban's, was about—assuming that he was the archdeacon.[54] The archdeacon was presumably trying to exercise rights over St Helen's and, probably, other Worcester churches. But as the oldest and most prestigious of their holdings, St Helen's signified the rights of the monks over all their churches.

The *actum* says that the monks were basically in the right. The members of the synod declared that these were their rights both in Wulfstan's day and in that of his predecessor, Ealdred; and between 1066 and 1080 (probably nearer the former) the monks obtained a writ that guaranteed these rights which, they claimed, came from Oswald. Now, only the bishop could have infringed what the monks called their *consuetudines*. One of the rights the monks were claiming was the power to appoint the incumbent of St Helen's. The admission by the wise men that the monks were only claiming their due, and Wulfstan's tardy acceptance of these claims, point to the early years of Wulfstan's pontificate as the likely date for the forgeries that were designed to show that Wynsige's appointment as *prepositus* was part of the original conversion of the community. After Wulfstan had accepted the main part of the monks' claims, the circumstances of Wynsige's appointment became academic at Worcester and the question does not seem to have been raised again.

The wise men seemed to concede that when Oswald converted his cathedral community he created the *mensa* of the monks—though they did not use this not especially common term. Were they right? Let us note first that their knowledge is convincingly detailed. They thought that Oswald took the holdings which the existing community owned in severalty and communalized them, thus fulfilling the third of Odo of Cluny's prescriptions. Such a programme was probably dictated by circumstances: Oswald was not pursuing a

---

[54] That archdeacons could be rectors of churches is shown by *English Episcopal Acta*, III, ed. C. R. Cheney and E. John (Oxford, 1986), no. 394. The difficulty remains that an archdeacon of Worcester called Ailric was named in the *actum* as one of the seniors consulted by Wulfstan. E. Mason, *St Wulfstan of Worcester*, (Oxford, 1990), 165, n. 38, suggests that there was more than one archdeacon of Worcester in Wulfstan's day.

programme of radical confiscation; and the new monks now simply possessed communally what they had before held as individual prebends. Some confirmation is offered by Domesday Book, read in conjunction with Oswald's *læns*. In 1086 the Domesday clerks found it necessary to distinguish the estates that pertained *as usum abbatis* or *episcopi* from those that pertained *ad usum monachorum*. The earliest trace of this terminology is found in Oswald's *læns*. Many of these were granted to laymen to help Oswald fulfil his obligations to the king as *archiductor* of Worcester. They were mostly granted for three lives and then returned to the *mensa* of the bishop. It is difficult to avoid the conclusion that Oswald did convert his cathedral community into a monastery, and that the consequences were still reverberating two centuries later.[55]

[55] The text for this chapter, on which Eric John was working in the last months of his life, was left in some disarray, and was revised to its present form by R.G. Had its author lived longer, the result would doubtless have been more finely tuned.

12

UNITY, ORDER, AND OTTONIAN KINGSHIP
IN THE THOUGHT OF ABBO OF FLEURY[1]

Alison Peden

At the turn of the year 996–7 the emperor Otto III asked Gerbert of Aurillac, in exile at the imperial court from the archbishopric of Reims, to 'fan our spirit with the flame of your knowledge' and to 'explain to us the book on arithmetic'—the de luxe copy of Boethius, *De Arithmetica* made for Charles the Bald which Gerbert is thought to have presented to Otto.[2] It is not just the academic interests of the young emperor that are notable, but also their implications for our understanding of the Ottonian vision of political unity and imperial order. Henry Mayr-Harting has demonstrated the fundamental importance of art as an articulation of Ottonian reflection on the regime;[3] his new work on the scholarship of Cologne shows that engagement with the liberal arts was considered a vital element of rulership of any kind: lordship over a part of the cosmos requires understanding of its structure, values, and ultimate destiny. Thus liberal arts studies are a valid source for the concerns and perspectives which directed the thinking of church leaders, the court, and the emperor himself.[4]

To some extent we have here another example of the well-recognized Ottonian refinement of Carolingian tradition. Since the time of Alcuin the terms *potestas* and *sapientia* (defined in terms of the seven liberal arts) had been closely connected in political thought, and the link had been developed in the court circle of Charles the Bald, for whom Solomon was the ideal model.[5] Perhaps influenced by this continental perspective, Asser reported that King Alfred had

---

[1] This paper was inspired by the Edwards Lecture given by Professor Henry Mayr-Harting at the University of Glasgow on 1 February 1996. I have also profited from discussions of earlier versions of it at the Denys Hay Seminar at Edinburgh University and at the Centre for Medieval and Renaissance Studies at Glasgow University.

[2] *Die Briefsammlung Gerberts von Reims* no. 186, ed. F. Weigle, MGH Die Briefe der deutschen Kaiserzeit II (Berlin, Zurich, and Dublin, 1966), 222; cf. F. Mütherich, 'The Library of Otto III' in *The Role of the Book in Medieval Culture*, ed. P. Ganz, 2 vols. (Turnhout, 1986), II, 11–25; here 20–1.

[3] H. Mayr-Harting, *Ottonian Book Illumination: An Historical Study*, 2 vols. (London, 1991).

[4] H. Mayr-Harting, 'Ruotger, the Life of Bruno and Cologne Cathedral Library', in *Intellectual Life in the Middle Ages: Essays Presented to Margaret Gibson*, ed. L. Smith and B. Ward (London and Rio Grande, 1992), 33–60.

[5] Alcuin, *De Grammatica*: PL 101, col. 853; id., *Epistolae* 121, 170, ed. E. Dümmler, MGH Epistolae Karolini Aevi IV (Berlin, 1895), 177, 279; cf. N. Staubach, *Rex Christianus. Hofkultur und Herrschaftspropaganda im Reich Karls des Kahlen* II (Cologne, Weimar, and Vienna, 1993), 9–15, 105–97, 221–53.

bewailed the fact that he had been created 'lacking in divine learning and knowledge of the liberal arts'.[6] The whole discourse on wisdom was elevated in neoplatonic terms by John Scottus, who argued for the king's cosmic and mediatory role in the providential procession of creation and its ultimate reversion to God (*processio* and *reditus*).[7] He was drawing on sources which unequivocally claimed a numerical, ordered structure for the universe. Boethius had asserted that mathematical reasoning was 'the original pattern in the mind of the creator', and that understanding of it was the basis of all wisdom.[8] Order and unity in the cosmos, studied mathematically, would provide not just a model for earthly programmes of rule, but an understanding of the larger whole of which all kingdoms should be integrated parts.

The pursuit of wisdom is set firmly in the context of the seven liberal arts in a poem found in a ninth-century manuscript from Fleury: Wisdom sits on a throne in a seven-columned palace, weighing all things by numbers, dividing, joining, and measuring. Unity and God stand at the origin of numbers and creation; there is one God, one baptism, one truth, one faith.[9] This was precisely the thrust of Abbo of Fleury's thought in the second half of the tenth century. As scholar, teacher, and then abbot (from 988 to 1004) at St Benoît-sur-Loire, he was able to infuse his vision of the church with a knowledge of the arts that he had built up steadily from his youth.[10] The most impressive display of his mastery of them was made in his *Commentary on the Calculus of Victorius of Aquitaine*, which probably dates from the early 980s, just before his spell as a teacher at Ramsey Abbey (985–7).[11] Victorius' *Calculus*, written in the mid-fifth century, was a set of multiplication tables for integers and fractions from × 2 to × 50, prefaced by a brief discussion of the fact that unity is indivisible, but that everything else is composite and divisible. Later, tables of subtraction and addition, square numbers, proportions of different fractions, and notes on weights and measures were added.[12] Abbo's aim was not just to expound the arithmetic of the tables, but to show that their numerical patterns revealed the

[6] Asser, *De Rebus Gestis Aelfredi*, 76, ed. W. H. Stevenson (Oxford, 1904), 60; cf. A. Scharer, 'The Writing of History at King Alfred's Court', *Early Medieval Europe*, 5:2 (1996), 177–206; here 196.

[7] Staubach, *Rex Christianus*, 91–104.

[8] Boethius, *De Arithmetica* I.2, ed. G. Friedlein (Leipzig, 1867), 12.16–17: 'Hoc enim fuit principale in animo conditoris exemplar.'

[9] Bern, Burgerbibliothek, 358, fols. 56–7, ed. K. Strecker, MGH Poetae Latini Medii Aevi IV.1 (Berlin, 1899), 249; cf. M. Mostert, *The Library of Fleury: A Provisional List of Manuscripts* (Hilversum, 1989), 74.

[10] Haimo, *Vita Abbonis*: PL 139, cols. 387–414; P. Cousin, *Abbon de Fleury-sur-Loire* (Paris, 1954).

[11] My edition is forthcoming with the British Academy; references will be given to the section and paragraph numbers of the edition, and to the text in Berlin, Deutsche Staatsbibliothek, MS. Phill. 1833 (*s.* x^ex, Fleury) (hereafter **F**). Cf. G. R. Evans and A. M. Peden, 'Natural Science and the Liberal Arts in Abbo of Fleury's Commentary on the Calculus of Victorius of Aquitaine', *Viator*, 16 (1985), 109–27.

[12] Partial editions in G. Friedlein, 'Victorii Calculus ex codice Vaticano editus', *Bulletino di Bibliografia e di Storia delle Scienze Matematiche e Fisiche*, 4 (1871), 443–63; id., 'Der Calculus des Victorius', *Zeitschrift für Mathematik und Physik*, 16 (1871), 42–79.

order of creation and thus something of the mind of God. His *Commentary* is subtitled 'Tractatus de numero, mensura et pondere', and this signals the text which determined Abbo's perspective: 'God created all things according to number, measure, and weight' (Wisdom 11.21). The text was well-cited by Abbo's time,[13] but in his *Commentary*—probably reflecting the influence of one of Abbo's major sources, the *De Statu Animae* of the fifth-century Claudianus Mamertus[14]—it gives a contemplative depth to what could have been a dry liberal arts treatise. The love of wisdom, he says, draws us 'from visible things through invisible ones to the ineffable unity of the Trinity'. Quoting Claudianus, he claims that 'the pattern of the unity of the Trinity' (*unitae specimen Trinitatis*) is present from the top to bottom: in God, who is supremely one and three; in the soul, whose triple powers of memory, intellect, and will judge, and so in some way become susceptible of (*capax existit*) threefold number, measure, and weight; and in corporeal things, in which number, measure, and weight are also present.[15]

Victorius, then, set the agenda for Abbo: to reveal the relationship between unity and plurality, between the source and principle of number and the corporeal and incorporeal things in which number may be found. This involved an investigation not only of unity but also of order, both arithmetical and cosmological. Abbo's sense of a conceptual and actual order permeating all things was deep and imaginative. He delighted in its visual manifestation in the tables of the *Calculus*, just as he did in his arrangement of *computus* data.[16] However, the authority he claimed for his perception of order rested on the value and power he attributed to unity.

Abbo conceived of unity in the Boethian sense, as the source of all number but not number itself, an abstract form which is the principle of measure, grasped only by reason.[17] Moreover, unity is the source of all being, in that the existence of things is inseparable from their unity: it is what enables them to 'be'.[18] Arithmetically this is shown in the way that unity prevents the division of

---

[13] I. Peri, '*Omnia mensura et numero et pondere disposuisti*: die Auslegung von Weish. 11,21 in der lateinischen Patristik', in *Mensura. Mass, Zahl, Zahlensymbolik im Mittelalter*, ed. A. Zimmermann, I (Berlin and New York, 1983), 1–21; it was cited by Abbo's pupil, Byrthferth of Ramsey, in his *Enchiridion*, I.1, ed. P. S. Baker and M. Lapidge (Oxford, 1995), 8.90; cf. S. C. McCluskey, *Astronomies and Cultures in Early Medieval Europe* (Cambridge, 1998), 154.

[14] Claudianus Mamertus, *De Statu Animae*, II. 4, ed. A. Engelbrecht, CSEL 11 (Vienna, 1885), III.5–6.

[15] *Commentary*, II.7, 16; **F**, fols. 8r, col. b: 'amor sapientiae . . . a visibilibus per invisibilia ad inennarrabilem Trinitatis unitatem consurgit'; and 9r, cols. a–b; cf. Claudianus Mamertus, *De Statu Animae*, II.6, ed. Engelbrecht, 119.5–25.

[16] F. Wallis, 'Images of Order in the Medieval *Computus*', in *Acta XV: Ideas of Order in the Middle Ages*, ed. W. Ginsberg (Binghamton, 1990), 45–68; here 54–7.

[17] *Commentary*, III.5, 30; **F**, fols. 9v, col. b, 12v, col. b; cf. Boethius, *De arithmetica*, I. 7,16; II.1, ed. Friedlein, 16.18–26, 33.6–7; 79.24–5; Macrobius, *Commentarii in Somnium Scipionis*, I.6.7–8, ed. J. Willis (Leipzig, 1970), 19.24–31.

[18] *Commentary*, III.3; **F**, fol. 9v, col. a; cf. Boethius, *Contra Eutychen*, IV, ed. E. K. Rand and S. J. Tester, *The Theological Tractates* (London and Cambridge, Mass., 1973), 94.36–9; id., *Commentum II in Isagogen*, I.10, ed. G. Schepss and S. Brandt, CSEL 48 (1906), 162.2–3.

odd numbers: Abbo shows how you cannot divide seventeen in half without using fractions, because there is a 'one' on either side of the two eights.[19] Unity preserves the existence of odd numbers from division and change, and so maintains 'sameness', the constant, defined quality associated with eternity and God, as opposed to the divisible, changeable, and mortal nature of 'difference', found in even numbers.[20] Unity was thus charged with supreme metaphysical value.

The power of unity was manifested by its generating of the dynamic procession of numbers and creation and its drawing them back to itself. Plato had established an intimate connection between number and the cosmos in the *Timaeus*, in which harmonic ratios were said to be woven into the World Soul, which shaped matter. Abbo used Calcidius' exposition of this text to demonstrate the flow of numbers like a river from unity, 'understood as Mind or Intelligence or God himself'.[21] Ordered multiplicity resulted from this creative dynamic, of which the arithmetical evidence was not just an image, but a constitutive part. In Abbo's view, saying that all numbers were generated from unity was another way of saying that God created all things.[22]

For Abbo, as for his neoplatonic sources, unity was not only the source of all number and creation but also its goal: multiplicity and otherness must be gathered back into oneness. Plurality is reduced to unity, Abbo declared, through its ordering according to number, measure, and weight.[23] Just as order was revealed in the systematic generation of multiples and ratios, so order was paramount in the resolution of such composites. Abbo was inspired by Boethius to demonstrate this arithmetically in tables showing that 'inequalities' such as multiples, superparticulars (e.g. $1\frac{1}{2}:1$), superpartients (e.g. $1\frac{2}{3}:1$), and so on could be systematically produced from three equal terms, and then the numbers so generated reduced back to equality by reversing the formula.[24] The point Abbo stressed was the regularity and order of the process: each type of inequality is generated in one way alone; they are not mixed up in a disorderly fashion. The resolution of these composites from one type to the next also proceeds according to the sequence and nature of their generation.[25] These are

[19] *Commentary*, III.11; **F**, fol. 10v, cols. a–b.

[20] Cf. Boethius, *De Arithmetica*, II.28, 31–2, ed. Friedlein, 117.26–119.11; 122.24–126.17; A. White (Peden), 'Boethius in the Medieval Quadrivium', in *Boethius: his Life, Thought and Influence*, ed. M. T. Gibson (Oxford, 1981), 162–205; here 177.

[21] *Commentary*, III.1; **F**, fol. 9r, col. a: '. . . mens sive intelligentia vel ipse Deus intelligi posset'; cf. Calcidius, *Commentarius in Timaeum*, XXXII, XXXIX, ed. J. H. Waszink (London and Leiden, 1962), 82, 88.12–89.2; Plato, *Timaeus*, 35a–37c.

[22] Cf. *Commentary*, III.3; **F**, fol.9v, col. a: '. . . qui investigans naturam unitatis praetendit rationem mundani principii.'

[23] *Commentary*, III.6; **F**, fol. 10r, col. a: 'Pluralitas eorum hac concordia ad unitatem reducitur quia numeri, mensurae et ponderis aequo examine dispensatur.'

[24] *Commentary*, III.20–7; **F**, fols. 11v, col. b–12r, col. b; Boethius, *De Arithmetica*, I.32; II.1, ed. Friedlein, 66.18–72.19; 77.1–79.28. Cf. White, 'Boethius', 170.

[25] *Commentary*, III.22; **F**, fol.11v, col. b: 'Et quid mirum si diversorum generum species non vulgo nec confuse permiscentur sibi in procreationis serie, cum nec unius generis nisi multiplicis ex se invicem prodire possint?'

composites made by 'will', but Abbo points out that 'natural' composites display the same ordered progression, such as the moon's cycle from new to full to new again every twenty-eight days.[26] The power and value of this cyclical ordering by number, measure, and weight was that it both drew what was divisible and changeable back to unity and sameness, and also represented that sameness and eternity in a repeatable figure. Similarly, Faith Wallis has shown that Abbo's innovation in the study of the *computus* was to recast the data as great cycles which proceed out and back with measured steps, immune from the irregularities of linear historical time.[27] It was part of his whole enterprise of presenting the cosmos and its order as the object of contemplation in the quest for wisdom.

The fundamental assumption of this enterprise was that wisdom embraces all branches of knowledge and study, and so, just as Abbo draws on any art that may be appropriate to his immediate task, he also infuses all his works with a characteristic vision of unity and order—his own 'wisdom'. The timeless values he perceived in the structure and numerical order of the cosmos elevated his views of king, church, and society to the status of ideals which were nonetheless prescriptive. This gave depth to an otherwise conventional alignment of heavenly and earthly kingdoms in Abbo's works: wisdom prompts the exercise of virtues which strengthen and increase the earthly and heavenly kingdom (in the *Commentary*); piety makes the kingdom prosper in the present and leads the king to a better celestial realm (in the *Collectio Canonum*); while in his *Passio Sancti Edmundi*, Edmund (king of East Anglia) is confident that the King of Kings pities his fate as earthly ruler and will take him to rule in eternal life.[28] Ideal earthly rulership thus acquires a timeless quality by its orientation towards eternal values.

Abbo's inclination towards writing about eternal values (and lack of historical evidence about his subject) led him to portray King Edmund as an ascetic philosopher, only pushed at the last into a heroic warrior's death.[29] The king's detachment from the world of crisis and flux was mirrored in his outward form, pictured by Abbo in almost late-antique imperial terms: 'He had an appearance worthy of a ruler, which the tranquil devotion of his most serene heart

[26] *Commentary*, III.16; F, fol. 11r, cols. a–b; cf. Evans and Peden, 'Natural Science', 117–8.

[27] F. Wallis, 'Colours, Crosses, Acrostics: Abbo of Fleury as a Designer of Computus Tables', paper delivered to the Annual Meeting of the Medieval Academy of America, 30.3.95. I am most grateful to Professor Wallis for letting me see a draft of her paper. Cf. also Wallis, 'Images of Order', 57; E.-M. Engelen, *Zeit, Zahl und Bild. Studien zur Verbindung von Philosophie und Wissenschaft bei Abbo von Fleury* (Berlin and New York, 1993), 5–6; 36–8; 100.

[28] *Commentary* II.2; F, fol.7v, col. b: 'Haec disciplinabiliter moribus virtutum exercitia suggerit, quibus terrena et caelestis respublica augetur et crescit'; *Collectio Canonum*, III, PL 139, col. 478; *Passio Sancti Eadmundi*, 9, ed. M. Winterbottom, *Three Lives of English Saints* (Toronto, 1972), 78.37–9.

[29] *Passio*, Praefatio, 3–4, 8–9, ed. Winterbottom, 68.31–2; 70.9–71.19;74.23–78.42. Cf. M. Mostert, *The Political Theology of Abbo of Fleury* (Hilversum, 1987), 162–6, 189.

continually beautified.'[30] In Abbo's view, Edmund's ordered virtue was crowned by his virginity, the distinguishing mark of monks and the basis for their claim to head the social hierarchy.[31] Abbo wrote that Edmund's virginity ensured his miraculous corporeal incorruptibility after death, made even more remarkable by the discovery that his severed head had been reunited to his body, leaving only a thin red line as witness to his martyrdom.[32] Edmund was a 'man of integrity'; the Horatian phrase Abbo used, 'integer vitae',[33] would perhaps have had numerical resonance for him. Although neither he nor Boethius used the word *integer* as a noun to mean 'a whole number', it is found in this sense at least by the late eleventh or early twelfth century.[34] For Abbo, Edmund was 'one', a number which another Abbonian source, Macrobius, said was most aptly joined with the 'virgin' number, seven.[35] In his death he was brutally divided, but the power of his virginal 'integrity' brought him back to wholeness and unity. The term Abbo used for this was <*caput*> *redintegratum*, not perhaps an unusual word, but the very one he had used in the *Commentary* when describing the addition of fractions (after their subtraction) in a *Calculus* table.[36] Abbo had found a powerful solution to the problem of the defeated king in the unity of the ideal ruler himself, which could triumph over the fissile world of time.

In Abbo's thought, the ideal ruler guarantees the unity and order of society against the forces of division and confusion. This was principally for the interests of the church, and involved the whole body of Christians, which Abbo conceived as a hierarchy with well-defined aptitudes and responsibilities. Christian order dominates the first part of his *Liber Apologeticus*, written in 994 to King Hugh Capet and his son Robert, to explain the riots at St Denis over the proposed appropriation of monastic tithes by the bishops, which Abbo was alleged to have instigated, and to protest at his excommunication by Gerbert.[37] A clear distinction between the three orders (monastic, clerical, and lay) was, he felt, vital to the correct assignment of resources and powers, and especially the preservation of monastic tithes. When Abbo accused the bishops of 'tangling the lines' of the church's patrimony, and again when in a letter he accused them

[30] *Passio*, 3, ed. Winterbottom, 70.9–10: 'Nam erat ei species digna imperio, quam serenissimi cordis iugiter venustabat tranquilla devotio.'
[31] Abbo, *Liber Apologeticus*: PL 139, 463–5; cf. J. Batany, 'Abbon de Fleury et les théories des structures sociales vers l'an mil', in *Études ligériennes d'histoire et d'archéologie médiévales*, ed. R. Louis (Auxerre, 1975), 9–18; here 15.
[32] *Passio*. 14, 17, ed. Winterbottom, 82.1–14; 86.3–87.9.
[33] Ibid. 11, ed. Winterbottom, 79.6; cf. Horace, *Carmina*, I.22.1.
[34] In Ralph of Laon's *De Semitonio*, ed. A. M. Peden, '"De semitonio": Some Medieval Exercises in Arithmetic', *Studi Medievali*, 3rd series, 35 (1994), 367–403; here 391.
[35] Macrobius, *Commentarii*, I.6.10, ed. Willis, 20.12–15.
[36] *Passio*, 14, ed. Winterbottom, 82.4; F, fol. 17v, col. a: 'Hinc . . . de assibus ponderum minutias subtrahere curavit, et ita ad instituendum quid subtractum quid relictum sit, quadam disciplina collegit. Denique eodem tenore ipsas summas recolligens docuit ordinem redintegratae coacervationis iuxta subductas partes demonstratae recisionis.' Cf. P. Brown, *The Cult of the Saints* (Chicago, 1981), 79–85.
[37] Mostert, *Political Theology*, 48–51; Batany, 'Abbon', 9–10.

of wrongly diverting church endowments, he used the text from Proverbs 22.28: 'Do not overstep the boundaries which your forefathers set up.'[38] To a mind which delighted in the precise and regular order of numbers these words had particular force. In his *Commentary* Abbo pointed out how rare were 'perfect' numbers, that is, those which were exactly equal to the sum of their factors and did not exceed them. In the same way, he remarked, perfect men must take care lest they 'overstep the boundaries which the excellent rulers of the earthly state have set up'.[39] Christian order required limitation and stability, the 'sameness' which Abbo found in unity and odd numbers, not the shapeless infinity of disorder.[40]

Abbo thought that rulers had an urgent duty to maintain the distinctions of Christian society, not just to protect monastic rights, but to preserve the Church itself. He argued that the Church's unity (and therefore existence) depended on it not being wrongly appropriated by separate individuals for personal gain, for scripture proved that it belonged to Christ alone. Abbo maintained that it was not he who was heretical in his stance on church reform but the bishops, who had confounded lay and clerical boundaries and 'made worldly what is holy'.[41] As Marco Mostert has pointed out, contemporary exegesis of the text from Proverbs on boundaries interpreted it as an injunction not to stray from orthodox doctrine.[42] For Abbo, this meant not defying the correctly defined order of Christian society; transgress its boundaries in doctrine and deed and you will create that most dangerous fragmentation, heresy. This was his answer to those who accused church reformers themselves of attacking the Church; it would also provide an orthodox perspective on the anti-hierarchical heretics of northern France who appeared a generation later, much more insidious than simoniacal bishops.[43]

If the king's office was to defend the unity of the Church by temporal power, the pope was its spiritual guarantor; both served Christendom by co-operating in their tasks. The pope's spiritual authority was supreme, as head of the body of Christ, and so bishops were subordinate to his rulings.[44] Abbo had made this ordering to a single spiritual ruler a reality in his conflicts with Bishop Arnulf of Orléans, and with the archbishop of Reims. He refused an oath of fealty to the

[38] *Liber Apologeticus*: PL 139, col. 461; *Epistola* XIV: PL 139, col. 440. Cf. *Epistola* V: PL 139, col. 424, where Abbo used the same text to justify respect for papal authority.

[39] *Commentary*, III.18; **F**, fol. 11v, col. a: 'Quos tamen ubique obsessos circumvallant reliqui ceu adversarii, innotescentes neminem perfectum debere esse securum, qui nisi adeptis virtutibus circumspiciat, utrimque habet quo cadat, vel cessando a bono opere vel transgrediendo terminos quos posuerunt obtimi rectores mundanae reipublicae.'

[40] Cf. Boethius, *De Arithmetica*, I. 32, ed. Friedlein, 66.7–18.

[41] *Epistola*, XIV: PL 139, cols. 440–1: 'in templo Dei fit saeculare quod sanctum est'; *Liber Apologeticus*: PL 139, cols. 465–8.

[42] Mostert, *Political Theology*, 116.

[43] R. I. Moore, *The Origins of European Dissent* (London, 1977), 25–38; Batany, 'Abbon', 10–11, Mostert, *Political Theology*, 92–3.

[44] *Liber Apologeticus*: PL 139, col. 467; cf. Mostert, *Political Theology*, 124–9.

former, claiming to be subject to the pope alone, and denied the right of the Council of Verzy in 991 to depose the latter (another Arnulf), who had been accused of treacherous support for the Carolingians. Only the pope, Abbo maintained, had the power to remove him. Abbo held out against the appointment of his replacement, Gerbert, to the see for six years, only obtaining papal reinstatement of Arnulf in 997 when visiting Gregory V in person.[45] The pope, however, was in Spoleto, not Rome, having been driven out of the city by Crescentius, leader of the local aristocracy. Abbo responded to the crisis with a complex acrostic poem, *Otto Valens*, addressed to Otto III, who was campaigning against the Slavs on the eastern frontiers. He pleaded with Otto to return to Italy and be, like his father and grandfather, 'a champion in a perilous time' (l. 33: *diro sub tempore victor*).[46] Otto had been crowned emperor on 21 May 996, and the thrust of Abbo's poem is that his centre of gravity must now be Rome. The poem's new editor, Scott Gwara, suggests that when Abbo said he hoped Otto would be *tractabilis* (l. 28), he punned on its double sense 'peaceable' and 'able to be drawn (back)'.[47] Otto should leave the 'wars of an exile' (l. 26) and be drawn back to his birthright. Empires might expand to far frontiers, but their rulers must return to the centre to defend the unity of the Christian world.

The question of how far the needs of Rome should take priority over Germany was an issue of contemporary debate, and in this case a sharp dilemma for the likes of Gerbert.[48] It was part of a wider consideration of the nature of imperial rule, which touched all levels of Ottonian culture, from the chancery to the illuminations of Otto III's gospel books.[49] Henry Mayr-Harting has shown that the latter may well have been contemplated primarily by Otto III himself, in the profound reflection on his role for which his education and religious culture had fitted him.[50] Here was an emperor who seemed to take seriously the acquisition of wisdom through the liberal arts, including—and perhaps especially—arithmetic. He was particularly interested in the demonstration of Boethius' principle that inequalities were generated from three equal terms and resolved back into them, which (as shown above) Abbo had expounded in his *Commentary*. He seems to have obtained a version from Notker of Liège, and then acquired the clearer one which Gerbert had originally sent to Constantine of Fleury.[51] He may also have had a compilation of texts

---

[45] Mostert, *Political Theology*, 36, 46–8, 55–7.

[46] *Otto Valens*, ed. S. Gwara, 'Three Acrostic Poems by Abbo of Fleury', *Journal of Medieval Latin*, 1 (1991), 203–35; here 213–4, 228.

[47] Ibid. 231.

[48] *Epistola*, 219 (to Otto III), ed. Weigle, 260: 'Si Scythas relinquimus, metuo, si Italos non adimus, reformido.'

[49] T. Reuter, *Germany in the Early Middle Ages* (London and New York, 1991), 279–80; Mayr-Harting, *Ottonian Book Illumination*, I, 60–80, 105–25, 157–78.

[50] Mayr-Harting, *Ottonian Book Illumination*, I, 176–7.

[51] N. Bubnov, *Gerberti Opera Mathematica* (Berlin, 1899), 297, n. 1; texts: 297–9 (Notker); 32–5 (Gerbert); cf. White, 'Boethius', 169–71.

on the abacus made at a Lotharingian centre.[52] No doubt such an interest was at least partly inspired by Gerbert, who had retired from the struggle at Reims to the imperial court in 997. While he and Abbo were bitterly opposed in church politics (for all Abbo's declaration of continuing friendship[53]), they shared a vision of unity and order from their common use of Boethius. Gerbert traced the ordered growth of composites from unity and their resolution to their origins in arithmetic and geometry, and demonstrated it on the abacus. These disciplines opened the mind's eye to the nature of the cosmos, he argued, and so to God's wisdom itself.[54]

The court culture of Otto III would thus have been receptive to Abbo's thought. The timeless detachment of Abbo's ideal world of numbers or the suffering King Edmund is also a distinctive feature of the representation of kings in Ottonian art;[55] his concern with the ordering of the many to the one—however quixotic a notion in Ottonian political practice[56]—was to be found not only in Gerbert's mathematical writing but also in the measured procession (or perhaps return) of the four personified provinces to their one emperor in the famous illumination in the Reichenau Gospel Book of Otto III.[57] Finally, Abbo's orchestration of ideals of unity and order for the specific purposes of church reform resonate with the more spiritual purposes of Otto III's *Renovatio* perceived by Schramm's critics.[58] It is true that Abbo's personal contact with imperial circles was made only indirectly, via Otto's uncle Pope Gregory V; he deployed rhetorical praise of the emperor as a reformer, not as a political propagandist. Nevertheless, the appetite of the court for ways to articulate imperial ideals was considerable, and it is not unthinkable that Abbo's *Commentary*, the most comprehensive of his treatments of wisdom, unity, and order, would have been regarded as a fitting addition to the Ottonian library. Is there any manuscript evidence to support this?

A manuscript of Victorius' *Calculus* with Abbo's *Commentary* from the early eleventh century survives in Bamberg, Staatsbibliothek, Class. 53, fols. 1r–46r. It is written in a German hand, but has no other definite signs of provenance.[59] The see of Bamberg was founded by the Emperor Henry II in 1007, who endowed it

---

[52] Bubnov, *Gerberti Opera*, 225–44; id., *Arithmetische Selbständigkeit der europäischen Kultur* (Berlin, 1914), 37, 236.

[53] Abbo, *Epistola*, I: PL 139, col. 420.

[54] J. V. Navari, 'The Leitmotiv in the Mathematical Thought of Gerbert of Aurillac', *Journal of Medieval History*, 1 (1975), 139–50.

[55] Mayr-Harting, *Ottonian Book Illumination*, I, 68, 117.

[56] D. A. Warner, 'Ideals and Action in the Reign of Otto III', *Journal of Medieval History*, 25 (1999), 1–18; here 9, 12.

[57] Munich, Bayerische Staatsbibliothek, Clm. 4453, fols. 23v and 24r: Mayr-Harting, *Ottonian Book Illumination*, I, 158–62; pls. XX–XXI.

[58] Warner, 'Ideals', 4.

[59] F. Leitschuh, *Katalog der Handschriften der königlichen Bibliothek zu Bamberg* I.2 (Bamberg, 1895), 59–60.

with a library which included books once owned by Otto III, some of which remain at Bamberg today.[60] One group comprises Frankish manuscripts which Otto had received as gifts from Gerbert,[61] and might once have included a copy of Abbo's *Commentary* which became the exemplar of Bamberg, Class. 53. Alternatively, the *Commentary* may have travelled independently to Germany. Berno, abbot of Reichenau 1008–48, had stayed at Fleury during Abbo's rule in the 990s,[62] and the musical works for which he became famous reflect not only an Abbonian facility with arithmetical theory (including an interest in the mathematical role of unity) but also Abbo's mode of dialectical argument.[63] He could well have brought the *Commentary* to Reichenau, and introduced it, if not to Otto III in his final years, then to the circle of his patron, Henry II. One suggestive feature of the Bamberg manuscript, which could constitute only the most tenuous link to Otto III, is the presence after Abbo's *Commentary* (on fols. 46v–47r) of tables of the regular constitution of multiples from three equal terms, the exercise which seems to have interested the emperor particularly. They are found in only one other of the seven extant manuscripts of the *Commentary*, Bernkastel-Kues, Hospitalbibliothek, 206, fols. iv–41r (*s*. xi, Germany), which was at St Mary and St Corbinianus, Freising, by the thirteenth century at least.[64] This manuscript is very close textually to the Bamberg copy, and suggests that the work was beginning to circulate in Ottonian cultural centres. A third, unfinished eleventh-century German copy of the *Commentary*, (Karlsruhe, Landesbibliothek, 504, fols. 85r–99r) has a fourteenth-century *ex libris* of the monastery of St Michael's, Bamberg, another foundation which benefited from Henry II's manuscript endowment. Abbo's *Commentary* is accompanied in the manuscript by quadrivial works which include those of Berno of Reichenau and his pupil, Hermannus Contractus.[65] Perhaps the manuscript was already at St Michael's at an early date; if so, it would constitute further evidence of the reception of Abbo's *Commentary* into ecclesiastical houses within the imperial ambit.

Abbo's *Commentary* was dedicated to his fellow monks, not to Otto III, whom he addressed only in the poem *Otto Valens*. This was characteristic of late Ottonian culture, which saw, in contrast to the Carolingian period, almost no

---

[60] H. Fischer, 'Die königliche Bibliothek in Bamberg und ihre Handschriften', *Zentralblatt für Bibliothekswesen* 24 (1907), 364–93; Mütherich, 'The Library', 12–13; Mayr-Harting, *Ottonian Book Illumination*, I, 54–5.

[61] Fischer, 'Die königliche Bibliothek', 385–91; Mütherich, 'The Library', 19–21; R. McKitterick, 'Ottonian Intellectual Culture in the Tenth Century and the Role of Theophanu', *Early Medieval Europe*, 2: 1 (1993), 53–74; here 61.

[62] A. van de Vyver, 'Les Oeuvres inédites d'Abbon de Fleury', *Revue Bénédictine*, 47 (1935), 125–69; here 139, 143, n. 2.

[63] e.g. *Prologus in Tonarium*, ed. M. Gerbertus, *Scriptores Ecclesiastici de Musica Sacra*, II (St Blasien, 1784), 65b; *De Mensurando Monochordo*, ed. J. Smits van Waesberghe, *Bernonis Augiensis Abbatis de Arte Musica Disputationes Traditae, Divitiae Musicae Artis Collectae*, ser. A, VI. A (Buren, 1978), 72.

[64] J. Marx, *Verzeichnis der Handschriftensammlung des Hospitals zu Cues* (Trier, 1905), 192–3.

[65] Van de Vyver, 'Les Oeuvres', 139; *Die Handschriften der Badischen Landesbibliothek in Karlsruhe*, IV (Wiesbaden, 1970), 92–4; Fischer, 'Die königliche Bibliothek', 372–3.

contemporary works dedicated to the emperor except laudatory poems.[66] But the *Commentary*'s vision of unity and order is of a piece not only with the rest of Abbo's thought, but also with Ottonian imperial aspirations. Monk and emperor considered themselves engaged in a common enterprise: to build up the house of Wisdom on the columns of the seven liberal arts, so that a united Christendom might be properly ordered to the glory of God.

[66] Mütherich, 'The Library', 22–3; McKitterick, 'Ottonian Intellectual Culture', 54–5, 61.

13

AN OTTONIAN SACRAMENTARY IN OXFORD

Martin Kauffmann

A reconsideration of Oxford's most important Ottonian illuminated manuscript seems appropriate in a volume dedicated to Henry Mayr-Harting, whose ground-breaking contextual study of Ottonian illuminated manuscripts reminded the scholarly world that Ottonian books were made by and for real people in particular religious and political situations, people who may even have gone so far on occasion as to talk to one another.[1] Oxford, Bodleian Library, MS. Canon. Liturg. 319, a sacramentary,[2] was first described in detail in the early twentieth century,[3] and was subjected to close examination in the mid-1960s by two liturgical scholars, who reached markedly different conclusions as to its origins (pls. 8–10, 12, 14, 16, and 18).[4] Since then considerable progress has been made by palaeographers and art historians in the study of Ottonian manuscript production, much of which has implications for our understanding of the Oxford sacramentary. The aim of this essay is briefly to reconsider the question of its place of origin and early travels, and to look more closely than has been done hitherto at the full-page miniatures it contains. Inevitably this will involve studying the relationship between our manuscript and others to which its decoration is closely linked; at the same time, it is important to consider the contents of the Oxford manuscript in their own right, rather than merely as links in a textual and iconographic chain.

Early in its life, as we shall see, Canon. Liturg. 319 was taken to Aquileia. As well as giving it a place in the larger story of the influx of Ottonian manuscripts to Italy, this explains why Oxford was to become its eventual resting-place. That manuscripts with an Italian provenance rank second only to those from the British Isles in the Bodleian Library's collections of illuminated manuscripts[5] is due very largely to the library's purchase in 1817 of a majority of the

---

[1] H. Mayr-Harting, *Ottonian Book Illumination: An Historical Study*, 2 vols. (London, 1991).

[2] F. Madan, *A Summary Catalogue of Western Manuscripts in the Bodleian Library at Oxford, vol. IV (Collections Received During the First Half of the 19th Century)* (Oxford, 1897), no. 19408.

[3] C. Foligno, *Di alcuni Codici Liturgici di Provenienza Friulana nella Biblioteca Bodleiana di Oxford* (Cividale del Friuli, 1914), 6–7 (first published in the *Memorie Storiche Forogiuliesi*, 9 (1913)).

[4] D. H. Turner, 'The "Reichenau" Sacramentaries at Zürich and Oxford', *Revue Bénédictine*, 75 (1965), 240–76; R. Bauerreiss, 'Ein altbayerisches Sakramentar des XI. Jahrhunderts in Oxford (Canon. Lit. 319)', *Studien und Mitteilungen zur Geschichte des Benediktinerordens*, 76 (1965), 85–95.

[5] As may be appreciated from O. Pächt and J. J. G. Alexander, *Illuminated Manuscripts in the Bodleian Library, Oxford*, 3 vols. (Oxford, 1966–73). Canon. Liturg. 319 is vol. I, no. 25.

manuscripts which had been collected by Matteo Luigi Canonici (1727–c.1805), a Jesuit who endured two suppressions of his Order and the loss of his first collection before retiring to Venice and building up a second.[6] The present red leather binding of the manuscript, with its characteristic decorative endpapers, was in all likelihood made for Canonici.[7] The circumstances in which it left Aquileia are not known; the only published reference to it before it entered Canonici's possession is one of 1748, which was copied on to the flyleaves of the book (fols. iii recto–v recto).[8]

The contents of Canon. Liturg. 319 may be summarized as follows:[9]

A. 1. (fols. iv–15r). Prefatory gradual (*Breviarium antiphonalis missarum*) and sanctoral, including provisions for the feasts of St Benedict and St Pelagius, and a series of Alleluias *per circulum anni*, ending with those of the common.

2. (fols. 15v–24r). Calendar, entitled *martyrologium per circulum anni*.

3. (fol. 24r). *Oratio sancti Ambrosii ante missam*, followed by other prayers.

4. (fols. 24v–27r). *Ordo missae*.

5. (fols. 27v–29r). Votive masses (added later in the eleventh century).

B. 1. (fols. 29v–36r). Introduction and Canon of the Mass.

2. (fols. 36r–161v). Masses of the temporal and sanctoral combined, with the service for baptism on Holy Saturday (fol. 85r), but omitting the Sundays after Easter, the Ascension, Pentecost, and the season of Advent.[10] The first part of the Exultet (fols. 79v–80r) is provided with neums.

3. (fols. 161v–164r). Common of saints.

---

[6] I. Merolle, *L'Abate Matteo Luigi Canonici e la sua Biblioteca. I manoscritti Canonici e Canonici-Soranzo delle biblioteche Fiorentine* (Rome/Florence, 1958).

[7] For the Canonici bindings, see J. B. Mitchell, 'Trevisan and Soranzo: Some Canonici Manuscripts From Two Eighteenth-Century Venetian Collections', *Bodleian Library Record*, 8:3 (1969), 125–35. The damage to the outer corners of the last few leaves (fols. 260–5) was probably caused by metal fittings from a previous binding. No similar marks are to be seen on fol. 266, which must therefore have been placed in its present position only when the manuscript was rebound. There is similar damage at the front of the manuscript (fols. 1–3), with the addition of a fifth mark in the middle of the page, presumably representing a central boss.

[8] The note (not in Canonici's hand) refers to L. A. Muratori, *Liturgia Romana Vetus*, 2 vols. (Venice, 1748), I, col. 70: 'Sunt et alii in Italia vetustissimi Codices ejusdem Gregorianae Liturgiae. An ex iis aliquem adservaret insignis Aquilejensis Patriarchalis Ecclesia, a Cl. V. Dominico Berroli, ejusdem Ecclesiae Canonico, sum percontatus. Retulit ille, haberi illic elegantissimum Codicem, cujus aetas spectare videtur ad Saeculum Christi Nonum, aut Decimum. En ejus titulum: *In Christi nomine incipit Liber Sacramentorum de circulo anni, a sancto Gregorio Papa Romano editum, qualiter Missa Romana celebratur. Hoc est in primis Introitus* etc.' The title in the manuscript actually reads (fol. 29v): *In nomine domini incipit Liber Sacramentorum de circulo anni expositus a sancto Gregorio Papa Romano. editus ex authentico libro bibliothecae cubiculi scriptus. qualiter missa romana celebratur. Hoc est in primis introitus.*

[9] See the descriptions in Turner, 'Reichenau Sacramentaries', 256–60, and S. J. P. van Dijk, 'Handlist of the Latin Liturgical Manuscripts in the Bodleian Library', I: 'Mass Books', unpublished typescript (Oxford, 1957), 12.

[10] Turner lists the saints' days which appear (excluding those normally found in the *Hadrianum* and supplement) on p. 260.

4. (fols. 164r–165r). Mass *in dedicatione aecclesiae.*

5. (fols. 165r–167r). Masses for the Sundays after Easter.

6. (fol. 167r). Mass for the Sunday after Ascension.

7. (fols. 167r–175v). Masses for the twenty-four Sundays after the octave of Pentecost.

8. (fols. 175v–178v). Masses for Advent.

9. (fols. 178v–245v). Votive Masses for each day of the week; *orationes pro pec-catis* (fol. 181r), *cottidianae* (fol. 185r), *matutinales* (fol. 188v), *uespertinales* (fol. 189r); further votive masses (fol. 192r), several with the epistle, gospel, and the opening words of the parts to be sung by the choir (with musical cues), and including one *pro salute uiuorum uel mortuorum* (fol. 207v), mentioning those *quorum corpora in hoc monasterio requiescunt,* and another *in monasterio* (fol. 208v).

10. (fols. 245v–263v). Masses for the Dead and (fol. 257r) *obsequium circa morientes.*

11. (fols. 263v–265r). Added (eleventh-century) material in space originally left blank: rubrics are included, but the spaces left for initials have not been filled.

12. (fol. 266). A leaf from another German sacramentary of the first half of the eleventh century.[11]

The basis of the sacramentary is the *Hadrianum* and supplement: that is, the text, supposedly composed by Gregory the Great, sent by Pope Hadrian to Charlemagne; and the Carolingian additions which expanded the festive sacramentary sent from Rome into a book suitable for the daily liturgical needs of churches throughout the Carolingian empire.[12] Derek Turner, who had previously contributed a liturgical chapter to C. R. Dodwell's reconsideration of the place of Reichenau in the history of Ottonian manuscript illumination,[13] compared the sacramentary of Canon. Liturg. 319 to three other sacramentaries from the abbey of Reichenau on Lake Constance, the abbey to which the illumination of this section of the manuscript had been attributed.[14] He concluded that it had no material of local significance in common with them. The calendar, which he argued did not originally belong with the sacramentary, was another matter. A *terminus post quem* for the calendar is given by the presence of St Adalbert (23 April), who died in 997. In the calendar Turner identified

---

[11] Brief physical details of the MS are given in the appendix.

[12] É. Bourque, *Étude sur les Sacramentaires romains*, part II, vol. II (Vatican City, 1958), 267, no. 210; K. Gamber, *Sakramentartypen. Versuch einer Gruppierung der Handschriften und Fragmente bis zur Jahrtausendwende* (Beuron, 1958), 144.

[13] C. R. Dodwell and D. H. Turner, *Reichenau Reconsidered: A Re-assessment of the Place of Reichenau in Ottonian Art* (London, 1965).

[14] Zürich, Zentralbibliothek, MS. Rheinau 71; Paris, Bibliothèque nationale de France, MS. lat. 18005; and Florence, Biblioteca Nazionale, MS. B.R. 231.

several entries which spoke of Reichenau,[15] as well as other Insular monastic saints whose presence could be explained by the influence of Reichenau's neighbour St Gallen. However, the calendar omits the dedication feast of Reichenau on 16 August. Instead it has a *Dedicatio ecclesiae sanctae Mariae* on 29 March, and a *Dedicatio sancti Nicolai* on 17 December. Turner could locate no documented monastic chapel or church dedicated to St Nicholas at this date in the region of Reichenau.[16] And although several monastic houses in the diocese of Constance honoured the Virgin Mary as their principal patron, he could find no other evidence to link Canon. Liturg. 319 to any of them. Although there are two calendars from St Gallen which have a Marian dedication on the same day, the Oxford calendar lacks all the major St Gallen dedication feasts.[17]

Turner noted, but could not explain, the presence of one original obit in the calendar, *Heinricus marchio* on 23 June. This must be margrave Henry I von Babenberg of Austria, who died in or after 1018 (giving an even more useful *terminus post quem*), and was buried at Melk, at that time the seat of the Austrian rulers but not yet a house of Benedictines. The Oxford manuscript has no other obvious connection with Melk. To Romuald Bauerreiss, whose article appeared shortly after that of Turner, which it criticized in certain respects, this entry provided the springboard for a very different analysis of the calendar.[18] Bauerreiss was himself a Benedictine monk in Munich, and his article was unambiguously entitled 'Ein altbayerisches Sakramentar'. Contrary to Turner, he believed that the calendar and the sacramentary in Canon. Liturg. 319 had always belonged together, and had been made not in the area of Lake Constance but in Bavaria or upper Austria—though he too was unable to link the two dedications to any particular foundation.[19]

Apart from the obit of *Heinricus marchio*, almost all the evidence brought into play by Bauerreiss belongs not to the original calendar but to its additions. These include the obits of six patriarchs of Aquileia;[20] of the mother (Bilihilt or

---

[15] For instance SS Pirmin, Pimenius, Senesius and Theopontus, Valens, Genesius, Fortunata and her brothers, and Januarius and his companions.

[16] K. Meisen, *Nikolauskult und Nikolausbrauch in Abendlande. Eine kultgeographisch-volkskundliche Untersuchung*, 2nd edn. (Düsseldorf, 1981).

[17] E. Munding, *Die Kalendarien von St. Gallen. Aus XXI Handschriften. Neuntes bis elftes Jahrhundert*, 2 vols. (Beuron, 1948–51).

[18] The calendar is printed by Bauerreiss on pp. 86–90.

[19] A. G. Watson, *Catalogue of Dated and Datable Manuscripts c.435–1600 in Oxford Libraries*, 2 vols. (Oxford, 1984), no. 270, follows Bauerreiss in believing that the manuscript was originally made in Upper Austria, and suggests that the obit of *Heinricus marchio* is an addition in the original hand, presumably because it is placed towards the right-hand edge of the line. He therefore dates the manuscript to the period 997–1018. The obit is certainly in the original hand; I am inclined not to agree with this interpretation of its placing, especially as the original scribe of a manuscript made for export would presumably not have been in a position to add an obit once the manuscript had gone to its intended destination.

[20] They are, in chronological order of their patriarchates: John on 19 July, Poppo on 28 September, Eberhard on 13 November, Gotebold on 27 December, Rabinger on 18 February, and Sigehard on 12 August. See the entries in *Necrologium Aquileiense*, ed. C. Scalon (Udine, 1982).

Pilihild) and brother (Friedrich) of the latest of the six, Sigehard;[21] of the emperors Henry II and Henry III;[22] of the counts Otto and Sirus;[23] of an abbess Reginlinda;[24] and of the nun Hadauuich.[25] There are also added entries for several saints venerated at Aquileia.[26] Turner and Bauerreiss agreed in considering Sigehard as the most likely source of the additions: the anniversary of his consecration as patriarch (15 June 1068) is in the same hand as many of the other additions, but his obit (12 August 1077) is in a different hand.[27] Sigehard came from a south-east Bavarian noble family; Bilihilt and Reginlinda are found in necrologies and confraternity books from Seckau, Salzburg, Seeon, and Mondsee.[28] Turner continued (rightly, it seems to me) to regard the original entries in the calendar as distinct from the additions, though he could not account for the calendar's transfer to Aquileia. Bauerreiss, dismissing the Reichenau and St Gallen saints in the calendar as insignificant, and seeming to ignore the absence of the liturgical features in the sacramentary which would have been necessary to support his thesis, argued that the whole manuscript must have had its origins somewhere close to the Sigeharding *Stammesgebiet*, such as Mondsee.

In trying to build a picture of the origins and first destination of Canon. Liturg. 319, it is not only the liturgical evidence of its contents which can be put to use. Since Turner and Bauerreiss wrote, there have been major advances in the palaeographical study of Ottonian centres of manuscript production. Hartmut Hoffmann has identified six scribes in the Oxford manuscript.[29] He argues that each of the two main sections of the book, the calendar and sacramentary, was written by a single scribe in the first quarter of the eleventh century: hand A wrote the original text of fols. 1v–27v, line 14; hand D wrote the original text of fols. 31r–263v, line 7 (pl. 8). Hoffmann places both these main scribes at Reichenau. Hand A is also found on fols. 1r–131v of London, British Library, Arundel 390, a manuscript of the chronicle of Regino of Prüm; hand D can be identified with the first scribe of Munich, Bayerische Staatsbibliothek,

---

[21] On 23 October and 29 August respectively.   [22] On 20 July and 5 October respectively.

[23] On 22 August and 21 July respectively.

[24] She is described as an abbess on 4 February, but as a nun on 3 May; the latter entry is explicitly an obit. If these are not two different women, it is possible that the first reference might be to the date of her installation as abbess.

[25] On 28 September, probably the *monaca nostra* who appears in the necrology of S. Maria di Aquileia: see C. Scalon, 'Fonti e ricerche per la storia', in *Il Friuli dagli Ottoni agli Hohenstaufen* (Udine, 1985), 162.

[26] Hermagoras and Fortunatus on 12 July; Felix and Fortunatus on 14 August; Thecla, Erasma, and Dorothea on 25 September.

[27] The belief that another of the patriarchs, Eberhard, had been a canon of Reichenau, and was thus the most likely means by which the book could have travelled, seems to have rested on a confusion between *Augustanus* and *Augiensis*, the adjectival form of Reichenau. Eberhard was a canon of Augsburg; Reichenau had no canons. See F. Ughelli, *Italia Sacra*, V, 2nd edn. (Venice, 1720), col. 56.

[28] C. Scalon, *Produzione e Fruizione del Libro nel Basso Medioevo. Il caso Friuli* (Padua, 1995), 4–5.

[29] H. Hoffmann, *Buchkunst und Königtum im ottonischen und frühsalischen Reich*, 2 vols. (Stuttgart, 1986), I, 331, 335–6, 416–8, 420; II, Ill. 162–3, 247–8.

Clm. 23338, an illustrated gospel lectionary.[30] Hands B, C, and E were responsible for the additions on fols. 27v, line 16[31]–28v, line 17; fols. 28v, line 18–29r; and
fols. 263v, line 9[32]–265v respectively. According to Hoffmann, these three
scribes are all localizable to Freising in the second quarter of the eleventh century.[33] Crucially, this palaeographical analysis yokes calendar and sacramentary
more firmly to each other, each containing Reichenau script (albeit by different
hands) with later Freising additions, one of whom (hand C) crossed over from
the end of the quire containing the calendar to the first leaf of the new quire
containing the beginning of the sacramentary. This hand is also to be found
inserting corrections in the text of the sacramentary, for example at fol. 202r.

Thus a picture begins to emerge of a manuscript produced at Reichenau but
intended for use elsewhere. Liturgically speaking, Freising, where the additions
seem to have been made, is not a possible first destination for the manuscript. Is
there any other plausible first destination that could yield a satisfactory explanation for the manuscript's liturgical features? It is worth reconsidering the case
for Murbach in Alsace, with which Reichenau entered into a confraternity in
828.[34] Murbach was dedicated to the Virgin Mary, St Michael, St Peter and St
Paul, and St Leger (or Leodegarius), bishop of Autun.[35] Canon. Liturg. 319 has
a Mass for St Leger in the sanctoral. It is clearly important, as a proper preface
is provided along with the collect, secret, and postcommunion. However, the
content of this Mass differs in some repects from that found in the eleventh-
century missal from Murbach, now Colmar, Bibliothèque municipale, MSS.
443–4.[36] Furthermore, the Oxford manuscript lacks other local feasts found in

---

[30] Although (as we shall see) the illumination of this MS is also related to Canon. Liturg. 319, it does
not appear to have been executed by the same artist. See A. S. Korteweg, 'Das Evangelistar Clm 23338
und seine Stellung innerhalb der Reichenauer *Schulhandschriften*', in *Studien zur mittelalterlichen Kunst
800–1250. Festschrift für Florentine Mütherich zum 70. Geburtstag*, ed. K. Bierbrauer, P. Klein, and W.
Sauerländer (Munich, 1985), 125–44.

[31] Line 15 is a rubric.   [32] Line 8 is a rubric.

[33] He compares hand C to hand U of London, British Library, Harley 2728 (Lucan), and hand E to
hand A of Berlin, Staatsbibliothek, Savigny 2 (*Collectio duodecim partium*).

[34] M. Barth, *Handbuch der elsässischen Kirchen im Mittelalter* (Archives de l'Église d'Alsace, 27–9,
NS 11–13 (1960–3)), cols. 885–97.

[35] Other houses dedicated to St Leger included Masmünster in Alsace (for which see Barth,
Handbuch der elsässischen Kirchen, cols. 801–7), and Lucerne (a subject of Murbach) in the diocese of
Constance.

[36] J.-B. Pitra, *Histoire de Saint Léger* (Paris, 1846), 510–11; V. Leroquais, *Les Sacramentaires et les mis-
sels manuscrits des bibliothèques publiques de France*, I (Paris, 1924), 131–3, nos. 54–5. This (perhaps 'southern') version of the Mass is the one found in books from Switzerland, the earliest being Zürich,
Zentralbibliothek, Rheinau 30: ed. A. Hänggi and A. Schönherr, *Sacramentarium Rhenaugiense* (Fribourg, 1970), 194–5, nos. 885–9. The Oxford elements which differ from the Colmar missal follow
another (perhaps 'northern') version of the Mass for St Leger, found in the *Missale Gothicum*, generally
thought to be from Autun and to date from the first half of the 8th century: *Missale Gothicum. Das gal-
likanische Sakramentar (cod. Vatican. Regin. Lat. 317) des VII.–VIII. Jahrhunderts*, ed. L. C. Mohlberg,
2 vols: facsimile and commentary (Augsburg, 1929), II, 130–1, nos. 425–31. I am indebted to Nicholas
Orchard of the Courtauld Institute, University of London, not only for detailed instruction in the historical development of the Mass for St Leger, but also for much other patient explanation of matters
liturgical.

the Colmar missal: Walburga, Boniface, Germanus and Remigius, Gall, and Januarius. The only other local feasts it does contain are for St Amarinus, abbot of Doroang in the Vosges, who was venerated in Alsace; St Alban of Mainz; and St Verena, a hermitess near Solothurn and later near Zurzach in the Aargau. Our volume is unlikely, then, to be a copy of a Murbach book made at Reichenau for Murbach; but might it possibly be an adaptation, made at Reichenau for Murbach, of an exemplar from somewhere else? It is unclear what measure of similarity we are entitled to look for in such a case; the production of a liturgical book for another monastic house may well have been a textually complicated procedure, if no single model had been provided. This may go some way to explaining the relative paucity of local feasts in the sanctoral.

It seems, therefore, that Canon. Liturg. 319 was originally made at Reichenau, certainly after 997 and probably after 1018, for use at another house; exactly which house will remain obscure until the liturgical evidence of the sacramentary can be convincingly linked to the two dedication feasts in the calendar.[37] For reasons unknown it was fairly soon taken to Freising, and from Freising to Aquileia, which it seems to have reached before 1077. The fact that Canon. Liturg. 319 demonstrably reached Aquileia in the eleventh century is itself of considerable cultural interest. At least two other richly illuminated Ottonian manuscripts, a sacramentary and a gospel book, both from Fulda, are known to have done the same, and are now in Udine.[38] Most of the patriarchs of Aquileia up to the thirteenth century were themselves German. The Fulda Gospels were used as an oath book when new bishops of the province swore allegiance to the patriarch. Whilst Italy is often seen as a rich storehouse of artistic models, it is clear that objects and books of artistic value could also travel from Germany to Italy, and not only via the traffic of rulers and churchmen to and from Rome. Most of the Ottonian manuscripts which reached Italy had not originally been produced for Italian destinations. They were given as diplomatic or fraternal gifts, or as a means of liturgical incorporation by reforming centres, or as tokens of Ottonian liturgico-political colonization.[39]

So far in the discussion of the circumstances in which Canon. Liturg. 319 might have been produced, no account has been taken of its decoration. There

---

[37] These feasts do not appear in the two surveys by M. Barth: 'Aus dem liturgischen Leben der Abtei Murbach', *Freiburger Diözesan-Archiv*, 73 (1953), 59–87; and 'Mittelalterliche Kalendare und Litaneien des Elsass', *Freiburger Diözesan-Archiv*, 86 (1966), 352–443.

[38] Udine, Archivio Capitolare, MS 1 (sacramentary) and MS 2 (gospels). In neither case was Aquileia the first destination of the manuscript. See W. Böhne, 'Das Fuldaer Sakramentar in Udine', *Archiv für mittelrheinische Kirchengeschichte*, 43 (1991), 327–62; E. Palazzo, *Les Sacramentaires de Fulda. Étude sur l'iconographie et la liturgie à l'époque ottonienne* (Münster, 1994), 206–10, 230–1. The Egbert Psalter now in Cividale (Museo Archeologico Nazionale, Cod. 136) reached Aquileia only in the thirteenth century: F. J. Ronig, 'Der Psalter des Trierer Erzbischofs Egbert in Cividale', in *Egbert, Erzbischof von Trier 977–993. Gedenkschrift der Diözese Trier zum 1000. Todestag*, ed. F. J. Ronig, 2 vols. (Trier, 1993), 163–8.

[39] I. Siede, *Zur Rezeption ottonischer Buchmalerei in Italien im 11. und 12. Jahrhundert* (St Ottilien, 1997).

is little difficulty in identifying the group of illustrated manuscripts to which the main illumination of the sacramentary belongs, though its exact relationship to the other members deserves attention. The leading members of this group (known as the 'Liuthar group' after the scribe of the Aachen Gospels) mostly have imperial connections: the Aachen Gospels themselves of *c*.996, the Munich Gospels of Otto III of *c*.998–1001, the Bamberg Apocalypse, and the 'Pericopes Book' of Henry II of *c*.1007–12.[40] The later examples, of which Canon. Liturg. 319 is one, and which are sometimes referred to as *Schulwerke*, all have stylistic and iconographical links to the core Liuthar group and to each other, but were evidently made for a variety of different contexts.[41] Their dating, both absolutely and relatively, is very largely a matter of conjecture: they are generally assigned to the period *c*.1020–40, with a further group of related manuscripts, known as the Bernulphus group, assigned to *c*.1040–75.[42] It will only be possible to judge the originality of the illumination in the Oxford sacramentary if we are aware of the traditions to which it conforms or from which it can be seen to depart.

As well as its miniatures, Canon. Liturg. 319 also contains five full-page initials or monograms, and ten smaller, three-, four-, or five-line decorated initials (pls. 8 and 9).[43] Once again, these are of the same distinctive type as those found in the other Liuthar group manuscripts.[44] The initials, which are framed and set against a purple ground, are of gold, with bright red, blue, and green infill. Gold branchwork, with a consistent repertoire of knobs and terminals, grows out of the initial forms, and is connected to the frame, sometimes by elaborate knotting devices. The frames themselves contain decorative panels of acanthus or

[40] Respectively, Aachen Cathedral Treasury (E. G. Grimme, *Das Evangeliar Kaiser Ottos III. im Domschatz zu Aachen* (Freiburg im Breisgau, 1984)); Munich, Bayerische Staatsbibliothek, Clm. 4453 (F. Dressler, F. Mütherich, and H. Beumann, *Das Evangeliar Ottos III.*, 2 vols.: facsimile and commentary (Frankfurt am Main, 1978)); Bamberg, Staatsbibliothek, Cod. Bibl. 140 (A. Fauser, *Die Bamberger Apokalypse* (Wiesbaden, 1958)); and Munich, Bayerische Staatsbibliothek, Clm. 4452 (H. Fillitz, R. Kahsnitz, and U. Kuder, *Zierde für ewige Zeit. Das Perikopenbuch Heinrichs II.* (exhibition catalogue, Munich: Bayerisches Nationalmuseum, 1984)).

[41] Augsburg, Städtische Kunstsammlungen, Maximiliansmuseum, Cod. 15a (gospel lectionary); Cologne, Dombibliothek, Col. Metr. 12 (gospel lectionary of Hillinus); Cologne, Dombibliothek, Col. Metr. 218 (Limburg Gospels); Erlangen, Universitätsbibliothek, MS. 12 (gospels); Hildesheim, Dombibliothek (Bibliotheca Beverina), Hs. 688 (orationale); Lille, Bibliothèque des Facultés catholiques, s.n. (gospel lectionary); Munich, Bayerische Staatsbibliothek, Clm. 4454 (gospel lectionary); Munich, Bayerische Staatsbibliothek, Clm. 23338 (gospel lectionary); Nuremberg, Stadtbibliothek, Cent. IV,4 (gospel lectionary); Paris, Bibliothèque nationale de France, MS. lat. 18005 (sacramentary); Vienna, Österreichische Nationalbibliothek, Cod. 573 (*Vita sancti Uodalrici*); Wolfenbüttel, Herzog-August-Bibliothek, Cod. Guelf. 84, 5 Aug. 2° (gospel lectionary).

[42] A. S. Korteweg, 'Der Bernulphuscodex in Utrecht und eine Gruppe verwandter spätreichenauer Handschriften', *Aachener Kunstblätter*, 53 (1985), 35–76.

[43] Details of the initials are given in the appendix.

[44] There is nothing to prove that the same artist was responsible for both the miniatures and the initials; but it is worth observing the degree of decorative co-ordination between the two, for instance in the columns, capitals, and acanthus-filled arches which frame both the miniature of the Women at the Tomb on fol. 95v and the full-page initial on the other side of the opening at fol. 96r.

1. Oxford, Bodleian Library, Auct. D. II. 14, fol. 39ᵛ. Page size: c.249 x 195 mm. See ch. 3.

ILLe homo qui dici
turibs
Lutum fecit et un
xit oculos meos
et dixit mihi
uade ad natatoriu
siloae et laba
et abii et laui
et uidi
et dixerunt ei
ubi est ille
ait nescio
adducunt eum ad pha
risaeos qui caecus
fuerat
erat autem sabbatu
quando lutum fe
cit ihs
et aperuit oculos eiu
iterum ergo inter
rogabant eum pha
risaei
quomodo uidisset
ille autem dixit eis
Lutum posuit mihi
super oculos
et laui et uideo
dicebant ergo ex
pharisaeis quidam

NON est hic homo adô
quia sabbatum non cus
todit
alii dicebant
quomodo potest ho
mo peccator haec
signa facere
et schisma erat in eis
dicunt ergo caeco
iterum
tu quid dicis de eo qui
aperuit oculos tuos
ille autem dixit quia
profeta est
non crediderunt er
go iudaei de illo quia
caecus fuisset et ui
disset
donec uocauerunt
parentes eius qui
uiderat
et interrogauerunt
eos dicentes
hic est filius uester
quem uos dicitis quia
caecus natus est
quomodo ergo nunc
uidet
responderunt eis

2. Oxford, Bodleian Library, Auct. D. II. 14, fol. 149ᵛ. See ch. 3.

3. London, British Library, Cotton Nero D. iv, fol. 95^r. The Lindisfarne Gospels: Incipit to Mark. Page size: c.340 × 250 mm. See ch. 4.

ENERANDA NOBIS dne huiusest diei festuitas· inqua sca di genitrix mortem subiit temporalem . nec tamen mostis nexibus deprimi potuit .quae filium tuum dese genuit incarnatu cuius intercessione qs· ut mostem euadere possimus animarum · feund·

AMULORUM TVO rum qs dni delictis igno sce· et qui placere deactibus ntis non ualemus· genttricis filii tui dni di nostri intercessione saluem· feund dnm ntm · ub ueniat dne plebi tuae di geniti eis oratio· quam et sip conditione car

8. Oxford, Bodleian Library, Canon. Liturg. 319, fol. 138ʳ. Sacramentary: Feast of the Assumption of the Virgin. Page size: c.245 x 180 mm. See ch. 13.

9. Oxford, Bodleian Library, Canon. Liturg. 319, fol. 30ᵛ. Sacramentary: *vere dignum* monogram
See ch. 13.

10. Oxford, Bodleian Library, Canon. Liturg. 319, fol. 31ᵛ. Sacramentary: *Te igitur* Crucifixion. See ch. 13.

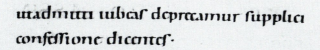

11. Paris, Bibliothèque nationale de France, lat. 18005, fol. 21ʳ. Sacramentary: *Te igitur* Crucifixion. Page size: *c*.230 × 185 mm. See ch. 13.

12. Oxford, Bodleian Library, Canon. Liturg. 319, fol. 38ᵛ. Sacramentary:
Nativity and Annunciation to the Shepherds. See ch. 13.

13. Munich, Bayerische Staatsbibliothek, Clm 4452, fols 8ᵛ–9ʳ. Pericopes Book of Henry II: Nativity and Annunciation to the Shepherds. Page size: c.423 × 315mm. See ch. 13.

14. Oxford, Bodleian Library, Canon. Liturg. 319, fol. 95^v. Sacramentary:
Holy Women at the Tomb. See ch. 13.

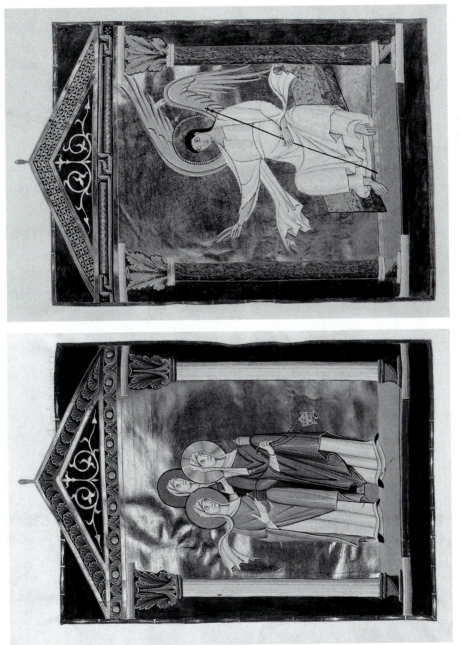

15. Munich, Bayerische Staatsbibliothek, Clm 4452, fols. 116^v–117^r. Pericopes Book of Henry II: Holy Women at the Tomb. See ch. 13.

16. Oxford, Bodleian Library, Canon. Liturg. 319, fol. 110ᵛ.
Sacramentary: Ascension. See ch. 13.

17. Paris, Bibliothèque nationale de France, lat. 18005, fol. 89ᵛ.
Sacramentary: Ascension. See ch. 13.

18. Oxford, Bodleian Library, Canon. Liturg. 319, fol. 115ᵛ.
Sacramentary: Pentecost. See ch. 13.

19. Wolfenbüttel, Herzog-August-Bibliothek, Cod. Guelf. 84,5 Aug 2°, fol. 61ʳ.
Gospel lectionary: Pentecost. Page size: 278 x 185 mm. See ch. 13.

20. London, British Library, Cotton Vitellius C. III, fol. 5ʳ. See ch. 24.

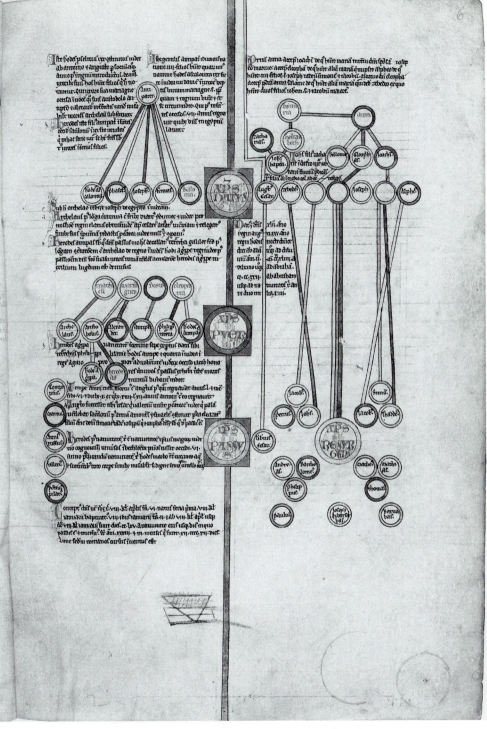

21. Oxford, Bodleian, Laud. misc. 151, fol. 6ʳ. See ch. 24.

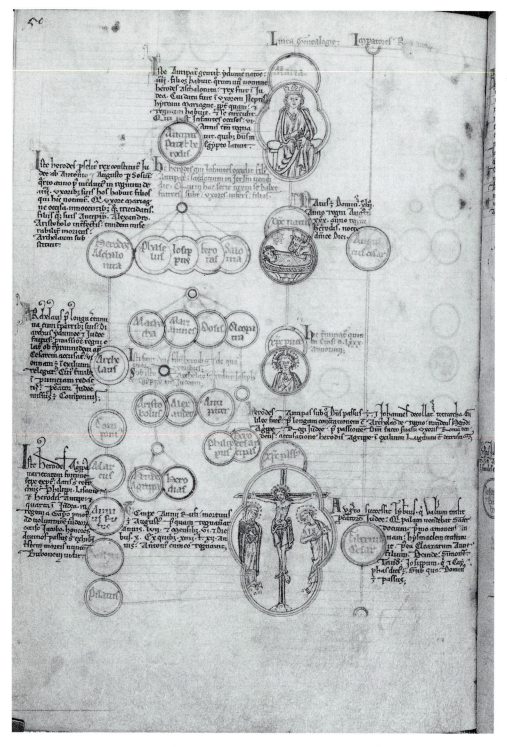

22. London, British Library, Cotton Faust. B. vii, fol. 51ᵛ. See ch. 24.

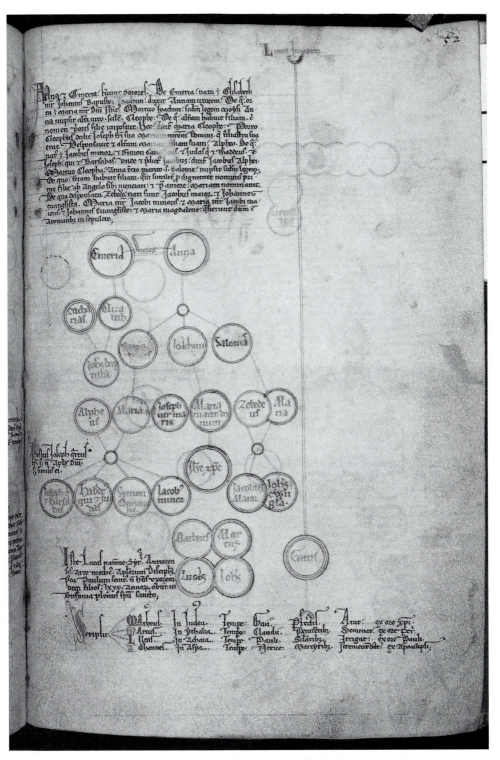

23. London, British Library, Cotton Faust. B vii, fol. 52ʳ. See ch. 24.

24. Oxford, Bodleian Library, Ashmole 1524, II, fol. 55ᵛ. See ch. 24.

geometric and ribbon motifs. The combination of dynamism and stability in these letters marks them out as a high point in the development of initial ornament.[45] But scholars have identified in the later manuscripts a gradual subsidence of energy and invention.[46] The initials have a tendency to become more compact, more isolated spatially; the networks by which they are linked to the frame become simpler, or disappear altogether. In this respect it is striking that one initial in Canon. Liturg. 319, that on fol. 111r opposite the miniature of the Ascension, is different from the others, being linked to the frame not by a knot but by a single tendril.

The production of the Liuthar group of manuscripts has for a long time been attributed to Reichenau. This assessment has not gone unchallenged, notably by Dodwell and Turner.[47] Dodwell found no mention of manuscript illumination in the encomium of Abbot Witigowo's artistic achievements, no notable illuminated manuscripts surviving from the remains of the abbey library, and no proof that the surviving wall paintings at Reichenau were carried out by Reichenau monks rather than by itinerant secular artists. He found reason, on the other hand, to think that the 'Reichenau' style of decorated initial was produced elsewhere, and that the inscription identifying the makers of the famous Codex Egberti[48] as Reichenau monks should be taken to imply that they were working away from home. Having also adduced plentiful evidence for the cultural, religious, and artistic importance of Trier, Dodwell suggested that many of the manuscripts traditionally attributed to Reichenau had in fact been produced at Trier, albeit sometimes by members of the Reichenau community.

Though the relationship between Reichenau and Trier was clearly complex and close, as the career of the artist known as the Gregory Master makes clear, these conclusions have not found general acceptance.[49] Critics have pointed to the difficulties of arguments from silence with respect to the praise of manuscript production; to the loss of the Reichenau treasury, where illuminated liturgical books might have been kept; to the wall paintings which would seem to identify Reichenau as an artistic centre; to the relationship between Reichenau and the Ottonian court; to a continuity of development that argues for a living tradition within a single centre, rather than for the copying of inert

[45] H. Jantzen, 'Das Wort als Bild in der frühmittelalterlichen Buchmalerei', *Historisches Jahrbuch*, 60 (1940), 507–13; A. J. Schardt, *Das Initial: Phantasie und Buchstabenmalerei des frühen Mittelalters* (Berlin, 1938).

[46] See e.g. D. Miner, 'A Late Reichenau Evangeliary in the Walters Gallery Library', *Art Bulletin*, 18 (1936), 168–85.

[47] Bauerreiss had also contributed an article on this question, before he came to write specifically about Canon. Liturg. 319: 'Gab es eine Reichenauer Malschule um die Jahrtausendwende?', *Studien und Mitteilungen zur Geschichte des Benediktinerordens*, 68 (1957), 40–72.

[48] Trier, Stadtbibliothek, MS 24, before 985: ed. H. Schiel, *Codex Egberti der Stadtbibliothek Trier*, 2 vols.: facsimile and commentary (Basle, 1960). The origin of the Codex Egberti was of central importance to Dodwell, since he argued that the (in his view mistaken) attribution of most of the members of the Liuthar group to Reichenau relied mainly upon their iconographic dependence on that manuscript.

[49] A useful summary is provided by Mayr-Harting, *Ottonian Book Illumination*, I, 202–9.

models; and finally to the fact that the identification of monks as members of
the Reichenau community might be taken as a sign not that they were working
away from home, but that their products were consciously intended for presentation elsewhere. This latter observation finds support in the palaeographical
observations of Hartmut Hoffmann. More than half the manuscripts identified
in his catalogue of books containing Reichenau script are liturgical, but many
of them, to judge from their contents and later history, were made for use
elsewhere.[50]

Liturgical evidence for connections with Reichenau, though bound to be
sparse in a group which consists mostly of gospel books and lectionaries, is not
entirely lacking in manuscripts of especial relevance to the Oxford sacramentary. One member of the Liuthar group, not yet mentioned, contains indu-
bitable liturgical evidence of a Reichenau origin. This is a troper, now Bamberg,
Staatsbibliothek, Cod. Lit. 5, closely datable to the years 1000–2, and containing a series of Reichenau saints in its sequences. Once at Bamberg, a prayer to
St George referring to Reichenau was altered to reflect its new situation. The
Masses for Reichenau saints in the sacramentary now in Paris, as well as the
Reichenau saints in the litany, suggest that it was made at the island monastery,
but the Trier saints in the calendar imply that it was made for export to Trier—
just as the Oxford sacramentary was made at Reichenau for export.[51] Henry
Mayr-Harting also argues for the specifically Reichenau connections of the
particular variant of the prayer *Veneranda* (the normal Ottonian collect for the
feast of the Assumption of the Virgin Mary) found not only in members of
the Liuthar group and followers, Canon. Liturg. 319 (pl. 8) among them, but
also in manuscripts of the earlier 'Anno' and 'Ruodpreht' groups.[52]

The earliest Reichenau manuscripts, the members of the Anno group, contain depictions of the evangelists and of Christ in Majesty, as well as dedication
images; but they do not in general contain New Testament illustrations. These
only begin to appear in numbers in the manuscripts of the Ruodpreht group,[53]
something of immense significance in the history of biblical illustration in
medieval Europe.[54] Another highly important development of Ottonian book

[50] *Buchkunst und Königtum*, I, 303–7 (analysis of script), 307–51 (catalogue of manuscripts).

[51] F. Avril and C. Rabel, *Bibliothèque nationale de France. Manuscrits enluminés d'origine germanique.
Tome I: X^e–XIVe siècle* (Paris, 1995), no. 83, with earlier literature.

[52] Mayr-Harting, *Ottonian Book Illumination*, I, 208–9.

[53] The phases of development at Reichenau are named after the scribes or artists whose names appear
in dedication pictures. Thus Anno is associated with the Gero codex (Darmstadt, Landes- und Stadtbibliothek, MS 1948) and the phase of *c*.965–75, and Ruodpreht with the Egbert Psalter (Cividale,
Museo Archeologico Nazionale, cod. 136) and the MSS of *c*.975–95.

[54] Its ramifications are beyond the scope of the present study, as is the question of the influence of a
hypothetical late antique illustrated gospel lectionary on the development of Ottonian New Testament
cycles, as propounded in A. Weis, 'Die spätantike Lektionar-Illustration im Skriptorium der
Reichenau', in *Die Abtei Reichenau. Neue Beiträge zur Geschichte und Kultur des Inselklosters*, ed. H. Mau-
rer (Sigmaringen, 1974), 311–62. Hugo Buchthal speculated on the possible influence of a set of feast pic-

illumination—basic to the scenes we shall be examining—is the verticality of the compositions, which mostly fill an entire page of a book whose height exceeds its width. The importance of this development was articulated by Otto Demus, who identified it as an aspect of the influence of Byzantium.[55]

The Liuthar manuscripts (in which term I mean to include the so-called *Schulwerke*) include a variety of types of book. Though the iconography of an individual scene may well reappear in different kinds of book (say a gospel lectionary and a sacramentary) without much alteration, the cycle of illustrations as a whole in the Oxford sacramentary should properly be compared with the same kind of liturgical book. From the Carolingian period onwards, two points in the canon of the Mass—the beginning of the preface, and the beginning of the canon itself—formed the principal (and sometimes the only) sites for decoration in a sacramentary or missal.[56] Canon. Liturg. 319 follows the Carolingian practice of placing the canon at the beginning of the book; but later in the eleventh century it was usually moved to the middle, before the Easter Mass, the most important feast in the Church calendar. The only other sacramentary in the same group is the one in Paris already mentioned, which contains eight miniatures, as opposed to Oxford's five: the Adoration of the Magi, the Presentation in the Temple, and the Dormition and Assumption of the Virgin are the additional three. Their degree of decoration and illustration marks out the Oxford and Paris sacramentaries as relatively luxurious productions.[57]

Thus the Crucifixion, not the Nativity, is the first full-page miniature to be found in Canon. Liturg. 319. Fol. 30v (pl. 9) contains a full-page VD monogram (*Vere dignum*, the beginning of the preface); the Crucifixion appears on fol. 31v (pl. 10).[58] The opening words of the canon, *(T)e igitur*, are written in gold capitals; the letter T forms the cross of the Crucifixion, linking Christ on the cross to the sacrifice of the Mass. The Greek *tau* had been understood since early Christian times as a symbol of the cross (though the T in this manuscript is not in the *tau* form); the earliest surviving example of this pictorial transformation of the *Te igitur* initial into a crucifix occurs in the Gellone sacramentary of the late eighth century.[59]

tures from a Byzantine lectionary: 'Byzantium and Reichenau', in *Byzantine Art, An European Art: Lectures*, ed. M. Chatzidakis (Athens, 1966), 45–60.

[55] *Byzantine Art and the West* (New York, 1970), 90–4.

[56] R. Suntrup, '*Te igitur*-Initialen und Kanonbilder in mittelalterlichen Sakramentarhandschriften', in *Text und Bild. Aspekte des Zusammenwirkens zweier Künste in Mittelalter und früher Neuzeit*, ed. C. Meier and U. Ruberg (Wiesbaden, 1980), 278–382; O. Pächt, *Book Illumination in the Middle Ages: An Introduction*, trans. K. Davenport (London, 1986), 36, 42.

[57] Of the later eleventh-century sacramentaries in the Reichenau tradition, one has the same selection of scenes as the Oxford MS (Paris, Bibliothèque nationale de France, MS. Smith-Lesouëf 3); one has the same selection as the Paris sacramentary (Bologna, Biblioteca Universitaria, Cod. 1084); and two (Einsiedeln, Stiftsbibliothek, Cod. 113 and 114) have only the Crucifixion.

[58] Both are reproduced in colour in Pächt, *Book Illumination*, col. pls. XVI (fol. 30v) and XVII (fol. 31v).

[59] Paris, Bibliothèque nationale de France, MS. lat. 12048, fol. 143v.

Reichenau gospel books and gospel lectionaries present the Crucifixion as a narrative scene, with other figures such as Longinus and Stephaton around the cross. Sometimes the page is also divided in two, and another scene, usually Christ before Caiaphas, is paired with it. This narrative emphasis inevitably makes the focus on the Crucifixion less intense. But in Reichenau sacramentaries, where as we have seen the image lies at the beginning of the canon, the heart of the liturgical re-creation of the sacrifice, Christ is presented on the cross alone, or attended only by the Virgin Mary and St John. In Canon. Liturg. 319, as in the Paris sacramentary (pl. 11), Christ is shown alive, with his eyes open, clean-shaven (as in most of the Reichenau representations), straight in posture, and clothed in a long tunic and pallium—though not in the *collobium*, the full-length tunic of purple silk with gold embroidery worn by the Byzantine emperors, which Christ wears in the Codex Egberti (fol. 83v) and the Pericopes Book of Henry II (fol. 107v). None of the possible symbols of divinity and eternity—the hand of God, angels, the sun and moon—are shown, though in Paris, attached to the frame, are eight crowned bust figures of uncertain significance, which have sometimes been identified as the beatitudes. The isolated figure of the crucified continued to appear later in the century in sacramentaries and missals from Reichenau and elsewhere, as seen for instance in the two missals from Einsiedeln and in the sacramentary now in Bologna.[60]

Henry Mayr-Harting has explored the variety of Ottonian depictions of the Crucifixion, and related them to the absorption of the ideal of humility into the Ottonian ideology of rule.[61] The Crucifixion could be represented as the culminating triumph of Christ or as the climax of his suffering. The most triumphalist Ottonian depiction is the Uta Codex from Regensburg,[62] where Christ is arrayed in a golden crown, wearing clothes of imperial purple and a stole indicative of his sacral kingship, whilst he rests his feet on a *suppedaneum*. To his right are the personifications of the sun, grace, and the church; to his left, the corresponding figures represent the moon, the law, and synagogue. Life and death are at the base of the cross. At the other pole, manuscripts from Cologne consistently emphasize the suffering humanity of Jesus. In the gospel book from Cologne now in Giessen,[63] his eyes are closed; he is clothed not in a long tunic but only in a loincloth; blood flows from his wounded hands and side. In the wooden Gero Crucifix in Cologne Cathedral Christ's body is also slightly twisted to the side; but as Henry Mayr-Harting observes, the suffering is

---

[60] All three are illustrated in W. Vogler, *Das goldene Buch von Pfäfers (Liber aureus). Vollständige Faksimile-Ausgabe im Originalformat des Codex Fabariensis 2 des Stiftarchivs Pfäfers im Stiftsarchiv St. Gallen. Kommentar* (Graz, 1993), Ill. 16, 22, 40.

[61] Mayr-Harting, *Ottonian Book Illumination*, I, 126–39.

[62] Munich, Bayerische Staatsbibliothek, Clm. 13601, fol. 3v: Mayr-Harting, *Ottonian Book Illumination*, I, pl. XVIII.

[63] Giessen, Universitätsbibliothek, Cod. 660, fol. 188r: Mayr-Harting, *Ottonian Book Illumination*, I, fig. 81.

restrained, noble, and serenely accepted, not abject or expressionistic. The Crucifixions depicted in manuscripts from Reichenau (which in the 920s had acquired a double relic of the Holy Cross and the Holy Blood) are usually somewhere in the middle of this spectrum, not triumphal in spirit but still preserving the divine dignity. The exception is the extraordinary image in the Aachen Gospels (p. 468), where Christ is shown dead on the cross, his body twisted and his head slumped; the spear pierces his side whilst the legs of the thieves are broken.

The most common method of depicting the Nativity in the Liuthar group and its followers is to place the scene in the top half of the page, with the Annunciation to the Shepherds below. This is the Byzantine pattern, adopted already in the Codex Egberti (fol. 13r). At Reichenau there were two different ways of representing the angelic element in the Annunciation to the Shepherds. In some cases, including Canon. Liturg. 319 (fol. 38v, pl. 12)[64] and the gospel lectionary now in Wolfenbüttel (fol. 63v), three half-figure angels are shown immediately below the crib. In others, such as the Paris sacramentary (fol. 27v), the news is given by one large angel standing on a hill, whilst the half-figure angels fly down towards the Nativity from the top of the page. These two types could be combined, as in Munich Clm. 23338 (fol. 1v), where there are two half-length angels below the crib, the third having been transposed into the single larger angel who announces the news. It is immediately clear that the two sacramentaries in the group, though they share some particular features, are not consistently closer to each other in iconographical detail than they are to the gospel books or lectionaries of the same group. By far the most impressive visualization is to be found in the Pericopes Book of Henry II, where the Annunciation to the Shepherds is on the left-hand side of an opening, with the Nativity opposite (pl. 13). The portrayal of the angel of the Annunciation, with its towering size, its high position, its windswept garments, the huge spread of its wings, and its domineering glance, is with justice described by Henry Mayr-Harting as the apogee of angelic power in Ottonian art.[65] He goes on to relate the stress on majesty, rule, and hierarchy in this manuscript, which was commissioned by Henry II from Reichenau for his new cathedral church at Bamberg, to the ruler's own influence and the ritual which had formed part of his struggle to assert his claim to the throne against determined opposition. Despite the numerous motifs Canon. Liturg. 319 shares with its grander forebear (such as the gesture of the shepherd on the left who holds up his hand in recognition of the news), its world is by comparison positively domestic.

Whilst in Byzantium the Resurrection of Christ was represented by the scene of the Harrowing of Hell or Descent into Limbo, at Reichenau the

---

[64] The miniature in MS. Canon. Liturg. 319 occurs at the opening of the Mass for Christmas Day.

[65] *Ottonian Book Illumination*, I, 187; II, 120; *Perceptions of Angels in History. An Inaugural Lecture Delivered in the University of Oxford on 14 November 1997* (Oxford, 1998), 10–11 and fig. 1.

Resurrection is consistently represented by the scene of the holy women approaching the angel sitting on the empty tomb. In Canon. Liturg. 319 the scene takes place under an arch supported by columns with acanthus capitals (fol. 95v, pl. 14).[66] The distinctive trumpet-shaped flowers, each emerging from the last, which decorate the arch, form part of the Reichenau decorative repertoire: compare, for instance, the decorated arch above St John the Evangelist in the Wolfenbüttel lectionary (fol. 4v). Below the arch, the three women stare from the left towards the angel on the right, who sits on the coffin lid, none of the rest of the tomb being visible. Two of the women hold jars of ointment, and the foremost swings a censer. The angel, who is distinctly larger in scale, is seated almost frontally, but turns his head towards the women, and blesses them with his right hand; in his left he holds a staff.

The text in Matthew's Gospel (28.1–7) mentions only two women, but the three of the version in Mark's Gospel (16.1–8) is most common in Ottonian art, and even a version with four is known, perhaps licensed by the other women mentioned in Luke 24.10. The basic composition is common to almost all the representations of the scene from Reichenau,[67] and the discrepancies between the Oxford version and those found elsewhere are mostly minor.[68] In its tight composition, and in the omission of most of the usual stage props—the built-up tomb, the winding-sheet, the sleeping guards—the Oxford sacramentary seems to follow the Pericopes of Henry II. But there the angel confronts the three women from the monumentally dignified distance of a separate page, as the scene is spread across an opening (pl. 15), in an extreme example of that book's daring use of statuesque figures and expansive gestures against spacious gold backgrounds. The gold grounds of Ottonian art, which derived from Byzantium and which put paid to the last vestiges of the late antique atmospheric sky, lend its miniatures qualities of spacelessness and timelessness, giving the actions of the characters a ritual significance. Yet the figures in Canon. Liturg. 319, in their smaller size and darting animation, seem to breathe a less refined air, even when (as here) that air is golden.

In the depiction of the Ascension the Reichenau manuscripts again adopt variants of three main types.[69] First there is the late antique version found in the

[66] The miniature occurs at the opening of the Mass for Easter Sunday. It is reproduced in colour in A. G. and W. O. Hassall, *Treasures from the Bodleian Library* (London, 1976), pl. 5.

[67] Many are reproduced in P. Bloch, 'Das Reichenauer Einzelblatt mit dem Frauen am Grabe im Hessischen Landesmuseum Darmstadt', *Kunst in Hessen und am Mittelrhein*, 3 (1963), 24–43.

[68] The first Mary sometimes turns her head, as in the Bernulphus Codex in Utrecht (fol. 113v); the angel may sit more sideways-on, as in the Bamberg Troper (fol. 82r); an architectural setting may be included, into which, as in the Hildesheim orationale (fol. 56v), the sleeping guards are sometimes incorporated; and usually the sarcophagus proper is shown, at an angle to the diagonally slanting lid, whilst in the Oxford scene the lid appears to float.

[69] As classified by U. Nilgen, 'Das Himmelfahrtsbild im Perikopenbuch Heinrichs II.', in *Sancta Treveris. Beiträge zu Kirchenbau und bildender Kunst im alten Erzbistum Trier. Festschrift für Franz J. Ronig zum 70. Geburtstag*, eds. M. Embach, C. Gerhardt, W. Schmid, A. Schommers, and H.-W. Stork (Trier, 1999), 467–90.

Codex Egberti (fol. 101v), in which Christ is viewed in profile within a mandorla, stepping up to take the hand of God which emerges from a cloud. In the
second type, which derives from Byzantium and is seen already in the Poussay
Pericopes of the late tenth century,[70] Christ stands frontally in the mandorla,
often holding a cross or cross staff in one hand and a book in the other. The
cross staff may derive from the tradition of Christ trampling the beasts in illustration of Psalm 90—though Nilgen speculates also on the possible importance
of monumental apse compositions of Christ in Majesty to this type. Finally,
Christ can also be shown frontally not in a mandorla but as if standing on a
cloud, as first found in the Pericopes of Henry II (fol. 131r); in such renderings
he often blesses with one hand and holds a cross staff in the other. In some versions of this type, such as that in the Augsburg lectionary, rays are shown emanating from the cloud. The artist of Canon. Liturg. 319, obviously aware of both
these traditions and perhaps bewildered by the choice, chose to try to combine
these possibilities by placing Christ on a cloud but still enclosing him within an
oval mandorla (fol. 110v, pl. 16).[71] Christ's contrapposto stance, which in the
Oxford version affects only his feet, is in any case common to both types. The
half-angels in the sky on either side of Christ, who gesture towards him, are not
found in the Codex Egberti or in the Poussay Pericopes; but once they had
appeared in the Pericopes of Henry II, they became a standard element of the
scene, whatever other choices an artist had made (pl. 17). In Canon. Liturg. 319,
as in many other cases, they appear as if leaning over the garden wall of heaven,
an effect caused partly by the colour differentiation of the earthly and heavenly
spheres (the background is gold below, but pink above).

   The basic disposition of the human and angelic witnesses below, divided into
two halves by the *terra undulata*, is common to all these Ascension scenes. The
Virgin Mary is not present in the biblical account, but had for long been present, sometimes even central, in Byzantine depictions. In general the variations
in the depiction of the witnesses in the Reichenau manuscripts, such as the
presence or absence of the tree in the middle, and the number of disciples, do
not correspond to the different ways of presenting Christ. Mayr-Harting has
observed a particular variant, which is found in the Oxford sacramentary, by
which one of the angels on the ground puts his arm around the shoulder of
St Peter. He suggests that it is a motif transposed from scenes in which a patron
saint ushers a pope or ruler into the presence of Christ.[72] This is another detail
that is found in some of the manuscripts but not in others. Thus the artists of
these miniatures did not simply adopt one of several 'packages' on offer, complete in all its details; rather, they adopted a basic type, and then seem to have
gathered ideas for the details of each scene from the various previous versions.

---

[70] Paris, Bibliothèque nationale de France, MS. lat. 10514, fol. 66v.
[71] The miniature occurs at the opening of the Mass for Ascension Day.
[72] *Ottonian Book Illumination*, I, 22.

This kind of variation would presumably not have been possible if these manuscripts had been copied in different places, each from a single exemplar. Instead the relationships between them are complex: the consistent affiliation of all the scenes in a manuscript to a single earlier model can be observed only very occasionally. Since it is unrealistic to imagine that all the different versions remained in one place—we have seen that books were made at Reichenau as gifts, or to satisfy outside commissions—the art historian is thrown back, in attempting to speculate on the scriptorium practices that made such transmission possible, on to that vital but strangely elusive stage prop of his trade, the model book.[73]

The final miniature is of Pentecost (fol. 115v, pl. 18).[74] The apostles are seated in a single row, following the usual Reichenau composition.[75] They have haloes, but no tongues of fire licking their heads,[76] and the rays of the Spirit descend from Heaven above. Sometimes, as in the Bamberg Apocalypse (fol. 73r) and the Paris sacramentary (fol. 94v), the haloed dove is shown flying down from the arc of Heaven from which the rays emanate (they are not shown actually emanating from the dove). But at the centre of the emanation in the Oxford scene is the blessing hand of God in front of a golden cross, supported on each side by the half-figure of an angel; the ends of the cross are three-pronged, like the rays of the spirit themselves. Some versions show only the hand; elsewhere, as in the Wolfenbüttel lectionary (pl. 19), the angels appear without a hand.

These differences are no doubt capable of theological interpretation; but it would seem unlikely that the variations represent any conscious desire on the part of artists or patrons to make subtle statements about the mode of descent of the Spirit. They are of a quite different order from the telling detail found in the Paris sacramentary of the bowl of bread below the seated apostles, obviously an echo of the bowl of bread in front of the apostles in the Codex Egberti (fol. 103r), where it is actually labelled *communis vita*. This is a clear reference to the sharing of goods in common by the apostles, whence derives the monastic ideal of the common life; Mayr-Harting points to the emphasis on this theme in the Gorze monastic reform and the part played in that movement by Archbishop Egbert in Trier.[77] What then of the object which extends from Peter to Paul in the centre of the row of Apostles in Canon. Liturg. 319? Is it a cloth spread over their knees, a reference to the long linen cloths described by ritual orders to be spread over the altar, and thus a signifier of monastic eucharistic devotion?[78] This seems plausible by comparison with the scenes of Christ

[73] R. W. Scheller, *Exemplum: Model-book Drawings and the Practice of Artistic Transmission in the Middle Ages (ca. 900–ca. 1470)* (Amsterdam, 1995).
[74] The miniature occurs at the beginning of the Mass for Pentecost.
[75] Although there are examples, e.g. Munich Clm. 23338 (fol. 104v), of the apostles arranged in four groups of three in each lobe of a quatrefoil frame, with the dove of the Holy Spirit in the centre.
[76] On the whole haloes and fire were considered to be alternatives: the combination of the two is rare.
[77] *Ottonian Book Illumination*, I, 84; II, 79–80.   [78] Ibid., II, 80, 236, n. 74.

preaching to the seated apostles in the Codex Egberti.[79] Or is the Oxford object
in fact a scroll, an artist's variation on the book held by Peter and Paul in some
other versions, such as the Bamberg Apocalypse and the Wolfenbüttel lectionary, designed to show that the emanation of the spirit is in harmony with
the spread of the gospel? Such an identification is supported by the fact that in
the Oxford miniature one apostle to the left holds a rolled-up scroll, one behind
Peter has a closed book, and a third on the extreme right is holding an open
book. It is unlikely that every variation should be expected to carry the same
weight of interpretation.

Comparisons with other closely related manuscripts may seem to run the risk
of reducing the appreciation of this individual book. In fact the opposite is
surely the case: just as individuals can better be understood in the context of
their families and friendships, so the true assessment of a book's character is
possible only by a full understanding of its near relations. The leading members
of the Liuthar group of manuscripts are mostly linked to imperial commissions,
and their imagery has been interpreted as having quite direct connections to the
concerns of their illustrious patrons. It may be that certain fashions were inau-
gurated in conscious homage to the prestige of these books produced for
rulers—or for rulers to give away. But any consideration of those 'royal' books
must also take into account that in many cases very similar images were considered suitable for a variety of other (mainly ecclesiastical) audiences. If we are
correct to see Reichenau as a centre of fine book production and decoration over
what, for any one scriptorium, must be counted a comparatively long period of
time, then we should think not only in terms of imperial fashions, but also of the
ability of the one centre to 'colonize' a variety of patrons and recipients by the
dispersal of manuscripts—manuscripts whose decoration and illustration,
whatever the variations of detail, remain strikingly unified. Canon. Liturg. 319
must always have been a special book; but its owners would probably have seen
others like it, and would have recognized and approved of the similarity of this
book to them.

APPENDIX

Physical Details of MS. Canon. Liturg. 319

Material: parchment, the hair side (on the outside of the quire) occasionally very mot-
tled, but never rough.

Measurements: 240–5 × 175–80 mm.

Number of leaves: 6 paper + 2 modern parchment + 266 + 2 modern parchment + 2
paper, foliated viii + 270 (there are two fol. 42s, but no fol. 197).

---

[79] e.g. on fol. 29r.

Ruling: in hard point; section A of the text has 22 ruled lines for 22 lines of text, the order in 2 columns, the calendar in one, ruled space 155–60 × 110–20 mm. Section B of the text has 17 ruled lines for 17 lines of text, single column, ruled space 155–60 × 100 mm (110 including the left-hand margin ruled for initials).

Collation: I–III⁸ (fols. 1–24), IV⁴ (fols. 25–8), V–VI⁸ (fols. 29–43, two leaves foliated 42 in error), VII⁶ (fols. 44–9), VIII¹² (fols. 50–61), IX⁴ (fols. 62–5), X¹² (fols. 66–77), XI² (fols. 78–9), XII¹² (fols. 80–91), XIII⁴ (fols. 92–5), XIV¹² (fols. 96–107), XV⁴ (fols. 108–11), XVI¹² (fols. 112–23), XVII⁴ (fols. 124–7), XVIII¹² (fols. 128–39), XIX⁴ (fols. 140–43), XX¹² (fols. 144–55), XXI⁴ (fols. 156–9), XXII¹² (fols. 160–71), XXIII⁴ (fols. 172–5), XXIV¹² (fols. 176–87), XXV⁴ (fols. 188–91), XXVI¹² (fols. 192–204, misfoliation results in a single leaf numbered 197–8), XXVII⁴ (fols. 205–8), XXVIII¹² (fols. 209–20), XXIX⁴ (fols. 221–4), XXX¹² (fols. 225–36), XXXI⁶ (fols. 237–42), XXXII–XXXIII⁸ (fols. 243–58), XXXIV⁸⁻¹ ⁺ ¹ (fols. 259–66, one leaf cancelled after fol. 265, fol. 266 attached to a stub). No quire signatures or catchwords.

Initials and rubrication: Five full-page initials or monograms: fols. 30v (the *Vere dignum* monogram), 39r (*Concede quaesumus omnipotens deus*), 96r (*Deus qui hodierna die*), 111r (*Concede quaesumus*), and 116r (*Deus qui hodierna die*). Each except the first faces a full-page miniature. Fols. 29v–30r written in gold capitals. Eleven 3-, 4-, or 5-line decorated initials (with the feasts whose texts they begin): fols. 44r (Epiphany), 123v (Nativity of St John the Baptist), 126v (Sts Peter and Paul), 138r (Assumption of the Virgin and its vigil), 142v (Nativity of the Virgin), 150r (Michael), 155v (All Saints), 165v (first Sunday after Easter), 167r (first Sunday after the octave of Pentecost), 192r (Trinity Sunday). 1-, 2-, 3-, and 4-line plain gold initials throughout; rubricated, with preparatory notes giving the text of the rubrics still visible in the margins.

14

EVENTS THAT LED TO SAINTHOOD: SANCTITY AND THE REFORMERS IN THE ELEVENTH CENTURY

Kathleen G. Cushing

Few historians would look to measure the eleventh-century reformers in terms of sanctity, especially those associated with Pope Gregory VII. Indeed, an abiding image of the Gregorian reforming circle is of men of practical expediency who preferred the harsher lines of polemic and law to the finer spiritual leanings of contemplation and salvation that are generally thought to characterize sanctity. Though this clearly is a one-sided view of the religious vision of the reformers, it is a stereotype that persists in modern historiography. Somewhat more surprising, it is a view that also finds support in the Lives of some eleventh-century reformers.

This image of action, however, may prove deceptive. Closer readings of the *vitae* of eleventh-century reformers reveal that while they may have been 'men of action' negotiating their way through tumultuous events rather than holy men of contemplation, they were inevitably acted *upon* by the authors of their Lives. Although this is true of all Christian hagiography where rhetorical and other needs led biographers to claim any number of fictitious deeds, it is important to take into account how the special circumstances of eleventh-century reform may have animated these authors. Clearly, the hagiographic repertoire included models for active men in the world.[1] The construction of sanctity in the *vitae* of eleventh-century reformers such as Ariald of Milan and Anselm of Lucca, however, appears to depend less upon traditional hagiographic strategies than on the broader context in which they were shown to operate. Whether there is a new form of 'reform sanctity' to be found in contemporaneous *vitae* has yet to be fully established. Using the *Vita et Passio Sancti Arialdi* and the *Vita Anselmi Episcopi Lucensis* as test cases, however, I wish to suggest that a new model of sanctity was indeed being proposed, one more in keeping with hagiographers' desire to show that the entire reforming movement was of

---

[1] e.g. the Lives of Martin, Gregory I, and Boniface, where active lives were combined with contemplation and personal sanctity.

itself a holy exercise.[2] Here, sanctity was not necessarily tied to place;[3] rather, it was associated with events and deeds played out on a public, polemical stage as part of the universal institutional reform of the Church and its spiritual life.

This is not to deny the role of traditional models in these and other eleventh-century Lives. More important, though, are the authors' attempts not simply to mediate between customary archetypes and their new ideals, but also to resonate with different audiences. In traditional hagiography the saint becomes the servant of a specific place or community. In the new hagiography of a movement, however, the locus of the cult is as much universal as personal. To put it another way, the 'locus' is the servant of the righteous cause, but the cult is actually the exaltation and perpetuation of the movement. In this light, the Lives not only function as commemorative, didactic hagiography, providing sainted figures for specific communities, but they also, more interestingly, try to sanctify the reform movement itself by situating the sanctity of the individual within the events of the struggle for reform. The cults of Ariald and Anselm in Milan and Mantua, therefore, operate on two levels and have at least two audiences. For the hagiographers and reform-minded individuals, the cult was the reform movement embodied in the saint; for the *populus*, the cult focused on the tangible body and his/her service to the needs of their communities. Through their devotion to the tangible, however, they also necessarily revered the reform movement.

Little is known of the life and career of Ariald, apart from the account of his hagiographer, Andreas of Strumi, and the often hostile witness of the Milanese chroniclers, Arnulf and, especially, Landulf Senior.[4] Born at Cucciago, a village near Milan, around 1010, Ariald belonged to a family of modest proprietary landowners, though Andreas claimed he was of noble birth.[5] What with familial circumstances, Ariald was apparently marked for an ecclesiastical career at an early age, though not surprisingly Andreas emphasized his precocious religiosity.[6] After initial schooling, probably in the nearby *pieve* of San Vittore di Varese, Ariald later went to the cathedral school in Milan, apparently taking orders as a deacon. Following the peripatetic lifestyle that was then becoming

[2] *Vita et Passio Sancti Arialdi*, MGH Scriptores XXX, 2 (Leipzig, 1934), 1047–75; *Vita Anselmi Episcopi Lucensis*, MGH SS XII (Leipzig, 1925), 1–35.
[3] Though a specific physical site (or sites) would be necessary for burial.
[4] Arnulf, *Liber Gestorum Recentiorum*, ed. C. Zey, MGH Scriptores Rerum Germanicarum LXVII (Hannover, 1994); *Landulfi Historia Mediolanesis*, MGH SS VIII (Leipzig, 1925), 32–100. On the problems of Landulf Senior, see C. Violante, *La Pataria milanese e la riforma ecclesiastica (1048–57)* (Rome, 1955), 15–16, 178–213; H. E. J. Cowdrey, 'The Papacy, the Patarenes and the Church of Milan', *TRHS*, 5th ser., 18 (1968), 25–48; O. Capitani, 'Storiografia e riforma della chiesa in Italia: Arnolfo e Landolfo Seniore di Milano', in *La storiografia altomedioevale*, 2 vols. (Spoleto, 1970), II, 557–629; and B. Stock, *The Implications of Literacy: Written Language and Models of Interpretation in the Eleventh and Twelfth Centuries* (Princeton, 1983), 174–214.
[5] *Vita et Passio Sancti Arialdi*, 2, 1050. Arnulf described his origins as 'humiliter': 3. 8, 175.
[6] *Vita Arialdi*, 3, 1051.

fashionable among young clerks in northern Italy, Ariald subsequently travelled 'in diversis terris', acquiring the degree of master of liberal arts.[7]

Ariald began his campaign as a reformer by preaching against married clergy in Varese in early 1057.[8] Meeting with little success, he went to Milan, where together with the notary, Landulf Cotta, he recommenced public preaching against clerical marriage and concubinage, urging his audience to boycott the ministrations of married priests.[9] Though detractors disparaged his preaching style, he was able, despite a soft voice, to tap the force of public indignation and attracted many adherents—to the dismay of the established Ambrosian clergy.[10] A violent clash was soon forthcoming. On 10 May 1057, during a procession in honour of San Nazario, Ariald called for the end of concubinage and clerical marriage. Citing a little-known but precise provision of Justinian, and perhaps alluding to a canon from the Council of Pavia in 1022, he formulated a *phytacium de castitate servanda* that the clergy were to sign under threat of death.[11] The ensuing struggle in the piazza disclosed an important change in tactics.[12] No longer would the Pataria simply boycott the services of compromised clerics; they would take sterner measures, even using force to prevent them from participating in the Mass.[13]

After this the Patarene campaign was extended to include simony, a natural result of preoccupations with clerical marriage because of its implications for the misuse of ecclesiastical resources.[14] With the support they were able to muster and their strong connections at Rome, the Pataria split Milanese society, pitting family against family, brother against brother.[15] The death of Landulf Cotta and the appointment of his brother Erlembald as the pope's lay representative in 1061 deepened the already widening gulf between the archbishop of Milan, Guido, and the reformers.[16]

Matters came to a head with the excommunication of Guido by Pope Alexander II on 9 March 1066. A violent anti-Patarene reaction ensued, and during an attempt to flee south to Rome, Ariald was imprisoned in a castle belonging to Guido's niece, Oliva, on an island in Lago Maggiore. In that

---

[7] Ibid. 4, 1051. Cf. Arnulf, 3. 8, 175; Landulf Senior, 3. 5, 76.

[8] *Vita Arialdi*, 4, 1051–2; cf. Landulf Senior, 3. 5–6, 72.   [9] Ibid.

[10] e.g. *Vita Arialdi*, 13, 1058; 18, 1062; 26, 1074. Cf. Stock, *Implications*, 215–17, 235–40.

[11] Arnulf, 3. 10, 178–9. Cf. *Constitutiones et Acta Publica*, MGH Leges, sectio IV.1 (Hannover, 1893), no. 34, 73; and *Vita Arialdi*, 4–5, 1052–3.

[12] Landulf Senior, 3. 8–10, 79–80; Arnulf, 3. 10, 179. Cf. Violante, *La Pataria milanese*, 175–213, esp. 184–9.

[13] Ariald and Landulf were subsequently excommunicated by Archbishop Guido of Milan at a synod at Fontaneto in November 1057—something Andreas ignores. Cf. Landulf Senior, 3. 16, 84; Arnulf, 3. 11, 179–80.

[14] *Vita Arialdi*, 10, 1055–57; Landulf Senior, 3. 5–6, 77–8; Arnulf, 3. 12, 180–1. Cf. Violante, 181–6.

[15] *Vita Arialdi*, 10, 1056. Cf. Landulf Senior, 3. 10, 14, pp. 80–1, 82; Arnulf, 3. 12, 15, pp. 180, 188–89.

[16] A brief respite came with Peter Damian's legation in 1059, when the Milanese church agreed to penance and compromise. *Die Briefe des Petrus Damiani*, 2. 65, ed. K. Reindel, 4 vols., MGH Briefe der deutschen Kaiserzeit V, 1–4 (Munich, 1983–93), 228–47.

obscure setting Ariald was assassinated on 27 June 1066 by unreformed priests (laymen having refused to set hands on him). His body was thrown into the lake. When it floated to the surface some ten months later the body was escorted back to Milan by Erlembald on 17 May 1067, where it was venerated in the cathedral for ten days. On 27 May Ariald was popularly acclaimed as a saint, his status as a martyr subsequently being recognized by Alexander II.

Written around 1075 by a Vallombrosan monk, Andreas of Strumi, the *Vita Arialdi* was ostensibly fashioned for a specific audience. Composed at the request of Abbot Rodulf (1073–6), it was intended as a work of edification for the Vallombrosan congregation, whose founder, John Gualbertus, had led a similarly spirited campaign for reform in Florence.[17] The first section of the Life (cc. 1–18) treats the Pataria's early phases, the second (cc. 19–26) is concerned with Ariald's martyrdom, and the third with a possibly apocryphal correspondence between Andreas and a Patarene priest named Sirus who claimed intimate acquaintance with Ariald. Andreas employed the well-known hagiographic model of the saint as popular agitator, emphasizing Ariald's asceticism and strong leadership among the reform community. Furthermore, Ariald is depicted as a living example of Christ, not only in terms of prayer and reform activity, but also—indeed especially—in his persecution and martyrdom, which like Christ's involved a betrayal by one of his own.[18]

The *Vita Arialdi*, however, is not merely a hagiographical life written to foster a local cult: it is also a polemical work designed to enshrine a particular ideology. Andreas deploys a range of narrative devices, such as 'verbatim' accounts of Ariald's sermons, the corroboration of reliable witnesses, and the correspondence with Sirus, which outline and seek to justify the wholly novel methods with which Ariald intimidated his opponents. After all, it had been Ariald's ability to mobilize urban crowds that had made radical measures possible. These included liturgical boycotts, and the use of force both to separate clerics from their wives or concubines and to constrain them from altars, churches, and especially benefices. Despite the frightening nature of these tactics, Andreas recounts them in a matter-of-fact way. While the tactics may have been novel, Andreas was more interested in situating Ariald and the righteousness of his cause in the context of reform than in addressing any specific critics.[19] Yet Andreas was concerned to buttress the authenticity of his account beyond simply relying on witnesses such as Ariald's brother Marchio, his servant Bonovisino, and even the testimony of Sirus. Accordingly we find Andreas intruding himself into the narrative in order to verify the events he recorded.

---

[17] *Vita Arialdi*, prolog., 1, 1049–50.

[18] e.g. *Vita Arialdi*, 10, 1056; 17, 1062; 20, 1065; 23, 1071. Cf. C. Alzati, 'Tradizione e disciplina nel dibattio tra ambrosiani e patarini a Milano nell'età di Gregorio VII', *Ambrosiana ecclesia: studi su la chiesa Milanese e l'ecumene cristiana fra tarda antichità e medioevo* (Milan, 1993), 187–206; Capitani, 'Storiografia', 572–5; and Cowdrey, 'The Papacy, the Patarenes', 28–9.

[19] It is often seen in relation to Arnulf.

He thereby reveals himself as a player within the struggle of Ariald as well as his hagiographer.[20]

In the *Vita*, Ariald is in many ways a typical reforming 'man of action'. Events and images of action are crowded into the text; Ariald leads by word, deed, and moral example. Reform itself is often depicted in active terms. In Ariald's sermons, the struggle against simony becomes an active religious duty; inaction entails acquiescence, and even implicates the passive Christian in the crime.[21] His supporters are to be God's agents, and all sectors of his audience have a role to play: they are all to fight (*pugnare*); laymen are to give alms to repel (*repellere*) and to destroy (*dispergere*) simony.[22] Ariald not only organizes his adherents as a quasi-sect, but also creates in his *canonica* (the church he established in Milan) what Karl Leyser termed a 'counter-church', where the injunction to boycott the ministrations of married clergy could be translated into action—action that included sacking the houses of alleged culprits.[23] Ariald's insistence on the communal life in the *canonica* is also suggestive of activity. Here, *vita communis* did not simply provide a framework for the pursuit of individual perfection, but also shaped a community that would act as a barrier against the havoc that married clergy and simonists had brought into the Church.[24] Even in death he remained a potent force, uniting, albeit briefly, the diverse social and religious strands of Milan into a single web.[25]

The actions and events, especially as they were 'completed' by martyrdom, are more important components than any personal virtues in the construction of Ariald's sanctity in Andreas's text. The mundane miracles, and the fact that they appear only in the correspondence with Sirus that comprises an appendix to the Life itself, reflect this. There are just three miracles (one in life and two posthumous), the first of which is an unexceptional liturgical one. The second miracle was a standard curative one: a paralytic who is healed during the translation of Ariald's coffin from Lago Maggiore to Milan. The third miracle entailed both punishment and redemption. A man 'puffed up with pride', blaspheming at Ariald's tomb, was afflicted with severe visceral pain and was cured only after humbling himself with penance.[26]

---

[20] e.g. *Vita Arialdi*, prolog., 1049–50. Cf. 8, 1054, where he confesses that while he cannot be precise as to the succession of events in the attack on Landulf, he testifies to seeing the weapon; and the 2nd letter to Sirus, 1074–5.

[21] See K. J. Leyser, 'On the Eve of the First European Revolution', in his *Communications and Power in Medieval Europe: The Gregorian Revolution and Beyond*, ed. T. Reuter (London, 1994), 1–20, here 2.

[22] *Vita Arialdi*, 10, 1056. For a different analysis (to which I am indebted), see Stock, *Implications*, 151–240.

[23] Leyser, 'On the Eve', 2; Cf. *Vita Arialdi*, 9, 1055; 11–12, 1057–8. For the *canonica*: 6, 1053; and Cowdrey, 'The Papacy, the Patarenes', 30.

[24] *Vita Arialdi*, 4, 1051–2; 12, 1058.

[25] Ibid. 23, 1071. Cf. Stock, *Implications*, 216–17; and Cowdrey, 'The Papacy, the Patarenes', 39–48, on the paradox that the ultimate failure of the Patarenes opened the way for real reform in Milan.

[26] For Ariald's miracles: *Vita Arialdi*, 1074–5.

The circumstance that there are only three 'generic' miracles should alert us to the fact that the Life proposes a new or at least different form of sanctity. In many ways the Life is an anti-miracle work.[27] Indeed, the structure of the text is such that Andreas needs to be prompted by Sirus's letter to recount these traditional proofs of sanctity. This is important, in that Andreas seeks, deliberately it seems, to contrast the unexceptional quality of Ariald's personal miracles with miraculous events that are associated with reform. Yet, if Ariald's personal miracles were greater, then we might be in danger of confusing the individual (Ariald) with the movement (reform). Consider, for instance, the attack on Landulf Cotta, which was intended to frighten Ariald into silence. Landulf's miraculous healing is depicted by Andreas not so much as a sign of favour to Landulf in particular, but as an indication that God would not allow any of his servants to suffer in a righteous cause—one implicitly personalized by Ariald.[28] More telling is the account of a punitive expedition against Ariald's estates, and the church he constructed there. This was another attempt to intimidate Ariald personally and, more importantly, to impede his 'cause', for the church was an important force for bringing reform from the *contado* into the city. Not only were some of the instigators blinded by the 'just judgement of God', but instead of destroying Ariald's vineyards and trees, the expedition devastated those of Ariald's neighbours.[29] Miraculously though, their trees and vines continued to blossom and bear fruit even though scorched. Andreas explicitly comments (after testifying to having seen the blossoms) that God would not permit his *causam* to be demolished or any harm to come to his true servants.[30] Even more instructive is the curious insistence in the final chapter on the miraculous repetition of the number 'ten' in the life, work, and death of Ariald. For ten years Ariald vigorously led the campaign on behalf of Christ. Ten was the number of mutilations and profanities suffered by his body (eight during martyrdom, two afterwards). For ten months his body had lain in the lake. For ten days he was venerated in the Ambrosian cathedral. In the tenth year after these events Erlembald also suffered martyrdom, and the *Vita* was written.[31] For Andreas, this was not coincidence but providence. Like the other miraculous events, it was the signature of the presence of God in the life of one of his servants, whose cause rather than simply his personal virtues underlay his sanctity.

Anselm of Lucca was perhaps the most important of Gregory VII's supporters. Bishop of Lucca from 1073 to 1086, nephew of Alexander II, spiritual advisor to

---

[27] For the reserved use of miracles in 'reformist circles': A. Murray, 'The Temptation of Hugh of Grenoble', in *Intellectual Life in the Middle Ages: Essays Presented to Margaret Gibson*, ed. L. Smith and B. Ward (London, 1992), 81–101, here 87–9; P. Toubert, *Les Structures du Latium médiéval*, 2 vols. (Rome, 1972), II, 823–25.

[28] *Vita Arialdi*, 8, 1054.   [29] Ibid. 9, 1055.

[30] Ibid.: 'O mira Domini pietas! suam demoliri causam permisit, servi vero sui optime tutari novit.'

[31] Ibid. 26, 1072.

Matilda of Tuscany, papal legate in Lombardy, polemicist and canon lawyer, Anselm seems to typify the Gregorian 'man of action'.[32] Born around 1040, probably in Milan, Anselm belonged to a noble family that had its principal seat in that city, but may also have had rights in Baggio.[33] While there is little information regarding his early life, Anselm was probably educated in Milan under the patronage of his family, perhaps becoming a canon at the cathedral.[34] Though the *Vita Anselmi* is largely silent on his education, only noting his good knowledge of grammar and acquaintance with dialectic, it is arguable that Anselm may also have been a peripatetic scholar, possibly travelling to study with Lanfranc at either Bec or St Étienne in Caen.[35] Appointed to the see of Lucca in the spring of 1073, Anselm's episcopacy was characterized by a bitter and ultimately unsuccessful attempt to reform his cathedral canons.[36] After a protracted struggle, Anselm was expelled from his bishopric in the summer of 1080 by the supporters of Henry IV and Wibert of Ravenna. He then joined Matilda's entourage and played an integral role in the resistance to Henry IV. Though his hagiographers stopped short of portraying him as a 'fighting bishop', Anselm travelled with the Matildine *fideles sancti Petri*, and may have been present at a number of battles. Dying on 18 March 1086 in Mantua, Anselm's wish to be buried at the Benedictine monastery of San Benedetto di Polirone (where his body had immediately been taken by Matilda) was countermanded by Bonizo of Sutri, who insisted that Anselm be buried as befitted one of Gregory VII's bishops. His body was then returned to Mantua, where many miracles were immediately recorded.[37]

The *Vita Anselmi Episcopi Lucensis* was written shortly after Anselm's death, probably by a member of his episcopal *familia* or an associate of Matilda. Unusually, it lacks a prologue or dedication. It is clear, in any event, that the author had ostensibly one ambition: to foster Anselm's cult with a view to his canonization—which occurred in 1087. Yet, like the *Vita Arialdi*, the Life sought to exalt not merely the man but also his cause, and looked to provide a considered justification of the motives that inspired the reformers in their struggle against Henry IV. The author did not, therefore, aim to produce a simple work of edification nor a portrait of a holy man growing in spiritual life towards sanctity. His intention was rather to embody reform, to locate and articulate Anselm's personal sanctity within the context of the reform movement itself. In many ways, it was less a Life than an exaltation of the figure and deeds of a sainted Gregorian bishop, as the following example demonstrates.

Between 18 March and 21 April 1073 Anselm was designated bishop of Lucca by Alexander II, and was sent in the company of Bishop Meginhard of

---

[32] See K. G. Cushing, *Papacy and Law in the Gregorian Revolution: The Canonistic Work of Anselm of Lucca* (Oxford, 1998), 2–6.

[33] *Vita Anselmi Episcopi Lucensis*, 17, p. 18. Cf. Cushing, *Papacy and Law*, 43–4.

[34] *Vita Anselmi*, 2, p. 13.   [35] See Cushing, *Papacy and Law*, 46–8.   [36] Ibid. 55–61.

[37] *Vita Anselmi*, 40, p. 24.

St Rufino to be invested by the king.[38] Yet, according to the anonymous author of his *Vita*, Anselm began to have serious doubts about the propriety of receiving investiture from the king, and decided to seize any opportunity to depart without being invested. Then, in the next chapter, the Life wholly contradicts itself, noting that after the death of Alexander and the elevation of Gregory VII, Anselm was elected to the bishopric of Lucca, and was subsequently consecrated by Gregory. The text then records that, after perusing books of diverse authorities, Anselm began to consider himself damned for having received his office from the king. Finding the situation insupportable, Anselm used the pretext of a visit to Rome to leave his bishopric, and entered an unnamed, supposedly Cluniac, monastery. Shortly afterwards, so this text says, Anselm was recalled by Gregory VII, who restored him to his bishopric, allowing him to continue wearing the monastic habit.

This account of Anselm's 'crisis' over investiture is indicative of problems in the *Vita Anselmi*. While it is a good 'reform' story, it is obviously faulty in detail, and contracts events that were drawn out over at least two years.[39] It is, however, an important incident in the construction of Anselm's sanctity. Though of brief duration, the monastic retirement was evidently an important event not only for Anselm but also for his hagiographer, writing in the context of the clash over lay investiture. Anselm wore the monastic habit for the rest of his life, and devoted himself to ascetic practices. In less personal terms though, Anselm's investiture crisis made him for other bishops a symbol of the grave error of accepting royal investiture. It provided, at the same time, a valuable guide to how one could nevertheless be reconciled with the Church. Most important of all, the confused events surrounding Anselm's election provided his hagiographer with an opportunity to display a man whose desire for a secluded contemplative life was outweighed by his obedience to Gregory VII, and was sacrificed to the burden of an active life in a cause of righteousness.

Unlike the *Vita Arialdi*, the *Vita Anselmi* is crowded with personal miracles, dating from the return of Anselm's body to Mantua until 7 June 1087, when the text breaks off. Underlining the work's role in propagating the saint's cult, more than half of the text (cc. 41–84) is devoted to cataloguing Anselm's posthumous miracles, along with the authoritative testimony of a range of reliable witnesses, including the author himself, as well as letters of Matilda and Bishop Ubald of Mantua. The beneficiaries are a socially and geographically diverse group. However much the 'locus' of the cult may have been fixed in Mantua, Anselm clearly was not intended simply to be a saint for that city. Many of the miracles are generic curative ones associated with prayer and devotions at Anselm's tomb. These include miraculous restoration of sight, the cure of paralysis, toothaches, lameness, arthritis, muteness, and many more too numerous to

---

[38] *Vita Anselmi*, 2–4, pp. 13–14.   [39] Cushing, *Papacy and Law*, 48–55.

recount here.[40] Other curative miracles derived from contact with Anselm's personal possessions, as in the case of a demon exorcised from a boy who had drunk water in which Anselm's ring had been dipped.[41] Others were effected by objects which had come into contact with him. Thus, Matilda's headache was cured when she touched a piece from the wooden table on which Anselm's body had been laid out; while on another occasion her eyesight was miraculously restored when she pressed against her eyes parchment on which Anselm had written some Psalms.[42]

Significant though these miracles are by their sheer variety and number, they are not, however, the basis for the construction of Anselm's sanctity, but are rather its proof. The same can be said of the bishop's many ascetical practices, which are lovingly recounted by the Anonymous. These include the standard topoi of private devotions, reading, abstinence, deprivation of sleep, and even details of how little Anselm chewed his meagre daily ration of bread so that he might not enjoy it.[43] Yet such commonplaces of hagiography may also have had a didactic and polemical value in the context of late eleventh-century episcopal culture, revealing how Anselm had successfully negotiated the tension between action and contemplation according to the model of Gregory I's *Regula Pastoralis*.

At the same time, the miracles in the *Vita Anselmi*, as in the *Vita Arialdi*, can be divided into those which are personal and those which pertain to reform. The copious posthumous miracles are offset by what might be termed 'miracles of reform', many of which occurred while Anselm was still alive.[44] These were effectively miracles of healing and conversion, but of a different kind. Here, the cure entailed moving from what was perceived and described as the wrong side (i.e. schismatic, heretical, or imperial) to the good side (orthodox and papal). The Anonymous recounts a number of instances in which Anselm's teachings and writings not only shamed the Wibertine opposition but also brought them back to the ranks of the faithful.[45] Anselm strengthened the resolve of the *fideles sancti Petri* (even granting them remission of sins), and on one occasion to his presence among them in battle is attributed the reintroduction of catholic bishops in the place of usurping schismatics.[46]

Yet, in many ways, Anselm the individual is curiously absent from his own *Vita*. He is a 'figure' who is often shown in relation to events and to other people, notably Matilda, whom he guided in all things secular and spiritual, and to whom he had been committed by Gregory VII as Christ had commended the Virgin to John.[47] That said, he does appear as a 'man of action' in the midst of events—for instance, in the struggle against his cathedral canons, where he

---

[40] *Vita Anselmi*, 43 ff., pp. 25 ff.   [41] Ibid. 51, p. 27.   [42] Ibid. 79–80, p. 34.

[43] Ibid. 27, p. 21.

[44] To which Ekkehard of Aura also testifies: *Chronicon Universale*, 24, MGH SS VI (Leipzig, 1925), 204.

[45] e.g. *Vita Anselmi*, 26, p. 21. Cf. Bernold of Constance, *Chronicon*, MGH SS V (Leipzig, 1925), 441–5.

[46] *Vita Anselmi*, 11, 23–4, pp. 16, 20–1. Cf. Bernold, *Chronicon*, 443, though not named.

[47] *Vita Anselmi*, 12, p. 17.

cajoles, rebukes, and even states that he would prefer to see all the churches utterly empty than for them to be filled with irregular canons.[48] We see him undertaking papal missions, as in the case of his legation to Milan after the reconciliation of Gregory and Henry at Canossa.[49] We see him at his most energetic after the expulsion from Lucca in the midst of the Matildine *fideles sancti Petri* in their campaign against Henry IV.[50] Most important for his hagiographer are Anselm's efforts, both in word and deed, to compel the schismatics to penance and reconciliation.[51]

Above all, it is Anselm's perceived connection with Gregory VII, and especially with the cause that the pope symbolized, which is of paramount importance for his hagiographer. Not only is Anselm most often depicted in this context, but his sanctity is effectively constructed in terms of this relationship. According to the Anonymous, Anselm strove in all things to follow Gregory, to be his most diligent disciple and imitator.[52] All of Anselm's actions, the ascetic topoi, and the miracles that testify to the righteousness of his cause, are to be seen in the light of this crucial relationship. As the Anonymous wrote: '[Gregory] was the source; [Anselm] was the stream that flowed from him and watered the arid ground. [Gregory] was the head that governed the entire body; [Anselm] was the zealous hand that carried out what had been imposed.'[53] By stressing the perfect devotion of Anselm to Gregory and his cause (which was implicit in everything Anselm did, wrote, or said), his hagiographer endeavoured to demonstrate how Anselm's life had been consecrated to the promotion of reform. In the *Vita Anselmi*, therefore, Anselm's hagiographer had constructed not only an icon for the reform movement, but also an archetype of a sainted bishop who operated within and was a focal point in the 'sacred space' that was the reform movement.

Both Ariald and Anselm were men of action. Of this there is little doubt, for on one level their *Vitae* delineated the events and deeds by which they were led to personal sanctity. Yet in a wider sense, in the construction of sanctity by their respective hagiographers, Ariald and Anselm were also symbols of reform, whose very sanctity derived from their undertaking of that holy cause. In contrast to earlier saints' lives, which saw the projection of the individual holy man as an end in itself even while assimilating them to an ideal, the *Vitae* of Ariald and Anselm subsumed their subjects, both textually and physically, into the greater cause of the reform movement. Ariald's martyrdom, Anselm's acceptance of an active life of obedience, their own personal miracles, but especially the aura of the miraculous that surrounded them, were in the end merely testimonies to the sanctified and sanctifying reform movement—the righteous cause that had brought the favour of God to earth through their agency.

---

[48] *Vita Anselmi*, 31, p. 22.   [49] Ibid. 16–17, p. 18. Cf. Arnulf, 5. 9, 230.
[50] *Vita Anselmi*, II, 23–4, 29–31, pp. 16, 20–1, 22.   [51] Ibid. 24–5, pp. 20–1, and esp. 26, p. 21.
[52] Ibid. 3, p. 14: '. . . ut sequeretur iste in omnibus.'   [53] Ibid. 32, p. 22.

15

PASTORALE PEDUM ANTE PEDES APOSTOLICI POSUIT: DIS- AND REINVESTITURE IN THE ERA OF THE INVESTITURE CONTEST

Timothy Reuter

Historians of the eleventh-century church are familiar with the public renunciations by bishops of the symbols of office followed by their return by the pope, acting either in consistory or in council: the first and most spectacular example took place at the Council of Reims in 1049, when Leo IX received an episcopal submission in this way, as we shall see. The action might seem to need no explanation, and it has certainly received none, but it does raise several interesting questions, in particular what it meant and why people began using it in this period. We may begin by looking at some detailed examples, and then move on to elucidate the meaning and the prehistory of this ritual, and the methodological questions it raises.

We can start with texts which refer to the practice in general terms. Some time in the mid-1080s a cleric in the *regnum Teutonicum*, probably in Verdun, wrote a small treatise in letter form, now found in the collection of the so-called 'Regensburg rhetorical letters'.[1] The author was concerned with various questions about canon law, papal authority, and the validity of orders. Towards the end of a long chain of argument he takes up the question of reinvestiture.[2] He begins with a type of argument used frequently in the Investiture Contest polemic: either A or B; but not A; therefore B. He then continues:

---

[1] For the background see C. Märtl, 'Regensburg in den geistigen Auseinandersetzungen des Investiturstreits', *Deutsches Archiv für Erforschung des Mittelalters*, 42 (1986), 145–89, at 156–7.

[2] 'Constat, secundum quod Dominus et salvator noster promisit, spiritum sanctum super apostolos descendisse, eos igne sui amoris non solum inflammasse, verum et capaces omnis scientię fecisse. Aut enim pleniter super eos descendit, aut aliquam exceptionem fecit. Si aliquam exceptionem fecit, minime omnium linguarum scientiam dedit. Si minime omnium linguarum scientiam dedit, frustra in universum mundum predicare evangelium misit. Sed non frustra misit. De omni namque natione quos ad vitam predestinavit, traxit ad fidem. Igitur omnium linguarum scientiam dedidit nullaque exceptione facta pleniter super eos descendit. Valde repugnans est, sanctos apostolos plenitudinem sancti spiritus habere et, quod modo apud modernos inventum est, non habuisse, episcopos scilicet episcopalem reddere virgam et recipere secreto, quasi in hac symoniacę hereseos inustio extincta sit; ad huiusque sancti spiritus iniurię similitudinem, qui in hoc altari, quia non legitime accedunt, ministrare non debent, ad aliud transmutatione facta transferuntur, quasi duo incestuosi dicerent: "tu meam, ego mutuo tuam uxorem accipio"': *Briefsammlungen der Zeit Heinrichs IV*, ed. C. Erdmann and N. Fickermann, MGH Die Briefe der deutschen Kaiserzeit V (Weimar, 1950), no. 8, pp. 311–12.

It is quite unacceptable to claim that the holy apostles have the fullness of the Holy Spirit and at the same time, as is now done by some contemporaries, have not had it, as when bishops return the episcopal staff and secretly receive it, as if by doing so the fire of simoniacal heresy were extinguished. This is the same kind of insult to the Holy Spirit as when persons who may not serve one altar because they did not lawfully come to it are set to serve another, much as if two incestuous men should say to one another: 'you take my wife, I'll take yours.'

The general meaning and thrust of the passage are clear enough, though the nuances, especially at the end, may be more elusive. But this much is certain: the author claims that simoniacal bishops laid down their staff of office and then got it back—from whom?—in secret, thus retrospectively freeing their accession to office of all stain.

The next passage is less problematic. Ivo of Chartres (1090–1116) wrote a letter to Archbishop Josceran of Lyons in 1111/12, after Paschal II had issued the *pravilegium* for Henry V and then withdrawn it and condemned investitures.[3] Josceran maintained the extreme positions of his predecessor Hugh, which Ivo was concerned to correct.[4] Investiture, he argues, cannot be a heresy, for if it were, then someone who had renounced it could not repeat the act without great danger. 'But I have seen many honourable men in Gaul and Germany who have extinguished this blemish by doing some kind of satisfaction, returning their staff of office and then receiving from the pope's hand the invesititures they had renounced.' Here the action is described as public and well known; according to Ivo several French and German bishops had carried it out. This is confirmed by a passage written by Gerhoh of Reichersberg in the 1140s,[5] about

---

[3] The controversy is best followed in U.-R. Blumenthal, '*Patrimonia* and *regalia* in 1111', in *Law, Church and Society: Essays in Honor of Stephan Kuttner*, ed. K. Pennington and R. Somerville (Philadelphia, 1977), 9–20; 'Opposition to Pope Paschal II: Some Comments on the Lateran Council of 1112', *Annuarium Historiae Conciliorum*, 10 (1978), 82–98; 'The Correspondence of Pope Paschal II and Guido of Vienne, 1112–1116', in *Supplementum Festivum: Studies in Honor of Paul Oskar Kristeller*, ed. J. Hankins, J. Monfasani, and F. Purnell (Binghamton, NY, 1987), 1–11. For Ivo's views on investitures, see A. Becker, *Studien zum Investiturproblem in Frankreich* (Saarbrücken, 1955), 99–110, 143–51; H. Hoffmann, 'Ivo von Chartres und die Lösung des Investiturstreites', *Deutsches Aarchiv für Erforschung des Mittelalters*, 15 (1959), 393–440.

[4] 'Investitura vero illa, de qua tantus est motus, in solis est manibus dantis et accipientis, quae bona et mala agere possunt, credere vel errare in fide non possunt. Ad haec, si haec investitura heresis esset, ei renuncians sine vulnere ad eam redire non posset. Videmus autem in partibus Germaniarum et Galliarum multas honestas personas purgato isto nevo per quamlibet satisfactionem pastorales virgas reddidisse et per manum apostolicam refutatas investituras recepisse. Quod summi pontifices minime fecissent, si in tali investitura heresim et peccatum in Spiritum sanctum latere cognovissent': Ivo of Chartres, *Epistola ad Joscerannum Lugdunensem episcopum*, ed. E. Sackur, MGH Libelli de Lite II (Hannover, 1892), 643–4.

[5] 'Vidimus nos oculis nostris quosdam episcopos a simoniacis regibus investitos, qui poenitentia seu vera seu falsa ducti retulerunt pretium sanguinis, id est ipsum episcopatum ad domnum apostolicum abrenuntiantes tali administrationi, ad quam non erant canonice promoti. Qua satisfactione utcunque purgati per domnum apostolicum denuo jussi administrare temporalia et spiritualia episcopatuum bona, ita de ipsis procuraverunt agrum in sepulturam peregrinorum ut essent studiosi aedificatores et ditatores coenobiorum in sepulturam, et requiem peregrinorum Christi pauperum': Gerhoh of Reichersberg, *Tractatus in Psalmum IX*, PL 193, col. 785.

the confirmation in office of bishops who had been invested by 'simoniac' kings. The rite was carried out by popes who restored them to office after they had done penance and performed 'some kind of satisfaction'. Gerhoh was probably thinking of the regularization of such positions at the end of the Investiture Contest, presumably at Lateran I, which he is known to have attended.[6]

These are general accounts, but individual cases give us more detailed information. The earliest and best known of these appears in the fullest contemporary account of the dramatic events at the Council of Reims in 1049,[7] when the assembled prelates were urged by a deacon, acting as Leo IX's mouthpiece, either to confess their guilt openly or else to clear themselves of all suspicion, should they have come to their offices through simony.[8] Most of the bishops claimed—probably not wholly truthfully in all cases—that they were innocent; but a few whose guilt was more notorious or whose consciences were more tender were unwilling to risk an immediate response. Amongst these was Bishop Hugh of Nevers. After asking for time to consider, he returned to make a public declaration that his parents had bought the bishopric for him without his knowledge, and that he had performed a number of acts contrary to canon law. Since he feared for the salvation of his soul, he wished to place his office at the pope's disposal, and while saying this he laid his staff at the pope's feet. Leo, moved by Hugo's repentance, had him confirm by oath his claim that he had been ignorant of his parents' simoniacal transaction, and then restored his bishopric to him, using a *different* staff to do so.

We have here the three elements which we shall meet repeatedly: surrender of office, symbolized by laying down or handing over of the staff; compurgation by oath; restoration to office through return of the staff. Anselm of Reims's *relatio*, incidentally, appears to be the only account which mentions the use of a

---

[6] P. Classen, *Gerhoch von Reichersberg: eine Biographie* (Wiesbaden, 1960), 26–7, 412–13 (dating of treatise to the mid-1140s).

[7] 'Post haec ad episcopos sermone converso, commonuit eos sub anathemate apostolicae auctoritatis, ut si quilibet eorum ad sacros ordines per simoniacam haeresim pervenisset, vel praemio quemlibet ad eamdem dignitatem promovisset, publica confessione patefaceret. ... omnes surrexerunt in ordine, secundum verba priorum purgantes se ab hujuscemodi suspicione, quatuor tantummodo exceptis, Lingonensi scilicet, Nivernensi, Constantiensi, Nannetensi: quorum causa eo die ad discutiendum relicta, diaconus sermonis cursum ad abbates qui aderant vertit . . . Mane . . . Nivernensis episcopus surgens, pro suo episcopio plurimum pecuniae confessus est a parentibus datum fuisse, se tamen ignorante; eoque adepto, nonnulla ecclesiastic̄ae religioni contraria commisisse: unde se asserebat divinae ultionis vindictam pertimescere. Ideoque, si domno papae et praesenti conventui dignum videretur, idem officium velle dimittere, potiusquam in ejus retentione animam suam pessumdare. Quae ubi dixit, pastorale pedum ante pedes ipsius apostolici posuit. Ille vero tanti viri flexus devotione, favente synodo, eumdem, quod absque consensu suo eadem pecunia data fuerit, sacramento comprobare fecit, sicque illi per aliud pedum ministerium episcopale reddidit': Anselm of Reims, *Historia Dedicationis Ecclesiae Beati Remigii Remensis*, cc. 26–27, 31, ed. J. Hourlier, in *La Champagne bénédictine. Contribution à l'année Saint Benoît (480–1980)*, Travaux de l'Académie Nationale de Reims, 160 (Reims, 1981), 181–297, here 238, 240, 246–8.

[8] On the background to the council and Leo's policies, see G. Tellenbach, *The Church in Western Europe from the Tenth to the Early Twelfth Century*, trans. T. Reuter (Cambridge, 1993), 188–90.

fresh staff for such an act. It is usually implied that the same staff was used,[9] though the end of the passage quoted above from the Regensburg rhetorical letter, with its rather dark sexual metaphor, may also refer to the use of a fresh staff; it certainly cannot be referring to translations in the conventional sense.

A similar case occurred in the early years of Alexander II's pontificate (1061–73). Bishop Fulco of Cahors was accused of simony, and returned his ring and staff to a papal legate called Hugo (probably *not* Hugh of Cluny, even though he was also active as papal legate around this time and in this region), who deposed him at a synod in Toulouse, probably early in 1062.[10] This may be a description of the deposition itself: Hugh forced Fulco to renounce his office publicly by surrendering ring and staff, the symbols of the office. Later Fulco went to Rome, where he cleared himself of the accusations through *inquisitio* and an oath of compurgation. Alexander thereupon returned ring and staff to him and so restored him to office.[11] The differences between the two accounts Alexander II gave of this are worth noting. One letter, to a colleague of Fulco's, talks only of a false suspicion. It is the other, addressed to the church of Cahors itself, which offers the details which are of interest to us: the three elements we observed in the case of the bishop of Nevers are again present.

The case of Frothar of Nîmes in 1064/5 is similar in outline.[12] Like Fulco, Frothar had been accused of simony. Like Fulco, Frothar was apparently deposed by the papal legate Hugh. Unlike Fulco, however, Frothar immediately

---

[9] On the question of whether bishops had one or more staffs of office, see below, p. 206.

[10] T. Schieffer, *Die päpstlichen Legaten in Frankreich vom Vertrage von Meersen (870) bis zum Schisma von 1130* (Berlin, 1935), 64–5, is inclined to suppose that the Hugh is not Hugh of Cluny; A. Kohnle, *Abt Hugo von Cluny (1049–1109)* (Sigmaringen, 1993), 83–4, is more positive. The association with the Council of Toulouse (and the dating of the latter to 1062) is by no means certain.

[11] 'Alexander II Petro Aniciensi episcopo. Fulconem Carturcensem episcopum, symoniace heresis macula fallaci obiectione quorundam invidia maculatum, districte super hoc expurgacionem facere fecimus, eumque studiosissima investigatione examinavimus. Quem ante altare sancti Petri et sacrosanctum corpus eius, tactis sanctis euuangeliis, inmunem ab huiusmodi criminis illata culpa evidentissime reperientes, eum episcopali dignitati et honori restituimus': Alexander II to Peter of Le Puy, JL 4481 (1062), ed. S. Löwenfeld, *Epistolae pontificum Romanorum adhuc ineditae* (Leipzig, 1885), 39, no. 71. 'Clero et populo Caturcensi. Qualiter per apostolice sedis legatum Hugonem, virga et anulo suo reddito, episcopali fuerit officio privatus Fulco episcopus vester, vobis credimus non esse ignotum; ideoque, qualiter nunc pristinae dignitati per humilitatem nostram sit restitutus, utile nobis visum est vobis omnibus notificandum. Tactis namque sacrosanctis euuangeliis coram collegio nostrorum fratrum nostraque presentia ante corpus sancti Petri se purificavit, quod neque per se neque per aliquam interpositam personam ante ordinationem suam precium, se sciente, dederit vel promiserit pro adipiscendo episcopatu; et sic apostolica auctoritate pontificali dignitati, gradui ac officio eum per anulum et virgam integriter restituimus': Alexander II to the clergy and people of Cahors, JL 4482, ibid. 40, no. 72.

[12] 'Goifrido Narbonensi archiepiscopo. Presentium lator Hugoni, predecessoris nostri pape Nicolai legato, episcopalis dignitatis insignia se confessus est sponte sua reddidisse, anulum videlicet et virgam. Quem cum percunctati essemus, conscientiae suae nobis penitus enucleare secretum, adeptum Nemosiensem episcopatum infra legitimos se protulit annos, extra suam conscientiam a patre pro eodem data pecunia. Quia vero Romane aecclesie, ut ipse multique cum eo testabantur, sponte se accusans paruit nuntio, visum est nobis, misericordia cogente, eius humilitati pie condescendere atque pristine dignitati per nostram reinvestiture confirmationem eundem Froterium restituere. Reddidimus ergo sibi die palmarum anulum et episcopatus baculum': Alexander II to Wifrid of Narbonne, JL 4549 (1064), Löwenfeld, *Epistolae*, 45–6, no. 90.

confessed that his assumption of office had been simoniacal, since his parents had paid for the bishopric without his knowledge because he was too young (compare the excuse offered by Hugh of Nevers). Alexander stressed that Frothar—whom Theodor Schieffer described as a 'notorious simonist', though I have found no other evidence for this—had laid down his office 'freely' (*sponte*).[13] Here a compurgation would obviously have been inappropriate: formally, Frothar's appointment was simoniacal. Alexander might perhaps have demanded an oath as Leo had with Hugh of Nevers, but he says rather that he had been moved by pity, and describes the restoration as an act of grace. The result was a 'reinvestiture': 'we restored his former dignity to that same Frothar by the confirmation of our reinvestiture.' It was, moreover, a demonstratively public reinvestiture, on Palm Sunday, at a time of the ecclesiastical year when the reconciliation of sinners and penitents played a prominent part in the life of the Church.[14]

The next example lies over a decade later. In the months following Canossa Gregory VII had renewed his attempts to promulgate his programme in west Francia, and his legate, Hugh of Die, had held a council for this purpose in Autun in September 1077.[15] Several northern and central French bishops had ignored Hugh's summons, mainly because they rejected the centralizing practices of Gregory and his legate. Hugh, who practised the 'off-with-his-head' style of management, promptly suspended them all. Gregory VII now faced problems of presentation and news management: he had to avoid both disavowing his legate and affronting the entire French episcopate. In almost all cases he did this by lifting the sanctions while insisting that the charges should be heard before the legate. Our sources for all of this are an unclearly worded report by Hugh and a synodal protocol in Gregory's register.[16] Hugh made no distinction between the different cases,[17] but Gregory appears to have reacted slightly differently to one case, that of Richard of Bourges. Since he had resigned by laying down ring and staff, but had done so in anger rather than by

---

[13] Schieffer, *Legaten*, 65; a mixed picture of Frothar's activities as prelate can be gained from E. Magnou-Nortier, *La Société laïque et l'église dans la province ecclésiastique de Narbonne (zone cispyrénéenne) de la fin du VIII*ᵉ *à la fin du XI*ᵉ *siècle* (Toulouse, 1974), 373, 408, 462, 474, 481–2.

[14] See on this the forthcoming study by S. Hamilton, *The Practice of Penance, c.900–c.1050* (London, 2000).

[15] R. Schieffer, *Die Entstehung des päpstlichen Investiturverbots für den deutschen König* (Stuttgart, 1981), 162–7; J. Engelberger, *Gregor VII. und die Investiturfrage: quellenkritische Studien zum angeblichen Investiturverbot von 1075* (Cologne, 1996), 250–1.

[16] 'Richardus Bituriensis archiepiscopus, quia irato animo et non synodali iudicio dimisit ecclesiam suam, virgam et anulum recepit promittens se de obiectis coram legato nostro satisfacere': Gregory VII (Synodal notice?), *Das Registrum Gregorx VII.*, V 17, ed. E. Caspar, MGH Epistolae Selectae II, 1, (Berlin, 1920–3), 378–80.

[17] Hugh's report, *Recueil des Historiens des Gaules et de la France*, ed. M. Brial, revised L. Delisle, vol. XIV (Paris, 1877), 613–14, no. 79, simply says that Richard had been suspended for contumacious non-appearance; on Hugh as legate see P.-R. Gaussin, 'Hugues de Die et l'épiscopat franco-bourguignon (1075–1085)', *Cahiers d'Histoire*, 13 (1968), 77–98.

synodal judgement, his office was restored by ring and staff on his promise to clear himself before the legate. Again we find the triple sequence: voluntary renunciation of the symbols of office, promise—as here—or oath, restitution through the symbols of office. Gregory's claim that Richard had renounced his office 'in anger, not through synodal judgement' presumably underlined the fact that this was not a *res iudicata*; had it been, restoration might not have been so simple.

Our last example is well known to English church historians: it is that of the bishop of Thetford / Norwich, Herbert Losinga. Despite respectable origins, Herbert had a very unrespectable reputation as a simonist at the start of his career, though he later redeemed this in office.[18] The precise details of his renunciation of office are somewhat problematic. William of Malmesbury's account implies that there had been a considerable lapse of time between his consecration and his journey to Rome to visit Urban II, but that cannot easily be squared with the other known facts.[19] We know that he was consecrated in early 1091; we also know that William Rufus confiscated his pastoral staff at an assembly in early 1094.[20] The king's action must surely have been a response to Herbert's journey. It is very unusual, possibly unique—there is certainly no other well-known example of a bishop's being suspended by a king in this way—and it can most easily be explained by pointing to the consequences for William of Herbert's action. Not only was it an implicit accusation of the king himself, but Herbert had been restored by a pope whom Rufus had not yet recognized, and so prejudiced a royal position. Herbert must, therefore, have visited Urban between early 1091 and the end of 1093; the only difficulty is that Urban was hardly in Rome at all in this period except in the final months of 1093, when Herbert is known to have been elsewhere. Presumably William of Malmesbury, writing a generation later, thought that Urban had indeed been in Rome.[21] His report does not mention a *purgatio* or *satisfactio*: Herbert simply repents of his youthful sins, goes to Rome, renounces his simoniacally acquired ring and staff, and then receives them again 'by the indulgence of the most merciful see'.

---

[18] On Herbert see J. W. Alexander, 'Herbert of Norwich, 1091–1119: Studies in the History of Norman England', *Studies in Medieval and Renaissance History*, 6 (1969), 119–227.

[19] 'Post hunc diebus Willelmi junioris emit episcopatum Tetfordensem Herbertus cognomento Losinga, quod ei ars adulationis impegerat, ex priore Fiscanni, et ex abbate Ramesiae factus episcopus, patre suo Rotberto ejusdem cognominis in abbatiam Wintoniae intruso. Fuit ergo vir ille magnus in Anglia simoniae fomes, abbatiam episcopatumque nummis aucupatus, pecunia scilicet regiam sollicitudinem inviscans, et principum favori promissiones non leves assibilans. Veruntamen erroneum impetum juventutis abolevit penitentia, Romam profectus severioribus annis, ubi loci simonicum baculum et anulum deponens, indulgentia clementissimae sedis iterum recipere meruit; quod Romani sanctius et ordinatius censeant, ut ęcclesiarum omnium sumptus suis potius serviant quam quorumlibet regum usibus militent': William of Malmesbury, *Gesta Pontificum*, II, 74, ed. W. Stubbs, RS (London, 1870), 151.

[20] Alexander, 'Herbert of Norwich', 136; *The Chronicle of John of Worcester*, ed. P. McGurk, vol. III (Oxford, 1998), 68–71 (HPL text, drawing on a version of the *Anglo-Saxon Chronicle* closely related to 'E').

[21] Alexander, 'Herbert of Norwich', 127–9.

There is a fundamental problem in assessing these cases, because on the one hand we have real symbolic actions based on metonymy, and on the other we have descriptions in which metonymy and metaphor also play an important role. As the latter are our only guide to the former, we cannot be certain about what 'really happened'. At the extremes, there are two diametrically opposed possibilities. The first is that no resigning bishop in the eleventh and twelfth centuries actually laid down ring and staff. The sources which appear to say that they did are simply using an obvious metaphor for episcopal office in describing resignations whose details are unknown to us. The second possibility is that the symbolism of ring and staff was such an obvious one that it was probably a component of *all* such actions—resignation, deposition, restitution—even when our sources do not explicitly mention it.

We can probably exclude the first possibility, since we have cases where the details imply reality rather than metaphor. When Anselm of Reims writes that Hugh of Nevers was restored to office using *another* staff, or when Alexander II writes that he restored Frothar of Nîmes on Palm Sunday, then we presumably have staffs and rings which really existed and changed hands. Nevertheless, we cannot entirely exclude the possibility that some of these examples are mere metaphor. In the case of Herbert Losinga, for example, it is conceivable that any or all of Herbert's renunciation, his restitution, and his deprivation by William II are described in metaphorical terms in our sources. The other possibility, that there was a more general use of the symbolism than is now reflected in our sources, is not so easily excluded. It will be recalled that only one of Alexander II's letters about Fulco of Cahors mentions the symbolic details. Had the compilers of the *Collectio Britannica* chosen to select the other one alone, we should not now know that the symbolism had been used. Ivo, Gerhoh, and the author of the Regensburg rhetorical letter write about the practice as if it were commonplace. Although we now know of only a handful of such cases, there are a number of others where the symbolism was probably used, even though it is not explicitly mentioned.

Consider first the case of Gerard II of Cambrai. This is slightly different from those we have examined so far, because Gerard had not yet been consecrated when, with troubled conscience, he sought out Gregory VII, and so he cannot have aimed at restitution. But the sequence of action was very similar.[22]

---

[22] 'Gerardus Cameracensis electus ad nos veniens, qualiter in eadem Camaracensi [*sic* ed.] ecclesia ad locum regiminis assignatus sit, prompta nobis confessione manifestavit non denegans post factam cleri et populi electionem donum episcopatus ab Henrico rege se accepisse, defensionem autem proponens et multum nobis offerens se neque decretum nostrum de prohibitione huiuscemodi acceptionis, nec ipsum Henricum regem a nobis excommunicatum fuisse aliqua certa manifestatione cognovisse. [after being instructed] ad satisfaciendum promptus donum, quod accepisse visus est, continuo in manus nostras refutavit et omnino causam suam nostro iudicio . . . reliquit. Pro cuius humiliatione et maxime, quoniam canonicam ęlectionem in eo precessisse audivimus, ad misericordiam moti sumus . . . ad promotionem eius discrete moderationis consideratione assensum prebere non indignum duximus. Attamen, ne istud aliis . . . ad exemplum vel occasionem quęrendę misericordię in posterum fore debuisset, illud constituimus,

Gerard had received the 'gift' (*donum*) of the bishopric from Henry IV, claiming not to have known that Gregory had prohibited such practice and excommunicated Henry.[23] When Gregory enlightened him, Gerard renounced the bishopric. Gregory was nevertheless prepared to be lenient, especially as Gerard had been canonically elected. He gave permission for Gerard's consecration, provided that he could clear himself by an oath taken before the assembled province of Reims (Gregory's account is addressed to the archbishop of Reims). There is no mention of ring and staff here; yet should we really understand 'renounced into our hands' in a purely metaphorical sense? Is it not likely that Gerard, who would certainly have received the *donum* from Henry IV by accepting ring and staff, renounced it in the same way?

Another example is the case of the bishops of Soissons and Beauvais in the early years of Urban II's pontificate. Once again we have a synodal or consistorial protocol, which survives in the *Collectio Britannica*.[24] This tells how Henry of Soissons, after having received investiture from Phillip I, came to Rome *sponte*, that is, without having been summoned or accused. There he had to renounce something (the bishopric? the episcopal insignia?) into the pope's hands, 'without hope of restitution'. The pope later decided, 'for the needs of the church', to restore him to office, and he had to swear an oath best characterized as an oath of loyalty, similar to that taken by metropolitans when receiving the *pallium*.[25] The bishop of Beauvais was dealt with in a similar manner. Again there is no mention of ring and staff, but we have a renunciation of office coupled with the *in manus/manibus resignavit* formula, an oath, and a restitution. It seems likely that the symbols were used, even if they are not explicitly mentioned.

My intention is not here to go through all the cases of deposition and restitution of bishops in the eleventh and early twelfth centuries showing that the

---

ut coram te et confratre nostro Remensi archiepiscopo et aliis comprovincialibus episcopis . . . se per sacramentum purgare debeat . . .': Gregory VII to Hugo of Die, *Das Registrum Gregors VII.*, IV, 22, ed. Caspar, 330–1. Hugh subsequently consecrated Gerard: Engelberger, *Investiturfrage*, 250 with n. 120.

[23] On this see Schieffer, *Investiturverbot*, 129, 142–4; Engelberger, *Investiturfrage*, 163–80.

[24] '<H>anricus Suessionensis episcopus Romam sponte veniens, quia a rege Francorum investituram acceperat, iudicio domini pape [episcopatum *added by editors*] in ipsius manibus refutavit absque spe recuperationis. Cui postea necessitate exigente ecclesie, nolenti et recusanti idem episcopus [episcopus *MS.*; episcopatus *editors*] per dominum Urbanum papam restitutus est, et hoc ipse sacramento astrictus est: "Ego Hanricus Suessionens(is) episcopus ab hac hora [*added by editors*] in antea fidelis ero beato Petro et tibi, domine meus papa Urbane, et tuis successoribus canonice intrantibus et Romane ecclesie. Legatum huius apostolice sedis cum honore recipiam, quem certum legatum agnoscam, et in suis necessitatibus adiuvabo. Vocatus autem ad sinodum, aut ad tuam aut legatorum tuorum veniam, nisi prepeditus canonico inpedimento. Excommunicatis ab hac sede me sciente non communicabo. Consecrationibus eorum, qui investituram recipiunt episcopatuum vel abbatiarum de laica manu me sciente non interero. Sic me Deus adiuvet et hec sancta evvangelia." Tunc etiam de Belvacensi episcopo idem actum est': R. Somerville with S. Kuttner, *Pope Urban II, the* Collectio Britannica *and the Council of Melfi (1089)* (Oxford, 1996), 99–101. On the bishop of Beauvais here named, see Michael Horn, 'Zur Geschichte des Bischofs Fulco von Beauvais (1089–1095)', *Francia*, 16 (1989), 176–84.

[25] Somerville and Kuttner, *Urban II*, 100–1, discuss the relationship to other oaths; see also T. Gottlob, *Der kirchliche Amtseid der Bischöfe* (Bonn, 1936), 42–9.

symbols of ring and staff might have played a part; it is simply to argue that the symbolism was widespread, and that cumulatively the sources might suggest that the use of ring and staff was becoming the norm. Yet it was a novelty: the first explicitly documented example of this symbolic sequence appears to be the case of Hugh of Nevers in 1049. As we shall see, there are precedents which help to explain it, but the symbolism itself was not used in this form in Merovingian or Carolingian times: this is not simply an argument from silence, since we have positive indications that other symbolic sequences were used in appropriate contexts.[26] In spite of this, the sequence appears as fully worked out and self-explanatory on its first appearance, suggesting that the general symbolic basis had already been firmly established. So where did it come from?

Ring and staff had long been symbols of episcopal office.[27] Isidore of Seville referred to the ring as a symbol of sacramental power, and to the staff as the symbol of rule.[28] The ring is said to have been derived from a seal-ring (the symbolism of the ring for the bishop's 'marriage' to his diocese dates from the ninth and tenth centuries, and is not as old as the ring itself). The staff is thought to derive from late antique staffs of office, though this is not absolutely certain. Given the prevalence of the shepherd metaphor in the New Testament, one might have expected a direct transfer from literature to symbolism, but the earliest recorded episcopal staffs were apparently not crooks (though of course late antique and early medieval shepherds' staffs may not have been either), but had either a knob or a small cross at the top. Crooks are recorded for abbatial staffs from the seventh century onwards, and for episcopal staffs somewhat later. In the course of the ninth century the transfer of staff and ring became part of the ceremony of episcopal installation, and from the end of the ninth century we have reports of the staff being used by kings for the investiture of bishops.

The tenth and early eleventh centuries provide numerous examples of the staff as a symbol of the bishop's jurisdictional power. In the course of the Gandersheim dispute, Willigis of Mainz made a visible renunciation in favour of the bishop of Hildesheim by handing over a staff.[29] This was also how the bishop of Würzburg renounced his rights over part of the diocese of Bamberg, and how the archbishop of Magdeburg acknowledged the restoration of the

---

[26] See below at nn. 34 ff., esp. n. 35.

[27] The following paragraph synthesizes T. Klauser, *Der Ursprung der bischöflichen Insignien und Ehrenrechte* (Krefeld, 1949), 17, 22; R. Bauerreiß, 'Abtsstab und Bischofsstab', *Studien und Mitteilungen zur Geschichte des Benediktinerordens*, 68 (1957), 215–26; P. Salmon, *Mitra und Stab: die Pontifikalinsignien im römischen Ritus* (Mainz, 1960; first published in French, Rome, 1955), 20, 29–33, 61–74; V. Labhardt, *Zur Rechtssymbolik des Bischofsrings* (Cologne, 1963), 13–14, 25–51; O. Engels, 'Der Pontifikatsantritt und seine Zeichen', *Settimane di studi*, 33 (1987), 707–70, at 754–64, H. Keller, 'Die Investitur. Ein Beitrag zum Problem der "Staatssymbolik" im Hochmittelalter', *Frühmittelalterliche Studien*, 27 (1993), 51–86, at 61–6.

[28] Isidore of Seville, *De Ecclesiasticis Officiis*, 2.5.12, ed. C. M. Lawson, CCSL 113 (Turnhout, 1989), 60: 'Huic autem, dum consecratur, datur baculus ut eius indicio subditam plebem uel regat uel corrigat . . . Datur et anulus propter signum pontificalis honoris uel signaculum secretorum . . .'

[29] Thangmar, *Vita Bernwardi Episcopi*, c. 43, ed. G. H. Pertz, MGH SS IV (Hannover, 1841), 777.

diocese of Merseburg after its twenty-year unification with his see.[30] It is not certain that these are *episcopal* staffs. Staffs of all kinds played an important role in contemporary legal practice, and some of the staffs mentioned may have been the normal short *festuca* used for transfers of rights and property, though the use of terms like *ferula* and *baculum* suggests otherwise.[31] But there is at least one absolutely clear-cut case. Towards the end of his life the aged bishop Ulrich of Augsburg began to transfer the administration of his diocese to his nephew Adalbero. This became general knowledge when Adalbero appeared in public bearing Ulrich's staff.[32] That raises the question of how it could be identified as specifically Ulrich's: it is not clear whether abbots and bishops normally had more than one staff, though if not it would have been awkward to give them away in legal transactions. Staffs were certainly not transpersonal symbols of the see in the way that some crowns and swords symbolized kingdoms, since they were often buried with their holders, but that does not exclude the possibility of multiple *episcopalia*.[33]

From the ninth century onwards ring and staff also played a role in the deposition of bishops, though how this was done depended on whether the deposee was physically present or not. When the Patriarch Photius was deposed in 869 his staff was publicly broken, as was that of Pope Benedict V in 964.[34] The graphic description of the deposition of episcopal 'invasors' at southern French councils in the 890s reveals that the ceremonial of episcopal consecration was reversed: the robes torn, the staffs broken over their heads, the rings pulled with dishonour from their fingers.[35] The return of the staff was also used in depositions in the twelfth century, for example in those of Henry of Verdun in 1129 or Brun of Strasbourg in 1131.[36] Whether such a symbolism was also used with voluntary resignations is less clear; most of the episcopal resignations of the early Middle Ages

---

[30] Thietmar of Merseburg, *Chronicon*, ed. R. Holtzmann, MGH SRG, NS (Berlin, 1935), VI, 1 and VII, 24, pp. 274, 426 (Merseburg); VI, 30, p. 310 (Würzburg).

[31] L. Carlen, 'Stab', *Handwörterbuch zur deutschen Rechtsgeschichte*, vol. IV (Berlin, 1990), cols. 1838–44, provides a convenient survey of their widespread use.

[32] Gerhard, *Vita Uodalrici Episcopi Augustensis*, cc. 21–3, ed. G. Waitz, MGH SS IV (Hannover, 1841), 407–9.

[33] See e.g. W. Watts, *Victoria and Albert Museum: Catalogue of Pastoral Staves* (London, 1924); E. Mason, 'St Wulfstan's Staff: A Legend and its Uses', *Medium Ævum* 53 (1984), 157–79. J. Petersohn, *'Echte' und 'falsche' Insignien im deutschen Krönungsbrauch des Mittelalters: Kritik eines Forschungsstereotyps* (Stuttgart, 1993), has recently argued strongly for multiple rather than unique regalia, and it seems likely that his arguments apply to episcopalia as well.

[34] Salmon, *Mitra und Stab*, 62; Engels, 'Pontifikatsantritt', 762.

[35] The complex history of these councils, often referred to in the literature as Nîmes 886, has been elucidated by I. Schröder, *Die westfränkischen Synoden von 888 bis 987 und ihre Überlieferung* (Munich, 1980), nos. 9–10, pp. 122–38; for the reverse ritual of deposition see W. Brückner, 'Devestierung', *Handwörterbuch zur deutschen Rechtsgeschichte*, vol. I (Berlin, 1971), cols. 724–6. Note that Frodoin of Barcelona, who was spared deposition, asked for mercy by appearing in bare feet and in sackcloth, i.e. by performing a *deditio* (see below at n. 45), not by surrendering his staff and receiving it back.

[36] M. Meyer-Gebel, *Bischofsabsetzungen in der deutschen Reichskirche vom Wormser Konkordat (1122) bis zum Ausbruch des Alexandrinischen Schismas (1159)* (Siegburg, 1992), 102, 105, 117–18.

Part of their force came from the bishop's voluntary admission of guilt. Modern German, though not English, law recognizes in certain cases the notion of
a voluntary self-accusation (for example when taxes have been improperly
withheld). One still has to pay a fine, but there are no proceedings or convic-
tions. The thought behind the examples discussed above is similar. Those formally condemned as simoniacs lost their office, but if they anticipated
condemnation by making a voluntary confession and placing their office at
their superiors' disposition they had a chance of restitution. As the somewhat
irritated author of the Regensburg rhetorical letter noted, they acted as if the
action wiped out the taint of simony: papal authority served as a kind of spiritual dry-cleaning for stained office.

Another concept which played a part was the idea of receiving the symbols of
office from an unimpeachable source, in order to guarantee the unimpeachabil-
ity of the office itself. We can find such thinking in other contexts. The abbots
of Cluny, and in consequence also the abbots of the congregation of Hirsau,
took their staffs of office either from their dying predecessor or with their own
hands from the altar on which it had been laid.[43] Radulf Glaber has an anecdote
about an abbot who had stolen a horse to present it to the emperor Henry III.[44]
Its owner complained to Henry, who promptly gave the abbot a dressing-down.
'Lay down that staff, which you apparently think you bear thanks to the generosity of a mere mortal.' Henry then took the staff and placed it in the hand of a
statue of Christ. 'Now go and take it from the hand of the omnipotent King,
and in future do not act as the debtor of any mortal, but bear it freely, as is proper
for the holder of so high an office.'

The prehistory of the eleventh-century symbolic sequence of dis- and reinvestiture thus explains it to a large extent, but how did it come to be used for the
first time? How could people be certain that it would be generally understood?
To answer this we have to consider the role of symbolic action in these societies
in a more general sense.[45] I have argued elsewhere that medieval politics were
often expressed in a metalanguage with its own vocabulary and grammar, sub-
suming natural language, dramatic scripts, and props—symbolically laden
objects and locations.

Historians often call statements in this metalanguage 'rituals', but the term is
best reserved for those statements where the precise 'wording' is significant. For
example, there are many different ways in which one can symbolically express

[43] H. Jakobs, *Die Hirsauer* (Cologne, 1960), 79–87; M. Hillebrandt, 'Abt und Gemeinschaft in Cluny
(10.–11. Jahrhundert)', in *Vom Kloster zum Klosterverband: Das Werkzeug der Schriftlichkeit*, ed. H. Keller
and F. Neiske (Munich, 1997), 147–72 at 154–5.
[44] Radulf Glaber, *Historiarum Libri Quinque*, V, 24, ed. J. France, *Rodulfi Glabri Historiarum Libri
Quinque* (Oxford, 1989), 251–2.
[45] For a fuller exposition of what follows see T. Reuter, '*Velle sibi fieri in forma hac*: symbolisches Han-
deln im Becketstreit', in *Formen und Funktion öffentlicher Kommunikation im Mittelalter*, ed. G. Althoff
(Sigmaringen, 2001), at nn. 6 ff.

preceded the bishop's entry into a monastery, and since they were legall
lematic we do not normally have a detailed account of what happened.
There is a very early provision laying down the use of such symbolis
restoration of bishops in the Fourth Council of Toledo (633), which de
that a bishop who had been unlawfully deposed at an earlier synod v
reinstated by the public return of the symbols of office before the altar.
also used as a confirmation when the status of a bishop's installation wa
ful. After Ebo of Reims had been reinstated in 840, he sent new rings ai
to his two suffragans consecrated during the period of his 'deposition'.[3]
Arnulf, archbishop of Milan, wanted to force Bishop Alrich of Asti to a
ledge his power as metropolitan in 1008—the bishop had been nomin
Henry II and consecrated by Pope Sergius IV in contempt of the ri
Milan—he made him 'lay down the staff and ring of the bishopric
assumed on the altar of the holy confessor [Ambrose], which afterwa
took up again in due form with the permission of the archbishop'.[40]

The reinvestor in these cases was not the pope, however. Popes did indee
secrate bishops on occasions in the ninth, tenth, and eleventh centuries
example in the case of new foundations and for those few bishoprics whicl
not part of a province. They were also the consecrator of last resort, shou
metropolitan be unable to act or unreasonably withhold his consent. But our
are not really consecrations; they are not even reordinations, as known fror
later eleventh century in the case of those who had been consecrated by simo
because there is no unction and no laying on of hands.[42] We are dealing
actions designed to restore a disturbed state of affairs, not to create a new on

---

[37] G. Caron, *La renuncia all'ufficio ecclesiastico nella storia del diritto canonico dalla età apostolica
riforma cattolica* (Milan, 1946), 86–8, 94–5, assembles most of the early medieval examples.
[38] 'Episcopus, presbyter aut diaconus si [a] gradu suo iniuste deiectus in secunda synodo inno
repperiatur, non potest esse quod fuerat nisi gradus amissos recipiat, ut si episcopus fuerit coram al
de manu episcoporum orarium, annulum et baculum': Toledo IV (633), c. 28, *Concilios Visigóti
Hispano-Romanos*, ed. J. Vives (Barcelona, 1963), 202–3.
[39] Charles the Bald to Nicholas I, ed. W. Hartmann, *Die Konzilien der karolingischen Teilre
860–874*, MGH Concilia IV (Hanover, 1998), 242.
[40] Arnulf of Milan, *Liber Gestorum Recentium* II, 19, ed. C. Zey, MGH SRG LXVII (Hannover, 19
142–3. The bishop had to enter the city with bare feet, carrying a book, and his brother and accomp
Manfred, margrave of Asti, was carrying a dog, a well-known humiliating punishment, so we are clea
dealing with a public surrender; see below, n. 45, on the public *deditio*; and on the carrying of dogs,
K. J. Leyser, 'Ritual, Ceremony and Gesture: Ottonian Germany', in id., *Communications and Power
Medieval Europe: The Carolingian and Ottonian Centuries*, ed. T. Reuter (London, 1994), 189–213, at 1
[41] I intend to publish a separate study of this complex topic. For some eleventh-century examples s
e.g. JL 4017 (Besalú, 1017: consecration of first bishop of newly founded see); JL i.539 (Troyes, 1050: coi
secration of bishop after previous bishop translated to Sens); JL 4265 and I.544 (Le Puy, 1053: consecra
tion of bishop in opposition to king); JL 5484 (Arras, 1093: archbishop to send the bishop to Rome to b
consecrated if others object); JL i.679 (Auxerre, 1095: consecration of bishop against opposition of kin
and metropolitan).
[42] L. Saltet, *Les Réordinations: étude sur le sacrement de l'ordre* (Paris, 1907), 186–7, 231–42, 260; J
Gilchrist, '*Simoniaca haeresis* and the Problem of Orders from Leo IX to Gratian', in his *Canon Law in
the Age of Reform, 11th–12th Centuries* (Aldershot, 1993), IV, 209–35.

submission, but we have a *ritual* of submission only when there is a precisely prescribed sequence of actions fixed in expectation (for example when one can express submission *only* by taking one's boots off, clothing oneself in sackcloth and ashes, and throwing oneself at the feet of one's opponent or superior).[46] Our dis- and reinvestitures were probably not a ritual in this narrower sense. But they were a statement in this metalanguage, whose native speakers were fluent in it, and could thus react to a new situation by uttering new 'sentences'. What Hugo of Nevers did (or was instructed to do) was almost certainly new; but it was immediately comprehensible to those who observed it.

All we now have as evidence of this metalanguage is recorded in ordinary language, and hence in a kind of indirect speech: we lose much of the detail and nuance. This increases for us the polysemy which was in any case present in such utterances (and may often have been intended). This in turn increases the probability that we may misinterpret actions which contemporaries would have found it quite impossible to misunderstand. In effect, we are presented with film stills. They may look very similar, but may nevertheless have been parts of rather different narratives. Moreover, they are blurred and grainy: there may be significant elements which elude our attention.

It is now generally accepted that in medieval political life public submissions were preceded by negotiations behind the scenes, in which the details of the dramatization to follow were agreed amongst the parties.[47] That probably happened in many of our cases; but in 1049 there may have been a genuinely spontaneous act—otherwise it is hard to explain how Hugh of Nevers could take this particular route while others did not. This illustrates the point made about details and nuances: if Anselm of Reims's account were fuller we might be in a position to explain why Hugh escaped where others were deprived of office, 'without hope of recuperation'. On the other hand, the use of a second staff by Leo IX may suggest preparation even on this first known occasion, unless we assume that Leo simply borrowed a fresh staff from one of the other bishops present, or that he normally had a few spares in the robing-room when he attended councils. It is easier to discern at a general level that symbolic actions were significant than it is to work out their precise implications. This particular symbolic action seems to have retained its significance only for a short period. An exhaustive search of the twelfth- and thirteenth-century evidence might yield more examples, but it seems likely that the increasing juridification of

[46] G. Althoff, 'Das Privileg der *deditio*. Formen gütlicher Konfliktbeendigung in der mittelalterlichen Adelsgesellschaft', in his *Spielregeln der Politik im Mittelalter: Kommunikation in Frieden und Fehde* (Darmstadt, 1997), 99–125; see also G. Koziol, *Begging Pardon and Favor* (Ithaca, 1992); T. Reuter, 'Unruhestiftung, Fehde, Rebellion, Widerstand: Gewalt und Frieden in der Politik der Salierzeit', in *Das Reich der Salier*, ed. S. Weinfurter, 3 vols. (Sigmaringen, 1991), III, 297–325, at 320–3; K. Schreiner, 'Nudis pedibus', in *Formen und Funktion öffentlicher Kommunikation im Mittelalter*, ed. Althoff.

[47] G. Althoff, 'Demonstration und Inszenierung. Spielregeln der Kommunikation in mittelalterlicher Öffentlichkeit', in his *Spielregeln*, 229–57 (article first published 1993); see also G. Althoff, *Otto III.* (Darmstadt, 1997), 105–13.

church life from 1150 onwards meant that the surrender of ring and staff came to seem inappropriate. The last case known to me is that of Becket, who is said to have resigned his see into Alexander III's hands after the Council of Northampton; Alexander took three days to think it over before restoring the archbishopric to Becket—but quietly and without fuss or symbolism.[48] We are moving towards the more bureaucratic world of the late medieval bishop.

[48] William FitzStephen, *Vita S. Thomae*, c. 68, ed. J. C. Robertson, *Materials for the History of Thomas Becket*, 7 vols., RS (London, 1875–83), III, 76.

16

THE RELIGIOUS PATRONAGE OF
ROBERT AND WILLIAM OF MORTAIN

Brian Golding

The book of benefactors to St Albans (*c.*1380) is an extraordinary and unique compilation intended to commemorate all the significant benefactors of that great Benedictine house. Not only does it summarize the grants, but over 200 patrons are portrayed in naive miniatures.[1] Amongst the men and women so memorialized we find Robert of Mortain and Almodis his wife, as well as Alured, Robert's steward and a prominent vassal.[2] At first sight this is appropriate, for some time between 1086 and his death in 1095 Count Robert granted half a hide in Redbourne and a virgate in Codicote (Herts.). Moreover, one of Robert's daughters, Mabel, was buried in the abbey.[3] Yet all is not as it seems. Redbourne was one of the least productive of Robert's manors and had already been subinfeudated by 1086, while the land in Codicote had originally belonged to the abbey and had been appropriated by the count's men. Robert's grant should therefore be seen as a restitution rather than a gift. Moreover Robert's tenant, Robert fitzIvo, had taken a hide of the abbot's land in Langley, which was now in the count's hands. In other words, in these transactions the abbey was a net loser.[4] By the time the book of benefactors was compiled the ambiguities surrounding Robert's grant had perhaps been forgotten by the monks of St Albans; to their late-eleventh century predecessors they would have been clear enough.

When Robert came to have dealings with them he was perhaps the wealthiest magnate in England. Even before the conquest his possessions in

---

[1] London, British Library, MS Cotton Nero D. vii. See L. F. Sandler, *Gothic Manuscripts, 1285–1385* (London, 1986), 180–1; and K. L. Scott, *Later Gothic Manuscripts, 1390–1490* (London, 1996), 236–9.

[2] London, British Library, MS Cotton Nero D. vii, fols. 93v, 94.

[3] W. Dugdale, *Monasticon Anglicanum*, ed. J. Caley, H. Ellis, and B. Bandinel, 6 vols. (London, 1846), II, 220; E. Cownie, *Religious Patronage in Anglo-Norman England, 1066–1135* (Woodbridge, 1998), 87, 176; see also *Victoria History of the County of Hertfordshire*, ed. W. Page (London, 1908), II, 367.

[4] *Domesday Book, seu Liber Censualis Willelmi Primi Regis Angliae*, ed. A. Farley, H. Ellis, *et al.* 4 vols., Record Commission (1783–1816), II, 135b [hereafter: DB]; see also B. Golding, 'Robert of Mortain', *ANS* 13 (1991), 119–44, at 139–40. Spoliation of abbeys was not confined to Norman seizures of the property of Anglo-Saxon monasteries. King Harold II was notorious for such behaviour and Orderic Vitalis provides many examples of similar depredations in Normandy (A. Williams, 'Land and Power in the Eleventh Century: The Estates of Harold Godwineson', in *ANS 3* (1981), 171–87, at 181–3: C. Harper-Bill, 'The piety of the Anglo-Norman Knightly Class', in *ANS* 2 (1980), 63–77, at 64).

Normandy, both of the patrimonial lands of his father, Herluin de Conteville, and of the highly strategic county of Mortain that commanded the south-west of the duchy, made him a key figure in the polity of his half-brother, Duke William.[5] The Norman conquest catapulted him into even greater prominence and he and his son William held vast honours in southern and south-western England, especially in Cornwall, Somerset, the rape of Pevensey (Sussex), and the honour of Berkhamsted (Herts.).[6] But this great lordship survived for less than forty years. William of Mortain joined the baronial rebellion against Henry I. In 1104 all his lands in England were confiscated, and following his capture two years later at the battle of Tinchebrai his estates in Normandy were also forfeit and he himself was imprisoned. Though he may have been released in 1118, he was certainly back in the Tower of London in 1129–30. According to Bermondsey tradition he became a monk there in 1140.[7] The tenurial redistribution that followed his fall was substantial. Many of the carved-up estates passed to the supporters, including former Mortain tenants, of the victorious king, while Mortain itself was granted to the king's nephew, Stephen of Boulogne.[8]

As counts of Mortain and great landholders in post-conquest England, Robert and William were in a position to show substantial generosity to religious houses throughout their lands. Such giving was of course expected, and the counts of Mortain are in no way unusual in the scope of their benefactions. Yet their giving was not indiscriminate, and its direction was dictated by many considerations, both dynastic and pious. While in some instances it is not difficult to detect the dynamic behind the giving, too often it is impossible to establish the motives and the mechanisms from the sparse and restrained formulae of the counts' charters. Until the end of the century choice was limited to

[5] For the early history of the duchy, see esp. C. Potts, 'The Earliest Norman Counts Revisited: The Lords of Mortain', *Haskins Society Journal*, 4 (1993), 23–36, which significantly revises D. Douglas, 'The Earliest Norman Counts', *EHR* 61 (1946), 129–56 and J. Boussard, 'Le Comté de Mortain au XIᵉ siècle', *Le Moyen Age*, 58 (1952), 253–79. Potts examines the Norman–Breton border, along which the early counts of Mortain were active, in 'Normandy or Brittany? A Conflict of Interests at Mont Saint Michel (966–1035)', *ANS* 12 (1990), 135–56.

[6] The most recent discussion is Golding, 'Robert of Mortain', 118–44.

[7] See William of Malmesbury, *Gesta Regum Anglorum: The History of the English Kings*, ed. R. A. B. Mynors, R. M. Thomson, and M. Winterbottom, 2 vols. (Oxford, 1998), I, 725; Orderic Vitalis, *Historia Ecclesiastica*, ed. M. Chibnall, 6 vols. (Oxford, 1969–80), VI, 58, 84 [hereafter: OV], and Anglo-Saxon Chronicle, s.a. 1104–6. According to Henry of Huntingdon (*Historia Anglorum: The History of the English People*, ed. D. Greenway (Oxford, 1996), 698) he was blinded. For his later fate see Golding, 'Robert of Mortain', 122, and W. Hollister, 'Royal Acts of Mutilation', in his *Monarchy, Magnates and Institutions in the Anglo-Norman World* (London, 1986), 291–301, at 298–9. See *Pipe Roll 31 Henry I*, ed. J. Hunter (Record Commission, 1831), 143. According to Leland (*Joannis Lelandi Antiquarii De Rebus Britannicis Collectanea*, ed. T. Hearne, 6 vols. (London, 1774), III, 255) he was buried at Bermondsey, though Grestain tradition had it that he was buried at Grestain, and recorded his epitaph (C. Bréard, *L'Abbaye de Notre-Dame de Grestain* (Rouen, 1904), 33). The Bermondsey annals, which, though much later in date, perhaps record earlier memories, tell how he was freed from the Tower through a miracle of the Holy Cross (*Annales Monastici*, ed. H. R. Luard, 5 vols., RS (1864–9), III, 432 and 436).

[8] OV, VI, 42.

Benedictine houses; thereafter other opportunities were offered as the 'new' orders, and especially the Augustinians, provided competition. If the choice of order was limited, that of location was not. Anglo-Norman magnates could choose to continue their patronage of Norman or other continental abbeys, which often involved the creation of dependent houses in England: alternatively they might choose to endow existing English communities, or to found new independent ones, as happened for example at Shrewsbury. Yet for political and economic reasons new foundations on this side of the Channel were comparatively rare, and the first generation of colonists tended to continue their patronage of abbeys founded by their ancestors. The grants of the post-conquest counts of Mortain fall into three main classes: first, those made to the abbey founded by Robert's father at Grestain, the *caput* of the estates acquired through Herluin's elevation in the 1030s; secondly, those made to communities established in Robert's lordship of Mortain; and thirdly, those made to foundations in England, most of which were linked with either Grestain or Mortain and which were frequently associated with honorial centres.

Although other religious houses in Normandy and beyond received small benefactions, the counts concentrated their largesse on Grestain and Mortain, and it was at Grestain, at the heart of his inherited estates and which was intended as the family mausoleum, that Robert chose burial rather than at either of his foundations at Mortain.[9] According to seventeenth-century belief, which may reflect earlier traditions, Grestain was founded by Herluin (who had become a leper), as the result of a vision in which the Virgin advised him that, if he wished to recover his health, he should go to a spring and restore a nearby ruined chapel dedicated to herself at Grestain, and establish a priest there. Then, healed but apparently still deformed, he was again told by the Virgin to found a monastery at the site. This done, Herluin was completely restored.[10] Though this account is apocryphal, it is not impossible that the site was once occupied by an earlier church, as was the case at a number of other Norman monasteries such as St Wandrille or St Évroul.[11] In fact the abbey does

---

[9] For Robert's grants or confirmations to Fleury, Lessay (where he held fraternity rights), and St Stephen's, Caen see *Gallia Christiana*, 16 vols. (Paris, 1715–1865), XI, 476–7, 917, and instr. 73; *Regesta Regum Anglo-Normannorum: The Acta of William I (1066–1087)*, ed. D. Bates (Oxford, 1998), no. 49, p. 232. That Robert also entered the confraternity of St Martin-le-Grand in London demonstrates an ambiguity towards English foundations in the same way as does his daughter's burial at St Albans (J. A. Green, *The Aristocracy of Norman England* (Cambridge, 1997), 424).

[10] A. du Monstier, *Neustria Pia, seu de omnibus et singulis abbatis et prioratibus totius Normanniae* (Rouen, 1663), 528.

[11] On the re-foundation topos in southern France, see A. G. Remensnyder, *Remembering Kings Past: Monastic Foundation Legends in Medieval Southern France* (Ithaca and London, 1995), 44–50. Remensnyder cites a very similar twelfth-century *vita* relating the foundation of Sainte-Enimie by a leprous Merovingian princess. For other Norman examples see Harper-Bill, 'Piety of the Anglo-Norman Knightly Class', 71–2. The *fontaine de Saint-Benoit* which lay to the west of the conventual buildings at Grestain, and which was presumably the site of the original foundation, was the object of an annual procession (Bréard, *L'Abbaye de Notre-Dame*, 184, 193).

seem to have been founded by Herluin in 1050, though William of Jumièges gave Robert as the founder and the Grestain necrology recorded Odo of Bayeux as *fundatoris eius loci*.[12] Such assumptions were understandable, for while Herluin's initial foundation was small, the benefactions that followed from Robert and William in both Normandy and England combined to establish a community of some wealth. Herluin probably ended his life as a monk at Grestain, presumably as an *ad succurrendum* entrant. In the mortuary roll of Matilda, daughter of William the Conqueror and abbess of La Trinité, Caen, *Herluino monacho* appears first in a list of names for whom prayers are requested, followed by Robert of Mortain and his wife Matilda.[13] While Robert might well be claimed as a far more generous patron than his father—he had, after all, many more resources—Odo's support was very limited, being confined to six bordars in Fiquefleur and Crémanfleur and twenty acres in order to make a saltern.[14] There is some doubt, indeed, whether during its first years Grestain, which is said to have been colonized by monks from St Wandrille and Préaux, even had abbatial status, and it is only its second leader, Geoffrey, a monk from St Sergius, Angers, who is first styled abbot.[15] This promotion may well have been a consequence of the substantial increase in benefactions given by Robert. A significant number of these grants brought commercial advantage to the monks. They included rights and fisheries on the River Seine, salt-works, mills, tithes from the count's fairs and mills: all would be appropriate grants from a magnate who took a considerable interest in the economic exploitation of his properties on both sides of the Channel.[16]

Even though no original charters survive, a recently discovered *pancarte*, dating from 1082—which can be supplemented by two confirmation charters of King Richard I issued on 14 November 1189, one for the abbey's properties in Normandy and one for those in England—gives a clear picture of the abbey's benefactions and indicates that most derived from the counts and their tenants.[17] Indeed, it is likely that some at least of these donors (such as the de

---

[12] Bréard, *L'Abbaye*, 599.

[13] L. Delisle, *Rouleaux des morts du IXe au XVe siècles* (Paris, 1886), 207. However, in the roll of Vital, Robert appears at the head just in front of his father (ibid. 289).

[14] Bréard, *L'Abbaye de Notre-Dame*, 28. These grants do not appear in Richard I's confirmation charter of 1189.

[15] *Neustria Pia*, 529; Bréard, *L'Abbaye de Notre-Dame*, 34–43, where it is suggested that this Abbot Geoffrey could perhaps be identified with Geoffrey, chaplain of the count of Mortain, who gave all the churches, tithes, and lands he had received from the count in Normandy to Grestain. The relationship with Préaux seems to be demonstrated in an annual procession at the feast of the Assumption, when monks from Préaux came to Grestain (ibid. 186). See also Bates, 'Notes sur l'aristocratie normande. II. Herluin de Conteville et sa famille', *Annales de Normandie*, 23 (1973), 21–38, at 25–6.

[16] *Regesta Regum Anglo-Normannorum*, no. 158, pp. 521–2; Bréard, *L'Abbaye de Notre-Dame*, 26–7, 120–8; Golding, 'Robert of Mortain', 133–5.

[17] Richard I's charters are published in Bréard, *L'Abbaye de Notre-Dame*, 199–209 and the *pancarte* of 1082 in *Regesta Regum Anglo-Normannorum*, no. 158, pp. 517–26. It is discussed in D. Bates and V. Gazeau, 'L'Abbaye de Grestain et la famille d'Herluin de Conteville', *Annales de Normandie*, 40 (1990), 5–30, at 24–30.

Cahagnes, or the L'Aigle family, which had supported Henry I against Robert of Bellême, and which had acquired the Mortain barony of Pevensey in chief) may have protected the foundation after the confiscation of William's estates in 1104 and his final downfall in 1106 when, according to the editors of *Gallia Christiana*, Henry I at first wished to appropriate the abbey's property into the royal demesne.[18] As will be seen later, other Mortain foundations were endangered by the new regime. Nor were fears of appropriation groundless: the nuns of Almenèches lost lands that had been given to them by Roger of Montgomery in Sussex which were then granted to a royal supporter.[19]

Herluin's initial endowment was closely concentrated around Grestain, which was situated only a few kilometres from Conteville. However, Robert's first grant to the abbey (a moiety of the estate and church of Muneville-sur-Mer on the south-west of the Cotentin) was made prior to his father's death and was taken from his lands as count of Mortain.[20] But, once Robert had inherited his father's patrimony, all his grants were taken from it, his lands of Mortain being employed to support his foundations in Mortain itself. Such a division made obvious sense for benefactor and communities alike. Within the *pancarte*, Robert's English benefactions are arranged in two groups, separated by unrelated grants from other donors of Norman lands.[21] This may indicate that the estates were given at two or more distinct times. These lands were rather scattered, though there was a concentration in the rape of Pevensey, where Grestain established a cell at Wilmington, a few miles inland and to the west of Pevensey itself. The first grants comprised a group in East Anglia: the vills of Creeting (St Olave and St Peter) and Brettenham in Suffolk, together with the tithes of Combs in the same county, and Robert's holding in Sawston (Cambs.). There is no indication as to how these lands were administered: certainly no dependent priory was created here.[22] The second group is much longer and probably conceals a number of grants made at different times. The most significant are the lands given in the rape of Pevensey: all were granted prior to 1086, when they appear in Domesday as Grestain's holdings. These comprised fifteen hides in Wilmington, six in Frog Firle, and two in Beddingham, together with its church, and one house (unrecorded in Domesday) in Pevensey itself.[23] These were substantial benefactions. Grestain had almost the entire estate of Wilmington under its control, though Battle Abbey already possessed six virgates here. Frog Firle had never been in Robert's demesne: most of

---

[18] *Gallia Christiana*, XI, 555.   [19] OV, VI, 32.   [20] Bréard, *L'Abbaye de Notre-Dame*, 26.

[21] Ibid. 28–30; *Regesta Regum Anglo-Normannorum*, no. 578, pp. 517–26.

[22] Yet not all these lands were granted at the same time: the Creeting estates amounting to 3 carucates were in the hands of Grestain by 1086 (DB, II, 291b); Brettenham was still then a demesne manor of 4 carucates. Grestain held 2 hides in Sawston of the count (DB, I,193a). The fact that Bernay had a small dependent priory in neighbouring Creeting St Mary may have precluded Grestain developing one of its own.

[23] Richard I's confirmation charter also refers to the grant of pannage and herbage, together with materials to build the priory's churches and houses and for firewood from the great forest of Pevensey.

Grestain's land here had been appropriated by Robert from the canons of St John's, Lewes, who had received it from Queen Edith.[24] The two hides in Beddingham had been granted by Edward the Confessor to Wulfnoth the priest, and almost certainly constitute the endowment of the minster and its priest.[25]

The other properties are a mixed bag. Before 1086 ten hides were granted in Connock (Wilts.), a large grant that was presumably farmed out by the abbey, since it was far from its own central interests and those of Robert himself.[26] The remainder were lands that had been associated with Matilda, Robert's first wife, and some of which seem to have constituted her dowry. Her father, Roger of Montgomery, had given her thirty-two hides in England, identified—though the figures do not quite add up—as eight in Harrington (Northants.), eleven in Marsh Gibbon and six in Ickford (Bucks.), two at Langborough (Glos.), and three-and-a-half at *Tomstonam* and three virgates at Clendon (Northants). All of these lands had been held by Alured, Robert's steward, for £15 per annum. Following Matilda's death Alured continued as tenant, paying the same rent to Grestain. Robert also granted a house in London, which his wife had formerly held of him. Two other properties involved complicated exchanges. Kempton (Middx.) had apparently been held by Matilda of her husband, then exchanged with him for 10s. per annum, a rent he now granted to Grestain, while Robert recovered Pendley (Herts.), which Matilda had held of the king from Grestain, and which he had then given to Grestain in exchange for Fiquefleur and the proceeds of half of its market, together with a moiety of a saltern which he had kept in his own possession.[27]

Though, as its recent editors have pointed out, the *pancarte* often gives fuller information than the 1189 charters, this is really only true of the sections dealing with the Norman benefactions.[28] In general the importance of Richard I's confirmation charter lies both in the occasional richer detail it provides of Robert's grants and in its revelation of the extent to which Robert and William's tenants patronized their lords' foundation. It also establishes that in addition to the lands listed in the *pancarte* as formerly belonging to Matilda, she was also responsible for the grant of the estate at Connock and Beddingham.[29] The *pancarte* only refers to one grant by a tenant—a post-mortem benefaction by Ralph de Vautorte, of his manor of Norton-sub-Hamdon (Somerset)—but the royal charter makes it clear that many more tenants were associated as patrons.[30] Robert fitzIvo, a leading tenant of Robert in the south-west, gave his

[24] DB, I, 21b. The *pancarte* lists 3 hides in Frog Firle, but the confirmation of Richard I and Domesday establish that 6 hides were given.
[25] DB, I, 20b. I am indebted to John Blair for his advice on this matter.   [26] DB, I, 68b.
[27] The earlier grant of half of the market and saltern is found in an earlier section of the *pancarte*.
[28] D. Bates and V. Gazeau, 'L'Abbaye de Grestain', 7–8.
[29] Such benefactions accord well with her reported generosity to Marmoutier (see below, p. 219).
[30] This manor was in Grestain's hands by 1086 (DB, I, 92b).

Domesday manor of Frithelstock (Devon.) sometime after 1086.[31] Alured *pin-cerna* gave his demesne tithes in Charlston (Sussex) and his son William granted four acres to the west of Pevensey church.[32] William of Mortain was if anything even more generous to Grestain (at least in England) than his father had been. Yet many of these grants represent his disinvestment of *spiritualia*, though these were sometimes accompanied by other properties. Such grants were relatively cheap, and their possession by the laity was increasingly difficult to defend. Thus he gave eleven churches, as well as tithes in ten other manors.[33] Of these the most significant was the gift of all the churches, the castle chapel, tithes, and the land of Geoffrey the chaplain in Berkhamstead.[34] It may be that the monks of Grestain were expected to provide for the spiritual needs of the comital castle, even though Grestain did not develop a cell here.

Though the family monastery was already well established at Grestain, it is clear that Robert wished to create a new ecclesiastical, as well as a political, centre of power at his own *caput* of Mortain. Such a move paralleled his brother the king's patronage and development of Caen rather than Rouen: the ducal family—William at Caen, Odo at Bayeux, and Robert at Mortain—was moving west. In 1082 Robert established two religious houses in Mortain itself: one (founded in conjunction with his wife, Matilda) was a collegiate church dedicated to St Évroul and situated in the castle of Mortain; the other, a cell of Marmoutier, was based at the church of Notre-Dame. We do not know what personal motives or incentives prompted such generosity at this point; and it is, of course, likely that both foundations were already well in hand before their formal constitution in 1082. There is some evidence that St Évroul was the earlier foundation, but neither foundation charter survives in its primitive form, and their evidence is contradictory. The foundation of St Évroul, established within the castle and staffed by secular canons, reflects a pattern symptomatic of the pious giving of eleventh-century Norman lords.[35] Robert was careful to stress how, in providing for the dean, he is observing canonical practice (*sicut instituto deposcit canonica*). It was presumably intended to cater both for the spiritual, and perhaps also the secretarial, needs of the count and his household: it also provided a school, for the charter went on to prohibit any other school in

---

[31] DB, I, 104b.

[32] For Alured's patronage of Montacute, see below, p. 224.

[33] The churches were largely found in the rape of Pevensey (East and West Dean and Frog Firle, where the manor was already held by Grestain), Northamptonshire (Blakesley, Grafton Regis, *Butebroc*, Helmdon), as well as Drayton Beauchamp (Bucks.), Berkhamsted (Herts.), *Bradeslewes* and *Stokes* (unidentified). On this trend in general see B. Kemp, 'Monastic Possession of Churches in England in the Twelfth Century', *JEH* 31 (1980), 133–60.

[34] Geoffrey was perhaps the castle chaplain.

[35] The most important study of these foundations is L. Musset, 'Recherches sur les communautés de clercs séculiers en Normandie au XIe siècle', *Bulletin de la Société des Antiquaires de Normandie*, 55 (1959–60), 5–38. Castle collegiate foundations were also found in post-conquest England. Examples include Roger of Montgommery at Arundel, Robert de Beaumont at Leicester, and Henry of Warwick at Warwick (see J. A. Green, *The Aristocracy of Norman England* (Cambridge, 1998), 402).

the Mortain valley and stipulated that if one was found its books should be confiscated by the canons and placed in their treasury.[36] The canons were certainly expected to be in Robert's company, when they were to be treated as his chaplains, and whenever he was in Mortain the dean, cantor, custodian of the church, and master of the school were to be entertained at his table. The foundation of St Évroul is known only from a lengthy fourteenth-century copy of a charter, which interpolates later grants by both counts William and Stephen.[37] There is some indication that there was an earlier church of St Évroul, and Robert's grant may represent a re-foundation and resiting within his castle.

Though Robert provided for the cantor and thirteen prebends, it is clear that the foundation was a collaborative act involving the count and his vassals, under his active encouragement. While Robert alone was responsible for the dean's endowment, his vassal Robert de Cuves established the cantor at the count's request, and the count added a sum of £32 Le Mans and, as an additional incentive, released Robert's son for two years from his obligation to provide castle-guard at Mortain. It is once again noteworthy that Count Robert's own grants were predominantly of proceeds from fairs (especially tolls), mills, churches, and tithes, while the college's landed endowments came primarily from the tenants. The foundation was reinforced with extensive jurisdictional privileges and freedoms from most ecclesiastical exactions, whilst at the same time Robert ensured that legal cases should be heard before his court. In addition to Robert's family, the charter was witnessed by King William, Roger de Beaumont, Roger of Montgommery, and almost all the Norman bishops: William, archbishop of Rouen, and the bishops of Bayeux, Évreux, Coutances, and Lisieux. The same bishops also consecrated the collegiate church, perhaps at the same time as the charter was issued in its original form. This impressive array of witnesses demonstrates the prestige attached to the foundation, which Robert probably intended to rival that of his father at Grestain. Robert's patronage was continued both by his son, who endowed another prebend, and by Stephen of Boulogne. Yet, in spite of the fact that the counts proved such great patrons of St Évroul, they granted but little of their English property to this community, the recorded grants being limited to William's manor of Langford (Wilts.) and his annual payment of £10 from the tolls of Pevensey.[38]

A further indication of the status Robert hoped to gain for St Évroul is

[36] See J. Fournée, *La Spiritualité en Normandie au temps de Guillaume le Conquérant*, Le Pays Bas-Normand: Société d'Art et d'Histoire, 186 (1987), 32, citing L. Delisle, *La Classe agricole en Normandie*, 177. See also B. Jacqueline, 'Écoles et culture dans l'Avranchin, le Mortainais et le Cotentin au temps de saint Anselme', in *Les Mutations socio-culturelles au tournant des XIᵉ–XIIᵉ siècles* (*Colloque du Bec*, 1982), ed. R. Foreville (Paris, 1984), 203–12, at 206–7.

[37] *Regesta Regum Anglo-Normannorum*, no. 215, pp. 676–85, and Boussard, 'Le Comté de Mortain', 258–68.

[38] Boussard, 'Le Comté de Mortain', 266. Langford was a demesne manor in 1086, valued at £5 in 1086 (DB, I,68b).

indicated by his promotion of the cult of William Firmatus. Firmatus was a native of Tours, where he became a canon and teacher then lived as a hermit accompanied by his mother, before undertaking a lengthy pilgrimage to the Holy Land, when he was allegedly—and most improbably—consecrated a bishop at Constantinople. He returned to France to live as a hermit at Mantilly, not far from Mortain, where he was supported by Count Robert. According to the saint's *Vita*, though he hated towns he often came into Mortain to pray, probably at St Évroul.[39] Following his death, two canons of St Évroul rushed to the funeral from Gorron, one of Robert's castles, and then conveyed the news to Robert. Shortly afterwards the neighbouring towns of Domfront and Mayenne planned to obtain William's body *cum violentia*, but a crowd loyal to Robert seized it and bore it in triumph to Mortain, where it was displayed with honour and became the centre of pilgrimage, while the dedication of the church was later changed to that of the new saint.[40]

Robert and his wife also created a small cell of Marmoutier at Mortain by granting that abbey the church of Notre-Dame and the prebend which canon Norgod had created from his own holdings for St Évroul, providing due compensation for the latter's loss. This foundation was on a much smaller scale than St Évroul, and virtually all of Robert's grant was confined to properties and tithes within Mortain itself, as well as the right to the burial of all those in the 'vill of St Évroul'.[41] Yet Robert seems to have anticipated that the new foundation might become independent of Marmoutier, for in 1088 he granted the cell a prebend in St Évroul on condition that its abbot, if it became an abbey, should perform his liturgical obligations at the collegiate church, and reciprocally, should the dean of St Évroul wish to be received as a monk he should be accepted without gift.[42]

However, the priory was quite well provided for in England. A rare insight into the process of pious benefaction beyond the often arid diplomatic of charters is provided in a royal notification showing how when Robert's first wife, Matilda, died her grieving husband and brother in law, King William, distributed her goods to monasteries and the poor. One of Marmoutier's monks who was at Mortain, and who was astute enough to attend the countess's funeral, acquired the grant of Piddle Hinton (Dorset), a manor of ten hides that

[39] The *vita* of William by Stephen, bishop of Rennes and former cantor of St Évroul, is printed in *Acta Sanctorum, April III*, 336–43. For doubts on his authorship see J. van Moolenbroek, *Vital l'ermite, prédicateur itinérant, fondateur de l'abbaye normande de Savigny* (Assen–Maastricht, 1990), 54–6.

[40] *Acta Sanctorum, April III*, 342. By contrast, Grestain is not known to have had any significant shrine. That a cult was established early at St Évroul is witnessed both by the recorded miracles, at least one of which must date from the time of Count Robert, and by an early grant.

[41] *Regesta Regum Anglo-Normannorum*, no. 205, pp. 642–6. He did also grant the land in Helleville held by his tenant, William de Lestre (ibid., no. 204, pp. 641–2). See also *Calendar of Documents Preserved in France, Illustrative of the History of Great Britain and Ireland*, Vol. I, *A.D. 918–1216*, ed. J. H. Round (London, 1899) (hereafter *CDF*), no. 1208, p. 436. Following Robert's death, Count William granted them the castle chapel of Hayes-du-Puits, on condition that the monks served it (ibid.).

[42] Ibid., no. 1207, pp. 435–6.

Matilda had held of her husband.[43] Land was also given in the rape of Pevensey. Here Robert's sheriff, Walter de Ricardeville, had seized lands in Withyham and Blackham in which Notre-Dame already had an interest. In return for a confirmation of the property, the monks responsible for the administration of these properties tendered £10 Le Mans to Robert, who also promised that the monks should have Withyham which they currently held at fee farm for £7. On his death William sold the property to the monks for an additional £23 and a very fine horse.[44] Between 1100 and 1104 William also attempted to found another cell of Marmoutier at Wingale (Lincs.), on condition that the monks of Marmoutier find twenty monks—a substantial complement—to serve the new foundation.[45]

Up till now the counts' foundations were of a 'traditional' nature: the patron-age of Benedictine and collegiate houses. But the favour shown to Firmatus is indicative of their awareness and reception of new expressions of monastic spirituality. The border region between Britanny, Maine, and Normandy was famous for its hermits.[46] Though Firmatus represented an 'old-style' eremitism, typified by a solitary, often peripatetic, life of asceticism rather than the newer expression of the holy life, usually marked by evangelistic fervour and the attraction of followers, frequently women or marginals, which often co-alesced into cenobitic communities, it is likely that he influenced the new gener-ation of local hermits—men such as Bernard of Tiron, Robert of Arbrissel, and Vital of Savigny, all of whom went on to found monastic groups. Vital's ties with Robert were long-standing. He was born at Tierceville, a comital manor near Conteville, half of which had been granted to Grestain by Robert. It is pos-sible, though there is no certainty, that Vital was educated at Grestain and then at Bayeux under the patronage of Odo, who may have been responsible for his further education at Liège and then for bringing him to the attention of Robert.[47] According to Claude Auvry, prior of Savigny early in the eighteenth century, Vital was taken from the service of Odo of Bayeux by Robert of Mortain, who wished to make Vital his chaplain; certainly the *Vita* makes it

[43] *Regesta Regum Anglo-Normannorum*, no. 207, pp. 648–9. For other examples of gift-giving at funerals see Cownie, *Religious Patronage*, 163. Matilda was buried at Grestain: did she die at Mortain, being afterwards transferred to Grestain?

[44] *CDF*, no. 1205, pp. 434–5.

[45] Ibid., no. 1210, p. 437. The history of this foundation is confused. According to Domesday the church of Wingeham (identified by Foster as Wingale priory) held 1½ carucates in Owersby, which was part of the lands of Roger of Poitou. In the Lindsey Survey of 1115–8 the lord of this land was Stephen, count of Mortain, who had acquired many of Roger's estates (*The Lincolnshire Domesday and the Lindsey Survey*, ed. C. W. Foster and T. Longley, Lincoln Record Soc., 19 (1924), 91, 245). Robert of Mortain did not hold any lands in Domesday in 1086. Moreover, by the early thirteenth century Wingale Priory was a dependency of Sées, not Marmoutier (*The Victoria History of the County of Lincolnshire*, ed. W. Page (London, 1906), II, 241).

[46] See, in general, L. Raison and R. Niderst, 'Le Mouvement érémitique dans l'Ouest de la France à la fin du XIᵉ siècle et au début du XIIᵉ', *Annales de Bretagne*, 53–5 (1946–8), 1–45; and see the comments in Geoffrey Grossus' *vita* of Bernard of Tiron (PL 172, cols. 1380–1).

[47] For these hypotheses see van Moolenbroek, *Vital l'ermite*, 148–53.

clear that Vital had returned to his native western Normandy and that his reputation had reached Robert.[48] That Vital was a trusted member of the count's
familia is suggested by the story in Stephen de Fougère's *Vita* of the saint that
tells how he intervened in a dispute between the count and his wife when he
found her crying after Robert had beaten her.[49] Vital's role as a mediator is also
indicated by Orderic Vitalis's account of how he served as an—unsuccessful—
negotiator prior to the battle of Tinchebrai.[50] Vital was also a canon of Robert's
collegiate foundation, a post he may have held concurrently with his position as
chaplain.[51] Some time shortly before Robert's death, and perhaps in 1093, Vital
left the college and established himself as a hermit at the unidentified site of
Dompierre, where he remained till the foundation of Savigny in 1112. Though
Savigny was founded well after the death of Robert and the imprisonment of
his son, there is some further evidence to indicate the counts' support for Vital's
activities. Count William has traditionally been regarded as the founder in 1105
of a community of religious women under the direction of Vital's sister. This
foundation has now been disproved, but it does seem likely that the counts were
behind the establishment of a *congregatio pauperum hominum* at the church of
La Trinité, Mortain, whose lands later formed the nucleus of the endowment
of the nunnery of 'les Blanches'.[52] These lands were conveyed to the abbey of
St Étienne, Caen, by Vital some time before Savigny was founded, and were only
recovered through the good offices of Henry I in 1118; and Van Moolenbroek
has suggested that the original transfer to Caen occurred shortly after Count
William's fall, when all his monastic foundations were under potential threat
from the victorious king. Henry's interference in 1118 reinforced his claim to be
the legitimate successor of the count.[53]

So far I have considered the counts' patronage of Norman communities.
They were also patrons, though much more ambivalently, of English religious
houses. Few of Robert's English benefactions can be regarded as made only in
pious expectation of heavenly reward. We have already seen how at St Albans,
though he gave with one hand, he took rather more with the other. So too in

---

[48] C. Auvry, *Histoire de la congrégation de Savigny*, ed. A. Laveille, Societé de l'Histoire de Normandie, 30:1 (1896), 38; *Vitae BB. Vitalis et Gaufridi*, ed. E. P. Sauvage, *Analecta Bollandiana*, I (1881),
362–3.

[49] *Vitae BB. Vitalis et Gaufridi*, 352–4: see also Golding, 'Robert of Mortain', 122–3.

[50] *Vitae BB. Vitalis et Gaufridi*, ed. Sauvage, 363–4; for a wonderful nineteenth-century evocation of
Vital's friendship with the count and his family, see the illustration in H. Sauvage, *Saint Vital et l'abbaye
de Savigny dans l'ancien diocèse d'Avranches* (Mortain, 1895), between pp. 23 and 24. OV, VI, 86. Cf. *Vita*,
366–8. He is also known to have been present at the Council of London in 1108.

[51] OV, IV, 330.

[52] For the fullest discussion see van Moolenbroek, *Vital l'ermite*, 128–45, 173–80, 347, n. 89. The
endowment consisted of lands in the suburb of Mortain focused on the church of St Hilaire, but other
lands were granted in the neighbourhood, including Surdeval and Tinchebrai, as well as 10 librates of
unidentified lands at *Thenuh* in England. The best edition of the charter is now van Moolenbroek, *Vital
l'ermite*, 319–22. The count's vassals who were associated with their lord's foundation are identified, ibid.
348, n. 99. For the alleged foundation of a nunnery see *Gallia Christiana*, XI, 555.

[53] van Moolenbroek, *Vital l'ermite*, 266–7.

Cornwall. Most of the existing communities lost land to Robert following the
conquest, and even his treatment of the canons at Launceston and St Michael's
Mount, where he was to develop two small priories, was cavalier. There was a
small community of canons at *Lanscaveton* (St Stephen's by Launceston) which
was probably of relatively recent foundation.[54] These canons had apparently
already suffered some vicissitudes, the Exon Domesday recording that in 1066
the four hides of its Launceston estate were held by Earl Harold.[55] But these
problems were exacerbated under the new regime. By 1086 the estate's value had
halved since 1066: worse, the canons' market, valued at 20s., had been moved by
Robert into his castle. His promise to the canons of the rights of a free borough
must have counted for little given the loss of the market, for which his compensation of 20s. was scant indeed.[56] Such aggressive economic predation is a feature on Robert's English estates: a few miles away the creation of a market at the
count's castle of Trematon had led to the ruin of a market held by St German's.[57]
Apart from confirming the canons' lands in and around Launceston, he did
little more than grant two-and-a-half hides of land taken from the royal manor
of Pendrim and grant the tithes from some demesne manors.[58] Nor is there any
indication that Count William had any interest in the canons, though he did
issue a confirmation of lands and liberties of both Launceston and St Petroc's,
Bodmin.[59]

   The counts of Mortain were also associated, though more tentatively, with
another Cornish foundation, St Michael's Mount. The early history of the
community here is obscure, but it would seem that a group of canons similar to
those found at St Stephen's Launceston had once occupied the site. By 1086, of
the two hides St Michael's held in Truthwall the count of Mortain had appropriated one to himself.[60] The canons may already have been subject to Mont
St Michel, for an intriguing but probably authentic charter, which can probably
be dated to the early 1030s, recorded in the twelfth-century cartulary of Mont
St Michel, shows the exiled Edward the Confessor, styling himself 'king of the
English', granting *Vennesire* and the port of *Ruminella* with their appurtenances
to the monks, as well as confirming the site of 'sanctum michaelem qui est iuxta
mare'. *Vennesire* can very likely be identified with Winnianton hundred on the
west side of the Lizard peninsula. *Ruminella* is more difficult. Suggestions have
included a misreading of Truthwall, which makes sense in the light of that

   [54] See the discussion in *Cartulary of Launceston Priory (Lambeth Palace MS. 719): A Calendar*, ed.
P. L. Hull, Devon and Cornwall Record Soc., NS, 30 (1987), pp. xi–xiii; L. Olson, *Early Monasteries in
Cornwall* (Woodbridge, 1989), 95–6.
   [55] DB, IV, 206b: Olson, *Early Monasteries*, 94.
   [56] These 'compensations' are found in a charter of Reginald de Dunstanville (*c.*1154–65): the reference
to a 'free borough' seems anachronistic for the late eleventh-century (*Cartulary of Launceston Priory*, ed.
Hull, no. 11, pp. 9–10).
   [57] See Golding, 'Robert of Mortain', 133–5.
   [58] *Cartulary of Launceston Priory*, ed. Hull, no. 3, pp. 2–4; DB I, 120a.
   [59] *Cartulary of Launceston Priory*, ed. Hull, no. 14, pp. 11–12.
   [60] DB I, 120b, 125a. See also Olson, *Early Monasteries*, 89–90.

manor's later association with the community; while its port has variously been identified as Marazion, Ruan Minor, and, most recently, Old Romney (Kent), where there was certainly a royal port in the eleventh century, but which is clearly very far from the Penwith peninsula, and where there is no evidence that the monks ever had later interests or claims.[61] If this charter is genuine it indicates the prior existence of a native community in Cornwall that was then ceded to Mont St Michel—though it was probably only incorporated as a cell *c*.1135.[62] While it is uncertain if this grant took effect immediately, the monks may have had control over St Michael's Mount by the time of the conquest, perhaps administering it through a local representative, who might be identified with Brictmer, described as a priest in Exon Domesday, who held Truthwall TRE.[63] The Mount's possession by Mont St Michel might explain why the Exon Domesday refers to the *canons* of virtually all of the pre-conquest Cornish communities, but only to the *lands* of St Michael.[64]

The date of Robert's grants to Mont St Michel has been much debated, particularly since these have implications for dating Robert's acquisition of Cornwall. I have argued elsewhere that Robert's first grant was made *c*.1070.[65] This gave half-a-hide of land and a Thursday market, to which was afterwards added three acres in Meneage in Traboe. This seems a very small amount of land and may be a scribal error; it certainly is contradicted by an entry in the Otterton customal which lists Robert's grants as lands sufficient for two ploughs in Tremayne, for three ploughs in both Traboe and Lesneage, and for two ploughs in Tregevis and Carvallack, and additional pasture.[66] This grant was followed by another, made perhaps twenty years later, in which Robert and his second wife, Almodis, ceded the manor of Ludgvan, held by Richard fitzTurold, and the land in Truthwall held by Blohin the Breton, which Robert had earlier taken from the monks. He also granted two fairs on the mainland opposite the Mount.[67] However, the charter makes it explicit that this transaction was a *conventio*, whereby in return for the land the monks of Mont St Michel gave the considerable sum of £60 Caen.[68] Though this suggests the resolution of some

[61] The most detailed discussion and recent publication of this charter is S. Keynes, 'The Aethelings in Normandy', *ANS* 13 (1991), 173–205, at 190–3, 204. See also *The Cartulary of St Michael's Mount*, ed. P. L. Hull, Devon and Cornwall Rec. Soc., NS, 5 (1962), pp. x–xiii. The only suitable harbour along this coast was on the island of St Michael's Mount: this lay within the manor of Truthwall.

[62] *Cartulary of St Michael's Mount*, ed. Hull, pp. xvii–xviii.   [63] DB IV, 208b.

[64] Which Hull perceived as arguing against a pre-conquest Celtic community (*Cartulary of St Michael's Mount*, p. xi).

[65] See Golding, 'Robert of Mortain', 126–8.

[66] *Cartulary of St Michael's Mount*, ed. Hull, no. 1, pp. 1–2, xviii–xix. See also *CDF*, no. 729, p. 265, where it is apparent that some of these lands were the subject of dispute with lay tenants.

[67] See O. J. Padel, 'The Names Marazion and Market Jew', in *The Charter Town of Marazion*, ed. C. North and J. Palmer (Marazion, 1995), 7–9.

[68] *Cartulary of St Michael's Mount*, ed. Hull, app. II, p. 62. For the suggestion that these lands had earlier been granted to Mont St Michel by Robert's *antecessor*, Count Brian, seized by Robert, and then released on this payment, see D. Matthew, *The Norman Monasteries and Their English Possessions* (Oxford, 1962), 36–7; Golding, 'Robert of Mortain', 127–8.

dispute, perhaps occasioned by Robert's earlier seizure of property, nevertheless there is no evidence that the monks ever gained possession of the lands, though they did retain the markets.[69] Nor is there any evidence that thereafter the counts of Mortain took much interest in the community. Just as Mont St Michel was peripheral to the concerns of the family in Normandy, so too St Michael's Mount lay at some distance from the chief estates of the family in England. Most of the Mortain demesne manors in Cornwall were concentrated in the more fertile eastern part of the shire and were grouped around Launceston and Liskeard: the counts had no castle, no *caput*, and probably no ambitions in the far west.[70] This may be significant. The counts of Mortain often established their religious foundations in close association with a castle, as at Launceston, Montacute, and Pevensey (where Wilmington Priory was in an adjacent parish and was probably expected to fulfil a similar function). The importance of the relationship between castle, monastery, and borough in the colonization of post-conquest England was formulated by le Patourel.[71] Though there was nothing out of the ordinary in the pattern of Mortain patronage, nowhere perhaps is this symbiosis as apparent as on the Mortain honors: indeed, this model of development is also found across the Channel at Mortain itself, where the count had his castle, two religious establishments, and a flourishing market centre, already possessing its suburb, the *neufbourg*.

William's pious giving in England was concentrated on his foundation of the Cluniac priory of Montacute. Following William de Warenne's foundation of Lewes in 1077, the Cluniacs received considerable patronage from the highest echelons of the Anglo-Norman aristocracy, and William's choice reflects this popularity.[72] However, William's support of the Cluniacs was more considerable than that of many of his contemporaries. Not only did he found Montacute, he also granted Lewes demesne lands in Ripe (Surrey) and a hide of land in Ripe and one virgate in Laughton (Sussex), while his vassal Alured granted the church and other properties in East Grinstead and the tithe of Preston (Sussex), and William de Cahagnes granted three hides in Langney (Sussex).[73] And of course, it was at Cluniac Bermondsey that he found final refuge and died.[74]

[69] *Cartulary of St Michael's Mount*, ed. Hull, app. II, pp. 62 and xvii.
[70] Golding, 'Robert of Mortain', 129.
[71] J. le Patourel, *The Norman Empire* (Oxford, 1976), 317. That it was a common practice for Norman lords to establish small religious communities at, or even in, their castles had long been recognized: see e.g. M. Chibnall, 'The Norman Monastic Plantation in England', in *La Normandie bénédictine au temps de Guillaume le Conquérant (XIᵉ siècle)* (Lille, 1967), 402, 404–5; Matthew, *Norman Monasteries*, 56–7. See also J. Martindale, 'Monasteries and Castles: The Priories of Saint Florent de Saumur in England after 1066', in *England in the Eleventh Century*, ed. C. Hicks (Stamford, 1992), 135–56, and M. W. Thompson, 'Associated Monasteries and Castles in the Middle Ages: A Tentative List', *Archaeological Journal*, 143 (1986), 305–21, esp. 308–11.
[72] This trend is discussed in B. Golding, 'The Coming of the Cluniacs', *ANS* 3 (1981), 65–77.
[73] *CDF*, no. 391, pp. 509–13.
[74] In 1086 Robert held a hide of the royal demesne in Bermondsey (DB, I, 34a). This land was in the

Montacute was the site of the discovery during Cnut's reign of the Holy Cross relic which had then been transferred to Waltham Abbey by Tovi the Proud.[75] The place was, therefore, already sanctified, and William's decision to found a house at the foot of the hill where one of the holiest relics had been discovered may have been partly influenced by a desire to appropriate this consecrated place for the new Norman order. Moreover, Montacute had long been a centre of Mortain power. Robert had already received the estate and built a castle there by 1069, and some time later had established a small town.[76] Just as at Launceston, a leading Mortain centre of military and administrative authority was now associated with a religious foundation, located immediately to the east of the castle and close to Bishopston, the original centre of the settlement.[77] Yet there is one significant difference between Launceston and Montacute: Launceston remained the centre of administrative and political power within Cornwall for generations; at Montacute William appears to have decided to cede comital authority altogether. Not only did he endow the priory with some of his most prosperous manors, he also gave up the entire settlement at Montacute, its church, borough and market, its mill, the vineyards and orchards, and most surprisingly of all, the castle that his father had built a generation before. Such an abdication seems unparalleled.[78]

Moreover, the history of the foundation presents a number of problems. It is usually dated to *c*.1102, though the foundation charter is undated. It cannot, however, be considered as later than 1104. Christopher Brooke has even suggested that the foundation should be attributed to Robert of Mortain and dated *c*.1078. This argument is based on a statement in the fourteenth-century annals of Montacute.[79] Though William is said to be the founder, the first abbot, Walter, is recorded as dying in 1087, and William himself is said to have died in 1088. Brooke's hypothesis is that Robert was the founder, William confirmed that foundation in 'his' foundation charter, and that confusion thence arose between father and son.[80] This is ingenious but unconvincing. As he acknowledges, 'no great reliance' can be placed upon the annals which, though they generally date Cluniac foundations correctly, get the date of Domesday hopelessly wrong. But the most telling evidence against an earlier date for the foundation lies in the total silence of Domesday. Had Montacute been founded

---

hands of the priory by the mid-twelfth century and presumably came into its possession after 1104. This might explain why William ended his life as a monk here (*The Victoria Historia of the County of Surrey*, ed. H. E. Malden (London, 1912), IV, 20).

[75] *The Waltham Chronicle*, ed. L. Watkiss and M. Chibnall (Oxford, 1994), pp. xiii–xvii, xxxiii–xxxvi, 2–16.

[76] Golding, 'Robert of Mortain', 125–6, and 'Coming of the Cluniacs', 74–5.

[77] See aerial photograph in *The Archaeology of Somerset*, ed. M. Aston and I. Burrow (Bridgewater, 1982), 122.

[78] See Golding, 'The Coming of the Cluniacs', 74–5.

[79] London, British Library, MS Cotton, Tiberius A. x, fols. 145–76.

[80] *The Heads of Religious Houses: England and Wales, 940–1216*, ed. D. Knowles, C. N. L. Brooke, and V. C. M. London (Cambridge, 1972), 121 and nn. 1 and 3.

almost a decade before 1086, the community would surely have found a mention amongst the entries relating to the not-inconsiderable properties granted by the count of Mortain and his tenants in Somerset, Dorset, and Devon.

The most significant endowments, which appear first in the charter, were Montacute, Tintinhull, and Creech (which was still part of the royal demesne in 1086). In 1086 Tintinhull was the most valuable of Robert's Somerset manors, being assessed at £16, while Montacute, though less productive, was the *caput* of the honour. Both were demesne manors, though some land in Montacute was held by members of the castle garrison.[81] Both, too, had been acquired with dubious legality. Montacute had been taken from Athelney Abbey and Tintinhull had been seized from Glastonbury, and though the abbeys had each been granted another manor in exchange, their value was less than half that of the lands they lost.[82] But the majority of the other endowments in the foundation charter were in fact grants made by William's tenants, as a later confirmation charter of Henry II makes clear.[83] Chief amongst these tenants were two leading members of the comital household: Alured *pincerna* and Ralph the chancellor.[84] The latter had clearly been well rewarded for his clerical services: his grant of the tithes of nine churches in Somerset and Dorset, as well as the manor of Thorne, suggests that he had been granted all these churches by his lord. Another cleric, Geoffrey, the count's chaplain, who gave the church of Brimpton, had presumably been similarly rewarded.

According to Leland, William founded a small priory, 'a 3 or 4 in number' (*sic*), and endowed it with the lordships of Montacute, Tintinhull, and Creech (St Michael). Following William's rebellion and imprisonment, these lands were taken from the monks by the king, causing them great hardship until the king himself offered the lands back, together with further endowments, on condition that they moved to *Lamporte*, 'wher at that tyme he entendid to have made a notable monasterie'. The monks, however, begged to stay at Montacute, and Henry made his proposed foundation at Reading instead.[85] Nevertheless, as Leland notes elsewhere, though William was the *primus fundator*, thereafter

---

[81] DB, I, 91b, 93a. See Golding, 'Robert of Mortain', 130.

[82] Golding, 'Robert of Mortain', 140. A later, muddled Glastonbury tradition referred to William I's foundation of Montacute on a site then known as 'Lodgaresburgh' and greatly exaggerated the scale of Glastonbury's holding in both Tintinhull and at Montacute itself, where there is no supporting evidence that that abbey ever held property (J. P. Carley, *The Chronicle of Glastonbury Abbey: An Edition, Translation and Study of John of Glastonbury's* Chronica sive Antiquitates Glastoniensis Ecclesie (Woodbridge, 1985), 41, 91, 109, 123, 139, 155).

[83] *Two Cartularies of the Augustinian Priory of Bruton and the Cluniac Priory of Montacute in the County of Somerset*, ed. by members of the Council, Somerset Record Soc., 8 (1894), no. 9, pp. 125–6.

[84] For these tenants see Golding, 'Robert of Mortain', 136, 138–9.

[85] J. Leland, *The Itinerary of John Leland*, ed. L. T. Smith, 5 vols. (London, 1907–10), I, pt. ii, 158, cited in *The Heads of Religious Houses*, ed. D. Knowles *et al.*, 121. See also C. N. L. Brooke, 'Princes and Kings as Patrons of Monasteries', in *Il Monachesimo e la Riforma Ecclesiastica (1049–1122)*, Miscellanea del Centro di Studi Mediovali, 6 (Milan, 1971), 125–52, at 137. Lamport is presumably Langport (Somerset), a royal burh in 1086 (DB, I, 86a).

'from the time of Henry I the kings of England were *fundatores*'. Henry's intervention as patron is witnessed by his confirmation charter, where the monks'
property is described as being 'in mea propria manu . . . sicut propria et pura
elemosina mea, et sicut proprium dominicum meum'. Moreover, the rubric to
this charter in the Montacute cartulary styles Henry as *fundator*.[86] Here, then,
as also at Grestain and Mortain, William's fall had endangered his pious
giving. Survival was a close-run thing, dependent upon the victorious king's
will.[87]

But this was not all that endangered the well-being of the monasteries
under his patronage. The successors to the fragmented Mortain inheritance
had, for the most part, different religious priorities. Rather than favouring the
old family's foundations, they made their own. While tenants of Robert and
William of Mortain might and did support the foundations of their lords, that
loyalty did not extend to following generations.[88] This is well illustrated by an
examination of the Mortain tenants in Somerset who might have been expected
to patronize Montacute. Though Alured *pincerna* was a generous patron of
Montacute, to which he granted lands and churches in all the south-western
counties, his son William gave nothing, while his grandson Richard merely
confirmed Alured's grant of half the tithes of Chiselborough, Cloford, and
Norton by Taunton.[89] Even though the *caput* of their honour, Chiselborough,
was only 3 miles from the priory, neither proximity nor tenurial association
seem to have counted for much. Robert de Beauchamp I, who had succeeded
Robert fitzIvo, a Mortain Domesday tenant, gave his property at Nynehead
(Somerset), but that was all. Bretel de St Clair granted one hide in Bishopstone:
again this was the sole grant of the family.[90] Richard de Monte Acuto, the son
of Robert's Domesday tenant Drogo, gave land to Montacute but chose to be
buried at nearby Bruton.[91] The family of Ansgar I Brito made no grants to
Montacute at all, though they were benefactors of another Cluniac house,
Bermondsey.[92] Those who had profited from Count William's fall had, of
course, even less cause to support his foundations. So, for example, we find
Walter Espec, who had done well for himself out of Mortain estates in
Yorkshire, founding the Cistercian abbeys of Rievaulx (where he ended his

[86] Leland, *Collectanea*, I, 81; *Monasticon Anglicanum*, II, 165–6. Such royal intervention to save the religious foundation of a rebel is also seemingly found at Shrewsbury after the fall of Robert de Bêlleme in
1102 (Green, *Aristocracy of Norman England*, 428).

[87] The counts of Mortain may also have been instrumental in the foundation of a small dependency
of Montacute at St Carroc in Cornwall, but this house is only first mentioned during the reign of Henry
II and its history remains extremely obscure (Leland, *Itinerary*, I, 206; Olson, *Early Monasteries*, 98).

[88] For a subtle recent overview, see E. Cownie, 'Religious Patronage and Lordship: The Debate on
the Nature of the Honor', in *Family Trees and the Roots of Politics: The Prosopography of Britain and France
From the Tenth to the Twelfth Century*, ed. K. S. B. Keats-Rohan (Woodbridge, 1997), 133–46.

[89] *Two Cartularies*, ed. Council, nos. 9, 169, 180, pp. 125–6, 185, 191. Alured was also a patron of another
Cluniac priory, Lewes, to which he gave his church of East Grinstead (Sussex) (*CDF*, no. 1391, p. 510).

[90] *Two Cartularies*, ed. Council, no. 9, p. 126.   [91] *Complete Peerage*, ix. 75.

[92] *Monasticon, Anglicanum* V, 96 (*bis*), *Regesta* i. no. 36; *Annales Monastici*, ed. Luard, III, 434.

life as a monk) and Warden, the Augustinian priory of Kirkham, and a Savignac house at Byland.[93]

Even in the early days of the Norman settlement support from the counts' tenants had not always been forthcoming. In 1086 Richard fitzTurold, lord of Cardinham, was second only to Reginald de Vautorte among Robert's tenants in Cornwall—indeed, his lands were worth rather more than Reginald's—yet neither he nor his descendants favoured either of the Mortains' Cornish foundations.[94] Rather, they concentrated on their own foundation of Tywardraeth, an alien priory of St Sergius and Bacchus, Angers.[95] Those tenants who in the first couple of generations did support their lords' foundations did not confine their grants to these communities. Alured *pincerna* was a patron of Grestain and Montacute, but he also favoured Lewes, Shaftesbury nunnery, where his daughter was a nun, and St Albans.[96] While Alured's son William is also found as a modest benefactor of Grestain, his grandson Richard has no ties with the abbey, but did continue the family connection with Lewes, giving additional land in East Grinstead.[97] Another leading tenant of Robert of Mortain, William de Cahagnes, who held principally in Northamptonshire and Sussex, patronized a different set of communities altogether. He was a benefactor of Lewes and Pipewell, but made grants to none of his lord's foundations.[98] His son, Hugh, also patronized Lewes, where he later became a monk.[99] Later in the century Ralf II de Cahagnes gave the

---

[93] P. Dalton, *Conquest, Anarchy and Lordship: Yorkshire 1066–1154* (Cambridge, 1994), 99–100; D. Baker, 'Patronage in the Early Twelfth Century: Walter Espec, Kirkham and Rievaulx', *Traditio— Krisis—Renovatio aus Theologischer Sicht. Festschrift Winifred Zeller*, ed. B. Jaspert and R. Mohr (Marburg, 1976), 92–100.

[94] The family's support was limited to Richard's son William's compensation and restoration of lands he and his son-in-law, Reginald of Dunstanville, had seized from Launceston during the anarchy: *Cartulary of Launceston Priory*, ed. Hull, pp. xi, xvii–xix, nos. 244, 246, 251–2 (pp. 93, 94–5).

[95] On Tywardraeth, see G. Oliver, *Monasticon Dioecesis Exoniensis* (Exeter, 1846), 33–47.

[96] London, British Library, MSS. Harley 61, fol. 23 and Cotton Nero D vii, fols. 94, 98v. He gave Shaftesbury 5 hides in Shilvinghampton (Dorset) before 1089 and his manor of Norton-le-Clay (Yorks.) and the tithes of his adjacent demesne manor of Cundall, together with a *pallium*, to St Albans. See K. Cooke, 'Donors and Daughters: Shaftesbury Abbey's Benefactors, Endowments and Nuns, *c*.1086–1130', *ANS 12* (1990), 29–45, at 36, 40; L. F. Salzmann, 'Some Sussex Domesday Tenants I: Alvred Pincerna and his Descendants', *Sussex Archaeological Collections*, 57 (1915), 162–79, at 163.

[97] London, British Library, MS Cotton Vespasian F. xv, fol. 43b. See Salzmann, 'Sussex Domesday Tenants I', 165 and n.

[98] L. F. Salzman, 'Sussex Domesday Tenants III: William de Cahagnes and the Family of Keynes', *Sussex Archaeological Collections*, 63 (1922), 180–202, at 182; J. H. Round, 'Some Early Grants to Lewes Priory', *Sussex Archaeological Collections*, 40 (1896), 58–74, at 70–1; London, British Library, MS Cotton Caligula A xiii, fol. 27. The Pipewell connection was continued by William's grandson, who granted land in Cold Ashby (London, British Library, Add. Ch. 7540).

[99] Salzmann, 'Sussex Domesday Tenants III', 184; Round, 'Some Early Grants', 67; BL, MS Cotton Vespasian F xv, fol. 137. See also Hugh's son, Richard's, confirmation charter to Lewes (fol. 64). They were both also patrons of Luffield Priory (*Luffield Priory Charters*, ed. G. R. Elvey, 2 vols., Buckinghamshire Records Soc., 15, 18 (1958, 1975), I, nos. 24–6, pp. 36–7; II, nos. 292–4, pp. 1–3; see also 'Sussex Domesday Tenants III', 187–8; Cambridge, University Library Ee 1.1, fol. 274I).

church of Cahagnes, as well as churches on four of his English estates, to Merton Priory.[100]

Robert and William of Mortain have long been underestimated. Robert is for ever tarred with William of Malmesbury's harsh assessment that he was— by contrast with his quick-witted brother Odo—a man 'of stupid and dull intellect'.[101] William is the loser, who threw away his vast inheritance by unwise rebellion and ended a blinded prisoner. Yet such assessments are unjust: Robert was sufficiently able and trustworthy to be granted vast estates in both Normandy and England, estates which he seemingly administered with entrepreneurial skill; while William was praised, albeit not unequivocally, by contemporary chroniclers. To Henry of Huntingdon he was 'a most upright man, righteous in spirit and impetuous in action', to William of Malmesbury, though his treacherous rebellion caused by his avarice brought its deserved award, yet he was a man of 'lively mind and youthful energy with some things to recommend him'; and the Hyde chronicler wrote that he was 'young in age but vigorous in strength and fierce in spirit, steadfast in justice and very rich in his possessions on both sides of the Channel'.[102]

Robert's shrewd administration of his properties and William's avarice may perhaps provide a clue to an understanding of their religious patronage. The counts made no grandiloquent gestures of personal piety. Neither emulated the example of many of their aristocratic contemporaries and entered the religious life on their deathbed. William did not follow his lord, Duke Robert, to Jerusalem. As far as we know, only one of their children entered the religious life—Robert's daughter Sybil, who became abbess of Notre-Dame, Saintes. Perhaps there was no pressure for oblation, since there were no surplus heirs thus to be disposed of. While it would be too cynical to dismiss the counts' support of William Firmatus and Vital of Savigny as self-serving, undoubtedly Robert saw the economic benefits of William's relics to his new foundation. Their support of religious foundations was calculated charity. They gave few large estates, but many churches. This pattern, so noticeable in the pious giving of Count William, was no doubt encouraged by new and more rigid attitudes towards lay possession of such property; but these grants were also relatively cheap for the donor, bringing spiritual rewards and perhaps temporal advantage too, when local priests close to comital castles could be employed as honorial administrators for comparatively low outlay. The counts' pious giving in both Normandy and England reflected that of the Anglo-Norman aristocracy in general. They had to balance pressures to maintain and extend ancestral ties with monasteries in their homeland, while at the same time patronizing

---

[100] 'Sussex Domesday Tenants III', 186, 189, 192–3; London, British Library, MS Cotton Tiberius E v, fol. 178.

[101] William of Malmesbury, *Gesta Regum Anglorum*, I, 506.

[102] Henry of Huntingdon, *Historia Anglorum*, ed. Greenway, 453: William of Malmesbury, *Gesta Regum, Anglorum*, I, 724; *Liber Monasterii de Hyda*, ed. E. Edwards, RS (London, 45, 1866), 306.

English houses, new and old, in order to consolidate and demonstrate their authority as colonizers in their new territories. In the first one or two generations after the conquest that tension could best be reconciled by the establishment of alien priories dependent on the Norman mother house. Robert and William recognized, as did their contemporaries at Shrewsbury and Belvoir, for example, the advantages of a close association of their religious foundations with comital *capita*.

Robert and William were shrewd investors in this world and for the next: unfortunately this acumen was not also reflected in their political judgements. William's failure to back Henry I against Duke Robert was a fatal blunder for which he paid with his liberty and estates. His fall almost brought down the family's religious communities in the ruin: their survival now depended on the king and, if their long-term prosperity was to be assured, on the continuing patronage of the successors to the Mortain lands. This could not be guaranteed.

17

RANULF FLAMBARD AND
CHRISTINA OF MARKYATE[1]

R. I. Moore

He [Ranulf Flambard] had the unsuspecting girl brought into his chamber where he himself slept, which was hung with beautiful tapestries, the only others present with the innocent child being members of his retinue. Her father and mother and the others with whom she had come were in the hall apart giving themelves up to drunkenness. When it was getting dark the bishop gave a secret sign to his servants and they left the room, leaving their master and Christina, that is to say, the wolf and the lamb, together in the same room. For shame! The shameless bishop took hold of Christina by one of the sleeves of her tunic and with that mouth which he used to consecrate the sacred species, he solicited her to commit a wicked deed.[2]

The story of Ranulf Flambard's overture to the young Theodora, later to be known by her name in religion as Christina of Markyate,[3] and of how she frustrated it by persuading him to allow her to bolt the door 'for even if we have no fear of God, at least we should take precautions that no man should catch us in the act', and doing so from the outside after making her escape, is understandably a popular one with writers and lecturers, and generally loses nothing in the telling. Ranulf was no longer, in William of Malmesbury's phrase, *totius regni procurator* ('manager of the whole kingdom') as he had been under William Rufus,[4] but he was still bishop of Durham, one of the wealthiest and

---

[1] I am grateful to my colleague A. E. Redgate, a friend and pupil of Henry Mayr-Harting, for comments on a draft of this paper.

[2] *The Life of Christina of Markyate*, ed. C. H. Talbot (Oxford, 1959; repr. with minor amendments, 1987), 40–3.

[3] For Christina's family and the chronology of her life I follow Talbot's introduction at pp. 10–15. The Life does not make it clear when she adopted the name Christina. *Pace* Thomas Head's valuable 'The Marriages of Christina of Markyate', *Viator*, 21 (1990), 75–100, at 85, the biographer's assertion that she 'deserved (*meruerit*) to be known by the name of her creator' for her steadfastness in resisting the consummation of her marriage though apparently deserted even by her spiritual adviser Sueno (*Life*, 56–7), does not necessarily mean that she was known by it from that time: she was addressed as Theodora in a vision and by her sister some time later, just before she ran away from home (ibid. 90–1). At this point she took refuge with the anchoress Alfwen at Flamstead, abandoning the silk dress and luxurious furs which she had worn in her father's house for a religious habit, and living in concealment for two years (ibid. 92–5). This would have provided both a religious and a practical occasion for changing her name, the latter perhaps accounting for the rather puzzling *nomen sibi Christinam accepit ex necessitate* of the opening paragraph (ibid. 34–5).

[4] William of Malmesbury, *De Gestis Pontificum Anglorum*, ed. N. E. S. A. Hamilton, RS (London,

most independent magnates of the kingdom, long since recovered from the disgrace and humiliation which the beginning of the new reign and the distrust of the new king had almost inevitably brought for the greatest servant of the old one, and the obvious scapegoat for the king's unpopularity.[5] Besides the elements of comedy and titillation in the story, there could hardly be a more touching image of defiance of the brutalities of conquest than a 16-year-old girl successfully fending off the man whose name—more than any except that of William Rufus himself, and despite the judicious reappraisal of modern scholarship[6]—stubbornly continues to evoke them. Yet, even allowing for the selectivity of memory and the improvements which doubtless occurred to the ageing Christina as she told the story to the anonymous monk of St Albans to whom we owe her Life,[7] the text does not quite bear out that impression. Certainly, though Christina may have feared that 'if she openly resisted him, she would certainly be overcome by force', 'attempted rape'[8] is a stronger description than the text will support. Though its recent use obviously reflects late twentieth-century distaste for the abuse of power for sexual ends, it echoes an older stereotype of the licence and inclinations of 'feudal' magnates in relation to young women 'of the people' which this story should encourage us to question, at least occasionally. The term more commonly employed, 'seduction,'[9] is nearer the mark, but it does not altogether prepare us for Ranulf's response to his somewhat ignominious rebuff:[10] he continued his journey to London, and 'on his return came to Huntingdon, bringing with him silken garments and precious ornaments of all kinds'—which Christina, of course, rejected with contumely. Nevertheless, that sounds more like courtship—even, conceivably, with a hint of apology for its over-hasty beginning. At the least it suggests that Ranulf's interest was neither impetuous nor furtive, and therefore—no small point for such a man—that he was prepared to risk whatever loss of face his failure, in the circumstances, would imply.

Perhaps, then, the risk was not so very great. The acquaintance, it will be recalled, arose from Ranulf's connection with Alveva (Ælfgifu), the sister of

---

1870), 274; quoted by Frank Barlow, *William Rufus* (London, 1983), 201, n. 173; similar characterizations from all the leading Anglo-Norman chroniclers are collected and discussed in ibid. 200–1, and by R. W. Southern, 'Ranulf Flambard' in his *Medieval Humanism and Other Studies* (Oxford, 1970), 183–205, at 184–5.

[5] Southern, 'Ranulf Flambard', 196–9.

[6] In addition to Southern's classic paper cited above, see esp. Barlow, *William Rufus*, 193–210 and *passim*, and H. S. Offler, 'Rannulph Flambard as Bishop of Durham', *Durham University Journal*, 64 (1971).

[7] Cf. Christopher Brooke, *The Medieval Idea of Marriage* (Oxford, 1989), 144–8, who suspects 'an element of fantasy' in the Flambard story.

[8] Christopher Holdsworth, 'Christina of Markyate', in *Medieval Women*, ed. Derek Baker, *Studies in Church History, Subsidia* 1 (Oxford, 1978), 185–305, at 198; Sharon Elkins, *Holy Women in Twelfth-Century England* (Chapel Hill, 1988), 28–9.

[9] Southern, 'Ranulf Flambard', 203; Brooke, *Medieval Idea of Marriage*, 144–5; Head, 'Marriages', 82; Barlow, *William Rufus*, 197.

[10] The epithet is borrowed from Southern, 'Ranulf Flambard', 186.

Christina's mother Beatrix. The text says simply that he had her (*habuerat*), but the relationship was not a transient one. It began when Ranulf was still 'justiciar of the whole of England, holding second place after the king', so before 1099 and probably before Christina's birth, *c.*1096–8. There were children (*filios*) by the union, and it seems that Ranulf took his obligations to them seriously, if Barlow was correct in identifying one of them as the 12-year-old boy for whom he tried to secure the bishopric of Lisieux, to the indignation of Ivo of Chartres, and another as Elias, clerk in Henry I's household and prebendary of St Paul's.[11] Southern's description of Ranulf's connection with Alveva as a marriage,[12] even allowing for the uncertainties attending that state in the 1090s, is not altogether easy to reconcile with the *Life*'s statement that 'afterwards he gave her in marriage (*in uxorem*) to one of the citizens of Huntingdon and for her sake held the rest of her kin in high esteem', but it does justice to the evidently public and respectable character of the liaison. Ranulf made it his habit to stay with Alveva and her husband on his journeys between London and Northumbria, and it was on one such occasion, probably around 1114, when 'Autti, his friend [and Alveva's brother-in-law], had come as usual to see him', that 'the bishop gazed intently at his beautiful daughter'. It does not sound as though Autti objected very strongly to the gaze, for he and his wife would hardly have become so drunk as not to notice the prolonged absence of their daughter in their host's bedroom, and Christina's conviction at the moment of crisis that it would be useless to call her parents because 'they had already gone to bed' is not entirely convincing, unless there was an unexpectedly high level of soundproofing even for a substantial town house. It can hardly have been without their knowledge that Ranulf renewed his advances with the expensive gifts from London. Nor was his friendship with Autti and Beatrix soured either by his own or by Christina's behaviour, since he responded to her second rebuff by arranging her marriage to Burthred, another of his connections among the English nobility of the vicinity. Her biographer's (and presumably, therefore, her own) attribution of this involvement to Ranulf's malicious determination to 'gain his revenge by depriving Christina of her virginity, either by himself or by someone else' may sound pruriently plausible to the post-Freudian mind, but a more obvious explanation is that he considered it consonant with his patronal relationship with her family to help secure an advantageous match for their eldest daughter, even though she had rejected his own offer of protection. In any case, the enthusiasm with which both parents urged the consummation of the marriage over the next couple of years provided ample opportunity for the trial—and the triumph—of Christina's resolve.

In short, there was evidently mutual and continuing advantage in the connection that had been created through Alveva. Perhaps the social eminence of her family, *ex anglis nobilibus antiquis atque potentibus* ('of ancient and powerful

---

[11] Barlow, *William Rufus*, 202.   [12] Southern, 'Ranulf Flambard', 186, 191.

English nobles'),[13] offered something of glamour or standing, as well as a good deal in helpful contacts among the conquered, to the low-born Norman who had risen so high. The shrewd observation that 'some kind of legitimation was to be sought in the co-option of the support of native heiresses and saints'[14] has wide application, and the standing of Christina's family, as well as her own distinction, was later implicitly acknowledged in Archbishop Thurstan's suggestion that she might enter Marcigny or Fontevrault,[15] two of the smartest convents in Europe. Certainly Ranulf had a great deal to offer in return to Saxons of high rank who were making their way back to the wealth and standing which they had enjoyed before the conquest.

In that light, the famous bedroom scene prompts the suspicion that Autti's family would not have been averse to seeing Christina succeed to the position that had brought her aunt wealth, a good marriage in the town, and friends, perhaps even sons, in high places. Christina preferred, of course, to dedicate her life to Christ, and eventually inherited the hermitage of Roger, a monk of St Albans who had lived the solitary rule under the obedience of his abbot. She might have preferred a monastic life from the outset if it had been open to her.[16] But, as Henry Mayr-Harting showed in his classic paper on the functions of the recluse in this period,[17] her refusal to succeed to Alveva's position by no means required her to dishonour her family or turn her back on friends and community. In her chosen life Christina achieved fame and influence far wider than Alveva's, not least through her intimacy with another great Norman prelate, Abbot Geoffrey of St Albans, whom King Stephen sent to Rome to secure papal confirmation of his election to the throne, and who was repeatedly advised by Christina on his relations with the royal court through the dangerous years that followed.[18] It was Geoffrey who built a priory at Markyate for Christina, and most probably his successor, Abbot Robert, who commissioned for her the great psalter whose obits commemorated her family and friends, including her parents, her brothers and her sister—and Alveva.[19]

If this reading is correct, it might seem that Christina did not so much refuse to take over the duties of her aunt as insist on reinterpreting them for a new generation, in a manner better suited to the sensibilities of a reformed church, a more elevated conception of female influence and the standing of her family, and even a more dignified representation of the relationship between Norman

---

[13] *Life*, ed. Talbot, 82. For the likely milieu of Christina's pre-conquest forebears, see Robin Fleming, 'Rural Élites and Urban Communities in Late Saxon England', *Past & Present*, 141 (1993), 3–37.

[14] Henrietta Leyser, *Medieval Women* (London, 1995), 200.   [15] *Life*, ed. Talbot, 126.

[16] Ibid. 15; Holdsworth, 'Christina of Markyate', 187; but her parents, once reconciled to her refusal to marry, could certainly have afforded the necessary dowry—if they had been willing, or anxious, for her to leave the neighbourhood.

[17] Henry Mayr-Harting, 'Functions of a Twelfth-Century Recluse', *History*, 60 (1975), 337–52.

[18] *Life*, ed. Talbot, 161–71.

[19] Ibid. 24–5; Otto Pächt, C. R. Dodwell, and Francis Wormald, *The St. Alban's Psalter* (London, 1960), 27–8.

administration and a prosperous English bourgeoisie. In that case, even if scepticism of the sensational details of her story were justified,[20] it would have remained a salutary and instructive example of the qualities which enabled the hermits and recluses who were, as Mayr-Harting insisted, to be found in or near so many communities in early twelfth-century England, to provide the indispensable bridge between conquered and conquerors. As he showed, the acquisition and deployment of spiritual power might, in these circumstances, require not only pre-eminent virtue, but also a measure of toughness, even bloody-mindedness, in the most unexpected ways. Christina, still in her teens, kept the keys to her father's strongbox.[21] She was fitted and destined, by family, talent, and upbringing, to assume a place among the leadership of the English community in Huntingdon, to which its relations with the Normans were obviously of crucial importance, and was no doubt expected to accept the responsibilities that went with it. Her mother's fury at her obdurate determination to resist the marriage which Ranulf arranged perhaps reflected not only the chagrin of disappointed social ambition, but also a sense of betrayal that her child should reject such a role. But Christina did not reject it. She was more fortunate than Alveva had been in the space for negotiation that was open to her as to the form her mediation should take, as well as skilful and determined in the use to which she put it over a long and distinguished life. Her rejection of Ranulf Flambard's bed may remind us how another young woman from Hertfordshire, Elizabeth Bennet, declined Lydia's offer to get husbands for all her sisters before the end of the winter: 'I thank you for my share of the favour, but I do not particularly like your way of getting husbands.'[22] Elizabeth, as it turned out, had a better way of her own.

---

[20] Brooke, *Medieval Idea of Marriage*. H. S. Offler declared himself sceptical of the whole story, but gave no reason, and saw none to doubt Ranulf's Huntingdon connection: *Durham Episcopal Charters, 1071–1152*, ed. H. S. Offler, Surtees Soc., 179 (1968), 105. In general the Life, the object of so much enthusiastic interest in recent years, has stood the scrutiny very well: see, for example, the confirmation of some of its most original elements offered coincidentally and quite independently by William of Malmesbury's account of a confrontation between Bishop Robert Bloet of Lincoln and the hermit Roger because the latter was giving shelter to a virgin who had escaped from her husband: *De Gestis Pontificum*, 314, noticed by Elkins, *Holy Women*, 31–2.

[21] *Life*, ed. Talbot, 73.

[22] Jane Austen, *Pride and Prejudice*, ed. R. W Chapman, c. li: World Classics (Oxford, 1929), 305.

18

FUNCTIONS OF A TWELFTH-CENTURY RECLUSE REVISITED: THE CASE OF GODRIC OF FINCHALE

Susan J. Ridyard

It is a summer day, early in the twelfth century. A group of peasants from the countryside around Finchale, near Durham, look with fierce resentment at the grain slowly ripening on the very spot where they, and their fathers before them, have been accustomed to pasture their sheep and cattle. It has been planted by a newcomer—brought in and given the land by the Bishop of Durham—a would-be hermit named Godric, a useless individual who shuns their company while threatening their livelihood. The peasants' anger has been simmering all through the spring; and now, just as the grain is ripening, they decide to do something to drive the newcomer away. They herd together their sheep and cattle; then they lead the animals to their accustomed pasture and loose them among the hermit's grain. The crop is ruined; what better way to show the newcomer that he is not wanted, that life in that valley will be made intolerable for him?[1] The peasants who organized this protest could never have imagined the entirely different events which took place many years later— exactly how many, our sources leave unclear. The hermit is still there. But he is old and infirm, and his small fields are far too much for him to handle. He looks to the peasants of a neighbouring hamlet for help; and they come, gladly, with their own oxen, to plough the fields for the holy man.[2] The gulf which separates these two episodes is much more than one of years; it is one of understanding, of two different ways of thinking about the hermit and his place in society. In the first episode he is a stranger, an intruder, a violator; in the second he is loved and respected, a valued, perhaps a necessary, member of a local society. It is the purpose of this paper to consider how he came to be thus valued.

It is a privilege to publish in a volume of essays honouring Henry Mayr-Harting a paper inspired by his seminal article of 1975, 'Functions of a Twelfth-

---

[1] Reginald of Durham, *Libellus de Vita et Miraculis S. Godrici Heremitae de Finchale*, ed. J. Stevenson, Surtees Soc. (London, 1847), 74–5 (hereafter, *Godric*). I am grateful to S. A. J. Bradley, Marjorie Chibnall, and Charles Perry for commenting on a draft of this paper.

[2] Ibid. 265.

Century Recluse',[3] which examines the place in society of the anchorite Wulfric of Haselbury. In this study Professor Mayr-Harting, himself inspired by the work of Peter Brown, was one of the first scholars to examine holy men not simply as spiritual virtuosi isolated in cell or cloister, but as individuals whose spiritual gifts held meaning within the broader society in which they lived. In addressing the question 'what did the holy man mean to a local community?', Mayr-Harting broke down the barriers between hagiography and social history, pointing the way to a continuing discussion of the complex relationships between holy individuals and the society which recognized their holiness. The present contribution to the discussion explores this relationship through a reading of Reginald of Durham's richly detailed Life of St Godric. In particular, it addresses the place of the recluse in the lives of lay people—the peasants, townspeople, and 'fighting men' of northern England.

It is appropriate to begin with a word about the hermit and his biographer. Reginald was prompted to write Godric's Life by Prior Thomas of Durham and the Cistercian abbot, Ailred of Rievaulx.[4] His interests are explicitly hagiographical: he presents Godric as a saint and, more specifically, as a Durham saint—a man shaped by devotion to St Cuthbert, supported by the bishop and monks of Durham, and whose life reflected and complemented that of the Durham monks. We see Godric, in short, through Reginald's very specific monastic lens. The question then arises of where, in Reginald's presentation, is the 'real' Godric, and where we should draw the line between Godric's actions and understanding and the meaning which Reginald attaches to them. This is a problem which is brilliantly explored in Frederick Buechner's novel *Godric*;[5] but it eludes the precise answers which the historian would like to give. We do know, however, that Reginald began work on his Life well before Godric's death in 1170 and spent much time with Godric in his later years. He wrote for people who knew Godric, some of whom had been present on occasions which Reginald describes: the Godric he presented must have been recognizable to this audience. In general, then, we can see Reginald's accounts of Godric's practices and encounters with others as descriptions of historical events. We can also begin to distinguish the narrative of an event from Reginald's interpretation of it, expressed in the authorial comments which frame each episode. More problematic are the many passages where Reginald seeks to present Godric's exact words: recognizing the difficulty of accurately recording speech, I treat these passages not as verbatim record but rather as offering important insights into the themes upon which Godric repeatedly touched in his 'teaching', and into the ways in which he responded to the needs of others.

Reference to Godric's 'teaching' recalls us to the central paradox of his life and those of other medieval recluses. The life of the recluse by definition

---

[3] *History*, 60 (1975), 337–52. Cf. P. Brown, 'The Rise and Function of the Holy Man in Late Antiquity', *Journal of Roman Studies*, 61 (1971), 80–101.
[4] *Godric*, 269.   [5] Frederick Buechner, *Godric* (New York, 1980).

centred on withdrawal from the world, yet he or she came to occupy an extremely important place in relation to the world. The recluse came to be recognized as a holy individual, and as such became a focus for the hopes and concerns of what was often a much wider community than that to which he or she had formerly belonged. Having rejected the world, the recluse was restored to it—as an object of reverence and a figure of authority.[6] Some would-be recluses perhaps anticipated this new status; others doubtless did not. Few, if any, could have known in advance how they would respond to the resulting tension between the solitary vocation and the demands of society. From Reginald's *Life of Godric* we gain a vivid picture of this tension and its resolution. We see not only northern peasants reconciling themselves to the hermit, but also the hermit reconciling himself to society. Initially violently hostile to human contacts, Godric came gradually to accept them, perhaps even to see service to others as integral to his service of God. Eventually he divided his life between days of silence, specifically designated as such, and days of speech—days when he shared with others those words which, I would argue, were at the heart of his ministry.[7]

Godric's entry to the solitary life, according to Reginald, was the result of a long personal search—perhaps for a life more fulfilling than that of the trader, in which he had spent his youth, perhaps for a life of greater service to God. Having chosen the solitary life, Godric embraced it with the utmost seriousness. Reginald develops this theme with relish, seizing the opportunity to show his subject's conformity to the eremitical, and specifically the Cuthbertine, tradition of holiness. Moved especially by Cuthbert's example, we are told, Godric sought a solitary place; he lived in dread of human company—so much so that he would throw himself into thorn bushes to hide when he saw people approaching. Dissociating himself from humankind, he brought himself into conformity with nature. Rejecting human company, he shared his dwelling with snakes; rejecting human food, he lived on grass and leaves.[8] He was doubtless aware that this way of life might attract attention: as a pilgrim in the Holy Land he had himself been drawn by their reputation for holiness to visit hermits; and in England he had served a kind of 'apprenticeship' with a Durham hermit, Ailric.[9] With this experience, he may not have been surprised when his presence at Finchale began to attract attention; but he was disappointed and distressed.

The hostile attention of the peasants with which this paper opened was, perhaps from the beginning, only one side of the coin. While those whose livelihood was threatened considered how to drive him away, others began to seek out the solitary who had established himself nearby. The first—undated—encounter which Reginald describes casts some light on the tentative forging of

[6] Cf. Mayr-Harting, 'Functions', 340–1.   [7] *Godric*, 137.
[8] Ibid. 30–72, on Godric's vocation and ascetic withdrawal.   [9] Ibid. 57–8, 44–52.

links between Godric and the local population. A woman from the village of Lummeley, no more than a mile away, would not rest until she had seen the hermit.[10] She did not, however, want to go empty-handed; so she made bread and cheese and took these as an offering to him. For his part, Godric did not want to sadden her by spurning her offering. He accepted it, but later offered it up to God, along with his prayers for the woman. The incident suggests the tremendous fascination—perhaps a mingled curiosity and reverence—with which at least some people regarded the presence of a hermit in their vicinity. In Godric's response to the woman we see an attempt to reconcile the eremitical vocation with the human impulse to avoid giving pain. In offering both the gift and his prayers to God, he admits an element of reciprocity into his relationship with the woman, thus tacitly, and perhaps subconsciously, acknowledging that by virtue of his spiritual vocation he might indeed have a place in the lives of others.

A more dramatic and especially crucial moment in the working out of Godric's place in the lives of others came after he had lived as a solitary for some twenty years.[11] One day as he knelt in prayer Godric became aware that three people (two women and a man) were waiting outside his oratory. In his dread of human company he prolonged his devotions, hoping that they would go away. But when he finally emerged they were still waiting, and the man and one of the women put down a sack at his feet. Inside was a small girl—dead. Godric was stunned: realizing that these parents believed he had the power to restore their child to life, he was overcome by a sense of inadequacy. Mentally he shrank from the responsibility and power they attributed to him; physically he fled, leaving the grieving adults and going off to work in his fields. What he found when he returned was perhaps even more disturbing; the adults had gone home, leaving the dead child inside the oratory—apparently for Godric either to revive or to bury. Recoiling from either looking at or touching the sack, Godric turned to prayer. For two days and three nights he prayed that God would restore the child to life; early on the third day he looked up and saw her crawling toward the altar. That same day she was restored to her parents, who swore that they would say nothing about this miracle during Godric's lifetime. Eventually, however, Godric himself broke silence. He discussed the episode at length with Reginald, and did so in terms which suggest that he perceived it as a critical moment in his spiritual life. For the first time, it seems, he was forced to confront the full implications of his own reputation for holiness. Although he denied it, others believed that he had the power to raise the dead. No doubt he realized that, even if this miracle did remain secret, other people would seek him out, requesting and expecting his aid. Somehow he must reconcile that being sought with his own commitment to the solitary life.

There was, perhaps, a connection between this miracle, with its profoundly

---

[10] Ibid. 73.   [11] Ibid. 132–5; see below, n. 12.

important implications, and the establishment of what for Godric was the most
significant relationship of his later life. It was after this, according to Reginald,
that Godric recognized his need for spiritual guidance and placed himself under
the direction of the priors of Durham, who became, with their monks, a constant
presence in his life. Reginald notes in particular that the priors were accustomed
to 'screen' those who wished to speak to Godric. The hermit would receive only
people who had the prior's permission to visit him; these arrived carrying a
wooden cross as a token of the prior's approval.[12] Much is unclear about Godric's
relationship with the community of Durham. Did the initiative come from
Godric, as Reginald implies, or from the priors, seeking to control a local hermit
and benefit from his presence? Were the arrangements for screening Godric's
visitors applied consistently and for the rest of Godric's life, or for a more limited
time? Did the priors employ any consistent principles in deciding who might
visit the hermit and who might not? Despite these unanswered—and perhaps
unanswerable—questions, Godric's new relationship with the priors does suggest that the hermit was coming to terms with the demands which society was
going to place upon him. The priors' 'screening' of his visitors may have been
intended to limit their number; it also had the effect of reinforcing Godric's
authority in his dealings with those who did appear at his door.

Reginald provides an important, though selective, account of those who were
able to visit the hermit, their concerns, and Godric's responses to them. The lay
people who capture his attention are men and women who turned to Godric in
times of crisis. Their stories allow Reginald to develop the hagiographical
theme of Godric's ability to alleviate suffering through prayer, prophecy, or
spiritual counsel; they take the modern reader to the heart of the human experience of suffering and anxiety. At the same time, however, this emphasis upon
crisis tends to obscure, or to reveal only incidentally, another important facet of
Godric's relations with others—the fact that many of these relationships were
long-lasting, born of or sustained in periods of normality, though finding their
most dramatic expression in circumstances of crisis.

Many of the episodes related by Reginald centred on illness and the fear of
death. When a man of Laudon, already devoted to Godric, became so ill that
the *medici* despaired of him, he sent a messenger to seek the hermit's prayers.[13]
Godric responded with an encouraging message and a gift of food which he had
blessed; after eating the food the man recovered. What happens here is familiar
to all readers of saints' Lives. A sick individual turns in despair to a person

[12] *Godric*, 135–7. Victoria Tudor ('The Priory and its Hermits', in *Anglo-Norman Durham, 1093–1193*,
ed. David Rollason *et al.* (Woodbridge, 1994), at 74–5) dates Godric's arrival at Finchale to 1112 or 1113,
and suggests that his close relationship with the monks began under Prior Roger (?1138–49) and was formalized after Roger's death; she sees Godric's new status as that of an 'associate monk' of Durham. This
dating suggests that his independent life at Finchale lasted for at least twenty-five years. If the establishment of this relationship with Prior Roger did indeed have anything to do with the episode of the dead
girl, then this must have taken place more than twenty years after Godric's arrival at Finchale.
[13] *Godric*, 180–1.

believed to be holy; that person's words bring hope and consolation, while his or her gift, sanctified by association, is believed to effect a miraculous cure. Where we begin to get a glimpse of Godric the individual is in the nature of his message to the sick man. God, he says, will spare him for a few more years, *in which he will be able to atone for his sins.* Here Godric converts the man's physical need into an occasion to address also his spiritual need, encouraging him to prepare for the death which will eventually come. On his recovery, the man vows a pilgrimage to St James. He also visits Godric, to express his gratitude and seek reassurance that he will indeed be able to complete his pilgrimage. On his return he visits Godric again, reporting that all has worked out as the hermit foresaw. What Reginald describes here is not simply a conventional curative miracle. It is a situation in which such a miracle is a pivotal event in a relationship between Godric and the local man which lasts for some time and in which Godric, through the power of his words, brings about significant changes in the man's spiritual life.

A similar instance of Godric's ministry to a layman facing death concerns a wealthy follower of William, bishop of Durham (1143–52).[14] Visiting Godric for the first time, he is troubled when the hermit predicts that just as they have never seen one another before, so they will not meet again before death. Soon afterwards the man becomes seriously ill and sends to Godric for guidance. The hermit replies that he will die before the feast of John the Baptist, and urges him to prepare for death by doing penance and by distributing his possessions to the poor. A dominant theme in Reginald's account, here as elsewhere, is that of Godric's foreknowledge. Equally significant, however, is the establishment of a relationship in which the man looks to Godric, not only to share this foreknowledge, but also for guidance in preparation for death. The clear implication is that as a result of Godric's words he was able to face death with the knowledge that he stood in a right relationship with God.

One period when death and life seemed to hang in the balance was that surrounding childbirth. A certain Henry, from Scotland, sought Godric's prayers after his wife had suffered three miscarriages.[15] Both husband and wife were grieving over this loss of three sons, and both were afraid that the repeated misfortune was a sign of God's judgement on them. Godric sent to the woman his own girdle, with instructions to wear this when about to give birth to ensure a safe delivery. He also gave advice which directly addressed the couple's concern with sin and judgement. He explained, acknowledging with respect the man's fear, that such misfortunes could often be the result of sin, and he advised the couple to do penance before having sex. In offering this advice, he provided the couple with a means to alleviate their dread of judgement; and it is perhaps no surprise that there were no further miscarriages.[16]

---

[14] Ibid. 217–18.   [15] Ibid. 218–19.
[16] The infertility of Roger de Brundun's wife was cured in the same way: ibid.

Like the threat of death and the dangers of childbirth, the prospect and experience of travel caused anxiety and led people to rely on the hermit. A knight from Tynedale came to commend himself to Godric's prayers before setting out for the royal court.[17] And the man of Laudon discussed above felt the need for Godric's reassurance that he would be able to complete his vowed pilgrimage. In both cases Godric's blessing or reassurance—perhaps especially valued because of his gift of foreknowledge—allayed anxiety and provided renewed confidence. Moreover, the anxiety evoked by long journeys was not confined to the travellers themselves; those left behind suffered as well. On one occasion Godric spoke with a father from Chester-le-Street whose son had gone on pilgrimage to St James, presumably at Compostella.[18] He had been gone for so long that his father was sure he was dead; he went to seek Godric's prayers for the young man's soul. His grief was especially strong because, like the girl restored to life by Godric, his son was an only child. In the event, Godric in a sense restored this 'child' too, prophesying that the son was alive and would be home within a week. For the father, it appears, the consolation of knowing that a holy man would be praying for his son was enough to draw him to Godric's hermitage; he must have returned home with an infinitely greater consolation. So too must the woman who came to Godric fearing that she had lost her husband and two of her sons.[19] First, the father and one son had sailed to Norway; then, when they failed to return, the other son had set out to look for them. What followed for their mother and brothers was several years of silence and then rumours, first that the elder son was dead, then that both were dead. Coming to Godric in grief for the loss of her sons, the mother learned that both were alive—and not only that; both had left England as paupers and both were now doing well. Godric gave no indication that the mother would have the consolaton of seeing them (or her husband!) again; but she could return home happy in the knowledge of her sons' well-being.

It is clear from the stories of Henry and of these parents who feared for their children that it was not only those concerned for their own safety who turned to Godric. All these individuals were driven to him by anxiety for others, in each case family members with whose well-being Godric's visitor was intimately involved: there could be no happiness for these supplicants so long as the threat of a son's death, a life without children, or perhaps a wife's death hung over them. Familial relationships were crucially significant for the men and women who came to Godric, as for many of those who had recourse to other living saints and, later, their shrines. Moreover, far from indicating that marriages were impersonal arrangements and children valued primarily as sources of future labour and income, such sources suggest that both men and women felt tremendous emotional attachment to their spouses and suffered immense sorrow at the loss of children, especially of only children.

---

[17] *Godric*, 302.   [18] Ibid. 268.   [19] Ibid. 349–50.

This does not mean, however, that family relationships were without conflict. In two especially interesting episodes we see something of the tensions of family life. In one we are taken into the home of a very poor—but, Reginald emphasizes, religious—man, who comes in tired and cold from his work and sits down by the fire to get warm.[20] His wife, trying to cook vegetables, starts to grumble about him and, provoked, he picks up a stick and beats her about the head. The next day he visits Godric, on some business which Reginald does not specify. When Godric asks if things have calmed down at home, he says simply that all is well, not understanding—or pretending not to understand—the hermit's meaning. But Godric, smiling, reveals that he knows all about the episode of the previous day and rebukes the man for beating his wife. He extracts a promise that this transgression will not be repeated, and only then is the man allowed to depart with Godric's blessing. The episode provides a fascinating glimpse into the everyday conflicts that can arise within a family, and which in this case are specifically associated with the misery of cold and poverty. Perhaps also we see a tension within the man himself—between the cold, tired worker who lashes out at his wife and the *vir devotus*, the man of genuine piety, who turns naturally to Godric in time of need and who is embarrassed and ashamed to discover that the hermit knows of his wrongdoing. The implication is that Godric's words were able to alleviate these tensions, restoring, at least temporarily, the husband and wife to harmony and the husband to peace with himself.

The second incident concerns a family of very different social status. A knight, already well known to Godric, seeks his prayers as he faces an important lawsuit.[21] When he gets home he gives his wife two *solidi*, with instructions to send them to Godric. She, however, deceives him by keeping the money for herself. About two years later, the lawsuit still dragging on, the knight sends a servant to ask again for Godric's prayers. Godric sends back what must have been a very disturbing message: he reminds the knight that two years earlier he had vowed the money to Godric and John the Baptist; the money has never reached him, but has been fraudulently kept by the wife; and he points out that the case would have been decided in the knight's favour long ago had Christ not been angered by this wrongdoing. On receiving this message both the knight and his wife are profoundly shaken; Godric receives the promised money; and the lawsuit is settled to the knight's satisfaction.

The knight of this episode was not alone in turning to Godric when facing the legal system. Like illness and travel, legal entanglements produced anxiety and fear which brought people to the hermit's door. The knight sought Godric's prayers in a lawsuit concerning theft of his land. For others there was even more at stake. Ethelwold, a steward of the bishop of Durham, was accused of squandering his lord's goods and was required to prove his innocence in a duel.[22] In

---

[20] Ibid. 291.   [21] Ibid. 278–9.   [22] Ibid. 189–91.

his fear he began to seek help from the 'servants of God', and the day before the duel he came to Godric and commended himself to the hermit's prayers. The following day he was killed in the combat—an outcome which on one level, and surprisingly, seems to cast doubt on the efficacy of Godric's prayers. But this was only a part of the story. Ethelwold lost his life, but through Godric he regained something which may have been almost equally important to him— his reputation. Godric shared with the Durham monks his knowledge that the steward, though suffering in purgatory, was not suffering for wasting the bishop's lands. He was no saint, but he was innocent of the crime for which he died.

The dangers of travel, the complexities of family relationships, the anxiety of legal proceedings: all were present in Godric's meeting with a noble *mater-familias* who came from some distance to seek his friendship and aid.[23] She explained that her husband had been away for two years; nobody had heard from him, and so she believed he must be dead. Meanwhile one of her relatives, a knight, had died; she was the rightful heir to his rich estate but had been unable to obtain possession of it. Godric calmed her, saying that she would obtain the land, and also that her husband would return—she would meet him unexpect-edly on a bridge. She went home reassured, and soon afterwards, on her way to Durham to plead concerning the land, she did indeed meet her husband on a bridge; he, a *miles strenuus*, accompanied her and won possession of the inherit-ance for her. We see here a series of interrelated problems. A long absence causes those left behind to fear for the traveller's life; the problem is exacerbated by lack of communication. Meanwhile legal problems arise, and a woman alone is unable to cope with them. In despair she seeks Godric's friendship; his words offer the hope that in normal circumstances her husband's presence would pro-vide. It is striking that Godric's first act on this woman's arrival was to persuade her to sit down and eat; like many others who sought spiritual refreshment from the hermit, she was welcomed also with earthly hospitality. Such hospitality plainly served a practical need; perhaps it also did more than this, establishing a bond between Godric and his guest and, symbolically, holding out the promise of spiritual succour to come.

For some of those who surrounded the hermit, physical succour itself was what mattered: charity to the poor formed a significant part of Godric's min-istry to others. The poor—although they remain nameless and without a his-tory in Reginald's narrative—were frequent visitors to his dwelling, and he shared with them the offerings that people brought him.[24] Perhaps this concern for the poor stemmed from suffering which Godric had experienced or wit-nessed as a youth struggling to make a living as a pedlar, or during his later travels. Perhaps also his trading experience enhanced his understanding of those who, having gained some wealth, worried about how to keep it. Mayr-Harting

---

[23] *Godric*, 299–300.   [24] e.g. ibid. 74, 136.

suggests that both Wulfric of Haselbury and Godric may have acted as 'primitive bankers', allowing local people to deposit money or valuables with them for safe keeping in the hope that, even in troubled times such as the 1130s, no one would violate the dwelling of a holy man.[25] In Godric's case we learn of what seem to have been such arrangements only when the hope proved misplaced. On one occasion an Englishman, Ælfhere, attempted to rob Godric after hearing that many people had entrusted their wealth to him; and in a more ambiguous passage we read that the riff-raff, as Reginald plainly regarded them, from the army of King David of Scotland raided Godric's cell and demanded his treasure—some of which, if he customarily helped other people safeguard their wealth, may not have been 'his' at all.[26] In addition to these tantalizing hints that Godric helped people keep their wealth securely, we see just one instance of him acting as 'mentor' to an aspiring trader. A maker of carved and painted images came in despair from Durham, where he was trying unsuccessfully to sell his images at St Cuthbert's fair.[27] Godric accepted one image as an offering and then sent him back with a reassurance that he would sell everything before the day's end—perhaps with a warning that he would sell nothing without trying. Like Wulfric, and like the holy men of late antiquity discussed by Brown, Godric here responds not—or not only—to the destitute, but also to those who seek, with both hope and trepidation, to profit from new economic opportunities.[28]

In his many-faceted contribution to the lives of others Godric was assisted by a number of servants, who catered to his practical needs, ran errands for him, helped him minister to the poor, and supported him in his hospitality to visitors. Godric's relationship with these servants was not an easy one, for the servants could be lazy, rebellious, even dishonest; but Godric was no less concerned with the spiritual well-being of this 'captive audience' than with that of individuals who willingly sought his guidance. Sharing with them everyday events rather than occasional visits, he repeatedly used those events in order to educate and reform. Two examples are especially telling. One Sunday a monk and priest of Durham came as usual to celebrate Mass for Godric.[29] In conversation afterwards, Godric began to complain that those who were supposed to serve him were in fact squandering his goods. When his principal *minister* heard this and attempted to discredit Godric, the hermit revealed to the priest that a man whom he had seen with his own eyes had been in effect a receiver of stolen goods, taking grain given to him by this same servant. The servant made excuses: he had sent the grain to Newcastle in exchange for salt. Godric,

<hr>

[25] Mayr-Harting, 'Functions', 342–4. [26] *Godric*, 102–3, 114–16.
[27] Ibid. p. xlii.
[28] Mayr-Harting, 'Functions', 340; Brown, 'Rise and Function'; also. P. Brown, 'Arbiters of the Holy', in his *Authority and the Sacred: Aspects of the Christianisation of the Roman World* (Cambridge, 1995), 55–78, where he examines the holy men of late antiquity from a somewhat different perspective.
[29] *Godric*, 195.

however, knew a lie when he heard one—and knew that the servant had actually sent the grain to some women living in *Ebbecestre*. The servant, flushing, finally admitted his fault and confessed to the priest all that he had done. It was surely no accident that Godric chose this occasion to reveal the servant's wrongdoing. Not only might a shaming before the priest be more effective than a private one; the priest's presence made possible a full confession, which carried with it the possibility of real and lasting reform.

On another occasion we find Godric enjoying a visit from a citizen of Durham with whom he has close and affectionate ties.[30] Godric calls his servant, says that this visitor must not be allowed to leave empty-handed, and sends the young man to look for a fish to give to the man's family. The servant argues. How can Godric give away food when he does not have enough for himself? And surely he knows that there are no fish in the pond? And why does he not stop making his servants run hither and thither on what are bound to be fruitless errands? Godric is firm: he rebukes the servant for complaining and for doubting that God will provide, then he shares his foreknowledge that the servant will indeed find two large salmon, one—the younger and better—for the visitor, the other for Godric and his servants. For Reginald, the episode is significant primarily as one of miraculous provision and prevision. But it is also an example of Godric's ministry to his servants: an everyday quarrel becomes an occasion for the hermit to teach some simple but essential Christian lessons. Most importantly, he calls the servant to have faith in God's care for his people; but his words also emphasize the importance of hospitality and of bonds between men, the need for obedience and humility, and the virtue of self-denial, as the best of what God provides is reserved for the visitor. Also significant is the fact that Godric's exchange with his servant seems to have taken place in the visitor's presence. The servant, then, is not the only beneficiary of Godric's teaching: rather, Godric seizes the opportunity which the youth's recalcitrance provides to expound Christian principles which might be of value to the visitor as well. Godric is deeply concerned with the spiritual welfare of the rebellious young man, whom he nevertheless addresses as *carissime*. He also perhaps recognizes that his servants might act as mediators between himself and others: through conversations with and stories about these men who share his daily life, he can communicate Christian teachings to those who visit his cell.

Since Godric's visitors included both men and women, it is appropriate to ask what light his Life might cast on women's lives and on gender relations in medieval England. This is indeed the most important area in which recent scholarship encourages, perhaps even requires, us to ask some different questions from those addressed over twenty years ago in Mayr-Harting's study of Wulfric. What, first, seem to have been Godric's own perceptions of women, and what was the nature of his response to their needs?

---

[30] *Godric*, 123–4.

From the encounters discussed above, it is plain that women as well as men actively sought Godric's friendship and support. It may be significant that at least some of Godric's female visitors came bearing gifts. Some men did so too; but the bringing of gifts may have been considered particularly important by women—or considered by men as an attribute of women. The first woman brought food, an offering which, in light of Caroline Bynum's work, we can see to be wholly appropriate; since food was the primary resource which women controlled, the special preparation and offering of food can be seen as a specifically female way of expressing reverence.[31] Another woman brought an extremely valuable offering—a bull.[32] None of this suggests, however, that it was *necessary* for women to bring offerings in order to gain access to the hermit. The episode of the bull makes clear that this was far from the case. Godric, foreseeing the woman's arrival, instructs her through his servant to take the bull and offer it to St Cuthbert in Durham, for he does not need it. When she returns he explains that she had no need to bring an offering in order to speak with him; she needed only to come with a faithful heart. In this case Godric states explicitly that the woman will be freed from the unspecified trouble which has brought her. Elsewhere too he acknowledges women's concerns and offers encouragement: he reassures one woman that her husband—and lands—will be restored; another that her sons are alive and prospering; others that they will safely give birth; and, most dramatically, he restores a dead daughter to life. He even intervenes to support a woman without her asking; by correcting the man who has struck his wife, he makes himself the protector of the woman.

But Godric's approval of women was not undiscriminating. While rebuking the 'wife-beating' husband, he allows him to defend himself by explaining how her complaints have provoked him. And the woman who keeps for herself the money destined for Godric is plainly considered a troublemaker, threatening her husband's standing not only in this world but also in the next. In addition, Godric twice encounters the devil in the form of a woman[33]—evidence of misogyny, it might seem, until one realizes that the devil also appears to Godric several times as a man of unspecified status, and as a pauper, a pilgrim, and a peasant, all male.[34] If we were to read the appearance of the devil in female form as evidence of 'prejudice' against women, we must equally assume that Godric was prejudiced against paupers and pilgrims.

These encounters with the devil in the form of a woman do seem, however, to hold the key to Godric's perceptions of the female. In the first the devil berates Godric for his indifference to women, asking why he avoids their company; was he not himself born of a woman, a product of the sexual act? Godric's response is clear: he does not avoid all women, but only the wicked. Good

---

[31] Ibid. 73; C. Bynum, *Holy Feast and Holy Fast: The Religious Significance of Food to Medieval Women* (Berkeley, 1987).
[32] *Godric*, 239–40.   [33] Ibid. 242, 354.   [34] Ibid. 107–8, 248–9, 104, 234–5, 243.

women he cherishes and speaks with often.[35] The second encounter more clearly articulates Godric's perception of what constitutes wickedness in a woman; here the devil appears as a woman of more than human beauty whose obvious goal is to seduce him.[36] What these and other passages suggest is that Godric's relations with others are governed by considerations not of gender but of morality and of faith. He understands neither men nor women as being 'good' or 'bad' by virtue of their gender; rather, he evaluates individuals according to their actions and the faith which underlies them. He recognizes, moreover, that within one individual both virtue and sin might play a part—that a religious man is quite capable of striking his wife, that a normally virtuous wife might hold on to money destined for another. In such cases, the essence of his ministry is to reveal and correct the sin, thus supporting his acquaintances in their somewhat shaky steps toward salvation.

In addition to illumining Godric's own attitudes, Reginald's Life prompts a few reflections on gender relations within northern English society. We learn, first, something of the expectations which men and women had of one another. For women, childbearing and child-rearing were obviously of primary importance.[37] So too was keeping of the home—food preparation, and in a more affluent household management of servants.[38] The evidence of the woman who kept for herself the money intended for Godric indicates the obedience and loyalty due from wife to husband; disaster follows when the wife flouts these expectations. For men, the right to command obedience and loyalty from their wives is matched by the expectation that they themselves will provide protection—in the negative sense of refraining from abuse and in the more positive sense of providing financial and legal support. These expectations are, of course, wholly conventional; and Godric himself shares and supports them in his perceptions of and advice to others.

While relationships between husbands and wives were characterized in part by conventional expectations, there was a more affective side to at least some of the marriages which Reginald describes. This is most striking in the case of Henry, whose wife suffered three miscarriages and who came himself to seek comfort from Godric. This, together with the crucial episode of the dead girl, suggests that crises in the lives of women and children were by no means dismissed as only marginally significant by men. Rather, we see men and women bound together by concern for each other and for their children. Moreover, it is not only among spouses that we find men actively concerned for the well-being of women: a monk of Durham seeks Godric's prayers on behalf of two women, one who has become sick after childbirth and the other suffering from constipation.[39]

[35] *Godric*, 242.   [36] Ibid. 354.   [37] Esp. ibid. 218–19.
[38] Ibid. 73, 291 (food), 278–9 (the woman expected to send, presumably through a servant, money to Godric).
[39] Ibid. 255, 256.

The role of this Durham monk as mediator between Godric and the two women reminds us that, although this paper focuses on the recluse's place in the lives of lay people, his relations with the Durham monks and with other religious were also extremely important. In numerical terms, many more religious than lay people seem to have been among Godric's associates, and I hope to examine his relations with these fellow-religious elsewhere. For present purposes, however, one question demands attention: can anything be learned from Godric's dealings with other religious which enhances our understanding of his ministry to lay people?

The mutual support of Godric and the Durham monks is striking and in some ways comparable to the relationship which Mayr-Harting detected between Wulfric and the parish priest of Haselbury Plucknett. In the terms of Aviad Kleinberg's recent work, the Durham monks might be seen as the 'impresarios' who helped to create and maintain Godric's reputation as a living saint.[40] And among these monks Reginald himself is especially important: frequently we find him drawing Godric out, persuading him to explain his visions and prophecies for his biographer's own edification and that of other monks—and, of course, for the wider audience which will eventually read Reginald's Life.

Explaining his visions and prophecies: this constitutes an important part of Godric's ministry to other religious and is what primarily differentiates his relations with these men and women from his interactions with lay people. Both lay people and religious came to Godric for guidance and for help in times of crisis; but it was almost exclusively with other religious that Godric shared his own deepest spiritual experiences. In a passage which refers specifically to Godric's miraculous knowledge of distant events, but which seems also to have a wider application, Reginald articulates the distinction thus: to the simple, Godric spoke only of that which would benefit the soul; from spiritual men, presumably his fellow-religious, he kept nothing hidden.[41]

Reginald's presentation of this distinction, of course, implies a hierarchy of values: Godric's simple conversations with lay people are contrasted with his 'higher' discourse with other religious. We might take away from this account an impression of Godric responding somewhat condescendingly to his lay visitors while thinly disguising his impatience to get back to his monastic companions. A more appropriate conclusion, however, might be this: that Godric possessed a remarkable ability to speak to each individual about the subjects which mattered to him or her, and in language which he or she would find intelligible and appealing. While in general this resulted in his addressing religious and lay people in different ways, it did not necessarily do so. For instance,

---

[40] Aviad Kleinberg, *Prophets in Their Own Country: Living Saints and the Making of Sainthood in the Later Middle Ages* (Chicago, 1992).

[41] *Godric*, 131.

Godric, more astute in his perception of individual needs than his monastic biographer, realized that discourse about the sacred mysteries of his visions could not by itself sustain all his monastic companions—that they might also have needs not unlike those of the laity. And so it was wholly characteristic that once on the feast of John the Baptist he made the miraculous provision of a salmon the occasion for a 'sermon' on the saint's goodness addressed both to his own servants and to some visiting monks.[42] The monks, no less than the *ministri*, might benefit from the simple lessons which Godric was able so skilfully to draw from daily life. And for Godric, perhaps, the 'highest' discourse was simply that which was effective in meeting the needs of the individuals to whom he spoke.

It is in this ability to gauge and respond to the needs of others that we find the key to understanding the affection with which Godric came to be regarded. As he came gradually to accept that he did indeed have a place in the lives of others, he seems to have given his mind to how best he might serve those who sought him out. He did so through his words, simple, clear, and carefully judged, which Reginald himself recognizes as making him like a priest—and in some ways more effective than a priest—in his dealings with others.[43] Through his words he brought comfort to those on the brink of death, calm to those torn by anxiety for themselves or others, consolation following the loss of a loved one. Through his words he called people to repentance, restoring their confidence in the possibility of grace. Through his words he reminded those around him of the enduring goodness of God and, as Reginald emphasizes, brought joy into their lives.[44] If we look for testimony to that joy, we find it in the enduring quality of many of the relationships which Godric formed and in the language of friendship in which his Life abounds. The voice of hostility, shrill at first but less insistent than that of those who clamoured for the hermit's attention, faded away entirely as Godric grew from being an untried intruder to become a living saint in the region around St Cuthbert's shrine.

---

[42] *Godric*, 159–61.   [43] Ibid. 138.   [44] Ibid.

19

ROBERT OF LEWES, BISHOP OF BATH, 1136–1166: A CLUNIAC BISHOP IN HIS DIOCESE

Frances Ramsey

The twelfth-century English church was notable for bishops of distinguished quality, and amongst such figures as Anselm and Becket, Henry of Blois and Theobald, Robert of Lewes cannot hope to rank highly. Yet he is not without interest. He was a Cluniac monk, one of only a handful to attain episcopal office in this period,[1] and so the question arises as to whether there was anything specifically monastic, or more particularly Cluniac, about the way in which he ran his diocese. He was also almost certainly the author of the *Gesta Stephani*, and thus a man of scholarly as well as administrative capacity.[2] And while his involvement in ecclesiastical politics and affairs of state was limited, the records of his diocesan activities are good. They provide an important glimpse of a local church beginning to adapt to the challenges of Gregorian reform.[3]

Robert of Lewes was of Flemish descent, though born in England, and became a monk at Lewes in Sussex, the first and most important Cluniac house in the country.[4] The dates of his birth and his entry into religion are not known. The first certain chronological points of reference come when Henry of Blois gave him administrative responsibilities at Glastonbury, where Henry was abbot from 1126, and followed this by procuring the see of Bath for him in 1135–6. It is also possible that Robert spent a brief period as prior of Winchester. A fifteenth-century Wells historian suggests that such was the case, and the 1130 Pipe Roll provides some corroboration, mentioning an otherwise unknown Robert, prior of Winchester.[5] So in the two religious houses where he made most impact, in both material and monastic terms, Henry of Blois's right-hand man was probably the future bishop of Bath.

[1] David Knowles, *The Monastic Order in England*, 2nd edn. (Cambridge, 1963), App. XII, 709–10.

[2] See *Gesta Stephani*, ed. and trans. K. R. Potter with introduction and notes by R. H. C. Davis (Oxford, 1976), pp. xviii–xxxviii.

[3] *English Episcopal Acta, X: Bath and Wells, 1061–1205*, ed. Frances M. R. Ramsey (London, 1995) provides a collection and study of his *acta*.

[4] *Florentii Wigorniensis Monachi Chronicon ex Chronicis*, ed. B. Thorpe, 2 vols., English Historical Soc. (London, 1848–9), II, 95; 'Historiola de Primordiis Episcopatus Somersetensis', *Ecclesiastical Documents*, ed. J. Hunter, Camden Soc., OS, 8 (London, 1840), 23.

[5] *Collectanea I: a Collection of Documents from Various Sources*, ed. T. F. Palmer, Somerset Record Soc., 39 (Frome and London, 1924), 62; *The Pipe Roll of 31 Henry I*, ed. J. Hunter, Pipe Roll Soc. (London, 1929), 38.

Henry of Blois, Robert's patron, was brother of King Stephen and a fellow-Cluniac. Abbot of Glastonbury from 1126 and bishop of Winchester from 1129 (in which office he was vilified by St Bernard as 'the old wizard of Winchester'),[6] he may also have been prior of Montacute, the only Cluniac house in the diocese of Bath.[7] Robert's dependence on him highlights a central point of interest in the episcopate: to what extent one may identify him with essentially old-fashioned, 'black monk' aspirations in church government and organization, and to what extent he responded to newer ideals when they manifested themselves within his diocese.

Bishop Robert's most celebrated and perhaps most characteristic activities concern the church of St Andrew at Wells. An episcopal see had been founded there in 909 on the division of the bishopric of Sherborne, and the new diocese's boundaries were those of the shire of Somerset. During the episcopate of Bishop John of Tours (1088–1122), however, Wells had lost its cathedral status to the monastery of St Peter at Bath. 'Andrew gave way to Simon, brother yielded to brother, the lesser to the greater', as William of Malmesbury puts it[8]—a comment which glosses over the more mundane reasons, economic and military, which lay behind this and other relocations of cathedral churches following the Council of London in 1075. In contrast to the position in some other dioceses, though, the church of Wells was able (with difficulty) to maintain something of its identity and independence, and in the early thirteenth century successfully reasserted its claim to be a cathedral church: the bishopric was subsequently that of 'Bath and Wells'. There were two main reasons for this, and both involve Bishop Robert to a considerable degree. One concerns the endowment of the church of Wells and the organization of its estates; the other, the part which the canons of Wells came to play in the administration of the diocese. Of these two, the second is the less remarkable: a similar phenomenon occurred in most English dioceses in the course of the twelfth century. Robert's reconstitution of the church of Wells, however, represents a noteworthy and imaginative adaptation of the organization of the canons' estates as he found it in 1136.

Wells was one of a number of English cathedral churches which had been reformed in the late eleventh century by a Lotharingian bishop. Bishop Giso (1061–88) had been responsible for the construction of a number of communal buildings—including a refectory and a dormitory—for the clergy of his cathedral church. He had also imposed on them the quasi-monastic Rule of St Chrodegang. Some of the fullest sources for the estates of the church of Wells in Giso's time remain suspect, but there is enough evidence in charters and the Domesday survey to show that he worked assiduously to build up the canons' holdings; and we know that under the Rule of St Chrodegang these

---

[6] *English Episcopal Acta, VIII: Winchester, 1070–1204*, ed. M. J. Franklin (London, 1993), p. xxxvii.

[7] Knowles, *Monastic Order*, 282, n. 3.

[8] 'Cessit enim Andreas Simoni, frater fratri, minor majori', *Willelmi Malmesbiriensis Monachi de Gestis Pontificum Anglorum Libri Quinque*, ed. N. E. S. A. Hamilton, RS 52 (London, 1870), 196.

would have been held communally and managed by a provost (*prepositus*).[9] At Wells a certain Isaac appears with this title in Giso's time.[10] However, between the end of Giso's episcopate and the beginning of Robert's the canons were to face difficulties. John of Tours, who moved his cathedral from Wells to Bath, was for obvious reasons concerned to reduce the status of the church at Wells. The tradition maintained by the earliest history of the bishopric, probably composed at Wells in the second half of the twelfth century, is that he destroyed the canons' communal buildings, and gave his steward, Hildebert, a substantial part of the church's revenues. Hildebert's son, the archdeacon John, succeeded in enforcing his claim to the usurped lands and tightened his control by also acquiring the provostship. However, he seems to have died during the vacancy immediately preceding Robert of Lewes's election (that is, between August 1135 and March 1136), and his brother and heir, Reginald, was persuaded to relinquish his claim in exchange for a favourable deal in the re-foundation of the church, as we shall see.[11] The dispute reared its head again in the 1160s,[12] but by then the canons' estates were managed on a very different basis.

One episcopal charter is of supreme importance for our knowledge of Robert of Lewes's work at Wells and, by extension, of his attitudes towards church government and pastoral concerns. This is the deed which established the secular chapter, headed by a dean and including several other dignitaries, and which divided the estates of the church into prebends for the endowment of individual officers and canons. The original does not survive, but there are several copies in the Wells registers, the fullest dating from *c*.1500 and the earliest (a slightly less complete text) from *c*.1240.[13] It is a document which merits close scrutiny, not least because Joseph Armitage Robinson, who wrote with great authority and scholarship on the early history of Wells (and who, as dean of the church, had more than a merely academic interest in the origins of the secular chapter there), believed that the transmitted text, dated to the first year of Robert's episcopate, could not be authentic. His view was that the substance of the charter as recorded in the Wells registers could not have been written until 1159, that circumstantial evidence would suggest that the foundation of the secular chapter itself did not take place until the early 1140s, and that the witness list (datable to 1136) was a spurious addition.[14] The document is certainly problematic, but these claims need re-examination in the light of a fuller knowledge of Robert's

---

[9] There is a confirmation of the lands of the see purporting to have been issued by Edward the Confessor in May 1065 which exhibits some extraordinary diplomatic forms and whose content is at variance with much of what else is known about the estates of the church in the period; and there is an apparently autobiographical account of Giso's efforts on behalf of the canons in an early history of the see which again it is hard to accept at face value. For a very useful compendium of all the sources relating to Bishop Giso, see Simon Keynes, 'Giso, Bishop of Wells (1061–88)', *ANS* 19 (1996), 203–71.

[10] See e.g. 'Historiola', ed. Hunter, 19.   [11] Ibid., 21–2.

[12] *Calendar of the Manuscripts of the Dean and Chapter of Wells*, ed. W. H. B. Bird and W. P. Baildon, 2 vols., Historical Manuscripts Comm. (London, 1907–14), I, 39–40.

[13] *Acta*, ed. Ramsey, no. 46.

[14] J. Armitage Robinson, *Somerset Historical Essays* (London, 1921), 56–61.

acta and the history of the see more generally. Moreover, it is crucial to establish the exact timing of the foundation of the secular chapter if one is to understand Robert's ambitions for one of the most important churches of his diocese.

In its basic diplomatic elements the charter causes no concerns. It begins with the simple inscription, 'Universis sancte matris ecclesie filiis', followed by the bishop's name and style. Although the name and style more commonly follow the address in Robert's *acta*, there is sufficient fluidity of form that no serious question can be raised over the document's authenticity on this score; and while the omission of 'dei gratia' from the style 'Bathon[iensis] ecclesie minister humilis' is unusual, it is not a unique occurrence. The greeting 'salutem in domino' reveals the influence of the papal chancery, and is used fairly often in Bishop Robert's *acta*. Along with a number of his other more solemn productions, the enacting clauses are introduced both by a pious preamble setting out the bishop's duty to drive out all evil from the churches in his care and to stamp out any hint of discord, and by a more circumstantial *narratio* stating that the bishop had found the church oppressed by the provostship, and had determined to ordain a dean and to establish the offices, liberties, and customs of the canons 'more aliarum ecclesiarum Anglie bene ordinatarum'. There follows a series of extremely interesting clauses providing for the endowment of a dean, precentor, and subdean, together with a prebend reserved for the fabric and ornaments of the church of Wells. In addition, prebends were created for fifteen canons, with a further four to be founded on the death of Reginald, the heir of John the archdeacon who had usurped the canons' estates, who was now made the precentor of the church. At the end of the deed is a corroboration clause making mention of the bishop's seal. There is no pronouncement of an ecclesiastical sanction against those who might violate the terms of the charter. This is as one might expect: although *sanctiones* are found in Robert's *acta*, they are relatively rare, and there is undoubtedly an increasing emphasis during his episcopate on 'bureaucratic' forms of enforcement, notably sealing (Robert was the first bishop of Bath who can be shown to have used a seal). Thus, in terms of authenticity, so far so good.

One of the central problems raised by Armitage Robinson, however, concerns the witness list. This sets out a roll-call of bishops, and leads one to suppose that the document was issued at Stephen's Easter court, held at Westminster in March 1136 (Easter Sunday was 22 March). A *terminus ante quem* is provided by the subscription of William, archbishop of Canterbury, who died in November 1136. The king's formal granting of the temporalities of the see of Bath to Robert of Lewes took place at the Easter court, and the royal grant of confirmation is witnessed by all except two of the bishops who witness the Wells statute.[15] These two are Roger de Clinton, bishop of Coventry, and

---

[15] *Regesta Regum Anglo-Normannorum*, III, ed. H. A. Cronne and R. H. C. Davis (Oxford, 1968), no. 46.

William Warelwast, bishop of Exeter. In the case of Roger de Clinton, one cannot determine from any other source whether or not he was present at the Easter court that year, but it seems as likely as not. Over William Warelwast, however, greater doubts hang. Armitage Robinson was firmly convinced that he could not have attended Stephen's Easter court in 1136, being blind and confined to his see; and this contributed to his conclusion, 'that the Ordinance itself [that is, Robert's charter] in the form in which we have it was thus approved by [the witnesses] is demonstrably untrue'. Of William Warelwast's blindness there is no uncertainty, but it was a long-term condition and did not prevent him from, for instance, travelling to Rome on royal business in 1120 (Hugh the Chantor reports that he was the victim of a cruel jibe about the blind leading the blind).[16] Whether he was confined to his see in March 1136 is harder to establish, and Armitage Robinson (uncharacteristically) gave no evidence in support of his view. The Annals of Plympton provide the best account of the final period of the bishop's life; and yet the obit notice given there only records the fact that he died on 28 September 1137 and had, 'in infirmitate extrema', surrendered his ring and pastoral staff to Henry of Blois, received chrism from Robert, bishop of Bath, and accepted a canon's habit from Geoffrey, prior of Plympton.[17] This, of course, leaves open the possibility that he might have travelled to Westminster in the March of the previous year.

What, then, of the claim that the substance of the statute could not have been written until 1159, and that it had taken until the early 1140s to implement the new constitution? The first problem arises as a result of the inclusion in Robert's deed of the prebend of Hewish; for a later document confirms that there had been a dispute over the church's estate at Hewish and that it was only in November 1159 that it was successfully established as a prebend. Nevertheless, the 1159 deed which notifies Theobald, archbishop of Canterbury, of the foundation of the prebend makes it clear that Bishop Robert had been allocating the land at Hewish to his clerks, that his concern is that the estate has been held 'without certain title', and that it might on the demand of unnamed 'potentes' pass into lay jurisdiction.[18] A case heard before the Curia Regis in 1220 over two knights' fees in Kenn and Hewish suggests that the origin of the problem may have lain in a dispute between the bishop and the earl of Gloucester, whose influence was strong in northern Somerset.[19] In 1220 Matthew of Clevedon alleged that on the death of his grandfather, William of Clevedon, a knight of the earl of Gloucester, Bishop Robert had seized the land and that successive generations of episcopal tenants had held it ever since. Whether all this compromises

---

[16] Hugh the Chantor, *The History of the Church of York, 1066–1127*, ed. C. Johnson (Edinburgh, 1961), 85–7.

[17] F. Liebermann, *Ungedruckte anglo-normannische Geschichtsquellen* (Strassburg, 1879), 27.

[18] *Acta*, ed. Ramsey, no. 50.

[19] *Curia Regis Rolls . . . Preserved in the Public Record Office* (London, 1922–), IX, 132–8; *Earldom of Gloucester Charters*, ed. R. B. Patterson (Oxford, 1973), nos. 20 n., 48, 115.

absolutely the authenticity of Robert's seemingly earlier statute is hard to determine. A prebend is apparently given a second foundation, which does not
inspire confidence, but there is circumstantial evidence for a dispute over the
estate at Hewish which might explain the reasons for this and show the first
foundation to have been a statement of intent—over-optimistic rather than
actually spurious. Lay occupation of prebendal land cannot have been uncommon, particularly given the circumstances of Stephen's reign (we know that
lands in Somerset which pertained to the church of Salisbury suffered in this
way);[20] and to re-found a prebend which had never been held with security by
the church of Wells seems a logical enough step. Furthermore, if Robert's deed
did date from the late 1150s or early 1160s, one might expect it to reflect more
fully the constitution of that time. By then several more dignitaries are known
to have appeared at Wells (a treasurer by 1158 at the latest, and a succentor before
Robert's death in 1166); yet these are not mentioned in the document; and
prebends which we know to have been established later in the episcopate are
similarly omitted.[21]

Finally, what of the circumstantial evidence for the existence of the secular
chapter at Wells? Here too a straightforward answer is elusive. Armitage
Robinson argued that the necessary work must have taken some years, that
there is no formal evidence of the chapter's existence until 1146, and that one
should trust the statement given in the 'Historiola' that Henry of Blois was
papal legate at the time when he assisted Robert in the recovery of the canons'
estates from Reginald, the heir of John the archdeacon (which necessarily
preceded the new foundation). Henry's legation lasted from March 1139 until
September 1143, and so Armitage Robinson has the secular chapter come into
being in the early 1140s.[22] What one has to set against this is a charter from the
bishop for the monks of Bath which is explicitly dated to the first year of the
episcopate and which is witnessed by Ivo, dean of Wells.[23] There is also a charter for Bruton, witnessed by the dean and convent of Wells, datable to the brief
period when William de Moyon was earl of Somerset and Dorset, that is
June/July 1141 x *c*.1142.[24] This, of course, is just about within Armitage Robinson's limit. The 'Historiola' was probably compiled in the late twelfth or
early thirteenth century and, although its chronology for the Anglo-Saxon
period is problematic, it seems to be well informed on Robert's episcopate. To
misdate the bishop of Winchester's period as legate would be an easy mistake
to make.[25]

---

[20] *Acta*, ed. Ramsey, no. 43.
[21] The prebend of West Lydford was created in or after 1151, and King Stephen gave the churches of
North Curry and North Petherton for prebends in the period 1143 x 1154: ibid., no. 48; *Regesta*, III, ed.
Cronne and Davis, no. 924.
[22] Armitage Robinson, *Somerset Historical Essays*, 61.
[23] Armitage Robinson rejects the date without explanation.   [24] *Acta*, ed. Ramsey, no. 21.
[25] Archbishop Theobald was incorrectly addressed as legate in one of Bishop Robert's own *acta*
(ibid., no. 50 n.).

There are no insuperable objections, then, to Robert's charter having been given in the form in which we have it at Stephen's Easter court in 1136. This would have been an appropriate setting for the re-foundation of the chapter, something which was clearly of importance to Henry of Blois and Robert of Lewes. Henry certainly used this occasion to promote the interests of both Glastonbury and Winchester,[26] where Robert was probably also involved in the reforming work; and given that both men already had considerable interests in Somerset, they may have been able to begin on the plans for Wells shortly after Bishop Godfrey of Bath's death in August 1135.[27] Crucially, there seems to be proof of the existence of a dean of Wells in the first year of Robert's episcopate. On the other hand, not every provision in the document was fully implemented early in his episcopate. Nevertheless, it is certain that the document is not the kind of later fabrication whose purpose is to confer respectability on the constitution of the day;[28] and it must at the very least reflect the situation quite early in Robert's episcopate. As such it provides extremely useful, detailed evidence of his work at Wells.

The way in which the estates of the church of Wells were divided into individual prebends reveals unusual features, which reflect the communal management of the property established by Giso. In several cases a degree of this communal management was retained even though the estates were being divided between individual canons. Thus, the extensive property held by the church in Wedmore was apportioned so as to provide endowment for the dean and subdean of Wells, the fabric and ornaments of the church, and five further prebends.[29] Another large estate, Winsham, was treated in a similar manner, with a single canon being made responsible for the management of all the revenues from the town of Winsham and for the payment of a further two canons. When the very generous single prebend granted to Reginald, the brother of John the archdeacon, was finally divided on his death into endowments for the precentor and four other canons, a similar arrangement was instituted. Interestingly, those canons charged with the payment of others were known at Wells as *prepositi*,[30] a clear connection with the organization imposed by Bishop Giso under the Rule of St Chrodegang. As well as the individual endowment of dean, precentor, subdean, and canons, the statute makes some more general

---

[26] *Regesta*, III, ed. Cronne and Davis, nos. 341, 945–9.

[27] We do not know the date of Robert's election or consecration as bishop, only that of the grant of the temporalities of the see, which took place in March 1136. The 'Historiola' places the death of John the archdeacon, essential for the restoration of the canons' estates, in the vacancy after Godfrey's death.

[28] Just such a document exists at Salisbury in the *Institutio* of St Osmund, shown to have been composed (mostly) 60 or 70 years after the initiative which it claimed to describe: Diana Greenway, 'The False *Institutio* of St Osmund', in *Tradition and Change: Essays Presented to Marjorie Chibnall*, ed. D. E. Greenway, C. J. Holdsworth, and J. E. Sayers (Cambridge, 1985), 77–101.

[29] Of these, four canonries were effectively to be a charge upon estates held by the dean in Wedmore, Mudgley, and Mark, in that he was required to pay four canons 100s. each per annum, retaining any excess for himself.

[30] See e.g. *Calendar of the Manuscripts of the Dean and Chapter of Wells*, ed. Bird and Baildon, I, 58.

grants: a prebend, as has been mentioned, assigned to the fabric and ornaments of the church, the gift of land at [North] Wootton and a tithe of the bishop's vines there,[31] and the allocation of the churchscots and tithes paid to the church of Wells to provide bread for those canons attending matins.

One can discern in Robert's work at Wells some of the ideals of the Gregorian reform movement—the desire, for instance, to provide adequately for priests and to regularize their lives to some degree. The provision for resident canons and the beginnings of the common fund speak of the bishop's pastoral concerns. This strikes one the more forcibly since Robert was not himself a secular priest. One also sees that increasing administrative burdens were being placed on bishops. Robert of Lewes clearly needed to find sufficient emoluments to pay his clerical staff. As the bishop of a monastic see, canonries were not available to him in his cathedral church, and Robert evidently used the prebends at Wells to fulfil this function. Several of those who—judging by their frequent attestation of the bishop's charters—must have been members of his household, held canonries. Master Alvred, the only clerk known for certain to have drafted one of the bishop's charters, witnesses on a number of occasions as a canon of Wells, as do the bishop's kinsman Stephen, and clerks named Edward and Paris.[32] There is some evidence that Robert's patronage may have been rather constrained: there are several cases of clerks being promised prebends which were yet to fall vacant. An otherwise unknown Master E., for example, had been ordained deacon by Robert and paid an annual stipend of forty shillings, with the assurance of being collated to the next prebend to fall vacant. Unfortunately for him, no prebend became available until after Robert's death, and a royal servant, Thomas de Erlegh, then managed to take possession of it.[33] Robert even had temporarily to assign the prebend of Biddisham, which was supposed to be reserved for the upkeep of the fabric and ornaments of the church of Wells, to one of his clerks; and again there was an assurance that a more orthodox arrangement would be made when possible. The clerk in this case was Herbert of Ilchester, the son of Richard of Ilchester, and later bishop of Salisbury (by which time he was usually known as Herbert Poore). His presence in Robert's household shows that it was a place of training and education for younger clerks who might be destined for a career in ecclesiastical administration.[34]

The bishop's documents also reveal a more 'literate mentality' in comparison with those of his predecessors. As already mentioned, Robert of Lewes is the first bishop of Bath known to have used a seal. This practice was linked with other

---

[31] There are today vineyards at North Wootton on the south-facing slopes of the spur between Launcherley Hill and Worminster Sleight, and since no other hill in the vicinity has the right aspect this is presumably the site of Bishop Robert's vines.

[32] *Acta*, ed. Ramsey, no. 28 ends with an attestation by 'Aluredo canonico Well' qui praesentem composuit chartam'. For a full analysis of Bishop Robert's household, see ibid., pp. xli–xlvi.

[33] Ibid., p. xlv.   [34] Ibid., no. 52.

'modern' features of episcopal diplomatic such as the use of the first-person plural, the move away from 'liturgical' characteristics such as the anathema and the *apprecatio* 'amen', and the imitation of the papal chancery.[35] Of thirty-nine surviving texts, only three end with *apprecationes* and a mere seven have sanction clauses. There is only one example of Robert's referring to himself in the first-person singular. Amongst the surviving original *acta*, about half are rather formal, old-fashioned productions written in what are essentially book-hands, but the rest are in charter-hands, all to some extent cursive, and one employs the papal tittle twice in the first line.

It is well known that bishops in this period faced a greater weight of administration than their predecessors, and responses such as the employment of highly educated secular clerks, often *magistri*, and the increasing use of formulaic documentation can be seen in virtually every English diocese by the mid-twelfth century. A more unusual theme emerges from Robert of Lewes's dealings with the monastic orders in his see. Here, as in his work at Wells, he espoused 'modern' causes, promoting in particular the Augustinians: his own Cluniac background does not seem to have caused him to favour the interests of black monks. There exists, for instance, just one charter issued by Bishop Robert for Montacute, the only Cluniac house in his diocese, and one for Monkton Farleigh, just over the border into the diocese of Salisbury. In both cases these are general confirmations of the priories' possessions, and the documents end with imprecations rather than witness lists. This might indicate monastic authorship, and thus no initiative on the part of the bishop.[36] Robert's relations with his cathedral priory at Bath seem to have been entirely harmonious: he sponsored a building programme there, and was remembered as a benefactor of the monks. He did not, however, make a full restoration of the monks' estates as they had stood before their alienation by his predecessor, Bishop John; and one has to conclude that, despite some generous acts, monastic interests were subordinate to episcopal concerns.[37] The careers of other monk-bishops, notably that of Theobald at Canterbury, point in the same direction.[38]

If Bishop Robert can be said to have sponsored a particular cause within his diocese, it was that of the Augustinians. Bruton Priory, founded in the late 1120s or early 1130s by William de Moyon, seems to have been especially favoured. There survive seven confirmations of grants to the house,[39] and the five of these which bear witness lists are attested by members of the bishop's household, suggesting that they reflect his own initiative. In one case the charter is explicitly

---

[35] On the diplomatic of Bishop Robert's *acta* and its context, see ibid., pp. lxxiv–lxxxi.

[36] Ibid., nos. 39–40.

[37] Ibid., pp. xxvi–xxvii; *Two Chartularies of the Priory of St Peter at Bath*, ed. W. Hunt, Somerset Record Soc., 7 (London, 1893), II, 808.

[38] A. Saltman, *Theobald, Archbishop of Canterbury* (London, 1956), 56–89.

[39] *Acta*, ed. Ramsey, nos. 20–2, 24–5, 28–9.

said to have been composed by one of the bishop's clerks.[40] In addition, the bishop gave the canons of Bruton two churches from the episcopal estates, those of Banwell and Westbury-sub-Mendip, and wrote to the bishop of Bayeux on their behalf concerning properties in his diocese.[41] No other institution, except the church of Wells, received this degree of attention from Robert of Lewes. His patron, Henry of Blois, also espoused the Augustinian cause, notably in his converting the church of Twynham into a house of regular canons.[42] On one occasion Robert even acted as an informal representative for the canons of Lanthony in relation to their church at Prestbury, a case in which he had no formal jurisdiction.[43]

A number of incidents relating to the anchorite Wulfric of Haselbury offer insights into Robert of Lewes's spiritual and pastoral concerns, and his reaction to 'Cistercian' practices when they manifested themselves in his diocese. The Life of the anchorite, written by John of Ford, records that Wulfric's asceticism was moderated on the express orders of the bishop, who told him to use a pillow made of hay on his uncomfortable bed of branches.[44] On Wulfric's death in 1154 Robert visited Haselbury, where an ugly dispute was raging over where the holy man should be buried. The bishop prevented the monks of Montacute from obtaining the body as they had demanded, spoke to the people to calm them down, and buried Wulfric in his cell.[45] The church of Haselbury was briefly established as a house of Augustinian canons at around this time, and it may have been their interests which the bishop had in mind when he kept at bay his fellow-Cluniacs from Montacute.

There is perhaps one further route into the mind and person of Robert of Lewes. In a compelling piece of historical detective work, R. H. C. Davis made a strong case for the bishop's authorship of the *Gesta Stephani*.[46] Davis's argument was based on the author's very evident knowledge of, and emotional attachment to the West Country, particularly Bristol and Bath, on his involvement with the party of Henry of Blois, and on his near-obsession with the importance of bishops. Although one can raise the problem of the author's changing political views,[47] or suggest that a learned member of the bishop's household might have had similar loyalties, local attachments, and views on the episcopal office, it must also be said that the work makes a great deal of sense as

[40] *Acta*, ed. Ramsey, no. 21.   [41] Ibid., nos. 23, 26, 30.
[42] In this case we are fortunate to know something of the provisions made for the pastoral care of parishes dependent on Twynham (essentially perpetual vicarages were set up). On this and more general issues relating to Henry of Blois and the monasteries of his diocese, see M. J. Franklin, 'The Bishops of Winchester and the Monastic Revolution', *ANS* 12 (1989), 47–65.
[43] *The 'Acta' of the Bishops of Chichester, 1075–1207*, ed. H. M. R. E. Mayr-Harting, Canterbury and York Soc. 130 (London, 1964), no. 38.
[44] *Wulfric of Haselbury, by John, Abbot of Ford*, ed. Dom Maurice Bell, Somerset Record Soc., 47 (Frome and London, 1933), 18.
[45] Ibid., 124–5, 129.
[46] R. H. C. Davis, 'The Authorship of the *Gesta Stephani*', *EHR* 77 (1962), 209–32.
[47] See e.g. Jim Bradbury, *Stephen and Matilda: The Civil War of 1139–53* (Stroud, 1996), 142.

the production of a Cluniac monk. It reflects the cultural world of Cluny in two important respects. The first is in its self-conscious classical style. Cluny under Peter the Venerable (after a less fertile period in the second half of the eleventh century) saw a great flourishing of literature, history, and theology, and a contemporary could refer to the monks as 'cowled poets'.[48] Robert of Lewes's patron, Henry of Blois, is known to have collected classical statuary, to have used an antique cameo gem as his counterseal, and was referred to as 'the Cicero of his day'.[49] The author of the *Gesta Stephani* is well versed in the classics, and writes as though addressing a classical audience: he follows a description of the city of Bath with the comment 'Quae civitas Batta uocatur, quod ex Anglice linguae proprietate trahens uocabulum, Balneum uocatur'; Woodchester in Gloucestershire is rendered 'castellum de silva'; and he employs classical Latin terms in contexts where other, less pretentious, forms would be more common ('summus antigraphus' for chancellor, 'legionarii' and 'centenarii' for soldiers, 'togati cives' for townsmen). King Stephen is praised for facing his afflictions with the steadfastness not only of Saul and the Maccabees, but of Alexander and Hercules as well.[50]

The other respect in which the *Gesta Stephani* reveals a frame of mind which may well be Cluniac in its formation is in its pessimistic moralizing. Although common to the Christian tradition as a whole, there is perhaps a notably strong moral theme to much Cluniac literature and art, whether one thinks of Odo of Cluny's lengthy *Occupatio*, concerned with the catastrophic effects of sin on human society, of the capitals of the choir at Cluny, with their representations of the Virtues, or more generally of the way in which tenth- and eleventh-century Cluny sought to set itself up as a bulwark against what its leaders perceived as the vices of the day.[51] In the *Gesta Stephani* one is bombarded with examples of how individual moral failings have led to personal downfall or disaster, and the author's explanation of the state of civil war into which the country fell rests entirely on the people's misdoings. His opening section describes the apparently inexplicable 'iniquitas', 'peruersitas', and 'dissensio' which followed the peaceful reign of King Henry. Men were sick in soul, and through robbery and the desire for vengeance depleted the kingdom of its resources.[52] Somewhat later in the work the author briefly abandons his narrative to return again to this

[48] Joan Evans, *Monastic Life at Cluny, 910–1157* (Oxford, 1931), 108–12.

[49] Lena Voss, *Heinrich von Blois, Bischof von Winchester* (Berlin, 1932), 135; *Acta, viii*, ed. Franklin, p. lxxix; G. Zarnecki, 'Henry of Blois as a Patron of Sculpture', in *Art and Patronage in the English Romanesque*, ed. S. Macready and F. H. Thompson (London, 1986), 159–72; N. Riall, *Henry of Blois, Bishop of Winchester: A Patron of the Twelfth-Century Renaissance* (Winchester, 1994).

[50] *Gesta Stephani*, ed. Potter and Davis, pp. xxx, 68–70.

[51] On Odo's *Occupatio* (*Odonis Abbatis Cluniacensis Occupatio*, ed. A. Swoboda (Leipzig, 1900)), see Raffaello Morghen, 'Monastic Reform and Cluniac Spirituality', in *Cluniac Monasticism in the Central Middle Ages*, ed. Noreen Hunt (London, 1971), 11–28. There is a detailed analysis of the capitals in Francis Salet, *Cluny et Vézelay: L'Oeuvre des sculpteurs* (Paris, 1995), 25–46.

[52] *Gesta Stephani*, ed. Potter and Davis, 2–4.

theme. Internecine strife had been visited on England in punishment for the sins of the people. The populace was 'luxu et otio dissolutus, luxuria et ebrietate eneruatus, fastu et arrogantia tumefactus'; their leaders were worse, indulging in every debauchery dangerous to the soul, and even Stephen's military skill was of no avail in achieving peace, since God was merciless in his anger. There was no solution but for the Ethiopian to change his skin.[53] Individual motivation and action, and the author's judgement of those who feature in his narrative, are always approached in similar, moral terms. William of Corbeil, the archbishop of Canterbury, would have been a better pastor had he distributed his wealth in alms; Robert of Bampton was gluttonous and a drunkard; Baldwin de Redvers exhibited arrogant, threatening behaviour; Geoffrey Talbot was frenzied and cruel, inspired by the poison of his hatred; the men of Bristol fell on the property of the king's supporters with covetousness and trickery.[54] The moralizing is such an overt and consistent strand in the author's thinking, and his pessimism about human nature is so great, that to find acceptable motives for the behaviour of many of the key figures of the period one has to look elsewhere.[55] But their prominence in the work would be entirely consistent with the particular outlook on human affairs fostered and promoted within Cluniac culture.

Much of what one can establish about the episcopate of Robert of Lewes at Bath falls into an established pattern. He ran his diocese with the assistance of a household of clerks whose numbers were clearly increasing and whose salaries he had to find from new sources—from the newly created prebends at Wells, whose foundation must rank as the most notable achievement of his period in office. Here he self-consciously followed the example of other English sees,[56] many of which had undergone a similar development in the post-conquest period. The forty or so *acta* which give us the best evidence of his activities are not yet strictly formulaic, but while retaining fluidity of form they nevertheless reveal a growing concern with providing authenticated written records of many kinds of transaction. These, both in their nature and in sheer numbers, reflect the increasingly bureaucratic world occupied by members of the episcopate, and—the documents are so different from anything produced by either of his immediate predecessors—the speed of response to change. More unusually, there is from the diocese of Bath convincing evidence that already some of the prime concerns of the Third and Fourth Lateran Councils (of 1179 and 1215 respectively) were beginning to be addressed. Bishop Robert seems to have made it his business to support and regulate the lives of priests, whether the secular clergy at Wells or the Augustinian canons of Bruton (and, briefly, Haselbury), presumably for the same reasons that his successors would ordain vicarages and scrutinize the financial arrangements of appropriated benefices.

---

[53] *Gesta Stephani*, ed. Potter and Davis, 84–6.   [54] Ibid., 10, 28, 30–2, 58, 62–4.
[55] Hence the essay question Henry Mayr-Harting posed to his undergraduates: 'Can a case be made for the barons of Stephen's reign?'
[56] *Acta*, ed. Ramsey, no. 46, lines 8–17.

And while it was not to be until twenty years after Robert's death that a clerk or canon with official responsibility for teaching appeared in the chapter at Wells,[57] it can be shown that his own household served as a place of teaching and training for younger clerks. The bishop's own monastic background and wider intellectual concerns, if one accepts his authorship of the *Gesta Stephani*, are further proof that the twelfth-century English church could draw upon men of varied and considerable talent to staff even the lesser dioceses, and in some senses justify Robert's own view of the role of and importance of bishops, whom he regarded as 'the pillars that hold up God's house . . . the small lions that support Solomon's famous laver'.[58]

---

[57] Peter of Winchester, variously described as *magister scolarum* and *cancellarius*, witnessed episcopal deeds in the 1180s: ibid., 214.

[58] *Gesta Stephani*, ed. Potter and Davis, 156.

20

KING HENRY II AND THE MONKS OF BATTLE: THE BATTLE CHRONICLE UNMASKED

Nicholas Vincent

As defined by the introduction to its most recent edition, 'The Chronicle of Battle Abbey is a roughly chronological account of legal and administrative affairs of Battle Abbey, a Benedictine monastery in Sussex, from the foundation of the house in the late eleventh century until the 1180s'.[1] It survives today in a single, incomplete manuscript: London, British Library, Cotton Domitian A ii. It has twice been printed, most recently by Professor Eleanor Searle, much of whose career was spent in the study of Battle Abbey, its lands and records.[2] Professor Searle judged that the Chronicle was composed towards the end of the reign of King Henry II, drawing for its earliest materials upon late eleventh- and early twelfth-century narrative and administrative records, but from the 1130s onwards representing the work of a single man, 'the chronicler', who could himself recall an event that took place during the time of Abbot Warner (1125–38).[3] The manuscript breaks off in mid-sentence, recounting a lawsuit of 1176. But elsewhere the chronicler refers explicitly to an event of 1184. Given her dating of the script of the sole surviving manuscript to the late twelfth century, this suggested to Professor Searle that the chronicler himself died or ceased writing towards the end of the reign of Henry II, and that the missing folios of the manuscript would have carried the narrative no further than 1189.[4]

If the Chronicle has a theme it lies in the desire to prove that Battle was an exempt house, freed from subjection to the authority of the local diocesan—the bishop of Chichester—by virtue of a series of royal privileges issued by the

---

[1] *The Chronicle of Battle Abbey*, ed. and trans. Eleanor Searle (Oxford, 1980) [henceforth: *Battle Chronicle*], 1. I am deeply indebted to Martin Brett, Michael Clanchy, Kate Dailinger, Sir James Holt, Robert Patterson, Richard Sharpe, and Christopher Whittick for their assistance in the writing of this paper, and to Henry Mayr-Harting who was kind enough to read a preliminary version, little knowing where it was to be published. The paper was first delivered, in a much abbreviated form, to a conference organized by Michael Gervers at the Collegium Budapest in March 1999. Sadly, Professor Eleanor Searle died before I could communicate my findings to her. I have no doubt that she would have responded with appropriate vigour.

[2] For the earlier printing, valuable for its publication of various related Battle Abbey charters, see *Chronicon Monasterii de Bello*, ed. J. S. Brewer, Anglia Christiana Society (London, 1846).

[3] *Battle Chronicle*, 8–12.

[4] Ibid. 9, 23–8. The final folio in the MS (fol. 130) ends a gathering, but was clearly followed by a continuation, now lost.

abbey's founder, King William I, and his successors, Henry I and Henry II. It has long been recognized that this claim to exemption was based upon forgery. In 1932 F. M. Stenton and David Knowles demonstrated that the majority of Battle's surviving charters issued in the names of William I and Henry I are forged, including every single charter earlier than 1154 that purports to award exemption from the diocesan authority of Chichester.[5] Professor Searle herself published a detailed study of these forgeries in 1962, in which she suggested that they were concocted in the 1150s, at a time when Battle's exemption was subject to appeal by Bishop Hilary of Chichester in a protracted dispute heard before the court of King Henry II, reported at length in the Battle Chronicle.[6] As Searle suggested, the forgeries were probably commissioned by Battle's abbot, Walter de Lucy (1139–71), the brother of Henry II's justiciar, Richard de Lucy. However, according to Searle and to all earlier commentators, the chronicler, identified as a monastic lawyer personally engaged in Battle's litigation before the royal courts, was not directly implicated in, and may even have disapproved of, the forging of the abbey's exemption.[7] In Searle's judgement, the chronicler provides an honest account of the process by which King Henry II was persuaded to accept the exemption and privileges of Battle Abbey, albeit that this process was founded upon earlier forgeries. Read in this light, the Chronicle remains a source of fundamental significance for our knowledge of Henry II's court. As such, it has been widely exploited by social, legal, and diplomatic historians for its wealth of details, including lengthy reported speeches that throw light upon the personality and government of King Henry II, upon the development of legal and documentary forms, and upon the relationship between Church and State both before and after the Becket conflict of the 1160s.

In what follows, I hope to demonstrate that this accepted picture of the Chronicle and its writer is erroneous; indeed, that henceforth we would be ill advised to accept anything from the Chronicle as the unvarnished truth. In particular, by examining three stories, reported at length in the Chronicle, concerning Battle's litigation before the court of King Henry II, and by comparing these stories with the charters supposedly issued by Henry II, preserved as originals or as cartulary copies, I hope to show that forgery at Battle, far from ending in the 1150s, remained rife for many years thereafter. The author of the Battle Chronicle, far from disapproving of forgery, was himself a forger on a very grand scale. As a study in the fictitious manipulation of narrative history by

---

[5] Stenton, in a series of notes appended to D. Knowles, 'Essays in Monastic History IV', *The Downside Review*, NS, 31 (1932), 218–25, 431–6, at 431–2.

[6] E. Searle, 'Battle Abbey and Exemption: The Forged Charters', *EHR* 83 (1968), 449–80. The charters of William I have since been subjected to further analysis by David Bates, *Regesta Regum Anglo-Normannorum: The Acta of William I, 1066–1087* (Oxford, 1998), 130–73, nos. 13–25. Stefan Dohmen, 'Exemplarische Untersuchungen zur Rechtskraft des Privilegs', *Archiv für Diplomatik*, 42 (1996), 33–224, esp. 56, 68 ff., devotes considerable attention to the Battle dispute and privileges as part of a wider study of the evolution of diplomatic forms, as drawn to my attention by Michael Clanchy.

[7] *Battle Chronicle*, 21–3; Searle, 'Forged Charters', 451.

a religious community, I trust that my enquiry will be judged appropriate to a collection of essays devoted to belief and culture. Above all, I hope that it will find favour with this volume's honorand, in whose tutorials I first became acquainted with the world of the monastic chroniclers, and whose own earliest researches were devoted to the twelfth-century diocese of Chichester.

Let us begin with a survey of the various general judgements on the Chronicle passed by Professor Searle. In a review published in 1981 Martin Brett questioned several of Searle's conclusions as to the authorship and composition of the Chronicle.[8] In particular, he pointed out that the manuscript transmission of the text is far more complicated than Searle would allow, and that the main section of the Chronicle, covering the years 1066 to 1176 (which for ease of reference we will christen the 'Long Chronicle'), appears to have been used as the basis of a 'Short Chronicle' of Battle's eleventh-century foundation and endowment, preserved as a separate *libellus*, today bound up amongst the opening folios of the composite Cotton manuscript.[9] Searle attempted to prove that the order of the two chronicles in the manuscript reflects the dates of their composition, and that the 'Short Chronicle' was the first to be written.[10] Brett, and more recently Elizabeth van Houts, suggest on the contrary that the shorter account of the abbey's foundation is nothing more than an epitome of the opening portions of the 'Long' Chronicle, which runs from 1066 to 1176 and which in the manuscript is placed second.[11] They have also drawn attention to other Battle narratives, at least one of them now lost, demonstrating that there were several versions of the abbey's foundation history in circulation in the twelfth century.[12] As Searle herself recognized, the Cotton manuscript of the 'Long' Chronicle cannot be the chronicler's autograph, but is a subsequent copy incorporating numerous misreadings and at least one major disordering of material copied out of sequence.[13] Beyond this, and arguing for an even more complicated process of composition, Michael Kauffmann has sought to date the illuminated portrait of King William I with which the 'Long' Chronicle opens

[8] M. Brett, review of *Battle Chronicle*, in *Medium Aevum*, 50 (1981), 319–22.

[9] Brett, noting the composite nature of Cotton Domitian A ii, and in particular the break in script and quires between the 'Short' Chronicle, fols. 8–21v (printed as *Battle Chronicle*, 32–66), and the 'Long' Chronicle, fols. 22–130 (printed as *Battle Chronicle*, 66–335). There are several insertions in the MS that are not signalled as such in Searle's edition. See e.g. fol. 35r–v (*Battle Chronicle*, 96, lines 3–7, *et feretrum . . . suscepta sunt*), and fol. 68v (*Battle Chronicle*, 174, lines 3–5, *singulis . . . accomodauere*).

[10] *Battle Chronicle*, 7–8, 15–23.

[11] Brett, 'review', 320; E. M. C. van Houts, 'The Memory of 1066 in Written and Oral Traditions', *ANS* 19 (1997), 167 n.

[12] See here E. M. C. van Houts, 'The Ship List of William the Conqueror', *ANS* 10 (1988), 165–7, 177; 'The "Brevis Relatio de Guillelmo nobilissimo comite Normannorum", Written by a Monk of Battle Abbey', ed. E. M. C. van Houts, *Camden Miscellany 34*, Camden Soc., 5th ser., 10 (1997), 7–24, drawing attention to a lost *libellus*, *De Constructione Ecclesie Belli*, in the seventeenth century forming part of a Battle Abbey manuscript most of which, but not the *De Constructione*, survives today, divided between manuscripts at Hereford and Oxford.

[13] *Battle Chronicle*, 27, noting the inversion in the copying of fols. 48 and 49, perhaps taken from an exemplar with a similar inversion.

nearer to 1130 than to 1170, suggesting that at least the opening parchment quires of this copy may have been prepared before the writing of the narrative of events from the 1150s onwards.[14] This in turn only strengthens Martin Brett's proposition that the 'Long' Chronicle from the 1150s is not a through-composed unity but a hybrid drawing upon several shorter narratives, including an independent account of Battle's litigation between 1148 and 1157, subsequently brought together into one work and today bound up with the related 'Short' Chronicle with its foundation history.[15] To this extent, Brett argues, it may be vain to seek for a single author; whilst, even if such an author existed, there is little to support Searle's contention that the (Long) Chronicle is 'the case-book of a common lawyer', composed by an elderly monk who had served as the abbey's advocate. In reality the Chronicle shows surprisingly little interest in the technicalities of the law, concentrating instead upon a series of dramatic set pieces in which the abbey's charters were produced before the king. Again, as Brett points out, there is no reason to suppose that the chronicler was made uneasy by the forgery of Battle's earliest charters, of kings William and Henry I. On the contrary, page after page of the chronicle quotes from these charters verbatim and with approval.[16] To these observations one more should be added. Searle assumed that the 'chronicler' was writing towards the end of the reign of Henry II, but before 1189. In fact, the composition of at least part of the Chronicle may date from after, rather than before, the king's death, since in describing a case fought over the church of Mildenhall the Chronicle states that the canons of Leeds Priory withdrew their claim against Battle 'for the time of King Henry [d. 1189] and Abbot Walter [d. 1171]'.[17] We know from other sources that litigation over Mildenhall was revived in the time of Pope Celestine III (1191–8), and continued, with interventions by the monks of Bury St Edmunds, until at least 1206.[18] The chronicler's remarks here can leave little doubt that he was aware of the dispute's revival after 1191. In short, and in the absence of any decisive palaeographical evidence that might enable us to date the manuscript more closely, the main section of the chronicle appears to be a

---

[14] C. M. Kauffmann, in *English Romanesque Art 1066–1200*, ed. G. Zarnecki *et al.* (London, 1984), 91, no. 13, with illustration at p. 17, commenting on the initial at fol. 21r (*recte* fol. 22r), the beginning of the main, or 'Long' Chronicle printed as *Battle Chronicle*, 66, line 3. In the MS it is noteworthy that the text of the chronicle is written over the green wash decoration of the initial, and that the heading, *Incipit lib(er) de situ ecclesie Belli*, is crammed rather untidily into the space to the right of the initial, suggesting that the text was added later, perhaps considerably later, than the decoration of the initial.

[15] Brett, 'review', 322, admits that the various constituent elements of the composition can no longer be distinguished with any certainty, whilst suggesting (in part on the basis of a change of hand in the MS at fol. 84r, as remarked by Searle, *Battle Chronicle*, 27, and 208 from *Hoc igitur fine*), that the entire section of text printed as *Battle Chronicle*, 146–208 (fols. 57r–84r) may have begun life as a separate *libellus*. In the MS this section opens with an elaborately decorated capital *A* for *Anno ab incarnatione*, suggesting a distinct break from the preceding material.

[16] Brett, 'review', 322.

[17] *Battle Chronicle*, 228–9: *ad tempus quieuerunt a lite, domino scilicet rege Henrico et abbate Waltero superstitibus.*

[18] See *English Episcopal Acta VI: Norwich 1070–1214*, ed. C. Harper-Bill (Oxford, 1990), no. 332 n.

composite work, put together at some time between *c.*1170 and *c.*1210, incorporating several individual stories that may have begun life as separate *libelli*,
drawing upon a rich store of historical writing at Battle concerned with the
abbey's foundation and later dealings with the royal court.

Bearing these complications in mind, and passing over at least one other
remarkable feature not commented upon by Searle—the chronicler's quite
blatant failure to explain the process by which Battle became detached from its
obedience to Marmoutier, the mother house to which it had originally been
granted—I wish now to proceed to the Chronicle's account of events during the
reign of Henry II.[19] In particular, I wish to examine three of the principal set
pieces which together make up the bulk of the Chronicle's narrative after 1154,
comparing its account with the charters of Henry II to the abbey that survive
elsewhere in cartulary and chancery sources. All told, we have eight surviving
charter texts of Henry II to Battle, preserved in cartulary and chancery copies.[20]
Five of these eight texts are either paraphrased in the Chronicle or are directly
related to litigation which the Chronicle describes in detail. In addition, the
Chronicle refers to several further letters or charters of the king whose texts no
longer survive.[21] As I shall show, only one of the five surviving charters of
Henry II referred to in the Chronicle is indisputably genuine. One charter is an
undoubted forgery, and the three others are of very questionable authenticity.
Let us begin, however, with the genuine charter, first brought to light by the late
Vivian Galbraith,[22] and from there proceed via the questionable to the
undoubtedly forged texts of Henry II to which the Chronicle refers.

As part of an extended account of the election of Abbot Odo of Battle in 1175,
the Chronicle reports Odo's attempt to have his earlier charters of liberty and
exemption confirmed by the king. The abbot, who had been blessed by the
archbishop of Canterbury at Malling on 28 September 1175,[23] travelled thereafter to the royal court carrying with him a charter of King William I, Battle's

---

[19] For tantalizing glimpses of the dispute with Marmoutier, see *Battle Chronicle*, 46–7, 74–7, 114–17.

[20] All of these charters will be published in my forthcoming edition of the *acta* of King Henry II
(Oxford, forthcoming). In brief, they comprise: 1. a mandate for the restoration of fugitives and serfs,
dated at Westminster (1154 x 1158); 2. a general confirmation of lands and liberties, without place-date
(1154 x 1161, considered in detail below); 3. a quittance from shires, hundreds, toll, etc., dated at Canterbury (1155 x 1158); 4. a confirmation of 3 virgates of land at Barnhorne, dated at Clarendon (1155 x 1166, considered below); 5. a writ to John, count of Eu, over the land at Barnhorne, dated at Clarendon (1155 x 1166,
considered below); 6. a further confirmation of the land at Barnhorne, dated at Westminster (1155 x 1166,
considered below); 7. a general confirmation of lands and liberties, dated at Winchester (1175 x 1179, considered below); and 8. a grant of protection, dated at Ludgershall (1175 x 1188). Of these, nos. 4 and 7 survive as original engrossments. An original of no. 8 was apparently seen by Thomas Madox, *Formulare
Anglicanum* (London, 1702), 296, no. 510, but has since been lost. The remaining texts survive in both of
the principal Battle cartularies (San Marino, Huntington Library MS BA29, and London, Lincoln's
Inn, MS Hale 87), and in the case of nos. 2, 6, 7, and 8 in chancery enrolments of Oct. 1431, Feb. 1434, and
Nov. 1486: *Calendar of Patent Rolls 1429–36*, 174–5, 364–5; London, Public Record Office C56/12 (Con-
firmation Roll 2 Henry VII part 3), m. 1, no. 5.

[21] *Battle Chronicle*, 212–13, 244–5, 278–81, 284–5, 296–7, 312–15.

[22] V. H. Galbraith, 'A New Charter of Henry II to Battle Abbey', *EHR* 52 (1937), 67–73.

[23] *Battle Chronicle*, 300–7.

founder, 'which had decayed with age'. According to the Chronicle, the king was unwilling to confirm this charter without judgement of his court, but was won round after a speech in council from his justiciar, Richard de Lucy, brother of the previous abbot of Battle, Walter de Lucy (d. 1171). Calling for Master Walter of Coutances, whom the chronicler describes as chancellor, but who in fact was at this time discharging a subsidiary office in chancery:

The king ordered that a new charter be made in the royal name and sealed with his own seal, following the form of the old charter, and specifying that in the new charter it be stated that he had confirmed it for the love of God and at the petition of Abbot Odo, wishing the name and merit of the abbot to be recorded. Now, whereas in the charters and muniments given by various persons at different times concerning the same matter, it is the custom that the later documents mention the earlier ones, so that the latter seem to require the evidence of the former, for example in such words as *sicut carta illa, vel illius N., testatur*, the king would put in no such phrase, but himself dictated another phrase, never before employed (*antea inusitatam*), bearing witness in his own person concerning what he had seen in these words: *quoniam inspexi cartam Willelmi proaui mei, in qua prescripte libertates et quietancie et libere consuetudines ab eo prefate ecclesie concesse continebantur.*

The chronicler then goes on to report the king's explanation for this new formula, inserted so that the new charter might stand independently of its archetype, removing the necessity for both the earlier charter of William I and its confirmation by Henry II to be produced in evidence. The king is further-more said to have ordered that the new charter be written out and sealed with the royal seal in three separate exemplars, so that the monks would always have a copy at hand, even if one or two of the exemplars were in use elsewhere, pre-sumably so that the charter might be produced simultaneously before different sessions of the king's courts, meeting in eyre in other counties or in other places where the monks claimed lands or liberties.[24]

As Galbraith pointed out, the chronicler's account here is of fundamental significance to our understanding of the evolution of the instrument later to be known as the royal inspeximus, suggesting that the verb *inspexi* was first intro-duced to the charters of Henry II in 1175 or shortly thereafter, for very practical reasons. Some previous writers who had known of the Battle chronicler's remarks had dismissed them as mere fiction.[25] Such a dismissal had come to seem all the more justified once it became clear to modern historians that the monks of Battle were engaged in widespread forgery in the 1150s, attempting to invent for themselves an exemption from the local diocesan authority of the bishops of Chichester on the basis of spurious charters of kings William I and Henry I. The charter confirmed by Henry II in 1175 may well have been just such a forgery, supposedly issued by King William before 1089, but in fact

[24] Ibid. 308–13, the translation above being adapted from that by Searle.
[25] Thus Sir Thomas Hardy, in *Rotuli Chartarum* (London, 1837), p. v, dismissing the earlier notice afforded the chronicler's remarks by Lord Coke and Sir Francis Palgrave.

written some sixty years later.[26] It was Galbraith's achievement not only to refocus attention upon the chronicler's account of the new clause introduced in 1175, but to bring to light one of the three authentic exemplars which, as the chronicler claims, Henry II ordered to be written and sealed in favour of the Battle monks. This document, now British Library, Additional Charter 70981, is of undisputed authenticity, written in the hand of a royal chancery scribe identified by T. A. M. Bishop as scribe 'XL', active from at least 1163 until 1187, dated at Winchester, and witnessed by Geoffrey, bishop of Ely, and eight other courtiers. Since, in accordance with the chronicler's remarks, this surviving charter refers to Abbot Odo, and since it is witnessed by Richard de Lucy, who retired from court in April 1179 and died that August, it can be dated without doubt to the period between September 1175 and April 1179, probably to early in that period, shortly after Abbot Odo's consecration. Its identity with the charter described in the chronicle is supported by its contemporary endorsement *triplex*, suggesting that it was indeed produced in triplicate as the chronicler claims. Most significantly of all, its corroborative clause is more or less identical to that described by the chronicler: *quia inspexi cartam regis Willelmi proaui mei in qua prescripte libertates et quietancie et libere consuetudines ab eo prefate ecclesie concesse continebantur.*[27] Nor does the proof end here. Unknown to Galbraith, a duplicate exemplar of the same original survives in the East Sussex Record Office at Lewes, in more or less identical terms save for the omission of the last two witnesses, and written in yet another recognizable chancery hand, identified by Bishop as that of scribe 'XLV', whose career spanned the service of both Henry II and Richard I, from *c.*1175 to 1189.[28]

By proving the basic accuracy of the Battle Chronicle's account of the inspeximus charter granted by Henry II to Battle *c.*1175, Galbraith appeared to lend credence to others of the Chronicle's stories relating to seals, charters, and royal confirmations. However, as I have demonstrated elsewhere, the chronicler's account of the introduction of the inspeximus may be less reliable than Galbraith supposed.[29] In particular, and in potential contradiction of the chronicler's statement that the Battle inspeximus was an innovation, previously unknown (*antea inusitatam*), we find that at much the same date as the Battle charter of 1175, possibly even a few months earlier, a charter of Henry II with the

[26] The charter of William I confirmed in the 1170s is identified by Searle, 'Forged Charters', 462–3, as London, British Library, Cotton Charter xvi. 28, further discussed by Bates, *Regesta William I*, 147–9, no. 19, version 1.

[27] London, British Library, Additional Charter 70981, as printed by Galbraith, 'New Charter', 73. For the scribe, see T. A. M. Bishop, *Scriptores Regis* (Oxford, 1961), 52, no. 328 and pl. xxxiv(a). The charter had earlier been printed in the *Proceedings of the Society of Antiquaries*, 2nd ser., 3 (1867), 408–11, and see also B. Scofield, 'The Lane Bequest', *British Museum Quarterly*, 11 (1937), 73–6.

[28] Lewes, East Sussex Record Office, MS BAT7, and for the scribe see Bishop, *Scriptores Regis*, 37, no. 26 and pl. xxxvii(b).

[29] N. Vincent, 'The Charters of King Henry II: The Introduction of the Royal Inspeximus Revisited', *Dating Undated Medieval Charters*, ed. M. Gervers (Budapest and Woodbridge, 2000), 197–220.

selfsame clause *inspexi* was issued to Battle's arch-rival, the bishop of Chichester.[30] To discover both Battle and Chichester in possession of so unusual an instrument is most intriguing, and suggests either that the bishop insisted upon obtaining a privilege in emulation of the monks' charter, or that the monks copied the bishop. In either event, the survival of inspeximus charters of Henry II for both Battle and Chichester suggests that the award of Battle's charter was a more controversial event than the Chronicle allows, and certainly that the Chronicle tells us only part of the story. To this extent, the Chronicle's account and the undoubtedly genuine inspeximus charter of Henry II for Battle cannot in themselves be taken as proof that others of the abbey's stories and royal charters are genuine.

With this in mind, let us turn to another well-known story, placed by the Battle Chronicle at some point in the 1160s. In the time of Abbot Ralph (1107–24), so the Chronicle states, the monks of Battle obtained three measures of land at Barnhorne in Bexhill (Sussex) from a man named Ingram 'beacon-rider', a vassal of Withelard de Bailleul, obtaining written confirmations of their new estate from Withelard and from King Henry I. Later, however, the land was seized back by the Bailleul family, leading to a plea before King Henry II at Clarendon, at some time between 1163 and 1166. On this occasion the cyrographs of purchase and gift were read before the court, together with the charters of confirmation. Gilbert de Bailleul, the monks' opponent, objected that although he had heard the cyrographs of his ancestors read, he saw no seals appended to them. Richard de Lucy, the king's chief justiciar and the brother of Abbot Walter of Battle, asked whether Gilbert himself possessed a seal. When he answered that he did, the great man smiled: 'It was not the custom in the past', he said. 'for every petty knight to have a seal.' Gilbert continued to challenge the authenticity of the charters of his ancestors and of King Henry I shown in court. Taking the charter and the seal of his grandfather, King Henry I, into his own hands, Henry II turned to Gilbert: '"By God's eyes", he said, "if you could prove this charter false, you would make me a profit of a thousand pounds in England . . . If by a like charter and confirmation the monks could show this sort of right to Clarendon itself, which I dearly love, there would be no just way for me to deny it to them."' As a result, the monks won their plea. The king could not prove their charter false, and with the assent of his entire court, sent letters under his own seal to the four knights who governed the county of Sussex, demanding that they restore the land to the monks of Battle.[31]

---

[30] A charter of Henry II in favour of Bishop John of Chichester, confirming the bishop's rights of free warren as inspected in the charters of the king's predecessors: *sicut carta regis Willelmi et carte regis Henrici aui mei quas ego inspexi et carte mee testantur*: best preserved in PRO C53/125 (Charter Roll 12 Edward III) m. 22, in an inspeximus of 1338, whence *Calendar of Charter Rolls 1327–41*, 440, no. 5. This Chichester charter, unknown to Galbraith and undoubtedly genuine, was issued at Portsea in Hampshire between 1175 and 1179, and in theory could date from some six months before the earliest possible date for the inspeximus charter granted to Battle: Vincent, 'The Inspeximus', 109.

[31] *Battle Chronicle*, 210–19, here adapting the translation by Searle.

As Sir James Holt has remarked, this is an extremely fine story, treasured by social historians and by all good students of diplomatic alike.[32] Richard de Lucy's quoted remarks on the spread of knightly seals, the challenge to early, unsealed diplomas, and the king's obligation to confirm the charters of his ancestors have been widely cited by authorities on writing and the written word.[33] Some time ago Holt took an axe to at least part of the chronicler's story by suggesting that the instruments shown to Henry II, including the supposed charters of Ingram 'beacon-rider', Withelard de Bailleul, and a confirmation by Henry, count of Eu, known from originals or from copies in the Battle cartularies, are all of them fairly crude forgeries, manufactured in the mid-twelfth-century, probably at the time of the plea of 1163–6.[34] Holt further impugned the authenticity of the supposed confirmation charter of Henry I.[35] His remarks here are amply supported by an examination of the original charter of the king, recently brought to light in the East Sussex Record Office, and written in a peculiar hand, similar, if not identical, to the hands of a large number of early royal charters forged at Battle.[36]

As Holt was aware, the Battle cartularies also preserve copies of three writs or charters of Henry II, supposedly issued in response to the litigation of the 1160s. The first of these, issued at Clarendon with general address, survives also as an original in the East Sussex Record Office, confirming three virgates in Barnhorne together with its marsh as pleaded by Abbot Walter of Battle in accordance with his charter of Henry I, before the king at Clarendon.[37] The

---

[32] J.C. Holt, 'More Battle Forgeries', *Reading Medieval Studies*, 11 (1985), 75–86, at 75.

[33] See e.g. M. T. Clanchy, *From Memory to Written Record: England 1066–1307* (London, 1979), 22–3, 36. For a further case (1163) in which Henry II was confronted with a claim based upon unsealed documents, in this instance Anglo-Saxon diplomas, and in which he is said to have supported the claim on the basis of a sealed charter of Henry I confirming the earlier diplomas, maintaining that the charter and seal of Henry I might serve to warrant the unsealed archetypes, see *Gesta Abbatum Monasterii Sancti Albani*, ed. H. T. Riley (London, 1867), I, 150–1.

[34] Holt, 'Battle Forgeries', 75–86. For the Bailleul descent, in which Osbern, the Domesday tenant holding of the counts of Eu who themselves had seized Bexhill from the bishops of Chichester, was succeeded by his son Withelard (*fl. temp.* Henry I) and his grandson Geoffrey (*fl. temp.* Stephen), Geoffrey by his son Osbern or Osbert (m. Maza, *fl.* 1138 x 1153), Osbert by his son Gilbert (*fl.* 1166), and Gilbert by his son Geoffrey, all of them tenants both at Barnhorne and at Haverhill in Suffolk, held of the Clare earls of Hertford, see London, British Library, MS Harley 2110 (Castle Acre cartulary), fol. 108r (102r). For the family, native to Bailleul-sur-Eaulne (dép. Seine-Maritime), see L.C. Loyd, *The Origins of Some Anglo-Norman Families*, Harleian Soc., 103 (1951), 11.

[35] Holt, 'Battle Forgeries', 78–9: 'The charter of King Henry I is plainly a shabby, unconvincing piece of draftmanship.' The charter itself is printed from cartulary copies in *Regesta Regum Anglo-Normannorum*, ed. H. W. C. Davis, C. Johnson, H. A. Cronne, and R. H. C. Davis, 4 vols. (Oxford, 1913–69), II, no. 1061, p. 330, and by Holt, 'Battle Forgeries', 83–4, no. 4.

[36] Lewes, East Sussex Record Office, MS Ac.4795 (Deanery of Battle), no. 2, sealed *sur simple queue*, seal impression missing. There is a marked similarity here to the script of various of Battle's forged charters of King William I, especially in the characteristic capitalization of the *MARTINO* of *confirmasse Deo et sancto MARTINO et monachis de Bello*. For comparison, see the forgeries in British Library, Cotton Charter xvi. 28; Additional Charter 70980; Harley Charter 83.A.12, as described by Searle, 'Forged Charters', 454–6, 458–9, 462–3, nos. 1, 4, 8.

[37] Lewes, East Sussex Record Office MS Ac.4795 (Deanery of Battle), no. 3, with cartulary copies in

second notifies Count John of Eu of this decision,[38] and the third, issued at Westminster, again with general address, confirms the land in similar terms to the first of the three charters.[39] In accordance with the general verdict upon the Battle Chronicle—that it is a reliable source for litigation brought after 1154, using forgery only for its account of conditions before the reign of Henry II — Holt assumed that the three Barnhorne charters of Henry II were themselves entirely genuine, albeit that they were obtained as a result of the use of other, forged evidences. In fact there is good reason to regard even the Henry II charters with suspicion. To begin with, although supposedly issued before 1172, all three, including the surviving original, carry the *Dei gratia* clause, long recognized as a feature introduced to Henry II's charters only after 1172.[40] The original, sealed on a tongue (which itself is somewhat peculiar in a confirmation with general address), is written in an otherwise unknown hand, almost certainly of the twelfth century, but not recorded elsewhere in the king's chancery productions.[41] This original is unique amongst the more than 500 genuine surviving originals of Henry II in opening with the king's name, spelled not as the initial *H.* of *Henricus*, which is otherwise a universal practice, but as the four opening letters *Henr'*.[42] It refers to the charter of King Henry I as the *carta regis Henr(ici) aui mei quam vidi*, a formula which is extremely rare.[43] Moreover, its corroborative clause, which we would expect to open with some variation upon *Quare volo et firmiter precipio*, instead follows a different pattern, *Volo igitur et firmiter precipio*, recorded elsewhere in only a handful of examples.[44] For all of these

San Marino, Huntington Library MS BA29 (Battle cartulary), fol. 35r–v; London, Lincoln's Inn Library MS Hale 87 (Battle cartulary) fo. 17r.

[38] San Marino, Huntington Library, MS BA29, fols. 35v–36r; Lincoln's Inn, MS Hale 87, fol. 17v.

[39] PRO C66/436 (Patent Roll 12 Henry VI part 2), m. 33, in an inspeximus of 1434, as printed in *Calendar of Patent Rolls 1429–36*, 364–5, also in San Marino, Huntington Library, MS BA29, fol. 36r; Lincoln's Inn, MS Hale 87, fol. 17v.

[40] For a survey of the extensive literature on the *Dei gratia* clause, whose significance was first noted by Léopold Delisle, see Vincent, 'The Inspeximus', 98–9.

[41] I am grateful to Robert Patterson for his opinion here, albeit based upon a wholly lamentable xerox shown to him in great haste.

[42] For the convention, see Bishop, *Scriptores Regis*, 13. For a forged original of Henry II with the same spelling of the king's name, probably manufactured in the thirteenth century, see Hereford Cathedral Muniments, no. 2178, printed by R. B. Patterson, *The Original Acta of St Peter's Abbey, Gloucester c.1122 to 1263*, Bristol and Gloucestershire Archaeological Soc., Record Series, 11 (1998), 268–9, no. 352, where it is (in my opinion) wrongly described as a genuine charter produced outside the royal chancery. It is worth pointing out that an original charter of Henry I to Battle, supposedly issued at Worthing, witnessed by Robert, bishop of Lincoln, William the chaplain, and Eudo Dapifer (d. *c.*1120), not noticed in the *Regesta*, adopts the same peculiar spelling of the king's name *Henr'*, and the *Dei gratia* clause, which itself was commonly used in Henry I's chancery before 1135: Lewes, East Sussex Record Office, MS BAT1. A charter of Henry II to Shrewsbury Abbey, supposedly issued in 1155, preserves an equally suspicious rendering of the king's name, spelled out in full as *Henricus*: Oxford, Bodleian Library MS Shropshire Charter 86, whence *The Cartulary of Shrewsbury Abbey*, ed. U. Rees (Aberystwyth, 1975), I, 41–6, no. 36. Note here the otherwise unique reference to William, earl of Gloucester, as 'earl of Bristol'.

[43] See Vincent, 'The Inspeximus', 104–5.

[44] For the only other examples of this formula known, save for two of the three charters under discussion here, see *Cartularium . . . de Colecestria*, ed. S. A. Moore (Roxburgh Club, 1897), 24, 38–9; British

reasons, and most notably for its combination of a unique spelling of the king's name with the *Dei gratia* clause before 1172, the charter must be classified either as a poorly drafted original drawn up by the beneficiary, or as an outright forgery. If a forgery, then it casts doubt upon the two other Barnhorne charters of Henry II that are also found in the Battle cartularies, both of them employing *Dei gratia* before 1172, with the charter supposedly issued at Westminster also making use of the clause *cartam Henrici regis quam vidi*. None of these three charters, it should be noted, can be easily identified with the document which the chronicler describes as being addressed to 'the four knights who at that time, by the king's order, governed Sussex'. Professor Searle sought to identify these knights as 'local justiciars . . . acting in place of a sheriff in the county'.[45] In reality, the office of local justiciar was virtually defunct by the 1160s, and in Sussex there was a royal sheriff in office, Roger Hay, from Michaelmas 1163 until Easter 1170.[46] The Chronicle's reference to four knights appears at best a misunderstanding, and at worst an anachronism introduced because the chronicler was writing about a time and an event of which he had only second-hand knowledge.

Furthermore, as Holt himself was aware, the dispute over Barnhorne did not end in the 1160s with the award of Henry's charters.[47] There is evidence that the monks' tenure there was still in dispute in the 1190s,[48] and in 1203 it resulted in a plea being brought before the court of King John in which the grandson of Ingram 'beacon-rider', John of Northeye, claimed that his father, Reiner, under-tenant at Barnhorne, had been a minor in the wardship of his uncle, Alured de St Martin, at the time that the monks claimed that he had lost his suit at Clarendon. The monks produced their charter from Henry II, to be identified as the original charter whose authenticity we have called into question, demonstrating that the original itself was undoubtedly in existence by 1203 at the latest.[49] There is no record of the outcome of John of Northeye's plea, save

Library MSS Cotton Claudius C. xi (Ely cartulary), fol. 348r; Tiberius C. viii (Wymondham cartulary), fols. 16v–17r. The last of these is almost certainly forged.

[45] *Battle Chronicle*, 218 n.

[46] *List of Sheriffs for England and Wales*, List and Index Soc., 9 (1898), 135, in accordance with the sheriffs' accounts that can be traced in the pipe rolls. For the local justiciars, see H. A. Cronne, 'The Office of Local Justiciar in England under the Norman Kings', *University of Birmingham Historical Journal*, 6 (1957), 18–38, noting that in general only one justiciar operated in each county, not four, and D. M. Stenton, *English Justice Between the Norman Conquest and the Great Charter 1066–1215* (Philadelphia, 1964), 65–70, noting the abandonment of the system in the 1160s.

[47] Holt, 'Battle Forgeries', 81.

[48] For subsidiary claims at Barnhorne by the Icklesham family, settled by a charter of dubious authenticity supposedly issued by Robert of Icklesham whilst on crusade in the 1190s, see J. Sayers, 'English Charters from the Third Crusade', *Tradition and Change: Essays in Honour of Marjorie Chibnall*, ed. D. Greenway, C. Holdsworth, and J. Sayers (Cambridge, 1985), 207–13; *Battle Chronicle*, 218–20.

[49] For the plea of 1203, first referred to in 1199, in which the charter of Henry II that still survives as an original was paraphrased in court as the monks' chief evidence, see *Rotuli Curiae Regis*, ed. F. Palgrave, 2 vols. (London, 1835), II, 136; *Curia Regis Rolls of the Reigns of Richard I, John and Henry III*, 18 vols. (London, 1922–), II, 178–9. For subsequent litigation, suggesting that, despite the pleas of the 1160s

for the evidence that Battle retained possession of Barnhorne thereafter.[50] Nonetheless it opens up two further avenues of enquiry. To begin with, it should be noted that Barnhorne, within Bexhill, formed part of an estate that in the 1160s had only recently been restored by the counts of Eu to the overlordship of Bishop Hilary of Chichester. With this restoration, accomplished after 1148, the Bailleuls and their three knights' fees at Bexhill became subject to the bishops, with Bishop Hilary granting a charter of enfeoffment to Geoffrey de Bailleul, the ancestor of the Gilbert de Bailleul subsequently impleaded by Battle.[51] This in itself must set us on our guard, since it suggests that Battle's claim to possess land at Barnhorne, supported by charters of the counts of Eu, dated from a time, before 1148, when Barnhorne and Bexhill had been detained by the counts. In the 1160s, however, it was Bishop Hilary, not Gilbert de Bailleul, who was the rightful overlord of Barnhorne. To this extent, the Barnhorne dispute should be seen as part of the wider rivalry between Battle and Chichester, perhaps as the outcome of Bishop Hilary's attempt to win back a part of the Bexhill estate that had been alienated whilst in the hands of the counts of Eu.[52] By portraying the dispute as one merely between the monks of Battle and the family of Gilbert de Bailleul, and by glossing over the identity of Gilbert's overlord, the Battle chronicler may well be guilty of obscuring the dispute's true significance. In these circumstances, given that it was the bishop of Chichester,

and 1203, the descendants of Ingram and Reiner continued to hold land at Bexhill, see *Curia Regis Rolls*, XI, no. 2734; XII, no. 2476; *An Abstract of Feet of Fines relating to the County of Sussex*, ed. L. F. Salzmann, 2 vols., Sussex Record Soc., 2: 7 (1902–8), I, nos. 430, 499. For Ingram of Northeye as witness to a general confirmation of John, count of Eu, 1140 x 1170, in favour of the Battle monks, see London University Library, MS Fuller Collection I/28/1. It is conceivable that he is the same man as Ingram 'of Hastings', sheriff of Hastings early in the twelfth century: J. A. Green, *English Sheriffs to 1154*, Public Record Office Handbooks, 24 (1990), 81.

[50] The 40s. said to have been offered by John of Northeye to have a jury to decide upon his claims goes unmentioned in either the fine or the pipe rolls, suggesting that it may never have been paid.

[51] *Victoria County History: Sussex*, IX, 118, 120; *The Red Book of the Exchequer*, ed. H. Hall, 3 vols., RS (London, 1896), I, 200, 202; Sayers, 'English Charters from the Third Crusade', 208–9; *The Acta of the Bishops of Chichester 1075–1207*, ed. H. Mayr-Harting, Canterbury and York Soc., 56 (1964), 90, no. 23, and for Gilbert as the heir of Geoffrey, see *Recueil des Actes de Henri II roi d'Angleterre et duc de Normandie*, ed. L. Delisle and E. Berger, 3 vols. (Paris, 1916–27) (henceforth Delisle and Berger, *Recueil*), II, no. 746 (p. 386, lines 21 ff.). Given their subsequent reassignment to the Ballieul family by the bishops of Chichester, there can be little doubt that the 10 hides restored by the count to the bishop after 1148 represented the 10 hides held in 1086 by Osbern, ancestor of the Bailleuls, out of a total of 20 hides which the then count of Eu is said to have seized from the bishop of Chichester. The remaining 10 hides, which after 1148 seem not to have been restored to the bishopric, were in 1086 divided between the count's demesne and a series of tenants. The three fees held by Gilbert de Bailleul from the count of Eu in 1166 (*Red Book*, I, 203) are unlikely to represent Gilbert's Bexhill fees, but others of the lands which since at least the 1080s had been held by Gilbert's ancestors from the count.

[52] For the subsequent exercise of the bishop of Chichester's lordship at Barnhorne and its subsidiary estate at Buckholt, including an award of a chapel at Buckholt to John of Northeye, the Bailleul undertenant, by Bishop Seffrid, 1180 x 1204, and an episcopal confirmation of a grant of land at Barnhorne made to Battle in 1261/2, see *The Chartulary of the High Church of Chichester*, ed. W. D. Peckham, Sussex Record Soc., 46 (1946), nos. 336, 869, 1053, with an original of one of these grants, now San Marino, Huntington Library, MS BA Box 14 no. 1513, formerly BA42/22, and see also *Custumals of Battle Abbey in the Reigns of Edward I and Edward II*, ed. S. R. Scargill-Bird, Camden Soc., 2nd ser., 41 (1887), 24.

not the count of Eu, who was Gilbert's overlord at Barnhorne, we may well wonder why one of the charters of Henry II, preserved in the Battle cartularies and supposedly confirming the settlement made at Clarendon, should be directed to the count and not the bishop. Secondly, the mention of Alured de St Martin as the guardian and uncle of the Bailleul under-tenant at Barnhorne, Reiner of Northeye, renders the chronicler's claim that King Henry found in favour of the monks of Battle that much more improbable. Alured de St Martin was a prominent courtier of Henry II, and would surely have been in a position to resist any attempt to deprive his nephew and ward of the land, especially if the nephew had been a minor, incapable of defending himself when the land was impleaded at Clarendon.[53] To this extent, the evidence from all sources save for those controlled by Battle Abbey confirms our suspicion that the charters of Henry II over Barnhorne, and indeed the chronicler's entire account of the dispute, are very far from trustworthy.

If our suspicions here are justified, then the story of Barnhorne as recorded in the Battle Chronicle is shot through with forgery. Not only did the monks forge charters of their early benefactors and of Henry I, but the chronicler's entire account of the confirmation supposedly supplied for these forgeries by Henry II is itself yet a further piece of myth-making, intended to supply a context and circumstantial support for charters of Henry II that were themselves manufactured by the Battle monks. Such forgery within forgery would be by no means unique. In a notorious case, recently unravelled by Martin Brett, the monks of Rochester can be shown not merely to have forged charters attributed to their eleventh- and early twelfth-century benefactors, but to have gone on from this to forge inspeximuses, and even inspeximuses of inspeximuses, intended to prove that the initial forgeries had been confirmed by successive archbishops of Canterbury throughout the twelfth and thirteenth centuries.[54] Nor is the dispute over Barnhorne the only, or indeed the most blatant, example of such deceit to be found in the Battle Chronicle.

The most detailed of the chronicler's narratives, occupying nearly a quarter of his entire chronicle, concerns the process by which Abbot Walter de Lucy of Battle obtained confirmation of his liberties from Henry II between 1155 and May 1157. The case was a significant one, since the charters of King William for which Abbot Walter sought confirmation, all of them long since exposed as

---

[53] For Alured, a leading tenant of the counts of Eu, probably native to St-Martin-le-Gaillard (dép. Seine-Maritime), introduced to the Eu estates in England c.1160, certainly active at court by 1171, founder of the Cistercian abbey of Robertsbridge in Sussex, see *Report on the Manuscripts of Lord De L'Isle and Dudley Preserved at Penshurst Place*, vol. 1, ed. C. L. Kingsford, Historical Manuscripts Commission (London, 1925), 33–8, 57; L. Delisle, *Recueil des actes de Henri II roi d'Angleterre et duc de Normandie concernant les provinces françaises et les affaires de France: Introduction* (Paris, 1909), 354–5; Delisle and Berger, *Recueil*, I, nos. 413–14, 434; II, no. 713; *Battle Chronicle*, 314–15. For further proof of his close association with the Northeye family, the Bailleul undertenants at Barnhorne, see *MSS of Lord De L'Isle and Dudley*, I, 39–40, 54–5.

[54] M. Brett, 'Forgery at Rochester', *Fälschungen im Mittelalter*, MGH Schriften XXXIII (1988), IV, 397–412. Several of the charters of Henry II for Rochester belong to this pattern of forgery.

forgeries, were intended to exempt Battle entirely from the authority of the local diocesan, the bishop of Chichester. The story of these documents has been several times retold, most recently by Eleanor Searle, who deserves credit for the meticulous way in which she has traced and edited the forged materials upon which the abbey's claims were based.[55] Searle, rather surprisingly, professed ignorance as to the precise reason why the dispute between Battle and Chichester came to a head in 1155.[56] The Chronicle itself makes plain that the dispute was, at least in part, a personal one, sparked off by the failure of Bishop Hilary of Chichester to endorse the candidacy of Abbot Walter of Battle for the see of London, vacated at the death of Bishop Robert in September 1150.[57]

In 1155, according to the chronicler, the dispute between monks and bishop reached fever pitch, with the bishop threatening to excommunicate the Battle monks should they refuse to attend his episcopal synod when summoned. Abbot Walter, with his powerful contacts at court, showed the abbey's supposed charters of exemption granted by William I during a royal council held at London in Lent. Henry II promised to confirm these charters under his seal. However, Bishop Hilary complained to Theobald, archbishop of Canterbury, that the proposed confirmation would run contrary to Theobald's own privileges.[58] His motives here become obvious when we examine the Battle forgeries, which claim to award the same freedom from episcopal control to Battle as was enjoyed by the monks of Christ Church, Canterbury. The archbishops of Canterbury had never recognized any such exemption for their own cathedral monks, nor, so far as we can judge, had the Canterbury monks advanced any such claim to exemption in the past. That they did so now suggests a serious breakdown in their relations with the archbishop.[59] In 1155 it seems that the monks of Battle and Christ Church joined forces to launch a claim to exemption: a claim that threatened Archbishop Theobald even more seriously than it threatened Hilary of Chichester. Christ Church, after all, was the archbishop's cathedral church, whereas Battle was merely one convent amongst many within the diocese of Chichester.

As a result, the archbishop appealed to the king, asking that no royal charter of confirmation for Battle be sealed, pending discussion. The king refused to delay the sealing of the charter, but nonetheless commanded that it was not to be released from the keeping of the chancellor until it had been properly

[55] Searle, 'Forged Charters', 449–80; *Battle Chronicle*, 150–211, and cf. Bates, *Regesta of William I*, nos. 13–25.

[56] Searle, 'Forged Charters', 453; *Battle Chronicle*, 21–2.

[57] *Battle Chronicle*, 190–1, and for the London election, in which Abbot Walter's rival was widely accused of simony, an accusation referred to in the *Battle Chronicle*, see A. Saltman, *Theobald Archbishop of Canterbury* (London, 1956), 117–19.

[58] *Battle Chronicle*, 146–55. For the specific issues at stake here: the bishop's right to summon the abbot to attend and obey the diocesan synod; the bishop's claim to hospitality at Battle as a matter of right; and his claim to carry out the blessing of new abbots and to exact an oath of obedience, see *Battle Chronicle*, 148–9; Knowles, 'Essays in Monastic History IV', 224–5.

[59] For Theobald's often stormy relations with his monks, see Saltman, *Theobald*, 56–64.

discussed.[60] A meeting was duly convened at Lambeth between Bishop Hilary, Archbishop Theobald, and Thomas Becket, the chancellor. At Lambeth Henry II's confirmation charter was publicly read, 'until at a particular phrase in the reading—that the church of Battle be wholly free from all subjection to bishops, like Christ Church, Canterbury—a shout went up from all sides'.[61] The Chronicle itself reports that some complained that the phrase was contrary to the privileges of Canterbury, and others that it ran contrary to canon law—clearly because it was unheard of for a king, rather than a pope, to award immunity from episcopal authority. As a result of this uproar the chancellor took the charter away with him, to be stored in the king's chapel.[62] Thereafter, in the summer of 1155, whilst the king was besieging Bridgnorth—an event which carries us to June or July—he was once again approached by the abbot of Battle, who through handsome gifts and, according to the chronicler, as the result of intercessions by Battle's patron saint St Martin, at last obtained the king's agreement to release the earlier charter, a decision that is said to have been made on 10 July. The abbot returned in triumph to Battle, carrying with him Henry II's sealed confirmation.[63]

Let us pause here a moment to examine the confirmation charter of Henry II whose issue is said to have been so vigorously disputed. If the chronicler's account is to be believed, the charter referred to in the Chronicle is almost certainly the same charter of Henry II that survives in two of the Battle cartularies, and in chancery enrolments of 1431 and 1486.[64] By it, the king confirms the possessions of Battle and its dependencies at St Nicholas' Exeter and Brecon, listed in detail, reciting the circumstances in which King William I had come to found the abbey, and confirming the abbey's liberties, including quittance from most secular burdens, from assarts in the king's forests, 'and from all subjection and oppression of bishops or exaction of any other persons in perpetuity, free and quit in the same way as Christ Church, Canterbury'. In this it is modelled, more or less word for word, upon a forged privilege of King Henry I to Battle, which in turn borrows its reference to Christ Church, Canterbury, from an equally spurious diploma of William I.[65] Just as the forged charter of Henry I is addressed, inelegantly, to Archbishop William of Canterbury, bishops Roger of

<hr/>

[60] *Battle Chronicle*, 154–7, stating unambiguously that the charter was sealed at the king's command.
[61] Ibid. 156–9.   [62] Ibid. 158–9.   [63] Ibid. 158–61.
[64] PRO C66/431 (Patent Roll 10 Henry VI part 1), mm. 21–2, whence *Calendar of Patent Rolls 1429–36*, 174–5, and PRO C56/12 (Confirmation Roll 2 Henry VII part 3), m. 1, no. 5, also in the thirteenth-century cartulary in London, Lincoln's Inn, MS Hale 87, fols. 16v–17r, and the mid-fourteenth-century cartulary at San Marino, Huntington Library, MS BA29, fols. 34r–35r. Save for minor variations in spelling, and the fact that the Lincoln's Inn version is more heavily abbreviated, lacking the witnesses, the copies are all more or less identical.
[65] For the charter of Henry I, see *Regesta*, II, no. 1896; Searle, 'Forged Charters', 457–8, 471–2, no. 3. For the charter of William I, now London, British Library, Harley Charter 83A12, see Searle, 'Forged Charters', 454–5, 469–70, no. 1, with further proofs of forgery in Bates, *Regesta of William I*, 161–5, no. 22. The charters of Henry I and Henry II are conveniently printed side by side in Dohmen, 'Privilegs', 219–20.

Salisbury and Seffrid of Chichester, and 'all other barons, both French and English, and sheriffs and their ministers in whose sheriffdoms the church of St Martin at Battle has lands or other possessions', witnessed by Archbishop William and Bishop Seffrid; so Henry II's confirmation follows the same form of address, substituting Archbishop Theobald for the three bishops addressed in the charter of Henry I, and being witnessed by Archbishop Theobald, Thomas the chancellor, and Richard de Lucy. Unlike the Henry I exemplar, which is dated at Rouen, the Henry II confirmation carries no place of issue.

Of all the documents that we have considered so far, this supposed confirmation charter of Henry II is perhaps the most remarkable. It is also the most blatant forgery. It carries the *Dei gratia* clause in all surviving copies, despite being awarded long before 1172. Its failure to specify a place of issue and its use of the term *vicecomitatus* in the address are both most peculiar, although various of these features might be explained by the fact that it is so closely modelled upon the forged charter of Henry I.[66] Far more damning a proof of its forgery is the fact that it is both addressed to and witnessed by Archbishop Theobald. This in itself makes it virtually impossible for us to accept the charter as a genuine award of Henry II, since it is inconceivable that Theobald would have assented to an award that not only guaranteed the spiritual exemption of Battle Abbey by royal command, but at the same time extended precisely this same exemption to Theobald's own cathedral convent at Christ Church, Canterbury. By doing so, Theobald would, in effect, have resigned any claim to discipline or govern his own monks, whereas, on the contrary, we know that Theobald and his successors continued to claim extensive powers over their cathedral convent. To this extent, our document is about as improbable as an application to the Communist party signed and sealed by Senator Joseph McCarthy.[67]

We might bear in mind here that during the hearing at Lambeth in 1155 Bishop Hilary of Chichester is said to have complained that, although the abbey had shown its privilege of King William, there was nowhere any evidence that the privilege itself had been witnessed by or known to the bishop's

---

[66] The address to Henry II's charter reads, inelegantly but in imitation of the Henry I exemplar: 'Theobaldo Cant' archiepiscopo omnibusque episcopis, comitibus, baronibus Francis et Anglis et vicecomitibus et ministris eorum in quorum vicecomitatibus ecclesia sancti Martini de Bello terras habet vel possessiones aliquas salutem.' Elsewhere, at least two genuine writs of Henry II are addressed in the basic form *omnibus vicecomitibus in quorum vicecomitatibus X terras tenet salutem: Calendar of Charter Rolls 1257–1300*, 106; *The Manuscripts of the Duke of Rutland at Belvoir Castle*, vol. IV, Historical Manuscripts Comm. (London, 1905), 108, and cf. Delisle and Berger, *Recueil*, I, no. 181; Westminster Abbey Muniments, MS Domesday, fol. 458v, this last being of distinctly dubious authenticity. However, in all cases, save that of Battle, the formula presupposes an address to the sheriffs, or the sheriffs and their officials, not, as at Battle, to an archbishop and bishops as well as to the sheriffs.

[67] In her initial survey of the Battle forgeries, published in 1967, even Professor Searle appears to have entertained doubts about the authenticity of Henry II's charter, referring to it with the all-important caveat 'if genuine': 'Forged Charters', 459, n. 2. Since thereafter the authenticity of the charter became central to Searle's entire reading of the chronicle, it is easier to understand why she made no attempt to follow through her initial doubts to their natural conclusion. In her edition of 1980 the question of the charter's authenticity is not once addressed.

predecessors.[68] Not to be outwitted, by 1157 the monks of Battle went on to forge yet a further version of their supposed privileges, in which William I's charter was recast as one specifically directed to and witnessed by Archbishop Lanfranc and by Bishop Stigand of Chichester, thereby outflanking Bishop Hilary's objection.[69] The address to Theobald, and his supposed attestation to the confirmation charter of Henry II, appear to fit into a similar pattern of deceit.[70] The claim, stated in both the Chronicle and the supposed confirmation charter of Henry II, that Theobald recognized an exemption for the monks of Christ Church is rendered all the more unlikely by the fact that at precisely this time Theobald was engaged in a dispute over exemption with the neighbouring abbey of St Augustine's at Canterbury—a dispute from which he was to emerge largely victorious.[71] The Battle Chronicle itself refers to the claims of St Augustine's as having been debated before the king at Colchester in May 1157, shortly before the second hearing of the Battle dispute.[72] Two months later Theobald obtained the profession of obedience from the abbot of St Augustine's that he had long been seeking.[73]

This mention of the disputes of 1157 carries us on to the aftermath of the events of 1155 as narrated by the Chronicle. Bishop Hilary, so the Chronicle states, refused to accept the decision of 1155, and instead pursued his claim to obedience from the abbot of Battle, employing against Abbot Walter a papal mandate that Hilary had already solicited as part of the dispute of 1155. After further contention the case was once again carried before the king, during a council held at Colchester in May 1157. Here the chronicler deploys his considerable narrative powers, to 're-create' the speeches that were made by the opposing parties, devising a set piece that has quite rightly earned inclusion in all subsequent studies of the contending jurisdictions of king and papacy. Bishop Hilary, so the chronicler claims, delivered a speech that enraged the king by its references, in classically papal-canonical language, to the twin powers of Church and State, quoting Matthew 16.18 on the authority awarded by Christ to the popes via St Peter.[74] At the same time Richard de Lucy delivered a resounding panegyric, extolling the virtues of the Normans against the wily English.[75] The king, after much debate, forced a decision in favour of the

---

[68] *Battle Chronicle*, 158–9.

[69] Ibid. 194–7; Searle, 'Forged Charters', 458–9, 473–4, no. 4, subsequently replaced with an even more conclusive forgery: ibid. 465, 473–4, no. 10.

[70] Here the fact that the charter of Henry I upon which Henry II's charter is modelled, is indeed both addressed to and witnessed by Bishop Seffrid of Chichester, suggests that the Henry I charter was not in existence in 1155. This in turn would place the forgery of Henry II's confirmation in 1157 or later, even though the chronicler states specifically that Henry II's charter referring to the liberties of Christ Church, Canterbury, was issued in 1155.

[71] Saltman, *Theobald*, 64–75.   [72] *Battle Chronicle*, 180–1.

[73] Saltman, *Theobald*, 74–5. For the revival of St Augustine's claims in the 1180s, see E. John, 'The Litigation of an Exempt House, St Augustine's Canterbury, 1182–1237', *Bulletin of the John Rylands Library*, 39 (1957), 390–415.

[74] *Battle Chronicle*, 184–7.   [75] Ibid. 178–9, 182–3.

abbey's privileges, denouncing the bishop for his attempt to seek papal intervention, and persuading Bishop Hilary to deliver a complete and humiliating resignation of whatever diocesan authority he had claimed to exercise over the monks of Battle.[76]

For present purposes what is most striking about this hearing of 1157 is that it should ever have taken place. If the chronicler is to be believed, the king had already confirmed and reissued Battle's exemption by his charter of 1155. Yet, in reporting the revived dispute of 1157, the chronicler gives us to understand that the issues were debated as if no such confirmation had been granted. At the points when we would most expect it, whenever the 1155 charter is referred to in the pleadings of 1157, it is a document that had inspired as yet unresolved disputes.[77] Nowhere in these references to Henry II's confirmation charter is there any mention of the fact that the charter had already been engrossed, sealed, and dispatched to Battle, as the chronicler had earlier claimed. Nor is there any indication that in 1157, as the result of Battle's supposed victory, the king commanded the issue of a second royal confirmation that might be identified as the charter that still survives in the Battle cartularies. Even if he did, the confirmation preserved in the cartularies, with its mention of the liberties of Canterbury, would be no less suspicious a document, whether it be assigned to 1155 or 1157.

The only other documentary proof of Battle's victory of 1155–7, besides the Chronicle and the apparently forged charter of Henry II, is a letter of Archbishop Theobald, itself of very doubtful authenticity, reporting the debate that had taken place at Colchester in May 1157 and reciting, in words almost identical to those of the Chronicle, although without any reference to the liberties of Christ Church, the terms of the resignation of episcopal rights made by Bishop Hilary of Chichester.[78] Of course, it is possible that the correspondence between the Chronicle account and Theobald's letter reflects the fact that the chronicler was writing many years later, with Theobald's letter before him as he wrote. Set against this, however, there is good reason to doubt whether Theobald's letter is authentic. It may well be yet another forgery, all too suspiciously close to the report of the chronicler himself.[79] As to the supposed exemption of Christ Church, Canterbury, referred to in Henry II's Battle

---

[76] Ibid. 176–209. [77] See e.g. ibid. 174–8, 192–5, 202–7.

[78] Saltman, *Theobald*, 243, no. 11.

[79] Suspicions here focus upon the disjunction between the address, *uniuersis sancte matris ecclesie filiis*, and the opening of the charter proper, *Notum vobis facio fratres karissimi*. The archbishop might be expected to use 'brothers' in addressing his fellow bishops, but 'sons' when notifying the people at large. There is a further disjunction between the use of the first-person singular, and the account of Bishop Hilary's plea, heard *nobis omnibus audientibus*. The corroborative clause opens most oddly, *Quod ego etiam*, and employs a unique form in referring to the archbishop's legatine office: *auctoritate episcopali et sicut sancte Romane ecclesie lelegatus (sic) presenti scripto confirmo*. The attestation of Roger, archbishop of York, is unique amongst Theobald's charters, but might be explained, quite innocently, by the unique nature of the case. Further cartulary copies at San Marino, Huntington Library, add Thomas, the king's chancellor and archdeacon of Canterbury, and Richard de Lucy to the witness list. I am indebted to Martin Brett for a discussion of this charter, and for much sage advice.

charter of the 1150s, nothing more is heard. In 1175, in the aftermath of the distinctly frosty relations that had prevailed between Archbishop Becket and the Canterbury monks, the monks are said to have asked to investigate the charters of Battle as a means of establishing their own claim to liberties.[80] In the event, however, they let the matter drop. When Prior Odo of Christ Church was elected abbot of Battle in 1175, he deliberately proclaimed his obedience, both at Canterbury and Battle, to the then archbishop, Richard, a former monk of Christ Church.[81] From a source which for once lies beyond the range of the Battle forgeries, the chronicler Ralph of Diss tells us, most significantly, that in carrying out the blessing of Abbot Odo in 1175, Archbishop Richard specifically declared that he was acting by virtue of his powers as legate, disclaiming any future prejudice to the bishops of Chichester: a disclaimer that suggests that the archbishop himself did not recognize Battle's right to exemption from the authority of Chichester.[82] Fifty years later, after the most bitter of disputes between the Canterbury monks and their archbishops, the monks of Christ Church were to forge for themselves a whole catalogue of liberties which they claimed had been conferred upon them by St Thomas, now transformed by memory into the chief protector, rather than an absentee disturber, of their convent.[83] But even here they held back from any claim to the complete exemption that would still have lurked for them amongst the muniments of Battle.

What can we conclude from all this? That there was dispute over exemption between the bishops of Chichester and the abbots of Battle there is no doubt. Writing in 1170 to the pope, the former royal chancellor, now archbishop, Thomas Becket, included the Battle affair amongst the more scandalous events of recent times, as proof that the kings of England had long ignored the privileges of the Church, well before Becket's own dispute with Henry II. 'And what of the bishop of Chichester?', Becket writes; 'What did it avail him against the abbot of Battle that, despite papal privileges, when he denounced the abbot in the Curia, and pronounced the abbot excommunicate, he was immediately forced to make public peace with the abbot, without any act of absolution, and to receive him with the kiss of peace?'[84] Clearly, Bishop Hilary had been forced

---

[80] *Battle Chronicle*, 278–97, esp. 284–5, 296–7; and for the relations between Becket and Christ Church, see Richard Southern's beautifully crafted essay, *The Monks of Canterbury and the Murder of Archbishop Becket*, William Urry Lecture (Canterbury, 1985). In 1175 the chronicler states that the monks of Canterbury looked to Battle, in an attempt to recover liberties awarded in charters destroyed in the recent Canterbury fire. The claim is mendacious, since the muniments of Christ Church undoubtedly survived the fire.

[81] *Battle Chronicle*, 296–307.

[82] *Radulfi de Diceto Decani Lundoniensis Opera Historica*, ed. W. Stubbs, 2 vols., RS (London, 1876), I, 403: 'Odo prior Cantuariensis electus in abbatem sancti Martini de Bello, bellum statim circa sue promotionis initium indixit episcopo diocesiano. Nam a metropolitano benedictionem accepit. Quod sibi licere iure legationis asserens, archiepiscopus nil in preiudicium ecclesie Cicestrensis egisse dicebat.'

[83] C. R. Cheney, 'Magna Carta Beati Thome: Another Canterbury Forgery', in Cheney, *Medieval Texts and Studies* (Oxford, 1973), 78–110.

[84] *Materials For the History of Thomas Becket*, ed. J. C. Robertson, 7 vols., RS (London, 1875–85), VII, 242–3, no. 643, as cited in *Battle Chronicle*, 208–9 n. The excommunication referred to here is mentioned

in some way to bow to royal pressure in his dispute with Battle. But the precise details of this settlement Becket's letter leaves uncertain. Likewise, although we know that Battle possessed charters of liberties from King Henry II, used to obtain quittance from fines for assarts in the king's forests after 1165 and referred to in the Exchequer pipe rolls, we have no way of knowing if these charters of Henry II are the same as those recorded in the Battle cartularies.[85] Whether or not we believe the Battle chronicler's account of the charters supposedly issued by Henry II, and of the abbey's victory in its dispute over exemption, will depend very much upon the degree of trust that we can place in others of the chronicler's remarks. Almost our only evidence here is supplied by the Chronicle itself and by the surviving charters and privileges preserved amongst the Battle Abbey muniments, and in these circumstances it is hardly surprising that charters and chronicler should confirm one another's claims. By the same token, however, the very fact that so many of the charters—not merely the eleventh-century charters, but the later confirmations by bishops and kings—are either undoubted forgeries or subject to grave suspicion must now give rise to questions about the nature of the Chronicle itself. Is the Chronicle, as has previously been supposed, a basically reliable account of twelfth-century litigation founded upon spurious privileges of earlier kings? Or is it instead a far more complex composition, intended to supply a circumstantial context for forgeries, not only of the eleventh-century but of all subsequent periods? If, as I have suggested, at least two of the charters of Henry II which are described with such circumstantial detail in the Chronicle are themselves forgeries, then what trust can we place in any other of the chronicler's claims? Can we, for example, continue to credit Richard de Lucy's supposed remarks on knightly seals, Bishop Hilary's pronouncement on the two powers, or the speeches attributed to Henry II on royal dignity and the use of royal charters, when so much of the background to these stories appears to be distorted or invented?[86]

---

on several occasions by the chronicler, but in terms that make it difficult to establish the exact sequence of events. Some sort of sentence appears to have been passed against the abbot shortly after 1148, followed by excommunication in 1154, relaxed later that year at the request of Archbishop Theobald, renewed in 1156, and not finally relaxed until the Colchester meeting of May 1157: *Battle Chronicle*, 150-1, 152-7, 164-7, 200-3, 206-7.

[85] *Pipe Roll 13 Henry II*, Pipe Roll Soc., 11 (1889), 8, 132 (*per libertatem cartarum ecclesie de Bello*); *Pipe Roll 14 Henry II*, Pipe Roll Soc., 12 (1890), 45 (*per cartam regis*). For these forest pleas of the 1160s, which inspired the monks to the forgery of a wide-ranging forest charter of William I, see *Battle Chronicle*, 220-3; Searle, 'Forged Charters', 460-1, no. 5; Bates, *Regesta of William I*, 151-5, no. 20. Besides the suspicious documents considered above, the Battle cartularies recite at least three other writs of Henry II—on the restoration of fugitive serfs, on quittance from toll, and of protection—that may well be genuine: San Marino, Huntington Library, MS BA29 (Battle cartulary), fols. 35r, 36r–v; Lincoln's Inn, MS Hale 87 (Battle cartulary) fol. 17r–v. Note, however, that the cartularies add the *Dei gratia* clause to all of these writs, despite the fact that two of the three date from before 1158.

[86] H. Mayr-Harting, 'Hilary, Bishop of Chichester (1147–1169) and Henry II', *EHR* 78 (1963), 209–24, long ago drew attention to the fact that, for all his supposed defence of papal privilege in the Battle dispute, Bishop Hilary appears as an out-and-out royalist on all other occasions. In an attempt to trace papal/canonical thought in Hilary's other writings, Mayr-Harting (pp. 216–17n.) cites a final

As to the much-vaunted exemption claimed by Battle, whose triumph the chronicler sets out to establish: take away the eleventh-century privileges and most of the early episcopal charters of Battle, all of which have long been recognized as forgeries; take away, furthermore, most of the charters of Henry II and the letters of Theobald said to have been issued in 1157, and what remains? The only charter of undoubted authenticity referred to in the Chronicle is Henry II's inspeximus granted c.1175, traceable, thanks to Galbraith, to its original exemplars, written by scribes of the royal chancery. Yet even here the genuine charter only throws further doubt upon the other, suspect documents. It is surely significant that, whilst Henry II's genuine confirmation charter of the late 1170s awards immunity from royal and secular burdens, it should do so without any reference to Battle's supposed exemption from the authority of the bishops of Chichester. Why should the genuine charter of c.1175 so signally omit the very exemption which, according to the Chronicle, had been confirmed by the king in 1155 and reconfirmed in 1157, and which is to be found, clearly set out, in Henry II's purported charter of the 1150s preserved in the Battle cartularies? In 1175, it is true, Abbot Odo of Battle refused blessing from his diocesan, turning instead to the papal legate Richard, archbishop of Canterbury. In carrying out the ceremony, however, the archbishop specifically renounced any future prejudice to the rights of Chichester.[87] In the same way, when the abbey's privileges were renewed in authentic charters of King Richard I (7 January 1198) and King John (18 December 1211), no mention whatsoever was made either of the abbey's supposed exemption from the bishops of Chichester, or of the privileges of Christ Church, Canterbury.[88] Might it not be that episcopal exemption was omitted from Henry II's genuine charter of the 1170s and from all subsequent royal confirmations, precisely because no such exemption had been recognized by Henry II in the first place, just as no such exemption had been recognized by any of the king's eleventh- or twelfth-century predecessors, by any bishop of Chichester, or by any archbishop of Canterbury?[89] Certainly, Battle advanced a claim to exemption: a claim that was disputed from the 1150s onwards, and that in the 1230s was at last to be carried before the popes. On this latter occasion the

concord supposedly drawn up before Hilary in the court of Henry II, which echoes the Roman Law tag *dolo malo*. However, the fine itself is almost certainly a forgery, as I shall show elsewhere, and in any event a vague echo of the *Corpus Iuris Ciuilis*, even if proved, would hardly substantiate the Battle chronicler's claims that Hilary served as an advocate of papal (not civilian) law in 1157.

[87] *Diceto*, I, 403.

[88] For Richard I's charter, see *Calendar of Patent Rolls 1429–36*, 176. For John's, see William Dugdale and Roger Dodsworth, *Monasticon Anglicanum*, ed. J. Caley and others, 6 vols. (London, 1846), III, 247; *Cartae Antiquae Rolls*, ed. L. Landon and J. Conway Davies, 2 vols., Pipe Roll Soc., ns, 17: 22 (1939–60), I, no. 212.

[89] One piece of tangential evidence is worth noticing here: a sermon extolling the virtues of obedience and counsel which Odo, prior of Christ Church, Canterbury, and later abbot of Battle, recalls preaching to a synod of priests, and of which he later prepared a summary. This might suggest that either at Canterbury or Battle Odo was accustomed to attending the diocesan synod, contrary to the Battle/Christ Church claim to exemption: *The Latin Sermons of Odo of Canterbury*, ed. C. de Clercq and R. Macken (Brussels, 1983), 33–4, 318–20.

bishop of Chichester immediately appealed against the abbey, and, as a result of hearings before papal judges delegate, obtained a drastic reduction in Battle's supposedly complete exemption.[90] Meanwhile, in the absence of any unimpeachably authentic charter of a king, pope, archbishop, or bishop confirming Battle's exemption from episcopal authority, we may legitimately suggest that Battle Abbey and its chronicler were duplicitous in their claim that Battle was exempt, conjuring up a world of make-believe from royal and episcopal charters, which were forged and reworked and thereafter incorporated within a narrative account, the Battle Chronicle, itself composed to lend credence to monastic fantasy. If so, then the monks' enterprise was a remarkably successful one, that has defied detection for the past seven centuries, and in the process supplied historians of twelfth-century diplomatic with some of their best-loved, but perhaps least reliable stories.

No doubt the Chronicle will continue to find defenders. Undoubtedly, its author was well informed as to the names of Henry II's courtiers, and from the 1150s onward supplies accounts of the king's itinerary in England that, although unsubstantiated in detail, tally well with what else we know of the king's movements from the pipe rolls and other sources well beyond the control of the Battle monks. By no stretch of the imagination can the Chronicle be dismissed as fiction pure and simple. Likewise, there could be any number of explanations for the anomalies in Battle's charters of Henry II: for example, that they were produced by the beneficiary rather than the royal chancery, and that they therefore ignore certain standard practices in the use of *Dei gratia* or the spelling of the king's name. In the same way, it might be argued that even the supposed confirmation charter of the 1150s is genuine in parts, and that Archbishop Theobald, although set down as its addressee and witness, failed to spot, or was powerless to delete, its damning reference to the exemption of Christ Church, Canterbury. The chancery of Henry II was not some forerunner of the xerox machine, churning out uniformly worded charters according to a pre-programmed formula. Anomalies and unusual linguistic formulas abound. New forms, like the inspeximus, were in the process of evolving, and not every peculiar turn of phrase is to be read as proof of forgery or fraud.

So great is the margin for uncertainty that Richard Mortimer has questioned whether any act of forgery can be conclusively proved in the charters of Henry II. When confronted with diplomatic oddity, Mortimer warns us, the criteria for authenticity are so weak that we should almost never reject a document out of hand: 'The best approach is to think again that it might be genuine, and to try to imagine how it came about. And if that fails, suspend judgement.'[91]

---

[90] For the papally delegated settlement of 1234–5, see E. Searle, *Lordship and Community: Battle Abbey and its Banlieu, 1066–1538* (Toronto, 1974), 94–8.

[91] R. Mortimer, 'The Charters of Henry II: What Are the Criteria for Authenticity?', *ANS 12* (1990), 133–4, concluding a valuable discussion which is nonetheless, in my opinion, over-cautious in its approach to forgery.

Diplomatic is not an exact science, and forgery comes in a bewildering variety of shades, from the omission or addition of a few key words, to the creation *ex nihil* of a wholly spurious document.[92] Yet, by a combination of tests, linguistic, palaeographical, and historical, we can on occasion adopt a less penumbrous approach to forgery. We should certainly tread more warily in future, both in respect to the Battle Abbey charters and to the abbey's chronicle. The chronicler's account of the introduction of the inspeximus clause needs to be redrawn in light of the evidence from Chichester. At least four others of the Battle charters of Henry II should be treated with grave suspicion; the confirmation charter of the 1150s almost certainly as an outright forgery. What is needed now is a palaeographical and diplomatic analysis of all the surviving twelfth-century charters of Battle, to establish quite what proportion of them is forged or suspicious. Whether, in the meantime, we dismiss much of the Battle Chronicle as a work of monastic fantasy, and the Henry II charters as just one part of this wider deception, will depend very much upon our own particular prejudice.

[92] Here I would reject the demand made by Timothy Reuter, 'The Making of England and Germany', in *Medieval Europeans*, ed. A. P. Smyth (London, 1998), 65, that we adopt the more forthright distinction between the forged and the authentic that Reuter claims prevails on the continent, and that he would prefer to the Anglo-Saxon tendency to 'persist in the belief that it is possible to be slightly dead or partly pregnant'.

21

THE LETTER-WRITING
OF ARCHBISHOP BECKET*

D. J. A. Matthew

Historians constructing accounts of Becket's dispute with Henry II make extensive use of the lives written after his martyrdom. Traces of this hagiography inevitably resurface in even the most secular of writers. It may seem impossible now to recover a sense of the affair as it appeared in Becket's lifetime, when no one prominent in the controversy divined his potential for sanctity. His own letters do, however, offer a direct view of him through pre-martyrdom sources, and although they have been used to fill out the details of the exile, they have not hitherto been studied as a group. Professor Barlow, Becket's most recent biographer, assumes without argument that the letters were all written by Becket's staff because 'Thomas was certainly incapable of drafting anything beyond the simplest letter', although he admits the unlikelihood 'that anything of importance went out without its having been read to, and approved by, the archbishop'.[1] Even in this limited sense, Becket's responsibility for the letters sent out under his name would be inescapable. They cannot properly be regarded as propaganda turned out by his staff. Many of them were written to friends or supporters, and give the impression of being composed by a single, forceful author. Becket himself had much more control of the letters issued in his name than is commonly acknowledged.

None of Becket's letters from before his consecration at Canterbury survives, and only seventeen of nearly 200 extant letters were written before the exile, so what they record is his ordeal as archbishop.[2] After his death scholarly work on his letters was undertaken, if not completed, at Canterbury, where the monastic community identified Becket's sacrifice with its own interests. Yet the collection contains no letter from Becket to his monks comforting them for his absence. His only unofficial letter to the community (502) concentrated on deflecting the monks' criticism of his neglect of them by identifying the sources

---

* The numbers in the text are those of the letters in *Materials for the History of Thomas Becket*, ed. J. C. Robertson and J. B. Sheppard, RS 67, 7 vols. (London, 1881–85), V–VII.

[1] F. Barlow, *Thomas Becket* (London, 1986), 133 and 304, n. 30.

[2] A. Duggan, *Thomas Becket: A Textual History of His Letters* (Oxford, 1980), app. 1. Publication of her edition of the Becket letters, long awaited, is imminent. Dr Duggan kindly supplied me with the numeration of the letters in her own edition, but in the circumstances of this publication I am regretfully unable to use them. Her edition will of course resolve some of the issues raised in this paper.

of his troubles as Foliot and Roger of York, 'who had turned against his mother'—Canterbury. It was left to John of Salisbury to try to mollify those monks who would not understand why their lord and protector was not at Canterbury to defend them from the king's greedy commissaries.[3] The monks had no share in the original project to preserve Becket's correspondence. It was in exile that Becket himself perceived the value of an epistolary dossier. He was no longer able to act in person on the political stage, and had to manage his affairs by other means. The impetus to collect reflects, in particular, his appreciation of statements written in his favour by influential clergy. His own additions to the collection were most numerous when he exercised authority as papal legate. About half of all Becket's surviving letters come from 1169 and 1170.

The unevenness of distribution in time may impair the chances of writing the history of the exile from the letters alone, but they nevertheless offer invaluable clues to aspects of Becket's mind which had no attractions for the hagiographers. Becket obviously had occasion in them to comment on particular issues of importance or refer to them casually in passing, doing so in such a way as to reveal his own attitude. It seems strange, then, that more has not been made of the letters. They may not provide a comprehensive picture of the whole problem, but they are the nearest we shall ever get to grasping Becket's own view of his situation, and on that account alone they deserve close attention.

THE BECKET STYLE OF LETTER-WRITING

We cannot tell how many of his own letters Becket deemed unworthy of preservation; on the other hand, paradoxically, some letters that had certainly not been sent somehow survived in his care. One of these, to the cardinal legate William of Pavia (312), began by thanking him for his recent letter: *speciem mellis in initio propinantes, venenum in medio, oleum in fine,* (an offer of poison with its sugared opening and its oily close). Becket wisely sounded John of Salisbury about the wisdom of sending it. John naturally recommended writing more tactfully, so it is hard to understand why this unsent letter was not destroyed.[4] Was Becket reluctant to repudiate his real sentiments about the cardinal? It might also be useful to remember what cardinals were like, even if he tactfully agreed not to throw his scorn in their faces. When writing to Gratian, his agent at the papal curia (695), Becket referred to the need to keep transcripts of all the letters relating to his affair (*negotium meum*). In this way, Becket's dossier could therefore have been intended to contain not only the pieces the archbishop thought essential for his case—like evidence of papal support—but also

---

[3] *The Letters of John of Salisbury*, ed. W. J. Millor, H. E. Butler, and C. N. L. Brooke, 2 vols. (Oxford, 1979–86), II, ep. 205.
[4] Ibid., ep. 227; cf. Becket's letter to Cardinal William in 1170 (693).

reminders of what he had to contend within the curia. Such a dossier of confidential material is not likely to have been preserved with a view to eventual publication. To explain the collection we do not need to accept the argument that Becket had a disinterested respect for truth and hoarded every scrap of relevant evidence.[5]

The letter to Cardinal William illustrates an unmistakable aspect of Becket's style—namely his vehemence—and this provides a basis for tracing his responsibility for certain other letters. Comparing, for example, two letters written to Gilbert Foliot in 1169 pronouncing excommunication (479–80), we find that one was much milder than the other and presumably represented second thoughts. He was not so ashamed of the earlier one, however, as to suppress it altogether. His excuse for strong language, as he told the pope, was that it is a form of impiety to ignore manifest injuries to Christ (497). This characteristic of Becket's letters strengthens the impression that he wrote impulsively to correspondents, agents, or supporters, either because he was alarmed, or because he wished to relieve his feelings or initiate some course of action. Characteristically, he did not wait to see if ugly rumours were well founded before writing (285, 288, 314).

Notwithstanding some formal letters that are addressed generally (as, for example, to the English bishops and clergy), in most letters Becket made a direct personal approach, rendering the letters sufficiently individual to create a precise impression of how the archbishop envisaged his correspondents and felt he might best stir them into action on his account. More tactful secretaries were therefore only used on rare occasions. Variations in the letters Becket himself sent at any one time to the curia demonstrate his technique. There are about seven batches of this kind, obviously dispatched with the same courier and treating of similar business, often employing the same phrases. Yet for all that, each one is carefully tailored to suit the individual cardinal. Three sent in the autumn of 1166 were designed to awaken the vigilance of the curia to the expected arrival there of John of Oxford, Henry II's clever envoy (247–49). Conrad of Mainz was reminded that John had been Henry's representative to the imperial court, and Becket insinuated that John's intrigues had been responsible for Conrad's own exile from Germany. He flattered the cardinal of Pisa (who had been legate in France in 1162 and there advised Becket to accept the archbishopric) with classical quotations and learned allusions. He says that the messenger could give direct evidence about the state of the church in England because he was the brother of a priest imprisoned by John of Oxford's own bishop at Salisbury. The letter to Cardinal Hyacinth (later Pope Celestine III) was more political. Becket cited Caesar's comment on Pompey as one who would be invincible if he knew how to win as well as he knew how to fight, with

---

[5] Cf. A. Morey and C. N. L. Brooke, *Gilbert Foliot and His Letters* (Cambridge, 1965), 25, for Becket's 'determination to be remembered and justified by a plain unvarnished tale of the transactions'.

a pointed reference to the corruptibility of the curia. In a somewhat earlier letter (250) Cardinal Boso was reminded of the devotion of Canterbury and Archbishop Theobald to Rome in 1148, in an attempt to play upon Boso's assumed sympathy for Canterbury. (Sadly, Boso was so little involved with Thomas and Canterbury that he never mentioned the Becket affair until the murder and its aftermath: to judge from his history, the quarrel with the empire and the papal position in Italy drove other issues out of his mind.)[6]

All the letters betray Becket's doubts about the cardinals' reactions and his concern to find some way to elicit their sympathies. His most fulsome expressions come in letters to Conrad of Mainz, whom he calls the better part of his soul (442). Conrad was also an exile, and Becket naturally stressed the similarity of their cases, though he was not himself offered a cardinalate. Unlike Conrad, he steadfastly refused even to go to the curia in Italy. The development of his relationships there can be traced through these letters. When he first wrote to Cardinal Hyacinth (33) he did not regard him as a special friend, but from the autumn of 1166 (249) the letters become increasingly confident. In 1169 the letter to Hyacinth (585) is the most carefully argued of the batch. Becket gives the impression that, although well-disposed, Hyacinth needed to be convinced, not stampeded. The letters to the senior cardinal, the bishop of Ostia (later Pope Lucius III), are more distant. The individuality of his epistolary style to the curia is most marked in letters like those to Cardinal John of Naples, on whom he pinned no hopes. He even used the formal greeting to have a dig at John's alleged openness to bribery—so to run through temporal advantages without losing things eternal (617). Then he reminded John of their original meeting in the royal orchard at Orléans, where the king of France had commended Becket to the cardinal's protection. Rejecting John's opinion that Rome should be merciful to the bishop of London, whom Becket had excommunicated, Becket retorted sarcastically that Rome had not been merciful, but soft on sin: it more frequently showed mercy to sinners than it corrected those at fault. How well Becket knew what he was doing is conveyed by a letter to the pope, where he quotes 'the most eloquent orator':[7] the success of a speech chiefly depends on knowing beforehand who will be on the judgement seat and in the auditorium (666).

Becket wrote letters because he could not be present in person to argue his cause. Speaking in public was then the principal means of discussing public issues, and Becket must have been practised in the art until exile suddenly deprived him of an audience. His letters betray habits of speech, and in as much

[6] Duggan, *Textual History*, attributes the Boso letter (250) to early 1166. Contrary to what is usually stated, she believes that Boso was not an English nephew of Pope Adrian IV (who made him a cardinal) but came from Tuscany. Boso, *Vita Alexandri*, in *Liber Pontificalis*, ed. L. Duchesne (Paris, 1892); trans. G. M. Ellis with introduction by P. Munz (Oxford, 1973). A. Duggan, 'A New Becket Letter: *Sepe quidem cogimur*', *Historical Research*, 63 (1990), 86–99, published a letter to Cardinal Hyacinth written in the same vein as the one to Cardinal Hubert of Ostia (538), in Aug. 1169.

[7] Quintillian, bk. III, ch. 9, section 7.

as the letters are lively and personal, it is because he saw himself addressing, even haranguing, his audience. Take, for example, the common experience of speakers who try to meet expected objections and turn them to advantage: a speaker launched upon his main point may judge from the audience's reaction, or even from some passing thought of his own, that there is an objection he should meet head on, and as he deals with this challenge he sees his way to scoring an additional point. This phenomenon stands out in many of the letters, because Becket was unwilling to rewrite completely, with more control. In his critical letter to the bishop of Auxerre (638) he complained that, because the bishop had not adequately prepared the way, he had himself undertaken a journey to no purpose. Suddenly realizing how thankless his letter must appear, Becket paused to slip in a remark that he was nevertheless not ungrateful for the bishop's help. Then, thinking he had said enough, he capitalized on the bishop's good-will and immediately warned him to make arrangements more carefully in the future, reverting to the earlier tone of arrogant irritation. If Becket had paused to consider the bishop's likely reaction he would not have dashed off a letter like this. It reads as though his own feelings simply boiled over. In his mind Becket saw the bishop as a fool; he recognized that the bishop would be hurt by the outburst, but concluded self-righteously. Such things may pass in conversation, where the blows may be softened by other means; in writing, they leap to the eye.

Individual recipients will not have noticed what strikes a reader of the whole collection, the repeated use of familiar biblical quotations, particularly from the Old Testament: thorns in your side (*sagitta in latere*, Numbers 33.55); he trusts he can draw up Jordan into his mouth (Job 40.23); if there be any sorrow like unto my sorrow (Lamentations 1.12); the head of all evils (*incentor omnium malorum*, 2 Maccabees 4.1); blinded by gifts (Deuteronomy 16.19); his arrogance is greater than his strength (*arrogantia eius major sit quam fortitudo*, Isaiah 16.6). Such phrases turn up in letters that were written at about the same time presumably because they were then in Becket's mind; while others, like the cliché, 'God is no respecter of persons' (Acts 10.34), recur at different times. Becket repeatedly defended his outspokenness as being due to his fear of what would be demanded of him when he stood at God's tribunal—revealing that he saw himself as a man subject to judgement. He claims that he could have made peace at any time, but would not do so until he obtained justice (617). Most of his contemporaries, particularly amongst the clergy, wanted a settlement, and did not think in terms of justice, as Becket did. Equally, Becket stated on several occasions that he would not forgive until all his goods, to the last farthing, had been restored (e.g. 610). Even in his joyful letter to Alexander III announcing his reconciliation with Henry II in the summer of 1170, when he was most sanguine about the future, he reported his determination not to return to England until every last yard of church land had been recovered, *quamdiu de terra ecclesiae passum pedis abstulerit*, because the only proof of royal repentance was total restitution (684). To the cardinal bishop of Ostia he justified his intransigence on the grounds that withholding any of his property would be an example of lying malice: the king would in effect be persisting in error and adding to his offences by fresh deception (692). In the same letter, Becket refers to discussions about the terms of reconciliation in which he refused to make any concessions, demanding total restoration on the original terms. This is what he understood by justice. He himself was guiltless. Becket emerges from this discussion as an advocate, aiming to win a case in the courts and claiming that it was Christ himself who, in his person, was unjustly accused.

BECKET AS ROME'S SOLE CHAMPION IN ENGLAND

What is susceptible to more objective assessment is Becket's belief that Henry persecuted him for his devotion to Rome, and that Rome's own future in England was therefore at stake. In one letter to the papal official, Gratian, who kept his Roman dossier (533), and another to the pope himself (666), Becket borrowed the words of St Paul to the Romans, that neither death nor life nor anything else can separate us, not from the love of God, as in the original, but from our fidelity to the lord pope and the Church of Rome, even if (as he admits to Gratian, though tactfully, for once, not to the pope) the Church of Rome should utterly abandon us, which God forbid. The last phrase indicates Becket's recognition that he was not much loved at the curia. He lamented to Roger of Worcester how much patience he had to show there (496). Some letters to Alexander III suggest, however, that exasperation sometimes overcame any resolution to be patient. When papal legates arrived to settle the quarrel, Becket invariably intrigued against them. Of all the various legates, he only ever approved of Gratian himself (663). He always refused to submit to the judgement of legates, and insisted that only the pope could judge him (331); going so far as to tell Conrad of Mainz that he would rather die excommunicate than submit to any judgement outside the court of Rome (314). Yet he would not travel to Italy, on the grounds that Henry was planning to have him assassinated on his journey (538). Becket's determination to secure a complete vindication and to refuse any compromise made him abjectly dependent on Rome, whence alone such a solution could come. As he put it in a letter to Gratian, if Rome stretched out its chastizing hand it would promptly give us peace—*in retribuendo, nobis citissime quies dabitur* (609). Becket could not accept that, if Rome did not stretch out her terrible hand, it was because Rome did not agree with his assessment of the situation.

Becket was indifferent to the pope's awkward position with the emperor over the schism. If Rome did not espouse his own cause, it was not because of the political situation but rather because his enemies practised tricks and bribery, because the curia was corrupt, or because the pope himself was weak or mild. Alexander III might have the power to restrain Becket, but not, the archbishop insisted, to stay the right hand of God (642). He deplored the disagreeable consequences of exile—his poverty, the shortage of horses, dependence on the hospitality of others. Significantly, he perceived and resented how much these consequences put him at a disadvantage, and compared his situation as archbishop in exile to his standing as the king's former chancellor.[8] But in his abject circumstances Becket still would not humble himself to Henry II and accept reconciliation. He had no alternative strategy but to wait until Rome was in a position to restore him to England. In this way the conflict became a personal contest between Becket and Henry for influence in Rome; to Alexander, Becket admitted that he would have wrestled with the king almost until death—*cum rege Anglorum fere usque ad mortem in agone contenderimus* (590). In a sense, Rome was never able to do what Becket demanded. Though he chose to explain Henry's willingness to make up the quarrel at Fréteval on 22 July 1170 as a consequence of Roman threats of an interdict, this was an exaggeration. Henry had pulled off a very clever trick by getting the archbishop of York to crown the young king on 14 June. It made Becket desperate to effect a reconciliation, if worse damage to Canterbury's interests was not to follow.[9] When Becket did return to England, after six years in exile, it was not as Rome's triumphant champion.

Becket's own anxiety to corner Rome's support obliged him to represent himself at the curia as its sole friend in England. Although his case has been widely accepted, at the time its absurdity would have been manifest to everyone, not least the curia itself. Henry II maintained a steady flow of envoys to the curia, which flattered the Roman sense of its importance. He successfully evaded papal censure, even when criticized for negotiating with the schismatic emperor—a very great offence in the curia, which Becket never tired of enlarging upon; the pope also granted Henry II personal exemption from excommunication by Becket (285). Becket seethed about the curia, and commented sardonically that the only reason for its indulgence must be its hope that the king would hang himself with the rope he was given (497, 642). Nor could Rome regard Becket as the only English cleric eager for papal support. Gilbert Foliot himself served regularly as a papal judge-delegate, and acknowledged Becket's excommunication and the need to go to Rome for absolution.[10] Roger of York had been a consistent supporter of the papacy in general and Alexander III in particular since his own consecration, and for much the same reason as Becket: his archiepiscopal authority and the independence of his archbishopric from the claims of his rival depended on the grant of Roman favours.[11] Becket

[8] Becket frequently refers to his own straitened circumstances (329, 331, 444, 637, 643); but John of Salisbury says Becket was never in real poverty: *Letters*, ed. Millor *et al.*, II, ep. 294.

[9] Becket was not taken by surprise (648–51, 666), but Henry nevertheless achieved his purpose and rode out the ensuing storm.

[10] Morey and Brooke, *Gilbert Foliot*, ch. xi, pp. 211–2, 257–60, 280.

[11] The Becket MSS contain none of Roger of York's letters, so he is invariably, even now, portrayed

suffered over the fact that Rome gave comfort to his enemies, for instance, by absolving the bishop of London from the need to renew his profession of obedience to Canterbury in 1163 (35, 67). In the last month of his life Becket was still attempting to persuade the pope that the archbishop of York and bishops of London and Salisbury were all working to destroy and threaten Roman authority in England (722). The obedience of these prelates to Rome was never an issue for them; nor, on the other hand, did they consider the king an enemy of the Church, as Becket did.[12]

BECKET'S STAND FOR CANTERBURY

Becket's professions of devotion were a great burden for a pope preoccupied with concerns of his own in Italy. He saw plainly that Becket had no hopes of forcing Henry II to receive him back unless the papacy frightened the king into doing so, and that any such papal action was likely to create offence. At the curia Becket was perceived to be much more concerned about himself and the church of Canterbury than about Rome.[13] Phrases attesting to this commitment are scattered throughout his letters. He called Canterbury the head of the whole English kingdom (*caput... in regno*, 19); he enthusiastically repeated to the pope Henry II's own description of Canterbury as the most noble church of the whole West (684)—in the circumstances, a slight on Rome itself. Becket refused to be translated from such a church, when negotiators suggested this as a way out (359). He wrote to his representatives at Rome (Canterbury men themselves) that he would rather be killed than snatched away alive from the mother church at Canterbury, which had nourished him and raised him to what he was (359, 538). Becket's conception of his new office was not limited to humbling York (716): he saw Canterbury as the head of the entire English kingdom, and with himself at the helm, dedicated to the cause of leading the whole English people, king included, for their spiritual good (223). As Becket reminded Henry II, the king had made solemn promises at the time of his coronation to uphold Canterbury's privileges (154). Becket understood this to mean that the king owed obedience and submission to himself as archbishop of Canterbury (603, 649–50, 684). Princes should bow their head to bishops, not judge them (153).

Only the pope could confer what Becket wanted for Canterbury, namely, authority over the whole English church (York included), either by confirmation

as he seemed at Canterbury—disloyal, weak, corrupt, and time-serving. There are many documents showing that he was dutiful about consulting the papacy frequently on the business of his province. Publication of the edition of his *acta* by Marie Lovatt is imminent and I am grateful to her for exchanging views with me about his relations with Becket. A. Saltman, *Theobald, Archbishop of Canterbury* (London, 1955), 123–4, contrasts Theobald's attitude to the Canterbury–York dispute with Becket's.

[12] H. Mayr-Harting, 'Henry II and the Papacy 1170–1189', *JEH* 16 (1965), 39: 'The English church was far from agreed about how much it wanted to be free from the king in order to obey the pope.'

[13] Becket was told (55) that Alexander III regretted the privileges granted to Canterbury by Adrian IV.

of the primatial rights of Canterbury or by making him papal legate for the whole kingdom, as Theobald had been.[14] Naturally, Rome was not disposed to grant what Becket expected. Why should it delegate its own authority, or compromise its standing with other English clergy and its relations with the king, to please Becket? He asked for far more than his predecessors had ever received. Theobald, when granted a legatine commission for the whole kingdom, including York, was incontrovertibly the senior archbishop. In 1162 the situation was different, and the irritation of the curia can be imagined.

Becket's problems at Canterbury often seem to be overlooked by historians who are persuaded that Henry II had made his pliant chancellor, archbishop of Canterbury for the purpose of bending the English church to the king's will. Since there is no evidence for any such policy, and our impression of Henry's intentions is heavily dependent on what Becket alleged about them, this interpretation is speculative. Worse, much of it is based on demonstrably erroneous assumptions about the constitutional position of Canterbury. In 1162 Canterbury as such had no authority of the kind assumed by many modern writers. Such authority as Theobald had himself been able to exercise rested upon his seniority and upon his position as papal legate. Becket himself had no illusions about his power to browbeat the churches in England as archbishop, let alone as Henry II's instrument. In fact, he had good reason to be worried about his ability to maintain, in ecclesiastical terms, the standing of his predecessor. His alleged misgivings about accepting promotion to Canterbury are more easily understood as uneasiness about his new responsibilities there than as anticipating a quarrel with the king. By the end of his life Theobald may have achieved his aspirations for Canterbury, but his successor could not capitalize on those achievements. He knew that Theobald had begun as abbot of Bec, and had been brought over from Normandy to Canterbury in 1138 as a virtual nonentity, overshadowed by the king's brother, Henry, bishop of Winchester, who clinched his eminence by being appointed resident papal legate over the archbishop's head in 1139. It was papal, not royal support that had eventually given Theobald distinction in England, when in 1150 he had been made papal legate. While legate, Theobald had dexterously appointed his archdeacon at Canterbury, Roger, to the see of York and consecrated him. On Theobald's death Roger, who had been archbishop for seven years, so far from respectfully remembering his 'mother' at Canterbury, had no intention of continuing to submit to its jurisdiction; he promptly got from Rome a declaration of his right to perform coronations (310). Roger hoped to strengthen his position further

---

[14] John of Salisbury, *Letters*, ed. Millor *et al.*, II, ep. 205, indicates that Becket aspired to recover the powers of Lanfranc in the English church. As shown by A. Duggan, 'The Confirmation of Becket's Primacy', *Journal of the Society of Archivists*, 9 (1988), 197–209, the papacy never granted Becket as primate formal powers over York; the diocese of York was exempt from his jurisdiction even as papal legate, May 1166–8 and 1169–70. Becket was therefore never accorded by Alexander III the coveted privilege of a papal legation for the whole kingdom, granted to Theobald by Eugenius III, Anastasius IV, and Adrian IV.

when consecrating Becket in 1162. Though this was averted by the bishops of
the southern province, Roger, nothing daunted, obtained yet further privileges
from Rome, including confirmation of his traditional rights to carry his
archiepiscopal cross and to crown the king, as his predecessors had enjoyed them
(13).[15] The quarrel between York and Canterbury assumed fresh significance in
the summer of 1163, at the papal Council of Tours, where Becket tried to obtain
the canonization of Archbishop Anselm. York, needless to say, had taken strong
exception to such a move, and the pope had evaded Becket's pressure by referring the matter back to a council in England.[16] The earliest of Becket's surviving letters to the pope was written in October 1163, precisely to complain
because Roger had not only raised his cross in the southern province, but had
also appealed to Rome when Becket had denounced this insulting provocation
(27). Roger naturally became hated as a turncoat in Canterbury circles. However, the loyalty of other bishops could no more be taken for granted. In the
spring of 1163 Foliot, bishop of Hereford, was translated by the pope at the
king's request to London, and obstinately refused, with papal support, to renew
his oath of obedience to Canterbury (35, 67). He was also given special responsibility for the care of Henry II's soul by the pope (18, 19, 26), and when difficulties with the king arose the pope expected Foliot, not Becket, to deal with them
(37, 81). The archbishop felt that the traditional powers of his see were under
attack from the disloyal Roger and the shifty Foliot. Worse, under assault from
Rome itself, Canterbury's standing had declined in his first year.

Becket had to be seen at Canterbury, nevertheless, as the champion of its pretensions. He had only two real weapons: to use his influence with the king, his
friend, patron and lord; or to press his own special claims on the curia. In these
ecclesiastical disputes the king's support could never have been sufficient, even
in 1162, and from the beginning of his archiepiscopate Becket sought to culti-
vate influence at the curia. These intrigues were themselves enough to arouse
Henry II's suspicions, for Becket's assertion of his claims against the archbishop
of York, the bishop of London, and the abbot of St Augustine's (34, 35, 36) all
effectively impinged on Henry's own standing with these prelates. Irrespective
of any other possible disagreements, the archbishop's agenda for Canterbury
caused Henry considerable disquiet, particularly because of the secretive way in

---

[15] Anne Heslin (Dr Duggan), 'Coronation of the Young King in 1170', in *Studies in Church History* 2,
ed. G. J. Cuming (1965), 165–78, confirms the date of the papal bull for Roger *Quanto per carissimum* as 17
June 1161; Theobald had died on 18 April; Roger had acted promptly. The papal bulls for Roger, confirming his traditional right to carry his cross and crown kings, were issued on 11 June 1162, that is, after
Becket's consecration (3 June 1162). Roger interpreted the bulls to authorize the raising of his cross in the
southern province; when he did so Becket promptly complained to the pope. Alexander first suspended
Roger's privilege while further enquiries were made (41); consulting the text again, he found it did not
cover the whole kingdom (42). The papal letter about this to Becket (43) betrays both confusion and
embarrassment.
[16] For the question of Anselm's canonization, see R. Foreville, 'Regard neuf sur le culte de Saint
Anselme à Canterbury au xiie siècle', in *Spicilegium Beccense II: Les mutations socio-culturelles au tournant
du xie et xiie siècles* (Paris, 1984), 299–316.

which Becket conducted his negotiations, and not with the pope only. Had Henry known that Louis VII was offering to receive Becket as his *socius* in France (36), his suspicions of his archbishop's loyalty (29) would have seemed fully justified.

THE QUARREL WITH HENRY II

Becket's relationship with the king eludes complete historical understanding because we only know what Becket himself thought about it. For the important years of friendship, from 1154 to 1162, the letters fail altogether. Becket had been recommended by Theobald to Henry II as his chancellor, a comparatively unimportant post which Becket made more significant. He became not merely a minister but a friend and companion; his advancement to Canterbury shows that he had earned Henry's respect. How the two men's friendship turned sour is explained by Becket's hagiographers as the effect of his promotion in 1162.[17] This was not Becket's own view. According to a letter to his envoys in 1169, he expected his return to Canterbury to be on the terms enjoyed by Theobald and by himself, 'until we set out for the Council of Tours and as always before the king began to persecute us and the church' (*postea quando profecti sumus ad concilium Turonense et semper antequam rex nos et ecclesiam persequeretur*, 610). The trouble had therefore started after his return from Tours. Moreover, in Becket's view, any change had come about, not in himself since his consecration, but in the king.

The crisis in their relations developed at a time when a debate about the customs of the English church was opened in the autumn of 1163. Many features of the dispute about the customs still remain obscure. It is not known why Henry II insisted on having the customs put into writing. Possibly he was impressed to hear about papal law-making at Tours in May 1163, and decided that it would be appropriate to publish some 'laws' of his own. It also may be relevant that the two archbishops had returned from Tours set on confrontation, and when Roger raised his cross in the southern province both archbishops referred their quarrel to the pope. Becket's letter about this made no mention of any pending quarrel with the king. In October Henry did not have a draft of any programme for the reform of the English church up his sleeve; agreement on finding a form of words to define ancient customs took another four months. Becket certainly worried in several letters to the curia about his own difficulties with the king, but the pope's replies suggest that these related specifically to the rights of Canterbury. At the time Becket's inclination, moreover, was to consult in France rather than openly to challenge royal tyrannies in England. The pope urged

---

[17] M. Staunton, 'Thomas Becket's Conversion', *ANS* 21 (1998), 193–211, discussed the literary conventions the hagiographers worked with to provide 'an internally consistent picture of sanctity from birth to death'.

Foliot to extinguish Henry's *scintilla* of enmity to Becket. The implication is that disagreements were perceived as personal, and not a danger for the whole church.

Modern writers still persist in claiming that Henry II's proposals amounted to a plan for the resuscitation of the royal rights of his grandfather which Stephen had abjectedly surrendered. When the customs were at last put into writing, however, no protests were raised that they were not genuinely ancient, or that they had recently lapsed, nor even that they had been lawfully abrogated by the superior authority of canon law. The bishops, Becket included, objected not to the customs as such, but to having them put into writing. This conferred on them a new formal status as 'law', and potentially opened up the possibility of a conflict between two written rules. Worse still, the king insisted in January 1164 at Clarendon that the bishops should swear to observe the 'customs' without reservations (*absolute*). Why Henry made such an issue of this has hardly been considered. It probably represents a justifiable suspicion on his part that, without it, the bishops would find excuses to wriggle out of their commitment to the customs by pleading the superior 'law' of the church. In this sense the Constitutions of Clarendon deserve their reputation as a landmark in the history of England. They asserted that traditional English customs should prevail against the novelties of canon law. Henry II was quite prescient enough to realize that, unless some English customs were promptly accepted as 'laws', they would be vulnerable to clerical 'reform'. The innovations in ecclesiastical affairs came from the clergy, not from the crown. Henry defended royal rights on the only acceptable grounds—that they were ancient customs.[18]

When the matter came to a head at Clarendon in January 1164, and all the bishops objected to swearing as Henry required, the king nevertheless coerced them into compliance, apparently after a private discussion with Becket himself.[19] So far from objecting to papal influence, Henry immediately asked the pope to ratify the Constitutions and to make Roger of York papal legate for the kingdom. Though the pope declined to endorse the customs, he found it expedient to mollify Henry by offering Roger the legatine commission, only to backtrack when Becket protested. Even so, the pope dreaded the effects of Henry II's disappointment and urged Becket to show restraint (50, 51). At this stage the customs were not regarded by either the archbishop or the pope as grounds for quarrelling with Henry. The archbishop even reassured the king of

---

[18] F. Barlow, *Thomas Becket*, 66–9, and 'The Constitutions of Clarendon', *Medieval History*, 1 (1991), 39–52. Barlow has a quite different interpretation of Henry II's plans for reform. According to him, Henry II was in 1163 *still* attempting to restore law and order after Stephen's reign; he had identified malpractices in ecclesiastical jurisdiction and was aware of popular dislike of the newfangled archidiaconal courts. He 'engineered the election of Becket' to Canterbury 'with the intention of putting matters right'. See John of Salisbury, *Letters*, ed. Millor *et al.*, I, ep. 16, for Stephen's insistence on having the case of a criminous clerk judged *iuxta consuetudinem gentis nostrae*.

[19] *The Letters and Charters of Gilbert Foliot*, ed. A. Morey and C. N. L. Brooke (Cambridge, 1967), 233–4, ep. 170 (*Multiplicem*).

France that the dispute over the customs had been settled, but that Henry had become irate again when Becket was reported to have denigrated Henry to the pope and the king of France (46). Becket begged Louis VII at least to reassure Henry that this was not so.

It is genuinely difficult to understand how the situation deteriorated during the course of 1164. Becket's dossier of letters, so rich for the exile, provides little help. The pressure put on the archbishop at Clarendon to back Henry's scheme for the Constitutions suggests that until January 1164 the king still valued his support. Thereafter Henry's suspicions of Becket were easily revived: he cannot have been pleased when Becket thwarted his plans for getting Roger of York, as senior archbishop, made legate in the kingdom, and if he knew anything at all of Becket's persistent negotiations behind his back with the king of France and the pope, Henry would have felt his distrust justified. For whatever reason, the king found ways to make life very disagreeable for his archbishop, keeping him metaphorically on the run until November, when Becket literally fled. Was Henry surprised by Becket's departure, or had he manoeuvred to drive him out of the kingdom? Either way, by October the king no longer had any further use for his services. He had isolated Becket from both his bishops and his Canterbury vassals; Becket was completely at Henry's mercy, and was treated, as he complained, as a mere layman (*tanquam laicus*). He had lost his former influence as Henry's friend and adviser, and had forfeited any power he could reasonably have expected to enjoy as archbishop.

Becket's English contemporaries were well aware of the actual circumstances of his exile as the consequence of the breakdown of his relations with the king. Accepting that he had been humiliated and goaded into voluntary exile would have been understandably difficult for Becket, who preferred to present himself as a victim of royal tyranny. Once across the Channel, he went straight to the curia at Sens to obtain papal absolution from the oath he had taken at Clarendon (466), which he himself thereby identified as his key error. By leaving the kingdom and by appealing to the curia he had openly broken his oath and may have had this on his conscience, and in this way the customs may indeed be regarded as the cause of his exile; but they were not more important than this. When John of Salisbury defended Becket to the monks of Canterbury, he dared not 'place Becket on a par with his predecessors who are glittering with miracles in our church', but claimed that 'the cause which he defends I think no whit inferior to theirs', without specifying any assault on ecclesiastical liberty.[20] It is hardly a ringing endorsement of the view that the customs constituted an outrageous affront. In his own letters, however, Becket tended to identify 'the customs' as the source of the problem, referring to them in parenthesis as a kind of irritating reminder, particularly to the curia, of his wrongs which they either

---

[20] John of Salisbury, *Letters*, ed. Millor *et al.*, II, ep. 205; cf. ep. 247 on Becket in exile for justice and the church's liberty.

ignored or doubted (466). He even pathetically reported to a sceptical cardinal that Henry II himself referred to the Constitutions as the cause of his exile (467). Becket could not afford to let the customs be forgotten. They constituted his proof of Henry's determination to trample on ecclesiastical liberty. In France, where kings enjoyed no such powers over the Church, Becket would have found no difficulty in convincing clergy that such customs were tyrannical. In England, though, clergy were prepared to tolerate some degree of compromise with the crown over the application of canon law, because of the corresponding advantages they derived from good relations with a powerful kingship; but once in exile Becket himself would not compromise. He could not contemplate returning to an England where certain customs were observed, for they would have seriously compromised his power to exercise his own office as he saw fit. In a letter to his agents, referring to Henry's attempts to strengthen his control over England, Becket identified the restraint on his own right to excommunicate as the most pernicious of all those customs the king asserts against God (*quoniam inter iura consuetudinum quas vendicat contra Deum si credatur expertis manifeste cognoscatur hoc fere esse perniciosissimum*, 610). The clause restraining excommunication of royal tenants in chief until royal permission had been obtained was the first of the six offensive clauses that Becket, as legate, condemned in June 1166, although when announcing this to the cardinals he tactfully made the clause restraining appeals to Rome the first of his objections (196). Even at Vézelay, however, only six of the sixteen clauses were specifically denounced (195), and in 1169 Becket picked out only four when trying to remind the pope of their wickedness (643). Becket claimed in one letter that the pope had pronounced a condemnation of the Constitutions (309), but in another that he had only condemned some of them (452); while in a third letter he declared that the pope ought to have condemned them (538). Had the papacy ever condemned them *en bloc* in writing, Becket would hardly have allowed such a statement to get lost. Reading between the lines, Alexander III's most decisive action was to absolve Becket personally from his sworn oath to uphold them (466).

The clause limiting appeals was probably the one of greatest interest in Rome, although it simply barred disputes from being carried outside the kingdom without the king's knowledge. Since a major quarrel between the two English archbishops was brewing in October 1163, Henry's interest in the matter is as understandable as Becket's disapproval of any limitations put on his access to the curia—particularly when he suspected the king of favouring the claims of Roger of York as senior archbishop. Later, in exile, Becket's right to appeal to Rome became indispensable to him, while pronouncing sentences of excommunication against his enemies was his chief means of taking action. Becket took pride in his ecclesiastical censures, referring to 'our excommunicates' and stoutly defending his right to absolve them without papal authority.[21]

---

[21] His excommunicates: 269, 359, 494, 583, 684.

His coyness on this issue shows up in a letter to his favourite English bishop, Roger of Worcester, whom he had consecrated. Roger had ventured to suggest that he might have some access to the excommunicated in order to negotiate with them for peace. Becket professed amazement at a request for relaxation of the rules. Not even the pope could do that: although he could absolve the excommunicate, he had no power to permit contact with them while the sentence was in place (496). The Constitutions, then, had been objectionable in their form from the beginning, but some of them assumed additional importance for Becket in exile. This also applied to the clause regarded by modern writers (with different preoccupations) as the most important: criminous clerks. This was the only clause that could be used to make Becket appear as a champion of the whole clerical order. It was naturally of great interest to his hagiographers and their readers.[22]

Becket's interpretation of the statement of English customs as a programme of royal tyranny has impressed modern writers who have found reasons of their own for presenting Henry II as a reformer of English royal government. Nevertheless, it is implausible. In exile, Becket's only hope of recovering his self-respect, his church, and his hold over both Henry and the kingdom lay in convincing the pope that he was the sole defender of ecclesiastical freedom in England, indeed in Christendom, for again and again Becket argued that concessions to Henry encouraged other princes to follow his example.[23] If he interpreted concessions in this way, it was easier for him not only to present but also to understand his own case in such a light.

BECKET AND HENRY II

What really caused the total breakdown of relations between king and archbishop remains elusive. The archbishop's anguish is clear. His letters are most emotional when the king is mentioned, as when he exaggerates Henry's dealings with the emperor as indicating his disloyalty to Rome. Becket paints an ugly portrait of the king: even in his youth he was a liar, wily, suspicious, a blusterer who only respected a firm hand and enjoyed his worldly eminence. Becket

---

[22] In his letters Becket does not pay much attention to the problem of criminous clerks (235, 287). Its prominence in modern historical accounts reflects the view that Henry II developed a policy of tightening up the enforcement of law and order, a very modern, and secular, preoccupation. In the 1160s Becket's arguments on benefit of clergy were not considered stronger than Henry II's. R. M. Fraher, 'The Becket Dispute and Two Decretist Traditions: The Bolognese Masters Revisited and Some New Anglo-Norman Texts', *Journal of Medieval History*, 4 (1978), 347–68, showed that only after the martyrdom were Bolognese canon lawyers encouraged to extend the benefit of clergy beyond its traditional limits to cover criminal cases, and that conscientious English canonists were themselves slow to welcome this interpretation.

[23] A bad example: 246, 285, 287, 331, 463, 466, 501, 583, 585, 587, 643. Becket's supporters regretted that Henry was less susceptible than Louis VII to clerical persuasion. The network of friendship described in this volume by Julian Haseldine ('Thomas Becket: Martyr, Saint—and Friend?') was a French one which understood nothing of the peculiar position of the church in England.

also refers to Henry's impatience of long speeches, as though he had personal experience of lecturing the king and finding him unresponsive (603). In his view, Henry could never be defeated by softness.[24] How had Becket ever become so friendly with a young man like this? Whatever else the relationship involved—genuine, if half-reluctant, affection, soured later by Henry's scorn— we may interpret Becket's intentions as hoping to guide and direct this lovable but sinful king. By the time of his exile Becket recognized that he had himself lost all influence with the king. Henceforth Henry would only do what Becket required when constrained by the pope to do so. Becket's letters show such a variety of emotions as to suggest that he was capable of exaggerating Henry's ill-will. His report to the pope of their reconciliation in July 1170 goes to the other extreme in painting a scene of ecstatic affection. The violence of his lan- guage, his attempts at one time to transfer blame to counsellors and at others to judge Henry II harshly, do not give the impression that he ever reached a detached or objective view of the king, such as befitted one who aspired to be Henry's spiritual father in God. If the archbishop's reading of Henry's charac- ter was correct, it must have depended on their earlier relationship, when Becket's own age, experience, and perhaps hectoring manner had enabled him, even as mere chancellor, to exercise influence.

An extraordinary insight into his feelings for the king is provided by a letter to the bishop of Nevers, intended to help him negotiate with Henry. He warns the bishop that Henry will try to test his constancy and that he will only respect him if he proves totally incorruptible; otherwise the bishop will become a figure of scorn: *in contemptum in fabulam in derisum* (644). Echoes of this phrase appear in other letters (602, 666). Becket must here be drawing on his own incomparable experience of Henry. Was he reproaching himself for his weak- ness at Clarendon in January 1164, when he had agreed in a private discussion to swear to the customs *absolute*, to the consternation of his fellow bishops? This interview may have marked the turning-point of Becket's career. We do not know how Henry persuaded Becket: did he appeal to their old friendship, and so cause Becket to stumble in his archiepiscopal duty? Whatever the case, Henry had found Becket's weak spot and turned him, therefore, *in contemptum, in fabulam, in derisum*.

Henry's own few letters do not shed a comparable light on his attitude to Becket, or explain what appears to be the personal ferocity of his treatment of the unhappy archbishop. As a young man Henry had been much in Becket's company and subject to his influence. He probably still was in 1162 when, in imitation of the emperor Frederick, he raised his chancellor to the archbish- opric. If so, he was doubtless hurt when Becket resigned the chancellorship as incompatible with his new duties. By severing his ministerial dependence on

---

[24] Becket regarded himself as an expert on Henry II's character (331): Henry as a liar since youth (609), wily (602) suspicious (666), a blusterer (538,644), respectful only of a firm hand (466, 612, 666). Why Becket so loved the king (244) is not explained with comparable detail.

the king, he gave notice that he put other duties higher than Henry's. Far from intending Becket to run the English church for him like a twelfth-century Cranmer, Henry probably expected him to continue in his diplomatic role, like an English Rainald Dassel. Instead of remaining Henry's chancellor, though, Becket as archbishop saw himself as the king's spiritual adviser.[25] It may be that, as Henry had become more experienced, he had become less susceptible to the chancellor's pressure, and if that were the case, Becket could have perceived the archbishopric as a means of reinforcing his diminishing personal powers of persuasion. It is, however, extremely improbable that Henry made him archbishop in order to strengthen Becket's moral authority over himself or over the English church. Any attempt by Becket to assert his superior spiritual claims was more likely to provoke Henry's resentment. That after 1162 the king still required Becket to serve as his minister is perhaps indicated by the decision to hound the archbishop for his alleged maladministration as chancellor: even as archbishop Becket should not escape his royal master.[26] As archbishop, Becket himself might well have felt that he had acquired higher obligations, but Henry cannot reasonably be blamed for not anticipating this. To all intents and purposes, for the previous eight years Becket had been Henry's henchman. Henry had no reason to be emotionally confused by their relationship. Only his charge that the archbishop had crept away in November 1164 without warning or permission, to consort with his enemy Louis VII, surely betrays his sense of being personally betrayed.

Uncritical acceptance of Becket's own presentation of the case as one about ecclesiastical liberty ignores his real problem. At the heart of his preoccupations lies not Rome, or even Canterbury, but his own relationship with the king. The only way he saw of recovering his former authority with Henry was by getting Rome to act for him. Becket's own words deserve to be pondered with greater attention than they have hitherto received, as direct evidence about the man who wrote them. The principal reason for this comparative neglect is that after his death his legacy passed into the hands of those with a different agenda from his. They presented his murder as martyrdom; the miracles made him a saint. His real life on earth no longer held any significance for anyone. It came naturally to writers of his 'life' to focus on episodes in it which consolidated his new reputation for sanctity. Those who had known him best in life were probably the least well qualified to perform this function. John of Salisbury's meagre life has been described as 'almost perfunctory ... evidently felt from the start to be

---

[25] See Ralph de Diceto, *Ymagines Historiarum*, ed. W. Stubbs, 2 vols. RS 68 (London, 1876), I, 307–8, for Henry II's wish to have an archbishop as his chancellor as Frederick Barbarossa did. Henry may even have expected that Archbishop Becket as chancellor would be prepared to accept Roger of York's formal seniority as archbishop. By resigning after his reception of the pallium, Becket showed that he put his duty to his see before any commitment to Henry.

[26] Becket claimed that Henry II did not abandon these claims until the autumn of 1169 (583–4). No formal discharge had been issued. Becket relied on some verbal declaration or tacit understanding.

inadequate'.[27] Beliefs about Becket had been miraculously transformed by 1171, and the demands for information about him required not history but hagiography. The impact of these 'lives' can be discerned in historians still writing. This attitude cannot be dismissed in Becket's case as a mere consequence of twelfth-century credulity, since recent experience confirms that people are still ready to allow a terrible death to give the past life a new sheen. Belief in posthumous miracles may indicate an archaic form of piety, but the determination to read profound meaning into a life tragically cut short is one of the mainsprings of historical writing. The difference between beliefs now and then is that it is no longer acceptable, for serious historians at least, to evade the difficulties of explaining the past as it happened by invoking hindsight. However difficult it may be to recover a sense of events as they occurred without interpreting them in the light of later developments, the historian's duty to do so is unavoidable. Becket did not appear as a saint until after Henry II's henchmen had murdered him, and it is incumbent on historians not to confuse the actual course of his quarrel by making anachronistic assumptions about his sanctity.[28] Becket's letters are to all intents and purposes the only strictly contemporary evidence we have about his own state of mind at the time. They do not seem to have been adequately appreciated as evidence for the way he saw himself, his protagonists, or his cause, or for what they—perhaps inadvertently—disclose about his deeper anxieties.

[27] John of Salisbury, *Letters*, ed. Millor *et al.*, II, pp. lix–lx.

[28] John of Salisbury and Peter of Celle had enjoyed joking in private about Becket as archbishop, as Peter, only slightly abashed, was prepared to recall after Becket's death. They were both bemused by the way God had vindicated him by the miracles. In these circumstances Peter's reference to him as *preciossisimus martyr* surely has a sardonic edge: Peter of Celle ep. 124: PL 202, col. 573. L. K. Barker, 'A Lost Lactantius of John of Salisbury', *Albion*, 22 (1990), 21–37, esp. 36, n. 62; B. Ross 'Audi Thoma Henriciani nota: A French Scholar Appeals to Thomas Becket?', *EHR* 89 (1974), 333–8. See Haseldine, 'Thomas Becket', n. 12, for Peter's rebuff of Becket's clumsy attempt when chancellor to become one of his correspondents; and n. 9 for Peter's possibly playful report to the credulous Prior Benedict of Christ Church, Canterbury, of two 'miracles', one of which was too trivial even for Benedict to accept.

22

THOMAS BECKET: MARTYR, SAINT—AND FRIEND?

Julian Haseldine

Thomas Becket, arriving more than half a century too late for the investiture contest, has fired devotion and kindled confusion since his abrupt and complete conversion to the cause of the Church in 1162. The immediate issues of the conflict he engendered were obviously different. For many his claims were questionable and his stance provocative, yet his devotees included one of the most erudite and politically sophisticated scholars of the day, John of Salisbury. His cult rapidly overwhelmed Canterbury, the church whose resources his actions had so depleted. A people who had witnessed the royal authority of one of their greatest leaders, peacemakers, and lawgivers shaken, craved Becket's intercessions. The pope to whom he had been an inconvenience and an embarrassment, and who had pressed him repeatedly to compromise, canonized him with almost incautious haste. The turns of Becket's life and death have been analysed so often and so well that their paradoxical aspect no longer surprises. Alexander III's calculations as to where the interests of the papacy lay before and then after the martyrdom are not always hard to fathom; the study of John of Salisbury is virtually a sub-discipline in its own right; while Frank Barlow's recent biography of the archbishop himself masterfully elucidates every twist in the drama.[1] Yet it is worth reminding ourselves from time to time of the astonishing character of those familiar events, and of the insoluble enigma of Becket's personal resolution of the question of his loyalties after 1162 in which they had their origin. A scandalous choice for archbishop, a man who drove the course of his own martyrdom with dubious claims and admirable resolve, a martyr canonized through a combination of political calculation and uncontrollable popular devotion, Becket's legacy is difficult to assess.

In 1996 Henry Mayr-Harting published a short article in *The Times* in defence of a small but beautiful and significant piece of that legacy, the Limoges casket then to be sold at Sotheby's. Rather than rehearse the case for government intervention to preserve the national heritage, the article conveyed—to a wider readership than that which academics normally address—something of the import and fascination of that heritage, concluding: 'Let us

---

[1] F. Barlow, *Thomas Becket* (London, 1986).

hope, therefore, that Becket's casket, with its enamel scenes representing his martyrdom and ascent into Heaven, will stay in England to remind us of this great Anglo-Norman and of a passage in our history significant for all of Europe.'[2] Here in two columns is a distillation of some of the illuminating insights into Becket's character, his cause, and its reception which must be familiar to anyone who has had the good fortune to be a tutee of Henry. Two points were particularly evocative of my own Becket tutorial. First, that it was the church of Canterbury rather than the Church universal whose cause Becket initially embraced with such determination, and to whose rights he clung until he commended himself to St Alphege at his death. And secondly, that what elevated this local conflict to the highest political level was not only its adoption by influential Paris theologians (who eventually propagated Becket's cause most widely, as an instance of the greater struggle of the Church against earthly power), but also something more personal to Becket, without which such an elevation must surely have been unlikely: 'Becket was a truly charismatic man, or else he could hardly have retained the loyalties of so many highly intelligent and able supporters for so long, to the certain detriment of their careers. There was no disguising his distinction.'[3]

Many causes have been identified, many speculations offered, to explain Thomas Becket's dramatic rending of the political fabric of one of Europe's strongest kingships. The compromise of rulers will always be welcomed in some quarters. The relationship of the Church to earthly power was an issue of central significance and increasing theoretical complexity—Becket's cause was received in an intellectually and ideologically charged atmosphere. At the same time, was he playing the devout son of the Church to compensate for the circumstances of his election and to secure a degree of authority independent of that conferred by the king? Yet none of these arguments is sufficient to explain both the course chosen and the vital base of devoted support which made it all possible. One might compare St Anselm, his conscience touched by the words of his pope in Rome rather than by Kentish land disputes, racked by the spiritual turmoil of competing loyalties, friendships, and duties, working slowly towards a solution, a churchman of impeccable credentials, in a better position to take advantage of the sorts of factors seen to have assisted Becket, and at a time when the papacy was more vehement in its claims against earthly authority. Even his immediate concerns for the rights and lands of Canterbury were, as Southern has shown, closer to Becket's than is often acknowledged, yet he did not see these as putting him automatically in opposition to his king;[4] still

---

[2] *The Times*, 28 June 1996, p. 20, 'Hold on to Becket's casket: turbulent priest or saint, asks Henry Mayr-Harting'. On the reliquary casket, see also n. 52 below.

[3] Ibid.

[4] See R. W. Southern, *Saint Anselm: A Portrait in a Landscape* (Cambridge, 1990), 305–6. On St Anselm and the investiture controversy, see 232–4, 280–4.

less did he carry others with him on a provocative collision course.[5] If we want to understand why Becket not only chose but was able to go so much further from so much flimsier a base than Anselm, Henry Mayr-Harting's argument takes us to the heart of the political reality of the situation. It can be all too easy to avoid discussions of charisma—likewise of sanctity or the miraculous, or of friendship, and other phenomena whose impact on politics eludes contractual or constitutional analysis—but to do so can leave us trapped between two abstractions, a deceptively persuasive political reductionism, and a view of the world in which ideologies grow independently of human agency. It is the scholarly treatment of undeniably important yet difficult-to-schematize phenomena such as this which the overused expression 'bringing the past to life' should imply, and which Henry's pupils will recognize as a memorable facet of his inspirational teaching, even if they have not had the specific benefit of the Becket tutorial, so unexpectedly recalled by that short piece in *The Times*.[6]

Friendship, even of the formalized sort cultivated by the literate elites of medieval Europe, can often be as difficult to assess, yet as real in its impact, as charisma.[7] Here too, incidentally, it would be hard to find two characters more different than the two saint archbishops and defenders of Canterbury's rights, Anselm and Thomas. Anselm's letters are a testament to a world built around the cultivation of friendships which were for him a genuine—indeed, the most personal—meeting-point of the human and the divine in this world. His personality drew in others, commanding devoted loyalty certainly, but tempering its consequences with friendly wisdom. Becket, it appears, shed friends easily as he progressed in his career, inspiring loyalty rather than affection.[8] In life contemporaries recognized the potential martyr; in death he was accepted unhesitatingly and virtually universally as a saint; a friend he appears not to have been. That Becket seems to have been able to pursue his career without notable reliance on the carefully cultivated network of friendships that characterize so much political activity in this period may be another testament to the particular strength of his charisma. His cause, however, did not operate entirely outside the context of friendship. If he himself stood apart from, or above, his contemporaries, he was yet able to benefit—in a sense vicariously—from the friendships of his followers, reaching out beyond and complementing the loyal support of his closest core.

Becket and his devotees were sustained through many years of exile by

[5] Christopher Brooke spoke of John of Salisbury and Thomas Becket's return to England in 1170 as 're-enter[ing] Kafka's castle' (*The Letters of John of Salisbury*, ed. W. J. Millor, H. E. Butler, and C. N. L. Brooke, 2 vols. (Oxford, 1979–86), II, p. xliv); and of course, as we chose to forget during the Cold War, Kafka's heroes are complicit in, indeed the agents of, their own destruction.

[6] It must be stressed that this rough and brief paraphrase should not be taken as an adequate representation of Henry's arguments, merely as a subjective reflection on a couple of the points summarized in the article. It was also Henry who first suggested to me the possibilities for the study of friendship.

[7] See e.g. the papers and bibliography in J. P. Haseldine (ed.), *Friendship in Medieval Europe* (Stroud, 1999).

[8] Cf. e.g. Barlow, *Thomas Becket*, 25. On Anselm and friendship, see Southern, *Portrait*, 138–65.

sympathizers and supporters who, even if not directly threatened by Henry II, cannot have given their support, political or economic, lightly. We know who many of them were, but what were their motivations? We can pick up the trail with another tale of relics. By 1175 or 1176 there were relics of Thomas at Saint-Remi, Reims; they are mentioned in a letter from the abbot, Peter of Celle, to Benedict of Peterborough, then prior of Christ Church, Canterbury, reporting accounts of two miracles, only one of which made it into Benedict's collection.[9] In the first, a sick monk of the Carthusian house of Mont-Dieu (in the Ardennes) was healed by touching a record of the miracles (*carta miraculorum*) of Thomas Becket. This 'had come to us [Saint-Remi] from England, and to the brothers of Mont-Dieu from us'. The other account, which Peter himself doubted should be counted as a miracle, and which Benedict did not include, involved the loss of a chapterbook:

In our chapel a little book containing saints' days and the memorials of our dead which is read out in chapter happened to be stolen by I know not whom. On the next day, when I was urgently demanding that the reading be given in the usual way from that very same book, to the dismay of the chaplains the little book could not be found. But while I was scolding those same chaplains for the negligence and carelessness of their bad guardian-ship, one of them, called Robert Anglicus, who used to celebrate Mass frequently at the altar in which the relics of St Thomas are kept, blurted out these words: 'I shall certainly never believe that Thomas is a saint unless he returns our little book.' About a month later the book was returned to us. If this is a miracle, I confirm it to be true.

A trivial enough incident, as Peter himself suggested and Benedict clearly agreed. We are not told when the relics had arrived, but they had evidently been there for some time as their presence is not cause for comment. The place and date offer no real surprises given what we know of the rapid spread of the cult. Nonetheless, the letter offers an interesting glimpse into the quotidian mechanics of its propagation. As we trace the story back, however, Peter of Celle's interventions look more significant. He made one of the earliest and most unambiguous statements on the martyrdom. When John of Salisbury asked whether Becket should be honoured as a martyr in anticipation of papal authorization, Peter declared that, 'in what God disposes to do through him-self, he does not seek the help or authority of man'.[10] If we go back further again,

---

[9] PL 202, col. 594, no. 150 (translations from and dates of Peter of Celle's letters are from my forth-coming edition for Oxford Medieval Texts; the letters will be renumbered therein and a concordance to the PL edn. included). The first of these accounts was copied with only minor changes into Benedict's miracle collection: *Material For the History of Thomas Becket, Archbishop of Canterbury*, ed. J. C. Robertson and J. B. Sheppard, RS, 7 vols. (London, 1875–85) (hereafter *Mats.*), II, 252. Peter of Celle was abbot of Montier-la-Celle, Troyes, *c*.1145–62, abbot of Saint-Remi, 1162–81, and bishop of Chartres, 1181–3 (*Letters of John of Salisbury*, ed. Millor *et al.*, II, pp. ix–x, n. 1).

[10] PL 202, col. 570–1, no. 121, early 1171 ('. . . quod Deus per se facere disponit, hominis auxilium uel auctoritatem non querit.') John of Salisbury's request is *Letters*, ed. Millor *et al.*, II, 724–39, no. 305 (the famous letter 'Ex insperato . . .', addressed to John of Canterbury but evidently widely circulated), at pp. 736–8.

to Becket's lifetime, we find Peter of Celle not merely anticipating the papal position, but actually contradicting it. Where Alexander counselled compromise, Peter urged resistance.[11]

The open support of this respected abbot and spiritual guide was doubtless most valued; it also represented a significant extension beyond Becket's inner circle. But how it came about is intriguing in the light of the early history of relations between the two men. Peter had snubbed a formal request for friendship from Thomas some years before, when the latter was royal chancellor and Peter still abbot of Montier-la-Celle. The episode was neatly characterized by Beryl Smalley, who wrote that 'To receive a letter of spiritual direction from [Peter] conferred a certificate of piety'—an honour which Becket failed to attain, as this 'polite and cruel snub' showed.[12] In fact this was not the end of the story, but the evidence of another letter from the abbot to the chancellor not included in the PL edition does little to alter this picture.[13] It is an elaborate excuse for Peter's delay in sending some sermons requested by Thomas in his first approach. Thomas is called 'dearest lord and friend' but, in a letter whose theme is gratitude and repayment of service, Peter seems barely comfortable with, let alone enthusiastic about, the connection. Peter of Celle was by no means too humble to correspond with Becket—his contacts included Peter the

[11] See Peter of Celle's letters, 85 (PL 202, col. 532, also *Mats.* VI, 305–6, no. 352: 1167 mid-Nov. × Dec.) and 114 (PL 202, col. 563–5: 1169 Aug.–Nov., quoted below). It is interesting to compare him with Alexander III on the theme of the wicked times: Alexander III to Becket, June 1165, forbidding him to take further action against his adversaries before the following Easter: 'Quoniam dies mali sunt, et multa sunt pro qualitate temporis toleranda, discretionem tuam rogamus, monemus, consulimus et suademus, ut in omnibus tuis et ecclesie agendis te cautum, prouidum et circumspectum exhibeas . . .' (*Mats.* V, 179–80, no. 95, at 179). Alexander III to Becket on the appointment of the legates Gratian and Vivian in 1169, urging caution: 'Quapropter rogamus fraternitatem tuam atque monemus, quatenus malitiam et angustiam temporis diligenter considerans, et attendens quomodo maiores nostri tempora redemerunt propter dierum malitiam, ad recuperandam gratiam et amorem supradicti regis, omnibus modis, quantum saluo ordine et officio tuo fieri poterit, elabores . . .' (*Mats.* VI, 563–4, no. 491, at 564). Peter of Celle to Becket, possibly with reference to the same legation, drawing opposite conclusions from a consideration of the times: 'Dicunt enim: "Non debet archiepiscopus tam instanter sua repetere a rege Anglie ut dimittat reconciliationis pacem pro amissa pecunia." . . . Pensanda etiam sunt tempora et diuersi status temporum secundum quos mutantur merita causarum. Nam in primitiua ecclesia sola patientia locum habuit, ut auferenti tunicam dimitteret et pallium [cf. Matt. 5. 40, Luke 6. 29]. . . . Modo uero iam adulta ecclesia non licet filiis ecclesie quod aliquando licuit inimicis. Decet enim matrem [i.e. the 'adulta ecclesia', the present Church] corrigere filium [here Henry II] sicut decuit pupillam [i.e. the 'primitiva ecclesia'] tolerare aduersarium.'

[12] B. Smalley, *The Becket Conflict and the Schools* (Oxford, 1973), 113. The letter is PL 202, col. 426, no. 24 (also *Mats.* V, 3–4, no. 2): 'Rogastis de familiaritate et amicitia. Quod rogastis si admitteretis admirationi procul dubio habendum esset pro inequali rogantis et rogati fortuna. Que enim proportionalitatis habitudo inter abbatem Cellensem et cancellarium regis Anglie?' The letter is a model of complex ambiguity, its central theme being a possibly deliberately barbed reflection on Becket's *moderatio* and *humilitas* in terms of a struggle between *gloria* and *prosperitas*. As so often with letters of this period and style, the context of many of the allusions is lost, but given Becket's possible intention of improving his standing with men of religious reputation (cf. Barlow, *Thomas Becket*, 63), this was surely no pat formula, and quite possibly double-edged.

[13] J. Leclercq, 'Nouvelles lettres de Pierre de Celle', *Studia Anselmiana*, 43 (1958), 160–79, at 178–9, no. 6.

Venerable, St Bernard, and Henry of France, Louis VII's brother. But his choice of correspondents, at least as reflected in the letter collection which he left for posterity, was overwhelmingly monastic.[14] Reluctant and hesitant as these letters are, they mark nonetheless a notable exception to Peter's usual choice of correspondent. Similarly, the letters written during the years of the Becket conflict stand out against the monastic concerns and spiritual tone of the bulk of the collection.[15] From a figure of such evident repute and standing in the monastic world, this cannot be without significance. The common thread running through this story is John of Salisbury, an old friend of Peter, possibly since their student days. It was most likely John who first prompted Becket to write to Peter of Celle.[16] He was also a guest of Peter at Saint-Remi for most of his years of exile. Interesting as this is, it would be of limited consequence if it were simply a case of a friend of one of Becket's colleagues responding, perhaps a little reluctantly, to a formal advance from the worldly chancellor, and then later issuing formal statements of support for the exiled archbishop. The connection becomes more significant, however, when one considers who else in France rallied to Becket's cause.

We would surely be wrong to assume that it would have been easy for those living outside the Angevin dominions to offer their open and active support for Becket. His cause was never simple: it conflated a number of issues, including material rights, the primacy contest with York, and, of course, the boundaries of royal and ecclesiastical jurisdiction. Supporting Becket simply as a model of resistance to tyranny risked being identified with the view that any cause, no matter how local or material, was an issue of ecclesiastical liberty. Furthermore, taking a clear stance also invited the possibility of compromising or embarrassing Louis VII or Alexander III, both of whom had compelling political reasons for their equivocation.[17] The political alignments, no less than the ecclesiological positions, were too complex to be explained away simply as manifestations of partisan support for the causes of *regnum* or *sacerdotium*, or of Angevin–Capetian, or Anglo-French, rivalry. However far distant one was (and many of his French supporters were not that far distant), Becket raised difficult problems. Support for a cause so contentious and divisive, on a theological as well as a political level, had to be considered carefully. Furthermore,

---

[14] Like many letters of this period, Peter's survive in a carefully compiled sender's collection, a work of literature rather than a business archive.

[15] Peter was also better known as a peacemaker and mediator than as a fighter: cf. J. P. Haseldine, 'Friendship and Rivalry: The Role of *Amicitia* in Twelfth-Century Monastic Relations', *JEH* 44 (1993), 390–414.

[16] Both Thomas and John had been members of Theobald of Canterbury's household. On the early connections between John and Peter, see *Letters of John of Salisbury*, ed. Millor *et al.* I, pp. xvi–xix.

[17] Cf. Barlow, *Thomas Becket*, 134: 'Typically, although Thomas depended almost entirely on Alexander and Louis, he could not rely on either of them. For both he was a useful, but small, diplomatic asset, of value mostly because they could sacrifice him if it was in their interest so to do.'

enduring support is distinct from sympathy or public opinion, and its impact on events is of a different nature. Public opinion can surge rapidly at critical or opportune moments and affect events dramatically in the short term, but can dissipate or change its object with equal rapidity, as a result of threats or boredom and rival claims to its attention. Enduring support is often grounded in more established networks whose origins and operations are very different. Becket received sufficient support to sustain himself and his followers in exile through many years of near deadlock, with all the political pressures on the hosts which that entailed[18]—not to mention, no doubt, what modern journalists term 'compassion fatigue'. It seems reasonable, then, to seek evidence of the networks through which sustained and active support was articulated, separately from indications of sympathy or shifts of opinion. In his examination of the politics of the Alexandrine schism, Timothy Reuter made an important observation on the question of political networks:

Frederick [Barbarossa] was perhaps helped [in his conflict with Alexander III] by the absence of a network of intellectuals in Germany bound by ties of cultivated *amicitia* and formal letter-writing such as was capable of providing a kind of public opinion in England and northern France. Rather, there were a number of small groups and isolated individuals, whose impact could not be great.[19]

It was just such a network that helped Becket in northern France, furnishing the support of people who were indeed neither isolated nor without influence, and which was more substantial than public opinion. It is in this wider context that Peter of Celle's relations with Thomas Becket, and his friendship with John of Salisbury, take on greater significance.

A preliminary survey of some of the epistolary sources reveals interesting connections between Becket's active supporters in France and Peter of Celle's circle of friends—connections which for the most part long pre-date the Becket affair.[20] John of Salisbury, going ahead of Becket into exile, very soon settled at Saint-Remi, where Peter of Celle had recently been installed as abbot. There he remained, while Becket went to Pontigny and later to Sainte-Colombe, Sens. John's connections outside England fall roughly into three groups: old Canterbury acquaintances, contacts in the curia, and others in northern France.

---

[18] The Cistercians discovered what involvement meant when, in 1166, Henry II threatened to expel the order from his lands unless they expelled Thomas from his refuge in Pontigny (Barlow, *Thomas Becket*, 157).

[19] T. A. Reuter, 'The Papal Schism, the Empire and the West, 1159–1169', D.Phil. thesis (Univ. of Oxford, 1975), 177, quoted by kind permission of the author.

[20] These comments are based on a cursory examination of the Becket, John of Salisbury, and Peter of Celle letter collections. A systematic network analysis, in the context of other types of evidence, is needed, but even at this stage a clear pattern begins to emerge. The relevant characters are those from non-Angevin areas, excluding members of the curia (whose reasons for involvement are manifestly different) and, obviously, Becket's own clerks temporarily resident in France. Active supporters include those who wrote in support of Becket and those named in the sources as supporters or friends.

The key to the last group is Peter of Celle.[21] John corresponded with the Carthusian priors Simon of Mont-Dieu and Engelbert of Val-Saint-Pierre, both of whom were prominent members of Peter's circle; both were crucial negotiators for Becket in the later stages of the dispute, holding papal commissions to mediate. Of all those who acted in various diplomatic roles, they were among the most sympathetic to Becket.[22] It is also noteworthy that Simon of Mont-Dieu's main contact in the curia, Albert of Morra, was also Peter of Celle's key friend there during these years, as well as being among John of Salisbury's connections.[23] Peter is named in John's letters to other correspondents as a mutual acquaintance or the source of the contact, as for example with Bishop Guy of Châlons-sur-Marne, who offered support to the exiles, most probably at Peter's behest.[24] Peter again seems to be the crucial figure in John's first contact with Count Henry the Liberal of Champagne.[25] Peter is known to have attended Henry's court, and dedicated his treatise on monastic life to him, as well as involving him in the foundation of a Carthusian house—a project close to Peter's heart.[26] Henry the Liberal sent to the pope a letter written in his name by Herbert of Bosham, denouncing John of Oxford's mission to the curia, and is also named as a supporter of Becket by John of Poitiers, and may have been regarded by the pope as one of the more sympathetic of the French nobles.[27] Archbishop Henry of Reims (Henry of France, Louis VII's brother)

---

[21] In addition to the letters dating from the years of the Becket conflict, discussed below, most of the letters to France in John's early collection are addressed to Peter of Celle himself (eight letters, plus one to his provost, Thomas, leaving only one to a member of the chapter of Sens and one to Ralph of Sarre, a former member of Theobald's household then at Reims—*Letters of John of Salisbury*, ed. Millor *et al.*, I, nos. 19, 31–5, 111–12; 20; 17; 124). And reciprocally, with the exception of those involved with Lapley, an English dependency of Saint-Remi, all of Peter's contacts in England can be traced to John of Salisbury.

[22] See e.g. *Mats.* VI, nos. 451–2, 456, 464, 472 (pp. 488–91, 496–8, 516–8, 531–2); Barlow, *Thomas Becket*, 179; *Letters of John of Salisbury*, ed. Millor *et al.*, II, nos. 183, 206, 286 (pp. 208–11, 306–9, 628–31) and pp. xxxiv, xli, 209–11, n. 1; PL 202, nos. 46–7, 155 (cols. 467–72, 598–9).

[23] Albert, cardinal of San Lorenzo in Lucina from 1158, later Pope Gregory VIII. (Another of Peter's circle, Berneredus of Saint-Crépin, became a cardinal, but not until 1179.) Simon to Albert, 1169, *Mats.* VI, no. 465, pp. 518–9. The original contact may have been through Engelbert of Val-Saint-Pierre; Albert was evidently Engelbert's patron in some capacity (see Peter of Celle to Albert of Morra, PL 202, col. 532–3, no. 86). John to Albert, *Letters of John of Salisbury*, ed. Millor *et al.*, II, nos. 234, 316 (pp. 926–33, 776–7) and pp. xlv, 427, n. 1.

[24] Guy de Joinville: see *Letters of John of Salisbury*, ed. Millor *et al.*, II, no. 141 (1164–70), pp. 26–7, and no. 144 (1165), pp. 31–7, at pp. 36–7.

[25] *Letters of John of Salisbury*, ed. Millor *et al.*, II, no. 209, at pp. 316–17.

[26] On Peter's attendance at the court, see J. F. Benton, 'The Court of Champagne as a Literary Center', *Speculum*, 36 (1961), 551–91; the treatise is *De disciplina claustrali*, see the dedicatory letter at PL 202, cols. 1097–1100; on the attempted Carthusian foundation (*c*.1160), see PL 202, nos. 47–8, cols. 470–4. Peter took a particular interest in the Carthusian Order and frequently lent it his support; he was also involved in their first attempts to settle in Denmark in the 1160s, under the aegis of his friend Eskil of Lund (PL 202, nos. 20 (1157 x 61) and 144 *bis* (1162 x 1173/4), cols. 421–3, 588–9).

[27] Letter to the pope (1166–7): *Mats.* VI, 140–2, no. 280; letter of John of Poitiers: *Mats.* V, 197, no. 103; in some MSS Henry is the addressee of *Mats.* V, no. 136, p. 245 (1166), and see n. 1 (Alexander III to Louis VII, urging continued support for Becket). Henry was also involved in negotiating for Henry II with Louis VII over the political settlement of the kingdom (see e.g. *Letters of John of Salisbury*, ed. Millor *et al.*, II, 562–71)—another illustration of the complexity of the political context.

was a major figure in the politics of the region and a staunch supporter of Alexander III. Both Becket and John of Salisbury attempted to make contact with Henry in the early stages of the dispute, but the breakthrough evidently came through Peter of Celle, and thereafter Henry appears in the sources as a supporter.[28] Henry seems to have been a patron of Peter of Celle; he had supported him in earlier years when he was bishop of Beauvais and Peter abbot of Montier la-Celle,[29] and his translation to Reims was followed rapidly by Peter's election to Saint-Remi. The Reims connection remained an important one; Dean Fulk appears in the correspondence as a supporter and friend of the exiles (among whom Philip of Calne and Ralph of Sarre were offered refuge at the cathedral), and is named by John of Salisbury as a friend in connection with Peter of Celle.[30] Another important source of support was Soissons. Here the key figure is Abbot Berneredus of Saint-Crépin-le-Grand, one of Peter of Celle's closest *amici*, the recipient of many letters, and an intimate member of his inner circle.[31] Berneredus was one of those whom Becket wanted the pope to mandate to order Henry II to agree to his terms in 1170.[32] John of Salisbury recalled this inner circle on his return to England when he asked Peter to request on his behalf the prayers of their mutual friends Simon of Mont-Dieu, Engelbert of Val-Saint-Pierre, Guy of Saint-Nicaise, and Berneredus of Saint-Crépin.[33] Finally of course, there is William 'aux Blanches Mains', the archbishop of Sens, brother of Count Henry the Liberal, perhaps the most active French proponent of Becket and a key mover in the canonization.[34] Peter of Celle is not explicitly named as the point of first contact with William, who was a greater political player in his own right than many of the others and presumably had his own agenda. Nevertheless, his connections with the circle are significant. Peter

---

[28] Barlow, *Thomas Becket*, 96, on Becket's early attempts to contact figures in France. *Letters of John of Salisbury*, ed. Millor *et al.*, II, no. 136 (early 1164), at p. 8: 'Et quia Remensem adire non potui, litteras meas ad abbatem sancti Remigii amicissimum michi direxi, ut in hac parte suppleat vices meas.' This is not explicitly a request for an introduction, but Henry subsequently appears in the John of Salisbury and Becket correspondence as a supporter: see ibid. II, 34–5, 100–1, 630–1 (and note the comment at p. xix that he was 'in a sense John's patron' during the exile); *Mats.* VI, 384–5, 501–2; also Barlow, *Thomas Becket*, 252.

[29] PL 202, cols. 423–4, no. 21, March 1151 x 1162, probably 1151/2.

[30] See e.g. *Mats.* V, nos. 86 (1165) and 146 (date uncertain), pp. 165–6, 256–8; *Letters of John of Salisbury*, ed. Millor *et al.*, II, no. 179 (1166), at p. 188.

[31] Peter to Berneredus, PL 202, nos. 93–5, 97–9, 101–2, cols. 540–54. He was apparently well acquainted with Simon of Mont-Dieu and Engelbert of Val-Saint-Pierre, and there is evidence for at least one meeting of the three with Peter of Celle, at Mont-Dieu (PL 202, no. 155, cols. 598–9, at col. 599; unfortunately the letter can be dated no more closely than 1162 x 79). Count Henry of Soissons was also an early sympathizer who offered refuge to the exiles (*Mats.* V, 58).

[32] Barlow, *Thomas Becket*, 218 (the other was Stephen of Meaux, see below n. 38).

[33] *Letters of John of Salisbury*, ed. Millor *et al.*, II, no. 304 (Dec. 1170), at p. 722. Peter's reply, PL 202, no. 121 (early 1171), cols. 570–1, names the same characters plus the abbot of Montier-la-Celle. Saint-Nicaise stood within sight of Saint-Remi, which presumably explains the lack of correspondence with its abbot.

[34] On his career see *Letters of John of Salisbury*, ed. Millor *et al.*, II, 567–8, n. 28; on his support for Becket, see Barlow, *Thomas Becket*, 130, 158, 191–2, 198, 252–4.

of Celle had supported the young William at an early stage of his career; later William was involved by Peter in the affairs of Engelbert of Val-Saint-Pierre and of one of the Carthusian foundations in which Peter took such an interest, and was also the chief mover in John of Salisbury's election to Chartres.[35]

This accounts for virtually all of the recipients of John of Salisbury's letters outside the Angevin dominions who can be identified with certainty.[36] More interestingly, it accounts for a good number of those in France who can be connected with active support for Becket—perhaps more than half, and certainly most of the long-standing and significant players.[37] While there were clearly others involved who had only a tangential connection—or none that is evident—with the Peter of Celle–John of Salisbury circle,[38] it does provide links between Henry of France, William 'aux Blanches Mains', Simon of Mont-Dieu, Engelbert of Val-Saint-Pierre, Berneredus of Saint-Crépin and other Soissons figures, Guy of Châlons, Fulk of Reims, and Henry the Liberal. Furthermore, while the situation in the Angevin lands was necessarily different, there is no evidence for other areas of France comparable to that for the Sens–Reims region. Open sympathy for Becket in Flanders soon dried up; in Bourges support was clandestine and uncertain;[39] the prominent figure in Lyons was Archbishop Guichard, the former abbot of Pontigny, Thomas's first residence in exile; Cluny was compromised, its abbot, Hugh de Fraisans, deposed and excommunicated by Henry of Reims for supporting the antipope;[40] the bishop of Nevers sided with Henry II;[41] further south there was an indifference similar to that which Reuter noted concerning the Alexandrine schism.[42]

Significantly, almost all of the connections which can be traced to the Peter

---

[35] Peter supported William's candidacy for the provostship of Soissons sometime after 1154: PL 202, no. 5, cols. 408–9; on William's involvement with the Carthusians (1172) and in John of Salisbury's election (1176), see nos. 116–7, cols. 566–8.

[36] With the exception of old Canterbury friends in exile, e.g. Gerard Pucelle. Other recipients include the treasurer of Reims and the abbot of Saint-Médard, Soissons, who may well, given the geographical foci of Peter's circle, have been connected to it.

[37] Again, excluding exiles temporarily in the region and curial officials.

[38] e.g. Stephen of Meaux (see *Mats.* V, no. 143, pp. 253–4; VI, nos. 240, 437, pp. 38–40, 462–4; VII, nos. 613–14, 743, pp. 183–4, 446–7), Matthew of Troyes and William of Auxerre (see *Mats.* VII, nos. 543, 548, pp. 35–7, 44–5), and Almaric of Senlis and Matthew, precentor of Sens (see *Mats.* VI, nos. 241, 281, 438, pp. 40–2, 142–3, 464–7). Some others who are not known to have been part of this circle were friends or contacts of John of Salisbury: Abbot Ersin of Saint-Victor and Prior Richard (see *Mats.* V, 456–8) and Baldwin de Beuseberg, dean of Noyon (see *Letters of John of Salisbury*, ed. Millor *et al.*, II, 4–7). These were interventions of varying degrees of significance; a number of the letters were written by Herbert of Bosham in the names of others.

[39] On Peter de Chastres, archbishop of Bourges, whose letters were reported to have been found among Becket's secret papers in 1167, see Barlow, *Thomas Becket*, 165 and n. 42; *Mats.* VI, no. 283, pp. 145–9, at p. 147; and on Hubert Crivelli, who may have helped the exiles, Barlow, *Thomas Becket*, 37, 131. Cf. also *Mats.* V, no. 83, pp. 159–60.

[40] See G. Constable, 'The Abbots and Anti-Abbot of Cluny During the Papal Schism of 1159', *Revue Bénédictine*, 94 (1984), 370–400.

[41] Barlow, *Thomas Becket*, 191.   [42] Reuter, 'The Papal Schism', 193–5.

of Celle–John of Salisbury circle pre-date the Becket affair, in many cases by decades, and continue to be in evidence in relation to other matters during and after the conflict. Thus, Henry of Reims's connection with Peter of Celle can be traced back to at least 1151 and, although the details of the relationship are obscure, it is clear that Henry showed Peter particular favour and cannot have been without influence in his election to Saint-Remi.[43] The earliest known connection between Peter of Celle and William 'aux Blanches Mains' dates from 1154/8, when Peter supported his contested election to the provostship of Soissons.[44] As with Henry of Reims, not only is the connection a long-standing one but it pre-dates his election to the archbishopric, suggesting something more than a routine contact between an important abbot and a local metropolitan. The connection of the Carthusians, Simon of Mont-Dieu and Engelbert of Val-Saint-Pierre, with Peter of Celle possibly dated back to the 1140s or earlier; Simon may have been one of Peter's monks, and Engelbert was a one-time pupil of John of Salisbury.[45] Moreover, they had worked together before their 'double act' in the Becket negotiations: in around 1160 they went to meet Henry the Liberal to negotiate the foundation of a new Charterhouse on Henry's lands—negotiations mediated by Peter of Celle. Engelbert was also involved in the foundation of Val-Dieu (Carthusian, Sées), in which Peter had involved William 'aux Blanches Mains'.[46] Peter's connection to Berneredus of Saint-Crépin cannot be proved conclusively before the 1160s, but the tone and content of the earliest evidence strongly suggests a long acquaintance.[47]

One can view all this evidence from yet another perspective. Not only is there an almost complete overlap between John of Salisbury's connections in France and the circle of Peter of Celle, as well as a notable degree of overlap between active supporters of Becket and this circle, but the characters who emerge in these connections represent a significant proportion of Peter of Celle's closest and most frequent correspondents. Only eight recipients of letters in Peter's collection receive more than five letters each; five of these eight recipients are among the known Becket supporters. These include the prior and community of Mont-Dieu, Peter's favourite retreat and the location both of the meeting between Peter, Simon of Mont-Dieu, Engelbert of Val-Saint-Pierre, and Berneredus of Saint-Crépin, and of the healing miracle involving the *carta*

---

[43] PL 202, no. 21, 1151 x 62, most likely 1151/2. Both also had past connections with Saint-Martin-des-Champs and Clairvaux: on Henry's early life see *The Letters of Peter the Venerable*, ed. G. Constable, 2 vols. (Cambridge, Mass., 1967), II, 195–6; for Peter of Celle's connection with Saint-Martin-des-Champs, PL 202, no. 159, col. 603.

[44] See above and n. 35.

[45] Simon may be the monk named in PL 202, no. 42 (*c.*1154 or earlier), cols. 459–61, at 461; on Engelbert and John, see *Letters of John of Salisbury*, ed. Millor *et al.*, II, 310–11.

[46] On these foundations, see above and nn. 35 and 26.

[47] On the correspondence, see above n. 31.

miraculorum sent there from Saint-Remi.[48] What we would seem to have here is the concerted mobilization of an inner circle of long standing.

It seems reasonable to suggest then—and at this preliminary stage a suggestion is all that it can be—that there is evidence here for something more than a temporary coincidence of sympathy for one cause, influenced by public opinion or shared ecclesiological ideology. These were not characters thrown together by their support for Becket; rather, their mutual obligations as friends led them into varying degrees of involvement in the affair. In making directly for Reims at the beginning of his exile, John of Salisbury may have been thinking of more than the rich library and warm hospitality of his old friend, or simply of establishing a comfortable and politic distance between himself and his controversial master. He was, after all, risking—indeed sacrificing—much for Becket. Both Christopher Brooke and Anne Duggan have argued that while he did seek his own settlement with Henry II at an early stage, John's fundamental loyalty to Becket remained firm.[49] His choice of Reims may indeed have had as much to do with loyalty or usefulness to the cause as with caution and hedging. By going there he was placing himself at the centre of an established network which he knew could be relied upon for more than passing support. If Thomas Becket did not qualify for his 'certificate of piety' from Peter of Celle in the early years, it was John of Salisbury who procured for him his 'passport to piety', and access to the important northern French friendship circle which was so sustaining a complement to the dedication and devotion of his own followers and fellow exiles. That is not to say that this was a carefully laid scheme from the beginning instigated by a prescient John; rather, it was such networks which made up the fabric of the political world in which John operated and which he understood intimately. Thomas Becket still does not come out of this as a man blessed with the gift of friendship; indeed, the image persists of one who felt the loneliness of greatness. His charismatic appeal may not be readily appreciable from the surviving documents,[50] but something of his greatness is at least reflected in the admiration and loyalty of this circle of friends. And this is a story not without colour, from the intricate and tortured delicacy of Peter's early letters, through the ringing declarations of support, to the cosy domestic miracle of the lost

[48] The recipients of more than five letters each are: the prior and community of Mont-Dieu ('letters addressed to whole communities are not uncommon in this period'), Berneredus of Saint-Crépin, Albert of Morra, John of Salisbury and Richard of Salisbury (John's brother, and a fellow exile); the others in this category are Pope Alexander III, Eskil of Lund, and Bishop John of Saint-Malo (who died before the crisis broke). On the meeting at Mont-Dieu, see above n. 31.

[49] *Letters of John of Salisbury*, ed. Millor *et al.*, II, p. xix; A. Duggan, 'John of Salisbury and Thomas Becket', in *The World of John of Salisbury*, ed. M. Wilks, *Studies in Church History, Subsidia* 3 (Oxford, 1994), 427–38.

[50] To quote the article in *The Times* again: 'David Knowles once wrote that in history there are those such as Cicero or Abraham Lincoln whose personality reveals itself in every word they wrote or spoke, and others whose charm and power were felt by their contemporaries but whose surviving words do not conduct "the magnetic spark". He put Becket among the latter.'

book. The volume itself may be safe yet: it is possible that it is still in Reims.[51] The Limoges reliquary is certainly safe, preserved for the nation by the intervention of the British government after—aptly for Thomas—an unprecedented political furore.[52] It is now on display in the Victoria and Albert Museum, and is rightly deemed to be an important part of the nation's heritage.

---

[51] Bibliothèque municipale 346: H. Loriquet, *Catalogue général des manuscrits des bibliothèques publiques de France. Départements*, vol. 38 (Paris, 1904), 428–40. The book certainly contains a martyrology and obits, as well as prayer associations, a copy of the Rule, and other material.

[52] I am grateful to Marian Campbell of the Metalwork Department of the Victoria and Albert Museum for answering my enquiries about the recent history of the casket. The political intervention was unprecedented in part because the casket had not been in the country for 50 years prior to the sale, and so would not normally have required an export licence. The Victoria and Albert Museum's information sheet on the casket gives details of the purchase, funding, and donors; the press coverage was most detailed in *The Times*, which published numerous articles (many by Dalya Alberge) and leading articles (13, 15, 28, 29 June 1996, at least one article every day between 2 and 6 July 1996, and 12 and 18 July 1996); on the casket itself see *The Medieval Treasury: The Art of the Middle Ages in the Victoria and Albert Museum*, ed. P. Williamson, 2nd edn. (London, 1996), 178–9.

23

TWO CONCEPTS OF TEMPTATION*

Henrietta Leyser

He asked Abba Joseph of Panepho, 'What would I do when the passions assail me? Should I resist them, or let them enter?' The old man answered, 'Let them enter, and fight against them.' Poemen returned to Scetis where he remained (as a hesychast). Now someone from Thebes came to Scetis and said to the brothers, 'I asked Abba Joseph, "When a passion draws near, should I oppose it or allow it to enter?" He answered me, "Absolutely do not let the passions enter, but cut them off at once."' When Abba Poemen learned that Abba Joseph had spoken to the Theban in such a manner, he arose, went to see him in Panepho, and said, 'Abba, I confided my thoughts to you; and you have said one thing to me, and another to the Theban.' The old man replied, 'Do you not know that I love you?' He answered, 'Certainly'.—'And did you now say, speak to me as you would speak to yourself?' 'Indeed', Poemen replied. Then the old man said, 'When the passions enter and you give and receive blows while contending with them, they will make you stronger. Surely, I spoke to you as to myself. But there are others who should not let the passions draw nigh: they must cut them off instantly.'[1]

My two concepts of temptation—a title suggested by Isaiah Berlin's *Two Concepts of Liberty*—are, of course, already very ancient by the twelfth century. A search for their origins would take us back beyond the deserts of Egypt and the wilderness of Galilee to the Promised Land, even to the Garden of Eden itself; and everywhere we would find the same question hovering over the figure of the Tempter: what is the source and rationale of his power? The Old Testament has more than one answer. The God of Isaiah makes 'light and darkness, good and evil'; Job's God holds a court which Satan, returning from 'roaming the earth', is expected to attend as a loyal and obedient servant; yet when we reach David's God in the First Book of Chronicles we find God and Satan in quite separate, even opposing camps. From then on, in the words of Neil Forsyth, 'the way was open for the rapid and spectacular rise to power of the independent evil ruler of human affairs'.[2]

---

* I offer here the abbreviated text of a lecture first delivered at St Peter's College, Oxford, in 1993 at a seminar organized by Henry Mayr-Harting on the twelfth century. It was followed by one of the many memorable teas that I have enjoyed with Henry.

[1] *Apophthemagata Patrum, Alph.*, Joseph Panephysis, n. 3: PG 75, cols. 228D–30A; quoted by I. Hausherr, *Spiritual Direction in the Early Christian East*, trans. A. P. Gythiel (Kalamazoo, 1990), 7. I owe this reference to Anthony Lappin. I also owe thanks to Timea Szell for her critical reading of my first draft and to Richard Gameson for superhuman patience.

[2] N. Forsyth, *The Old Enemy: Satan and the Combat Myth* (Princeton, 1987), 122.

The relationship between God and the Devil profoundly affects, even if it does not precisely determine, my two concepts. Briefly, I see temptation as being perceived, on the one hand, as the terrible legacy of Eden, as an ever-present plague to be both fought and avoided, while on the other it is accepted as part of the human condition, however painful, a means of spiritual growth and therefore of positive value. All sorts of intermediate positions are, of course, possible, but as far as the twelfth century is concerned there is, I hope to argue, a case for making a sharp contrast between the temptation you could well do without, and the temptation which does you good.

Let us begin with contrasting accounts of the temptations of Hugh, bishop of Lincoln († 1200). In Adam of Eynsham's *Magna Vita Sancti Hugonis* Hugh, in his first years as a Carthusian, is severely assailed by temptations: 'the tempter', he would recall, 'direct[ed] all the ancient weapons of his infernal armoury against a new recruit to this holy warfare and in particular, as if from a very powerful crossbow, he shot bolts which, he hoped, I could not resist, since they were part of myself. I mean that he aroused my carnal lusts.'[3] To his horror, years later, as Hugh is about to become prior of England's first Charterhouse, such temptations return: angels of darkness seek to lure him into 'the dark night of evil consent'.[4] They are decisively overcome and Hugh is never again put through such ordeals; as bishop he will be able to tell Adam how confidently he can 'invite devout matrons and widows to eat at his table and even sometimes reverently embrace them';[5] a saying of his, about women and the Incarnation, should, according to Adam, be remembered because of its beauty. Compare this account with the lurid version given in Hugh's *Metrical Life*, where tempt-ation would seem to have no value beyond adding a certain spice to the story. In the *Metrical Life* we find that even before Hugh enters the Charterhouse he has met a woman, a supermodel:

her hair rivalled gold, some of it was disguised by her attire, as though not venturing to be seen, but some of it strayed about her ivory neck. The tresses were propped back by the ear, which was delicate and whorled like a conch-shell. . . . The black line of the eye-brow curved into an arch, with not a hair out of place. . . . Her eyes sparkled like a pair of emeralds. . . . The lips were suffused . . . with rose-red. . . . From this censer proceeded the mouth's breathing: it had the fragrance of new incense and of longstored balm.[6]

Hugh, we are assured, is able to repel this 'serpentine' woman—when she touches him he takes 'a sharp knife and cuts out the small portion of his flesh affected'[7]—but there are just too many other women about, and it is to escape

---

[3] *Magna Vita Sancti Hugonis*, bk. I, c. 9: *The Life of St Hugh of Lincoln*, ed. D. Douie and H. Farmer, 2 vols. (Oxford, 1985), I, 28.

[4] Ibid., II, c. 2; ed. Douie and Farmer, I, 50.

[5] Ibid., IV, c. 9; ed. Douie and Farmer, II, 48.

[6] ll. 171–93: *The Metrical Life of Saint Hugh*, ed. and trans. C. Garton (Lincoln, 1986), 18.

[7] ll. 246–57: *The Metrical Life*, ed. Garton, 23.

the snake-like coils with which they are ensnaring his companions that, leaving
the latter apparently to their fate, he decides to become a Carthusian. As a
young monk Hugh will next be both tempted and cured much as in the *Magna
Vita*, but with this difference: there is not the slightest hint or indication that
Hugh later in his life had any particular sympathy for women or that he had
learnt anything from his temptations beyond the agonistic teaching of the
Fathers: 'no war, no victory.'

These suggestive accounts of Hugh's trials and temptations can be compared
with experiences of 'positive' temptation among Hugh's monastic contemporaries in England. First, we find Gilbert of Sempringham († 1189), an earnest
young man back from the schools of Paris, with a family living to look after.
What happens? He is smitten by the beauty of his landlord's daughter; worse
still, he has a dream that he 'put his hand into this girl's bosom and was unable
to draw it out'.[8] Overcome with anxiety, he tells his dream to his fellow
lodger—a priest—only to discover that he too is being 'affected by the same
trouble'.[9] Neither resort to rolling in nettles (a proven solution), but they do
decide to live elsewhere. What does not happen is the forswearing of all female
company. Quite the contrary: Gilbert will go on to found a double order, a
twelfth-century novelty. It will start with a small community of seven women,
one of whom is the landlord's beautiful daughter. Years later, when Gilbert is an
old man and his order has a dozen houses, one of the nuns (so Gerald of Wales
tells us) lusts after him. Gilbert meets the temptation head on with a response
as dramatic as it is unexpected. Off come his clothes; 'hairy, emaciated,
scabrous, and wild', he points at a crucifix and tells the whole community of
nuns 'behold the man who should be duly desired by a woman consecrated to
God and a bride of Christ'.[10]

Ailred of Rievaulx's story is in its way no less astonishing than Gilbert's.
Ailred, he himself tells us, had had a riotous adolescence: 'Recall,' (he writes to
his sister) 'my rottenness when a cloud of lust was emitted from my slimy concupiscence and from the gushing up of puberty, and there was no one to snatch
me away and save me.'[11] Once he has become a Cistercian monk at Rievaulx,
Ailred submits himself to standard ascetic practices, such as total immersion in
ice-cold water, but the outcome is startling and innovative. Both as abbot of
Rievaulx and as the author of the *Speculum Caritatis*, Ailred champions a
daring programme of friendship. Friendships, according to Ailred, lead us to
God. Their spiritual value does not, however, preclude the physical. Physical

---

[8] *Vita Sancti Gilberti*, c. 4: *The Book of St Gilbert*, ed. R. Foreville and G. Keir (Oxford, 1987), 17.
[9] Ibid., c. 4: *Book of St Gilbert*, 19.
[10] Gerald of Wales, *Gemma Ecclesiastica* I, 17: *Giraldi Cambrensis Opera*, ed. J. S. Brewer, J. F. Dimock,
and G. F. Warner, 8 vols., RS 21 (London, 1861–91), II, 247–8. Quoted by G. Constable, 'Ailred of
Rievaulx and the Nun of Watton', in *Medieval Women*, ed. D. Baker (Oxford, 1978), 205–26, at 222.
[11] Ailred of Rievaulx, *De Institutione Inclusarum*, ed. and trans. C. Dumont, *La Vie de recluse*,
SC 76 (Paris, 1961), 148.

attraction may be instantaneous; in itself it is neither good nor bad: 'An elegant appearance, a pleasant way of speaking, a mature bearing, and a comely countenance easily invite and ensure attachment, even if one does not know what kind of a person this is.'[12] Caution but not prudery is advised: physical attachment should be 'neither rejected utterly nor allowed just as it gushes out'.[13] Special care must be taken with relationships between older and younger men and between men and women, though here too Ailred's optimism breaks through:

when our attachment, however rational or even spiritual extends itself to someone of suspect age or sex, it is extremely advisable that it be held back within the bosom of the mind and not permitted to spill over into inane compliments or soft tenderness, unless perhaps, because of this the attachment may occasionally develop maturely and temperately until virtue loved and praised may be more fervently practised.[14]

The identification of Ailred's sources—notably Cicero, St Augustine, and Ambrose—undoubtedly helps the reader to comprehend more fully his teaching; yet it would be a mistake to imagine that we can understand his life only through the lens of this intellectual heritage. In the illness of his last years, so Walter Daniel tells us, Ailred is surrounded in his cell by his monks:

every day they came to it and sat in it, twenty or thirty at a time, to talk together of the spiritual delights of the Scriptures and of the observance of the order. There was no one to say to them, 'Get out, go away, do not touch the Abbot's bed'; they walked and lay about his bed and talked with him as a little child prattles with its mother. . . . He did not treat them with the pedantic imbecility habitual in some silly abbots who, if a monk takes a brother's hand in his own, or says anything that they do not like, demand his cowl, strip, and expel him. Not so Ailred, not so.[15]

Those ice-cold baths seem a long way off.

These examples, and others that could be given, come from the new monastic orders of the twelfth century.[16] The nature and development of these orders are, of course, closely bound up with what has been called 'the discovery of the individual'. These topics are indeed central to my theme, but much has already been written about both,[17] and I give here only the briefest summary. The more introverted piety of the twelfth century sees the focus of prayer shift from society to self. The monks of the new orders are concerned now not so much with the waging of liturgical warfare as with meditative piety. Sin is to be fought

---

[12] Ailred of Rievaulx, *Liber de Speculo Caritatis*, c. 15, ed. C. H .Talbot, CCCM 1 (Turnhout, 1971), iii. For the translations here and below see Aelred of Rievaulx, *The Mirror of Charity*, trans. E. Connor (Kalamazoo, 1990).

[13] Ibid., c. 27.   [14] Ibid., c. 28.

[15] *Vita Ailredi*, c. 31: *Walter Daniel's Life of Ailred*, ed. F. M. Powicke (Edinburgh, 1950), 40.

[16] Robert of Arbrissel's alleged practice of chastely sleeping with women is a case in point. See J. Smith, 'Robert of Arbrissel: *Procurator Mulierum*', in *Medieval Women*, ed. Baker, 175–84.

[17] For 'the discovery of the individual' see, above all, C. Morris, *The Discovery of the Individual, 1050–1200* (London, 1972) and C. W. Bynum, 'Did the Twelfth Century Discover the Individual?', in her *Jesus as Mother: Studies in the Spirituality of the High Middle Ages* (Berkeley, 1982), 82–109.

through self-knowledge. The externalization of evil, as Guy of Chartreuse recognized, is seen to be an evasion: 'the cause of our bad qualities we must
attribute to ourselves and not to the things with which we sin. All they do is to
test us out—they show us our hidden nature but they do not make us what we
are.'[18]

   To concentrate on the new orders of the twelfth century is not, of course, to
claim that the demons who stalked the cells and cloisters of such orders—
whether at Chartreuse, Sempringham, or Rievaulx—were of a totally different
breed from those to be found at say, Cluny or St Emmeram, where Otloh († *post*
1070) was so sorely tempted,[19] or at Guibert de Nogent's house of St Germer.
Demons were not, so far as we can tell, discriminating about their targets; their
aim was to be everywhere. A glance at the pages of Caesarius of Heisterbach
will show how quickly demons of every shape and size had found their way into
Cistercian imaginations: they are legion; they flit about the church glittering
with a sinister light; they appear as dragons, as huge Ethiopians, as mere
shadows, as toads the size of hens. They are dreadful teases, busily attempting
to promote gluttony, vanity, and weariness in prayer. They hide under beds
telling monks not to get up, catch the voices of over-proud singers and collect
them in a sack, conjure up illusory dishes of meat. A grim game is being played
out, over and over again. Humans ought to win—they need only remember that
'the Devil is like a lion or a bear fastened to a stake, which can growl around
within the range of his chain, but cannot injure anyone unless he catch that
person within his circle'.[20] So long as the human does not consent to the Devil's
suggestions he will not get caught; but the Devil is, of course, a master of
disguise and an infinitely artful tactician. Even then, in many situations
humans hold trump cards. The skill consists in playing the right hand: prayer,
confession, or the sign of the cross can all fail, whereas a simple *benedicite* may
send the demon scuttling away.

   Demons such as these are never likely to be out of a job; by the sixteenth century, according to some estimates, Satan was employing 7,004,000 of them.[21]
All the same, despite the Devil's resilience and powers of endurance, it will not
do to underestimate the extent to which in the twelfth century his position had
been challenged. Once upon a time he had had clear, well-defined, and easily
understood rights over mankind; the theology behind them was dualistic, but it
made sense. St Anselm's attack on it in *Cur Deus Homo* 'destroyed a satisfying

---

[18] *Guigues Ier Prieur de Chartreuse, Les Meditations*, ed. 'un Chartreux', SC 308 (Paris, 1983), 238.
[19] Otloh of Saint Emmeram, *Libellus de Suis Temptationibus, Varia Fortuna et Scriptis:* PL 146, 29–58.
[20] *Caesarii Heisterbacensis Monachi Dialogus Miraculorum*, ed. J. Strange, 2 vols. (Cologne, 1851), I, 336.
But cf. Caesarius' story of the angel who 'is said to have delivered a female recluse in France from the
temptations of the flesh and then restored them again because they were good for her soul', as noted by
Henry Mayr-Harting in his inaugural lecture, *Perceptions of Angels in History* (Oxford, 1998), 18.
[21] See the tracts on demonology cited by J. Delumeau, *La Peur en occident (XVI–VVIII siecles): Une cité
assiegée* (Paris, 1978), 251.

triangle of divine, demonic and human rights, and had left Man and God facing each other with no go-between to bridge the gap'.[22] Two extreme responses were now possible—and both would be heard. On the one hand there was the arch-conservative, Manichaean solution whereby the Devil was attributed with even more power than he had had before; such a view, however dour, at least made moral choices look relatively simple. On the other hand there was Peter Abelard's interpretation which, however attractive in theory, in practice made the whole business of being human a great deal more demanding. For, according to Abelard:

we are justified in the blood of Christ and reconciled to God by this singular grace shown to us in that his son received our nature and in this nature left us an example by word and deed of enduring until death. In doing this he so bound us to himself in love that being enflamed by so great a divine grace we will not fear to endure all things for his sake.[23]

The diminution of the Devil's role in the scheme of things as presented both by Anselm and by Abelard has frequently been seen as liberating; in the long run doubtless it was, but at the time it could have had quite the opposite effect. The burden of personal responsibility—how best to follow Christ's example, how to endure sufficiently or love adequately—which teaching such as Abelard's raises could be both daunting and confusing. No longer was the world made up of sinful laymen and women whose only chance of being saved was through the prayers of monks; now every Christian found him or herself able to be both saint and sinner. The message of the Fourth Lateran Council of 1215 was inclusive: 'if someone falls into sin after having received baptism he or she can always be restored through true penitence. For not only virgins and the continent but also married persons find favour with God by right faith and good actions and deserve to attain to eternal blessedness.'[24]

   The new scenario, to be at all tolerable, required and found for itself a new system for the management of sin and a new assertiveness in promulgating the Church's teaching—needs which the Fourth Lateran Council was expressly intended to meet. The council opened, exceptionally, with a solemn declaration of faith to which all present subscribed and which is crystal-clear about the origins of evil: 'The Devil and other demons were created by God naturally good, but they became evil by their own doing. Man, however, sinned at the prompting of the Devil.'[25] The creed is equally emphatic in its teaching about the Incarnation: Christ became incarnate through the action of the whole Trinity

---

[22] R. W. Southern, *Saint Anselm: A Portrait in a Landscape* (Cambridge, 1990), 210. For the text see *Sancti Anselmi Opera*, ed. F. S. Schmitt, 5 vols. (Seckau, Rome, and Edinburgh, 1938–61), II, 37–133.

[23] *Commentaria in Epistolam Pauli ad Romanos: Petrus Abaelardus, Opera Theologica*, I, ed. E. M. Buytaert, CCCM II (Turnhout, 1969), 117–8; quoted by Southern, *Saint Anselm*, 210.

[24] *Decrees of the Ecumenical Councils*, 2 vols., ed. N. P. Tanner (London and Washington, 1990), I, 230–1.

[25] Ibid. I, 230.

in common, he was born with human flesh, he died and suffered according to his humanity, he rose in the flesh as will all Christians—'with their own bodies, which they now wear'.[26] The definition of transubstantiation which follows is not only a reaffirmation of the humanity of Christ; it is also a proclamation of the sacramental role of matter—of bodies, of bread, and of wine.

The need to rebut Manichaean heresy clearly lies at the heart of the incarnational theology so firmly propounded by Lateran IV; if we ask why it was that this dualist heresy was at the time attracting so much support, one answer must surely be that it was the response of conservatives to the deeply felt anxieties about sin and temptation, salvation and the Devil, which reformers, popes, and theologians alike had generated.[27] Transubstantiation, the doctrine of Purgatory, and the institution of regular confession formed the basis of the counterattack. I would like here to focus on confession, looking closely at *Omnis Utriusque Sexus*, the twenty-first decree of the Lateran Council by which it became obligatory for all the faithful of either sex to confess their sins at least once a year and thereafter to take communion. In the words of the decree:

Let them reverently receive the sacrament of the eucharist at least at Easter unless they think, for a good reason and on the advice of their own priest, that they should abstain from receiving it for a time. Otherwise they shall be barred from entering a church during their lifetime and they shall be denied a christian burial at death. Let this salutary decree be frequently published in churches, so that nobody may find the pretence of an excuse in the blindness of ignorance. If any persons wish, for good reasons, to confess their sins to another priest let them first ask and obtain the permission of their own priest; for otherwise the other priest will not have the power to absolve or bind them. The priest shall be discerning and prudent, so that like a skilled doctor he may pour wine and oil over the wounds of the injured one. Let him carefully enquire about the circumstances of both the sinner and the sin, so that he may prudently discern what sort of advice he ought to give and what remedy to apply, using various means to heal the sick person. Let him take the utmost care, however, not to betray the sinner at all by word or sign or in any other way. If the priest needs wise advice, let him seek it cautiously without any mention of the person concerned. For if anyone presumes to reveal a sin disclosed to him in confession, we decree that he is not only to be deposed from his priestly office but also to be confined to a strict monastery to do perpetual penance.[28]

The importance of *Omnius Utriusque Sexus* for the story of temptation hardly needs underlining. It is now not only the sin itself but its prehistory, the story of each temptation, that has to be considered: who, what, where, with what help, why, how, when, were all questions that would be asked. The secrecy of the confessional, the freedom—however relative—to choose a priest, the priest's need

[26] *Decrees*, ed. Tanner, I, 230.
[27] For an analysis of the contrast between Catholic and Cathar rituals of penance and the marked absence of individual confession among Cathar communities, see now P. Biller, 'Confession in the Middle Ages: Introduction', in *Handling Sin: Confession in the Middle Ages*, ed. P. Biller and A. J. Minnis (York, 1998), 3–33, at 20–1.
[28] *Decrees*, ed. Tanner, I, 245.

to use 'various means' to heal the sinner, the penitent's own estimate of his or her worthiness to receive communion at Easter, all of this is about an individualization of sin that stands in sharp contrast to the penitential practices of the early Middle Ages. Nonetheless, it must be remembered that the decree of 1215 is itself a compromise, the outcome of decades of controversy. Twelfth-century theologians might agree that penance consisted of infusion of grace, contrition of heart, confession of mouth, and satisfaction of deeds, but they were divided about which of these elements mattered most. For Abelard, true contrition was itself sufficient; a view which today, when formal confession is often seen as oppressive, a vexatious instrument of 'social control', commands widespread support. In 1215, on the other hand, the provision for priestly absolution and penance will have looked quite different: it helped to assuage the burden of guilt which notions of sin and contrition had imposed, to mitigate the sense of shame, to spare those blushes which previous theologians had proclaimed to be necessary for the remission of sin.

The twenty-first decree of 1215 was both the outcome of decades of debate and the occasion for manual upon manual on its proper execution. Let us consider just one text which reflects these new (as well as old) ways of thinking about sin and the temptation to sin: the *Ancrene Wisse*, a treatise written originally for three English anchoresses of the early thirteenth century.

The eight sections of *Ancrene Wisse* concern devotions, the custody of the senses, the regulation of inward feelings, temptations, confession, penance, love, and external rules. The section on temptation, on the kinds of temptation there are, and on how the anchoress faced with them may find 'various sorts of comfort and manifold remedies', is by far the longest.[29] The anchoress must realize that temptations are an unavoidable part of holy life; but this is no reason for her to be unduly alarmed, or to act like a sick man who will not allow anyone to touch his sore or to cure him. On the contrary, she must accept spiritual comfort and understand that through her temptations 'she can and should be all the more confident of salvation'.[30] Temptations come both from God and the Devil; those from God test the anchoress's love and fear of God and require 'patience; that is long-suffering' to withstand them; temptations that come from the Devil include 'various vices or the desire for them', that must be resisted with 'wisdom and spiritual strength'.[31] In this discussion of temptation the author freely mixes notions drawn from both old and new theological concepts—on the one hand the treatise gives us the first vernacular discussion of 'inwit', that is, of personal conscience; on the other the Devil still has something of a pre-Anselmian mentality and can be tricked accordingly. But what is especially interesting about the Devil, as has been shown by Linda Georgianna, is

---

[29] *Anchoritic Spirituality: Ancrene Wisse and Associated Works*, trans. A. Savage and N. Watson (The Classics of Western Spirituality, 1991), 157.
[30] Ibid. 114.   [31] Ibid. 115.

his capacity to mimic both the priest of the confessional and the anchoress herself. If the priest is a skilled doctor, so too, in his own way, is the Devil. He has at his disposal 'boxes full of his medicines'—'think now of the number of his phials'[32]—so he can be sure of finding an appropriate dose. Thus he may well tempt an anchoress to fast too much, or to become over-concerned with almsgiving. The choice given to the anchoress in these instances, and I quote Georgianna, is not 'holiness *versus* sin; in this world of subtle process, holiness can *become* sin'.[33] In such a world the need for self-awareness and the confessional would seem to go hand-in-hand.

The *Ancrene Wisse*, because of its stress on personal conscience, needs to be recognized (according to Georgianna) as a reflection of the renaissance of the twelfth century.[34] But this renaissance has of late been re-examined. R. W. Southern's age of humanism has been offset by R. I. Moore's image of a persecuting society, by a view of a harshly authoritarian culture increasingly intolerant of its minorities.[35] A look at the twelfth century through the eyes of the tempted may suggest how demanding, even threatening, humanism could be. If the Devil is given only an offstage role, if it is through one's own inheritance that sin flourishes, if it is because of original sin that one is open to temptation, then considerable vigilance over the self is called for. The persecution of Jews and of heretics may, arguably, be understood as a form of distraction, however horrific, a way of focusing attention and blame on the alleged depravity of others.

If the twelfth-century renaissance has, then, its dark side, this is all the more reason to remember those such as Guy of Chartreuse who welcomed what one may call the challenge to the self, who did not attempt to externalize evil, to pass it on to someone else, who accepted that temptation could be a challenge, a part of the twelfth century's concern with self-knowledge and new learning. For such people Christ was teacher, model, and even pupil. This was why, according to St Bernard, Christ had assumed the form of a man rather than that of an angel. Only by laying himself open to 'human wretchedness' could he expect men to turn to him, to entrust their weaknesses to him, and at the same time to be merciful to each other: 'he wanted to suffer and to be tempted and to share all our human miseries "except sin" (Heb. 4.15) —for that is what it is to be "like his brothers in all things"—so that he might learn by his own experience to be merciful and to suffer with us in our sufferings and temptation.'[36] For Christ too, in the twelfth century, temptation was not to be shunned; rather, it was a necessary part of learning what it was to be human.

---

[32] *Ancrene Wisse*, trans. Savage and Watson, 31.

[33] L. Georgianna, *The Solitary Self: Individuality in the Ancrene Wisse* (Cambridge, Mass., 1981), 133.

[34] Ibid. 6.

[35] Cf. e.g. R. W. Southern, 'Medieval Humanism', in his *Medieval Humanism and Other Studies* (Oxford, 1970), 30–60, with R. I. Moore, *The Birth of a Persecuting Society* (Oxford, 1987).

[36] *Sancti Bernardi Opera*, ed. J. Leclercq, and C. H. Talbot and H. Rochais, 8 vols. (Rome, 1957–77), III, 23.

24

PETER OF POITIERS'S *COMPENDIUM IN GENEALOGIA CHRISTI*: THE EARLY ENGLISH COPIES[1]

Stella Panayotova

The balance between scholarship and teaching which challenges modern academics and inspires their students was part of the ideal image of the twelfth-century *magister*. As the chancellor of the University of Paris (1193–1205), Peter of Poitiers incarnated this image, uniting his preference for speculative theology with his interest in sacred history, and combining his fame as one of the most eloquent preachers of the twelfth century with his devotion to the teaching of *sacra pagina*.[2] To his concern for his students we owe the *Compendium in Genealogia Christi*, genealogical tables with brief entries on Christ's ancestors, biblical personages, and contemporary rulers. Together with Peter Lombard's *Magna Glossatura* and Peter Comestor's *Historia Scholastica*, the *Compendium* provided an indispensable tool for the study of the Bible; in manuscripts it often accompanies the Bible or *Historia Scholastica*. This explains why it often remains unrecorded: in a large volume containing a long, authoritative text, the *Compendium* is easily overlooked—especially when unillustrated. A typical example is the copy found at the end of the thirteenth-century Bible, Cambridge University Library, Dd. 8. 12.[3]

The *Compendium* has been discussed in the light of Bible illustration[4] and in relation to universal chronicles,[5] but no serious attempt has been made to

---

[1] The illustrations are reproduced by permission of the British Library and the Bodleian Library, Univesity of Oxford.

[2] P. S. Moore, *The Works of Peter of Poitiers* (Notre Dame, Ind., 1936), 118–22; B. Smalley, *The Study of the Bible in the Middle Ages*, 3rd edn. (Oxford, 1983), 209–15.

[3] The MS is not listed in Hans-Eberhard Hilpert, 'Geistliche Bildung und Laienbildung: Zur Überlieferung der Schulschrift *Compendium historiae in Genealogia Christi (Compendium veteris testamenti)* des Petrus von Poitiers († 1205) in England', *Journal of Medieval History*, 11 (1985), 315–31; the *Compendium* is not noted in the description of the MS in N. Morgan, *Early Gothic Manuscripts 1190–1250*, 2 vols. (London, 1982–8), I, no. 44.

[4] O. Pächt and J. J. G. Alexander, *Illuminated Manuscripts in the Bodleian Library*, 3 vols. (Oxford, 1966–73), III, 429; W. Monroe, 'A Roll-Manuscript of Peter of Poitiers' Compendium: Cleveland Museum of Art MS 73. 5', *The Bulletin of the Cleveland Museum of Art* (1978), 92–107; Morgan, *Gothic Manuscripts*, II, 91–2.

[5] A. de la Mare, *Catalogue of the Collection of Medieval Manuscripts Bequeathed to the Bodleian Library, Oxford, by James P. R. Lyell* (Oxford, 1971), 214.

distinguish between the different versions of the text. Scholars have assigned copies to the original or the interpolated recension on the basis of Philip Moore's studies of the text.[6] Yet, a survey of the codices and rolls in English libraries alone reveals the existence of more than two versions. The rich spectrum of recensions is understandable in view of the wide dissemination and long-lasting popularity of the *Compendium*, and may explain why such a brief text has not yet received a modern critical edition.[7]

The purpose of this paper is to distinguish between the different versions recorded in the oldest English copies of the *Compendium*. It will outline the early stages in the development of the text while taking into consideration the presence (or absence) of diagrams and illustrations. In Appendices I and II the passages which help to distinguish between the original and the interpolated versions will be transcribed from the earliest most complete manuscripts, to facilitate reference. The occurrence of these passages in thirty English copies dated between the late twelfth and the late thirteenth centuries will then be tabulated in Appendix III (Table I), as will the presence of illustrations and diagrams (Table II). With the exception of four manuscripts which I have not yet had the opportunity to study,[8] the tables include the twelfth- and thirteenth-century English copies of the text known to me.[9] Finally, peculiarities of the text, illustrations, and layout will be discussed, and observations will be made on the relationship between individual manuscripts.

The passages listed in the appendices are the most typical, but by no means the only features which distinguish the interpolated versions of the text from the original. The presence or absence of diagrams and illustrations may also

---

[6] Moore, *Works*, 188–96. For instance, a roll in the Cleveland Museum of Art has been described as 'a standard, uninterpolated Compendium manuscript' (Monroe, 'Compendium', 95). However, the last membrane contains the entries on the Virgin, Christ, and St Anne's family which, it will be demonstrated below, were added to the original version and became an integral part of the early interpolated recension.

[7] *M. Petri Pictaviensis Galli Genealogia et Chronologia Sanctorum Patrum . . . que a Iulio Caesare, usque ad nostra tempora continuata est ab Hulderico Zuinglio Iuniore . . .* (Basel, 1592), 1–12; H. Vollmer, *Deutsche Bibelauszüge des Mittelalters zum Stammbaum Christi mit ihren lateinischen Vorbildern und Vorlagen*, Bibel und deutsche Kultur, I (Potsdam, 1931), 127–88. An edition by William Raymond Johnson was planned in 1979, but abandoned in 1985: see *Speculum*, 54 (1979), 213, and 60 (1985), 239.

[8] Cleveland Museum of Art, MS 73. 5; New York, Pierpont Morgan Library, MS M. 628; New York, collection of Robert S. Pirie; Philadelphia, Free Library, s.n. See Monroe, 'Compendium', 92–105; Morgan, *Gothic Manuscripts*, I, 92; II, 180; C. de Hamel, 'Medieval and Renaissance Manuscripts from the Library of Sir Sydney Cockerell (1867–1962)', *British Library Journal*, 13:2 (1987), 186–210, esp. 208.

[9] Cambridge, Christ's College, MS 5; Corpus Christi College, MSS 29; 83, and 437; Fitzwilliam Museum, MS 253; University Library, MSS Dd. 1. 16; Dd. 8. 12; and Ff. 3. 7; Edinburgh, University Library, MS 18; Eton College, MS 96; Liverpool, National Museums and Galleries on Merseyside, MS Mayer 12017; London, British Library, MSS Add. 11758; 14819; 24025; and 60628; Cotton Faust. B. vii; Cotton Vit. C. iii; Fairfax 13; Harley 658; Royal 4 B. vii; Royal 8 C. ix; Royal 14 B. ix; Oxford, Bodleian Library, MSS Ashmole 1524; Auct. D. 4. 10; Bodley 164; Lat. th. b. 1; Laud. Misc. 150; and 437; Rawlinson C. 563; Salisbury Cathedral Library, MS 60. I would like to thank the librarians at the institutions listed above, and in particular Mr Nick Baker, Dr Michelle Brown, Ms Suzanne Eward, and Ms Ann Stewart, for their assistance.

indicate different stages in the development of the text. The diagrams of Noah's Ark, the mansions in the desert, the Tabernacle, and *habitatio regis et sacerdotum* were designed by Peter of Poitiers as mnemonic devices supplementing the genealogical tables. Highly informative and often aesthetically pleasing, they reveal the pedagogical advantages of the visual representations, as well as their vital role in organizing and elucidating a large body of factual material.[10] Apart from two manuscripts that lack Noah's Ark,[11] all the copies of the original version contain the four diagrams. They are also present in almost all of the interpolated copies examined here.[12] By contrast, the illustrations of biblical personages and scenes, and of world rulers, were seemingly not among the components which Peter of Poitiers considered essential: though a feature of many interpolated copies, they are found in only one manuscript of the original version and in one of the copies with ad hoc additions.[13] The use of other didactic schemes together with the genealogical tables in the lecture room or in the study may have led to the inclusion of the former in copies of the *Compendium*. Trees of virtues and vices, attributed to Peter of Poitiers by Alberic of Trois Fontaines († 1251), often supplement the Genealogy.[14] The virtues are also a component of another pictorial scheme found in the *Compendium*, the seven-branched candlestick.[15] The treatise which usually accompanies the image and explains its symbolic meaning may have been a part of the work *De Vitiis et Virtutibus* that was attributed to Peter of Poitiers by Alberic.[16] However, the diagrams of *virtutes*, *vicia*, and *candelabrum* can hardly have originated with the *Compendium*. The schemes of virtues and vices, which had a textual and visual tradition independent of the *Compendium*,[17] do not appear in any of the copies of the original version, and the candlestick features in only one of them. Their presence at the beginning or the end of several interpolated copies, as well as on the reverse of rolls, indicates that they were associated with the later stages in the development of the *Compendium*.[18]

[10] M. Evans, 'The Geometry of the Mind', *Architectural Association Quarterly*, 12:4 (1980), 32–55.

[11] Cambridge, Corpus Christi College, MSS 29 and 437.

[12] See Appendix III.

[13] Cambridge, Christ's College, MS 5; London, British Library, Royal 8 C. ix.

[14] MGH Scriptorum XXIII, ed. G. H. Pertz (Hannover, 1874), 886: 'Obiit magister Petrus Pictavinus . . . qui pauperibus clericis consulens excogitavit arbores historiarum Veteris Testamenti in pellibus depingere, et de vitiis et virtutibus similiter compendiose disponere.' They are found in Cambridge, Christ's College MS 5; London, British Library, Royal 14 B. ix; and Harley 658. See Morgan, *Gothic Manuscripts*, II, 180.

[15] See Appendix III.   [16] Moore, *Works*, 168–9.

[17] A. Katzenellenbogen, *Allegories of the Virtues and Vices in Medieval Art* (London, 1939); E. Greenhill, *Die geistigen Voraussetzungen der Bilderreihe des Speculum virginum*, Beiträge zur Geschichte der Philosophie und Theologie des Mittelalters, 39:2 (Münster, 1962).

[18] The trees of virtues and vices combined with *manus meditationis* and the Wheel of Sevens on the verso of a fifteenth-century roll copy of the *Compendium* (Cambridge University Library, Dd. 3. 56) are in the tradition of the *Speculum Theologiae*, a collection of theological diagrams compiled by the Franciscan Johannes Metensis in the last quarter of the thirteenth century. L. F. Sandler, *The Psalter of Robert De Lisle* (London, 1999), 23–7, 107–15.

The gradual textual and visual expansion of the *Compendium* in late twelfth-and thirteenth-century English copies is summarized in the tables. The material presented in them gives the following picture. Seven of the thirty copies contain the original text alone. The remaining twenty-three copies show various stages of interpolation. These range from the ad hoc addition of text and glosses in the margin; through the insertion of passages at the beginning or end of the text, but as part of the original design and not as an afterthought; to an interpolated version with the additions appearing as an integral part of the text; culminating in a heavily interpolated version transforming the *Compendium* into a part of a larger chronicle. For the sake of clarity, in the tables each stage is represented by a group of manuscripts headed by Royal 8 C. ix, Dd. 1. 16, Cotton Faust. B. vii, and Eton College, 96 respectively. Yet, it is my hope that these stages will illustrate for the reader the natural development of a text which, for the time being, eludes any rigorous attempt for classification and division into strictly defined recensions.

Some of the manuscripts mark important stages in the process of interpolation and deserve further consideration. Among the earliest is British Library, Cotton Vit. C. iii. It contains the original version, to which the scribe added three marginal glosses on fol. 5r (pl. 20). A comment on παρασκευή ascribed to Remigius of Auxerre is added in the lower margin: 'paracheue [*sic*] interpretatur preparatio dominice passionis'. The other two glosses refer to Cain. The first, inserted in the inner margin ('Creatura creatori recte optulit, sed non recte divisit, quia se diabolo offerens'), is continued in the lower margin by the second, which is structured as a distinction with seven subdivisions: 'I. Se diabolo offerens; II. Fratri invidit; III. Dolose egit vocans in agro; IV. Occidit;' and so on. Most interestingly, in an interpolated copy of the *Compendium* from the first half of the thirteenth century these two glosses are united in a single passage and inserted in the main text after the usual entry on Cain.[19]

A clear example of the first stage of interpolation is the early thirteenth-century copy of the original version, British Library, Royal 8 C. ix. The scribe responsible for the interpolations seems different from, but contemporary with, that of the main text. He wrote comments on Christ's disciples, the Fathers, and the early Christian writers and popes on fols. 13v–16r, at the end of the original text. In the margins of fol. 12v he also added entries on St John the Baptist, the Virgin, and St Anne.[20] The same material, with minor variations, features in Edinburgh 18 and Fairfax 13, but in contrast to Royal 8 C. ix, here the

---

[19] 'Creatura creatori recte obtulit, set non recte divisit, primo diabolo se offerens, secundo fratri invidit, tertio dolose egit vocando eum in agro, quarto occidit eum, quinto per taciter [*sic*] negavit, sexto desperavit, septimo dampnatus nec penitenciam egit' (Fitzwilliam Museum, MS 253, fol. 1r).

[20] 'Iohannes Baptista filius Zacharie . . .'; 'Maria que interpretatur domina sive illuminatrix . . .'; 'Anna et Emerita fuerunt sorores . . .'.

interpolated passages are included after the original version.[21] Although added at the end of the genealogy, these passages were written by the scribes responsible for the main text and were therefore part of the original design. This suggests that they were either absent from the exemplar and copied from a different source, or featured in the exemplar in the form of ad hoc additions.

Apart from these standard additions, less common interpolations appear in several copies of the *Compendium*, demonstrating the manifold possibilities for extending its textual and visual contents. The theme of Creation occurs in four thirteenth-century copies, Add. 11758, Harley 658, Royal 4 B. vii, and Fairfax 13.[22] The elements of God's Creation, with the corresponding days marked by small Roman numerals, are listed in a single line before the prologue in Harley 658. In Add. 11758 they received the same prominent position at the beginning of the text, and a more elaborate description in two stanzas. In the remaining two manuscripts the theme is summarized in a diagram. In Royal 4 B. vii the diagram is appended to the *Compendium* together with a passage on the three-fold interpretation of scripture and the importance of understanding and memorizing the historical sense. In Fairfax 13 it follows the prologue, thus becoming part of the *Compendium* itself, and contains brief descriptions of each day, encircled and linked to *Deus* in the central medallion. The larger circle of the sixth day enclosing the names of Adam, Eve, and the animals is also used as the first circle of the genealogical line. Fairfax 13 thus presents a rare example of an interpolation that is integrated into the visual content of the *Compendium*, rather than being added as a verbal preface or appendix.

The most unusual miscellaneous material added to the original version is found in Bodleian Library, Auct. D. 4. 10. Alongside and beneath the prologue two different hands, seemingly contemporary with the scribe of the main text, inserted: passages on Adam and Eve's ability to conceive without experiencing carnal pleasure, and on their children; a moralizing interpretation of Abel's name; Peter Riga's verses on Abel's death as a prefiguration of Christ's sacrifice;[23] and an excerpt, probably from Augustine, on the typological relationship between Adam and Christ. Verses on the apostles and on St Anne's family follow at the end of the genealogy.[24] With the exception of the entry on Adam's

---

[21] 'Primum Anna accepit Joahim . . .'; 'Quinque fuerunt Anne . . .'; 'Beata virgo Maria mater domini XII annorum fuit . . .'; 'Conceptus est Dominus . . .'; 'Quadragesimo secundo anni [*sic*] regni Augusti . . .'; 'Prima etas . . .'; followed by interpretations of the names of the Virgin ('Maria que interpretatur domina sive illuminatrix . . .'), St John the Baptist ('Iohannes Baptista filius Zacharie . . .'), and Christ's disciples ('Symon Petrus . . .').

[22] It is also found in a fifteenth-century roll, Cambridge University Library, MS Dd. 3. 56.

[23] This is an excerpt from *Liber Genesis* of Peter Riga's *Aurora*, 429–36, with an interpolation from the second recension of Aegidius inserted after line 430: cf. *Aurora Petri Rigae*, ed. Paul E. Beichner, 2 vols. (Notre Dame, Ind., 1965), I, 43–4.

[24] The first eight lines of the interpolation on the apostles are elegiacs from Peter Riga's *Recapitulationes*, 475–82: cf. *Aurora Petri Rigae*, II, 625. I am grateful to Dr Greti Dinkova-Bruun for identifying

children,[25] the remaining texts have not been recorded in any of the other copies examined here.

Certain physical aspects of our manuscripts merit consideration. Alberic of Trois Fontaines informs us that Peter of Poitiers's genealogical tables were depicted on animal skins;[26] and internal evidence reveals that numerous manuscripts were copied from rolls or from codices which preserved the features characteristic of rolls. The splitting of names between roundels at the bottom of one page and at the top of the following one is a common feature indicating the end of a scroll membrane in the exemplar.[27] The same is suggested by the numerous semi-roundels at the bottom and top of pages, the majority of which were left blank.[28] In copying from roll to codex, the lines which linked the annulets in the genealogical tables were likely to occupy different positions on each page, which made it difficult for scribes and readers alike to follow the sequence and to distinguish between the genealogy of Christ's predecessors and the subordinate lines of Jewish priests and judges or world rulers. To avoid confusion, the lines in numerous manuscripts were shaded in different colours. In Corpus Christi, 29 they were also marked with letters at the bottom and top of pages, and sigla were used to link texts which ran over to the verso or the next folio. In Christ's College, 5 the supplementary lines were indicated by the letters 'e', 'f', 'g', and 'h', the letter 'a' being reserved for Christ's genealogy.

these passages. I have been unable to identify the remaining eight hexameters on the apostles and the nine hexameters on St Anne's family:

> Petrus ego celi portas reserabo fideli.
> Qui fueram Saulus modo dicor nomine Paulus.
> Plus me dilexit qui me sub pectore vexit.
> Vexor morte artis que dat mihi gaudia lucis.
> Occubui gladio Christi sic hostia fio.
> Patrem nescivi, patremque videre cupivi.
> Terre prostratus vivus sum decoratus.
> De tempo stratus vivo sum astra beatus.

> Anna tribus Ioachim, Cleophe, Salomeque Marias
> tres parit. Has ducunt Ioseph, Alpheus, Zebedeus.
> Christum prima, Ioseph, Iacobum cum Symone Iudam
> altera, que sequitur Iacobum parit atque Iohannem.
> Ex Ioachim, Cleopha, Saloma tres Anna Marias
> quas genuit iunxit Ioseph, Alpheo, Zebedeo.
> Unius hec mater, hec quatuor, illa duorum.
> Natu maiorem Iacobum cognosce minorem
> ob quod post natus prius est de nave vocatus.

[25] Also present in British Library, Royal 1 B. x (s. xiv), which was used as an example of the interpolated version in Moore, *Works*, 189–96.

[26] See n. 12.

[27] e.g. Cambridge, Christ's College, MS 5; Corpus Christi College, MSS 29 and 437; British Library, Cotton Vit. C. iii and Royal 4 B. vii.

[28] e.g. British Library, Cotton Faust. B. vii and Bodleian Library, Ashmole 1524.

Despite the measures that were taken to avoid mistakes, the interference of Tituvilus, the demon of scribes, is often recorded in copies of the *Compendium*. His damaging work was facilitated by the complex layout of the genealogical tables. The splitting of names between roundels on consecutive pages was often continued in manuscript copies where it was not actually necessary. For example, Antipater received two annulets ('Anti'–'Pater') on fol. ixv of Bodley 164, while the second part of Phalech's name appears in the first roundel on fol. 194v of Royal 4 B. vii ('lech'), although the last roundel on the recto contains his full name.

A similar copying error can be seen in Cotton Vit. C. iii. Lamech's name appears twice in the genealogical tables on fol. 5r and is linked via sigla to a corresponding text on both occasions (pl. 20). The content of the two passages is identical, but the abbreviations differ, suggesting that the scribe was using two exemplars.[29]

The schema of St Anne's family presented a serious challenge. In Fairfax 13 the annulets for the names of St Anne, her sister 'Esmeria', and the latter's daughter 'Elyzabeth', were drawn on one level, as if all three were sisters. Furthermore, St Anne is missing from her own family tree: the annulet designed for her name contains 'Maria' instead. An even more striking mistake appears in Bodleian Library, Laud. Misc. 151 (pl. 21). The annulets which should have encircled the names of St Anne's three daughters were left empty. As in numerous other copies, the female names were to be added in red ink once the remaining texts had been inserted; but our scribe did not finish his text.[30] However, since all three of St Anne's daughters were named Mary, this would not have caused any confusion had the scribe copied the names of her husbands in the usual order. Yet here Cleophas occupies the middle position, most often reserved for Joseph, while the rest of the scheme remains unaltered. The annulet which stems from Cleophas is linked with the one containing *Christus resurgens*, thus making the Virgin Cleophas's daughter! A scribe working under pressure and running out of time or patience at the end of his text might be forgiven a lapse of concentration. The fact that no medieval reader corrected such a flagrant error is more striking.

Many of these errors help to establish links between manuscripts, especially when supported by similarities in textual recension, illustration or layout. As mentioned above, the splitting of Antipater's name between two annulets on fol. ix v of Bodley 164, a manuscript of the mid-thirteenth century, indicates an exemplar in which the two annulets were on different pages. One such

---

[29] One of them may have been the source of the comment on Cain's sin and the distinction which were added in the margins of fol. 5r and mentioned above.

[30] It lacks the passages on the Virgin and Sts Mathias, Paul, and Barnabas. Perhaps they were to be written on fol. 6v which now contains the sketch of the seven-branched candlestick, but whose ruling pattern is the same as that of the entire *Compendium*.

manuscript is Bodleian Library, Laud. Misc. 270, a copy of early thirteenth-century date. The general layout of the rather crudely executed Bodley 164 is very similar to that of Laud. Misc. 270, which is, however, masterfully designed and elegantly decorated. In both manuscripts the *Compendium* appears in its original version, the first two annulets containing Christ's name are not marked *natus* and *puer*, but the third and fourth annulets are rubricated *passus* and *resurgens*; furthermore, the diagrams of *tabernaculum* and *habitatio regis et sacerdotum* are identical. Yet the differences in the word order within individual entries and in the names at the beginning and the end of each page rule out a direct relationship between the two manuscripts. Though not identical to Laud. Misc. 270, the exemplar of Bodley 164 shared many specific features with it.

A similar case is presented by two manuscripts in Corpus Christi College, Cambridge. MS 29 is a large, early thirteenth-century copy of the *Historia Scholastica* which is prefaced by a full-page drawing of the seven-branched candlestick, along with the *Compendium* whose genealogical tables are neatly outlined in red, tinted in yellow and brown, and marked by letters. By contrast, MS 437 is a very small Bible of the second half of the century that is preceded by one of the most heavily abbreviated and least attractive copies of the *Compendium*, links between annulets being drawn without a ruler and names being connected to the corresponding passages by black, tremulous lines. Nevertheless, the two manuscripts contain the original version of the text and display an almost identical layout page by page. Among the most significant similarities are the division of Thare's name between two circles, the position of the diagrams of *mansiones* and *tabernaculum*, the omission of Noah's Ark (most unusual for copies of the original version), the order of the Roman emperors, and the design of the schema of St Anne's family, which is identical down to the smallest detail. The differences in scale and colour cannot obscure the relationship between the two manuscripts.

The textual and visual connections between Cotton Faust. B. vii, Corpus Christi College, 83, and Cleveland Museum, 73. 5, have already been noticed.[31] What has escaped attention is the even closer relationship between Cotton Faust. B. vii (pls. 22–3) and another early thirteenth-century copy of the interpolated version, Ashmole 1524 (pl. 24). Although its illustrations were never executed, the blank medallions provided for them correspond in their location on the pages, their inscriptions, and their shapes and sizes to those in the Cotton manuscript. The two copies share the same colour scheme; the interpolated text on Cain, which is a feature of Cotton Faust. B. vii (and Corpus Christi, 83) also appears in the Bodleian manuscript. Furthermore, the schema of St Anne's husbands and the accompanying texts (which are left out in Corpus Christi, 83) are included in both Cotton Faust. B. vii and Ashmole 1524. Now the Bodleian

---

[31] Morgan, *Gothic Manuscripts*, I, 91–2; Monroe, 'Compendium', 97–8. I plan to examine the relationship between these MSS in a future study.

manuscript does not contain the two diagrams of Noah's Ark (which are found in their usual place within the text of Corpus Christi, 83), but it has the *tabernaculum* and *mansiones* (which are missing in the Cambridge manuscript) outlined at the end of the text.[32] These anomalies are explained by the place of the three diagrams in Cotton Faust. B. vii: they are absent from the main text, but appear on fol. 43r, before the Trinity diagram (fol. 43v), Peter Riga's *De Operibus Septem Dierum* (fol. 44r–v), and the *Compendium* (which begins on fol. 45r). The similar approach to the images provides strong evidence that Ashmole 1524 was copied from Cotton Faust. B. vii.

A study of later copies of the *Compendium* may reveal further relationships between manuscripts, and shed more light on the development of the text in England. The fact that there is no necessary correlation between date of production and the recension copied makes their evidence all the more valuable. Some fifteenth-century copies, such as the roll manuscript Dd. 3. 56 at Cambridge University Library, preserve the original version of the text with fewer interpolations than manuscripts dating from as early as the end of the twelfth century, for instance Dd. 1. 16 in the same library. The latter is the oldest surviving English copy of the *Compendium* known to me, but it already has the standard additions inserted at the appropriate places as integral parts of the text.[33] It seems that the expansion of the *Compendium* began at the very early stage of its dissemination and was conditioned by its close association with Peter Comestor's *Historia Scholastica*. In eight of the manuscripts surveyed here, Peter of Poitiers's Genealogy accompanies *Historia Scholastica*, which would have encouraged, and provided ample material for, expansion.[34]

While *Historia Scholastica* was the work most commonly coupled with the *Compendium*, there were various other texts frequently accompanied by it. What was then the context in which the *Compendium* was disseminated in England? The majority of the manuscripts studied here point to the learned environment in which it was copied. When associated with Bibles,[35] biblical concordances,[36] and versified Bibles, such as Peter Riga's *Aurora*,[37] the *Compendium* would have played the role of a teaching and reference tool in accordance with its author's intentions. In the company of exegetical works, and speculative and moral theology, this primary function was probably extended into a more specialized scholarly use. The features indicating this most clearly

[32] The sketches appear on fol. 56v.
[33] The earliest known English copies of the original version are slightly later in date—the beginning of the thirteenth century. It is not impossible that still earlier copies may yet come to light.
[34] Cambridge University Library, Dd. 1. 16 and Ff. 3. 7; Christ's College, 5; Corpus Christi College, 29; Bodleian Library, Bodley 164; Laud. Misc. 151; Laud. Misc. 270; British Library, Royal 8 C. ix. The latter was discussed above as a clear manifestation of the earliest stage of interpolation.
[35] Cambridge University Library, Dd. 8. 12; Corpus Christi College 437; Bodleian Library, Auct. D. 4. 10.
[36] Bodleian Library, Auct. D. 4. 10; Salisbury Cathedral Library 60.
[37] Cambridge, Corpus Christi College 83; British Library, Cott. Faust. B. vii.

are the sigla, the distinctions, and the glosses. All three were established as vital components of the apparatus in twelfth-century glossed Bibles and commentaries. The sigla link the names in the annulets to the passages in the text referring to them (pl. 20).[38] The distinctions summarize passages on St Anne's family in Salisbury 60, on world rulers and their domains in Fitzwilliam 253, and on the Evangelists in Cotton Faust. B. vii (pl. 23). Glosses are found in one copy of the *Compendium* only, Harley 658, and it is notable that among the various texts this manuscript contains there are *quaestiones, glossae, expositiones*, and *notae* on various biblical books. In view of its miscellaneous material, which includes chronologies, computistics, mystical and exegetical tracts, a map of Jerusalem, *schema cerebri* and *schema primatum qualitatum*, tables of the virtues, vices, the Muses, and the winds, diagrams of metres, of *anima* and *sapientia*, and *arbor consanguinitatis* and *arbor affinitatis*, it is hardly an exaggeration to describe Harley 658 as an encyclopaedia of thirteenth-century knowledge. Peter of Poitiers's *Compendium* was one of its vital components.

Designed as a meeting-point of teaching and scholarship, Christ's Genealogy was used not only in the classroom or for private study. In its capacity as a reference tool it entered yet another realm, that of moral theology and preaching. It is found together with sermons in Salisbury Cathedral Library, 60 and in Bodleian Library, Ashmole 1524.[39] Whether drawn on membranes for poor students, penned in scholars' and preachers' working copies, or decorated in elaborate manuscripts for wealthy patrons, Peter of Poitiers's *Compendium* fostered Christian belief through specialized intellectual knowledge. Without rising to the status of a cultural emblem, it embodied, in its own practical way, the quintessential ideal of the High Middle Ages, the equilibrium between *ratio* and *fides*.

APPENDIX I

Passages Characteristic of the Original Version

The entries on Adam and Cain follow the prologue, while those on Sts Mathias, Paul and Barnabas surround the last annulet with Christ's name in the genealogical tables.

a. Adam

Adam in agro damasceno formatus et in paradisum unde IIIIor flumina oriuntur translatus cum femine de costa dormientis facte nomine sicut et ceteris rebus imposito de Christo et ecclesia prophetasset. Et eidem de comedendo pomo adquievisset, pro disconvenientia nuditatis factis perizomatibus a Domino de paradiso collocatis cherubim

---

[38] e.g. Cambridge, Christ's College MS 5; Corpus Christi College MS 29; Salisbury Cathedral Library MS 60; Eton College 96; British Library, Cotton Vit. C. iii; Harley 658; and Fairfax 13.

[39] Its connection with devotional texts (British Library, Royal 4 B. vii) and mystical literature (Harley 658) is less straightforward.

et flammeo gladio post increpationem eiectus, de terra maledicta in sudore vultus sui panem adquirit (Royal 4 B. vii, fol. 194r).

b. Cain

Caim agricola dolens sua munera et non fratris fuisse reprobata licet a Domino increpatus fratrem septiformi peccato interfecit. Postea vagus et instabilis super terram factus est, postquam a Domino est maledictus (Royal 4 B. vii, fol. 194r).

c. Christ

Natus est autem Dominus XLIIo anno regni Augusti, XXXmo anno regni Herodis nocte dominice diei (Royal 4 B. vii, fol. 199r).

d. Sts Paul and Barnabas

Paulus et Barnabas in Antiochia a Spiritu Sancto sunt segregati XIIIo anno a passione Domini et ascendentes in Eirusalem [*sic*] ad Petrum et Iacobum qui eis manus imposuerunt XIIIIo anno ad predicandum profecti sunt. Quibus postea separatis, Paulus post longam predicationem Romam veniens, postquam XII annis in libera custodia sub Nerone manserat, XIIII anno Neronis passus est eodem die quo et Petrus (Royal 4 B. vii, fol. 199r).

e. St Mathias

Mathias loco Iude substitutus est supra quem cecidit sors cum ipse cum Ioseph fuit electus inter ascensionis dies et pentecostes (Laud. Misc. 270, fol. 6v).

APPENDIX II

Passages Characteristic of the Interpolated Versions

The expanded passages on Adam and Cain signal an early interpolated version. Any additional texts indicate later developments; their presence is marked in the tables, but because of their variety and considerable length they cannot be transcribed here. The entries on the Virgin and Christ are the earliest texts to be appended to the original version in the form of marginal glosses or additions at the end of the genealogy. The same applies to the texts explaining St Anne's family tree, although the diagram of the family itself belonged to Peter of Poitier's initial plan. The passage on the Eight Ages tends to appear at the beginning of the *Compendium*, although without a fixed place.

a. Adam

Adam in agro damasceno formatus et in paradysum unde quatuor flumina oriuntur translatus cum femine de costa dormientis facte nomine sicut et ceteris rebus imposito de Christo et ecclesia prophetasset et eidem uxori sue a serpente seducte de comedendo pomo adquievisset, pro disconvenientia nuditatis factis perizomatibus a Domino de paradyso collocatis cherubim et flammeo gladio post increpationem abiectus, de terra maledicta in sudore vultus sui panem adquirit (Cotton Faust. B. vii, fol. 45r).

b. Cain

Chaym agricola dolens sua munera et non fratris fuisse reprobata licet a Domino increpatus fratrem septiformi peccato interfecit. Postea vagus et instabilis super terram factus postquam a Domino maledictus. Signo tamen, scilicet tremore capitis, ei imposito, ut sic sciretur punitus a Domino et excomunicatus [*sic*] et etiam indignus misericordia ne interficeretur (Cotton Faust. B. vii, fol. 45r).

c. St Anne

Quinque fuerunt Anne. Prima mater Samuelis. Secunda uxor Raguelis. Tercia mater Tobie. Quarta filia Phanuel. Quinta mater matris Domini Ihesu Christi (Royal 14 B. ix, roll).

Primum accepit Anna Ioachim de quo habuit Mariam matrem Domini sponsam Ioseph. Eo mortuo accepit Cleopham de quo habuit aliam Mariam que nupsit Alpheo de quo habuit IIIIor filios, scilicet, Ioseph, Taddeum, Simonem et Iacobum. Mortuo autem Cleopha, accepit Salome de quo habuit aliam Mariam quam dedit Zebedeo, ex quo habuit duos filios Iohannem, scilicet [Evangelistam], et Iacobum maiorem (Royal 14 B. ix, roll).

Anna et Emerita fuerunt sorores. De Emerita nata est mater Iohannis Baptiste. Ioachim duxit Annam in uxorem de quo nata est mater Domini Ihesu. Mortuo Ioachim, Cleophas duxit Annam et genuit ex ea alteram Mariam que dicitur Maria Cleophe. Puero Cleophas dedit Iosep [*sic*] fratri suo Mariam matrem Domini que filiastra sua erat. Desponsavit et alteram Mariam filiam suam Alpheo de qua natus Iacobus minor et alius Iosep [*sic*], unde dicitur Iacobus Alphei. Mortuo Cleopha, Anna tercio marito Salome nupsit, que genuit terciam Mariam de qua desponsata Zebedeo nati sunt Iacobus maior et Iohannes Evangelista. Maria mater Iacobi minoris et Maria Iacobi et Iohannis Evangeliste et Maria Magdalene quesierunt Dominum cum aromatibus in monumento (Royal 8 C. ix, fol. 12v).

d. The Virgin

Beata Virgo Maria mater Domini XII annorum fuit quando per Spiritum Sanctum angelo nunciante concepit. Et Dominus Ihesus Christus XXX annorum erat cum baptizatus erat a Iohanne in Iordane. Tribus quoque annis predicavit et tribus mensibus. Postea crucifixus, mortuus et sepultus, tercia die resurgens, per XL dies conversatus est cum discipulis in terris. Quadragesimo die resurrectionis ascendit in celum et sedit ad dexteram Patris. Quinquagesimo die Spiritum Sanctum apostolis dedit ad robur. Dederat enim ante ad facienda miracula et ad dimittenda peccata. Vixit autem Beata Virgo Maria post passionem Domini annis II in domo beati Iohannis Evangeliste. Postea assumpta est in celum. Et facti sunt omnes dies illius anni XLVII et tres menses (Royal 14 B. ix, roll).

e. Christ

Conceptus est Dominus noster Ihesus Christus VIII Kalendis aprilis feria VI, natus feria prima VIII kalendis, baptizatus VIII idus ianuarii. Sunt dies CCLXV a nativitate eius in quo passus est et crucifixus. Sunt anni XXXIII et III menses qui sunt XII CCCC et XII dies (Harley 658, fol. 38v).

Quadragesimo secundo anni [*sic*] regni Augusti natus est Dominus anno Herodis XXXo nocte dominice diei (Harley 658, fol. 38v).

f. The Eight Ages

Prima etas fuit ab Adam usque ad Noe. Secunda a Noe usque ad Abraham. Tercia ab Abraham usque ad David. Quarta a David usque ad transmigracionem Babilonis. Quinta usque ad Christum. Sexta a Christo usque ad finem seculi. Hec sex sunt viventium. Septima est quiescentium que incipit a passione Domini. Octava erit resurgentium que incipiet a die iudicii et durabit usque in sempiternum. Nota quod non dicuntur etates propter numerum annorum, sed millenarium ut quidam volunt scilicet propter quedam mirabiliora quae facta sunt in quarumlibet inicio. Nam in principio prime facta est mundi constructio. Principio secunde mundi per diluvium purgacio. In principio tercie instituta est contra originale peccatum circumcisio. In principio quarte regum inunctio. In principio quinte populi Dei in Babilonem transmigracio. In principio sexte filii Dei incarnatio. In principio septime ianue celestis apercio. In principio octave erit corporum resurrectio et bonorum et malorum plena remuneracio (Royal 14 B. ix, roll).

APPENDIX III

Tables

In the tables the manuscripts are divided into five groups representing the original version and four early stages of interpolation; the order within the groups is chronological. The abbreviations stand for original entry (or.), interpolated entry (int.), diagram (d) of St Anne's family, and texts (t) on it. Otherwise the presence or absence of a feature is signalled by + or − respectively.

T ABLE I. *Texts*

MSS	Adam	Cain	Christ	Paul + Barnabas	Mathias	St Anne	Virgin	Eight Ages
Royal								
4 B. vii	or.	or.	or.	+	−	d	−	−
Christ's								
College 5	or.	or.	or.	+	+	d	−	−
Corpus								
Christi 29	or.	or.	or.	+	+	d	−	−
Corpus								
Christi 437	or.	or.	or.	+	+	d	−	−
Ff. 3. 7	or.	or.	or.	+	+	d	−	−
Laud.								
Misc. 270	or.	or.	or.	+	+	d	−	−
Bodley 164	missing	missing	or.	+	−	d	−	−
Royal 8 C. ix	or.	or.	or.	+	−	d + t	+	−
Auct. D. 4. 10	or.	or.	or.	+	+	d + t	−	−
Cott. Vit.								
C. iii	or.	or.	or.	+	+	d	−	−
Fairfax 13	or.	or.	or.+ int.	+	−	d + t	−	−
Edinburgh 18	or.	or.	or.+ int.	−	−	t	+	+
Add. 11758	or.	or.	or.	+	+	d + t	−	+
Dd. 1. 16	or.	or.	or.+int.	+	+	d + t	+	+
Harley 658	or.	or.	or. + int.	+	+	d + t	+	−
Laud.								
Misc. 150	or.	or.	or. + int.	−	−	d + t	−	+
Lat. th. b. 1	or.	or.	or. + int.	+	+	t	+	+
Royal 14 B. ix	or.	or.	or. + int.	+	+	d + t	+	+
Dd. 8. 12	or.	or.	or. + int.	+	+	d + t	+	−
Cott. Faust.								
B. vii	or. + int.	or. + int.	or.	−	−	d + t	−	−
Ashmole 1524	or. + int.	or. + int.	or.	+	+	d + t	−	−
Corpus								
Christi 83	or. + int.	or. + int.	or.	−	−	−	−	−
Salisbury 60	or. + int.	or. + int.	or. + int.	+	+	d + t	+	−
Fitzwilliam								
253	or. + int.	or. + int.	or.	+	+	d + t	+	−
Mayer 12017	or. + int.	or. + int.	or. + int.	+	+	d + t	+	+
Rawlinson 563	or.	or. + int.	or. + int.	+	+	d + t	+	+
Eton								
College 96	or. + int.	or. + int.	missing	missing	missing	missing	missing	−
Add. 60628	or. + int.	or. + int.	or. + int.	+	−	d + t	+	−
Add. 14819	or. + int.	or. + int.	or. + int.	+	+	d	+	−
Add. 24025	or. + int.	or. + int.	or. + int.	+	+	d	+	−

TABLE 11. *Images and diagrams*

MSS	Noah's Ark	*Mansiones*	*Tabernaculum*	*Habitatio*	Biblical illustrations	*Candelabrum*
Royal 4 B. vii	+	+	+	+	−	−
Christ's College 5	+	+	+	+	+	
Corpus Christi 29	−	+	+	+	−	+
Corpus Christi 437	−	+	+	+	−	−
Ff. 3. 7	+	+	+	+	−	−
Laud. Misc. 270	+	+	+	+	−	−
Bodley 164	missing	+	+	+	−	−
Royal 8 C. ix	+	+	+	+	+	−
Auct. D. 4. 10	−	+	+	+	−	−
Cott. Vit. C. iii	−	+	+	+	−	−
Fairfax 13	+	+	+	+	−	−
Edinburgh 18	+	+	+	+	−	−
Add. 11758	+	+	+	+	−	−
Dd. 1. 16	+	+	+	+	−	−
Harley 658	+	+	+	+	−	−
Laud. Misc. 150	+	+	+	+	+	+
Lat. th. b. 1	+	+	+	+	+	+
Royal 14 B. ix	+	+	+	+	+	+
Dd. 8. 12	+	+	+	+	−	−
Cott. Faust. B. vii	+	+	+	+	+	−
Ashmole 1524	−	−	−	+	−	−
Corpus Christi 83	+	−	−	+	+	−
Salisbury 60	−	+	−	+	−	−
Fitzwilliam 253	−	+	+	+	−	+
Mayer 12017	+	+	+	+	+	+
Rawlinson 563	+	+	+	+	+	−
Eton College 96	+	missing	missing	missing	+	−
Add. 60628	+	+	+	+	+	+
Add. 14819	+	+	+	+	+	−
Add. 24025	+	+	+	+	+	−

25

THE SAINT AND THE OPERATION OF THE LAW: REFLECTIONS UPON THE MIRACLES OF ST THOMAS CANTILUPE

Valerie I. J. Flint

When historians of medieval law turn to the written record, they do not (as a rule) turn readily to collections of miracles. Such reluctance is, at first sight, understandable, for in that such collections are compelled by their very nature to laud the supernatural over the works of rational man, are necessarily prejudiced towards their subjects, and are often anecdotal and repetitive to boot, they appear to be the very antithesis of all that sober legal historians hold most dear. They are often relegated as evidence, therefore, to a status well beneath that given to laws, legal treatises, government documents, charters, biographies, and even monastic chronicles.[1]

This paper will seek to show that miracle collections in fact offer great advantages to historians of the law; advantages which may, on occasion, surpass those even of the favoured categories I have just named. This is especially true, I shall suggest, of collections in dossiers put together for the canonization of a saint. One of the most important of the aims of such dossiers is, after all, the confounding of sceptics. To such an enterprise trustworthy description is absolutely vital, together, where possible, with those small details whose judicious employment can lend an additional air of veracity to the whole. The compilers of such dossiers, then, devote special efforts to the production of an accurate and convincing record, encased in anecdote as it well may be. If, furthermore, the dossier is produced in a land distant from the examiners in Rome, it will be necessary for the advocates of the hoped-for saint to instruct the consistory there about particular elements of that country's condition or customs, the better to illuminate the achievements of their candidate. Should the subject be presented principally as a healer, for instance, then we may find in his or her

---

[1] Beyond the *Materials for the Life of Thomas Becket* one looks in vain for reference to canonization dossiers in even the most recent edition of Pollock and Maitland, magnificent as this classic study is: F. Pollock and F. W. Maitland (reissued by S. F. C. Milsom), *The History of English Law*, 2 vols. (Cambridge, 1968), I, 1. xix–xxii. R. F. Hunnisett, *The Medieval Coroner* (Cambridge, 1961) is deservedly the standard authority for this particular subject and will be cited frequently below, but he too felt no need to consult such records.

dossier information about the deficiencies of the medical profession which the miracle made good; if a provider, about the policies of local estate-holders; if a soldier, about the exigencies of contemporary warfare; and if engaged in active government, about government and the law. In sum, there *is* important material to be found in such collections, and its exploration is long overdue.

I propose here to offer a preliminary investigation of just one such canonization dossier, and to demonstrate the reliability and, above all, the richness of the information it has to give about the law of medieval England. The dossier is the one put together for the canonization of Thomas Cantilupe, bishop of Hereford 1275–82. Cantilupe was seen as a candidate for sainthood immediately upon his death, and his cause was promoted promptly by his friend and successor Richard Swinfield (bishop of Hereford 1283–1317). It met with little success, however, until King Edward I of England (1272–1307) took it up in 1305, with a letter to the then pope, Clement V. The enthusiasm of the king is itself indicative of the importance of the case. Pope Clement then appointed a commission to examine the matter in 1307, and the present dossier was offered to this commission. Thomas was eventually canonized in 1320.[2]

The Cantilupe dossier yields information about many different aspects of life in late thirteenth-century England. Cantilupe was many things to many people (including the loving owners of pet dormice[3]); but, as a bishop, nobleman, and good friend of the king, he was, together with his close adherents, deeply involved in the administration of English law. His dossier has in it eight miracle stories which contain direct reference to the secular criminal law current under Edward I; stories which, taken together, throw light upon the day-to-day operation of this law, upon the duties of the king's law officers, and upon the attitudes of the king's lay subjects towards their own responsibilities under it. Through their admiring accounts of the miraculous interventions of the would-be saint, moreover, the stories also inform us about how some sections of the English church viewed the king's criminal law (and perhaps about how Rome too was asked to view it). Such stories may add, then, to our understanding of the relations between church and state in England. This is perhaps their most important aspect.

In that the saint *does* feel the need to intervene in the day-to-day operations of the king's law, he may seem, at first sight, to be a critic of them. His actions do indeed signal anxieties about the administration of this law; but they seem helpful to it too. The subject of the relations of the medieval church and state in law and government is one especially dear to the heart of the dedicatee of this book of essays. This is my chief reason for reopening the matter here.

---

[2] On the campaign for the canonization of Cantilupe, see P. H. Daley, 'The Process of Canonisation in the Thirteenth and Fourteenth Centuries', in *St Thomas Cantilupe Bishop of Hereford: Essays in His Honour*, ed. M. Jancey (Hereford, 1982), 125–35.

[3] One of his resuscitation miracles involves the revival of such a dormouse, accidentally trodden underfoot: *Acta Sanctorum*, (henceforward *AS*), *Octobris* I, 675.

All eight stories tell of a death in doubtful circumstances. Six report upon the accidental deaths of children and young persons, and two upon the deaths of adults through a sentence of judicial execution. All of the victims are brought back to life through the power of Thomas Cantilupe.

In the first story of accidental death we hear of the drowning of a 5-year-old child named Joan. This tale, recounted by some of the participants,[4] is worth rehearsing in detail because of its charm as a vignette of village life, as well as for its telling information about contemporary legal procedures. Joan's parents had betaken themselves to a local tavern with a group of friends, leaving the children to play in the tavern garden. There was a large fish-pond, about six feet deep, in this garden. Joan and a friend called John were throwing stones into the pond when the little boy pushed the little girl, and she tumbled in and was drowned. John, it seems, ran away in understandable fright. Some time later the younger section of the revellers came out of the tavern and into the garden to sing for the assembled party in return for their drinks, 'secundum modum'. They arranged themselves around the pond to do so, and while awaiting their audience saw the child lying in the water.

At this point we learn what, in strict legality, should then have happened;

It was the custom in that part of the country, and indeed throughout the whole of England (except for the cities), that whoever first discovered a dead body (of one slain or drowned as it might be) had to publish the fact and raise the hue and cry. All those who heard it must follow the discoverer from vill to vill until they got to the place where those in charge of the area's jurisdiction lived. The discoverer had then to announce the said homicide or drowning, whereupon he would be held until he could produce a pledge that he would appear before the king's justices when they next came to those parts, and submit to judgement in their presence. Meanwhile, no one must move the body of the slain or drowned person from the place in which it was first found without calling in the king's officer in charge of the investigation of such events for, in the kingdom of England, such matter bore upon the rights of the crown. This was the case even when the king's officer lived so far away that he might not come before three months had passed. Should anyone do otherwise, he would commit an extremely grave offence. In this case, the pool where the body had been found would have been filled in.

The law was not, however, obeyed. No one person among the singers wanted to be the discoverer, for reasons evident from the passage quoted. A tavern servant proposed to tell his master, but was speedily restrained. The whole company decided instead to behave as though nothing untoward had happened and, later that night, to come back secretly and transfer Joan's corpse to a nearby river, the 'Lugge' (a river near Hereford still identifiable). The father of the little boy, who was among the singers, went so far as to carry John away and lock him up in his house when he heard the child trying to tell Joan's mother about the accident. The remainder of the tale attests to Cantilupe's miraculous powers—which was

---

[4] *AS* 610–12.

clearly the reason for its inclusion. John escaped from his father and finally told Joan's mother. The body was found and recovered by the women. Joan was prayed over by both the men and the women, and 'measured' to Thomas Cantilupe.[5] Then, when hope had been almost abandoned, Joan returned to life, sat up, and (an addition which adds a tremendous air of credibility) promptly told upon her friend.

The second story is also about a drowning.[6] The body of young William Lorimer is found in a river. Here the hue and cry *is* raised in careful accordance with the law, for the chief witnesses to the miracle are those who respond to it. Fortunately, the prayers and measuring to Thomas which immediately follow the discovery revive the corpse so quickly that there is no need for further action.

The third tale reinforces the description given in the first of how the law should in theory work, adds details, and tells again of the reluctance of those involved actually to observe this law.[7] In this tale a child is accidentally crushed to death beneath the wheels of his father's ox-cart. His parents are terrified of the *periculum et dispendium* which recourse to the king's justice would bring upon them. Should the death be announced publicly, we are told, they knew that they would be held in prison and their oxen and wagon confiscated whilst the king's officers investigated the matter. Thus they hide the boy in their bed while they think of what to do. Happily, they remember that Thomas Cantilupe works wonders in such matters, and so they measure the child to him and pray until daybreak. The child returns to consciousness, bruised but alive.

In the fourth tale[8] another little boy, Roger, falls one night from a bridge leading to the newly built castle of Conway, and, as the moat has not yet been filled with water, is dashed to death on the rocks below. The coroners arrive the very next day to conduct their investigations (so important a settlement evidently merited resident borough coroners). They pronounce the boy dead, but then John Seward, a citizen, climbs down into the moat, makes the sign of the cross over Roger with a penny offered to Thomas Cantilupe, and vows to make a pilgrimage to his shrine in Hereford should he revive the boy. Roger shows signs of life and the coroners suspend their enquiries forthwith. We learn from further witnesses that no one had dared to move the body before the arrival of the coroners, for this was against the law, and that the coroners, when they came, brought a clerk to record their findings. Interestingly, the coroners are named: Stephen of Ganvy and William of Nottingham, together with their clerk, William. All made a very careful investigation of the body so as to note

---

[5] The process whereby the body of one ill or dead was measured with a length of thread, and the thread subsequently offered to a saint (perhaps as the wick of a candle), is well attested in the Middle Ages. It appears to derive from pagan practice, and to have been thought, by some Christians, harmless enough to be allowed into their practice too: V. I. J. Flint, *The Rise of Magic in Early Medieval Europe* (Oxford, 1991), 314.

[6] *AS* 615.   [7] *AS* 621.   [8] *AS* 626–8.

the wounds. They had seated themselves, in fact, a little distance away to complete their notes when the said John Seward, not realizing that the coroners had forbidden anyone else to come down into the moat whilst the recording was going on, climbed down and performed his acts of mercy.

In the fifth and sixth tales we are assured once more that no one may bury a body without the king's licence, not even should the coroners take two days and two nights or three whole days to come.[9] The sixth story, of yet another drowning, spells out these requirements in further careful detail, and with a non-English audience very evidently in mind. It explains that the coroners take great trouble with their enquiries so as to safeguard the rights of the crown, and to make sure that the king's justices, when they make their visitations, have all the information which pertains to them ready to hand.[10] The body is, in this last case, measured to Thomas Cantilupe only after the coroner has arrived and declared the drowned girl dead.

From the last two stories of the eight, those of death by judicial execution, we learn much about the powers and potentially fatal errors both of local lords and of the king's justices themselves. In the first,[11] one William Crak (or Aprees) is accused of homicide by his lord, William de Braose (Brewes).[12] He is captured, imprisoned in the lord's castle of Swansea for fifteen days, questioned by his lord, and, in the face of vigorous protestations of innocence on his part, hanged. But William Crak had been on pilgrimage to the shrine of St Thomas at Hereford, had received a vision of the Virgin Mary and St Thomas whilst in prison, together with a promise that he would be saved, and had bent a penny to Thomas Cantilupe and carried it with him to the gallows. After a second effort to hang him (for the gallows broke during the first), William is pronounced dead, and the lord's wife requests the body for burial. She and her daughter measure it to Thomas with a thread from her daughter's purse;[13] and William miraculously comes back to life.

This story includes interesting extra scraps of information. First, William (for the revived victim himself was one of the witnesses recruited by the compilers of the dossier) complains that no one but his lord had accused him, and that no formal sentence of death had been pronounced upon him before he was taken to the gallows. A clear suggestion is made here that the lord had flouted a larger law, and that he would have done so with impunity but for the saint and

---

[9] *AS* 647, 671.

[10] '. . . coronarius, ad quem pertinet secundum legem regni modum et causam per infortunium morientium, seu etiam occisorum, inquirere, et quod inquisierit, regis iusticiariis nunciare, ut sciatur, qualiter ipsa pax regni, quae ad coronam regiam pertinet, vel etiam infringatur.'

[11] The tale of William Crak appears twice in the dossier, told by different witnesses: *AS* 633–5, 76.

[12] Lord of Gower 1290–1326. William Crak was accused of involvement in the burning of the castle of 'Ostremue' (*AS* 634), and of being taken, therefore, to his lord's castle at 'Sweyneseye'. Oystermouth and Swansea were major castles in the lordship.

[13] The story refers to William de Braose's first wife. Her name is unknown. William had two daughters by this marriage: Aline and Joan. G.E.C. *The Complete Peerage*, vol. II (London, 1912), 303–4.

the Virgin Mary. William Crak's complaint makes excellent sense in context. William de Braose was notorious for his excessive claims to, and exercise of, justice within the liberty of Gower.[14] King Edward I disciplined him for these delicts in the very year in which the king began to take a serious interest in Cantilupe's cause: 1305.[15] This account, with its happy ending, would then have been music to the ears of the king. Secondly, the story reveals a distinction between the treatment of non-nobles and nobles. The gallows collapsed in fact through the addition of a second victim: a Welsh noble, Trahern Ap Howel, whose friends had failed to pay William de Braose for his freedom. One lord, then, could expect money should he threaten another with hanging, seemingly regardless of the king's officers. Indeed, William de Braose had waited hopefully for this money for quite a while before adding Trahern to the gallows.[16] The Welshman, however, seems also to have been saved supernaturally from his fate, in accordance with the vision of the Virgin and Thomas Cantilupe vouchsafed to William,[17] and again, perhaps, to the relief of the king.

The final story is particularly poignant.[18] A woman, one Christina, sells her herd of pigs, along with an extra pig which had joined it long ago and had never been reclaimed. She is reported to the king's officers, imprisoned in the royal castle at Hereford, and sentenced to death for theft. Her children measure her to Thomas Cantilupe as she is taken to the prison, and measure her again as she makes her confession at the church of St Martin on her way to be hanged. She is then duly hanged, and her body remains on the gallows from Nones until Vespers, together with those of other victims. At Vespers Christina's body is taken down for burial in a cemetery—a privilege allowed by the city to the members of the confraternity of the hospital of St John, to which Christina belonged. Her son, daughter, and friends place her on a bier and carry her to that same church of St Martin in which she had made her confession and been measured for the second time to Thomas Cantilupe. When they reach it an onlooker declares that she has seen the body move, and asks that it be brought inside the church. Once inside, Christina is lifted from the bier and is able to explain to the assembled crowd (which seemingly includes the king's justices themselves) that Thomas Cantilupe had held her up by her feet at the gallows, and so saved her from death. She stays inside the church for three full weeks, fearing that if she leaves it the justices will have her recaptured. At the end of this time, with a cross in her hand, 'in accordance with the custom of the kingdom', and in the presence of these same justices, she solemnly abjures the realm and leaves for Ireland.[19]

[14] T. B. Pugh, *Glamorgan County History*, vol. III, *The Middle Ages* (Cardiff, 1971), 233.

[15] R. R. Davies, *Lordship and Society in the March of Wales* 1282–1400 (Oxford, 1978), 243, 264–5.

[16] This detail too is credible, for William de Braose was improvident and impecunious: ibid. 100.

[17] 'Et tunc dictus testis [William] iterum petiit a B. Maria praedicta, quid fieret de supradicto Trahern Ap Howel; et B. Maria respondit: Dimittatis eum.' *AS* 634.

[18] *AS* 638.

[19] '. . . et postmodum secundum consuetudinem regni accepta cruce in manu et in praesentia dictorum justiciarium ivit, abjurato regno Angliae . . . in Hyberniam; et ex tunc non vidit eam.' *AS* 638.

The picture sketched in by these stories is a singularly unified one. The king's justice was viewed by his subjects as inflexible and harsh, and the fact that it was a little less arbitrary than that of some of the king's lords did little to diminish its essential crudity. We might note, also, that particular pains are taken in every one of these stories to stress the predominance of misadventure, and the essential blamelessness of all the individuals involved. A great deal of circumstantial detail is adduced to make these points. The death of Joan, for example, is described as the result of a singularly innocent form of playfulness. John's efforts to report the accident show beyond doubt that he had meant no malice. The revelling parents might be held ultimately to blame, perhaps, but the fault, such as it was, seems by this account to have been singularly human, and so venial. A flooded ford and the lack of handrails to a nearby bridge brought about the drowning of William Lorimer.[20] A disastrous house fire had compelled the owners of the ox-cart to move their belongings, and had also distracted them as to the whereabouts of their son. Little Roger had often made the journey to see his father, who worked at Conway Castle, but this time it was dark. His mother was meanwhile dutifully attending the night-long obsequies of her husband's colleague, believing her son to be asleep. Tragedy here resulted from actions and habits which were in essence guiltless. Trahern was the victim of the failings of his friends; and William Crak had asserted his own innocence throughout. Christina was a member of a respectable confraternity and had been, or so it appears, a mere passive recipient of future trouble. Yet, for all this, the king's 'justice' was still deeply to be feared. In the last of the six stories about the miraculous resuscitation of children, that of a drowned girl laid out on the riverbank for the coroner's inspection, the woman who measures the girl to Thomas Cantilupe, clearly for reasons of the best, is described as acting *audacter* in the presence of the coroner.[21] In Christina's case (where the law had been followed to the letter), the penalty was clearly far too heavy for the crime.

Despite the incentives to accuracy I mentioned at the beginning of this discussion, instinctive prejudice might lead one still to expect some exaggeration in a document so clearly biased towards a cause; the exaggeration, perhaps, of the time a given victim lay dead before the saint was invoked, of the harshness of the penalties his intervention had rendered null, of the prevalence of accident, and of the blamelessness of the persons he helped. In fact, however, each of these stories corresponds with, and so usefully corroborates, the accounts of the operation of royal criminal justice legal historians have built up from other sources. The owners of the ox-cart, for instance, have in mind the law of *deodand*, whereby the instrument which brings about a death must be given to God through the intermediary of the king's officers, and presumably generally was so given. Sometimes the decision as to who will profit from the confiscation will await the justices in eyre, but the owners will still be deprived of their

---

[20] ' . . . et in lateribus pontis non erant aliqua appodiamenta'; *AS* 615.   [21] *AS* 671.

property from the very beginning of the enquiry.[22] The threatened filling in of the fish-pond in which Joan had drowned may have stemmed from this same law.

The activities of the king's coroners, as recorded here, are also in absolute accord with all we know of them from elsewhere; and the story of Roger gives a particularly pleasing account of the coroners and their clerk in action,[23] including their concern for the listing of wounds and the preparation of an accurate return as a check upon, and for comparison with, the presentments of the hundred jurors.[24] No one, certainly, may bury a body before the coroners have seen it, on pain of amercement. The remarks that coroners may live a long way away from the scene of the homicide, and might take a long time to respond to a call, are further testimony to the possibly grand and county-wide status of these officers, in contrast, perhaps, with that of the sergeant or bailiff of the hundred to whom the hue and cry of the tavern singers might, had it happened, have first appealed.[25] The duties of raising this hue and cry in the countryside and of following it from vill to vill until a royal officer is found are very well attested,[26] as is the prescribed fate (and consequent evasiveness) of the discoverer of the body.[27] He, and perhaps his four nearest neighbours, would have to find pledges. Should the 'first finders' or pledges fail to make themselves available to the eyre they could be amerced.[28] Since the eyre could take a long time to reach a given area, all might be held in alarming and extended suspense. Should any single person be under suspicion, he or she could be arrested and his or her moveables valued pending a successful prosecution.[29] Should an accusation be made, then a jury verdict on the matter might be both expensive and unreliable.[30]

The king's system of criminal justice, moreover, did indeed pay little attention to misfortune or blamelessness in matters of homicide, for all the efforts of some jurors,[31] and especially little when the persons involved were poor and

---

[22] On the law of *deodand*, particularly in the thirteenth century, see Pollock and Maitland, *History of English Law*, II, 473–74. Ox-carts often fell victim to it.

[23] For a parallel account see J. B. Given, *Society and Homicide in Thirteenth Century England* (Stanford, 1977), 11–12.

[24] Hunnisett, *Medieval Coroner*, 5, 8, 57–8.   [25] Ibid. 2, 55–6, 170–1.

[26] The remark in the first story that the cities arranged matters differently presumably refers both to the smaller distances involved and to the possibility of reporting first to the reeve, bailiff, or king's sergeant: ibid. 10.

[27] '. . . there is much evidence to show that the duties of "first finder" and his consequent chances of punishment for defaults tended to postpone the official "finding" and that the "first finder" in law, the man who ultimately raised the hue and cry, might often have been more correctly termed the "last finder", many having previously noticed the body in silence and hurried by': ibid. 10.

[28] Ibid. 11, 25–6, 60, and, for further evidence of the wide range of offences bringing amercement, 108–9.

[29] Given, *Society*, 10–11.

[30] On these dangers, see esp. R. D. Groot, 'The Early Thirteenth Century Criminal Jury', in *Twelve Good Men and True: The Criminal Trial Jury in England 1200–1800*, ed. J. D. Cockburn and T. A. Green (Princeton, 1988), 18–25.

[31] And these may well have been considerable; see e.g. T. A. Green, *Verdict According to Conscience* (Chicago, 1985), 25–32 ff.

could not buy the king's 'grace'.[32] The rights of the crown were, after all, money-making rights, and his officers were known to be appointed with the enforcement of such rights principally in mind.[33] Unnatural deaths, and the *deodands*, confiscations, amercements, and bribes they involved, made up the largest single item in their business.[34] Coroners were unpaid, and were no strangers to extortion or the perversion of justice in their own interests. They might charge heavily for holding a rapid inquest to speed burial, or for presiding over an abjuration. During the reign of Edward I, moreover, their meanness was a notorious cause of comment.[35] The last two stories of the eight provide similar supporting evidence. The failings of seigneurial justice are evident in the case of William Crak and, in that of Christina, so are those of the king's criminal justice itself when it *was* called into play.[36] Against such an array of alarming legal possibilities, the dismay of the young singers and of the ox-cart owners, and the sense of wrong felt by William Crak and Christina's family and friends, are readily understandable.

All of these stories, then, provide extra confirmation of a state of affairs recoverable from other sources. This fact alone might justify taking this type of evidence seriously, and encourage further recourse to it.[37] But there is more. In that canonization dossiers represent the attitude of certain sections of the *church*, they do more than merely corroborate the evidence of the secular record. They expand it in significant ways. With its explanations of *why* some of the king's subjects were so unwilling to have recourse to his system of justice, its concern for the vulnerability of the comparatively guiltless to the royal officers, its attention to the matter of misadventure, and, above all, its interest in the moment of intervention by the saint, this dossier draws an explicit contrast between the situation which existed in reality and that which might, with the help of the church, be brought about. It allows us a glimpse of the English church's contribution to the problem.

The dossier put together for the canonization of Thomas Cantilupe confirms that there were deficiencies in the contemporary operation of the king's criminal law, certainly; but it also adduces remedies for these deficiencies. It offers alternative means of addressing the problem of crime, means perhaps capable eventually of restoring the trust of the king's subjects in his law. There *is* a way of adjusting the balance between the rights of the crown and the just

---

[32] Pollock and Maitland, *History of English Law*, II, 483–4. Pardons for accidental homicide were widely available, but only at the end of a long and expensive process: Hunnisett, *Medieval Coroner*, 77–8.

[33] Hunnisett, *Medieval Coroner*, 2–3.   [34] Ibid. 104.   [35] Ibid. 118–25, 173.

[36] The sentence of hanging, particularly for theft, seems to have been more readily awarded in the early thirteenth century than in the early years of the reign of Edward I, but it was more rigorously enforced after the 1290s. See Groot, 'The Early . . . Jury', 17–18, and B. W. McLane, 'Juror Attitudes Toward Local Disorder', in Cockburn and Green, *Twelve Good Men* 36–8, 58. Women may have been especially vulnerable, for they could not offer proof by combat and the ordeal had been denied to them since 1215.

[37] The appearance of two coroners at the Conway inquest, for instance, seems to be an interesting variation of the rule that only one need attend: Hunnisett, *Medieval Coroner*, 135.

deserts of his people, the dossier seems to say. The way lies through the proper employment of the resources of the late thirteenth- and early fourteenth-century English Church; resources which might, at first sight paradoxically, be helpful to the king of England himself.

The resources offered seem intangible at first, to say the least. Correcting the injustices (or threatened injustices) reported in these stories requires the intervention of a practitioner who, though hopefully sainted, is dead, together with a miracle—a prescription not easily translatable into practical governmental terms. On this level, then, the dossier appears to offer a cheap propitiation of the credulous at the expense of all true improvement, and to be relevant only to persons made immune to facts by their Christian faith. In reality, however, its stories perform a far grander function. They identify real and enduring remedies for the observed deficiencies of the king's criminal law. Those who purveyed them should, then, be seen less as an obstacle than as a powerful reinforcement to the administration of this law.

The remedies to which the miracles in the eight stories direct us are four: ecclesiastical sanctuary, pilgrimage, confession, and the good offices of a well-connected bishop. And all of them are devised to allow the church to have a carefully administered corrective impact. The first remedy, the invocation of ecclesiastical sanctuary, confronts state methods directly. The others, which interpose differing means of discipline between the criminal and his or her punishment, approach the problem by a slightly more circuitous route. These last three measures provide for intervention at an earlier stage in the cycle of crime and its punishment than that at which the attendance of the king's officers would normally be required. This aspect is especially important.

Ecclesiastical sanctuary is advocated, as we saw, in the miracle of Christina's resuscitation from the gallows. As Cantilupe's miracle on Christina's behalf begins to take effect, she is brought into the church of St Martin. Three weeks later, and whilst still inside the church, she abjures the realm, thus evading her original sentence of death. All of the distinguishing features of sanctuary are present in this story. The three weeks during which she remains in the church fall squarely within the period allowed by the law of sanctuary,[38] as does the ceremony whereby, holding a cross, she solemnly abjures. Ceremonies of abjuration from sanctuary often prefaced outlawry and exile by the state, but Christina's abjuration is not a secular one. The ceremony is not performed before the coroner or coroners, nor are the witnesses to it summoned by them, as the king's law required.[39] Instead, this abjuration takes place before an

---

[38] From the twelfth century onwards a felon could claim sanctuary at an ordinary church for up to forty days: ibid. 37. Earlier kings had limited the time to thirty-seven days: D. Hall, 'The Sanctuary of St Cuthbert', in *St Cuthbert, His Cult and His Community to A.D. 1200*, ed. G. Bonner *et al.* (Woodbridge, 1989), 431–2.

[39] The composition of a body of witnesses might vary greatly, but, if the king's law was to be observed, they must act in obedience to the coroner: Hunnisett, *Medieval Coroner*, 41–2.

audience gathered in defiance of the royal officers and is enacted not with the consent of the justices, but in the face of the sentence of death pronounced by them. Christina feared, indeed, that these justices would have her recaptured if they could.[40]

Christina, moreover, appears to have owed her successful appeal to sanctuary primarily to the community. A local woman had had her taken into the church in the first place, and many others went in with her and stayed with her there. The sympathy of the local community was, as we now know, essential to the successful operation of sanctuary,[41] and this case provides us not merely with additional evidence of the power of the community in this sphere, but with a positive demonstration of how church and people might act together, even against the royal officers of the law.[42] The law by which Christina was judged and sentenced was, in sum, not that of the king, but that of the saint and the church in co-operation with the people. In this miracle, then, the intervention of Cantilupe is used actively to transfer a victim of the king's 'justice' to judgement of an available but contrasting kind. The line between secular and ecclesiastical sanctuary law is not always an easy one to draw, it is true; but the discomfiture of the king's justices in this incident is a clear indication that the real power here had passed to other hands. This miracle is employed both to promote a method of distinguishing and disciplining wrong which is distinct from that provided by the king, and to illuminate the superior features of this different process. The prayers, bendings of pennies, and measurings to Thomas Cantilupe which undid the deaths by accident, and with them the secular legal processes they entailed, may also perhaps best be understood within the context of the ecclesiastical and popular control of sanctuary. Objects associated with the saint act in these cases as a kind of mobile sanctuary, and are seen to procure improvements in the meting out of justice which are similar to those which were secured for Christina.[43] Sanctuary, in its many guises, intervenes in a wholly beneficial way in these miracles.

The second remedy, that of penitential pilgrimage, plays an important part in the other case of judicial execution—that of William Crak. The relations of his lord, William de Braose, with the church in his liberty were not perhaps of an

---

[40] Her case is similar in this respect to an 'extraordinary' one cited by Hunnisett. Here, a Northamptonshire thief was hanged for theft, carried to a church, revived, and abjured the realm without the permission of the justices: ibid. 38.

[41] For an excellent discussion of the importance of the local community in the operation of English sanctuary law, see G. Rosser, 'Sanctuary and Social Negotiation in Medieval England', in *The Cloister and the World*, ed. J. Blair *et al.* (Oxford, 1996), 57–79, esp. 64–5. I am indebted to Mr Kelvin Meek for drawing my attention to this article.

[42] As a publicly condemned thief, Christina should not strictly have been allowed sanctuary according to papal rulings upon the subject: P. Timbal Duclaux de Martin, *Le Droit d'asile* (Paris, 1939), 210–12. Local opinion, however, clearly thought differently.

[43] For interesting observations upon the use of mobile sanctuary, see Rosser, 'Sanctuary', 62, 66–7. Here, however, it seems to have been used less as prelude than as an adjunct to the establishment of localized sanctuary.

order to encourage William Crak to take to sanctuary in a nearby ecclesiastical building. He had recourse instead, then, to mobile sanctuary in combination with penitential pilgrimage to a tolerably distant shrine. As we saw, William is described in the dossier as having owed a measure of his salvation to the fact that he had bent a penny to Thomas Cantilupe when he was first imprisoned, and had carried the penny with him to the gallows. The rest is attributed to his having been on an earlier pilgrimage to the tomb of Thomas Cantilupe at Hereford. In an interesting addition to the first entry of the story in the dossier,[44] William is described as having made a promise of penance and reform of life on this pilgrimage, a promise which saved him even after (by this account) a third attempt by his lord to have him hanged. After his miraculous return to life, this second account goes on, William made yet another pilgrimage to Thomas's shrine, this time taking with him a repentant Lord William de Braose and also Lord William's wife.[45]

Penitential pilgrimage is represented here both as the foundation of that innocence which William claimed throughout, and as a means to the public chastening of his unjust lord. There is, furthermore, an extra dimension to this act of pilgrimage. In the dossier's first account of the affair we learn that William was saved both in accordance with the promise given by the Virgin and Thomas Cantilupe, whom he had seen in a dream in prison, and through the intercession of Lord William's wife. The latter had obtained William Crak's body and had prayed over it, and she and her daughter had measured it to Thomas. The intercession of the wife and daughter also, it seems, began the softening of the heart of the lord. The compassion of the female members of William de Braose's family, the intercession of the Virgin Mary, and penitential pilgrimage are linked together, then, in this particular miracle of salvation.

Tales of the merciful intercession of the Virgin, especially in the face of acts of judgement, were much favoured by the English church in the thirteenth century;[46] and this story should be placed within the context of these other accounts if its bearing upon the operation of the law is fully to be understood. By appealing to the compassionate and better part of human nature, the stories in which the Virgin procures mercy for wrongdoers, and obtains a relaxation of their sentences in return for promises of reform, sought to achieve a more profound change of behaviour than could ever be brought about by harsher methods. They stimulated the emotion of compunction in preference to the fear of punishment. Such judicial miracles, performed in company with

---

[44] *AS* 676. Further witnesses appear to have been called later in the proceedings.

[45] '. . . et postmodum dominus et domina dicti castri cum eo venerunt peregrini ratione dicti miraculi ad tumulum praedicti S.Thomae, et obtulerant ibi quasdam funras [?furcas] de cera, et funem cum qua fuit suspensus, quam apportavit insutam [?in sertam] ad collum suam': *AS* 634.

[46] See N. Morgan, 'Texts and Images of Marian Devotion in Thirteenth Century England', in *England in the Thirteenth Century: Proceedings of the 1989 Harlaxton Symposium*, ed. W. M. Ormrod (Stamford, 1991), 69–103.

penitential pilgrimage of the kind William Crak undertook, were, then, rather an inhibition to further wrongdoing than a sanction after the event. The image of the bare-breasted Virgin, which crowned the famous late thirteenth-century Hereford Map at the shrine of St Thomas Cantilupe,[47] may have served the same function. It too may have been designed to play a part in this deep process of reform.

Pilgrimage and remorse of this order elevated the function of shrines, for they allowed the images of compassion and the powers of the Virgin and the saint to intervene *before* the machinery of crime, its punishment, and the possible injustices associated with this punishment had begun relentlessly to turn. Penitential pilgrimage bears an apparent similarity to sanctuary and abjuration, for an abjuror will occasionally adopt the garb of the pilgrim, and the abjuror too will undergo the pilgrim's expiatory experience of travel. He might even be allowed to return as a result of it.[48] By tackling the problem of crime and its punishment so early in the cycle, however (almost as a rehearsal of the abjuration which might later be required by the law), penitential pilgrimage could perhaps obviate the need for these larger sanctions. William Crak clearly thought it should have done so in his case; and in the end, of course, it did. Cantilupe's intervention seems here to have been devised deliberately to point a contrast between the unjust prosecutor and the excessive penalty William suffered, and the role penitential pilgrimage and prayers to the Virgin could play in preserving an innocent man from these dangers. Their pilgrimage turned out, furthermore, to be profitable both to William and to his erring lord. In this way, pilgrimage to a shrine could both ameliorate the injustices of the current system, and actively supplement it. It could render persons both less inclined to break the law, and unwilling to operate this law unjustly. Its relevance to the positions both of William Crak and William, lord of Gower, is striking.

William Crak had promised reform; Christina of the pigs confessed. This brings us to the third of the remedies: many other stories in the dossier stress the importance of confession to a priest in the improvement of behaviour. Young Robert, heir to the earl of Oxford, for instance, fell prey to the sins of the flesh and their associated diseases. Contrition, together with a pilgrimage to, and confession at, Cantilupe's tomb, both healed and reformed him.[49] Confession is so obvious a means towards correction, and such an ecclesiastical one, that its potential influence upon the administration of the secular law may easily be overlooked. In truth, however, the importance of ecclesiastical confession in thirteenth-century England may perhaps best be understood by relating it to the functioning of the secular law. Crime and sin can be, after all, very

---

[47] It was perhaps already at the shrine when William Crak himself made his pilgrimages: V. I. J. Flint, 'The Hereford Map: Its Author(s), Two Scenes and a Border', *TRHS* 6th ser., 8 (1998), 19–43.
[48] Given, *Society*, 208.   [49] *AS* 670.

much alike.[50] In fact, ecclesiastical confession in the dossier has as specific and remedial a part to play vis-à-vis the law of the king as have the other measures we have reviewed. Christina's own confession in the church of St Martin was the preface to her being brought to sanctuary there and to her subsequent return to life; but in her case both authority and penalty are changed by the intervention of the saint.

Finally, the dossier allows us to look a little more closely at the good offices of a well-connected bishop. All of the stories cited here are about unnatural death. Miraculous returns from the grave are among the most spectacular of all miracles and provide, of course, excellent theatre; but here again, Thomas's miraculous resuscitations have specific points to make about the law. These particular accounts of unnatural deaths require that the dossier's compilers describe the working practices of the king's coroner, as we have seen; but they allow also the arraignment of the bishop against him. Put in another way, the deaths reported here permit Bishop Thomas successfully to defy the king's coroner when the activities of the latter fall short of the bishop's version of justice. The bishop-confessor treats death by misadventure or misjudgement in a manner quite unlike that offered by the coroner. It requires comfort, not penalty. Again, the miracles both introduce and fortify the alternative mechanisms offered by the church.

The idea of 'conflict between church and state', and the real battle between Henry II and Becket in the matter of the criminous clerks, loom as spectres behind all discussion of the king's criminal law in medieval England. All of the ecclesiastical sanctions mentioned in these stories, however, seem to be offered less as criticisms of, than as improvements to, the criminal law of King Edward I. The dossier is in no doubt about the king's ultimate right to try and to punish criminals. Cantilupe intervenes in only one case of judicial homicide, for instance, and that is to defeat the 'justice' of a Marcher lord to whom the king himself was hostile. In their efforts to remedy the inefficient and unpopular methods of some of the king's officers, however, and to put alternatives in their place, the miracles of Thomas Cantilupe actually offer significant reinforcements to government.

The alternatives, moreover, are conceived with a singular carefulness. All of those we have just discussed have echoes in measures favoured by the state. Edward I certainly had a use for sanctuary, for he incorporated English sanctuary into the prescriptions of his 1284 Statute of Wales.[51] Confession of a kind was required by the secular criminal law as it stood; before the coroner in

---

[50] The significance of the relationship between the two was indicated some years ago: T. Plucknet, *Edward I and the Criminal Law* (Cambridge 1960), 62–5. Plucknet was preoccupied, however, with the problems faced by the secular government, and had little to say about the contribution the church might make towards alleviating them.

[51] Rosser, 'Sanctuary', 70. *Statutes of the Realm*, I, 59.

sanctuary, for example, and also as a preface to the culprit's being allowed to abjure the realm or turn approver.[52] The process of abjuration of the realm from ecclesiastical sanctuary is similar to the process of outlawry in the county court.[53] When Edward I disciplined William de Braose in 1305, the first part of the penalty William had to undergo was to walk bare-headed and unarmed to the exchequer, like a pilgrim, and deliver an apology.[54] Parallels of this kind can help to bridge rather than deepen the gulf, by lessening the sense of confrontation. In being introduced at a different time, administered by a different authority, and, most important of all, in attracting a different penalty, the remedies the church advanced in these miracles seem in truth to have been a vital supplement to the king's administration of justice. The measures offered by the dossier do not, in short, seek to undermine the place of the king in the administration of the law so much as to shore it up against imminent disaster.

For it is not the king, but the king's so-called supporters and law officers, who bear the brunt of the dossier's criticisms. Evidently, their activities fall short of true justice and so alienate and terrify the lesser subjects of the king. By bringing churchmen to the fore *early* in the keeping of discipline, and intervening quickly in the cycle of crime and punishment, however, the church might marginalize these officers by rendering their harsh judgements unnecessary. Through such measures, the king's subjects might be reconciled with the king. The dossier gives us glimpses of such attempted reconciliations. It reports, for instance, that a number of the king's grand relatives joined Aniane, bishop of Bangor, and David, abbot of Margam, in the celebrations at the church in Conway which followed the revival of little Roger,[55] even though the miracle had in fact taken place, as we saw, in part as the result of disobedience to the coroners' commands. This augurs well for true co-operation with the king's law.

A great deal is said and written about the opposition between church and state in matters of law and justice; far less about the mutual interests they had to preserve. Those miracles of Cantilupe which concern the law, however, suggest that, under Edward I at least, the advantages of this co-operation were clearly recognized by both church and king. We noted that the support of King Edward was crucial to the success of the canonization of Thomas Cantilupe, and the interventions of Cantilupe in the king's law may help us to understand why. A saint and pilgrimage shrine of this stature might reach more deeply into the operation of the king's true justice than any of the other means he had.

The judicial miracles of Thomas Cantilupe thus offer us a new way of looking at the relations of church and state. In total contrast to his namesake,

[52] Hunnisett, *Medieval Coroner*, 3, 43, 45, 68–9; Rosser, 'Sanctuary', 68.

[53] Hunnisett himself describes such abjuration as 'tantamount to outlawry': Hunnisett, *Medieval Coroner*, 61–2, 64.

[54] M. Prestwich, *Edward I* (London, 1988), 536–8.   [55] *AS* 626–7.

Thomas Becket, Cantilupe is shown as supplementing, rather than competing with, the king's government. He replaces confrontation with an assistance both active and most cleverly conceived. Miracle collections of this type, then, *can* contain evidence of the first importance. Far from concerning themselves exclusively with the supernatural domain, they may be active vehicles for the church's intervention in the affairs of state. Thus, they deserve to be treated with the utmost seriousness by all who would understand this state's mechanisms. Perhaps Maitland and miracles might rejoice in each other's company after all.

INDEX OF MANUSCRIPTS

GENERAL INDEX

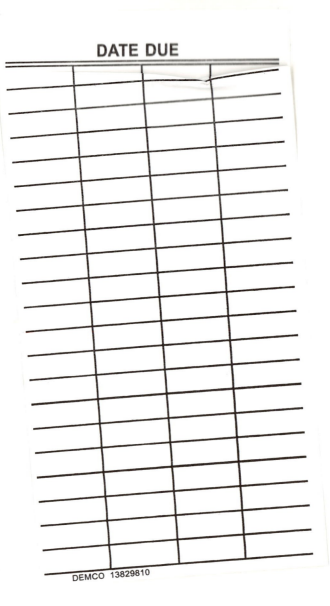

DATE DUE